SVETLANA ALEXIEVICH

The Unwomanly Face of War

Translated by Richard Pevear and Larissa Volokhonsky

PENGUIN BOOKS

PENGUIN CLASSICS

UK | USA | Canada | Ireland | Australia
India | New Zealand | South Africa

Penguin Books is part of the Penguin Random House group of companies whose addresses
can be found at global.penguinrandomhouse.com.

First published in Russian as *У войны не женское лицо* by Mastatskaya Litaratura,
Minsk 1985
First published in English as *War's Unwomanly Face* by Progress Publishers, Moscow 1988
This translation first published in the United States by Random House, an imprint and
division of Penguin Random House LLC 2017
This translation first published in Great Britain by Penguin Classics 2017
005

Printed in Great Britain by Clays Ltd, St Ives plc

A CIP catalogue record for this book is available from the British Library

ISBN: 978-0-141-98352-3

www.greenpenguin.co.uk

MIX
Paper from
responsible sources
FSC® C018179

Penguin Random House is committed to a
sustainable future for our business, our readers
and our planet. This book is made from Forest
Stewardship Council® certified paper.

CONTENTS

————

FROM A CONVERSATION WITH A HISTORIAN   ix

A HUMAN BEING IS GREATER THAN WAR   xi

————

"I DON'T WANT TO REMEMBER . . ."   3

"GROW UP, GIRLS . . . YOU'RE STILL GREEN . . ."   19

    Of Oaths and Prayers   20

    Of the Smell of Fear and a Suitcase of Candy   34

    Of Everyday Life and Essential Life   54

"I ALONE CAME BACK TO MAMA . . ."   71

"TWO WARS LIVE IN OUR HOUSE . . ."   91

"TELEPHONES DON'T SHOOT . . ."   99

"THEY AWARDED US LITTLE MEDALS . . ."   113

    Of Dolls and Rifles   117

    Of Death and Astonishment in the Face of Death   122

    Of Horses and Birds   126

"IT WASN'T ME . . ."   131

"I REMEMBER THOSE EYES EVEN NOW . . ."   141

"WE DIDN'T SHOOT . . ."   159

    Of Nice Little Shoes and a Cursed Wooden Leg   160

    Of the Special "K" Soap and the Guardhouse   168

    Of Melted Bearings and Russian Curses   176

"THEY NEEDED SOLDIERS . . . BUT WE ALSO
WANTED TO BE BEAUTIFUL . . ."   185

    Of Men's Boots and Women's Hats   186

    Of a Girlish Treble and Sailors' Superstitions   197

    Of the Silence of Horror and the Beauty of Fiction   207

"YOUNG LADIES! DO YOU KNOW: THE COMMANDER
OF A SAPPER PLATOON LIVES ONLY TWO
MONTHS . . ."   211

"TO SEE HIM JUST ONCE . . ."   225

    Of a Damned Wench and the Roses of May   226

    Of a Strange Silence Facing the Sky and a Lost Ring   239

    Of the Loneliness of a Bullet and a Human Being   247

"ABOUT TINY POTATOES . . ."   251

    Of a Mine and a Stuffed Toy in a Basket   253

    Of Mommies and Daddies   265

    Of Little Life and a Big Idea   271

"MAMA, WHAT'S A PAPA?"   281

    Of Bathing Babies and of a Mama Who Looks
        Like a Papa   281

    Of Little Red Riding Hood and the Joy of
        Meeting a Cat During the War   290

    Of the Silence of Those Who Could Now Speak   298

"AND SHE PUTS HER HAND TO HER HEART . . ."   303

    Of the Last Days of the War, When Killing
        Was Repugnant   303

    Of a Composition with Childish Mistakes
        and Comic Movies   312

    Of the Motherland, Stalin, and Red Cloth   317

"SUDDENLY WE WANTED
    DESPERATELY TO LIVE . . ."   323

FROM A CONVERSATION
WITH A HISTORIAN

—*At what time in history did women first appear in the army?*

—Already in the fourth century B.C. women fought in the Greek armies of Athens and Sparta. Later they took part in the campaigns of Alexander the Great.

The Russian historian Nikolai Karamzin* wrote about our ancestors: "Slavic women occasionally went to war with their fathers and husbands, not fearing death: thus during the siege of Constantinople in 626 the Greeks found many female bodies among the dead Slavs. A mother, raising her children, prepared them to be warriors."

—*And in modern times?*

—For the first time in England, where from 1560 to 1650 they began to staff hospitals with women soldiers.

—*What happened in the twentieth century?*

—The beginning of the century . . . In England during World War I women were already being taken into the Royal Air Force. A Royal

* The Russian poet and writer Nikolai Karamzin (1766–1826) was the author of a masterful twelve-volume *History of the Russian State.*

Auxiliary Corps was also formed and the Women's Legion of Motor Transport, which numbered 100,000 persons.

In Russia, Germany, and France many women went to serve in military hospitals and ambulance trains.

During World War II the world was witness to a women's phenomenon. Women served in all branches of the military in many countries of the world: 225,000 in the British army, 450,000 to 500,000 in the American, 500,000 in the German . . .

About a million women fought in the Soviet army. They mastered all military specialties, including the most "masculine" ones. A linguistic problem even emerged: no feminine gender had existed till then for the words "tank driver," "infantryman," "machine gunner," because women had never done that work. The feminine forms were born there, in the war . . .

A HUMAN BEING IS
GREATER THAN WAR

Millions of the cheaply killed
Have trod the path in darkness . . .

—OSIP MANDELSTAM[*]

FROM THE JOURNAL OF THIS BOOK

1978–1985

I am writing a book about war . . .

I, who never liked to read military books, although in my childhood and youth this was the favorite reading of everybody. Of all my peers. And that is not surprising—we were the children of Victory. The children of the victors. What is the first thing I remember about the war? My childhood anguish amid the incomprehensible and frightening words. The war was remembered all the time: at school and at home, at weddings and christenings, at celebrations and wakes. Even in children's conversations. The neighbors' boy once asked me: "What do people do under the ground? How do they live there?" We, too, wanted to unravel the mystery of war.

It was then that I began to think about death . . . And I never

---

[*]   Osip Mandelstam (1891–1938) was one of the greatest Russian poets of the twentieth century. The epigraph comes from "Lines on the Unknown Soldier" (1937–1938). Mandelstam died in transit to one of Stalin's hard-labor camps.

stopped thinking about it; it became the main mystery of life for me.

For us everything took its origin from that frightening and mysterious world. In our family my Ukrainian grandfather, my mother's father, was killed at the front and is buried somewhere in Hungary, and my Belorussian grandmother, my father's mother, was a partisan* and died of typhus; two of her sons served in the army and were reported missing in the first months of the war; of three sons only one came back. My father. The Germans burned alive eleven distant relations with their children—some in their cottage, some in a village church. These things happened in every family. With everybody.

For a long time afterward the village boys played "Germans and Russians." They shouted German words: *Hände hoch! Zurück! Hitler kaputt!*

We didn't know a world without war; the world of war was the only one familiar to us, and the people of war were the only people we knew. Even now I don't know any other world and any other people. Did they ever exist?

———

THE VILLAGE OF MY postwar childhood was a village of women. Village women. I don't remember any men's voices. That is how it has remained for me: stories of the war are told by women. They weep. Their songs are like weeping.

In the school library half of the books were about the war. The same with the village library, and in the nearby town, where my father often drove to get books. Now I know the reason why. Could it have been accidental? We were making war all the time, or preparing for war. Remembering how we made war. We never lived any other way, and probably didn't know how. We can't imagine how to live differently, and it will take us a long time to learn, if we ever do.

---

* A participant in a voluntary resistance movement fighting a guerrilla war against the Germans during World War II.

At school we were taught to love death. We wrote compositions about how we would like to die in the name of . . . We dreamed . . .

But the voices outside shouted about other more alluring things.

For a long time I was a bookish person, both frightened and attracted by reality. My fearlessness came from an ignorance of life. Now I think: If I were a more realistic person, could I throw myself into that abyss? What caused it all—ignorance? Or the sense of a path? For the sense of a path does exist . . .

I searched for a long time . . . What words can convey what I hear? I searched for a genre that would correspond to how I see the world, how my eye, my ear, are organized.

Once a book fell into my hands: *I Am from a Burning Village,* by A. Adamovich, Ya. Bryl, and V. Kolesnik.* I had experienced such a shock only once before, when I read Dostoevsky. Here was an unusual form: the novel was composed from the voices of life itself, from what I had heard in childhood, from what can be heard now in the street, at home, in a café, on a bus. There! The circle was closed. I had found what I was looking for. I knew I would.

Ales Adamovich became my teacher . . .

FOR TWO YEARS I was not so much meeting and writing as thinking. Reading. What will my book be about? Yet another book about war? What for? There have been a thousand wars—small and big, known and unknown. And still more has been written about them. But . . . it was men writing about men—that much was clear at once. Everything we know about war we know with "a man's voice." We are all captives of "men's" notions and "men's" sense of war. "Men's" words. Women are silent. No one but me ever questioned my grandmother.

* The novel *I Am from a Burning Village* (also known in English as *Out of the Fire*), by the Belorussian writers Ales Adamovich (1927–1994), Yanka Bryl (1917–2006), and Vladimir Kolesnik (1922–1994), chronicles the Nazi destruction of Belorussian villages during World War II. Adamovich was a novelist, critic, and philosopher who had fought as a partisan in 1942–1943 and became a forceful antiwar activist.

My mother. Even those who were at the front say nothing. If they suddenly begin to remember, they don't talk about the "women's" war but about the "men's." They tune in to the canon. And only at home or waxing tearful among their combat girlfriends do they begin to talk about their war, the war unknown to me. Not only to me, to all of us. More than once during my journalistic travels I witnessed, I was the only hearer of, totally new texts. I was shaken as I had been in childhood. The monstrous grin of the mysterious shows through these stories . . . When women speak, they have nothing or almost nothing of what we are used to reading and hearing about: How certain people heroically killed other people and won. Or lost. What equipment there was and which generals. Women's stories are different and about different things. "Women's" war has its own colors, its own smells, its own lighting, and its own range of feelings. Its own words. There are no heroes and incredible feats, there are simply people who are busy doing inhumanly human things. And it is not only they (people!) who suffer, but the earth, the birds, the trees. All that lives on earth with us. They suffer without words, which is still more frightening.

But why? I asked myself more than once. Why, having stood up for and held their own place in a once absolutely male world, have women not stood up for their history? Their words and feelings? They did not believe themselves. A whole world is hidden from us. Their war remains unknown . . .

I want to write the history of that war. A women's history.

AFTER THE FIRST ENCOUNTERS . . .

Astonishment: these women's military professions—medical assistant, sniper, machine gunner, commander of an antiaircraft gun, sapper—and now they are accountants, lab technicians, museum guides, teachers . . . Discrepancy of the roles—here and there. Their memories are as if not about themselves, but some other girls. Now they are surprised at themselves. Before my eyes history "humanizes" itself, becomes like ordinary life. Acquires a different lighting.

I've happened upon extraordinary storytellers. There are pages in their lives that can rival the best pages of the classics. The person sees herself so clearly from above—from heaven, and from below—from the ground. Before her is the whole path—up and down—from angel to beast. Remembering is not a passionate or dispassionate retelling of a reality that is no more, but a new birth of the past, when time goes in reverse. Above all it is creativity. As they narrate, people create, they "write" their life. Sometimes they also "write up" or "rewrite." Here you have to be vigilant. On your guard. At the same time pain melts and destroys any falsehood. The temperature is too high! Simple people—nurses, cooks, laundresses—behave more sincerely, I became convinced of that . . . They, how shall I put it exactly, draw the words out of themselves and not from newspapers and books they have read—not from others. But only from their own sufferings and experiences. The feelings and language of educated people, strange as it may be, are often more subject to the working of time. Its general encrypting. They are infected by secondary knowledge. By myths. Often I have to go for a long time, by various roundabout ways, in order to hear a story of a "woman's," not a "man's" war: not about how we retreated, how we advanced, at which sector of the front . . . It takes not one meeting, but many sessions. Like a persistent portrait painter.

I sit for a long time, sometimes a whole day, in an unknown house or apartment. We drink tea, try on the recently bought blouses, discuss hairstyles and recipes. Look at photos of the grandchildren together. And then . . . After a certain time, you never know when or why, suddenly comes this long-awaited moment, when the person departs from the canon—plaster and reinforced concrete, like our monuments—and goes on to herself. Into herself. Begins to remember not the war but her youth. A piece of her life . . . I must seize that moment. Not miss it! But often, after a long day, filled with words, facts, tears, only one phrase remains in my memory (but what a phrase!): "I was so young when I left for the front, I even grew during the war." I keep it in my notebook, although I have dozens of yards of tape in my tape recorder. Four or five cassettes . . .

What helps me? That we are used to living together. Communally. We are communal people. With us everything is in common—both happiness and tears. We know how to suffer and how to tell about our suffering. Suffering justifies our hard and ungainly life. For us pain is art. I must admit, women boldly set out on this path . . .

How do they receive me?

They call me "little girl," "dear daughter," "dear child." Probably if I was of their generation they would behave differently with me. Calmly and as equals. Without joy and amazement, which are the gifts of the meeting between youth and age. It is a very important point, that then they were young and now, as they remember, they are old. They remember across their life—across forty years. They open their world to me cautiously, to spare me: "I got married right after the war. I hid behind my husband. Behind the humdrum, behind baby diapers. I wanted to hide. My mother also begged: 'Be quiet! Be quiet! Don't tell.' I fulfilled my duty to the Motherland, but it makes me sad that I was there. That I know about it . . . And you are very young. I feel sorry for you . . ." I often see how they sit and listen to themselves. To the sound of their own soul. They check it against the words. After long years a person understands that this was life, but now it's time to resign yourself and get ready to go. You don't want to, and it's too bad to vanish just like that. Casually. In passing. And when you look back you feel a wish not only to tell about your life, but also to fathom the mystery of life itself. To answer your own question: Why did all this happen to me? You gaze at everything with a parting and slightly sorrowful look . . . Almost from the other side . . . No longer any need to deceive anyone or yourself. It's already clear to you that without the thought of death it is impossible to make out anything in a human being. Its mystery hangs over everything.

War is an all too intimate experience. And as boundless as human life . . .

Once a woman (a pilot) refused to meet with me. She explained on the phone: "I can't . . . I don't want to remember. I spent three years at war . . . And for three years I didn't feel myself a woman. My organism was dead. I had no periods, almost no woman's desires. And I was beautiful . . . When my future husband proposed to me . . . that was already in Berlin, by the Reichstag . . . He said: 'The war's over. We're still alive. We're lucky. Let's get married.' I wanted to cry. To shout. To hit him! What do you mean, married? Now? In the midst of all this—married? In the midst of black soot and black bricks . . . Look at me . . . Look how I am! Begin by making me a woman: give me flowers, court me, say beautiful words. I want it so much! I wait for it! I almost hit him . . . I was about to . . . He had one cheek burned, purple, and I see: he understood everything, tears are running down that cheek. On the still-fresh scars . . . And I myself can't believe I'm saying to him: 'Yes, I'll marry you.'

"Forgive me . . . I can't . . ."

I understood her. But this was also a page or half a page of my future book.

Texts, texts. Texts everywhere. In city apartments and village cottages, in the streets and on the train . . . I listen . . . I turn more and more into a big ear, listening all the time to another person. I "read" voices.

A HUMAN BEING IS greater than war . . .

Memory preserves precisely the moments of that greatness. A human being is guided by something stronger than history. I have to gain breadth—to write the truth about life and death in general, not only the truth about war. To ask Dostoevsky's question: How much human being is in a human being, and how to protect this human being in oneself? Evil is unquestionably tempting. Evil is more artful than good. More attractive. As I delve more deeply into the boundless world of war, everything else becomes slightly faded, more ordinary than the ordinary. A grandiose and predatory world. Now I understand the solitude of the human being who comes back from there. As if from another planet or from the other world. This human being has a knowledge that others do not have, that can be obtained only there, close to death. When she tries to put something into words, she has a sense of catastrophe. She is struck dumb. She wants to tell, the others would like to understand, but they are all powerless.

They are always in a different space than the listener. They are surrounded by an invisible world. At least three persons participate in the conversation: the one who is talking now, the one she was then, at the moment of the event, and myself. My goal first of all is to get at the truth of those years. Of those days. Without sham feelings. Just after the war this woman would have told of one war; after decades, of course, it changes somewhat, because she adds her whole life to this memory. Her whole self. How she lived those years, what she read, saw, whom she met. Finally, whether she is happy or unhappy. Do we talk by ourselves, or is someone else there? Family? If it's friends, what sort? Friends from the front are one thing, all the rest are another. My documents are living beings; they change and fluctuate together with us; there is no end of things to be gotten out of them. Something new and necessary for us precisely now. This very moment. What are we looking for? Most often not great deeds and heroism, but small, human things, the most interesting and intimate for us. Well, what would I like most to know, for instance, from the life of ancient Greece? From the history of Sparta? I would like to read how people talked at home then and what they talked about. How they went to war. What words they spoke on the last day and the last night before parting with their loved ones. How they saw them off to war. How they awaited their return from war . . . Not heroes or generals, but ordinary young men . . .

History through the story told by an unnoticed witness and participant. Yes, that interests me, that I would like to make into literature. But the narrators are not only witnesses—least of all are they witnesses; they are actors and makers. It is impossible to go right up to reality. Between us and reality are our feelings. I understand that I am dealing with versions, that each person has her version, and it is from them, from their plurality and their intersections, that the image of the time and the people living in it is born. But I would not like it to be said of my book: her heroes are real, and no more than that. This is just history. Mere history.

I write not about war, but about human beings in war. I write not the history of a war, but the history of feelings. I am a historian of the soul. On the one hand I examine specific human beings, living in a specific time and taking part in specific events, and on the other hand I have to discern the eternally human in them. The tremor of eternity. That which is in human beings at all times.

They say to me: Well, memories are neither history nor literature. They're simply life, full of rubbish and not tidied up by the hand of an artist. The raw material of talk, every day is filled with it. These bricks lie about everywhere. But bricks don't make a temple! For me it is all different . . . It is precisely there, in the warm human voice, in the living reflection of the past, that the primordial joy is concealed and the insurmountable tragedy of life is laid bare. Its chaos and passion. Its uniqueness and inscrutability. Not yet subjected to any treatment. The originals.

I build temples out of our feelings . . . Out of our desires, our disappointments. Dreams. Out of that which was, but might slip away.

ONCE AGAIN ABOUT THE same thing . . . I'm interested not only in the reality that surrounds us, but in the one that is within us. I'm interested not in the event itself, but in the event of feelings. Let's say— the soul of the event. For me feelings are reality.

And history? It is in the street. In the crowd. I believe that in each of us there is a small piece of history. In one half a page, in another two or three. Together we write the book of time. We each call out our truth. The nightmare of nuances. And it all has to be heard, and one has to dissolve in it all, and become it all. And at the same time not lose oneself. To combine the language of the street and literature. The problem is also that we speak about the past in present-day language. How can we convey the feelings of those days?

———

A PHONE CALL IN the morning: "We're not acquainted . . . But I've come from Crimea, I'm calling from the train station. Is it far from you? I want to tell you my war . . ."

Really?!

And I was about to go to the park with my little girl. To ride the merry-go-round. How can I explain to a six-year-old what it is I do? She recently asked me: "What is war?" How do I reply? . . . I would like to send her out into this world with a gentle heart, and I teach her that one shouldn't simply go and pick a flower. It's a pity to crush a ladybug, to tear the wing off a dragonfly. So how am I to explain war to the child? To explain death? To answer the question of why people kill? Kill even little children like herself. We, the adults, are as if in collusion. We understand what the talk is about. But what of children? After the war my parents somehow explained it to me, but I can't explain it to my child. Can't find the words. We like war less and less; it's more and more difficult to find a justification for it. For us it's simply murder. At least it is for me.

I would like to write a book about war that would make war sickening, and the very thought of it repulsive. Insane. So that even the generals would be sickened . . .

My men friends (as opposed to women) are taken aback by such "women's" logic. And again I hear the "men's" argument: "You weren't in the war." But maybe that's a good thing: I don't know the passion of hatred; my vision is normal. Unwarlike, unmanly.

There is a concept in optics called "light-gathering power"—the greater or lesser ability of a lens to fix the caught image. So, then, women's memory of the war is the most "light-gathering" in terms of strength of feelings, in terms of pain. I would even say that "women's" war is more terrible than "men's." Men hide behind history, behind facts; war fascinates them as action and a conflict of ideas, of interests, whereas women are caught up with feelings. And another thing: men are prepared from childhood for the fact that they may have to shoot. Women are not taught that . . . They are not prepared to do that work . . . And they remember other things, and remember differently. They are capable of seeing what is closed to men. I repeat once more: their war has smell, has color, a detailed world of existence: "They gave us kit bags and we made skirts out of them"; "I went into the recruiting office through one door wearing a dress, and came out through the other wearing trousers and an army shirt, with my braid cut off, and only a little lock left on my forehead . . ."; "The Germans gunned down the village and left . . . We came to the place: trampled yellow sand, and on top of it one child's shoe . . ." I had been warned more than once (especially by male writers): "Women are going to invent a pile of things for you. All sorts of fiction." But I'm convinced that such things cannot be invented. Who could they be copied from? If that can be copied, it's only from life; life alone has such fantasy.

Whatever women talk about, the thought is constantly present in them: war is first of all murder, and then hard work. And then simply ordinary life: singing, falling in love, putting your hair in curlers . . .

In the center there is always this: how unbearable and unthinkable it is to die. And how much more unbearable and unthinkable it is to kill, because a woman gives life. Gives it. Bears it in herself for a long time, nurses it. I understood that it is more difficult for women to kill.

———

MEN . . . THEY reluctantly let women into their world, onto their territory.

At the Minsk tractor factory I was looking for a woman who had served in the army as a sniper. She had been a famous sniper. The newspapers from the front had written about her more than once. Her Moscow girlfriends gave me her home phone number, but it was old. And the last name I had noted down was her maiden name. I went to the factory where I knew she worked in the personnel department, and I heard from the men (the director of the factory and the head of the personnel department): "Aren't there enough men? What do you need these women's stories for? Women's fantasies . . ." The men were afraid that women would tell about some wrong sort of war.

I visited a family . . . Both husband and wife had fought. They met at the front and got married there: "We celebrated our wedding in the trench. Before the battle. I made a white dress for myself out of a German parachute." He had been a machine gunner, she a radio operator. The man immediately sent his wife to the kitchen: "Prepare something for us." The kettle was already boiling, and the sandwiches were served, she sat down with us, but the husband immediately got her to her feet again: "Where are the strawberries? Where are our treats from the country?" After my repeated requests, he reluctantly relinquished his place, saying: "Tell it the way I taught you. Without tears and women's trifles: how you wanted to be beautiful, how you wept when they cut off your braid." Later she whispered to me: "He studied *The History of the Great Patriotic War* with me all last night. He was afraid for me. And now he's worried I won't remember right. Not the way I should."

That happened more than once, in more than one house.

Yes, they cry a lot. They shout. Swallow heart pills after I am gone. Call an ambulance. But even so they beg me: "Come. Be sure to come. We've been silent so long. Forty years . . ."

I realize that tears and cries cannot be subjected to processing, otherwise the main thing will be not the tears and cries, but the processing. Instead of life we're left with literature. Such is the material, the temperature of this material. Permanently off the charts. A human being is most visible and open in war, and maybe also in love. To the depths, to the subcutaneous layers. In the face of death all ideas pale, and inconceivable eternity opens up, for which no one is prepared. We still live in history, not in the cosmos.

Several times women sent back my transcribed text with a postscript: "No need for small details . . . Write about our great Victory . . ." But "small details" are what is most important for me, the warmth and vividness of life: a lock left on the forehead once the braid is cut; the hot kettles of kasha and soup, which no one eats, because out of a hundred persons only seven came back from the battle; or how after the war they could not go to the market and look at the rows of red meat . . . Or even at red cloth . . . "Ah, my good girl, forty years have already gone by, but you won't find anything red in my house. Ever since the war I've hated the color red!"

———

I listen to the pain . . . Pain as the proof of past life. There are no other proofs, I don't trust other proofs. Words have more than once led us away from the truth.

I think of suffering as the highest form of information, having a direct connection with mystery. With the mystery of life. All of Russian literature is about that. It has written more about suffering than about love.

And these women tell me more about it . . .

———

Who were they—Russians or Soviets? No, they were Soviets— and Russians, and Belorussians, and Ukrainians, and Tajiks . . .

Yet there was such a thing as Soviet people. I don't think such people will ever exist again, and they themselves now understand that. Even we, their children, are different. We want to be like everybody else. Not like our parents, but like the rest of the world. To say nothing of the grandchildren . . .

But I love them. I admire them. They had Stalin and the Gulag,* but they also had the Victory. And they know that.

I received a letter recently: "My daughter loves me very much; I am a heroine for her. If she reads your book, she will be greatly disappointed. Filth, lice, endless blood—that's all true. I don't deny it. But can the memory of it possibly engender noble feelings? Prepare one for a great deed . . . ?"

More than once I've realized:

. . . our memory is far from an ideal instrument. It is not only arbitrary and capricious, it is also chained to time, like a dog.

. . . we look at the past from today; we cannot look at it from anywhere else.

. . . they, too, are in love with what happened to them, because it is not only war, but also their youth. Their first love.

_____

I LISTEN WHEN THEY speak . . . I listen when they are silent . . . Both words and silence are the text for me.

—This isn't for print, it's for you . . . The older people . . . they sat on the train deep in thought . . . Sad. I remember how one major began talking to me during the night, when everybody was asleep, about Stalin. He had drunk a lot and became bold; he confessed that his father had already spent ten years in the camps without the right of correspondence.† Whether he was alive or not, no one knew. This major spoke terrible words: "I want to defend the Motherland, but I don't want to defend that traitor of the revolution—Stalin." I had

---

* Gulag is the Russian acronym for "Main Administration of Camps," i.e., the system of "corrective" forced labor camps instituted in the Soviet Union beginning in 1918.

† In Soviet legal terminology the phrase "without the right of correspondence" usually meant the prisoner had been executed.

never heard such words . . . I was frightened. Fortunately, by morning he disappeared. Probably got off . . .

—I'll tell you in secret . . . I was friends with Oksana, she was from Ukraine. It was from her that I first heard of the horrible hunger in Ukraine. Golodomor.* You couldn't even find a frog or a mouse—everything had been eaten. Half the people in her settlement died. All her younger brothers, her father and mother died, but she saved herself by stealing horse dung at the kolkhoz† stable by night and eating it. Nobody could eat it, but she did: "When it's warm it's disgusting, but you can eat it cold. Frozen is the best, it smells of hay." I said, "Oksana, Comrade Stalin is fighting. He destroys the saboteurs, but there are many." "No," she said, "you're stupid. My father was a history teacher, he said to me, 'Someday Comrade Stalin will answer for his crimes . . . '"

At night I lay there and thought: What if Oksana is the enemy? A spy? What am I to do? Two days later she was killed in combat. She had no family left, there was no one to send the death notice to . . .

I touch upon this subject carefully and rarely. They are still paralyzed not only by Stalin's hypnosis and fear, but also by their former faith. They cannot stop loving what they used to love. Courage in war and courage of thought are two different courages. I used to think they were the same.

———

THE MANUSCRIPT HAS BEEN lying on the desk for a long time . . .

For two years now I've been getting rejections from publishers.

---

* Golodomor ("holodomor" in Ukrainian) means "death by hunger." The term refers to the deliberately created famine of 1932–1933 in Ukraine, which cost many millions of lives.

† The Soviet acronym for "collective farm."

Magazines don't reply. The verdict is always the same: war is too terrible. So much horror. Naturalism. No leading and guiding role of the Communist Party. In short, not the right kind of war . . . What is the right kind? With generals and a wise generalissimo? Without blood and lice? With heroes and great deeds? But I remember from childhood: my grandmother and I are walking beside a big field, and she tells me: "After the war nothing grew in this field for a long time. The Germans were retreating . . . And there was a battle here, it went on for two days . . . The dead lay next to each other like sheaves. Like railroad ties. The Germans' and ours. After rain they all had tear-stained faces. Our whole village spent a month burying them."

How can I forget that field?

I don't simply record. I collect, I track down the human spirit wherever suffering makes a small man into a great man. Wherever a man grows. And then for me he is no longer the mute and traceless proletarian of history. With a torn-off soul. What then is my conflict with the authorities? I understood—a great idea needs a small human being, not a great one. A great one is superfluous and inconvenient for it. Hard to process. And I look for them. I look for small great human beings. Humiliated, trampled upon, insulted—having gone through Stalin's camps and treachery, these human beings came out victorious. They performed a miracle.

But the history of the war had been replaced by the history of the victory.

They themselves will tell about it . . .

SEVENTEEN YEARS LATER

2002—2004

I'm reading my old journal . . .

I'm trying to remember the person I was when I was writing this book. That person is no more, just as the country in which we then lived is no more. Yet it is that country that had been defended and in whose name people had died in the years '41 to '45. Outside the window everything is different: a new millennium, new wars, new ideas, new weapons, and the Russian (more exactly, Russian-Soviet) man changed in a totally unexpected way.

Gorbachev's perestroika began . . . * My book was published at once, in an astonishing printing—two million copies. This was a time when many startling things were happening, when we again furiously tore off somewhere. Again into the future. We still did not know (or else forgot) that revolution is always an illusion, especially in our history. But that would come later, and at the time everybody was drunk with the air of freedom. I began to receive dozens of letters daily, my folders were swelling. People wanted to talk . . . to finish talking . . . They became more free and more open. I had no doubt that I was doomed to go on writing my books endlessly. Not rewriting, but writing. A full stop immediately turns into an ellipsis . . .

———

I THINK THAT TODAY I would probably ask different questions and hear different answers. And would write a different book—not entirely different, but still different. The documents (the ones I deal with) are living witnesses; they don't harden like cooled clay. They don't grow mute. They move together with us. What would I ask more about now? What would I like to add? I would be interested in . . . I'm hunting for the word . . . the biological human being, not just the human being of time and ideas. I would try to delve deeper into human nature, into the darkness, into the subconscious. Into the mystery of war.

I would write about my visit to a former partisan fighter. A heavyset but still beautiful woman. She told me how her group (she was the oldest, plus two adolescents) went on a scouting mission and accidentally captured four Germans. They circled about in the forest with

* Gorbachev's perestroika: The "restructuring" begun in 1986 under Mikhail Gorbachev (1933–), the last General Secretary of the Communist Party and head of state until the dissolution of the Soviet Union in 1991.

them for a long time. Ran into an ambush. It became clear that they would not be able to break through with the captives and get away, and she made a decision—to dispose of them. The adolescents would not have been able to kill them; they had been wandering together in the forest for a few days, and when you spend that much time with a person, even a stranger, you get used to him, he becomes close—you know how he eats, how he sleeps, what kind of eyes and hands he has. No, the adolescents couldn't do it. That became clear to her at once. So she had to kill them. She recalled how she did it. She had to deceive her own people and the Germans. She supposedly went to fetch water with one German and shot him from behind. In the head. She took another to gather brushwood . . . I was shocked to hear her tell it so calmly.

Those who were in the war remember that it took three days for a civilian to turn into a military man. Why are three days enough? Or is that also a myth? Most likely. A human being in war is all the more unfamiliar and incomprehensible.

I read in all the letters: "I didn't tell you everything then, because it was a different time. We were used to keeping quiet about many things . . ." "I didn't confide everything to you. Not long ago it was impossible to speak about it. Or embarrassing." "I know the doctors' verdict: my diagnosis is terrible . . . I want to tell the whole truth . . ."

And recently this letter came: "For us old people life is hard . . . But not because our pensions are small and humiliating. What wounds us most of all is that we have been driven from a great past into an unbearably small present. No one invites us anymore to appear at schools, in museums, we are not needed anymore. In the newspapers, if you read them, the fascists become more and more noble, and the Red soldiers become more and more terrible."

Time is also the Motherland . . . But I love them as before. I don't love their time, but I do love them.

EVERYTHING CAN BECOME LITERATURE . . .

In my archives I was interested most of all in the notebooks where I wrote down the episodes crossed out by the censors. And my conversations with the censors as well. I also found there pages that I had thrown out myself. My self-censorship, my own ban. And my explanation— why I had thrown them out. Many of these and other things have been restored in the book, but I would like to give these few pages separately— they also make a document. My path.

FROM WHAT THE CENSORS
THREW OUT

—I just woke up in the night . . . It's as if somebody's . . . crying nearby . . . I'm at the front . . .

We're retreating . . . Beyond Smolensk some woman gives me her dress, and I manage to change my clothes. I'm alone . . . among men. I was wearing trousers, but now I march in a summer dress. Suddenly I begin to have my . . . woman's thing . . . It started early, probably from the agitation. From being nervous, upset. There was nowhere to find what I needed. I was embarrassed! So embarrassed! People slept under bushes, in ditches, on stumps in the forest. There were so many of us, there was no room in the forest for everybody. We went on bewildered, deceived, trusting nobody anymore . . . Where was our air force, where were our tanks? Everything that flew, drove, rumbled—was all German.

In that state I was captured. On the last day before I was captured, both of my legs got broken . . . I lay there and peed under myself . . . I don't know where I found strength to crawl away by night to the forest . . . The partisans chanced to pick me up.

I'm sorry for those who will read this book, and for those who won't . . .

———

—I was on night duty . . . Went to the ward of the badly wounded. There was a captain there . . . The doctors warned me before I started my shift that he would die during the night. Wouldn't make it till morning . . . I ask him: "How are things? Anything I can do for you?" I'll never forget it . . . He suddenly smiled, such a bright smile on his haggard face: "Unbutton your coat . . . Show me your breast . . . I haven't seen my wife for so long . . ." I was totally at a loss, I'd never even been kissed before. I gave him some answer. I ran away and came back an hour later.

He lay dead. And still had that smile on his face . . .

—Near Kerch . . . We went on a barge at night under shelling. The bow caught fire . . . The fire crept along the deck. Our store of ammunition exploded . . . a powerful explosion! So violent that the barge tilted on the right side and began to sink. The bank wasn't far away, we knew the bank was somewhere close by, and the soldiers threw themselves into the water. There was machine-gun fire from the bank. Shouts, moans, curses . . . I was a good swimmer, I wanted to save at least one of them. At least one wounded man . . . This was in the water, not on dry land—a wounded man perishes at once. Goes to the bottom . . . I heard somebody next to me come up to the surface, then sink down again. Up—then down. I seized the moment and grabbed hold of him . . . Something cold, slimy . . . I decided it was a wounded man, and his clothes had been torn off by the explosion. Because I was naked myself . . . Just in my underwear . . . Pitch dark. Around me: "Ohh! Aiie!" and curses . . . I somehow made it to the bank with him . . . Just then there was the flash of a rocket, and I saw that I was holding a big wounded fish. A big fish, the size of a man. A white sturgeon . . . It was dying . . . I fell down beside it and ripped out some sort of well-rounded curse. I wept from rancor . . . And from the fact that everybody was suffering . . .

———

—We were trying to get out of an encirclement . . . Wherever we went, there were Germans. We decided that in the morning we would fight our way through. We were going to die anyway, it was better to die with dignity. In combat. There were three girls with us. They came during the night to each of us who could . . . Of course, not everybody was able to. Nerves, you understand. That sort of thing . . . Each of us was preparing to die . . .

A few of us survived till morning . . . Very few . . . Well, maybe seven men, and we had been fifty, if not more. The Germans cut us down with machine-gun fire . . . I remember those girls with gratitude. In the morning I didn't find a one of them among the living . . . Never ran into them again . . .

FROM A CONVERSATION
WITH THE CENSOR

—Who will go to fight after such books? You humiliate women with a primitive naturalism. Heroic women. You dethrone them. You make them into ordinary women, females. But our women are saints.

   —*Our heroism is sterile, it leaves no room for physiology or biology. It's not believable. War tested not only the spirit but the body, too. The material shell.*

—Where did you get such thoughts? Alien thoughts. Not Soviet. You laugh at those who lie in communal graves. You've read too much Remarque . . . * Remarquism won't get you anywhere with us. A Soviet woman is not an animal . . .

———

—Somebody betrayed us . . . The Germans found out where the camp of our partisan unit was. They cordoned off the forest and the

* The German novelist Erich Maria Remarque (1898–1970) is best known for his novel *All Quiet on the Western Front* (1928), about the harsh experiences of German soldiers during World War I. His works were banned and publicly burned by the Nazis in 1933.

approaches to it on all sides. We hid in the wild thickets, we were saved by the swamps where the punitive forces didn't go. A quagmire. It sucked in equipment and people for good. For days, for weeks, we stood up to our necks in water. Our radio operator was a woman who had recently given birth. The baby was hungry . . . It had to be nursed . . . But the mother herself was hungry and had no milk. The baby cried. The punitive forces were close . . . With dogs . . . If the dogs heard it, we'd all be killed. The whole group—thirty of us . . . You understand?

The commander makes a decision . . .

Nobody can bring himself to give the mother his order, but she figures it out herself. She lowers the swaddled baby into the water and holds it there for a long time . . . The baby doesn't cry anymore . . . Not a sound . . . And we can't raise our eyes. Neither to the mother nor to each other . . .

—We took prisoners, brought them to the detachment . . . We didn't shoot them, that was too easy a death for them; we stuck them with ramrods like pigs, we cut them to pieces. I went to look at it . . . I waited! I waited a long time for the moment when their eyes would begin to burst from pain . . . The pupils . . .

What do you know about it?! They burned my mother and little sisters on a bonfire in the middle of our village . . .

—I don't remember any cats or dogs during the war, I remember rats. Big . . . with yellow-blue eyes . . . There were huge numbers of them. When I recovered from a wound, I was sent back to my unit from the hospital. The unit was stationed in the trenches near Stalingrad. The commander ordered: "Take her to the girls' dugout." I entered the dugout and first of all was surprised that there was nothing in it. Empty beds of fir branches and that's all. They didn't warn me . . . I left my knapsack in the dugout and stepped out. When I came back half an hour later I didn't find my knapsack. Not a trace of anything, no hair comb, no pencil. It turned out the rats instantly devoured everything . . .

In the morning they showed me the gnawed hands of the badly wounded . . .

Not even in the most horrible film did I see how the rats leave before the bombing of a town. This wasn't at Stalingrad . . . This was already near Vyazma . . . In the morning swarms of rats went through the town, heading for the fields. They sensed death. There were thousands of them . . . Black, gray . . . People watched this sinister spectacle in horror and pressed against the houses. And precisely at the moment when the rats disappeared from sight, the bombing began. Planes came flying. Instead of houses and basements only rubble was left . . .

—There were so many people killed at Stalingrad that horses stopped being afraid. Usually they're afraid of the dead. A horse will never step on a dead man. We gathered our own dead, but there were Germans lying about everywhere. Frozen . . . Icy . . . I was a driver, I transported crates of artillery shells, I heard their skulls crack under the wheels . . . the bones . . . And I was happy . . .

FROM A CONVERSATION
WITH THE CENSOR

—Yes, we paid heavily for the Victory, but you should look for heroic examples. There are hundreds of them. And you show the filth of the war. The underwear. You make our Victory terrible . . . What is it you're after?

—*The truth.*

—You think the truth is what's there in life. In the street. Under your feet. It's such a low thing for you. Earthly. No, the truth is what we dream about. It's how we want to be!

———

—We advance . . . The first German villages . . . We're young. Strong. Four years without women. There's wine in the cellars. Food. We'd catch German girls and . . . Ten men violated one girl . . . There weren't enough women, the population fled before the Soviet army, we found very young ones. Twelve or thirteen years old . . . If she cried, we'd beat her, stuff something into her mouth. It was painful for her, but funny for us. Now I don't understand how I could . . . A boy from a cultivated family . . . But I did it . . .

The only thing we were afraid of was that our own girls would find out about it. Our nurses. We were ashamed before them . . .

—We were encircled . . . We wandered in the forests, over the swamps. Ate leaves, tree bark. Some sort of roots. There were five of us, one a very young boy, just called up for the army. At night my neighbor whispers to me: "The boy's half dead, he'll die anyway. You get me . . ." "What do you mean?" "An ex-convict once told me . . . When they escaped from the labor camp, they purposely took a young man with them . . . Human flesh is edible . . . That's how they stayed alive . . ."

I didn't have strength enough to hit him. The next day we ran into some partisans . . .

—In the afternoon the partisans rode into the village on horseback. They led the village headman and his son out of their house. They beat them on the head with iron rods till they fell down. And finished them off on the ground. I sat by the window. I saw everything . . . My older brother was among the partisans . . . When he came into our house and wanted to embrace me—"Sister dear!"—I shouted: "Don't come near me! Don't come near me! You're a murderer!" Then I went dumb. Couldn't speak for a month.

My brother was killed . . . What would have happened if he had stayed alive? And come back home . . .

—In the morning the punitive forces set fire to our village . . . Only those who fled to the forest survived. They fled with nothing, empty-handed, didn't take even bread. No eggs or lard. During the night Aunt Nastya, our neighbor, beat her daughter because she cried all the time. Aunt Nastya had her five children with her. Yulechka, my friend, was the weakest. She was always sick . . . And the four boys, all of them little, also asked to eat all the time. And Aunt Nastya went crazy: "Ooo . . . Ooo . . ." And in the night I heard . . . Yulechka begged, "Mama, don't drown me. I won't . . . I won't ask to eat anymore. I won't . . ."

In the morning there was no Yulechka to be seen . . .

Aunt Nastya . . . We went back to the embers of the village . . . It had burned down. Soon Aunt Nastya hanged herself from the charred apple tree in her garden. She hung very, very low. Her children stood around her asking to eat . . .

FROM A CONVERSATION
WITH THE CENSOR

—This is a lie! This is slander against our soldiers, who liberated half of Europe. Against our partisans. Against our heroic people. We don't need your little history, we need the big history. The history of the Victory. You don't love our heroes! You don't love our great ideas. The ideas of Marx and Lenin.

—*True, I don't love great ideas. I love the little human being . . .*

FROM WHAT I THREW OUT MYSELF

—1941 . . . We were encircled. With our political instructor, Lunin . . . He read us the order, that Soviet soldiers do not surrender to the enemy. With us, as Comrade Stalin said, there are no prisoners, there are only traitors. The boys drew their pistols . . . The political instructor ordered: "Don't. Go on living, boys, you're young." And he shot himself . . .

And now it's 1943 . . . The Soviet army is advancing. We're moving through Belorussia. I remember a little boy. He ran out to us from somewhere under the ground, some basement, and shouted, "Kill my mama . . . Kill her! She loved a German . . ." His eyes were round from fear. An old woman in black ran after him. All in black. She was running and crossing herself: "Don't listen to the child. The child's gone crazy . . ."

—I was summoned to school . . . A teacher who had just returned from evacuation talked to me:

"I want to transfer your son to another class. In my class I have the best pupils."

"But my son has high grades."

"That doesn't matter. The boy lived under the Germans."

"Yes, it was hard for us."

"That's not the point. All those who were in occupied territories . . . They are under suspicion . . ."

"What? I don't understand . . ."

"He tells other children about the Germans. And he stutters."

"That's because he was frightened. The German officer who was billeted with us gave him a beating. He didn't like how my son polished his boots."

"You see . . . You yourself admit . . . You lived alongside the enemy . . ."

"And who let that enemy get as far as Moscow? Who left us here with our children?"

I was in hysterics . . .

For two days I was afraid the teacher would denounce me. But she kept my son in her class . . .

—During the day we were afraid of the Germans and the *polizei** and during the night of the partisans. The partisans took my last cow, I had only a cat left. The partisans were starved, angry. They took my cow, and I followed them . . . I walked about seven miles. I begged them to give it back. I left three hungry children at home by the stove. "Go back, woman!" they threatened. "Or else we'll shoot you."

Try finding a good man during the war . . .

People turned against each other. The children of the kulaks† came back from exile. Their parents had been killed, and they served the German forces. They took their revenge. One of them shot an old teacher in his cottage. Our neighbor. This neighbor had once denounced his father and had taken part in dispossessing him. He was a fervent Communist.

At first the Germans disbanded the kolkhozes and gave people the land. People breathed more freely after Stalin. We paid quitrent . . . Paid it accurately . . . And then they began to burn us. Us and our houses. They drove the livestock away and burned the people . . .

Aie, daughter dear, I'm afraid of words. Words are scary . . . I saved myself by doing good, I didn't wish evil on anyone. I pitied them all . . .

—I went with the army as far as Berlin . . .

I came back to my village with two Medals of Honor and some

---

*   German for "police," but the term was also applied to Russian collaborators.

†   Originally a term for wealthy independent peasant farmers; under the Soviets it became a derogatory label for any peasants who resisted the forced collectivization of agriculture. Kulaks were arrested and either shot or sent to hard labor in Siberia.

decorations. I spent three days there, and on the fourth my mother got me up early, while everybody was asleep: "Daughter dear, I've prepared a bundle for you. Go away . . . Go away . . . You have two younger sisters growing up. Who will marry them? Everybody knows you spent four years at the front, with men . . ."

Don't touch my soul. Write, as the others do, about my decorations . . .

—War is war. It's not some kind of theater . . .

They had our unit form up in a clearing; we stood in a ring. In the middle were Misha K. and Kolya M.—our boys. Misha was a brave scout, he played the accordion. And nobody sang better than Kolya . . .

They spent a long time reading the sentence: in such-and-such village they had demanded two bottles of moonshine, and at night . . . raped their host's two daughters . . . And in such-and-such village they robbed a peasant of an overcoat and a sewing machine . . . which they went and exchanged for drink at the neighbors' . . .

They were sentenced to be shot . . . The sentence was final and without appeal.

Who will do the shooting? The unit is silent . . . Who? We're silent . . . The commander himself carried out the sentence . . .

—I was a machine gunner. I killed so many . . .

For a long time after the war I was afraid to have children. I gave birth to a child when I calmed down. Seven years later . . .

But I still haven't forgiven anything. And I won't . . . I was glad when I saw German prisoners. I was glad that they were pitiful to look at: footwraps on their feet instead of boots, footwraps on their heads . . . They were led through the villages and they asked, "*Mother, give brot . . . Brot . . .*" I was astonished that peasants came out of their cottages and gave them—one a piece of bread, another a potato . . .

Boys ran after the column and threw stones . . . But the women wept . . .

It seems to me that I've lived two lives: one a man's, the other a woman's . . .

—After the war . . . Human life was worthless. I'll give you an example . . . I'm riding on a bus after work; suddenly there's shouting: "Stop thief! Stop thief! My purse . . ." The bus stops . . . A crowd forms at once. A young officer takes a boy outside, puts his arm on his knee and—whack!—breaks it in two. Jumps back on the bus . . . And we go on . . . Nobody defended the boy, nobody called a policeman. A doctor. The officer had his whole chest covered with combat decorations . . . I was getting off at my stop, he hopped down and gave me his hand: "Allow me, Miss . . ." Such a gallant one . . .

I've just remembered it . . . At the time we were all still people of the war, we lived by the laws of wartime. Are they human at all?

—The Red Army came back . . .

We were allowed to dig up the graves, to search for where our families had been shot. By an old custom you have to wear white next to death—a white kerchief, a white shirt. I'll remember it to my last breath! People went with white embroidered towels . . . Dressed all in white . . . Where did they get it?

We dug . . . Whatever we found and recognized we took. One brought an arm in a wheelbarrow, another a head in a cart . . . A man doesn't stay whole in the ground for long, they were all mixed up together. With clay, with sand.

I didn't find my sister, but I thought that a scrap of a dress was hers, it looked familiar . . . Grandfather also said, "Take it, there'll be something to bury." We put this piece of a dress into a little coffin . . .

We got a notice that my father was "missing in action." Others got something for those who had been killed, but my mother and I got a scare in the village council: "You're not entitled to any aid. It may be he's living in clover with some German Frau. An enemy of the people."

I began to look for my father under Khrushchev.* Forty years later, under Gorbachev, I received an answer: "Not listed in the records . . ." But his regimental comrade wrote to me and I found out that my father had died a hero. He had thrown himself with a grenade under a tank at Mogilev† . . .

It's a pity my mother didn't live to get this news. She died branded as the wife of an enemy of the people. A traitor. There were many like her. They didn't live to learn the truth. I went to mother's grave with this letter. Read it . . .

—Many of us believed . . .

We thought that after the war everything would change . . . Stalin would trust his people. But the war was not yet over, and the troop trains were already going to Magadan.‡ Troop trains with the victors . . . Those who had been captured, those who had survived the German camps, those whom the Germans had taken along to work for them—all those who had seen Europe—were arrested. Those who could tell how people there lived. Without Communists. What kind of houses they had and what kind of roads. And that there were no kolkhozes . . .

After the Victory everybody became silent. Silent and afraid, as before the war . . .

---

* Nikita Khrushchev (1894–1971), who became First Secretary of the Communist Party in 1953, at Stalin's death, and later served as premier, instituted the process of "de-Stalinization" of the Soviet Union, beginning with the 20th Party Congress in 1956.

† Mogilev, an old city in Belorussia, was taken by the Nazis in 1941 and retaken by the Soviets in 1944. Its large Jewish population was exterminated.

‡ A city and territory in the far east of Russia, which became the center for a vast labor-camp system established by Stalin in 1932.

———

—I'm a history teacher . . . Within my memory the history textbook has been rewritten three times. I taught children with three different textbooks . . .

Ask us while we're alive. Don't rewrite afterward without us. Ask . . .

Do you know how hard it is to kill a human being? I worked in the underground. After six months I was sent on a mission—to take a job as a waitress in a German officers' mess . . . I was young, beautiful . . . They hired me. I was supposed to put poison into the soup cauldron and leave for the partisans the same day. I had already grown used to them; they were the enemy, but I saw them every day, they said, "*Danke schön . . . Danke schön . . .*" It was hard . . . To kill is hard . . . To kill is more terrible than to die . . .

I've taught history all my life . . . And I never knew how to tell about that . . . In what words . . .

———

I HAD MY OWN war . . . I went a long way together with my heroines. Just like them, for a long time I did not believe that our Victory had two faces—one beautiful and the other terrible, all scars—unbearable to look at. "In hand-to-hand combat, when you kill a man, you look him in the eye. It's not like throwing bombs or shooting from a trench," they told me.

Listening to how a person killed or died is the same—you look him in the eye . . .

THE
UNWOMANLY
FACE
OF WAR

"I DON'T WANT
TO REMEMBER . . ."

———

An old three-story house on the outskirts of Minsk, one of those built hastily just after the war and, as it then seemed, not meant to last, now cozily overgrown with old jasmine bushes. With it began a search that went on for seven years, seven extraordinary and tormenting years, during which I was to discover for myself the world of war, a world the meaning of which we cannot fully fathom. I would experience pain, hatred, temptation. Tenderness and perplexity . . . I would try to understand what distinguishes death from murder and where the boundary is between the human and the inhuman. How does a human being remain alone with the insane thought that he or she might kill another human being? Is even obliged to? And I would discover that in war there is, apart from death, a multitude of other things; there is everything that is in our ordinary life. War is also life. I would run into countless human truths. Mysteries. I would ponder questions the existence of which I had never suspected. For instance, why is it that we are not surprised at evil, why this absence in us of surprise in the face of evil?

A road and many roads . . . Dozens of trips all over the country, hundreds of recorded cassettes, thousands of yards of tape. Five hundred meetings, after which I stopped counting; faces left my memory, only voices remained. A chorus resounds in my memory. An enormous chorus; sometimes the words almost cannot be heard, only the weeping. I confess: I did not always believe that I was strong enough for this path, that I could make it. Could reach the end. There were moments of doubt and fear, when I wanted to stop or step aside, but I no longer could. I fell captive to evil, I looked into the abyss in order to understand something. Now I seem to have acquired some knowledge, but there are still more questions, and fewer answers.

But then, at the very beginning of the path, I had no suspicion of that . . .

What led me to this house was a short article in the local newspaper about a farewell party given at the Udarnik automobile factory in Minsk for the senior accountant Maria Ivanovna Morozova, who was retiring. During the war, the article said, she had been a sniper, had eleven combat decorations, and her total as a sniper was seventy-five killings. It was hard to bring together mentally this woman's wartime profession with her peacetime occupation. With the routine newspaper photograph. With all these tokens of the ordinary.

. . . A small woman with a long braid wound in a girlish crown around her head was sitting in a big armchair, covering her face with her hands.

"No, no, I won't. Go back there again? I can't . . . To this day I can't watch war movies. I was very young then. I dreamed and grew, grew and dreamed. And then—the war. I even feel sorry for you . . . I know what I'm talking about . . . Do you really want to know that? I ask you like a daughter . . ."

Of course she was surprised.

"But why me? You should talk to my husband, he likes to remember . . . The names of the commanders, the generals, the numbers of units—he remembers everything. I don't. I only remember what happened to me. My own war. There were lots of people around, but you were always alone, because a human being is always alone in the face of death. I remember the terrifying solitude."

She asked me to take the tape recorder away.

"I need your eyes in order to tell about it, and that will hinder me."

But a few minutes later she forgot about it . . .

Maria Ivanovna Morozova (Ivanushkina)
CORPORAL, SNIPER

This will be a simple story . . . The story of an ordinary Russian girl, of whom there were many then . . .

The place where my native village, Diakovskoe, stood is now the Proletarian District of Moscow. When the war began, I was not quite eighteen. Long, long braids, down to my knees . . . Nobody believed the war would last, everybody expected it to end any moment. We would drive out the enemy. I worked on a kolkhoz, then finished accounting school and began to work. The war went on . . . My girlfriends . . . They tell me: "We should go to the front." It was already in the air. We all signed up and took classes at the local recruitment office. Maybe some did it just to keep one another company, I don't know. They taught us to shoot a combat rifle, to throw hand grenades. At first . . . I'll confess, I was afraid to hold a rifle, it was unpleasant. I couldn't imagine that I'd go and kill somebody, I just wanted to go to the front. We had forty people in our group. Four girls from our village, so we were all friends; five from our neighbors'; in short—some from each village. All of them girls . . . The men had all gone to the war already, the ones who could. Sometimes a messenger came in the middle of the night, gave them two hours to get ready, and they'd be carted off. They could even be taken right from the fields. (*Silence.*) I don't remember now—whether we had dances; if we did, the girls danced with girls, there were no boys left. Our villages became quiet.

Soon an appeal came from the central committee of Komsomol[*] for the young people to go and defend the Motherland, since the Germans were already near Moscow. Hitler take Moscow? We won't allow it! I wasn't the only one . . . All our girls expressed the wish to go to the front. My father was already fighting. We thought we were the only ones like that . . . Special ones . . . But we came to the re-

---

[*]   Soviet acronym for "League of Communist Youth."

cruitment office and there were lots of girls there. I just gasped! My
heart was on fire, so intensely. The selection was very strict. First of
all, of course, you had to have robust health. I was afraid they wouldn't
take me, because as a child I was often sick, and my frame was weak,
as my mother used to say. Other children insulted me because of it
when I was little. And then, if there were no other children in a household except the girl who wanted to go to the front, they also refused:
a mother should not be left by herself. Ah, our darling mothers! Their
tears never dried . . . They scolded us, they begged . . . But in our
family there were two sisters and two brothers left—true, they were
all much younger than me, but it counted anyway. There was one
more thing: everybody from our kolkhoz was gone, there was nobody to work in the fields, and the chairman didn't want to let us go.
In short, they refused us. We went to the district committee of Komsomol, and there—refusal. Then we went as a delegation from our
district to the regional Komsomol. There was great inspiration in all
of us; our hearts were on fire. Again we were sent home. We decided,
since we were in Moscow, to go to the central committee of Komsomol, to the top, to the first secretary. To carry through to the end . . .
Who would be our spokesman? Who was brave enough? We thought
we would surely be the only ones there, but it was impossible even to
get into the corridor, let alone to reach the secretary. There were
young people from all over the country, many of whom had been
under occupation, spoiling to be revenged for the death of their near
ones. From all over the Soviet Union. Yes, yes . . . In short, we were
even taken aback for a while . . .

By evening we got to the secretary after all. They asked us: "So,
how can you go to the front if you don't know how to shoot?" And we
said in a chorus that we had already learned to shoot . . . "Where? . . .
How? . . . And can you apply bandages?" You know, in that group at
the recruiting office our local doctor taught us to apply bandages. That
shut them up, and they began to look at us more seriously. Well, we
had another trump card in our hands, that we weren't alone, there were
forty of us, and we could all shoot and give first aid. They told us: "Go

and wait. Your question will be decided in the affirmative." How happy we were as we left! I'll never forget it . . . Yes, yes . . .

And literally in a couple of days we received our call-up papers . . .

We came to the recruiting office; we went in one door at once and were let out another. I had such a beautiful braid, and I came out without it . . . Without my braid . . . They gave me a soldier's haircut . . . They also took my dress. I had no time to send the dress or the braid to my mother . . . She very much wanted to have something of mine left with her . . . We were immediately dressed in army shirts, forage caps, given kit bags and loaded into a freight train—on straw. But fresh straw, still smelling of the field.

We were a cheerful cargo. Cocky. Full of jokes. I remember laughing a lot.

Where were we going? We didn't know. In the end it was not so important to us what we'd be. So long as it was at the front. Everybody was fighting—and we would be, too. We arrived at the Shchelkovo station. Near it was a women's sniper school. It turned out we were sent there. To become snipers. We all rejoiced. This was something real. We'd be shooting.

We began to study. We studied the regulations: of garrison service, of discipline, of camouflage in the field, of chemical protection. The girls all worked very hard. We learned to assemble and disassemble a sniper's rifle with our eyes shut, to determine wind speed, the movement of the target, the distance to the target, to dig a foxhole, to crawl on our stomach—we had already mastered all that. Only so as to get to the front the sooner. In the line of fire . . . Yes, yes . . . At the end of the course I got the highest grade in the exam for combat and noncombat service. The hardest thing, I remember, was to get up at the sound of the alarm and be ready in five minutes. We chose boots one or two sizes larger, so as not to lose time getting into them. We had five minutes to dress, put our boots on, and line up. There were times when we ran out to line up in boots over bare feet. One girl almost had her feet frostbitten. The sergeant major noticed it, reprimanded her, and then taught us to use footwraps. He stood over us and droned: "How am I to make soldiers out of you, my dear girls, and not targets for Fritz?" Dear girls, dear girls . . . Everybody loved us and pitied us all the time. And we resented being pitied. Weren't we soldiers like everybody else?

Well, so we got to the front. Near Orsha . . . The 62nd Infantry Division . . . I remember like today, the commander, Colonel Borodkin, saw us and got angry: "They've foisted girls on me. What is this, some sort of women's round dance?" he said. "Corps de ballet! It's war, not a dance. A terrible war . . ." But then he invited us, treated us to a dinner. And we heard him ask his adjutant: "Don't we have something sweet for tea?" Well, of course, we were offended: What does he take us for? We came to make war . . . And he received us not as soldiers, but as young girls. At our age we could have been his daughters. "What am I going to do with you, my dears? Where did they find you?" That's how he treated us, that's how he met us. And we thought we were already seasoned warriors . . . Yes, yes . . . At war!

The next day he made us show that we knew how to shoot, how to camouflage ourselves in the field. We did the shooting well, even better than the men snipers, who were called from the front for two days of training, and who were very surprised that we were doing their work. It was probably the first time in their lives they saw women snipers. After the shooting it was camouflage in the field . . . The colonel came, walked around looking at the clearing, then stepped on a hummock—saw nothing. Then the "hummock" under him begged: "Ow, Comrade Colonel, I can't anymore, you're too heavy." How we laughed! He couldn't believe it was possible to camouflage oneself so well. "Now," he said, "I take back my words about young girls." But even so he suffered . . . Couldn't get used to us for a long time.

Then came the first day of our "hunting" (so snipers call it). My partner was Masha Kozlova. We camouflaged ourselves and lay there: I'm on the lookout, Masha's holding her rifle. Suddenly Masha says: "Shoot, shoot! See—it's a German . . ."

I say to her: "I'm the lookout. You shoot!"

"While we're sorting it out," she says, "he'll get away."

But I insist: "First we have to lay out the shooting map, note the landmarks: where the shed is, where the birch tree . . ."

"You want to start fooling with paperwork like at school? I've come to shoot, not to mess with paperwork!"

I see that Masha is already angry with me.

"Well, shoot then, why don't you?"

We were bickering like that. And meanwhile, in fact, the German officer was giving orders to the soldiers. A wagon arrived, and the soldiers formed a chain and handed down some sort of freight. The officer stood there, gave orders, then disappeared. We're still arguing. I see he's already appeared twice, and if we miss him again, that will be it. We'll lose him. And when he appeared for the third time—it was just momentary; now he's there, now he's gone—I decided to shoot. I decided, and suddenly a thought flashed through my mind: he's a human being; he may be an enemy, but he's a human being— and my hands began to tremble, I started trembling all over, I got chills. Some sort of fear . . . That feeling sometimes comes back to me in dreams even now . . . After the plywood targets, it was hard to shoot at a living person. I see him in the telescopic sight, I see him very well. As if he's close . . . And something in me resists . . . Something doesn't let me, I can't make up my mind. But I got hold of myself, I pulled the trigger . . . He waved his arms and fell. Whether he was dead or not, I didn't know. But after that I trembled still more, some sort of terror came over me: I killed a man?! I had to get used even to the thought of it. Yes . . . In short—horrible! I'll never forget it . . .

When we came back, we started telling our platoon what had happened to us. They called a meeting. We had a Komsomol leader, Klava Ivanova; she reassured me: "They should be hated, not pitied . . ." Her father had been killed by the fascists. We would start singing, and she would beg us: "No, don't, dear girls. Let's first defeat these vermin, then we'll sing."

And not right away . . . We didn't manage right away. It's not a woman's task—to hate and to kill. Not for us . . . We had to persuade ourselves. To talk ourselves into it . . .

A few days later Maria Ivanovna would call and invite me to see her war friend Klavdia Grigoryevna Krokhina. And once again I would hear . . .

Klavdia Grigoryevna Krokhina
FIRST SERGEANT, SNIPER

The first time is frightening . . . Very frightening . . .

We were in hiding, and I was the lookout. And then I noticed one German poking up a little from a trench. I clicked, and he fell. And then, you know, I started shaking all over, I heard my bones knocking. I cried. When I shot at targets it was nothing, but now: I—killed! I killed some unknown man. I knew nothing about him, but I killed him.

Then it passed. And here's how . . . It happened like this . . . We were already on the advance. We marched past a small settlement. I think it was in Ukraine. And there by the road we saw a barrack or a house, it was impossible to tell, it was all burned down, nothing left but blackened stones. A foundation . . . Many of the girls didn't go close to it, but it was as if something drew me there . . . There were human bones among the cinders, with scorched little stars among them; these were our wounded or prisoners who had been burned. After that, however many I killed, I felt no pity. I had seen those blackened little stars . . .

. . . I came back from the war gray-haired. Twenty-one years old, but my hair was completely white. I had been badly wounded, had a concussion, poor hearing in one ear. Mama met me with the words: "I believed you'd come back. I prayed for you day and night." My brother had fallen at the front.

Mama lamented: "It's all the same now—to give birth to girls or boys. But still he was a man, he had to defend the Motherland, but you're a girl. I asked one thing of God, that if they disfigure you, better let them kill you. I went to the train station all the time. To meet the trains. Once I saw a girl soldier there with a burned face . . . I shuddered—you! Afterward I prayed for her, too."

In the Chelyabinsk region, where I was born, they were doing some sort of mining not far from our house. As soon as the blasting began—it was always during the night for some reason—I instantly jumped out of the bed and grabbed my coat first thing—and ran, I had to run somewhere quickly. Mama would catch me, press me to her, and talk to me: "Wake up, wake up. The war is over. You're home." I would come to my senses at her words: "I'm your mama. Mama . . ." She spoke softly. Softly . . . Loud talk frightened me . . .

The room is warm, but Klavdia Grigoryevna wraps herself in a heavy plaid blanket—she is cold. She goes on:

We quickly turned into soldiers . . . You know, there was no real time to think. To dwell on our feelings . . .

Our scouts took a German officer prisoner, and he was extremely surprised that so many soldiers had been killed at his position, and all with shots in the head. Almost in the same spot. A simple rifleman, he insisted, would be unable to make so many hits to the head. That's certain. "Show me," he asked, "the rifleman who killed so many of my soldiers. I received a large reinforcement, but every day up to ten men fell." The commander of the regiment says: "Unfortunately, I cannot show you. It was a girl sniper, but she was killed." It was our Sasha Shliakhova. She died in a snipers' duel. And what betrayed her was her red scarf. She liked that scarf very much. But a red scarf is visible against white snow. When the German officer heard that it was a girl, he was staggered, he didn't know how to react. He was silent for a long time. At the last interrogation before he was sent to Moscow (he turned out to be a bigwig), he confessed: "I've never fought with women. You're all beautiful . . . And our propaganda tells us that it's hermaphrodites and not women who fight in the Red Army . . ." So he understood nothing. No . . . I can't forget . . .

We went in pairs. It's very hard to sit alone from sunup to sundown; your eyes get tired, watery, your hands lose their feeling, your whole body goes numb with tension. It's especially hard in spring. The snow melts under you; you spend the whole day in water. You float in it; sometimes you freeze to the ground. We started out at daybreak and came back from the front line when it got dark. For twelve hours or more we lay in the snow or climbed to the top of a tree, onto the roof of a shed or a ruined house, and there camouflaged ourselves, so that the enemy wouldn't see where we were observing them from. We tried to find a position as close as possible: seven or eight hundred, sometimes only five hundred yards separated us from the trenches where the Germans sat. Early in the morning we could even hear their talk. Laughter.

I don't know why we weren't afraid . . . Now I don't understand it.

We were advancing, advancing very quickly . . . And we ran out of steam, our supplies lagged behind: we ran out of ammunition, out of provisions, and the kitchen was demolished by a shell. For three days we ate nothing but dry crusts; our tongues were so scraped we couldn't move them. My partner was killed, and I went to the front line with a "new" girl. And suddenly we saw a colt on "no man's land." Such a pretty one, with a fluffy tail . . . Walking about calmly, as if there wasn't any war. And I heard the Germans make some stir, having seen him. Our soldiers also started talking among themselves.

"He'll get away. Could make a nice soup . . ."

"You can't hit him with a submachine gun at such a distance . . ."

They saw us.

"The snipers are coming. They'll get him straight off . . . Go on, girls!"

I had no time to think; out of habit I took aim and fired. The colt's legs buckled under him; he collapsed on his side. It seemed to me— maybe it was a hallucination—but it seemed to me that he gave a thin, high whinny.

Only then did it hit me: why had I done it? Such a pretty one, and I killed him, I put him into a soup! I heard someone sob behind me. I turned; it was the "new" girl.

"What's the matter?" I asked.

"I'm sorry for the colt . . ."—and her eyes were full of tears.

"Oh, oh, what a sensitive nature! And we've gone hungry for a whole three days. You're sorry because you haven't buried anyone yet. Go and try marching twenty miles a day with a full kit, and hungry to boot. First drive Fritz out and later we can get emotional. We can feel sorry. Later . . . Understand, later . . ."

I look at the soldiers who just now had egged me on, shouted. Asked me. Just now . . . A few minutes ago . . . Nobody looks at me, as if they don't notice me; each of them drops his eyes and goes about his own business. Smokes, digs . . . One is sharpening something . . . And I can do as I like. Sit down and cry. Howl! As if I'm some sort of a butcher, who doesn't mind killing just like that. But I had loved all living creatures since childhood. We had a cow—I was already going to school—and it got sick and had to be slaughtered. I cried for two days. Couldn't calm down. And here—bang!—I shot a defenseless colt. What can I say . . . It was the first colt I'd seen in two years . . .

In the evening supper was served. The cooks: "Well, young sniper! Tonight we've got meat in the pot . . ." They set down the pots and left. And my girls sat and didn't touch the supper. I understood what it was about, burst into tears, and ran out of the dugout . . . The girls ran after me, started comforting me. Then quickly grabbed their pots and began to eat . . .

Yes, that's how things were . . . Yes . . . I can't forget . . .

At night we talked, of course. What did we talk about? Of course, about home, each told about her own mother, and the father or brothers who were fighting. And about what we would do after the war. And how we would get married, and whether our husbands would love us. Our commanding officer laughed.

"Eh, you girls! You're good all around, but after the war men will be afraid to marry you. You've got good aim; you'll fling a plate at his head and kill him."

I met my husband during the war. We were in the same regiment. He was wounded twice, had a concussion. He went through the whole war, from beginning to end, and was in the military all his life afterward. Was there any need for me to explain to him what war was? Where I had come back from? How I was? Whenever I raise my voice, he either pays no attention or holds his peace. And I forgive him, too. I've also learned. We raised two children; they've both finished university. A son and a daughter.

What else can I tell you . . . So I was demobilized, came to Moscow. And to get home from Moscow I had to ride and then go several miles on foot. Now there's a subway, but then it was old cherry orchards and deep ravines. One ravine was very big, and I had to cross it. It was already dark when I got to it. Of course, I was afraid to go across that ravine. I stood there, not knowing what to do: either go back and wait for dawn, or pluck up my courage and risk it. Remembering it now, it's quite funny. I had the war behind me, what hadn't I seen, corpses and all the rest—and here I was afraid to cross a ravine. I remember to this day the smell of the corpses, mingled with the smell of cheap tobacco . . . But then I was still a young girl. Riding on the train . . . We were coming home from Germany . . . A mouse ran out of somebody's knapsack, and all our girls jumped up; the ones on the upper bunks came tumbling down, squealing. And there was a captain traveling with us; he was surprised: "You're all decorated, and you're afraid of mice."

Luckily for me, there was a truck passing by. I thought: I'll hitch a ride.

The truck stopped.

"I need to go to Diakovskoe," I shouted.

"I'm going to Diakovskoe myself." The young fellow opened the door.

I got into the cabin, he put my suitcase into the back, and off we went. He sees I'm in uniform, with decorations. He asks: "How many Germans did you kill?"

I say to him: "Seventy-five."

He says a bit mockingly: "Come on, you probably didn't lay eyes on a single one."

Then I recognized him: "Kolka Chizhov? Is it you? Remember, I helped you tie your red neckerchief?"

Before the war I had worked for a time as a Pioneer leader in my school.*

"Maruska, it's you?"

"Me . . ."

"Really?" He stopped the truck.

"Take me home! What are you doing stopping in the middle of the road?" There were tears in my eyes. And in his, too, I could see. Such a meeting!

We drove up to my house, he ran with my suitcase to my mother, danced across the courtyard with this suitcase.

"Come quick, I've brought you your daughter!"

I can't forget . . . O-oh . . . How can I forget it?

I came back, and everything had to start over from the beginning. I had to learn to wear shoes; I'd spent three years at the front wearing boots. We were used to belts, always pulled tight, and now it seemed that clothes hung baggy on us, we felt somehow awkward. I looked at skirts with horror . . . at dresses . . . We didn't wear skirts at the front, only trousers. We used to wash them in the evening and sleep on them—that counted as ironing. True, they weren't quite dry, and they would freeze stiff in the frost. How do you learn to walk in a skirt? It was like my legs got tangled. I'd go out in a civilian dress and

---

* The All-Union Pioneer Organization, for Soviet children from ten to fifteen years old, was founded in 1922. It was similar to Scout organizations in the West.

shoes, meet an officer, and involuntarily raise my hand to salute him. We were used to rationing; everything was provided by the state, so I'd go to a bakery, take as much bread as I needed, and forget to pay. The salesgirl knew me, understood why, she was embarrassed to remind me, so I wouldn't pay, I'd take it and leave. Then I'd be ashamed of myself; the next day I'd apologize, take something else, and pay for it all together. I had to learn ordinary things over again. To remember ordinary life. Normal! Who could I confide in? I'd go running to a neighbor . . . To mama . . .

I also think this . . . Listen . . . How long was the war? Four years. Very long . . . I don't remember any birds or flowers. They were there, of course, but I don't remember them. Yes, yes . . . Strange, isn't it? Can they make a color film about war? Everything was black. Only the blood was another color, the blood was red . . .

Just recently, about eight years ago, we found our Mashenka Alkhimova. The commander of the artillery division was wounded; she crawled to save him. A shell exploded right in front of her . . . The commander was killed, she didn't make it to him, and both her legs were so mangled that we were barely able to bandage her. We had a hard time with her . . . We carried her to the first-aid station, and she kept asking: "Dear girls, shoot me dead . . . I don't want to live like this . . ." She begged and pleaded . . . So! They sent her to the hospital, and we went on advancing. When we started looking for her . . . the trail was already lost. We didn't know where she was, what had become of her. For many years . . . We wrote everywhere, and nobody could tell us. The "pathfinders" of Moscow's School No. 73 helped us. Those boys, those girls . . . They found her in a veterans' home, somewhere in Altai,* thirty years after the war. So far away. All those years she had been traveling from one invalid home to another, from one hospital to another, undergoing dozens of surgeries. She didn't even tell her mother she was alive . . . She hid from every-

---

* The mountainous Altai region is in central Asia, on the border of Russia, China, and Kazakhstan.

body . . . We brought her to our reunion. We were all bathed in tears. Then we brought her together with her mother . . . They met thirty years after the war . . . Her mother almost lost her mind. "I'm so happy that my heart didn't break from grief before now. So happy!" And Mashenka repeated: "Now I'm not afraid to meet people. I'm already old." Yes . . . In short . . . That's war . . .

I remember lying at night in the dugout. I am not asleep. Somewhere there is artillery fire. Our cannons are shooting . . . I really didn't want to die . . . I gave an oath, a military oath, that if need be I'd give my life, but I really didn't want to die. Even if you come home alive, your soul will hurt. Now I think: it would be better to be wounded in an arm or a leg. Then my body would hurt, not my soul . . . It's very painful. We were so young when we went to the front. Young girls. I even grew during the war. Mama measured me at home . . . I grew four inches . . .

Saying goodbye, she awkwardly reaches her hot arms out and embraces me:
   Forgive me . . .

"GROW UP, GIRLS . . .
YOU'RE STILL GREEN . . ."

———

Voices . . . Dozens of voices . . . They descended upon me, revealing the unaccustomed truth, and that truth did not fit into the brief formula familiar from childhood—we won. An instant chemical reaction took place: pathos dissolved in the living tissue of human destinies; it turned out to be a very short-lived substance. Destiny—is when there is something else beyond the words.

What do I want to hear decades later? How things were in Moscow or Stalingrad, descriptions of military operations, the forgotten names of captured heights and hillocks? Do I need stories about the movements of sites and fronts, about advances and retreats, about the number of blown-up troop trains and partisan raids—about all that has already been written in thousands of volumes? No, I am seeking something else. I gather what I would call knowledge of the spirit. I follow the traces of inner life; I make records of the soul. For me the path of a soul is more important than the event itself. The question of "how it was" is not so important, or not the most important; it does not come first. What disturbs and frightens me is something else: What happened to human beings? What did human beings see and understand there? About life and death in general? About themselves, finally? I am writing a history of feelings . . . A history of the soul . . . Not the history of a war or a state and not the lives of heroes, but the history of small human beings, thrown out of ordinary life into the epic depths of an enormous event. Into great History.

The girls of 1941 . . . The first thing I want to ask: Where did their kind come from? Why were there so many? How is it they decided to take up arms on a par with men? To shoot, mine, blow up, bomb—kill?

Pushkin asked himself this same question in the nineteenth century, publishing in his magazine The Contemporary *an excerpt from the notes of Cavalry Maiden Nadezhda Durova,* who took part in the war with Napoleon: "What were the reasons that made a young girl from a good aristocratic family leave her ancestral home, renounce her sex, take on labors and duties that even frighten men, and turn up on the battlefield—and what a battlefield! Napoleon's. What prompted her? Secret griefs of the heart? Inflamed imagination? An inborn irrepressible inclination? Love?"*

Well, so—what?! A hundred and some years later, the same question . . .

OF OATHS AND PRAYERS

Natalya Ivanovna Sergeeva
PRIVATE, NURSE-AIDE

I want to speak . . . to speak! To speak it all out! Finally somebody wants to hear us. For so many years we said nothing, even at home we said nothing. For decades. The first year, when I came back from the war, I talked and talked. Nobody listened. So I shut up . . . It's good that you've come along. I've been waiting all the while for somebody, I knew somebody would come. Had to come. I was very young then. Absolutely young. Too bad. You know why? I didn't even know how to remember . . .

A few days before the war my girlfriend and I were talking about the war; we were certain there wouldn't be any war. We went to the movies, there was a newsreel before the film: Ribbentrop and Molo-

---

*   The daughter of a Russian officer, Nadezhda Durova (1783–1866) disguised herself as a man and served in the Russian cavalry during the Napoleonic Wars, for which she was much decorated. Her memoirs, entitled *The Cavalry Maiden*, were published in 1836.

tov were shaking hands.* The words of the narrator stamped themselves on my memory: Germany is the faithful friend of the Soviet Union.

Before the month was out German troops were already near Moscow . . .

We were eight children in our family, the first four were all girls, I was the oldest. Papa once came home from work and wept: "I used to be happy that we had girls first . . . Brides-to-be. But now in every family someone is going to the front, and we have nobody . . . I'm too old, they won't take me; you're all girls, and the boys are still little." In our family this was keenly felt.

Courses for nurses were organized, and my father took me and my sister there. I was fifteen, my sister fourteen. He said: "This is all I can offer for our victory . . . My girls . . ." There was no other thought then.

A year later I wound up at the front . . .

Elena Antonovna Kudina
PRIVATE, DRIVER

During the first days . . . Total confusion in town. Chaos. Icy fear. Everybody was catching some sort of spies. People said to each other: "Don't believe provocations." Nobody could accept even the thought that our army had suffered a catastrophe, that it had been crushed in a few weeks. We had been told that we'd make war on other countries' territory. "We won't surrender an inch of our land . . ." And we were retreating . . .

Before the war there were rumors that Hitler was preparing to attack the Soviet Union, but such talk was strictly forbidden. Certain organizations saw to that . . . You know what I mean? The NKVD . . .

---

* The Molotov-Ribbentrop Pact, named for the foreign ministers of the Soviet Union and Germany, was a nonaggression pact signed in August 1939. It was broken by the German invasion of eastern Poland in June 1941.

The Chekists . . . * If people whispered, it was at home, in the kitchen, and in the communal apartments—only in their own room, behind closed doors, or in the bathroom with water running. But when Stalin began to speak . . . He addressed us: "Brothers and sisters . . ." Then everybody forgot their grievances . . . We had an uncle sitting in a labor camp, mama's brother, a railroad worker, an old Communist. He had been arrested at work . . . You know who arrested him? The NKVD . . . Our beloved uncle, and we knew he wasn't guilty of anything. We believed it. He was decorated after the Civil War . . .† But after Stalin's speech mama said: "We'll defend the Motherland and sort it out later." Everybody loved the Motherland.

I ran to the recruiting office at once. I had angina, I still had a high temperature. But I couldn't wait . . .

<hr>

Antonina Maximovna Knyazeva

JUNIOR SERGEANT, LIAISON

Our mother had no sons . . . There were five daughters. The announcement came: "War!" I had an excellent musical ear. Dreamed of studying at the conservatory. I decided that my ear would be of use at the front, that I'd be a liaison.

We were evacuated to Stalingrad. And when Stalingrad was besieged, we volunteered to go to the front. All together. The whole family: mother and five daughters; my father was already fighting by then . . .

<hr>

* NKVD is the abbreviation for People's Commissariat for Internal Affairs, a police agency that by the 1930s had become a vast internal security force, responsible for running the Gulag, among other things. The Cheka was the early secret political police force of the Bolsheviks.

† The Russian Civil War (1917–1922) was fought between various pro- and antirevolutionary factions, loosely known as the Reds and the Whites.

Tatyana Efimovna Semyonova
SERGEANT, TRAFFIC CONTROLLER

Everybody had one wish: to get to the front . . . Scary? Of course it was scary . . . But all the same . . . We went to the recruiting office, and they told us: "Grow up, girls . . . You're still green . . ." We were sixteen or seventeen years old. But I insisted and they took me. My friend and I wanted to go to sniper school, but they said: "You'll be traffic controllers. There's no time to teach you."

Mama waited at the station for several days to see us transported. She saw us going to the train, gave me a pie and a dozen eggs, and fainted . . .

Efrosinya Grigoryevna Breus
CAPTAIN, DOCTOR

The world changed all of a sudden . . . I remember the first days . . . Mama stood by the window in the evening praying. I never knew that my mother believed in God. She looked and looked in the sky . . .

I was mobilized; I was a doctor. I went out of a sense of duty. My papa was happy that his daughter was at the front. Defending the Motherland. Papa went to the recruiting office early in the morning. He went to get my papers, and he went early in the morning on purpose, so that everybody in the village could see that his daughter would be at the front . . .

Lilya Mikhailovna Butko
SURGICAL NURSE

Summer. The last day of peace . . . The evening before, we went to a dance. We were sixteen. We went around in a group; together we took one home, then another. We still hadn't broken up into separate couples. So we went, say, six boys and six girls.

And just two days later these boys, tank-school students, who had taken us home from the dance, were brought back crippled, bandaged. It was dreadful! Dreadful! If I heard someone laugh, I couldn't forgive it. How could anybody laugh, how could anybody be joyful, when such a war was going on?

Soon my father went to join the militia. Only my little brothers and I remained at home. My brothers were born in '34 and '38. And I told mama that I would go to the front. She cried, and I, too, cried that night. But I ran away from home . . . I wrote to mama from my unit. There was no way she could fetch me back from there . . .

Polina Semyonovna Nozdracheva
MEDICAL ASSISTANT

The command: Fall in . . . We lined up by height; I was the small-est. The commander comes, looks. Walks up to me: "What sort of Thumbelina is this? What are you going to do? Maybe you should go back to your mother and grow up a little?"

But I no longer had a mother . . . My mother had been killed dur-ing a bombing . . .

The strongest impression . . . For my whole life . . . It was during the first year, when we were retreating . . . I saw—we were hiding in the bushes—I saw one of our soldiers rush at a German tank with his rifle and beat the armor with the rifle butt. He beat, and shouted, and wept till he fell. Till a German submachine gun shot him. During the first year we fought with rifles against tanks and "Messers" . . . *

---

* Messerschmitts, German fighter aircraft.

Evgenia Sergeevna Sapronova

SERGEANT OF THE GUARDS, AIRPLANE MECHANIC

I begged my mama . . . I pleaded with her: only you mustn't cry . . . This didn't happen at night, but it was dark, and there was constant howling. They didn't cry, the mothers who were seeing their daughters off, they howled. But my mama stood as if made of stone. She controlled herself; she was afraid I would start crying. I was my mother's daughter; they pampered me at home. Now my hair was cut like a boy's, they left only a small lock in the front. She and my father didn't want me to go, but I lived for one thing only: To the front, to the front! To the front! These posters we now see in the museums— "The Motherland is calling!," "What have you done for the front?"— affected me very strongly. They were before our eyes all the time. And the songs? "Arise, vast country . . . Arise, for mortal combat . . ."

As we rode along, we were struck that dead people lay right on the platforms. The war was already there . . . But youth holds its own, and we sang songs. Even something merry. Some sort of silly couplets.

By the end of the war our whole family had taken part in it. Father, mama, sister—they all became railroad workers. They followed the frontline units and restored the tracks. And each of us got a medal "For victory": father, mama, sister, and I . . .

Galina Dmitrievna Zapolskaya

TELEPHONE OPERATOR

Before the war I worked as an army telephone operator . . . Our unit was stationed in the town of Borisov, where the war came during the first weeks. The head of the unit had us all line up. We were not in the service, we weren't soldiers, we were hired workers.

He says to us: "A cruel war is beginning. It will be very difficult for you, girls. Before it's too late, whoever wants to can go back home. Those who wish to stay at the front, step forward . . ."

And all the girls, all of them, stepped forward. There were about twenty of us. We were all ready to defend our Motherland. Before the war I didn't even like books about war. I liked to read about love. And now!

We sat at the telephones all the time, around the clock. Soldiers brought us pots, we'd have a bite, doze off for a bit right there by the telephones, and then put our earphones on again. I had no time to wash my hair, so I asked: "Girls, cut off my braids . . ."

Elena Pavlovna Yakovleva
SERGEANT MAJOR, NURSE

We went to the recruiting office time after time . . .

And when we came yet again, after I don't know how many times, the commissar almost threw us out: "If you had at least some profession. If you were nurses, drivers . . . What are you able to do? What will you do at the front?" But we didn't understand him. This question had never presented itself to us: what will we do? We wanted to go to war, that's all. It never dawned on us that to make war one had to be able to do something. Something specific. He took us unawares with his question.

I and several more girls went to nursing school. We were told that we had to study for six months. We decided: no, that's too long, it doesn't suit us. There was another school where the studies took three months. True, we reckoned three months was also long. But the program there was just about to end. We asked to be allowed to take the exams. There was one month of studies left. At night we got practical training in the hospitals, and during the day we studied. Altogether, we studied for a little over a month . . .

We were sent not to the front, but to a hospital. This was at the end of August '41 . . . Schools, hospitals, clubs were overcrowded with the wounded. But in February I left the hospital, you might say I ran away, deserted, it can't be called anything else. Without any documents, with nothing, I ran away on a hospital train. I left a note: "Not coming for my shift. Leaving for the front." That was all . . .

Vera Danilovtseva
SERGEANT, SNIPER

I had a rendezvous that day . . . I flew there on wings . . . I thought that day he would confess to me: "I love you." But he came all sad: "Vera, it's war! We're being sent from school straight to the front." He studied in a military school. Well, so I, of course, at once imagined myself in the role of Joan of Arc. Only to the front and only with a rifle in my hands. We had to be together. Only together! I ran to the recruiting office, but they cut me off sternly: "For now only medics are needed. And you have to study six months." Six months—that's completely crazy! I was in love . . .

They somehow persuaded me that I had to study. All right, I'll study, but not to be a nurse . . . I want to shoot! To shoot like he does. Somehow I was ready for that. The heroes of the Civil War and those who fought in Spain often came to our school. Girls felt equal to boys; we weren't treated differently. On the contrary, we had heard since childhood and at school: "Girls—at the wheel of the tractors!," "Girls—at the controls of a plane!" Well, and there was love as well! I even imagined we'd be killed together. In the same battle . . .

I had studied at the theater institute. Dreamed of becoming an actress. My ideal was Larissa Reisner.* A woman commissar in a leather jacket . . . I liked her because she was beautiful . . .

---

* Larissa Reisner (1895–1926) was a pro-Bolshevik Russian journalist and, after the revolution, a political commissar.

Anna Nikolaevna Khrolovich
NURSE

My friends, who were all older than me, were taken to the front . . . I cried terribly, because I was left alone, I wasn't taken. They told me: "You must study, little girl."

But my studies didn't last long. Soon our dean made an announcement: "Once the war is over, you'll finish your studies, girls. Now it's necessary to defend the Motherland . . ."

Our patrons from the factory saw us off to the front.* It was summertime. I remember the whole train was decorated with greenery, flowers . . . They gave us presents. I got some delicious homemade cookies and a pretty sweater. On the platform I danced a Ukrainian *gopak* with such enthusiasm!

We rode for many days . . . At some station we girls got off the train with a bucket, to fetch some water. We looked around and gasped: there were trains passing by one after another with nothing but girls in them. They were singing. They waved to us—some with scarves, some with forage caps. It became clear: there weren't enough men, they had all been killed . . . Or taken prisoner. Now we were to replace them.

Mama wrote a prayer for me. I put it into a locket; maybe it helped—I did come back home. Before combat I used to kiss that locket . . .

Antonina Grigoryevna Bondareva
LIEUTENANT OF THE GUARDS, SENIOR PILOT

I was a pilot . . .

When I was still in the seventh grade, a plane came flying to us. It

* Factories in the Soviet Union offered "patronage" to schools and orphanages, helping to train young people, sending them to summer camps, and so on.

was years ago, imagine, in 1936. Then it was a great novelty. And just then a slogan appeared: "Girls and boys—to the airplanes!" As a Komsomol member I was, of course, among the first. I signed up for the flying club at once. My father, to tell the truth, was categorically against it. Up to then in our family they had all been metallurgists, several generations of blast-furnace metallurgists. And my father thought that metallurgy was a woman's work, and piloting wasn't. The director of the flying club learned about it and allowed me to take my father for a flight in a plane. So I did. My father and I went up in the air together, and after that day he kept mum. He liked it. I graduated from the club with honors, I was good at parachuting. Before the war I had time to get married and give birth to a girl.

From the first days of the war there were various reorganizations in our club: the men were taken, and we, the women, replaced them. We taught the cadets. There was a lot of work, we worked from morning till night. My husband was one of the first to leave for the front. All I had left was a photograph: he and I are standing together beside a plane in pilot's helmets . . . I now lived together with my daughter; we lived all the time in the camps. How did we live? I would lock her up early in the morning, give her some porridge, and at four in the morning we already started flying. I would come back in the evening, and she would have eaten or not eaten; she would be all covered with that porridge. She didn't cry, she just looked at me. She had big eyes, like my husband . . .

At the end of 1941 I received a death notice: my husband had been killed near Moscow. He was a flight commander. I loved my daughter, but I left her with his family. And I started requesting to be sent to the front . . .

The last night . . . I spent it kneeling by my daughter's little bed . . .

Serafima Ivanovna Panasenko

SECOND LIEUTENANT, PARAMEDIC OF
A MOTORIZED INFANTRY BATTALION

I've turned eighteen . . . I'm so happy; it's my birthday. And every-body around shouts: "War!!!" I remember how people wept. As many as I met outside, they all wept. Some even prayed. It was unusual . . . People in the street praying and crossing themselves. In school they taught us that there was no God. But where were our tanks and our beautiful planes? We always saw them during parades. We were proud! Where were our commanders? Budenny . . . * There was, of course, a moment of perplexity. And then we began to think about something else: how to win the war.

I was a second-year student at the paramedical-obstetric school in the city of Sverdlovsk. I immediately thought: "Since it's war, I must go to the front." My papa was a longtime Communist; he had been a political prisoner before the revolution. He had instilled in us from childhood that the Motherland was everything, the Mother-land must be defended. I didn't hesitate: if I don't go, who will? I've got to . . .

Tamara Ulyanovna Ladynina

PRIVATE, FOOT SOLDIER

Mama came running to the train . . . My mama was strict. She never kissed us, never praised us. If we did something good, she just gave us a gentle look, that's all. But this time she came running, held my head and kissed me, kissed me. And looked in my eyes . . . Looked . . . For

---

* Semyon Budenny (1883–1973) was a Russian cavalry officer during World War I, became the leader of the Red Cavalry during the Civil War, served in various government positions, and was a close ally of Stalin's. He was one of the first Marshals of the Soviet Union, the high-est Soviet military rank.

a long time . . . I realized that I'd never see my mother again. I sensed it . . . I wanted to drop my kit bag and go back home. I felt sorry for everybody . . . My grandmother . . . And my little brothers . . .

Then music began to play . . . The command: "Fall out! Get on the train . . . !"

I kept waving for a long time . . .

Maria Semyonovna Kaliberda

SERGEANT MAJOR, LIAISON

I was assigned to a communications regiment . . . I would never have agreed to go into communications, because I didn't understand that that, too, meant fighting. A division commander came to us; we all lined up. Mashenka Sungurova was with us. This Mashenka Sungurova takes a step forward.

"Comrade General, allow me to address you."

He says: "Well, address me, then, address me, Soldier Sungurova."

"Private Sungurova requests to be relieved of service in communications and sent where the shooting is."

You understand, we were all in that state of mind. We had the idea that this communications thing was very puny; it even humiliated us. We just had to be on the front line.

The general's smile disappeared at once.

"My dear girls!" (And you should have seen how we looked then— without food, without sleep; in short, he spoke to us not as a commander, but as a father.) "You clearly don't understand your role at the front. You are our eyes and ears. An army without communications is like a man without blood."

Mashenka Sungurova was the first to give in.

"Comrade General! Private Sungurova is ready surefire to perform any task you give her!"

Afterward we called her "Surefire" till the end of the war.

. . . In June 1943 at the Kursk Bulge* we were handed the regimental banner, and our regiment, Detached Communications Regiment 129 of the 65th Army, consisted then of 80 percent women. And I want to tell you something, so that you get an idea . . . So that you understand . . . What was going on in our souls then. Because there probably will never again be such people as we were then. Never! So naïve and so sincere. With such faith! When the commander of the regiment received the banner and gave the command: "Regiment, before the banner! On your knees!"—we all felt so happy. We were trusted, we were now a regiment like all others, tank regiments, infantry regiments . . . We stood there and wept; we all had tears in our eyes. You won't believe me now, but my whole body had been so tense from the turmoil that I got sick, I came down with "night blindness." It was from lack of food, from nervous strain. But now my night blindness went away. You understand, the next day I was healthy, I got well, and it was because my whole soul was so shaken . . .

Xenia Sergeevna Osadcheva
PRIVATE, HOSPITAL MATRON

I just became an adult . . . On June 9, 1941, I turned eighteen, I became an adult. And two weeks later this cursed war began, even twelve days later. We were sent to build the Gagra-Sukhumi railroad. There were only young people. I remember the bread we ate. There was almost no flour in it, but all sorts of other things, mostly water. This bread lay on the table and left a little puddle of water. We used to lick it up.

In 1942 . . . I voluntarily applied to serve in Evacuation-Clearance Hospital No. 3201. It was a very big frontline hospital that belonged to the Trans- and North-Caucasian fronts and the separate Coastal Army. There were fierce battles, with a lot of wounded. I was as-

---

* A major battle took place in July-August 1943 at a salient ("bulge") around the city of Kursk, ending in a decisive Russian victory.

signed to distribute food—this was a round-the-clock duty; it would already be morning and time to serve breakfast, but we would still be handing out supper. Several months later I was wounded in the left leg—I hopped on the right one, but went on working. Then I was appointed to the post of matron, and also had to be there round the clock. I lived at work.

May 30, 1943 . . . At exactly one o'clock in the afternoon there was a massive airstrike in Krasnodar. I ran out of the building to see if the wounded had been sent off from the train station. Two bombs hit a shed where ammunition was stored. Before my eyes boxes flew up higher than a six-story building and exploded. I was thrown against a brick wall by the blast. I lost consciousness . . . When I came to it was already evening. I raised my head, tried to bend my fingers—they seemed to move. I cautiously unglued my left eye and went to my section, all covered with blood. In the corridor I met our head nurse, who did not recognize me at first and asked: "Who are you? Where from?" She came closer, gasped, and said: "Where have you been so long, Xenia? The wounded are hungry and you're not there." They quickly bandaged my head and my left arm above the elbow, and I went to fetch the supper. It was dark before my eyes; I was dripping sweat. I started serving supper and fell down. They brought me back to consciousness and all I heard was: "Quick! Hurry!" And again— "Quick! Hurry!"

A few days later they were still taking blood from me for the badly wounded. People were dying . . .

. . . I changed so much during the war that when I came home, mama didn't recognize me. People showed me where she lived, I went to the door and knocked.

There came an answer: "Yes, come in . . ."

I go in, greet her, and say: "Let me stay the night."

Mama was lighting the stove, and my two little brothers were sitting on the floor on a pile of straw, naked, they had no clothes. Mama didn't recognize me and said: "Do you see how we live, citizen? Go somewhere else before it gets dark."

I go up closer, and she again says: "Go somewhere else, citizen, before it gets dark."

I bend over her, embrace her, and murmur: "Mama, dear mama!"

Then they all just fell on me and burst out crying . . .

Now I live in Crimea . . . Here everything drowns in flowers, and every day I look out the window at the sea, but I'm worn out with pain, I still don't have a woman's face. I cry often, I moan all day. It's my memories . . .

OF THE SMELL OF FEAR AND
A SUITCASE OF CANDY

Olga Mitrofanovna Ruzhnitskaya
NURSE

I was leaving for the front . . . It was a magnificent day. Clear air and a sprinkle of rain. So beautiful! I stepped out in the morning and stood there: can it be I won't come back here again? Won't see our garden . . . Our street . . . Mama wept, clutched me, and wouldn't let go. I had already left, she caught up with me, embraced me, and wouldn't let go . . .

Nadezhda Vasilyevna Anisimova
MEDICAL ASSISTANT IN A MACHINE-GUN COMPANY

To die . . . I wasn't afraid to die. Youth, probably, or whatever . . . There was death around, death was always close, but I didn't think about it. We didn't talk about it. It was circling somewhere nearby, but kept missing. Once during the night a whole company conducted a reconnaissance mission in our regiment's sector. Toward morning it pulled back, and we heard moaning in no-man's-land. A wounded man had been left behind. "Don't go there, you'll be killed," the soldiers held me back. "Look, it's already dawn."

I didn't listen to them and crawled there. I found the wounded man. It took me eight hours to drag him back, tied with a belt by the hand. He was alive when we finally made it. The commander of the regiment learned about it, had a fit, and was going to arrest me for five days for being absent without permission. The deputy commander's reaction was different: "She deserves to be decorated."

At nineteen I had a medal "For Courage." At nineteen my hair was gray. At nineteen in my last battle I was shot through both lungs, the second bullet went between two vertebrae. My legs were paralyzed . . . And they thought I was dead . . .

At nineteen . . . My granddaughter's age now. I look at her—and don't believe it. A child!

When I came home from the front, my sister showed me my death notice . . . They had already buried me . . .

Albina Alexandrovna Gantimurova
SERGEANT MAJOR, SCOUT

I don't remember my mama . . . Only vague shadows remain in my memory . . . Outlines . . . Her face or her body when she bent over me. Close to me. So it seemed afterward. I was three years old when she died. My father served in the Far East, a career officer. He taught me to ride a horse. That was the strongest impression of my childhood. My father didn't want me to grow up a sissy. I remember myself from the age of five living in Leningrad with my aunt. During the Russo-Japanese War* my aunt was a nurse. I loved her like my mama . . .

What kind of girl was I? I'd jump from the second floor of our school on a bet. I loved soccer; I was always goalkeeper for the boys. When the Finnish War began, I kept running away to the Finnish War.† In 1941 I had just finished seventh grade and had time to apply to a technical school. My aunt wept: "It's war!" But I was glad I would go to the front and fight. How could I know what blood is?

The 1st Guards Division of the people's militia was being formed, and several of us girls were accepted in a medical battalion.

I phoned my aunt: "I'm going to the front."

From the other end came the reply: "Come home at once! Dinner's already cold."

I hung up. Later I felt sorry for her, terribly sorry. The siege began, the dreadful siege of Leningrad,‡ when half the city died, and she was there alone. A little old woman.

I remember I got leave to go home. Before going to my aunt I stopped at the grocery store. Before the war I was awfully fond of candy.

I said: "Give me some candy."

The salesgirl looked at me as if I was crazy. I didn't understand: what are food coupons, what is a siege? Everybody in the line turned

---

* The Russo-Japanese War was fought between February 1904 and September 1905 over conflicting territorial ambitions in Manchuria and Korea, and ended with Russian defeat.

† The Russo-Finnish War, also known as the Winter War, was fought between the Soviet Union and Finland from November 1939 to March 1940, following a Soviet invasion of Finland to "reclaim" extensive border territory around Leningrad.

‡ The siege of Leningrad by the German army began in September 1941 and ended in January 1944, after 872 days, with a toll of some 1.5 million lives of Russian soldiers and civilians.

to me, and my rifle was bigger than I was. When they gave them out to us, I looked at it and thought: "When will I grow big enough for this rifle?"

And suddenly everybody, the whole line, begged: "Give her candy. Take our coupons."

And they gave me candy.

They were collecting aid for the front in the streets. Big trays lay on tables right in the square; people came and took off, one a golden ring, another earrings . . . They brought watches, money . . . Nobody noted anything down, nobody signed anything . . . Women took off their wedding rings . . .

These are pictures in my memory . . .

And there was Stalin's famous Order No. 227: "Not a step back!" If you turn back, you're shot! Shot right there. Or else court-martialed and sent to the specially created penal battalions. Those who wound up there were as good as dead. Those who escaped from encirclement or captivity were sent to the filtration camps. Behind us moved the retreat-blocking detachments . . . Our own shot at our own . . .

These are pictures in my memory . . .

An ordinary clearing . . . It's wet, muddy after rain. A young soldier is on his knees. In glasses. For some reason they keep falling off; he picks them up. After rain. A cultivated boy from Leningrad. They had already taken away his rifle. We are all lined up. There are puddles everywhere . . . We . . . hear him beg . . . He swears . . . He begs not to be shot; his mother is alone at home. He begins to cry. And they shoot him on the spot—right in the forehead. With a pistol. A show execution: this is what will happen to people who waver. Even for a single moment! A single moment . . .

This order turned me into an adult at once. This you couldn't . . . For a long time we didn't remember . . . Yes, we won the war, but at what cost! At what terrible cost!

We stayed awake round the clock, there were so many wounded. Once none of us slept for three days and three nights. I was sent to the hospital with a truckload of wounded. I handed over the wounded, and the truck went back empty, so I could sleep. I returned fresh as a daisy, and everybody was falling off their feet.

I ran into the commissar.

"Comrade Commissar, I'm ashamed."

"What's the matter?"

"I slept."

"Where?"

I told him how I took the wounded in a truck, came back empty, and had a nice sleep.

"So what? Good for you! At least one of us can be normal; the rest of them are falling off their feet."

But I was ashamed. And with that kind of conscience we lived through the whole war.

They treated me well in the medical battalion, but I wanted to be a scout. I said I'd run away to the front line if they didn't let me go. They wanted to expel me from Komsomol for that, for not obeying military regulations. But I ran away even so . . .

My first decoration was the medal "For Courage" . . .

A battle began. A barrage of gunfire. The soldiers lay cowering. The order came: "Forward! For the Motherland!" They just lay there. Again the order, again they just lay there. I took off my cap so they could see: a girl's standing up . . . And they all stood up and we went into battle . . .

They gave me the medal, and that same day we went on a mission. For the first time in my life I had . . . our . . . women's thing . . . I saw blood and howled: "I'm wounded . . ."

There was a paramedic in the scouts with us, an older man. He came to me.

"Where are you wounded?"

"I don't know where . . . But there's blood . . ."

He told me all about it, like a father . . .

After the war I went scouting for some fifteen years. Every night. And dreamed things like that my submachine gun refused to shoot, or we were surrounded . . . I'd wake up grinding my teeth. Trying to remember—where are you? There or here?

When the war ended I had three wishes: first—to ride on a bus, instead of crawling on my stomach; second—to buy and eat a whole loaf of white bread; and third—to sleep in white sheets and have them make crinkly noises. White sheets . . .

Liubov Arkadyevna Charnaya
SECOND LIEUTENANT, CRYPTOGRAPHER

I was expecting a second child . . . I had a two-year-old son, and I was pregnant. Then—the war . . . And my husband was at the front . . . I went to my parents and had . . . Well, you understand? An abortion . . . Though it was forbidden then . . . How could I give birth? Tears all around . . . War! How could I give birth in the midst of death?

I finished the course in cryptography. They sent me to the front. I wanted to take revenge for this child I couldn't give birth to. My girl . . . I had expected a girl . . .

I requested the front line. They kept me at headquarters . . .

Valentina Pavlovna Maximchuk
ANTIAIRCRAFT GUNNER

They were leaving town . . . Everybody was leaving . . . At noon on June 28, 1941, we, the students of Smolensk Pedagogical Institute, also assembled in the courtyard of the printing house. It was not a long assembly. We left the city by the old Smolensk road in the direction of the town of Krasnoe. Observing caution, we walked in separate groups. Toward the end of the day the heat subsided, walking became easier, we went more quickly, not looking back. We were afraid to look back . . . We reached a stopping place and only then looked to the east. The whole horizon was enveloped in a crimson glow. From a distance of thirty miles it seemed to fill the whole sky. It was clear that it was not ten or a hundred houses burning. The whole of Smolensk was burning . . .

I had a new chiffon dress with ruffles. My girlfriend Vera liked it. She tried it on several times. I promised to give it to her as a wedding present. She was going to get married. There was a nice guy.

And here suddenly was this war. We were leaving for the trenches. Our possessions were all given to the superintendent of the dormitory. What about the dress? "Take it, Vera," I said when we were leaving the city.

She didn't take it. Why, you promised it to me as a wedding present. It got burned up in that fire.

Now we walked and kept looking back. It felt as if our backs were being roasted. We walked all night without stopping and at dawn came to our work. Digging antitank ditches. A sheer wall seven yards long and three and a half yards deep. I was digging and my shovel burned like fire, the sand looked red. Before my eyes stands our house with flowers and lilac bushes . . . White lilacs . . .

We lived in hovels on a flood meadow between two rivers. Hot and humid. Myriads of mosquitoes. We used to smoke them out before going to bed, but at dawn they would get in anyway; it was impossible to sleep peacefully.

I was taken to the field hospital from there. We lay on the floor next to each other. Many of us got sick then. I had a high fever. Chills. I lay there—I cried. The door to the ward opened, the doctor says from the threshold (he couldn't get any further, the mattresses were lying so close to each other): "Ivanova has plasmodium in her blood." Me, that is. She didn't know that for me nothing could have been scarier than this plasmodium, ever since I read about it in a textbook back in the sixth grade. And at that moment the radio played: "Arise, vast country . . ." I heard this song for the first time then. "I'll recover," I thought, "and go to the front at once."

They brought me to Kozlovka, not far from Roslavl, unloaded me on a bench. I sat there, holding on with all my might so as not to fall over, and heard as if through sleep: "This one?"

"Yes," the paramedic says.

"Take her to the dining room. Give her something to eat first."

And then I was in a bed. You should understand what it was to sleep not on the ground by a fire, not on a tarpaulin under a tree, but in a hospital, in the warmth. With a sheet. I didn't wake up for seven days. They said the nurses roused me and fed me, but I don't remember it.

When I woke up by myself after seven days, a doctor came, examined me, and said: "Sturdy organism; you'll pull through."

And I plunged into sleep again.

. . . At the front my unit, for its part, immediately got encircled. The food norm was two dry crusts a day. There was no time to bury the dead; we simply scattered sand over them. The faces we covered with forage caps . . . "If we survive," the commander said, "I'll send you to the rear. I used to think that a woman couldn't live like this even for two days. I imagine my wife . . ." I was so hurt I burst into tears. For me to sit in the rear at such a time was worse than death. I could stand it all with my mind and my heart, but physically it was more than I could take. The physical load . . . I remember how we carried the shells, carried the guns through the mud, especially in Ukraine, where the ground after rain or in spring was so heavy, like dough. To dig a common grave and bury our comrades after we hadn't slept for three days . . . even that was hard. We no longer wept, because in order to weep you also need strength, but we wanted to sleep. To sleep and sleep.

On watch I used to walk back and forth without stopping and recite poetry out loud. Other girls sang songs, so as not to collapse and fall asleep . . .

Maria Vasilyevna Zhloba

UNDERGROUND FIGHTER

We were transporting the wounded out of Minsk . . . I wore high-heel shoes, because I was short and embarrassed by it. One heel broke just as they shouted: "Assault!" And I ran barefoot, the shoes in my hand; a pity, they were beautiful shoes.

When we were encircled and saw that we couldn't break through, the nurse-aide Dasha and I climbed out of the ditch, no longer hiding, and stood up tall: better to have your head torn off by a shell than to be captured and brutalized. The wounded, those who were able, also stood up . . .

When I saw my first fascist soldier, I couldn't say a word, I lost speech. And they walked along young, cheerful, smiling. And wherever they stopped, wherever they saw a water pump or a well, they washed themselves. They always had their sleeves rolled up. They wash and wash . . . Blood all around, screaming, and they wash and wash . . . Such hatred of them rose up in me . . . When I came back home, I changed blouses twice. Everything in me protested against them being here. I couldn't sleep nights. Wha-a-t?! Our neighbor, Aunt Klava, got paralyzed when she saw them walking on our land. In her house . . . She died soon, because she couldn't bear it . . .

Maria Timofeevna Savitskaya-Radiukevich

PARTISAN LIAISON

The Germans rode into the village . . . On big black motorcycles . . . I stared at them all eyes: they were young, cheerful. They laughed all the time. They guffawed! My heart stopped at the thought that they were here, on our land, and laughing.

I only dreamed of revenge. I imagined that I'd be killed, and some-one would write a book about me. My name would remain. Those were my dreams . . .

I gave birth to a baby girl in '43 . . . By then my husband and I had gone to the forest to join the partisans. I gave birth to her in a swamp, on a haystack. I dried the swaddling clothes on my body: I would put them in my bosom, warm them up, and swaddle the baby. Every-thing around us was burning, villages were burned down with people in them . . . They rounded people up in schools, in churches . . . Poured kerosene . . . My five-year-old niece listened to our conversa-tions and asked: "Aunt Manya, when I burn up, what will be left of me? Only rubber boots . . ." That's what our children asked us about . . .

I myself gathered the charred remains . . . I gathered my friend's family. We found little bones, and if there was a bit of clothing left, just some little scrap, we recognized who it was. Each of us looked for his own. I picked up a small piece, my friend said: "It's mama's jacket . . ." And fainted. Some gathered the bones in a sheet, some in a pillowcase. In whatever they had. My friend and I had a hand-bag; what we gathered filled less than half of it. And we put it all into a common grave. Everything was black, only the bones were white . . . and the bone ash . . . I already recognized it . . . White as could be . . .

After that, whatever mission they sent me to, I wasn't afraid. My baby was small, just three months old, I used to go on missions with her. The commissar would send me off, and weep himself . . . I used to bring medications, bandages, serums from town . . . I would apply it under her arms and between her legs, swaddle her, and carry her. There were wounded men dying in the forest. I had to go. I had to! There were German and police guard posts everywhere, nobody could pass except me. With the baby. I had her swaddled . . .

It's horrible to tell about it now . . . Oh, so hard! To give the baby a temperature and make her cry, I rubbed her with salt. She'd get all red then, covered with rash, scream her head off. I'd go up to the guard: "Typhus, sir . . . Typhus . . ." They'd shout at me: "Away! Away!" so as to send me off quickly. I rubbed her with salt and put in some garlic. The baby was small . . . I was still nursing her . . .

Once we got past the guards, I'd go into the forest and weep my heart out. I'd shout! I was so sorry for my baby. And in a day or two I'd go again . . .

Elena Fyodorovna Kovalevskaya

PARTISAN

I discovered what hatred was . . . For the first time I discovered that feeling . . . How can they walk on our land! Who are they? My temperature went up from those scenes. Why are they here?

A column of prisoners of war passes, and hundreds of corpses are left on the road . . . Hundreds . . . Those who fell down exhausted were shot on the spot. They were driven like cattle. There was no more wailing over the dead. It was impossible to bury them, there were so many. They went on lying on the ground. The living lived with the dead . . .

I met my half sister. Their village had been burned down.

She had three sons, but they were no more. Their house had been burned down with the children in it. She used to sit on the ground and rock from side to side, rocking her grief. She would get up and not know where to go. To whom?

We all left for the forest: papa, my brothers, and I. Nobody urged us, nobody forced us, we went on our own. Mama stayed alone with the cow . . .

Anna Semyonovna Dubrovina-Chekunova

FIRST LIEUTENANT OF THE GUARDS, PILOT

I didn't even think twice . . . I had a profession that was needed at the front. I didn't think, didn't hesitate for a second. In general I met few people then who wanted to sit out that time. Wait till it was over. I remember one . . . a young woman, my neighbor . . . She told me honestly: "I love life. I want to powder my nose and put makeup on, I don't want to die." I didn't see any more like that. Maybe they kept quiet, hid themselves. I don't know how to answer you . . .

I remember I took the plants from my room and asked the neighbors, "Please water them. I'll be back soon."

I came back four years later . . .

The girls who stayed home envied us, and the women wept. One of the girls who went with me stood there. Everybody is weeping, and she's not. Then she took some water and wetted her eyes. Once, twice. With a handkerchief. See, I'm embarrassed, everybody's weeping. How could we understand what war is? We were young . . . It's now that I wake up at night in fear, when I dream that I'm in the war . . . The plane takes off, my plane, gains altitude, and . . . falls . . . I realize that I'm falling. The last moments . . . And it's so terrifying, until you wake up, until the dream evaporates. An old person fears death, a young one laughs. He's immortal! I didn't believe I could die . . .

Maria Afanasyevna Garachuk

PARAMEDIC

I finished medical school . . . I came back home, my father was ill. And then—the war. I remember, it was morning . . . I learned this terrible news in the morning . . . The dew hadn't dried on the leaves of the trees yet, and they were already saying—war! And this dew that I suddenly saw on the grass and the trees, saw so clearly—I remembered at the front. Nature was in contrast with what was happening with people. The sun shone brightly . . . Daisies bloomed, my favorites, there were masses of them in the fields . . .

I remember us lying somewhere in a wheat field; it was a sunny day. The German submachine guns go rat-a-tat-tat—then silence. All you hear is the wheat rustling. Then again the German submachine guns go rat-a-tat-tat . . . And you think: will you ever hear again how the wheat rustles? This sound . . .

Liubov Ivanovna Liubchik
COMMANDER OF A MACHINE-GUN PLATOON

My mother and I were evacuated to the rear . . . To Saratov . . . Somewhere there I took a three-month course in metal turning. We would stand at the lathes for twelve hours on end. We were starving. Our only thought was to get to the front. There would be rations there. Rusks and tea with sugar. They'd give us butter. Someone told us so, I don't remember who. Maybe the wounded at the train station? To save ourselves from starvation, well, and also, obviously, we were Komsomol girls. My girlfriend and I went to the recruiting office. We didn't tell them we worked at the factory. In that case they wouldn't have taken us. And so we enlisted.

We were sent to the Ryazan Infantry School. We graduated as commanders of machine-gun units. A machine gun is heavy; you have to drag it with you. You feel like a horse. It's night. You stand watch and listen to every sound. Like a lynx. Wary of every rustle . . . In war they say you're half man and half beast. It's true. There's no other way to survive. If you're just a human being—you won't stay whole. You'll get bashed in the belfry! In war you have to remember something about yourself. Something . . . Remember something from when a man was not quite a man yet . . . I'm not very educated, I'm a simple accountant, but that I know.

I got as far as Warsaw . . . And all on foot . . . The infantry, as they say, is the wartime proletariat. We crawled on our stomachs . . . Don't ask me any more . . . I don't like books about war. About heroes . . . We went sick, coughing, sleepy, dirty, poorly dressed. Often hungry . . . But we won!

Ulyana Osipovna Nemzer
SERGEANT, TELEPHONE OPERATOR

My father had been killed, that I knew . . . My brother was dead. And to die or not to die no longer had any significance for me. I only pitied my mama. She had instantly turned from a beauty into an old woman, very embittered by her lot. She couldn't live without my papa.

"Why are you going to the war?" she asked.

"To avenge papa."

"Papa wouldn't stand seeing you with a rifle."

My papa used to do my braids when I was little. Tied the ribbons. He liked beautiful clothes more than mama did.

I served as a telephone operator in the unit. I remember best how our commander shouted into the receiver: "Reinforcements! I'm asking for reinforcements! I demand reinforcements!" The same every day . . .

Anna Iosifovna Strumilina
PARTISAN

I'm not a heroine . . . I used to be a pretty girl, I was pampered when I was little . . .

The war came . . . I didn't want to die. Shooting was scary, I never thought I'd shoot. Oh, lord! I was afraid of the dark, of the dense forest. Of wild animals, of course . . . Oh . . . I couldn't imagine how someone could meet a wolf or a wild boar. I was even afraid of dogs in my childhood; a big German shepherd bit me when I was little, and I was afraid of them. Oh, lord! That's how I was . . . But I learned everything with the partisans . . . I learned to shoot—with a rifle, a pistol, and a machine gun. And now, if need be, I can show you. I'll remember. We were even taught what to do if there's no other weapon than a knife or a shovel. I stopped being afraid of the dark. And of wild animals . . . But I would avoid a snake, I'm not used to snakes. At night she-wolves often howled in the forest. And we sat in our dugouts and didn't mind. The wolves were vicious, hungry. We had these small dugouts, like burrows. The forest was our home. The partisans' home. Oh, lord! I began to be afraid of the forest after the war . . . I never go to the forest now . . .

I thought I'd sit out the war at home with my mama. My beautiful mama. Mama was very beautiful. Oh, lord! I'd never have ventured . . . Myself, no. Never . . . But . . . They told us . . . The town had been taken by the Germans, and I discovered that I was Jewish. And before the war we all lived together: Russians, Tatars, Germans, Jews . . . We were the same. Oh, lord! I'd never even heard this word "yids," because I lived with papa, mama, and books. We became like lepers, we were driven out everywhere. People were afraid of us. Some of our acquaintances even stopped saying hello to us. Their children stopped. The neighbors said to us: "Leave us all your things, you don't need them anyway now." Before the war we used to be friends. Uncle Volodia, Aunt Anya . . . * Lord!

Mama was shot . . . This happened a few days before we were supposed to move to the ghetto. There were orders hanging all over town: Jews are not allowed—to walk on the sidewalks, to have haircuts in barber shops, to buy anything in the stores . . . Mustn't laugh, mustn't sing . . . Oh, lord! Mama couldn't get used to it; she was always absentminded. She probably didn't believe it . . . Maybe she

---

* Russians often use "uncle" and "aunt" as terms of endearment, with no reference to family relations.

went into a store? Or somebody said something rude, and she laughed. As a beautiful woman . . . Before the war she sang in the philharmonic, everybody loved her. Oh, lord! I imagine . . . If she hadn't been so beautiful . . . our mama . . . She would still have been with me or with papa. I think about it all the time . . . Strangers brought her to us at night, dead. Already without her coat and shoes. It was a nightmare. A terrible night! Terrible! Somebody had taken off her coat and shoes. Her gold wedding ring. Papa's gift . . .

We had no home in the ghetto; we were put in the attic of someone's house. Papa took a violin, our most valuable prewar thing. Papa wanted to sell it. I had a bad case of angina. I lay in bed . . . Lay in bed with a high fever, and I couldn't speak. Papa wanted to buy some food; he was afraid I might die. Die without mama . . . Without mama's words, mama's hands. I was so pampered . . . so loved . . . I waited for him for three days, until some acquaintances told me that papa had been killed . . . They said it was on account of the violin . . . I don't know how valuable it was. As he was leaving, papa said: "It will be good if they give me a pot of honey and some butter." Oh, lord! I was left—without mama . . . without papa . . .

I went looking for papa . . . I wanted to find him even if he was dead, so we could be together. I was blond, not dark-haired; my eyebrows and hair were light, so no one in the town touched me. I came to the market . . . I met papa's friend there, he lived in a village by then, with his parents. Also a musician, like my father. Uncle Volodia. I told him everything . . . He put me on his cart, under a cover. There were piglets squealing, chickens clucking in the cart. We drove for a long time. Oh, lord! Till evening. I slept, woke up . . .

That's how I wound up with the partisans . . .

Vera Sergeevna Romanovskaya
PARTISAN NURSE

There was a parade . . . Our partisan detachment merged with units of the Red Army, and after the parade we were told to surrender our weapons and go and work on restoring the city. But it just didn't make sense to us: the war was still going on, only Belorussia had been liberated, but we were supposed to surrender our weapons. Every one of us wanted to go on fighting. And we went to the recruiting office, all our girls . . . I said that I was a nurse and asked to be sent to the front. They promised me: "All right, we'll register you, and if there's a need, we'll summon you. Meanwhile go and work."

I waited . . . They didn't summon me . . . I went to the recruiting office again. I went many times . . . And finally they told me frankly that there was no need, they already had enough nurses. What was needed was sorting bricks in Minsk . . . The city was in ruins . . . What kind of girls did we have, you ask? We had Chernova; she was pregnant, and she carried a mine at her side, next to where her baby's heart was beating. So go and figure what sort of people they were. For us there was no need to figure, that's just how we were. We were brought up that we and the Motherland were one and the same. Or another friend of mine, she went around town with her little daughter, and under her dress her little body was wrapped in leaflets. The girl would raise her arms and complain: "Mama, I'm hot. Mama, I'm hot." And in the streets there were Germans everywhere. *Polizei.* It was possible to deceive a German, but not a *polizei.* He was one of us, he knew your life, your insides. Your thoughts.

And so even children . . . We took them into our detachment, but still they were children. How to save them? We decided to send them back across the front line. But they escaped from the children's centers and returned to the front. They were caught on the trains, along the roads. They would escape again, and again return to the front . . .

History will spend hundreds of years trying to understand: What was it? What sort of people were they? Where did they come from? Imagine, a pregnant woman walking with a mine . . . She was expecting a child, yes . . . She loved, she wanted to live. And, of course, she was afraid. But she went . . . Not for the sake of Stalin, but for the sake of her children. Their future life. She didn't want to live on her knees. To submit to the enemy . . . Maybe we were blind, and I won't even deny that there was much then that we didn't know or understand, but we were blind and pure at the same time. We were made of two parts, of two lives. You must understand that . . .

Maria Vasilyevna Tikhomirova

PARAMEDIC

Summer was beginning . . . I finished medical school. Received my diploma. War! They summoned me to the recruiting office at once. The order was: "You have two hours to get ready, we're sending you to the front." I packed everything in one small suitcase.

What did you take to the war?

Candy.

What?

A whole suitcase of candy. In the village I was sent to after training school, they gave me some relocation money. So there was money, and I spent it all on chocolate candy, a whole suitcaseful. I knew I wouldn't need money at the front. And on top of the candy I put my class picture, with all the girls. I came to the recruiting office. The commissar asks: "Where do you want to be sent?" I say: "And where are you sending my friend?" She and I came together to the Leningrad region; she worked in a village ten miles away. He laughs: "She asked the same question." He took my suitcase, to carry it to the truck that was to take us to the station. "What have you got that's so heavy?" "Candy. A whole suitcaseful." He said nothing. Stopped smiling. I saw he was embarrassed, even somehow ashamed. He was no longer a young man . . . He knew where I was going . . .

Tamara Illarionovna Davidovich
SERGEANT, DRIVER

My fate was decided at once . . .

An announcement hung in the recruiting office: "Drivers needed." So I took a driving course. Six months long . . . They didn't pay any attention to the fact that I was a teacher (I had studied to be a teacher before the war). Who needs teachers in wartime? It's soldiers that are needed. There were many of us girls, a whole auto battalion.

Once during a drill . . . For some reason I can't remember it without tears . . . It was in spring. We finished shooting and were going back. I picked some violets. A little bouquet. I picked it and tied it to my bayonet. And went on like that.

We returned to the camp. The commander had us all line up and asked me to step forward. I did . . . I forgot that I had violets tied to my rifle. He began to scold me: "A soldier should be a soldier, not a flower picker . . ." He found it incomprehensible that I could think about flowers in such circumstances. A man was unable to understand it . . . But I didn't throw those violets away. I took them off and put them in my pocket. I got three extra turns of duty for them . . .

Another time I was standing at my post. At two o'clock in the morning they came to relieve me, but I refused. I sent my replacement to sleep: "You'll stand during the day, and I'll stand now." I would accept to stand there all night till dawn, just to hear the birds sing. Only at night was there something reminiscent of the former life. Peaceful.

When we were leaving for the front, we walked down the street, and people stood all along it: women, old people, children. And they were all crying: "Girls are going to the front." We were a whole battalion of girls.

I'm at the wheel . . . We pick up the dead after the battle; they're scattered over the field. All young. Boys. And suddenly there's a young girl lying there. Killed . . . Everybody falls silent.

Vera Iosifovna Khoreva
ARMY SURGEON

How I prepared to go to the front . . . You won't believe . . . I thought it wouldn't be for long. We'll defeat the enemy soon! I took one skirt, my favorite one, two pairs of socks, one pair of shoes. We were retreating from Voronezh, but I remember going to a store and buying another pair of high-heeled shoes. I do remember that we were retreating, everything was black, smoky (but the store was open—a miracle!), and for some reason I felt like buying a pair of shoes. Such elegant little shoes, I remember as if it were today . . . I also bought some perfume . . .

It was hard to renounce all at once life as it had been up to then. Not only my heart but my whole body resisted. I remember how happy I was when I came running out of the store with those shoes. I was inspired. And there was smoke everywhere . . . Rumbling . . . I was already in the war, but I still didn't want to think about it. I didn't believe it.

And there was rumbling all around . . .

OF EVERYDAY LIFE
AND ESSENTIAL LIFE

Nonna Alexandrovna Smirnova
PRIVATE, ANTIAIRCRAFT GUNNER

We dreamed . . . We wanted to go to war . . .

We were assigned seats in a train car, and classes began. Everything was different from the way we had pictured it at home. We had to get up early, and run around all day. But the former life still lived in us. We were indignant when the section commander, Sergeant Gulyaev, who had a fourth-grade education, taught us the regulations and mispronounced certain words. We wondered: what can he teach us? But he taught us how not to perish . . .

After the quarantine, before we took the oath, the sergeant major brought our uniforms: overcoats, forage caps, army shirts, skirts, and, instead of underwear, two long-sleeved men's shirts of unbleached calico, stockings instead of footwraps, and heavy American boots, iron shod at the heels and toes. By my height and constitution I turned out to be the smallest in the company, five feet tall, shoe size five, and, naturally, military industry did not provide for such tiny sizes, and America certainly did not supply us with anything that small. I was given a pair of size ten boots. I put them on and took them off without unlacing them, and they were so heavy that I dragged my feet on the ground as I walked. When I marched on stone pavement, my iron-shod boots made sparks, and my gait resembled anything but a marching step. It's awful to remember the nightmare of my first march. I was ready to do great deeds, but I wasn't ready to wear size ten boots instead of five. They were so heavy and ugly! So ugly!

The commander saw me marching and called me out.

"Smirnova, what kind of step is that? Haven't you been taught? Why don't you pick up your feet? Put in three extra turns of duty . . ."

I answered: "Yes, sir, Comrade First Lieutenant, three extra turns of duty!" I turned to go and fell down. I fell out of my boots . . . My feet were all bloody blisters . . .

Then it became clear that I could no longer walk. The company shoemaker, Parshin, was ordered to make me a pair of size five boots out of an old tarpaulin . . .

Antonina Grigoryevna Bondareva
LIEUTENANT OF THE GUARDS, SENIOR PILOT

And there was so much that was funny . . .

Discipline, regulations, insignia—we didn't master all this wisdom at once. We were standing guard by the plane. And the regulations say that if anyone comes, we should stop him: "Halt, who goes there?" My friend saw the regimental commander and shouted, "Halt, who goes there? Excuse me, but I'm going to shoot!" Imagine? She shouted, "Excuse me, but I'm going to shoot!" Excuse me . . . Ha-ha-ha . . .

Klavdia Ivanovna Terekhova
AIR FORCE CAPTAIN

The girls arrived at school with long braids . . . With their hair done up . . . I also had braids around my head . . . But how could we wash it? Where to dry it? Suppose you've just washed it, and there's an alarm, you have to run. Our commander, Marina Raskova, told us all to cut off our braids. The girls cut them and wept. Lilya Litvyak, later a famous pilot, couldn't bring herself to part with her braid.

I went to Raskova.

"Comrade Commander, your orders have been carried out, only Litvyak refused."

Marina Raskova, despite her feminine gentleness, could be a very strict commander. She sent me away.

"What kind of party organizer are you if you can't get your people to carry out an order! About-face, march!"

Dresses, high-heeled shoes . . . How sorry we were to put them away. It was boots during the day, and in the evening at least a little time in shoes in front of the mirror. Raskova saw it and a few days later came the order: pack all the women's clothes and mail them home. So there! But as a result we finished studying a new plane in six months instead of two years, as it would have taken in peaceful times.

In the first days of training we lost two teams. There were four coffins. All three of our regiments sobbed out loud.

Raskova stepped forward.

"Friends, wipe your tears. These are our first losses. There will be many of them. Clench your hearts like a fist . . ."

Later, at the front, we buried without tears. We stopped crying.

We flew fighters. The altitude itself was a terrible strain on a woman's whole body. Sometimes your stomach was pressed right up against your spine. But our girls flew and shot down aces, and what aces! You know, when we walked by, men looked at us with astonishment: "They're women pilots." They admired us . . .

Vera Vladimirovna Shevaldysheva
FIRST LIEUTENANT, SURGEON

In the fall I was summoned to the recruiting office . . . The commander received me and asked: "Do you know how to parachute?" I confessed that I was afraid. He spent a long time persuading me to become a paratrooper: handsome uniform, chocolate every day. But

I'd been afraid of heights since childhood. "And what about antiaircraft artillery?" As if I knew anything about antiaircraft artillery? Then he suggests: "Let's send you to a partisan unit." "And how can I write to mama in Moscow from there?" He takes a red pencil and writes on my assignment: "Steppe Front . . ."*

On the train a young captain fell in love with me. He spent a whole night standing in our car. He had already been burned by the war, had been wounded several times. He looked at me, looked, and then said: "Verochka, only don't lower yourself, don't become coarse. You're so delicate now . . . I've already seen everything!" And more in the same vein, meaning it's hard to come out pure from the war. From hell.

A friend and I spent a month traveling to the 4th Guards Army of the 2nd Ukrainian Front. We finally arrived. The chief surgeon came out for a few moments, looked us over, and led us to the surgery room: "Here's your operating table . . ." Ambulances were driving up one after another, big cars, "Studebakers." The wounded were lying on the ground, on stretchers. We only asked: "Who should we take first?" "The silent ones . . ." An hour later I was standing at my table, operating. And so it went . . . You operate around the clock, then take a short nap, quickly rub your eyes, wash—and go back to your table. And every third man was dead. We had no time to help them all. Every third man . . .

At Zhmerinka station we came under a terrible bombardment. The train stopped, and we ran. Our political commissar had had his appendix removed the day before, and that day he, too, ran. We sat in the forest all night, and our train was blown to pieces. In the morning German planes began combing the forest. Where to hide? I couldn't burrow into the ground like a mole. I put my arms around a birch tree and stood there: "Oh, mama, my mama! . . . Can it be I'll perish? If I survive, I'll be the happiest person in the world." When I told people

* The Steppe Front was a new formation, formed by the Soviet army on territory near the Ukrainian border after the German defeat at Stalingrad in February 1943.

afterward how I held on to the birch tree, they all laughed. I was such an easy target. Standing up tall, a white birch . . . Hilarious!

I met Victory Day in Vienna. We went to the zoo, I wanted so much to go to the zoo. We could have gone to see a concentration camp. They took everybody there to see it. I didn't go . . . Now it surprises me that I didn't go . . . I wanted something joyful. Funny. To see something from a different life . . .

Svetlana Vasilyevna Katykhina
PRIVATE IN A FIELD BATH-AND-LAUNDRY UNIT

There were three of us: mama, papa, and myself . . . My father was the first to leave for the front. Mama wanted to go with my father, she was a nurse, but he was sent in one direction, she in another. I was only sixteen . . . They didn't want to take me. I kept going to the recruiting office, and after a year they took me.

We traveled by train for a long time. Soldiers were returning from the hospitals with us, and there were also some young fellows. They told us about the front, and we sat listening open-mouthed. They said there would be shooting, and we sat and waited: when would the shooting begin? So that when we came we could say we had already been under fire.

We arrived. But they didn't give us rifles, they sent us to the cauldrons and tubs. The girls were all my age, loved and pampered in their families. I was an only child. But there we had to carry firewood, stoke the stoves. Then we took the ashes and used them in cauldrons instead of soap, because there was always a shortage of soap. The linen was dirty, full of lice. Bloody . . . In winter it was heavy with blood . . .

Sofya Konstantinovna Dubnyakova
SERGEANT MAJOR, MEDICAL ASSISTANT

To this day I remember my first wounded man. His face . . . He had a compound fracture of the middle third of the thigh bone. Imagine it, the bone sticking out, a shrapnel wound, everything turned inside out. That bone . . . I knew theoretically what to do, but when I crawled over to him and saw it, I felt faint, nauseous. And suddenly I hear: "Drink some water, dear nurse . . ." It was the wounded man speaking. He pitied me. I remember that picture as if it were now. When he said it I came to my senses: "Ah," I thought, "you damned Turgenev young lady! A man is perishing and you, tender creature, feel nauseous . . ." I opened a first-aid kit, covered up the wound—and felt better, and was able to give the man proper aid.

Now I watch films about the war: a nurse on the front line, she's neat, clean, not in thick pants, but in a skirt, a pretty forage cap on top of her head . . . Well, it's not true! How could we have pulled a wounded man out, if we were like that . . . You're not going to go crawling about in a skirt with nothing but men around. And to tell the truth, they issued us skirts only at the end of the war, for dressing up. We also got some knitted cotton underwear instead of men's shirts. We were so happy we didn't know what to do. We unbuttoned our tunics to show it off . . .

Anna Ivanovna Belyai
NURSE

A bombardment . . . They bombed and bombed, bombed and bombed and bombed. Everybody rushed and ran somewhere . . . I'm running, too. I hear someone moan: "Help . . . Help . . ." But I keep running . . . A few minutes later, something dawns on me, I feel the first-aid bag on my shoulder. And also—shame. Where did the fear go! I run back: it was a wounded soldier moaning. I rush to bandage him. Then a second, a third . . .

The battle ended during the night. In the morning fresh snow fell. Under it the dead . . . Many had their arms raised up . . . toward the sky . . . You ask me: what is happiness? I answer . . . To suddenly find a living man among the dead . . .

Olga Vasilyevna Korzh
MEDICAL ASSISTANT IN A CAVALRY SQUADRON

I saw my first dead man . . . I stood over him and cried . . . Mourned for him . . . Then a wounded man called to me: "Bandage my leg!" His leg was torn off, hanging out of the trouser leg. I cut the trouser leg off: "Put my leg down! Put it beside me." I did. If they're conscious, they won't give up their arm or leg. They take it along. And if they're dying, they ask that it be buried with them.

During the war I used to think I'd never forget anything. But things get forgotten . . .

Such a young, attractive fellow. And he lies there dead. I thought all the killed got buried with military honors, but they took him and dragged him into the hazel bushes. Dug a grave . . . Without a coffin, without anything, they put him in the ground and simply covered him over. The sun was shining brightly—on him, too . . . A warm summer day . . . There was no tarpaulin, nothing, they laid him out in his army shirt and jodhpurs, as he was, and it was all new, he had obviously arrived recently. So they laid him out and buried him. The hole was very shallow, just enough to lay him in. And the wound was small, a mortal one—in the temple, but there was little blood, and the man lay as if alive, only very pale.

After the artillery fire the bombing began. They bombed that place. I don't know what was left of it . . .

And how did we bury people in an encirclement? Right there, next to the trench we ourselves were sitting in, we put them in the ground—that's all. There was just a little mound. Of course, if the Germans came right after, or some tanks, they would trample it down at once. There would be ordinary ground left, not a trace. We often buried in the woods under the trees . . . Under the oaks, the birches . . .

Even now I can't go to the forest. Especially where there are old oaks or birches . . . I can't sit there . . .

Vera Borisovna Sapgir
SERGEANT, ANTIAIRCRAFT GUNNER

I lost my voice at the front . . . My beautiful voice . . .

My voice returned when I came back home. The family got together in the evening, we drank: "So, Verka, sing for us." And I began to sing . . .

I left for the front a materialist. An atheist. I left as a good Soviet schoolgirl, who had been well taught. And there . . . There I began to pray . . . I always prayed before a battle, I read my prayers. The words were simple . . . My own words . . . They had one meaning, that I would return to mama and papa. I didn't know any real prayers and didn't read the Bible. No one saw me pray. I did it in secret. On the sly. Cautiously. Because . . . We were different then, people lived differently. You understand? We thought and understood differently . . . Because . . . I'll tell you a story . . . Once a believer turned up among the new arrivals, and the soldiers laughed at him when he prayed: "Well, did your God help you? If he exists, how does he put up with all this?" They were unbelievers, like the man who cried at the feet of the crucified Christ, "If He loves you, why doesn't He save you?" I read the Bible after the war . . . Now I read it all the time . . . And that soldier, he was no longer a young man, he didn't want to shoot. He refused: "I can't! I won't kill!" Everybody agreed to kill, but he didn't. At that time . . . A terrible time . . . Because . . . They court-martialed him and two days later they shot him . . . Bang! Bang!

A different time . . . Different people . . . How can I explain it? How? . . .

Fortunately I . . . I didn't see those people, the ones I killed . . . But . . . All the same . . . Now I realize that I killed them. I think about it . . . Because . . . Because I'm old now. I pray for my soul. I told my daughter that when I die she should take all my medals and decorations, not to a museum, but to a church. Give them to the priest . . . They come to me in my sleep . . . The dead . . . My dead . . . Though I never saw them, they come and look at me. I keep searching with my eyes, maybe someone was only wounded, badly wounded, but could still be saved. I don't know how to put it . . . But they're all dead . . .

Maria Selivestrovna Bozhok
NURSE

The most unbearable thing for me was the amputations . . . They often amputated so high up that they'd cut off the whole leg, and I could barely hold it, barely carry it to the basin. I remember they were very heavy. I would take it quietly, so that the wounded man wouldn't hear, and carry it like a baby . . . A small baby . . . Especially if it was a high amputation, way above the knee. I couldn't get used to it. Under anesthesia the wounded men would groan or curse. Well-rounded Russian curses. I was always bloody . . . Blood is dark red . . . Very dark . . .

I wrote nothing to mama about it. I wrote her that everything was fine, that I had warm clothes and boots. She sent three of us to the front, it was hard for her . . .

Maria Petrovna Smirnova (Kukharskaya)

MEDICAL ASSISTANT

I was born and grew up in Crimea, near Odessa. In 1941 I finished tenth grade in the Slobodka high school, Kordymsky district. When the war began, I listened to the radio for the first few days. I realized that we were retreating. I ran to the recruiting office. They sent me home. I went there twice more and was refused twice more. On July 28 the retreating units passed through our Slobodka, and I went to the front with them without any call-up.

When I first saw a wounded man, I fainted. Later I got over it. When I went under fire to a wounded soldier for the first time, I screamed so loud that it seemed I drowned out the noise of the battle. Then I got used to it . . . Ten days later I was wounded. I extracted the shrapnel myself, and bandaged myself.

December 25, 1942 . . . Our 333rd Division of the 56th Army occupied an elevation on the approach to Stalingrad. The enemy decided to take it back at all costs. A battle began. Tanks attacked us, but our artillery stopped them. The Germans rolled back, and a wounded lieutenant, the artillerist Kostia Khudov, was left in no-man's-land. The orderlies who tried to bring him back were killed. Two first-aid sheepdogs (this was the first time I saw them) crept toward him, but were also killed. And then I took off my flap-eared hat, stood up tall, and began to sing our favorite prewar song: "I saw you off to a great deed," first softly, then more and more loudly. Everything became hushed on both sides—ours and the Germans'. I went up to Kostia, bent down, put him on a sledge, and took him to our side. I walked and thought: "Only not in the back, better let them shoot me in the head." So, right now . . . right now . . . The last minutes of my life . . . Right now! Interesting: will I feel the pain or not? How frightening, mama dear! But not a single shot was fired . . .

We could never have enough uniforms: they'd give us a new one, and a couple of days later it was all bloody. My first wounded man was First Lieutenant Belov, my last was Sergei Petrovich Trofimov, sergeant of a mortar platoon. In 1970 he came to visit me, and I showed my daughters his wounded head, where he still had a big scar. Altogether I carried 481 wounded soldiers from under fire. One of the journalists counted them up: a whole infantry battalion . . . We hauled men two or three times our weight. When they're wounded they're still heavier. You carry him, his weapon, plus there's his overcoat, boots. So you hoist some 180 pounds on your back and carry it. Unload it . . . Go for the next one, and again it's 150 or 180 pounds . . . Five or six times in one attack. And you yourself weigh a hundred pounds—like a ballet dancer. It's hard to believe now . . . I myself find it hard to believe . . .

Vera Safronovna Davydova
FOOT SOLDIER

It was 1942 . . . we were going on a mission. We crossed the front line and stopped by some cemetery. We knew the Germans were three miles away from us. It was during the night, and they kept sending up flares. With parachutes. These flares burn for a long time and light up everything far around. The platoon commander brought me to the edge of the cemetery, showed me where the flares were fired from, where the bushes were that the Germans might appear from. I'm not afraid of dead people, even as a child I wasn't afraid of cemeteries, but I was twenty-two, I was standing guard for the first time . . . In those two hours my hair turned gray . . . It was my first gray hair, I discovered a whole streak in the morning. I stood and looked at those bushes, they rustled and moved, I thought the Germans were coming from them . . . And something else . . . Some monsters . . . And I was alone . . .

Is it a woman's job to stand guard by a cemetery at night? Men took it all more simply, they were already prepared for the thought that they had to stand guard, had to shoot . . . But for us in any case it was unexpected. Or to make a twenty-mile march. With combat gear. In hot weather. Horses dropped dead . . .

Lola Akhmetova
FOOT SOLDIER, RIFLEMAN

You ask what's the most frightening thing in war? You expect me . . . I know what you expect . . . You think I'll say the most frightening thing in war is death. To die.

Am I right? I know your kind . . . Your journalist's tricks . . . Ha-ha-ha . . . Why aren't you laughing? Eh?

But I'll say something else . . . For me the most terrible thing in war was—wearing men's underpants. That was frightening. And for me it was somehow . . . I can't find the . . . Well, first of all, it's very ugly . . . You're at war, you're preparing to die for the Motherland, and you're wearing men's underpants. Generally, you look ridiculous. Absurd. Men's underpants were long then. Wide. Made of sateen. There were ten girls in our dugout, all wearing men's underpants. Oh, my God! Winter and summer. For four years.

We crossed the Soviet border . . . As our commissar used to say at political sessions, we were finishing the beast off in his own den. Near the first Polish village we got a change of clothes: new uniforms and . . . And! And! And! For the first time they issued us women's underpants and brassieres. For the first time in the whole war. Ha-ha-ha . . . Well, of course . . . We saw normal women's underwear . . .

Why aren't you laughing? You're crying . . . Why?

Nina Vladimirovna Kovelenova

SERGEANT MAJOR, MEDICAL ASSISTANT
IN AN INFANTRY COMPANY

They wouldn't send me to the front . . . I was too young, just barely sixteen. But they did accept a woman we knew, a paramedic. She was very upset and wept, because she had a little son. I went to the recruiting office: "Take me instead of her . . ." Mama didn't want me to go: "Nina, no, how old are you? Maybe the war will be over soon." Mama is mama.

The soldiers used to save things for me, one a dry crust, another a piece of sugar. They looked out for me. I didn't know we had a Katyusha rocket launcher under cover behind us. It started shooting. It shoots, there's thunder all around, everything's on fire . . . And I was so shocked, I was so frightened by this thunder and fire, that I fell into a puddle and lost my forage cap. The soldiers laughed: "What's wrong, Ninochka? What's wrong, dear girl?"

Hand-to-hand combat . . . What do I remember? I remember crunching . . . Once hand-to-hand combat begins, there's immediately this crunching noise: the breaking of cartilage, of human bones. Animal cries . . . When there was an attack, I'd walk along with the fighters, well, just slightly behind, virtually next to them. It all happened before my eyes . . . Men stabbing each other. Finishing each other off. Breaking bones. Sticking a bayonet in the mouth, in the eye . . . In the heart, in the stomach . . . And this . . . How to describe it? I'm too weak . . . Too weak to describe it . . . In short, women don't know such men, they don't see such men at home. Neither women nor children. It's frightful to think of . . .

After the war I went home to Tula. I used to scream during the night. Mama and my sister sat with me at night. I'd wake up from my own screaming . . .

Nina Alexeevna Semyonova
PRIVATE, RADIO OPERATOR

We came to Stalingrad. There was deadly combat going on there. It was the most deadly place . . . The water and the earth were red . . . We had to cross from one bank of the Volga to the other. Nobody wanted to listen to us: "What? Girls? Who the hell needs you here? We need riflemen and machine gunners, not radio operators." And there were lots of us, eighty in all. Toward evening the older girls were taken, but another girl and I were left behind. We were small. Hadn't grown up yet. They wanted to leave us in the reserve, but I set up such a howl . . .

In my first battle the officers kept pushing me off the breastwork, because I stuck my head up to see everything. There was some sort of curiosity, childish curiosity . . . Naïveté! The commander shouts: "Private Semyonova! Private Semyonova, you're out of your mind! Fuck it all . . . You'll be killed!" I couldn't understand that: how could I be killed, if I'd only just arrived at the front? I didn't know yet how ordinary and indiscriminate death is. You can't plead or argue with it.

Old trucks kept bringing people's militias. Old men and young boys. They were given two grenades and sent into the battle without a rifle. They were supposed to find themselves a rifle in battle. After the battle there was nobody to bandage . . . They had all been killed . . .

Ekaterina Mikhailovna Rabchaeva
PRIVATE, MEDICAL ASSISTANT

I went through the whole war from beginning to end . . .

When I was hauling my first wounded man, my legs nearly gave way under me. I was hauling him and whispering: "Only let him not die . . . Only let him not die . . ." I was bandaging him and weeping, saying something gentle to him. And the commander passed by. He yelled at me, even used some dirty language . . .

Why did he yell at you?

I shouldn't have pitied him, shouldn't have wept like that. I'd just wear myself out, and there were many wounded.

We drove along, dead soldiers lay there, cropped heads, green as potatoes from the sun . . . They were scattered like potatoes . . . As they ran, so they lay on the plowed field . . . Like potatoes . . .

Natalya Ivanovna Sergeeva
PRIVATE, NURSE-AIDE

I can't tell you where it was . . . In what place . . . Once there were two hundred wounded men in a shed, and I was alone. The wounded were brought straight from the battlefield, lots of them. It was in some village . . . Well, I don't remember, so many years have gone by . . . I remember I didn't sleep or sit down for four days. Each of them cried out: "Nurse . . . dear nurse . . . help me, dear girl!" I ran from one to another, and once I stumbled and collapsed, and instantly fell asleep. I was awakened by shouting. Our commander, a young lieutenant, also wounded, raised himself a little on his healthy side and shouted: "Quiet! I order you to be quiet!" He realized that I was exhausted, and everybody was in pain and calling to me: "Nurse . . . dear nurse . . ." I leaped up and ran—I don't know where, why. And then, for the first time since I got to the front, I wept . . .

And so . . . You never know your own heart. In winter some captive German soldiers were led past our unit. They walked along all frozen, with torn blankets on their heads, holes burnt in their overcoats. It was so cold that birds dropped in flight. The birds froze. A soldier was marching in that column . . . A young boy . . . There were tears frozen on his face . . . And I was taking bread to the mess in a wheelbarrow. He couldn't take his eyes off that wheelbarrow; he didn't see me, only the wheelbarrow. Bread . . . Bread . . . I broke a piece off a loaf and gave it to him. He took it . . . Took it and didn't believe it . . . He didn't believe it!

I was happy . . . I was happy that I wasn't able to hate. I was astonished at myself then . . .

"I ALONE CAME BACK
TO MAMA . . ."

I'm on my way to Moscow . . . What I know about Nina Yakovlevna Vishnevskaya at the moment takes up only a few lines in my notebook: at seventeen she left for the front, went through the war as a medical assistant in the 1st Battalion of the 32nd Tank Brigade of the 5th Army. Took part in the famous tank engagement near Prokhorovka, a confrontation between a total, on both sides—Soviet and German—of 1,200 tanks and self-propelled guns. It was one of the biggest tank battles in world history.

Her address was furnished to me by the schoolboys of Borisovo, who had gathered a lot of material for their museum about the 32nd Tank Brigade, which had liberated their town. Ordinarily the medical assistants in tank units were men, but here was a girl. I prepared to go at once . . .

I had already begun to think about how to choose among dozens of addresses. At first I took notes from everybody I met. They learned about me through the grapevine; they phoned each other. They invited me to their reunions, or simply to one of their homes for tea and cakes. I began to receive letters from all over the country; my address was also passed around. They wrote, "You're one of us, you're a frontline girl, too." I soon realized that it was impossible to write it all down; some other principle of search and selection was needed. What would it be? Having sorted the available addresses, I came up with a formula: to try to record women of various military professions. We all see life through our occupations, through our place in life or the events we participate in. It could be supposed that a nurse saw one war, a baker another, a paratrooper a third, a pilot a fourth, the commander of a submachine-gun platoon a fifth . . . Each of these women had her own radius of visibility, so to speak. One had an operating table: "I saw so many cut-off arms and legs . . . It was even hard to believe that somewhere whole men existed. It seemed they were all either wounded or dead . . ." (A. Demchenko, sergeant major, nurse). Another had the pots and pans of a field kitchen: "Sometimes after a battle there was no one left to eat . . . I'd cook a whole pot of soup, a pot of kasha, and there'd be no one to give it to . . ." (I. Zinina, private, cook); a third a pilot's cockpit: "Our camp was in the forest. I came back from a mission and decided to go to the forest; it was already summer, the strawberries were ripe. I walked down the path and saw a dead German lying there . . . Already black . . . I was so frightened. I'd been in the war for a year and had never seen dead people. Up there it's a different matter . . . When you fly you have one thought: to find your target, bomb it, and come back. We didn't see dead people. We didn't have this fear . . ." (A. Bondareva, lieutenant of the guards, senior pilot). And for a partisan fighter, war to this day is associated with the smell of a burning campfire: "We did everything on the campfire: baked bread and cooked food; we put jackets and felt boots near the remaining coals to dry. During the night we warmed ourselves . . ." (E. Vysotskaya).

But I wasn't left alone with my thoughts for long. The attendant brought tea. The people in my compartment began to introduce themselves noisily and cheerfully. On the table the traditional bottle of Moskovskaya appeared, some homemade snacks, and—as usual with us—a heart-to-heart conversation began. About our family secrets and politics, about love and hate, about leaders and neighbors.

I understood long ago that we are a people of roads and conversations . . .

I also told them who I was going to and why. Two of my fellow travelers fought—one went as far as Berlin as commander of a sapper battalion, the other spent three years as a partisan in the Belorussian forests. We began talking about the war at once.

Later I noted down our conversation as it was preserved in my memory:

—We're a vanishing tribe. Mammoths! We belong to the generation that believed there is something more in a life than human life. There is the Motherland and the great Idea. Well, and also Stalin. Why lie? You can't leave a word out of a song, as they say.

—There's that, of course . . . We had a brave girl in our unit . . . She used to go to the railroad to plant explosives. Before the war her whole family had been arrested: the father, the mother, and two older brothers. She had lived with her aunt, her mother's sister. She sought out the partisans from the first days of the war. We could see in our unit that she was asking for trouble . . . She wanted to prove . . . Everybody got decorated, but she not once. They wouldn't give her a medal, because her parents were enemies of the people. Just before our army came, her leg was blown off. I visited her in the hospital . . . She wept . . . "But now," she said, "everybody will trust me." She was a beautiful girl . . .

—When some fool from the personnel department sent me two girls who were commanders of sapper platoons, I sent them back at once. They were terribly upset. They wanted to go to the front line and make mining passages.

—*Why did you send them back?*

—For many reasons. First, I had enough good sergeants who could do what these girls had been sent for. Second, I thought there was no need for a woman to go to the front line. To that hellfire. There were enough men. I also knew that I'd have to dig them a separate dugout, to surround their commanders' activities with a heap of different girly things. A lot of bother.

—*So, in your opinion, women are out of place in war?*

—We know from history that Russian women in all times didn't only send their husbands, brothers, sons to the war, and grieve and wait for them. Princess Yaroslavna already climbed onto the rampart and poured melted pitch on the heads of the enemy.* But we men had a sense of guilt about girls making war, and it has stayed with me . . . I remember, we were retreating. It was autumn, it rained around the

---

*   Princess Yaroslavna is the wife of Prince Igor Svyatoslavich of Novgorod in the twelfth-century Old Slavic poem *The Lay of Igor's Campaign*.

clock, day and night. There was a dead girl lying by the road . . . She had a long braid, and she was all covered with mud . . .

—There's that, of course . . . When I heard that our nurses, being surrounded, shot at the enemy, defending the wounded soldiers, because they were helpless as children, I could understand that. But now picture this: two women crawl into no-man's-land with a sniper rifle to do some killing. Well, yes . . . I can't help feeling that that was a kind of "hunting," after all . . . I myself shot people . . . But I'm a man . . .

—*But they defended their native land. They saved the Fatherland . . .*

—There's that, of course . . . I'd go on a scouting mission with such a woman, but I wouldn't marry her . . . No . . . We're used to thinking of women as mothers and brides. The beautiful lady, finally.* My younger brother told me how he and some other boys shot stones from slingshots at captive Germans when they were led through our town. Our mother saw it and boxed his ear. And these Germans were greenhorns, the last scraps Hitler had recruited. My brother was seven years old, but he remembered mother looking at them and weeping: "May your mothers be struck blind: how could they let you go to war!" War is a man's business. What, don't you have enough men to write about?

—N-no . . . I'm a witness. No! Let's remember the catastrophe of the first months of the war: our air force was destroyed on the ground, our tanks burned like matchboxes. The rifles were old. Millions of soldiers and officers were captured. Several million! In six weeks Hitler was already near Moscow . . . University professors signed up to serve in the militia. Old professors! And girls were eager to get to the front voluntarily—a coward won't volunteer to go and fight. Those were brave, extraordinary girls. There are statistics: the losses at the front line among medical personnel were in second place after the

---

*   In 1904 the Russian symbolist Alexander Blok (1880–1921) published a collection of poems entitled *Verses About the Beautiful Lady,* expressing his spiritual-erotic vision of the eternal feminine.

losses in the riflemen's battalions. In the infantry. What is it, for instance, to haul a wounded man from a battlefield? I'm going to tell you.

We mounted an attack, and the Germans started to mow us down with submachine-gun fire. And our battalion was no more. Everybody fell. They weren't all killed, many were wounded. The Germans didn't let up. Quite unexpectedly a girl leaped out of the trench, then a second, a third . . . They started bandaging and carrying the wounded men away. Even the Germans went dumb with astonishment for a moment. By ten o'clock in the evening all the girls had been badly wounded, but each of them had saved as many as two or three men. They were meagerly decorated; at the beginning of the war decorations weren't just thrown around. A wounded man had to be saved along with his personal weapons. The first question in the medical unit was: where are the weapons? We didn't have enough of them then. Rifles, submachine guns, machine guns—they had to carry all that as well. In 1941 Order No. 281 was issued concerning decorations for saving soldiers' lives: for saving fifteen badly wounded men, carried from a battlefield along with their personal weapons—the medal "For Distinguished Service"; for saving twenty-five men—the Order of the Red Star; for saving forty—the Order of the Red Banner; for saving eighty—the Order of Lenin. And I just told you what it meant to save at least one wounded man . . . Under fire . . .

—There's that, of course . . . I also remember . . . Well, yes . . . We sent our scouts to a village where a German garrison was stationed. Two of them went . . . Then one more . . . Nobody came back. The commander summoned one of our girls: "You go, Liusya." We dressed her as a cowherd, led her to the road . . . What could we do? There was no other solution. A man would be killed, but a woman could get through. Right . . . But to see a rifle in a woman's hands . . .

—*Did the girl come back?*

—I forget her last name . . . I just remember her first name—Liusya. She was killed . . . The peasants told us afterward . . .

———

There was a long silence. Then we gave a toast to those who had been killed. The conversation took another turn: we talked about Stalin, how before the war he had destroyed the best commanders, the military elite. About the brutal collectivization and about 1937.* The camps and exiles. That without 1937 there would have been no 1941. There would have been no retreat all the way to Moscow. But after the war that was forgotten. The Victory overshadowed everything.

"*Was there love during the war?*" *I asked.*

—I met many pretty girls at the front, but we didn't look at them as women. Though, in my view, they were wonderful girls. But they were our friends, who dragged us off the battlefield. Who saved us, took care of us. I was hauled off wounded twice. How could I have bad feelings about them? But could you marry your brother? We called them little sisters.

—And after the war?

—The war ended, and they all turned out to be terribly defenseless . . . Take my wife—an intelligent woman, but she has bad feelings about girls who were in the war. She thinks they went to the war to find husbands, that they all had love affairs there. Though, in fact, since we're having a sincere conversation, they were mostly honest girls. Pure. But after the war . . . After all the dirt, and lice, and death . . . We wanted something beautiful. Bright. Beautiful women . . . I had a friend, at the front there was a wonderful girl, as I now understand, who loved him. A nurse. But he didn't marry her; he was demobilized and found another, prettier one. And he's unhappy with his wife. Now he remembers the other one, his wartime love; she would have been a good companion to him. But after the front he left her. Because for four

---

*   1937 was the height of Stalin's purges and the Moscow show trials; in June of that year there was also a secret trial of Red Army commanders, followed by their execution, and later in the year there was a massive purge of Red Army officers.

years he had seen her only in old boots and a man's padded jacket . . . We wanted to forget the war. And we forgot our girls, too . . .

—There's that, of course . . . We were all young. We wanted to live . . .

None of us slept that night. We talked till morning.

   . . . I made my way straight from the subway to a quiet Moscow courtyard. With a sandbox and children's seesaw. I walked and recalled the astonished voice on the phone: "You've come? And straight to me? You're not going to verify anything in the Veterans' Council? They have all my data, they've checked me." I was taken aback. I used to think that the sufferings a person goes through made him free; he belonged only to himself. He was protected by his own memory. Now I discovered: no, not always. Often this knowledge and even super-knowledge (there's no such thing in ordinary life) exist separately, as some sort of an emergency reserve or the specks of gold in layers of ore. You need to spend a long time removing the empty rock, rummaging together in the alluvial trifles, and in the end—a flash! A gift!

   Then what are we in reality—what are we made of, what material? How durable is it—that I want to understand. That is why I'm here . . .

   The door is opened by a short, plump woman. She offers me one hand in a manly greeting; the other is held by her little grandson. From his coolness and accustomed curiosity, I understand that there are frequent visitors to this house. They are expected here.

   The big room is uncluttered; there is almost no furniture. Books on a home-made shelf—mostly war memoirs, many enlarged military photographs; a tank helmet hangs on an elk horn; on a polished table there is a row of little tanks with gift labels: "From the soldiers of N. Unit," "From the students of tank school" . . . Beside me on the sofa "sit" three dolls—in military uniforms. Even the curtains and the wallpaper in the room are of khaki color.

   I realize that here the war hasn't ended and never will.

Nina Yakovlevna Vishnevskaya

SERGEANT MAJOR, MEDICAL ASSISTANT OF A TANK BATTALION

Where shall I begin? I've even prepared a text for you. Well, all right, I'll speak from the heart . . . This is how it was . . . I'll tell you as I would a friend . . .

I'll begin by saying that girls were accepted reluctantly into the tank forces. One could even say they weren't accepted at all. How did I get there? We lived in the town of Konakovo, in the Kalinin region. I had just passed my exams to go from junior high to high school. None of us understood then what war was; for us it was some sort of game, something from a book. We had been brought up on the romanticism of the revolution, on ideals. We believed the newspapers: the war would soon end in our victory. At any moment . . .

Our family lived in a big communal apartment. There were many families in it, and every day somebody left for the war: Uncle Petya, Uncle Vasya. We saw them off, and we, the children, were mostly overcome by curiosity. We went all the way to the train with them . . . Music played, women wept, but none of that frightened us; on the contrary, it amused us. The brass band always played the march "The Slav Girl's Farewell." We, too, wanted to get on the train and leave. To that music. The war as we pictured it was somewhere far away. I, for instance, liked uniform buttons, the way they shone. I was already taking courses to become a medical volunteer, but that was also like some sort of child's game. Then our school was closed, and we were mobilized to build defensive constructions. We were housed in a shed, in an open field. We were even proud that we had been sent to do something connected to the war. We were assigned to a battalion of weaklings. We worked from eight in the morning till eight in the evening, twelve hours a day. We dug antitank trenches. We were all girls and boys of fifteen or sixteen . . . And so once, as we were working, we heard voices, some shouting "Air raid!" and some "Germans!" The adults ran to hide, but we were interested in seeing German planes, in seeing what Germans were. They flew over us, but we couldn't see anything. We were even upset. After a while they turned and flew lower. We all saw black crosses. There was no fear; again there was only curiosity. And suddenly they opened machine-gun fire and started rattling away, and before our eyes our own boys and girls, with whom we had been studying and working, began to fall. We were petrified; we simply couldn't understand what was happening. We stood and watched . . . As if rooted to the spot . . . The adults ran up to us and threw us to the ground, and still there was no fear in us . . .

Soon the Germans came very close to our town; they were some seven miles away, we could hear the cannon fire. All of us girls ran to the recruiting office: we, too, had to go and defend the town, to be together. Nobody had any doubts. But they didn't take all of us; they took only the strong, sturdy girls, and above all those who were already eighteen. Good Komsomol girls. Some captain chose girls for a tank unit. He didn't even listen to me, of course, because I was seventeen, and I was only five foot three inches tall.

"An infantry soldier gets wounded," he explained. "He will fall to the ground. You can crawl to him, bandage him on the spot, or drag him to cover. It's not the same with a tank soldier . . . If he gets wounded inside the tank, he has to be pulled out of it through the hatch. How are you going to do that? Tank soldiers are all big and sturdy, you know. You have to climb up on the tank, it's being shelled, there are bullets, shells flying. And do you know how it is when a tank catches fire?"

"But I'm a Komsomol girl like all the others, aren't I?" I began to cry.

"Of course you're also a Komsomol girl. But a very small one."

And my girlfriends, the ones I studied with at school and at the medical courses—big, strong girls—were taken. I was offended that they were going and I was left behind.

I said nothing to my parents, of course. I went to see the girls off, and they took pity on me: they hid me in the back under a tarpaulin. We traveled in an open truck, all wearing different colored kerchiefs—black, blue, red . . . And I had mama's blouse tied on my head instead of a kerchief. As if I was going not to the war, but to an amateur concert. Quite a sight! Like a movie . . . I can't think of it now without smiling . . . Shura Kisseleva even took her guitar along. We rode for a while; the trenches were already in sight. The soldiers saw us and shouted, "Actors are coming! Actors are coming!"

We drove up to the headquarters. The captain ordered us to fall in. We all fell in; I was the last. The girls with their things, and me just so. Since I had left unexpectedly, I had nothing with me. Shura gave me her guitar: "So you won't be empty-handed."

The superior officer came out, and the captain reported to him: "Comrade Lieutenant Colonel! Twelve girls have arrived to serve under your command."

The man looked us over. "There are thirteen in all, not twelve."

The captain insisted, "No, twelve, Comrade Lieutenant Colonel." He was so sure there were twelve of us. Then he turned, looked, and asked me straight out, "Where did you come from?"

I answered, "I've come to fight, Comrade Captain."

"Step forward!"

"I've come with a friend . . ."

"You go to a dance with a friend. Here it's war . . . Come closer."

As I was, with my mother's blouse on my head, I went up to them. I showed my certificate as a medical volunteer. I began to beg: "Don't doubt, sirs, I'm strong. I worked as a nurse . . . I gave blood . . . Please, let me . . ."

They looked over all my papers, and the lieutenant colonel ordered, "To be sent home! In the first vehicle going that way!"

And till the vehicle came, they assigned me temporarily to a medical platoon. I sat and made cotton swabs. The moment I saw some vehicle approaching headquarters, I'd run into the forest. I'd sit there for an hour or two, the vehicle would leave, I'd come back out. And I did that for three days, until our battalion went into combat. The 1st Tank Battalion of the 32nd Tank Brigade . . . Everybody went to fight, and I was preparing dugouts for the wounded. Half an hour hadn't gone by before they started bringing the wounded . . . and the dead . . . One of our girls was killed in that battle. And they all forgot that I was to be sent home. They got used to me. The superiors no longer mentioned it . . .

Now what? Now I had to get into military dress. We were all given kit bags to put our things in. They were brand-new. I cut off the straps, ripped out the bottom, and put it on. It looked like a military skirt . . . Somewhere I found an army shirt that wasn't too ragged, put on a belt, and decided to show myself off to the girls. I had just started turning around before them, when the sergeant major came into our dugout, followed by the commander of the unit.

The sergeant major: "Ten-hut!"

The lieutenant colonel entered, and the sergeant said to him, "Comrade Lieutenant Colonel, permission to speak, sir! There has been an incident with the girls. I issued them kit bags to keep their things in, and they got into them themselves."

At this point the commander of the unit recognized me. "Ah, it's you, the 'stowaway'! Well, then, sergeant, we must put the girls in uniforms."

What did they issue us? Tank soldiers have canvas trousers with thick pads on the knees, but we got thin cotton overalls. The ground there was half mixed with metal, stones were sticking up every-where—so again we went around ragged, because we didn't sit in the tank, but crawled outside on the ground. Tanks often burned. A tank soldier, if he survives, is all covered with burns. We, too, used to get burned, because to pull them out of burning tanks we had to go into the fire. It's very hard to get a man through the hatch, especially a turret gunner. A dead man is heavier than a living one. Much heavier. I learned all that quickly . . .

We were untrained, didn't understand who was which rank, and the sergeant major kept teaching us that we were now real soldiers, had to salute anyone of higher rank, and go about trim, with buttoned overcoats.

The soldiers, seeing we were such young girls, liked to make fun of us. Once I was sent from the medical platoon to get some tea. I came to the cook. He looked at me.

"What have you come for?"

I say, "T-tea . . ."

"The tea isn't ready yet."

"Why not?"

"The cooks are washing in the cauldrons. Once they're done washing, we'll make tea . . ."

I believed him. I took it quite seriously, picked up my buckets, and went back. I met the doctor.

"Why are you coming back empty-handed? Where's the tea?"

"The cooks are washing in the cauldrons," I answered. "The tea isn't ready yet."

He clutched his head. "Which cooks are washing in the cauldrons?"

He went back with me, gave that cook a good going-over, and they poured me two buckets of tea.

I was carrying this tea, and I met the head of the political section and the commander of the brigade. I remembered at once how they taught us that we had to salute everybody, because we were rank-and-file soldiers. And here there are two of them. How am I to greet them both? I tried to decide as I went. When I came up to them, I set the buckets down, put both hands to my visor, and saluted the two of them. They had been walking along without noticing me, but when I did that they froze in astonishment.

"Who taught you to salute that way?"

"The sergeant major. He said we were to salute everybody. And there were two of you coming at once . . ."

For us girls, everything in the army was difficult. It was very hard for us to sort out the different insignia. When we came to the army, there were still diamonds, cubes, stripes, so just try figuring out what his rank is. They say, "Take this letter to the captain." And how can I tell he's a captain? The word itself slips out of your mind on the way. I go.

"Sir, the other sir told me to give you this . . ."

"What other sir?"

"The one who always wears a soldier's shirt. Without a tunic."

What we remembered was not whether this or that officer was a lieutenant or a captain, but whether he was handsome or not, red-headed, tall . . . "Ah, him, the tall one!" Of course, when I saw singed overalls, burned hands, burned faces . . . I . . . It's astonishing . . . I lost the ability to cry . . . The gift of tears, the woman's gift . . . When tank soldiers jumped out of burning vehicles, everything on them was burning. Smoking. They often had broken arms or legs. Those were very badly wounded. A man would lie there and ask, "If I die, write to my mother, write to my wife . . ." And I wasn't able. I didn't know how to tell someone about death . . .

When the tank soldiers picked me up with my legs crippled and brought me to a Ukrainian village—it was in the Kirovograd region—the woman who owned the cottage that housed the medical platoon kept repeating, "What a young lad!"

The tank soldiers laughed. "What do you mean 'lad,' granny, she's a girl!"

She sat down beside me and looked me over. "What do you mean 'girl'? That's not a girl. It's a young lad . . ."

My hair was cut short, I was wearing overalls, a tank helmet—a lad. She yielded me her warm place over the stove and even slaughtered a young pig, so I'd recover more quickly. And she kept pitying me. "Don't they have enough men, that they recruit such children? . . . Little girls? . . ."

From her words, her tears . . . I lost all courage for a while, I felt so sorry for myself, and for mama. What am I doing here among men? I'm a girl. What if I come home with no legs? I had all kinds of thoughts . . . Yes, I did . . . I don't conceal it . . .

At the age of eighteen, at the Kursk Bulge, I was awarded the medal "For Distinguished Service" and the Order of the Red Star; at nineteen, the Order of the Patriotic War, second degree. When fresh reinforcements arrived, all of them young boys, they were surprised, of course. They were also eighteen or nineteen, and sometimes they asked me mockingly, "What did you get your medals for?" or "Have you been in combat?" Or they would taunt me: "Can a bullet pierce the armor of a tank?"

One of them I later bandaged on the battlefield, under fire, and I even remember his last name—Shchegolevatykh. He had a broken leg. I was putting a splint on it, and he asked my forgiveness.

"Forgive me, dear nurse, for offending you that time. To be honest, I liked you."

What did we know about love then? If there was anything, it was a schooltime love, and schooltime love is still childish. I remember we once fell into an encirclement . . . We dug into the ground with our own hands, we had nothing else. No shovels . . . Nothing . . . We were pressed on all sides. We had already decided: that night we would either break through or die. We thought most likely we would die . . . I don't know if I should tell about this or not. I don't know . . .

We camouflaged ourselves. We sat there. We waited for night so as to try and break through somehow. And Lieutenant Misha T.— he was replacing our wounded battalion commander, he was about twenty—began to recall how he loved to dance, to play the guitar. Then he asked, "Have you tried it?"

"What? Tried what?" I was terribly hungry.

"Not what, but who . . . I mean baba!"*

Before the war there was a pastry called "baba."

"No-o-o . . ."

And I never had. We might die and not even know what love is like . . . We'd be killed that night . . .

* "Baba" is both a pastry and a familiar spoken Russian word for "woman."

"Oh, come on, you fool!" Then I finally understood what he meant.

We went to die for life, without knowing what life was. We had only read about it in books. I liked movies about love . . .

Medical assistants in tank units died quickly. There was no room provided for us in a tank; you had to hang on to the armor plating, and the only thought was to avoid having your legs drawn into the caterpillar tread. And we had to watch for burning tanks . . . To jump down and run or crawl there . . . We were five girlfriends at the front: Liuba Yasinskaya, Shura Kiseleva, Tonya Bobkova, Zina Latysh, and me. The tank soldiers called us the Konakovo girls. And all the girls were killed . . .

Before the battle in which Liuba Yasinskaya was killed, she and I sat in the evening hugging each other. We talked. It was 1943. Our division was approaching the Dnieper. She suddenly said to me, "You know, I'll be killed in this battle. I have some sort of premonition. I went to the sergeant major, asked to be issued new underwear, and he turned stingy: 'You got some just recently.' Let's go in the morning and ask together."

I tried to calm her down: "We've been fighting for two years; by now bullets are afraid of us." But in the morning she persuaded me to go to the sergeant major anyway, and we got him to give us new sets of underwear. So there she was in this new undershirt. Snow white, with laces . . . It was all soaked in blood . . . This white and red together, with crimson blood—I remember it to this day. That was how she had imagined it.

The four of us carried her together on a tarpaulin, she'd become so heavy. We lost many in that battle. We dug a big common grave. We put them all in it, without coffins, as usual, and Liuba on top. I still couldn't grasp that she was no longer with us, that I would never see her again. I wanted to take at least something from her to remember her by. She had a ring on her finger, gold or something cheap—I don't know. I took it. The boys held me back: don't you dare, it's bad luck.

But when we were taking leave of her, and each one threw a handful of earth into the grave, I threw some, too, and the ring fell off with it into the grave . . . to Liuba. Then I remembered that she loved that ring very much . . .

Her father went through the whole war and came back alive. Her brother, too. The men of her family came back . . . But Liuba was killed . . .

Shura Kiseleva . . . She was the prettiest of us. Like an actress. She got burned up. She hid the badly wounded among the hayricks, shelling began, the hay caught fire. Shura could have saved herself, but she would have had to abandon the wounded . . . She burned up with them . . .

I found out the details of Tonya Bobkova's death only recently. She shielded the man she loved from a mine fragment. The fragments take a fraction of a second to reach you . . . How did she have time? She saved Lieutenant Petya Boichevsky, she loved him. And he survived.

Thirty years later Petya Boichevsky came from Krasnodar. Found me. And told me all about it. He and I went to Borisov and found the clearing where Tonya was killed. He took some earth from her grave . . . Carried it and kissed it . . .

There were five of us girls from Konakovo . . . But I alone came back to mama.

Unexpectedly for me, Nina Yakovlevna bursts into poetry:

> A brave girl leaps onto the armor plating,
> And she defends her Motherland.
> She's not afraid of bullets or shells—
> Her heart is all aflame.
> Remember, friend, her modest beauty,
> When her body's borne away . . .

She confesses that she composed it at the front. I already know that many of them wrote verses at the front. Even now they are carefully copied out and kept in family archives—artless and touching. Hence their war albums—and they show me albums in every home—often resemble girls' diaries. Only there it's about love, and here it's about death.

I have a close-knit family. A good family. Children, grandchildren . . . But I live in the war, I'm there all the time . . . Ten years ago I tracked down our friend Vanya Pozdnyakov. We thought he had been killed, but it turned out he was alive. His tank—he was a commander—was destroyed by two German tanks at Prokhorovka, and they set fire to it. The crew were all killed, only Vanya was left—without eyes, burned all over. We sent him to the hospital, but we didn't think he would live. There wasn't a living spot on him. All his skin . . . all . . . It came off in big pieces . . . Peeled off. I found his address thirty years later . . . half a lifetime . . . I remember going up the stairs, my legs giving way under me: was it him or wasn't it? He opened the door himself, touched my face with his hands, recognized me: "Ninka, is it you? Is it you?" Imagine, after so many years he recognized me.

His mother is a little old woman, he lives with her; she sat with us at the table and cried. I was surprised.

"Why are you crying? You should rejoice that companions at arms have met again."

She replied, "My three sons went to the war. Two were killed; Vanya alone came home alive."

Vanya lost both eyes. She's been leading him by the hand ever since.

I asked him, "Vanya, the last thing you saw was that field at Prokhorovka, the tank battle . . . What do you remember of that day?"

And do you know what he answered?

"I regret only one thing: that I gave the command for the crew to leave the burning vehicle too early. The boys died anyway. But we could have destroyed one more German tank . . ."

That's what he regrets . . . To this day . . .

He and I were happy during the war . . . No word had been spoken between us yet. Nothing. But I remember . . .

Why was I left alive? What for? I think . . . As I understand, it's in order to tell about it . . .

My meeting with Nina Yakovlevna had a sequel, but in writing. Having tran-scribed her account from the tape recorder and chosen what astonished and im-pressed me most, I sent her a copy, as I had promised. Several weeks later a weighty registered package came from Moscow. I opened it: newspaper clippings, articles, official reports about military and patriotic work conducted by the war veteran Nina Yakovlevna Vishnevskaya in Moscow schools. The material I had sent was also returned; very little was left of it—a lot had been crossed out: the amusing lines about the cooks who washed in the cauldrons, and even the harm-less: "Sir, the other sir told me to give you this . . ." had been removed. And in the margins of the story about Lieutenant Misha T. stood three indignant ques-tion marks and a note: "I am a heroine for my son. A deity! What is he going to think of me after this?"

More than once afterward I met with these two truths that live in the same human being: one's own truth driven underground, and the common one, filled with the spirit of the time. The smell of newspapers. The first was rarely able to resist the massive onslaught of the second. If, for instance, besides the storyteller, there was some family member or friend in the apartment, or a neighbor (espe-cially a man), she would be less candid and confiding than if it was just the two of us. It would be a conversation for the public. For an audience. That would make it impossible to break through to her personal impressions; I would imme-diately discover strong inner defenses. Self-control. Constant correction. And a pattern even emerged: the more listeners, the more passionless and sterile the ac-count. To make it suit the stereotype. The dreadful would look grand, and the incomprehensible and obscure in a human being would be instantly explained. I would find myself in a desert of the past, filled with nothing but monuments.

Great deeds. Proud and impervious. So it was with Nina Yakovlevna: one war she remembered for me—"like a daughter, so you'll understand what we mere girls had to live through." The other was meant for a big audience—"the way other people tell and they write in the newspapers—about heroes and great deeds, so as to educate the youth with lofty examples." I was struck each time by this mistrust of what is simple and human, by the wish to replace life with an ideal. Ordinary warmth with a cold luster.

And I couldn't forget how we drank tea the family way, in the kitchen. And how we both wept.

"TWO WARS LIVE IN
OUR HOUSE . . ."

———

*A gray cinder-block house on Kakhovskaya Street in Minsk. Half of our city
has been built over with these nondescript high-rises, which turn gloomier by the
year. But all the same this one is special. "Two wars are living here in our one
apartment," I will hear, when the door is opened. Sergeant Major First Class
Olga Vasilyevna Podvyshenskaya fought in a naval unit in the Baltic. Her husband, Saul Genrikhovich, was a sergeant in the infantry.*

*Everything is repeated . . . Again I spend a long time studying the family
albums, carefully and lovingly designed and always put on display for guests.
And for themselves as well. Each of these albums has a title: Our Family, The
War, The Wedding, The Children, The Grandchildren. I like this respect for
their own lives, the well-documented love for what has been lived through. For
dear faces. It is quite rare that I meet with such a sense of home, with people
studying their forebears, their line, though I've already visited hundreds of
apartments, been with various families—cultivated and simple. Urban and
rural. Frequent wars and revolutions have probably broken our habit of main-
taining a connection with the past, of lovingly weaving the family web. Of looking far back. Of taking pride. We hasten to forget, to wipe away the traces,
because preserved facts can become evidence, often at the cost of life. No one
knows anything further back than their grandparents; no one looks for their
roots. They made history, but live for the day. On short memory.*

But here it is different . . .

*"Is this really me?" Olga Vasilyevna laughs and sits down beside me on the
sofa. She takes the photograph in which she is wearing a sailor suit with combat*

decorations. "Each time I look at these photos, I get surprised. Saul showed them to our six-year-old granddaughter. She asked me: 'Grandma, you were a boy first, right?'"

"Olga Vasilyevna, did you go to the front at once?"

My war began with evacuation . . . I left my home, my youth. On the way, our train was strafed, bombed; the planes flew very, very low. I remember how a group of boys from a vocational school jumped out of the train; they were all wearing black uniform jackets. Such a target! They were all shot. The planes flew just above ground . . . It felt as if they shot them and counted them off . . . Can you imagine?

We worked at a factory; they fed us there, it wasn't bad. But my heart was burning . . . I wrote letters to the recruitment office. One—a second—a third . . . In June of 1942 I was called up. We were transported to besieged Leningrad across Lake Ladoga on open barges under fire. Of my first day in Leningrad I remember the white night and a detachment of sailors marching in black uniforms. The atmosphere was tense, no one in the streets, only searchlights and sailors marching along wearing cartridge belts, like during the Civil War. Can you imagine? Something from a movie . . .

The city was completely encircled. The front was very close. Tram No. 3 took you to the Kirov factory, and the front began right there. When the weather was clear, there was artillery shelling. They pounded us with direct fire. Pounded, pounded, pounded . . . The big ships moored by the pier were camouflaged, of course, but even so the possibility of a hit was not excluded. We became smoke-screeners. A special unit of smoke camouflage was organized, commanded by a former commander of the division of torpedo boats, Captain Lieutenant Alexander Bogdanov. The girls mostly had secondary technical education or else one or two years of university. Our task was to protect the ships by covering them with smoke. When the shelling began, the sailors would say: "The girls better hurry up and hang the smoke. It feels safer." We went there in vehicles with a special mixture, while everybody was hiding in bomb shelters. In a way, we called the shelling down on ourselves. The Germans shelled this smoke screen . . .

We ate "siege" food, you know, but somehow we bore with it . . . Well, first of all, a matter of youth, that's important, and, second, we had the Leningraders for comparison. We were at least somehow provided for, there was some food, though minimal, but they collapsed from weakness. They died walking. Several children came to us, and we fed them a little from our meager rations. They weren't children, they were some sort of little old people. Mummies. They told us their siege menu, if I can call it that: soup made from leather belts or new leather shoes, aspic made from woodworker's glue, pancakes made from mustard . . . All the cats and dogs in the city had been eaten. The sparrows and magpies had disappeared. Even mice and rats were caught and eaten . . . They fried them somehow . . . Then the children stopped coming, and we waited a long time for them. They probably died. So I think . . . In winter, when Leningrad remained without heating, we were sent to break up the houses in one of the areas where wooden buildings still stood. The most painful moment was when you came up to the house . . . There stood a fine house, but the owners had either died or left, but most often had died. You could tell by the dishes left on the table, by the belongings. For maybe half an hour nobody could raise a crowbar. Can you imagine? We all stood and waited for something. Only when the commander came up and drove in his crowbar could we start knocking it down.

We did logging; we lugged boxes of ammunition. I remember I was dragging one box and fell flat on my face: it was heavier than I was. That was one thing. A second was how hard it was for us as women. Later on I became commander of a section. The section was all young boys. We spent the whole day on a motorboat. The boat was small, and there was no head on it. The boys could do the necessary overboard, and that was that. But what about me? A couple of times I held myself back so long that I just jumped overboard and swam around. They shouted: "Sergeant Major overboard!" And they pulled me out. That's such an elementary trifle . . . But was it such a trifle? I later had to be treated . . . Can you imagine? And the weight of the weapons? Also too heavy for a woman. They began by giving us rifles, and the rifles were taller than we were. Girls walked along, and the bayonets stuck two feet above their heads.

It was easier for men to adjust to it all. To that ascetic life . . . To those relationships . . . But we missed, we missed terribly our homes, our mothers, our comforts. There was a Muscovite among us, Natasha Zhilina; she received a medal "For Courage," and as a bonus she got leave to go home for a few days. When she came back we sniffed her. We literally lined up and sniffed her. We said she smelled like home. We missed home so much . . . We were so overjoyed at the mere sight of an envelope with a letter . . . In papa's handwriting . . . If there happened to be a moment of leisure, we embroidered something, some sort of handkerchiefs. They issued us footwraps, and we made scarves out of them and tied them on our necks. We wanted to do some women's work. There wasn't enough women's work for us; it was simply unbearable. You looked for any pretext to pick up a needle, to mend something, to take back your natural image at least for a time. Of course there was joy and laughter, but all that was not like before the war. It was some peculiar state . . .

The tape recorder records the words, preserves the intonation. The pauses. The weeping and embarrassment. I realize that, when a person speaks, something more takes place than what remains on paper. I keep regretting that I cannot "record" eyes, hands. Their life during the conversation, their own life. Separate. Their "texts."

"We have two wars here . . . That's just it . . ." Saul Genrikhovich enters the conversation. "We begin to remember, and I have the feeling that she remembers her war and I mine. I, too, had something like what she told about the house, or how they lined up to smell the girl who came from home. But I don't remember it . . . It flitted past me . . . It seemed like a trifle at the time. Nonsense. But she didn't tell you about the sailor caps yet . . . Olya, how could you forget such a thing?"

"I didn't. It's the most . . . I'm always afraid to call this story up from my memory. Each time . . . It was like this—at dawn our boats put out to sea. Several dozen of them . . . Soon we heard the battle begin. We waited . . . Listening . . . The battle lasted several hours, and there was a moment when it came very close to the city. But it died down somewhere nearby. Before evening I went to the shore: there were sailor caps floating down the Morskoy Canal. One after another. Sailor caps and big red stains on the waves . . . Splinters of wood . . . Our boys had been thrown into the water somewhere. As long as I stood there, these sailor caps kept floating by. I began to count them, but then I stopped. I couldn't leave and I couldn't look. The Morskoy Canal became a common grave . . .

"Saul, where's my handkerchief? I just had it in my hands . . . Well, where is it?"

"I memorized many of her stories and 'tagged' them, as they now say, for the grandchildren. Often I tell them not about my war, but about hers. I noticed it's more interesting for them," Saul Genrikhovich continues. "I have more specific military knowledge, but she has more feelings. And feelings are always more intense, they're always stronger than facts. We also had girls in the infantry. As soon as one of them appeared among us, we pulled ourselves together. You can't imagine . . . You can't!" He catches himself. "I also picked up that little word from her. But you can't imagine how good it is to hear a woman's laughter at war! A woman's voice.

"Was there love in the war? There was! The women we met there are excellent wives. Faithful companions. Those who married in the war are the happiest people, the happiest couples. We, too, fell in love with each other at the front. Amid fire and death. That makes for a strong bond. There were other things, I won't deny it, because it was a long war and there were many of us in it. But I mostly remember what was bright. Noble.

"I became better in the war . . . Unquestionably! I became better as a human being, because in war there is a lot of suffering. I saw a lot of suffering and I suffered a lot myself. There what's not most important in life is immediately swept aside, it's superfluous. There you understand that . . . But the war took its revenge on us. But . . . We're afraid to admit it to ourselves . . . It caught up with us . . . Not all our daughters' personal lives worked out well. And here's why: their mothers, who were at the front, raised them the way they themselves were raised at the front. And the fathers, too. According to the same moral code. At the front, as I've already said, you see at once how a person is, what he's worth. You can't hide there. Their girls couldn't imagine that life could be different than in their homes. They had not been warned about the world's cruel underside. And these girls, getting married, easily fell into the hands of swindlers, who deceived them, because it was all too easy to deceive them. This happened with many children of our friends from the front. And with our daughter, too . . ."

"For some reason we didn't tell our children about the war. We were probably afraid and took pity on them. Were we right?" Olga Vasilyevna ponders. "I didn't wear my ribbons. There was an occasion when I tore them off and never pinned them on again. After the war I worked as a director of a bread-baking factory. I came to a meeting and my superior, also a woman, saw my ribbons and said in front of everybody: 'Why have you pinned them on like a man?' She herself had the Order of Labor, and she always wore it, but for some reason she disliked my military decorations. When we were alone in the office, I explained it all to her in sailor fashion. She was embarrassed, but I did lose the wish to wear the decorations. I still don't pin them on. Though I'm proud of them.

"It was only decades later that the well-known journalist Vera Tkachenko wrote about us in the central newspaper *Pravda,* about the fact that women were also in the war. And that there are frontline women who have remained single, have not arranged their lives, and still have nowhere to live. And that we were in debt to these saintly women. And then little by little people began to pay more attention to these frontline women. They were forty or fifty years old, and they lived in dormitories. Finally they began to give them individual apartments. My friend . . . I won't mention her name, she might suddenly get offended . . . An army paramedic . . . Wounded three times. When the war ended, she studied in medical school. She had no family; they had all been killed. She lived in great want, had to scrub floors at night for a living. She didn't want to tell anybody that she was an invalid and was entitled to benefits. She tore up all her certificates. I asked her: 'Why did you tear them up?' She wept: 'And who would have married me?' 'Well, so,' I said, 'you did the right thing.' And she wept still louder: 'Those papers would be very useful to me now. I'm very ill . . . ' Can you imagine? She wept.

"To celebrate the thirty-fifth anniversary of the Victory a hundred sailors were invited to Sevastopol, the city of Russian naval glory—veterans of the Great Patriotic War from all the fleets, and among them three women. My friend and I were two of them. And the admiral of the fleet bowed to each of us, thanked us before everybody, and kissed our hands. How can I forget it?!"

"And would you like to forget the war?"

"Forget? Forget . . ." Olga Vasilyevna repeats my question.

"We're unable to forget it. It's not in our power." Saul Genrikhovich breaks the prolonged pause. "Remember, Olya, on Victory Day, we met an old, old mother, who had a little old poster hanging on her neck: 'Looking for Kulnev, Tomas Vladimirovich, reported missing in 1942 in besieged Leningrad.' You could tell by her face that she was well over eighty. How many years has she been looking for him? And she'll go on looking till her last hour. We're the same."

"And I'd like to forget. I want to . . ." Olga Vasilyevna utters slowly, almost in a whisper. "I want to live at least one day without the war. Without our memory of it . . . At least one day . . ."

I remember the two of them together, as in the wartime pictures, one of which they gave me. They're young in them, much younger than I am now. At once everything acquires a different meaning. It comes closer. I look at these young photos and already hear differently what I had just heard and recorded. The time between us disappears.

"TELEPHONES DON'T
SHOOT . . ."

———

They all meet me and talk to me differently . . .

Some start telling their story at once, while still on the phone: "I remember . . . I keep it all in my memory as if it was yesterday . . ." Others put off the meeting and the conversation for a long time: "I have to prepare myself . . . I don't want to wind up in that hell again . . ." Valentina Pavlovna Chudaeva is one of those who was fearful for a long time, reluctant to let me into her troubled world. For several months I called her every now and then, but one day we talked on the phone for two hours and finally decided to meet. At once—the very next day.

And so—here I am . . .

"We'll eat pies. I've been fussing about since morning . . ." the hostess greets me cheerfully on the threshold. "We can talk later. And weep our fill . . . I've lived with my grief for a long time . . . But first of all—the pies. With bird cherry. Like we make in Siberia. Come in.

"Forgive me for addressing you informally. It's a frontline habit: 'Hey girls! Come on, girls!' We're all like that, you know by now . . . You've heard . . . We haven't acquired any crystal, as you see. All that my husband and I have squirreled away fits into a tin candy box: a couple of orders and medals. They're in the cupboard, I'll show you later." She takes me inside. "The furniture's old, too, you see. We'd be sorry to get rid of it. When things live in the house for a long time, they acquire a soul. I believe that."

She introduces me to her friend Alexandra Fyodorovna Zenchenko, a Komsomol worker in besieged Leningrad.

I sit down at the set table . . . Well, so, if it's pies, let it be pies, the more so if they're Siberian, with bird cherry, which I had never tried before.

Three women. Hot pies. But the conversation immediately turns to the war.

"Only don't interrupt her with questions," Alexandra Fyodorovna warns me. "If she stops, she starts crying . . . And after the tears, she'll say nothing . . . So don't interrupt . . ."

Valentina Pavlovna Chudaeva

SERGEANT, COMMANDER OF ANTIAIRCRAFT ARTILLERY

I'm from Siberia . . . What prompted me, a girl from far-off Siberia, to go to the front? From the end of the world, as they call it. Concerning the end of the world, a French journalist asked me that question at a meeting. He looked at me so intently in the museum, I even became embarrassed. What does he want? Why does he stare like that? Then he came up and asked through the interpreter to have an interview with Mrs. Chudaeva. I, of course, became very nervous. I thought: Well, what does he want? Hadn't he listened to me at the museum? But he was evidently not interested in that. The first thing I heard from him was a compliment: "You look so young today . . . How could you have gone through the war?" I answered him: "That proves, as you see, that we were very young when we went to the front." But he was wondering about something else: how did I get to the front from Siberia—it was the end of the world! "No," I figured out, "evidently you're wondering why I, a schoolgirl, would go to the front, if there was no general mobilization." He nodded his head "Yes." "Very well," I said, "I'll answer that question." And I told him my whole life, as I'm going to tell it to you. He wept . . . The Frenchman wept . . . In the end he confessed, "Don't be offended, Mrs. Chudaeva. For the French, World War I caused a greater shock than World War II. We remember it; there are graves and monuments everywhere. But we know little about you. Today many people, especially the young, think it was only America that defeated Hitler. Little is known about the price the Soviet people paid for the victory—twenty million human lives in four years. And about your sufferings. Immeasurable. I thank you—you have shaken my heart."

. . . I don't remember my mother. She died young. My father was a representative of the Novosibirsk local party committee. In 1925 they sent him to his native village to get bread. There was great want in the country, and the kulaks hid the bread and let it rot. I was nine months old then. My mother wanted to go to the village with my father, and he took her along. She took me and my sister, because she had no one to leave us with. Papa once worked as a farmhand for that kulak, whom he threatened at the evening meeting: "We know where you hide the bread. If you don't hand it over yourself, we'll come and take it by force. We'll take it in the name of the revolutionary cause."

The meeting ended, and the family all gathered together. Papa had five brothers. Afterward none of them came back from the Great Patriotic War, and neither did my father. So they all sat down at the festive table—traditional Siberian dumplings. The benches stood along the windows . . . My mother sat between windows, one shoulder by a window, the other by my father, and my father sat where there was no window. It was April . . . At that time in Siberia you can still have frosts. Mother must have been cold. I understood that later, when I grew up. She stood up, threw father's leather jacket over her shoulders, and began to nurse me. At that moment a rifle shot rang out. They were aiming at my father, at his leather coat . . . Mother only managed to say "Pa . . ." and dropped me onto the hot dumplings . . . She was twenty-four years old . . .

Later my grandfather was chairman of the village council in that village. He was poisoned with strychnine; they put it in his water. I've kept a photograph of my grandfather's funeral. There is a cloth draped over his coffin with the inscription "Died at the hands of the class enemy."

My father was a hero of the Civil War, commander of an armored train, which fought against the rebellion of a Czechoslovakian corps. In 1931 he was awarded the Order of the Red Banner. At the time very few people were given that order, especially in Siberia. It was a great honor, and was greatly respected. My father was wounded nineteen times; there wasn't an unhurt place on his body. My mother told—not me, of course, but our relatives—that the White Czechs sentenced my father to twenty years of hard labor. She requested a meeting with him; at the time she was in the last month of pregnancy with Tasya, my older sister. There was such a long corridor in that prison, and they didn't let her walk down it to my father, they said, "Crawl, Bolshevik scum!" And she, just days before giving birth, crawled to my father along this long cement corridor. That's how they had their meeting. She didn't recognize my father; his hair was all gray. A gray-haired old man. He was thirty.

Could I sit there indifferently when the enemy again came to my land, if I had grown up in such a family, with such a father? I was of his blood . . . his dear blood. He had lived through so much . . . He was denounced in 1937; they wanted to slander him. To make him out as an enemy of the people. Well, there were those horrible Stalin purges . . . Yezhovshchina* . . . As Comrade Stalin said, when you chop wood, the chips fly. A new class struggle was proclaimed, so the country never stopped living in fear. In submission. But my father managed to be received by Kalinin,† and his good name was restored. Everybody knew my father.

My relatives told me about these things afterward . . .

And now it's 1941 . . . My last school bell just rang. We all had our plans, our dreams, we were young girls. After the commencement ball, we went for a boat ride down the river Ob to an island. So cheerful, happy . . . As yet unkissed, as they say. I'd never even had a boyfriend. We met the dawn on the island and went back . . . The whole city is seething; people are weeping. All around they repeat, "War!

---

*   Nikolai Yezhov (1895–1940) was head of the NKVD and directed the Great Purge of 1936 to 1938, which was called "Yezhovshchina" ("Yezhov's thing") after him.

†   Mikhail Kalinin (1875–1946), an early Bolshevik and close ally of Stalin's, became chairman of the All-Russian Central Executive Committee in 1919, a position he held until his retirement in 1946.

War!" Radios are turned on everywhere. We couldn't fathom it. What war? We were so happy, we had made such grandiose plans: who was going to study where, to become what. And suddenly—war! The grown-ups wept, but we weren't afraid; we assured each other that within a month we'd "beat the fascists' brains out." We sang prewar songs. Our army would certainly crush the enemy on their own territory . . . There wasn't a shadow of doubt . . . Not a shred . . .

We began to understand it all when death notices started to come back. I simply got sick: "So it was all lies?" The Germans were already preparing to parade on Red Square . . .

My father was not taken to the front. But he stubbornly haunted the recruiting office. Later my father went. And that with his health, his gray hair, his lungs: he had chronic tuberculosis. Just doctored a bit. And at what age? But he went. He joined the Steel Division, or Stalin Division, as it was called.* There were many Siberians in it. We also thought that without us the war wasn't right, that we, too, had to fight. Give us weapons at once! Our whole class ran to the recruiting office. On October 10 I left for the front. My stepmother cried a lot: "Valya, don't go . . . What are you doing? You're so small, so thin, what kind of fighter are you?" I had been rachitic for a long time, a very long time. It happened after my mother was killed. I didn't walk till I was five . . . Where did all this strength come from!?

We rode in freight cars for two months. Two thousand girls, a whole train. A Siberian train. What did we see as we approached the front? I remember one moment . . . I'll never forget it: a broken-down train station and sailors hopping about the platform on their hands. They had no legs or crutches. They walked on their hands . . . The platform was full of them . . . They also smoked . . . They saw us and laughed. Joked. My heart went thump-thump . . . Thump-thump . . . What are we getting into? Where are we going? We sang to cheer ourselves up, sang a lot.

There were commanders with us. They instructed us, encouraged

---

* Stalin took his name from the Russian word стаᴧь, "steel."

us. We studied communications. We arrived in Ukraine, and there we were shelled for the first time. Just when we were in the bathhouse for decontamination. When we came to wash, there was a man on duty there, in charge of the bathhouse. We felt shy with him there; well, we were girls, quite young ones. But once the shelling began, we all clung to him for safety. We got dressed any old way, I wrapped my head with a towel, I had a red towel, and we ran outside. A first lieutenant, also young, shouted, "Run to the shelter, girl! Drop that towel! It breaks cover . . ."

I ran away from him: "I'm not breaking any cover! Mama told me not to go out with a wet head."

He found me after the shelling: "Why didn't you obey me? I'm your commander."

I didn't believe him. "That's all I need, you as my commander . . ."

I argued with him like a kid. We were the same age.

We were issued big, thick overcoats. We were like wheat sheaves in them; we didn't walk, we waddled. At first there were no boots for us. What they had were men's sizes. Then they issued us other boots: the foot part was red, and the upper was black tarpaulin. We strutted around in them! We were all skinny; the men's army shirts hung loose on us. Those who could sew tailored them somehow. But we were girls; that wasn't enough for us! So the first lieutenant started taking measurements. We laughed and cried. The battalion commander came: "Well, has the first lieutenant issued you all your women's things?" The lieutenant says, "Measurements taken. They'll get everything."

And I became a radio operator in an antiaircraft unit. On duty at the command point, in communications. And maybe I would have stayed on as a radio operator for the rest of the war, if I hadn't received a notice that my father had been killed. My beloved papa was no more. The closest person I had. The only one. I started begging, "I want revenge. I want to pay them back for my father's death." I wanted to kill . . . I wanted to shoot . . . They tried to tell me that the telephone was very important in the artillery. But telephones don't shoot . . . I submitted a request to the commander of the regiment. He refused. Then, without thinking twice, I addressed myself to the commander of the division. Colonel Krasnykh came to us, lined us all up, and asked, "Where is the girl who wants to be a gun commander?" I stepped forward: thin, skinny neck, and on that neck a submachine gun hanging, a heavy submachine gun, seventy-one cartridges . . . I was obviously such a pathetic sight that he even smiled. Second question: "What do you want?" I said, "I want to shoot." I don't know what he thought. He said nothing for a long time. Not a word. Then turned sharply and left. "Well," I thought, "that's it, he'll refuse." The commander came running: "The colonel has given his permission . . ."

Do you understand that? Can it be understood now? I want you to understand my feelings . . . You can't shoot unless you hate. It's a war, not a hunt. I remember at political classes they read us the article "Kill Him!" by Ilya Ehrenburg.* As many times as you meet a German, so many times you kill him. A famous article, everybody read it then, learned it by heart. It made a strong impression on me. I carried it in my bag all through the war, that article and papa's death notice . . . Shoot! Shoot! I had to take revenge . . .

I completed a short-term course, very short-term—three months of studies. I learned to shoot. And I became an artillery commander. They sent me to the 1357th Antiaircraft Regiment. At first I kept bleeding from the nose and ears, my stomach was completely upset . . . My throat was so dry I was nauseous . . . At night it wasn't too bad, but in daytime it was very frightening. It seemed the plane was flying straight at you, precisely at your gun. About to ram you! Another moment and it would reduce you to nothing. It's all over! That wasn't for a young girl . . . Not for her ears, not for her eyes . . . First we had the eighty-five millimeters. They proved good around Moscow. Then they were sent against tanks, and we were given thirty-seven millime-

---

* Ilya Ehrenburg (1891–1967) was a prolific Soviet writer and journalist. His article "Kill Him!" (the actual title was simply "Kill!"), published in 1942, was widely read.

ters. That was at the Rzhevsk front . . .* There were such battles there . . . In spring the ice began to break up on the Volga . . . and what did we see? We saw a red-and-black ice block floating along, and on it two or three Germans and one Russian soldier . . . They had perished like that, clutching each other. They were frozen into this ice block, and the ice block was all bloody. All our Mother Volga was bloody . . .

She suddenly stopped. "I need to catch my breath . . . Or else I'll start sobbing, and our meeting will be ruined . . ." She turned to the window to get control of herself. A moment later she was already smiling. "Honestly, I don't like to cry. As a child I learned not to cry . . ."

"And listening to Valya, I remembered besieged Leningrad." Alexandra Fyodorovna, who had been silent till then, entered the conversation. "Especially one incident that astounded us all. They told us about an old woman who opened her window every day and threw water out with a dipper, and each time she managed to throw it further and further. First we thought: well, she's probably crazy, all sorts of things happened during the siege, and we went to her to find out what was the matter. Listen to what she said to us: 'If the fascists come to Leningrad, and set foot on my street, I'll scald them with boiling water. I'm old, there's nothing else I can do, so I'll scald them with boiling water.' And she practiced . . . Every day . . . The siege had just begun, there was still hot water . . . She was a very cultivated woman. I even remember her face.

"She chose a way of fighting for which she was still strong enough. Imagine that moment. The enemy was already close to the city, combat went on at the Narva Gates, the Kirov Factory was being shelled . . . Each person thought of doing something to defend the city. To die was too easy; you had to do something. To act. Thousands of people thought the same . . ."

"I want to find the words . . . How can I express it all?" Valentina Pavlovna asked either us or herself.

---

* The Rzhevsk front, around the town of Rzhev to the west of Moscow, was the scene of a series of battles from October 1941 to March 1943. The front came to be known as the "Rzhev meat grinder" owing to the immense loss of both military and civilian lives.

——

I came back from the front crippled. I had been wounded in the back by shrapnel. The wound wasn't big, but I had been thrown way off into a snowdrift. And for several days I hadn't dried my felt boots. Maybe there wasn't enough firewood, or it wasn't my turn to dry them at night. Our stove was small, and there were many of us. Before they found me, my feet got badly frostbitten. I was obviously covered with snow, but I could breathe, and an opening formed itself in the snow . . . A sort of pipe . . . The first-aid dogs found me. They dug into the snow and took my ear-flapped hat. My death passport was in it; we all had these passports: which family members to inform, and where. They dug me out, put me on a tarpaulin, my jacket was soaked with blood . . . But nobody paid attention to my feet . . .

I spent six months in the hospital. They wanted to amputate my leg, amputate it above the knee, because gangrene was setting in. And here I turned a little fainthearted, I didn't want to go on living as a cripple. What should I live for? Who needs me? No father, no mother. A burden in life. Who needs a stump like me? I'll strangle myself . . . And I asked the nurse-aide for a big towel instead of a small one . . . They all teased me in the hospital: "And here's granny . . . Old granny's lying here." Because when the head of the hospital saw me for the first time, he asked: "Well, and how old are you?" I said quickly, "Nineteen . . . I'll be nineteen soon . . ." He laughed: "Oh! That's old, old. A ripe old age." So the nurse-aide Aunt Masha also teased me that way. She said to me, "I'll give you the towel, because they're preparing you for surgery. But I'll keep an eye on you. I don't like your look, girl. Have you got something naughty in mind?" I said nothing . . . But I saw it was true: they were preparing me for surgery. And I didn't know what surgery was, I had never once been under the knife, not like now, when my body's a geographical map, but I could guess. I hid the big towel under my pillow and waited till everybody left or fell asleep. We had iron beds. I thought I'd tie the towel to the bed and strangle myself. If I had strength enough. But Aunt Masha didn't leave my side all night. She saved my young life. She didn't sleep . . . She saved foolish me . . .

My ward doctor, a young lieutenant, went after the head doctor and asked, "Let me try. Let me try . . ." And the head doctor: "What are you going to try? One of her toes is already black. The girl's nineteen. She'll die because of you and me." It turned out that my ward doctor was against the surgery. He suggested another treatment, new at the time. To inject oxygen under the skin with a special needle. Oxygen nourishes . . . Well, I don't quite know how it works, I'm not a medic . . . And he, this young lieutenant, persuaded the head doctor. They didn't cut off my leg. They started using that treatment. And after two months I began to walk. With crutches, of course; my legs were like rags, no support at all. I saw them, but I didn't feel them. Then I learned to walk without the crutches. They congratulated me: you've been born for the second time. After the hospital I was supposed to rest. Rest how? Where? I had no one. I went back to my unit, to my gun. There I joined the Party. At the age of nineteen . . .

I met Victory Day in East Prussia. For two days it was quiet, there was no shooting, then in the middle of the night a sudden signal: "Alert!" We all jumped up. And there came a shout: "Victory! Capitulation!" Capitulation was all right, but victory—that really got to us. "The war's over! The war's over!" We all started firing whatever we had: submachine guns, pistols . . . We fired our gun . . . One wiped his tears, another danced: "I'm alive, I'm alive!" A third fell to the ground and embraced it, embraced the sand, the stones. Such joy . . . And I was standing there and I slowly realized: the war's over, and my papa will never come home. The war was over . . . The commander threatened later, "Well, there won't be any demobilization till the ammunition's paid for. What have you done? How many shells have you fired?" We felt as if there would always be peace on earth, that no one would ever want war, that all the bombs should be destroyed. Who needed them? We were tired of hatred. Tired of shooting.

How I wanted to go home! Even if papa wasn't there, and mama wasn't there. Home is something greater than the people who live in it, and greater than the house itself. It's something . . . a human being should have a home . . . But I bow down to my stepmother . . . She met me like a mother. I've called her mama ever since. She waited for me, waited so much. Although the hospital director had written that my leg had been amputated, that I'd be brought to her a cripple. He wanted to prepare her. He promised that I could stay with her for a while, and afterward I'd be taken away . . . But she wanted me to come home . . .

She waited for me . . . I resembled my father very much . . .

We left for the front at the age of eighteen or twenty and came back at twenty or twenty-four. First there was joy, but then fear: what were we going to do in civilian life? There was a fear of peaceful life . . . My girlfriends had managed to finish various institutes, but what about us? Unfit for anything, without any professions. All we knew was war, all we could do was war. I wanted to get rid of the war as quickly as possible. I hastily remade my uniform coat into a regular coat; I changed the buttons. Sold the tarpaulin boots at a market and bought a pair of shoes. When I put on a dress for the first time, I flooded myself with tears. I didn't recognize myself in the mirror. We had spent four years in trousers. There was no one I could tell that I had been wounded, that I had a concussion. Try telling it, and who will give you a job then, who will marry you? We were silent as fish. We never acknowledged to anybody that we had been at the front. We just kept in touch among ourselves, wrote letters. It was later that they began to honor us, thirty years later . . . to invite us to meetings . . . But back then we hid, we didn't even wear our medals. Men wore them, but not women. Men were victors, heroes, wooers, the war was theirs, but we were looked at with quite different eyes. Quite different . . . I'll tell you, they robbed us of the victory. They quietly exchanged it for ordinary women's happiness. Men didn't share the victory with us. It was painful . . . Incomprehensible . . . Because at the front men treated us marvelously well; they always protected us. I've never encountered such an attitude toward women in peaceful life. When we retreated, we'd lie down to rest on the bare ground, they stayed in their army shirts and gave us their overcoats: "The girls . . . The girls need to be covered . . ." They'd find a piece of cotton wool or a bandage somewhere: "Take it, you might need it . . ." They'd share a last little rusk. We saw and knew nothing but kindness and warmth during the war. And after the war? I'm silent . . . Silent . . . What keeps us from remembering? The unbearableness of the memories . . .

My husband and I arrived in Minsk. We had nothing, not even a sheet, or a mug, or a fork . . . Two overcoats, two army shirts. We found a good map, mounted on cotton fabric. We soaked it . . . it was a big map . . . This cotton was our first sheet. Later, when our daughter was born, we cut it up for diapers. This map . . . I still remember, it was a political map of the world . . . And our daughter slept in a suitcase . . . The plywood suitcase my husband brought from the front served as a cradle. Besides love there was nothing in the house. I'll say that . . . Once my husband came: "Let's go, I saw a discarded old sofa" . . . And we went to get the sofa—at night, so that nobody would see us. How we rejoiced over that sofa!

All the same we were happy. I now had so many girlfriends! It was a hard time, but we were never downcast. We'd get food with our coupons and call each other: "Come, I got some sugar. We'll have tea . . ." We had nothing over our heads, nothing under us, no rugs, no crystal, nothing . . . And we were happy. Happy because we were still alive. We talked, we laughed. We walked in the streets . . . I admired things all the time, though there was nothing to admire— broken stones all around, even the trees were crippled. But we were warmed by the feeling of love. People somehow needed people; we all needed each other very much then. It was later that we separated, each on his own, in his own home, his own family, but then we were still together. Shoulder to shoulder, like in a trench at the front . . .

Now I'm often invited to meetings at the war museum . . . Asked to lead excursions. Yes, now. Forty years later! Forty! Recently I appeared before some young Italians. They asked me questions: What kind of doctor treated me? What were my illnesses? For some reason they wanted to know whether I consulted a psychiatrist. And what sort of dreams did I have? Did I dream about the war? A Russian woman who fought with weapons was a riddle to them. Who is this woman who not only saved people and bandaged wounds, but herself shot guns and blew things up . . . Killed men . . . They were also interested in whether I was married. They were sure that I wasn't. That I was single. And I laughed, "Everybody brought trophies home from war, and I brought my husband . . . I have a daughter. Now my grandchildren are growing up . . ." I haven't told you about love . . . I won't be able to, my heart isn't strong enough. Some other time . . . There was love! There was! Can a human being live without love? Survive without love? Our battalion commander fell in love with me at the front . . . During the whole war he protected me, wouldn't let anyone go near me, but once he was demobilized he sought me out in the hospital. Then he declared himself . . . Well, about love later . . . You come, be sure to come. You'll be my second daughter . . . Of course, I dreamed of having many children, I love children. But I have only one daughter . . . My dear daughter . . . I had no health, no strength. And I couldn't study—I was often sick. My feet, always my feet . . . They're my weak point . . . Before I retired I worked as a technician in the Polytechnical Institute. Everybody liked me, professors and students. Because there was a lot of love in me, a lot of joy. That's how I understood life, that's how I wanted to live after the war. God didn't make us for shooting, He made us for love. What do you think?

Two years ago our chief of staff, Ivan Mikhailovich Grinko, visited me. He retired long ago. He sat at this same table. I also baked pies. He talked with my husband, reminisced . . . Mentioned our girls. And I burst into tears: "Honor, you say, respect. But those girls are almost all single. Unmarried. They live in communal apartments. Who pitied them? Defended them? Where did you all disappear to after the war? Traitors!!" In short, I ruined their festive mood . . .

The chief of staff was sitting where you are now. "Show me," he pounded his fist on the table, "show me who offended you. Just show him to me!" He asked my forgiveness. "I can't say anything to you,

Valya, I can only weep." But there's no need to pity us. We're proud. Let them rewrite history ten times. With Stalin or without Stalin. But this remains—we were victorious! And our sufferings. What we lived through. This isn't junk and ashes. This is our life.

Not a word more . . .

Before I leave she hands me a packet of pies. "They're Siberian. Special. You can't buy them in any store." I also get a long list of addresses and phone numbers. "They'll all be glad to see you. They're waiting. I'll explain to you: it's terrible to remember, but it's far more terrible not to remember."

Now I understand why they speak all the same . . .

"THEY AWARDED US
LITTLE MEDALS . . ."

———

Every morning I open my mailbox . . .

My personal mail resembles more and more the mail of a recruiting office or a museum. "Greetings from the women pilots of the Marina Raskova Air Regiment." "I am writing to you on behalf of the women partisans of the Zhelezniak Brigade." "The women of the Minsk Underground congratulate you . . . We wish you success in the work you are beginning . . ." "The privates of the Women's Field Bath-and-Laundry Detachment address you . . ." In all the time of my search I have had only a few desperate refusals: "No, it's like a terrible dream . . . I can't! I won't!" or "I don't want to remember! I don't want to! It took me so long to forget . . ."

I remember yet another letter, with no return address: "My husband, a chevalier of the Order of Glory, got ten years in the labor camps after the war . . . That is how the Motherland met her heroes. The victors! He had written in a letter to his university friend that he had difficulty being proud of our victory— our own and other people's land was covered with heaps of Russian corpses. Drowned in blood. He was immediately arrested . . . His epaulettes were torn off . . .

"He came back from Kazakhstan after Stalin's death . . . Sick. We have no children. I don't need to remember the war, I've been at war all my life . . ."

Not everyone ventures to write down their memories, and not everyone succeeds in entrusting to paper their feelings and thoughts. "Tears hamper me . . ." (A. Burakova, sergeant, radio operator). And so the correspondence, against my expectations, provides only addresses and new names.

V. Gromova
MEDICAL ASSISTANT

I have enough metal in me . . . I carry a fragment from a wound I received near Vitebsk in my lung, within an inch of my heart. A second fragment in the right lung. Two in the region of the stomach . . .

Here is my address . . . Come. I cannot write more, I don't see anything for my tears . . .

V. Voronova
TELEPHONE OPERATOR

I have no big decorations, only medals. I don't know whether you would be interested in my life, but I would like to tell it to somebody . . .

Alexandra Leontievna Boiko
FIRST LIEUTENANT, TANKMAN

My husband and I lived in the Far North, in Magadan. My husband worked as a driver, I as a ticket collector. As soon as the war began, we both asked to be sent to the front. We were told to work where we were needed. Then we sent a telegram addressed to Comrade Stalin, saying that we were contributing fifty thousand rubles (a lot of money at the time, it was all we had) to the construction of a tank, and we both wanted to go to the front. We received an expression of gratitude from the government. And in 1943 my husband and I were sent to the Chelyabinsk tank training school, which we finished as externs.

In that school they also assigned us a tank. We were both senior driver mechanics, and a tank needs only one. The superiors decided to appoint me commander of an IS-122 tank, and my husband a senior driver mechanic. We went through the whole war as far as Germany. Both wounded. Have decorations.

There were quite a few girl tankmen of medium-sized tanks, but I was the only one who worked on a heavy tank. I sometimes think it would be good if some writer wrote about my life. I do not know how to do it myself . . .

I. A. Levitsky

COMMANDER OF THE 5TH SECTION OF THE 784TH ANTIAIRCRAFT ARTILLERY REGIMENT

1942 . . . I was made commander of a section. The regimental commissar warned me, "Bear in mind, Captain, you are taking charge not of an ordinary section, but a 'girls' section. It is half made up of girls, and they require a special approach, special attention and care." I knew, of course, that girls served in the army, but I could not picture it very well to myself. We career officers were apprehensive of "the weaker sex" being involved in military affairs, which from time immemorial had been considered men's work. Well, nurses, let's say— that was a usual thing. They had already proved themselves in World War I, then in the Civil War. But what would girls do in the antiaircraft artillery, where they would have to carry very heavy shells? How to place them in a battery where there is only one dugout, and there are men in the crew? They have to sit for hours at the controls, and they are metal, and the seats are also metal, and that's not good for girls. Where, finally, would they wash and dry their hair? A mass of questions arose, it was such an unusual thing . . .

I started going around the batteries, taking a closer look. I confess, I felt a little out of sorts. A girl is standing guard with a rifle, a girl is on the watchtower with binoculars—and here I've come from the front, from the front line. And they were so different—bashful, timorous, mincing, or resolute, fired up. Not all of them knew how to submit to military discipline; women's nature resists army rules. She would forget what she had been ordered to do, or else she would receive a letter from home and spend the whole morning weeping. You punish them, and another time you cancel the punishment—out of pity. I kept thinking, "These people will be the end of me!" But soon I had to abandon all my doubts. The girls became real soldiers. We walked a hard path together. Do come. We'll have a long talk . . .

The most diverse addresses—Moscow, Kiev, the town of Apsheronsk in the Krasnodar region, Vitebsk, Volgograd, Yalutorovsk, Suzdal, Galich, Smolensk . . . How can I include them all? The country is enormous. And here chance comes to my aid. An unexpected prompting. One day the mail brings me an invitation from the veterans of the 65th Army of General P. I. Batov: "We usually gather on May 16 and 17 in Moscow on Red Square. A tradition, and a ritual. Everyone who is still strong enough turns up. They come from Murmansk and Karaganda, from Alma-Ata and Omsk. From everywhere. From all over our boundless Motherland . . . In short, we'll be waiting . . ."*

. . . The Hotel Moscow. The month of May—the month of the Victory. Everywhere people embrace, weep, take pictures. I can't tell the flowers pressed to people's breasts from the medals and decorations pinned to them. I enter this stream, and it bears me up and carries me, draws me in irresistibly, and soon I find myself in an almost unfamiliar world. On an unfamiliar island. Among people I recognize or don't recognize, but I know one thing—I love them all. Usually they are lost among us and invisible, because they are already departing, there are fewer and fewer of them, and more of us, but once a year they gather together, in order to go back if only for a moment to their time. And their time is their memories.

On the seventh floor, room 52, Hospital No. 5257 has gathered. At the head of the table—Alexandra Ivanovna Zaitseva, military doctor, captain. She is glad to see me and happily introduces me to everybody as if she and I had known

* General Pavel Ivanovich Batov (1897–1985), a much-decorated general of the Red Army, commanded the 65th Army from 1942 to the end of the war, on the Don front, at Kursk, and later in Belorussia.

each other for a long time. Yet I had knocked on this door completely by chance. At random.

I write down: Galina Ivanovna Sazonova, surgeon; Elizaveta Mikhailovna Aizenstein, doctor; Valentina Vasilyevna Lukina, surgery nurse; Anna Ignatyevna Gorelik, senior surgery nurse; Nadezhda Fyodorovna Potuzhnaya, Klavdia Prokhorovna Borodulina, Elena Pavlovna Yakovleva, Angelina Nikolaevna Timofeeva, Sofya Kamaldinovna Motrenko, Tamara Dmitrievna Morozova, Sofya Filimonovna Semeniuk, Larissa Tikhonovna Deikun, nurses.

OF DOLLS AND RIFLES

—Ehh, girls, how vile it was, this war . . . When you look at it with our eyes. Simple women's eyes . . . As frightful as can be. That's why they don't ask us . . .

—Do you remember, girls, we were riding in the freight cars . . . And the soldiers laughed at how we held our rifles. We didn't hold them the way you hold a weapon, but like this . . . Now I can't even show it . . . The way you hold a doll . . .

—People wept, shouted . . . I hear the word "War!" And I think, "What war, if we have an exam tomorrow at the institute? An exam— it's so important. What kind of war can there be?"

A week later the bombings began; we were already saving people. Three courses in medical school meant something at such a time. But in the first days I saw so much blood that I began to be afraid of it. There's a half-doctor for you, there's "honors" in practical courses. But people behaved exceptionally well. And that was encouraging.

I told you, girls . . . The bombing was over, and I see the ground in front of me stirring. I run there and begin to dig. With my hands I felt a face, hair . . . It was a woman . . . I dug her out and began to weep over her. But she, when she opened her eyes, didn't ask what happened to her, she started worrying, "Where's my purse?"

"What do you want with your purse now? You'll find it."

"My papers are in it."

Her thoughts were not about how she was, whether she was hurt, but where her party card and military ID were. I immediately started looking for her purse. Found it. She laid it on her breast and closed her eyes. Soon the ambulance came, and we put her in. I checked once more whether the purse was there.

In the evening I came home, told my mother about it, and said I had decided to go to the front . . .

—Our troops were retreating . . . We all came out to the road . . . An elderly soldier walks by, stops at our house and bows very low before my mother. "Forgive me, mother . . . Try to save your girl! Aie, save your girl!" I was sixteen then, I had a very long braid . . . And black eyelashes—like this!

—I remember how we went to the front . . . A truckload of girls, a big covered truck. It was night, dark, and the branches brushed against the canvas, and we were so tense, it seemed like it was bullets, that we were under fire . . . The war brought about a change in words and sounds . . . The war . . . Ah, it's always right next to us now! You say "mama" and it's quite a different word; you say "home" and it's also quite different. Something was added to them. More love was added, more fear. Something else . . .

But from the first day I was convinced that they wouldn't defeat us. Our country is so big. Endless . . .

———

—Mama's girl . . . I had never left our town, never slept in anyone else's house, and I wound up as a junior doctor in a mortar battery. What it did to me! The mortars would begin to shoot—and I would go deaf at once. It was as if I was burned all over. I'd sit down and whisper, "Mama, dear mama . . . Dear mama . . ." We were stationed in the forest. I'd get up in the morning—it was quiet, dewdrops hanging. Can this be war? When it's so beautiful and so good . . .

They told us to wear uniforms, and I was five feet tall. I put the trousers on and the girls pulled them all the way up to my shoulders. So I wore my own clothes and tried to hide from the superiors. They put me in the guardhouse for violating army discipline . . .

—I would never have believed . . . I didn't know I could sleep while I walked. You march in a column and you sleep. You bump into the one marching ahead of you, wake up for a second, and fall asleep again. A soldier's sleep is sweet everywhere. Once, in the dark, instead of going straight I swerved to the side and walked into a field. I walked and slept, until I fell into some kind of ditch. Then I woke up and ran to overtake the others.

Soldiers sit during a halt—they have one hand-rolled cigarette for the three of them. One smokes, the other two sleep. Even snore . . .

—I'll never forget it: they brought a wounded man, took him off the stretcher . . . Someone felt his pulse, "No, he's dead." We stepped aside. And then the wounded man breathed. I knelt in front of him and heard him breathing. I sobbed and shouted, "Doctor! Doctor!" They roused the doctor, shook him, and he fell like a sheaf of wheat, he was so fast asleep. They couldn't rouse him even with sal ammoniac. He hadn't slept for three days before then.

And how heavy the wounded are in winter . . . The army shirts get stiff from blood and melted snow, the tarpaulin boots from blood and ice—impossible to cut. They're all cold, like the dead.

You look out the window—winter, indescribably beautiful. Magic white firs. You forget everything for a moment . . . Then again . . .

—It was a ski battalion . . . All tenth-graders . . . They were mowed down by machine guns . . . One of them was brought in; he was crying. And we're the same age, but already older from experience. You embrace him, "Dear child." And he: "If you'd been there, you wouldn't say 'child' . . . " He was dying and screaming all night long: "Mama! Mama!" There were two fellows there from Kursk; we called them "the Kursk nightingales." You come to wake him up, he's sound asleep, his lips wet with spittle. They were like little children . . .

—We stood at the operating table around the clock . . . You stand there, and your arms drop by themselves. Once my head sank down right onto the man I was operating on. Sleep! Sleep! Sleep! Our feet were swollen; they wouldn't get into the tarpaulin boots. Our eyes were so tired it was hard to close them . . .

My war has three smells: blood, chloroform, and iodine . . .

—Ohh! And the wounds . . . Big, deep, jagged . . . You could lose your mind . . . Fragments of bullets, grenades, shells in the head, in the guts—all over the body. Along with metal we take out uniform buttons, pieces of overcoats and shirts, leather straps. I remember one, his whole chest was turned inside out, you could see his heart . . . Still beating, but he was dying . . . I'm bandaging him for the last time and can barely hold back my tears. I must finish quickly, I think, and go to some corner and cry my fill. He says, "Thank you, dear nurse . . ." and he hands me some small metal object. I look: it's a crossed saber and rifle. "Why are you giving it to me?" I ask. "Mama said this talisman would save me. But I don't need it anymore. Maybe you're luckier than me?" He said it and turned to the wall.

By evening we had blood in our hair, it had soaked through the gown to our bodies, was on our caps and masks. Black, sticky, mixed with everything there is in a man. With urine, with excrement . . .

Another time one of them would call me, "Nurse, my leg hurts." But there was no leg . . . Most of all I was afraid of carrying the dead. The wind lifts the sheet, and he looks at you. If his eyes were open, I couldn't carry him, I had to close them . . .

—A wounded man was brought . . . He lay all bandaged on the stretcher; the wound was to the head, you could see almost nothing of him. Just a little. But I obviously reminded him of someone, and he addressed me, "Larissa . . . Larissa . . . Larochka . . ." Apparently a girl he loved. And that is my name, but I knew I'd never met this man before. Yet he was calling me. I went to him, didn't know what to think, kept looking at him. "You've come? You've come?" I took his hands, bent down . . . "I knew you'd come . . ." He whispered something, but I didn't understand what he whispered. Even now I can't talk about it calmly; when I remember it, tears come to my eyes. "When I was leaving for the front," he said, "I didn't have time to kiss you. Kiss me . . ."

So I bent down and kissed him. A tear welled up, ran off into the bandages, and vanished. And that was all. He died . . .

OF DEATH AND ASTONISHMENT
IN THE FACE OF DEATH

—People didn't want to die . . . We responded to every moan, every cry. One wounded man, when he felt he was dying, seized me by the shoulder, embraced me, and wouldn't let go. It seemed to him that if someone was next to him, if the nurse was there, life wouldn't leave him. He asked, "Just five more minutes of life. Just two more minutes . . ." Some died inaudibly, quietly; others cried out, "I don't want to die!" Men cursed: "Fuck it all . . ." One man started to sing . . . A Moldavian song . . . A man is dying, but he still doesn't think, doesn't believe he's dying. But you see this yellow, yellow color coming from under the hairline, you see the shadow moving first over the face, then down under the clothes . . . He lies dead, and on his face there's some sort of astonishment, as if he's lying there thinking, "How is it I'm dead? Can it be I'm dead?"

As long as he can hear . . . Till the last moment you tell him, no, no, how could you die? You kiss him, embrace him. There now, there now. He's already dead, eyes fixed on the ceiling, but I still whisper something . . . soothing him . . . The names are erased, gone from my memory, but the faces are still there . . .

—They bring the wounded . . . They're crying . . . Crying not from pain, but from impotence. It was their first day at the front; some of them hadn't fired a single shot. They weren't given any rifles, because in the first year of the war weapons cost their weight in gold. And the Germans had tanks, mortars, airplanes. Their comrades fell, they picked up their rifles. Grenades. They went into combat barehanded . . . Like into a fistfight . . .

And ran straight into tanks . . .

———

—When they were dying . . . The way they looked around . . . The way they . . .

—My first wounded man . . . A bullet had hit him in the throat. He lived for several more days, but he couldn't speak . . .

When an arm or a leg is amputated, there is no blood. There is clean white flesh; the blood comes later. To this day I can't cut up a chicken, if it's clean white flesh. It makes my mouth taste very salty . . .

—The Germans didn't take women soldiers prisoner . . . They shot them at once. Or led them before their lined-up soldiers and showed them off: look, they're not women, they're monsters. We always kept two bullets for ourselves, two—in case one misfired.

One of our nurses was captured . . . A day later we took back that village. There were dead horses lying about, motorcycles, armored vehicles. We found her: eyes put out, breasts cut off. They had impaled her on a stake . . . It was freezing cold, and she was white as could be, and her hair was all gray . . . She was nineteen years old.

In her knapsack we found letters from home and a green rubber bird. A child's toy . . .

—We retreat . . . They shell us. During the first year we kept retreating. The fascist planes flew very low, hunting down each person. It always seemed it was you he was after. I'm running . . . I see and hear that the plane is aiming at me. I see the pilot, his face, and he sees that we're young girls . . . It's a hospital train . . . He rattles away along the wagons, and even smiles. He's having fun . . . Such an insolent, terrible smile . . . A handsome face . . .

I can't stand it . . . I shout . . . I run into a cornfield—he's there; I turn toward the forest—he presses me to the ground. I reach the underbrush . . . I ran into the forest and hid in some old leaves. My nose bled from fear, I didn't know whether I was alive or not. I was alive . . . Since then I've been very afraid of planes. It's still far away, but I'm already afraid; I don't think of anything anymore, except that it's flying, where can I hide, where can I huddle, so as not to see and hear. To this day I can't stand the sound of planes. I never fly . . .

—Ehh, girls . . .

—Before the war I wanted to get married . . . to my music teacher. It was a crazy story. I was seriously in love . . . So was he . . . Mama didn't allow it: "You're too young!"

Soon the war began. I asked to be sent to the front. I wanted to leave home, to become an adult. At home they wept as they got me ready for the road. Warm socks, underwear . . .

I saw my first dead man on the first day . . . A stray fragment happened to fly into the schoolyard where our hospital was and mortally wounded our paramedic. And I thought: my mother decided I was too young to marry, but I'm not too young for the war . . . My beloved mama . . .

—We've just arrived . . . We set up the hospital, fill it with the wounded, and then the order: evacuate. We put some of the wounded in trucks, not all. There aren't enough trucks. They hurry us: "Leave them . . . Go without them . . ." You're getting ready to go, they look at you. Follow you with their eyes. There's everything in their look: humility, hurt . . . They ask, "Brothers! Dear sisters! Don't leave us to the Germans. Finish us off." So sad! So sad! Whoever can walk leaves with us. Those who can't—lie there. And you have no strength left to help any of them, you're afraid to raise your eyes . . . I was young, I cried all the time . . .

When we began to advance we didn't leave a single one of our wounded. We even picked up the German wounded. And for a while I worked with them. I got used to it, I bandaged them, it was all right. Then I'd remember 1941, when we had to leave our wounded, and what they did to them . . . How they treated them . . . We saw . . . It seemed I'd never be able to go near them . . . The next day I'd go and bandage them . . .

—We saved lives . . . But many were sorry they were medics and could only bandage, and hadn't taken up arms. Didn't shoot. I remember . . . I remember that feeling. I remember that the smell of blood on the snow was especially strong . . . The dead . . . They lay in the fields. Birds tore their eyes out, pecked their faces, their hands. Aie, an impossible life . . .

—Toward the end of the war . . . I was afraid to write letters home. I won't write, I thought, because what if I'm suddenly killed, and mama will weep that the war was over, and I died just before the Victory. Nobody talked about it, but everybody thought about it. We already sensed that we'd soon be victorious. The spring had already begun.

I suddenly saw that the sky was blue . . .

—What do I remember . . . What's imprinted in my memory? The silence, the extraordinary silence in the wards of the badly wounded . . . The worst . . . They didn't talk among themselves. Didn't call anyone. Many were unconscious. Most often they just lay there silently. Thinking. Looking off somewhere to the side and thinking. You call out to him and he doesn't hear.

What were they thinking about?

OF HORSES AND BIRDS

—We rode and rode . . .

There were two trains standing next to each other at the station . . . One with the wounded, and the other with horses. And then a bombardment began. The trains caught fire . . . We started to open the doors, to save the wounded, so that they could get away, but they all rushed to save the burning horses. When wounded people scream, it's terrible, but there's nothing more terrible than the neighing of wounded horses. They're not guilty of anything, they don't answer for human deeds. And nobody ran to the forest, everybody rushed to save the horses. All those who could. All of them!

I want to say . . . I want to say that the fascist planes flew just over the ground. Low, very low. Later I thought: the German pilots saw it all, can it be that they weren't ashamed? What were they thinking?

—I remember one time . . . We came to a village, and there were some dead partisans lying near a forest. What they had done to them I can't tell you, my heart won't bear it. They had been cut up into pieces . . . They were trussed like pigs. They lay there . . . and horses were grazing not far away. They must have been the partisans' horses; they even had saddles. Either they had escaped from the Germans and then came back, or the Germans hadn't managed to take them away—I don't know. They didn't go far. There was a lot of grass. I thought: how could those people do such things in front of horses? In front of animals? The horses had watched them . . .

—The field and forest were burning . . . The meadow was smoky. I saw burned cows and dogs . . . An unusual smell. Unfamiliar. I saw . . .

Burned barrels of tomatoes, of cabbage. Birds were burned. Horses . . .
Many . . . Many completely charred ones lay on the road. We also had
to get used to that smell . . .

   I realized then that anything can burn . . . Even blood burns . . .

—During a bombardment, a goat latched on to us. She lay down with
us. Simply lay down nearby and screamed. When the bombing ceased,
she went with us and kept clinging to people—well, she's alive, she's
also afraid. We came to a village and said to some woman, "Take her
out of pity." We wanted to save her . . .

—Two wounded men lay in my ward . . . A German and our badly
burned tank driver. I come to look at them: "How do you feel?"

   "I'm all right," our tank driver replies, "but he's in a bad way."

   "This fascist . . ."

   "No, I don't know, but he's in a bad way."

   They were no longer enemies, but people, simply two wounded
men lying next to each other. Something human arose between them.
I observed more than once how quickly it happened . . .

—How is it . . . How . . . Remember . . . Birds are flying in late
fall . . . Long, long flocks. Our artillery and the Germans' are firing,
and they're flying. How to call out to them? How to warn them:
"Not here! There's shooting here!" How?! The birds are falling, falling to the ground . . .

—They brought us some SS officers to be bandaged. A nurse comes to
me: "How are we to bandage them?"

   "Normally. They're wounded . . ."

And we bandaged them normally. Two of them later escaped. They were caught, and to keep them from escaping again, I cut the buttons off their long drawers . . .

—When they told me . . . These were the words: "The war is over!" I just sat on the sterilized table. The doctor and I had agreed that when they said "The war is over!" we'd sit on the sterilized table. Do something unbelievable like that. I never let anyone come near that table, not even within gunshot of it. I had gloves, I wore a mask, I had a sterilized smock on, and I handed over all necessary things: swabs, instruments . . . And now I just sat on that table . . .

What did we dream of? First, of course, of being victorious; second, of staying alive. One said, "Once the war is over, I'll give birth to a whole slew of children." Another: "I'll enroll in the university." Yet another: "I'll spend all my time at the hairdresser's. I'll dress up in pretty clothes and pamper myself." Or: "I'll buy nice perfume. Buy a scarf and a brooch."

And now that time had come. Everybody suddenly grew quiet . . .

—We took back a village . . . We looked for where to draw some water. We entered a courtyard where we noticed a well sweep. A carved wooden well . . . A shot man was lying in the yard . . . Next to him sat his dog. He saw us and began to whimper. It took us a while to realize he was calling us. He led us to the cottage . . . We followed him. On the threshold lay the man's wife and three children . . .

The dog sat next to them and wept. Really wept. Like a human being . . .

—We entered our villages . . . There were only stoves standing—that was all. Nothing but stoves! In Ukraine we came to villages where there was nothing, just watermelons growing. People ate nothing but these watermelons; it was all they had. They came to meet us and brought watermelons . . . Instead of flowers . . .

I returned home. In a dugout—my mother, three children, and a little dog, all eating boiled goosefoot. They boiled the goosefoot, ate it themselves, and gave it to the dog. And the dog ate it . . . Before the war we had so many nightingales, but for two years after the war nobody heard them. The earth was all overturned, the so-called ancestors' dung had been dug under. Plowed in. The nightingales appeared only in the third year. Where had they been? Nobody knows. They came back after three years.

People put up houses, then the nightingales came back . . .

—Whenever I see wild flowers, I remember the war. We didn't pick flowers then. And if we made bouquets, it was only when we buried someone . . . When we bid farewell . . .

—Ehh, girls, how vile it was . . . This war . . . Let's drink to the memory of our friends . . .

"IT WASN'T ME . . ."

———

What do you remember most?

You remember most the quiet, often perplexed human voice. The woman feels astonished at herself, at what happened to her. The past disappeared, it blinded her with its scorching whirl and vanished, but the human being remained. Remained in the midst of ordinary life. Everything around is ordinary except her memory. And I also become a witness. A witness to what people remember and how they remember, to what they want to talk about and what they try to forget or remove to the furthest corner of memory. Curtain off. How they desperately seek for words, yet wish to reconstruct what is gone in the hope that from a distance they may be able to find its full meaning. To see and understand what they hadn't seen and understood then. There. They study themselves, meet themselves anew. Most often it is already two persons—this one and that one, the young one and the old one. The one in the war and the one after the war. Long after the war. The feeling that I am hearing two voices at the same time never leaves me . . .

At that time, in Moscow, on Victory Day, I met Olga Yakovlevna Omelchenko. All the women were wearing spring dresses, bright scarves, but she wore an army uniform and an army beret. Tall, strong. She did not talk and did not weep. She was silent all the time, but this was some sort of special silence, which implied more than could be said, more than words. It was as if she talked to herself all the time. She no longer needed anybody.

We became acquainted, and afterward I came to see her in Polotsk.

*Before me yet another page of the war opened, before which any fantasy will
fall silent . . .*

Olga Yakovlevna Omelchenko

MEDICAL ASSISTANT IN AN INFANTRY COMPANY

Mama's talisman . . . Mama wanted me to be evacuated together with
her. She knew that I was eager for the front, and she tied me to the
cart on which our things were being transported. But I quietly untied
myself and left with a piece of that rope still on my arm . . .

Everybody was on the move . . . Fleeing. Where was I to go? How
to reach the front? On the road I met a group of girls. One of them
said to me, "My mother lives nearby, let's go to my place." We came
at night, we knocked. Her mother opened the door, looked at us, and
we were dirty, ragged. "Stay there in the doorway," she ordered. We
stood there. She brought enormous cauldrons, took all our clothes
off. We washed our hair with ashes (there was no soap anymore),
climbed on the stove,* and I fell fast asleep. In the morning this girl's
mother cooked cabbage soup, baked some bread from bran and potatoes. How tasty that bread seemed to us and how sweet the cabbage
soup! And so we stayed four days, and she fed us up. She gave us a
little at a time, otherwise she was afraid we'd eat too much and die. On
the fifth day she said, "Go." And before that a neighbor came. We
were sitting on the stove. The mother put her finger to her lips, so
that we'd be quiet. She hadn't told her neighbors that her daughter
had come back; she told everybody that her daughter was at the front.
This was her only daughter, but she didn't feel sorry for her. She
couldn't forgive the disgrace of her coming back. Of not fighting.

During the night she woke us up, gave us small bundles of food,
embraced each of us, and said, "Go . . ."

---

* Russian tile stoves are elaborate structures that include "shelves" for sleeping.

She didn't even try to keep her daughter home?

No, she kissed her and said, "Your father's fighting, you go and fight, too."

Back on the road this girl told me that she was a nurse, her unit had fallen into an encirclement . . .

For a long time I wandered from place to place and finally wound up in the city of Tambov and found a job in a hospital. The hospital was good; after going hungry for a long time I ate well, I became plump. And then when I turned sixteen, they told me that, like all the nurses and doctors, I could give blood. I started giving blood every month. The hospital constantly needed hundreds of liters, there was never enough. I gave a pint of blood twice a month. I was given a donor's ration: two pounds of sugar, two pounds of farina, two pounds of sausage, to restore my strength. I was friends with a floor attendant, Aunt Niura. She had seven children, and her husband had been killed at the start of the war. The oldest boy, who was eleven, went to the grocery store and lost their ration cards, so I gave them my donor's ration. One day the doctor said to me, "Let's attach your address, in case somebody suddenly turns up who has had a transfusion of your blood." We wrote out my address and stuck the label to the vial.

And a while later, two months, not more, I finished my shift and went to sleep. They came and roused me. "Get up! Get up, your brother has come."

"What brother? I don't have a brother."

Our dormitory was on the top floor. I went down, looked: there stood a handsome young lieutenant. I asked, "Who wants to see Omelchenko?"

He said, "I do." And he showed me the label the doctor and I had written. "Here . . . I'm your blood brother."

He brought me two apples, a bag of candy—it was impossible then to buy candy anywhere. My God! How tasty those candies were! I went to the head of the hospital: "My brother has come . . ." They gave me a leave. He said, "Let's go to the theater." It was the first time in my life I went to the theater, and with a young fellow, at that. A handsome young fellow. An officer!

He left several days later. He had orders to go to the Voronezh front. When he came to say goodbye, I opened the window and waved to him. I couldn't get a leave: just then a lot of wounded arrived.

I had never received letters from anybody; I had no idea what it was—to receive a letter. And suddenly they handed me a little triangle. I opened it, and there was written, "Your friend, commander of a machine-gun platoon . . . died a hero's death . . ." It was my blood brother. He was from an orphanage, and probably mine was the only address he had. My address . . . When he was leaving he kept asking me to stay in this hospital, so that after the war he could easily find me. "It's easy to lose each other during the war," he said. And a month later I received this letter, that he had been killed . . . And I was so frightened. I was struck to the heart . . . I decided to do all I could to go to the front and avenge my blood; I knew that my blood had been spilled somewhere there . . .

But it wasn't so easy to go to the front. I applied three times to the head of the hospital, and the fourth time I came to him and said, "If you don't let me go to the front, I'll run away."

"Very well. I'll give you an order, since you're so stubborn."

The most terrible thing, of course, is the first battle. It's because you don't know anything yet . . . The sky throbs, the ground throbs, your heart seems about to burst, your skin feels ready to split. I never thought the ground could crackle. Everything crackled, everything rumbled. Heaved . . . The ground heaved . . . It was more than I could take . . . How was I to live through all that . . . I thought I couldn't endure it. I was so terribly frightened, and then I decided: so as not to turn coward, I took my Komsomol card, dipped it in the blood of a wounded soldier, put it in my pocket over my heart, and buttoned it. And by doing that I made myself an oath that I had to endure, and above all not to turn coward, because if I did it in my first battle, I wouldn't be able to take a step afterward. I'd be removed from the front line and sent to the medical battalion. And I only wanted to be at the front line; I wanted sometime to see at least one fascist face-to-face . . . Personally . . . And we advanced, we walked through the grass, and the grass was waist high. Nothing had been sown there for several years. It was very hard to walk. This was at the Kursk Bulge . . .

After the battle the chief of staff summoned me. It was some sort of ruined hut, with nothing inside. There was one chair, and he was standing. He sat me in the chair.

"I look at you and think: what made you come to this hellfire? You'll be killed like a fly. It's war! A meat grinder! Let me at least transfer you to a medical unit. It's all very well if they kill you, but what if you're left without eyes, without arms? Have you thought of that?"

I reply, "I have, Comrade Colonel. And I ask you one thing: don't transfer me from the company."

"All right, go!" he shouted at me. I even got scared. And he turned to the window.

Heavy combat. Hand-to-hand . . . That is a horror . . . Not for a human being . . . They beat, they stab with a bayonet, they strangle each other. They break each other's bones. There's howling, shouting. Moaning. And that crunching . . . That crunching! Impossible to forget it . . . the crunching of bones . . . You hear a skull crack. Split open . . . Even for war it's a nightmare; there's nothing human in it. I won't believe anyone who says that war isn't terrifying. Now the Germans rise up and advance; they always march with their sleeves rolled up to the elbows. Another five or ten minutes and they attack. You begin to shake. To shiver. But that's before the first shot . . . And then . . . Once you hear the command, you no longer remember anything; you rise up with everybody and run. And you no longer think about being afraid. But the next day you can't sleep, you're afraid. You remember everything, all the details, and it dawns on you that you could have been killed, and you're insanely frightened. Right after an attack it's better not to look at faces; they're some sort of totally different faces, not like people usually have. They themselves cannot raise their eyes to each other. They don't even look at the trees. You go up to someone and he says, "Go a-way! A-way . . ." I can't express what it is. Everybody seems slightly abnormal, and there's even a glimpse of something bestial. Better not to see it. To this day I can't believe I stayed alive. Alive . . . Wounded and shell-shocked, but whole. I can't believe it . . .

I close my eyes and see it all again in front of me . . .

A shell hit the ammunition depot, and it caught fire. The soldier who was standing guard next to it got scorched. Turned into a black piece of meat . . . He kept jumping around . . . And everybody watched from the trench, and nobody budged, they were all at a loss. I grabbed a sheet, ran over, covered the soldier with it, and lay down on him. Pressed him to the ground. The cold ground . . . Like that . . . He thrashed about till his heart burst, then grew still . . .

I was all covered with blood . . . One of the older soldiers came up and embraced me. I heard him say, "The war will end, and if she's still alive, there'll be nothing human left of her anyway, it's all over." Meaning that I was in the midst of such horror, and living through it, at such a young age. I was shaking as if in a fit; they took me under the arms to the dugout. My legs wouldn't hold me up . . . I was shaking as if an electric current was running through me . . . I can't describe how it felt . . .

Then the battle began again . . . At the Sevsk the Germans attacked us seven or eight times a day. So that day I also carried the wounded with their weapons. When I crawled to the last one, his arm was completely smashed. Hanging by little pieces . . . by the sinews. He was all bloody . . . His arm had to be urgently amputated and bandaged, otherwise it was impossible to bandage him. But I had no knife or scissors. My kit was loose on my shoulder, and things had fallen out. What was I to do? I bit his flesh off with my teeth. I bit it off and bandaged him . . . I was bandaging, and the wounded man said, "Make it quick, nurse, I'll go and fight some more . . ." In delirium . . .

A few days later, when the tanks came against us, two men turned coward. They fled . . . The whole line wavered . . . Many of our comrades were killed. The wounded that I had dragged to a shell hole were taken prisoner. An ambulance was supposed to come for them . . . But when those two turned coward, panic set in. The wounded were abandoned. Later on we came to the place where they lay, some with their eyes put out, some with their guts ripped open . . . After I saw it my face turned black overnight. I was the one who had gathered them in one place . . . I . . . It frightened me so much . . .

In the morning the whole battalion lined up, those cowards were brought out and placed before us. The order that they be shot was read. Seven men were needed to carry out the sentence . . . Three men stepped forward; the rest stood there. I took a submachine gun and stepped forward. Once I stepped forward . . . a young girl . . . everybody followed me . . . Those two could not be forgiven. Because of them such brave boys were killed!

And we carried out the sentence . . . I lowered the submachine gun, and became frightened. I went up to them . . . they lay there . . . One had a living smile on his face . . .

I don't know, would I have forgiven them now? I can't tell . . . I don't want to lie. There are moments when I want to weep. But I can't . . .

I forgot everything in the war. My former life. Everything . . . And I forgot love . . .

The commander of the scout company fell in love with me. He sent me little notes through his soldiers. I came to see him once. "No," I said. "I love a man who was killed long ago." He moved very close to me, looked straight into my eyes, turned, and went away. There was shooting, but he walked on and didn't even duck his head . . .

Later—this was already in Ukraine—we liberated a big village. I thought: "I'll take a stroll, look around." The weather was clear, the cottages white. And outside the village—graves, freshly dug earth . . . The graves of those who fought for this village. I didn't know why, but I was drawn there. On each grave there was a photograph and a last name on a plank . . . Suddenly I saw a familiar face . . . The commander of the scout company who was in love with me. And his last name . . . And I felt so uneasy. Such great fear . . . as if he saw me, as if he was alive . . . And just then his men came to the grave, from his company. They all knew me; they had delivered his notes to me. Not one of them looked at me, as if I wasn't there. Invisible. Later, too, whenever I met them, it seemed to me . . . so I think . . . They wanted me to die, too. It was hard for them to see that I was . . . alive . . . I sensed it . . . As if I was guilty before them . . . And before him . . .

I came back from the war and fell gravely ill. For a long time I went from one hospital to another, until I happened upon an old professor. He began to treat me . . . He treated me more with words than with medications; he explained my illness to me. He said that if I had left for the front at eighteen or nineteen, my body would have been stronger, but since I had just turned sixteen—it was a very early age—I had been badly traumatized. "Of course, medications are one thing," he explained. "They may treat you, but if you want to restore your health, if you want to live, my only advice is: you should get married and have as many children as possible. Only that can save you. With every child your body will be reborn."

How old were you?

When the war ended, I was going on twenty. Of course I didn't even think of getting married.

Why?

I felt very tired, much older than my peers, even simply old. My friends went to dances, had fun, and I couldn't, I looked at life with old eyes. From another world . . . An old woman! Young fellows courted me. Mere boys. But they didn't see my soul, what was inside me. Here I've told you about one day . . . The fighting at Sevsk. Just one day . . . After which I had blood flow out of my ears during the night. In the morning I woke up as if after a grave illness. A bloody pillow . . .

And in the hospital? In the surgery room we had a big tub behind a screen where they put the amputated arms, legs . . . Once a captain came from the front and brought his wounded friend. I don't know how he got behind there, but he saw that tub and . . . fainted.

I can go on and on remembering. I can't stop . . . But what is the most important thing?

I remember the sounds of the war. Everything around booms and clangs, crackles from fire . . . In war your soul ages. After the war I was never young . . . That's the most important thing. To my mind . . .

Did you get married?

I got married. I gave birth to five sons and raised them. Five boys. God didn't give me girls. What surprises me most is that after such great fear and horror I could give birth to beautiful children. And I turned out to be a good mother and a good grandmother.

I recall it all now and it seems that it wasn't me, but some other girl . . .

I was on my way home, bringing four cassettes (two days of conversations) with "yet another war," having various feelings: shock and fear, perplexity and admiration. Curiosity and bewilderment, and tenderness. At home I retold some episodes to my friends. Unexpectedly for me, the reactions were all similar: "Too frightening. How could she stand it? And not go out of her mind?" Or: "We're used to reading about a different war. In that war there are clear distinctions: us and them, good and evil. But here?" But I noticed they all had tears in their eyes, and they all fell to thinking. Probably about the same things as I. There have been thousands of wars on earth (I read recently that they've counted up more than three thousand—big and small), but war remains, as it has always been, one of the chief human mysteries. Nothing has changed. I am trying to bring that great history down to human scale, in order to understand something. To find the words. Yet in this seemingly small and easily observable territory— the space of one human soul—everything is still less comprehensible, less predictable than in history. Because before me are living tears, living feelings. A living human face, which the shadows of pain and fear pass over as we talk. Occasionally a subversive hunch even creeps in of the barely perceptible beauty of human suffering. Then I get frightened of my own self . . .

There is only one path—to love this human being. To understand through love.

"I REMEMBER THOSE EYES
EVEN NOW . . ."

———

The search continues . . . But this time I don't have far to go . . .

The street I live on in Minsk is named after the Hero of the Soviet Union Vasily Zakharovich Korzh—participant in the Civil War, hero of battles in Spain, commander of a partisan brigade during the Great Patriotic War. Every Belorussian has read a book about him, at least in school, or seen a movie. He is a Belorussian legend. Having written his name hundreds of times on envelopes or telegram forms, I had never thought about him as a real man. The myth has long replaced the once-living person. Has become his double. But this time I walked down the familiar street with a new feeling: a half-hour trolleybus ride to the other end of the city, and I'll see his daughters—they both fought at the front—and his wife. Before my eyes the legend will come alive and turn into a human life, descend to earth. The great will become small. However much I love to look at the sky or the sea, still I'm more fascinated by a grain of sand under a microscope. The world in a single drop. The great and incredible life I discover in it. How can I call the small small and the great great, when both are so boundless? I've long ceased to distinguish between them. For me one human being is so much. There is everything in him—you can get lost.

I find the address I need—again a massive and unwieldy multistoried building. Here is entrance 3; in the elevator I press the button for the seventh floor . . .

The door is opened by the younger sister—Zinaida Vasilyevna. The same wide dark eyebrows and the stubbornly open gaze as her father's in the photographs.

———

"We're all here . . . My sister Olya came from Moscow this morning. She lives there. Teaches at Patrice Lumumba University. And our mama is here. So, thanks to you, we've all gotten together."

Both sisters, Olga Vasilyevna and Zinaida Vasilyevna Korzh, had been medical assistants in cavalry squadrons. They sat next to each other and looked at their mother, Feodosia Alexeevna.

It was she who began:

"Everything was burning . . . They told us to evacuate . . . We rode for a long time. We reached the Stalingrad region. Women with children moved to the rear, and men moved up. Combine drivers, tractor drivers, everybody went. Whole truckloads. One man, I remember, stood up and shouted, 'Mothers, sisters!! Go to the rear, harvest bread, so we can defeat the enemy!' And they all took their hats off and looked at us. And all we had time to bring with us were our children. We held them. Some in our arms, some by the hand. He begged, 'Mothers, sisters! Go to the rear, harvest bread . . . '"

During the whole time of our conversation she did not utter another word. Her daughters would quietly stroke her hand every once in a while to calm her down.

Zinaida Vasilyevna

We lived in Pinsk. I was fourteen and a half, Olya was sixteen, our brother Lenya thirteen. Just during those days we sent Olya to a children's sanatorium, and father wanted to go with us to the country. To his family . . . But in fact he didn't spend that night at home. He worked in the regional party committee, was summoned during the night, and came home only in the morning. He stopped in the kitchen, grabbed something to eat, and said, "Children, war has begun. Don't go anywhere. Wait for me."

We left by night. Father had a most precious souvenir from Spain—a hunting rifle, richly ornamented, with a cartridge belt. It was a reward for courage. He tossed the rifle to my brother. "You're the eldest now, you're a man, you must look after mama and your little sisters . . ."

We kept that rifle all through the war. Whatever nice things we had, we sold or exchanged for bread, but we kept the rifle. We couldn't part with it. It was our memory of father. He also threw a big sheepskin coat into the car with us. It was the warmest thing he had.

At the station we got onto a train, but before we reached Gomel, we came under heavy shelling. The command: "Off the train, into the bushes, lie flat!" When the shelling was over . . . First silence, then shouting . . . everybody ran . . . Mama and my brother managed to jump back onto the train, but I stayed. I was very frightened . . . Very! I had never been alone before. And here I was—alone. It seems I even lost speech for a time . . . I went dumb . . . Somebody asked me something, and I was silent . . . Then I attached myself to some woman and helped her to bandage the wounded—she was a doctor. They addressed her as "Comrade Captain." And I rode on with her medical unit. They were nice to me, fed me, but soon it occurred to them: "How old are you?"

I realized that if I told the truth they would send me to some children's home. I figured it out at once. But I no longer wanted to lose these strong people. I wanted to fight the way they did. It had been instilled in us—and my father had said—that we'd fight on foreign territory, that it was all temporary, that the war would soon end in victory. All that without me? Those were the childish thoughts I had. I told them I was sixteen, and they let me stay. Soon they sent me to training courses. I studied for about four months at these courses. I studied and at the same time took care of the wounded. Got used to the war . . . Of course we had to get used to it . . . I didn't study at the school, but right there, in the medical battalion. We were retreating and taking the wounded with us.

We didn't follow the roads; the roads were being bombed, shelled.

We moved across the swamps, along the waysides. We moved in a scattered way. Various units. Where they became concentrated, it meant they were giving battle. And so we went on, and on, and on. Went across the fields. What a harvest! We walked and trampled down the rye. And the harvest that year was unprecedented, the grain stood very tall. Green grass, bright sun, and dead men lying there, blood . . . Dead men and animals. Blackened trees . . . Destroyed train stations . . . Charred people hanging from black train cars . . . We went on like that as far as Rostov. I was wounded there during a bombardment. I regained consciousness on a train and heard an elderly soldier, a Ukrainian, barking at a young one, "Your wife didn't cry so bad giving birth as you're crying now." When he saw me open my eyes, he said, "But you cry away, dear, cry away. It'll make things easier. Go ahead." I remembered mama and wept . . .

After the hospital I was given a leave, and I tried to find my mama. And she was looking for me, and my sister Olya was looking for us both. Oh, miracle! We all found each other through some acquaintances in Moscow. We all wrote to their address, and so found each other. A miracle! Mama was living near Stalingrad in a kolkhoz. I went there.

It was the end of 1941 . . .

How did they live? My brother worked on a tractor; he was still quite young, thirteen years old. First he was a trailer hand, and when all the tractor drivers were taken to the front, he became a driver. He worked day and night. Mama followed the tractor or sat next to him. She was afraid he would get sleepy and fall off. The two of them slept on someone's floor . . . They didn't undress, because there was nothing to cover themselves with. That was their life . . . Soon Olya came; they gave her a job as an accountant. She wrote to the recruiting office asking to be sent to the front, and kept being refused. And we decided—I was already a seasoned warrior—that we'd go to Stalingrad together and find some unit there. We set mama at ease, by deceiving her that we were going to Kuban, the rich parts, where father had acquaintances . . .

I had an old uniform overcoat, an army shirt, two pairs of trousers. I gave one pair to Olya; she had nothing at all. We also had one pair of boots for the two of us. Mama knitted something like socks or slippers for us, out of sheep's wool, something warm. We walked forty miles on foot all the way to Stalingrad. One of us wore the boots, the other mama's slippers. Then we'd change. We walked through freezing cold. It was February; we were frozen, hungry. What did mama make for us for the road? She made a sort of aspic from boiled bones and several flatcakes. And we were so hungry . . . If we fell asleep and dreamed, it was only about food. Loaves of bread flew over me in my sleep.

We made it to Stalingrad, and there nobody wanted us. Nobody wanted to listen to us. Then we decided to go to Kuban, where mama had sent us, to the address papa had given. We got on some freight train. I put on the overcoat and sat, and Olya hid under the seats. Then we'd change places: I'd get under the seats and Olya would sit. They didn't touch the military. And we had no money at all . . .

We got to Kuban . . . a sort of miracle . . . Found the acquaintances. And there we were told that a volunteer Cossack corps was being formed. This was the 4th Cossack Cavalry Corps; later on it became a Guards corps. It was formed entirely of volunteers. There were people of all ages: seasoned Cossacks that Budenny and Voroshilov had once led to the attack,* and young ones as well. They took us. To this day I don't know why. Maybe because we asked so many times. And there was nothing else they could do with us. We were enlisted in the same squadron. Each of us was issued a uniform and a horse. Your horse had to be fed, watered, fully taken care of. Luckily when I was little we had a horse, and I got used to it and loved it. So when they gave me a horse, I mounted it—and wasn't scared at all. I didn't manage it right away, but I wasn't afraid. My horse was small,

---

*   For Budenny, see note, p. 30. Kliment Voroshilov (1881–1969) was a prominent military figure, one of the first five Marshals of the Soviet Union, and a member of the Central Committee of the Communist Party from 1921 to 1961. He played a major role in Stalin's Great Purge.

tail down to the ground, but it was quick, obedient, and I somehow learned to ride it quickly. Even showed off . . . Later I rode Hungarian and Romanian horses. And I came to love horses so much, and to know them so well, that even now I can't pass by a horse with indifference. I hug them. We slept under their feet. The horse would move its leg carefully, and would never step on a human being. It would never step on a dead man, and if a living man was only wounded, it would never go away and abandon him. Very intelligent animals. For a cavalryman, a horse is a friend. A faithful friend.

The first baptism in combat . . . It was when our corps took part in repelling tanks at the Cossack village of Kushchevskaya. After the battle of Kushchevskaya—it was the famous cavalry attack of the Kuban Cossacks—the corps was raised to the rank of a Guards corps. It was a dreadful battle . . . And for Olya and me—the most dreadful, because we were still very afraid. Though I had already fought and knew how it was . . . But still . . . When the cavalrymen went it was like an avalanche—capes flying, sabers bared, horses snorting, and a horse when it races is so strong . . . This whole avalanche went against the tanks, the artillery—it was like in an otherworldly dream. Unreal . . . And there were lots of fascists, lots more than us. They walked with their submachine guns at the ready, walked beside the tanks—and they couldn't hold out against it, you see, they couldn't hold out against that avalanche. They abandoned their submachine guns . . . Abandoned their cannons and fled . . . That was a picture . . .

Olga Vasilyevna

I was bandaging the wounded . . . There was a fascist lying there. I thought he was dead and paid no attention to him, but he was only wounded . . . And he wanted to kill me . . . I felt it, as if somebody nudged me, and turned around to him. I managed to knock the submachine gun away with my foot. I didn't kill him, but I didn't bandage him either, I left. He was wounded in the stomach . . .

Zinaida Vasilyevna

I was leading a wounded man and suddenly saw two Germans coming from behind a tankette. The tankette had been hit, but they must have had time to get out. A split second! If I hadn't managed to give them a burst, they would have shot me and the wounded man. It happened so unexpectedly. After the battle I went to them; they lay with their eyes open. I remember those eyes even now . . . One was such a handsome young German. It was a pity, even though he was a fascist, all the same . . . That feeling didn't leave me for a long time. You see, I didn't want to kill. There was such hatred in my soul: why had they come to our land? But when you yourself kill, it's frightening . . . There's no other word . . . Very frightening. When you yourself . . .

The battle was over. The Cossack hundreds were breaking camp, and Olya wasn't there. I was the last one to leave, I rode at the end, I kept looking back. It was evening. Olya wasn't there . . . I got word that she stayed to pick up the wounded. There was nothing I could do, I just waited for her. I'd lag behind my hundred, wait a little, then catch up with everybody. I wept: Can it be I lost my sister in the first battle? Where is she? What's happened to her? Maybe she's dying somewhere, calling me . . .

Olya . . . Olya, too, was all in tears . . . She found me at night . . . All the Cossacks wept when they saw us meet. We hung on each other's necks, unable to let go. And then we realized that it was impossible, it was unbearable for us to fight together. Better to separate. Our hearts wouldn't be able to stand it if one of us was killed before the other's eyes. We decided that I should ask to be transferred to another squadron. But how to part? How?

Afterward we fought separately, first in different squadrons, later even in different divisions. We would just send greetings, if the chance came along, to find out whether the other was alive . . . Death watched our every step. Lay in wait . . . I remember it was near Ararat . . . We were camped in the sands. Ararat had been taken by the Germans. It was Christmas, and the Germans were celebrating. A squadron was chosen and a forty-millimeter battery. We set out at around five and kept moving all night. At dawn we met with our scouts, who had set out earlier.

The village lay at the foot of a hill . . . As if in a bowl . . . The Germans never thought we could get through such sand, and they set up very little defense. We passed through their rear very quietly. We descended the hill, captured the sentries, and burst into this village, flew into it. The Germans came running out completely naked, only with submachine guns in their hands. There were Christmas trees standing around . . . they were all drunk . . . And in every yard there were no less than two or three tanks. Tankettes stood there, armored vehicles . . . All their machinery. We destroyed it on the spot, and there was such shooting, such noise, such panic . . . Everybody rushed about . . . The situation was such that each one was afraid of hitting his own men. Everything was on fire . . . The Christmas trees, too, were on fire . . .

I had eight wounded men . . . I helped them up the hill . . . But we committed one blunder: we didn't cut the enemy's communications. And the German artillery blanketed us with both mortar and long-range fire. I quickly put my wounded on an ambulance wagon, and they drove off . . . And before my eyes a shell landed on the wagon, and it was blown to pieces. When I looked, there was only one man left alive there. And the Germans were already going up the hill . . . The wounded man begged, "Leave me, nurse . . . Leave me, nurse . . . I'm dying . . ." His stomach was ripped open . . . His guts . . . All that . . . He gathered them himself and stuffed them back in . . .

I thought my horse was bloody because of this wounded man, but then I looked: he was also wounded in the side. I used up a whole individual kit on him. I had several pieces of sugar left; I gave him the sugar. There was shooting on all sides now; you couldn't tell where the Germans were and where ours. You go ten yards and run into wounded men . . . I thought: I've got to find a wagon and pick them all up. So I rode on, and I saw the slope, and at the foot of it three roads: this way and that way and also straight. I was at a loss . . . Which way to go? I had been holding the bridle firmly; the horse went wherever I pointed him. Well, so here, I don't know, some instinct told me, or I'd heard somewhere, that horses sense the road, so before that fork I let go of the bridle, and the horse went in a completely different direction from where I was going to go. He went on and on . . .

I sit there with no strength left; I no longer care where he goes. What will be will be. So he goes on and on, and then more and more briskly, he wags his head, I've picked up the bridle again, I'm holding it. I bend down and put my hand to his wound. He goes more and more cheerfully, then: whinny-whinny-whinny . . . As if he's heard somebody. I was worried it might be the Germans. I decided to set the horse free first, but then I saw a fresh trail: hoof prints, the wheels of a machine-gun cart; no less than fifty people had passed this way. Another two or three hundred meters and my horse ran smack into a wagon. There were wounded men in the wagon, and here I saw the remainder of our squadron.

Aid was already arriving, wagons, machine-gun carts . . . The order was to pick up everybody. Under bullets, under artillery fire, we picked them all up to a man—the wounded and the dead. I also rode in the cart. Everybody was there, even the man wounded in the stomach. We took them all. Only the dead horses were left behind. It was already morning; we rode on and saw—a whole herd lying there. Beautiful, strong horses . . . The wind stirred their manes . . .

One wall of the big room we're sitting in is all covered with enlarged prewar and wartime photos of the sisters. Here they are still schoolgirls—hats, flowers. The snapshot was taken two weeks before the start of the war. Ordinary childish faces, ready to laugh, slightly restrained by the importance of the moment and the wish to look adult. Now they are already in Cossack coats, cavalry capes. The picture was taken in 1942. A year's difference, but the face is not the same, the person is not the same. And this snapshot Zinaida Vasilyevna sent to her mother from the front: on her army shirt the first medal "For Courage." This one shows them both on Victory Day . . . I memorize the movement of the face: from soft, childish features to a confident woman's gaze, even a certain toughness, severity. It is hard to believe that this change took place in a few months, or years. Ordinary time performs this task much more slowly and imperceptibly. A human face is molded over a long time. The soul is slowly traced on it.

But the war quickly created its image of people. Painted its own portraits.

Olga Vasilyevna

We took a big village. Some three hundred houses. There was an abandoned German infirmary in the building of the local hospital. The first thing I saw was a big hole dug in the yard and some patients lying in it shot—before leaving, the Germans themselves shot their own wounded. They evidently decided that we would do it anyway. That we would do to their wounded what they did to ours. Only one ward was left, which they evidently didn't get to, didn't have time, or maybe they were abandoned because they all had no legs.

When we entered this ward they looked at us with hatred: they evidently thought we came to kill them. The interpreter said that we don't kill the wounded, we treat them. Then one of them even started to make demands: they'd had nothing to eat for three days, their bandages hadn't been changed for three days. I looked—in fact, it was horrible. They hadn't seen a doctor for a long time. The wounds were festering, the bandages were growing into the flesh.

Did you pity them?

I can't call what I felt then pity. After all, pity is compassion. That I didn't feel. It was something else . . . There was an incident with us . . . a soldier hit a prisoner . . . I found that intolerable, and I intervened, though I understood . . . It was a cry from his soul . . . He knew me, he was older, of course, he cursed. But he stopped hitting . . . He swore at me, "Have you forgotten, fuck it all! Have you forgotten how they, fuck it all . . ." I hadn't forgotten anything. I remembered those boots . . . When they set up in front of their trenches a row of boots with cut-off legs in them. It was in winter, they stood there like stakes . . . Those boots . . . That was all we saw of our comrades . . . What was left of them . . .

I remember some sailors coming to help us . . . Many of them were blown up by mines; we had stumbled into a big minefield. These sailors lay there for a long time. In the sun . . . The corpses puffed up, and because of their striped jerseys they looked like watermelons. Big watermelons on a big field. Giant ones.

I hadn't forgotten, I hadn't forgotten anything. But I couldn't hit a prisoner, if only because he was already defenseless. Everybody decided that for himself, and it was important.

Zinaida Vasilyevna

In battle near Budapest . . . It was winter . . . I was carrying a wounded sergeant, the commander of a machine-gun crew. I was wearing trousers and a warm jacket, a flap-eared cap on my head. I'm carrying him and I see this blackish snow . . . charred . . . I realize that it's a deep shell hole, which is what I need. I go down into the hole and there's someone alive—I sense he's alive, and I hear a metallic scraping . . . I turn and there's a wounded German officer, wounded in the legs, lying there and aiming his submachine gun at me . . . My hair had slipped from under my cap, and I also had a medical kit on my shoulder with a red cross . . . When I turned, he saw my face, realized I was a girl, and went, "Ha-a-ah!" His nerves relaxed, and he threw aside his submachine gun. He no longer cared . . .

And so the three of us are in the same hole—our wounded man, me, and this German. The hole is small, our legs touch. I'm all covered with their blood; our blood mingles. The German has such huge eyes, and he looks at me with those eyes. What am I going to do?

Cursed fascist! He threw the submachine gun aside at once, you see? That scene . . . Our wounded man doesn't understand what's going on, he clutches his pistol . . . reaches out and wants to strangle him . . . But the German just stares at me . . . I remember those eyes even now . . . I'm bandaging our man, and the other one's lying in blood, he's losing blood, one of his legs is completely smashed. A little longer and he'll die. I see that very well. And, before I finished bandaging our man, I tore up the German's clothes, twisted them into a tourniquet, bandaged him, and then went back to bandaging ours. The German says, *"Gut . . . Gut . . ."* He keeps repeating that word. Our wounded man, before he lost consciousness, shouted something at me . . . threatened . . . I caressed him, soothed him. When the ambulance came, I pulled them both out . . . and put them in. The German, too. You see?

Olga Vasilyevna

When men saw a woman at the front line, their faces became different; even the sound of a woman's voice transformed them. Once during the night I sat by a dugout and began to sing softly. I thought everybody was asleep and no one would hear me, but in the morning the commander said to me, "We didn't sleep. Such longing for a woman's voice . . ."

I was bandaging a tankman . . . The battle goes on, the pounding. He asked, "What's your name, girl?" He even paid me some compliment. It felt so strange to pronounce my name, Olya, amid this pounding, this horror . . . I always tried to look neat, trim. People often said to me, "Lord, how can she have been in battle, she's so clean." I was very afraid that if I was killed, I'd lie there looking unattractive. I saw many girls killed . . . In mud, in water . . . Well . . . How shall I . . . I didn't want to die like that. Sometimes I hid from shelling, not so much thinking they won't kill me this way, but just to hide my face. My hands. I think all our girls thought about it. And the men laughed at us, they thought it was funny. Meaning, it's not death they think about, but devil knows what, something stupid. Women's nonsense.

Zinaida Vasilyevna

Death can't be tamed . . . No . . . You can't get used to it . . . We were retreating from the Germans into the mountains. We had to leave five men badly wounded in the stomach. These wounds were deadly, another day or two and they would all die. We couldn't take them along, we had nothing to transport them in. They left me and another medical assistant, Oksanochka, with them in a shed, promising, "We'll come back in two days and take you." They came back in three days. We were with these wounded men for three days. They were fully conscious, robust men. They didn't want to die . . . And we had only some powders, nothing else . . . They asked to drink all the time, but they weren't allowed to drink. Some understood, but others cursed. There was all this foul language. One flung a mug at me, another a boot. Those were the most terrible days of my life. They were dying in front of our eyes, one after another, and we just looked on . . .

The first award . . . They awarded me the medal "For Valor." But I didn't go to collect it. I was offended. By God, it was funny! You see why? My friend was awarded the medal "For Military Services" and I got the medal "For Valor." She had only been in one battle, and I had already been at the battle of Kushchevskaya Station and several other operations. So I was offended: she got "Military Services" for one battle—a lot of service—and I only "For Valor," as if I had showed myself only once. The commander came and laughed when he found out what was the matter. He explained that "For Valor" was the biggest medal, almost an order.

Near Makeevka, in the Donbas region, I was wounded in the hip. A little fragment got in and sat there like a little stone. I felt blood, I folded an individual gauze pad and put it there. And I went on running around bandaging. I was embarrassed to tell anybody, a girl wounded, and where—in a buttock. In the behind . . . When you're sixteen, it's embarrassing to tell anybody. It's awkward to admit it. So I ran all over, bandaging, until I fainted from loss of blood. My boots were full of blood . . .

Our soldiers looked and evidently decided I had been killed. The orderlies would come and pick me up. The fighting moved on. A little longer, and I would have died. But some tankmen on reconnaissance came and saw a girl on the battlefield. I lay there without my cap, the cap had rolled off. They saw blood flowing from under me, meaning I was alive. They brought me to the medical battalion. From there to the hospital, first one, then another. Ahh . . . A quick end to my war . . . Six months later they transferred me to the reserves for reasons of health. I was eighteen . . . No longer in good health: wounded three times, plus a heavy concussion. But I was a young girl, and of course I concealed it. The wounds I talked about, but the concussion I concealed. Yet I did feel the aftereffects. I was hospitalized again. They gave me disability . . . And what did I do? I tore up those papers and threw them out; I didn't even go to get some money. For that I'd have had to go through all kinds of commissions, tell about myself: when I got the concussion, when I got wounded. Where.

In the hospital, the squadron commander and the sergeant major came to visit me. I liked the commander very much during the war, but at the time he didn't notice me. A handsome man, the uniform suited him very well. All men looked good in uniform. And what did women look like? In trousers, braids weren't allowed, we all had boys' haircuts. Only toward the end of the war did they allow us to have some sort of hairstyle, and not to cut it short. In the hospital my hair grew back. I could braid it, I looked better, and they . . . My God, it's so funny! They both fell in love with me . . . Just like that! We had gone through the whole war together, and there had been nothing of the sort, and now both of them, the squadron commander and the sergeant major, proposed to me. Love! Love . . . How we all wanted love! Happiness!

That was the end of 1945 . . .

After the war we wanted to forget it as soon as possible. In this our father helped me and my sister. He was a wise man. He took our medals, decorations, official acknowledgments, put it all away, and said, "There was a war, you fought. Now forget it. There was a war, but now a new life is beginning. Put on some nice shoes. You're both beautiful girls . . . You should study, you should get married."

Olya somehow couldn't get used to this different life all at once. She was proud. She didn't want to take off her soldier's overcoat. And I remember how father said to mother, "It's my fault that the girls went to war at such a young age. I hope it hasn't broken them . . . Otherwise they'll be at war all their lives."

They gave me some sort of special coupons for my decorations and medals, so that I could go to the military store and buy myself something. I bought a pair of rubber boots that were fashionable then, a coat, a dress, some ankle shoes. I decided to sell the overcoat. I went to the market . . . I came in a light-colored summer dress . . . With my hair pinned up . . . And what did I see there? Young fellows without arms, without legs . . . All fighting men . . . With orders, medals . . . Whoever has hands sells homemade spoons. Women's bras, underpants. Another . . . without arms, without legs . . . sits bathed in tears. Begs for small change . . . There were no wheelchairs then; they rolled around on homemade platforms, pushing them with their hands, if they had them. Some are drunk. Singing about an orphan, "Forgotten, abandoned." Such scenes. I left, I didn't sell my overcoat. And all the while I lived in Moscow, probably five years, I couldn't go to the market. I was afraid one of these cripples would recognize me and shout, "Why did you pull me out of the fire then? Why did you save me?" I remembered a young lieutenant . . . His legs . . . One was cut off by shrapnel, the other still hung on by something. I bandaged him . . . under the bombs . . . And he shouted at me, "Don't drag it out! Finish me off! Finish me . . ." You see? I was always afraid of meeting that lieutenant . . .

When I was in the hospital, there was a handsome young fellow. The tankman Misha . . . Nobody knew his last name, but everybody knew he was Misha . . . They amputated his legs and his right arm, all he had was the left one. They amputated high up by the hip, so he couldn't have prostheses. They rolled him around in a wheelchair. They made a high wheelchair specially for him and rolled him around, anyone who could. Many civilians came to the hospital to help with the care, especially of such badly wounded men as Misha. Women and schoolchildren. Even young children. This Misha was carried in their arms. And he didn't lose heart. He wanted so much to live! He was only nineteen, he hadn't lived at all yet. I don't remember whether he had any family, but he knew that he wouldn't be abandoned in his plight; he believed that he wouldn't be forgotten. Of course the war went all over our land, there was devastation everywhere. When we liberated villages, they were all burned down. All people had left was the land. Nothing but the land.

My sister and I did not become doctors, though that had been our dream before the war. We could have gone to medical school without exams; we had the right to do that as war veterans. But we had seen so much human suffering, so many deaths. We couldn't imagine seeing more of it again . . . Even thirty years later I talked my daughter out of studying medicine, though she wanted to very much. After decades . . . As soon as I close my eyes I see . . . Spring . . . We go around some field, just after a battle, looking for the wounded. The field is trampled all over. I come upon two dead men—a young soldier of ours and a young German. Lying in young wheat and looking into the sky . . . No signs of death on them yet. Just looking into the sky . . . I still remember those eyes . . .

Olga Vasilyevna

The last days of the war . . . I remember this . . . We were driving and suddenly there was music somewhere. A violin . . . For me the war ended that day . . . It was such a miracle: suddenly music. Different sounds . . . As if I woke up . . . We all imagined that after the war, after such oceans of tears, there would be a wonderful life. Beautiful. After the Victory . . . after that day . . . We imagined that all people would be very kind, would only love each other. They would all become brothers and sisters. How we waited for that day . . .

"WE DIDN'T SHOOT . . ."

———

There are many people in war . . . And many duties in war . . .

There is much work not only around death, but also around life. There is not only shooting and killing people, mining and demining, bombing and exploding, going into hand-to-hand combat—there is also laundering, cooking kasha, baking bread, cleaning cauldrons, tending horses, repairing machinery, planing and nailing down coffins, delivering mail, mending boots, supplying tobacco. Even during war life consists by more than half of banal things. And of trifles, too. It's unusual to think so, isn't it? "There are mountains of our ordinary women's work there," recalls nurse-aide Alexandra Iosifovna Mishutina. The army marched first, and behind it "the second front"—laundresses, cooks, auto mechanics, mailmen . . .

One of them wrote to me, "We're not heroes, we were backstage." What was there backstage?

OF NICE LITTLE SHOES AND
A CURSED WOODEN LEG

Tatyana Arkadyevna Smelyanskaya
MILITARY JOURNALIST

We walk through the mud. Horses sink into this mud or fall down dead. Big trucks stall . . . Soldiers drag artillery by themselves. Pull wagons with bread and linen. Boxes of tobacco. I see one box of tobacco tumble into the mud, followed by a well-rounded Russian curse . . . They cherish ammunition, they cherish tobacco . . .

My husband says to me, he repeats all the time, "Keep your eyes peeled! This is epic! Epic!"

Irina Nikolaevna Zinina
PRIVATE, COOK

Before the war I had a happy life . . . With papa and mama. My papa fought in the Finnish War. He came back with a finger missing on his right hand, and I asked him, "Papa, why is there war?"

War soon came, and I still wasn't quite grown up. We were evacuated from Minsk. They brought us to Saratov. There I worked on a kolkhoz. The chairman of the village council summoned me: "I think about you all the time, girl."

I was surprised. "What do you think, Uncle?"

"If it weren't for this cursed wooden leg! It's all this cursed wooden leg . . ."

I stood there; I didn't understand anything.

He said, "There's this letter, I have to send two people to the front, and I have nobody to send. I would've gone myself, except there's this cursed wooden leg. I can't send you, you're not local. But maybe you'll go? I've got two young girls here: you and Maria Utkina."

Maria was such a tall one, a fine girl, but not me. I was so-so.

"Will you go?"

"Will they give me footwraps there?"

We were all ragged, because we had no time to take anything with us!

"You're such a pretty one, they'll give you nice little shoes."

I agreed.

. . . They unloaded us from the train, and a fellow came to pick us up, sturdy, mustached, but nobody went with him. I don't know why, I didn't ask, I wasn't an activist and never pushed myself forward. We didn't like the fellow. Then a handsome officer came. A doll! He talked us into it, and we went. We arrived at the unit, and that mustached one was there, laughing. "So you snub-noses didn't want to come with me?"

The major invited us one by one and asked, "What can you do?"

One girl said, "Milk cows." Another: "At home I boiled potatoes and helped mama."

He calls me up: "And you?"

"I can do laundry."

"I see you're a good girl. Can you cook?"

"I can."

The whole day long I cooked food, and in the evening I had to do laundry for the soldiers. I stood guard. They shout, "Sentry! Sentry!"—and I can't respond. I don't even have strength enough to speak . . .

Svetlana Nikolaevna Liubich

MEDICAL VOLUNTEER

I went around on a hospital train . . . I remember I spent the whole first week crying: first, I missed mama, and also I wound up on the top shelf, where they put the luggage now. It was my "room."

How old were you when you went to the front?

I was in the eighth grade, but I didn't finish the school year. I ran away to the front. All the girls on the hospital train were my age.

What did your work consist of?

We took care of the wounded, gave them water, fed them, brought bedpans—all that was our job. I was on duty with an older girl. She tried to spare me at first: "If they ask for a bedpan, call me." There were badly wounded men: one without an arm, another without a leg. The first day I kept calling her, and then I remained alone, because she couldn't really stay with me day and night. So I stayed by myself. A wounded man called me, "Nurse, a bedpan."

I brought him a bedpan, and I saw he didn't take it. I looked: he had no arms. My brain was in a whirl; somehow I figured out what had to be done, but for several minutes I stood not knowing what to do. You understand me? I had to help him . . . And I didn't know what to do, I'd never seen it. They didn't even teach it in the courses . . .

Alexandra Semyonovna Masakovskaya

PRIVATE, COOK

I didn't shoot . . . I cooked kasha for the soldiers. They gave me a medal for that. I don't even remember about it: did I ever fight? I cooked kasha, soup for the soldiers. I carried cauldrons, pails. Very heavy . . . I remember our commander used to say, "I'd shoot all these pails . . . How are you going to give birth after the war?" And once he up and shot at all those pails. We had to find smaller ones in some village.

The soldiers would come back from the front line for some rest. The poor things were all filthy, exhausted, their hands and feet frostbitten. The Uzbeks and Tajiks were especially afraid of frost. In their parts it's always sunny, and here we had minus twenty to minus forty. The man couldn't get warm, I had to feed him, he couldn't bring the spoon to his mouth.

Maria Stepanovna Detko
PRIVATE, LAUNDRESS

I did laundry . . . I went all through the war with a tub. We did it by hand. Padded jackets, army shirts . . . They would deliver underwear, so worn out, infested with lice. White robes, you know, those camouflage ones. All bloody, not white, but red. Black from old blood. The first water is red or black—you can't launder in it . . . An army shirt without a sleeve, and with a big hole in the chest, trousers without a leg. You wash them with tears and rinse them with tears.

Heaps and heaps of these army shirts . . . Padded coats . . . My hands ache now as I remember it. In winter these coats were heavy, with frozen blood on them. I often see it in dreams now . . . A black heap of them . . .

Maria Nikolaevna Vasilevskaya
SERGEANT, RADIO OPERATOR

There were so many miracles during the war . . . I'll tell you . . .

Anya Kaburova is lying on the grass . . . Our radio operator. She's dying—a bullet hit her heart. Just then a wedge of cranes flew over us. Everybody raised their heads to the sky, and she opened her eyes. She looked: "What a pity, girls." Then paused and smiled: "Can it be, girls, that I'm going to die?" Just then our mailwoman, our Klava, comes running and shouting, "Don't die! Don't die! You've got a letter from home . . ." Anya doesn't close her eyes, she waits . . .

Our Klava sat next to her, opened the envelope. A letter from mama: "My dear, my beloved little daughter . . ." The doctor stands next to me, he says, "This is a miracle. A miracle! She lives contrary to all the laws of medicine . . ." They finished reading the letter . . . And only then did Anya close her eyes . . .

Vasilisa Yuzhnina
PRIVATE, HAIRDRESSER

My specialty . . . My specialty is men's haircuts . . .

A girl comes . . . I don't know how to cut her hair. She has luxuriant wavy hair. The commander enters the dugout. "Give her a man's haircut."

"But she's a woman."

"No, she's a soldier. She'll be a woman again after the war."

All the same . . . All the same, as soon as the girls' hair grew a little, I'd curl it during the night. We had cones instead of curlers . . . Dry pine cones . . . We could at least curl the forelock . . .

Anna Zakharovna Gorlach
PRIVATE, LAUNDRESS

I hadn't read many books . . . And I didn't know any fancy talk . . . We clothed the soldiers, laundered, ironed for them—that was our heroism. We rode on horseback, less often by train. Our horses were exhausted, you could say we got to Berlin on foot. And since we're remembering like this, we did everything that was necessary: helped to carry the wounded, delivered shells by hand at the Dnieper, because it was impossible to transport them. We carried them from several miles away. We made dugouts, built bridges . . .

We fell into an encirclement, I ran, shot, like everybody else. Whether I killed or not, I can't say. I ran and shot, like everybody else.

It seems I've remembered very little. But there was so much of everything! I'll remember . . . Come again . . .

Natalya Mukhametdinova
PRIVATE, BAKER

My story is a short one . . .

The sergeant major asks, "How old are you, girl?"

"Sixteen, why?"

"Because," he says, "we don't need minors."

"I'll do whatever you like. Even bake bread."

They took me . . .

Elena Vilenskaya
SERGEANT, CLERK

I was enlisted as a clerk . . . This is how they persuaded me to go work at headquarters . . . They told me: we know you worked as a photographer before the war, you'll be our photographer.

What I remember well was that I didn't want to take pictures of death. Of the dead. I took pictures when the soldiers were at rest—smoking, laughing—when awards were handed out. It's too bad I didn't have color film then, only black-and-white. Carrying the regimental banner . . . I could have taken a beautiful picture of that . . .

And today . . . Journalists come to me and ask, "Did you take pictures of the dead? The battlefield . . ." I began to look . . . I have few pictures of dead men . . . When someone was killed, the boys would ask me, "Have you got him alive?" We wanted to see him alive . . . Smiling . . .

Zoya Lukyanovna Verzhbitskaya
COMMANDER OF A UNIT IN A CONSTRUCTION BATTALION

We built . . . Built railroads, pontoon bridges, blinds. The front was close by. We dug the ground at night, so as not to be seen.

We cut down woods. My unit was mostly girls, all young. There were a few men, all from the reserves. How did we transport trees? We'd all pick one up and carry it. The whole unit carried one tree. We had bloody blisters . . . On our hands . . . on our shoulders . . .

Maria Semyonovna Kulakova
PRIVATE, BAKER

I finished teacher training . . . I got my diploma when the war was already going on. Because of the war they did not assign us to jobs but sent us home. I came home and a few days later was summoned to the recruiting office. Mama, of course, didn't want me to go. I was very young, only eighteen: "I'll send you to my brother and tell them you aren't home." I said, "I'm a Komsomol member." In the recruiting office they assembled us and said: Thus and so, we need women to bake bread at the front.

. This work was very hard. We had eight cast-iron ovens. We came to a devastated village or town and set them up. Having set up the ovens, we needed firewood, twenty or thirty buckets of water, five sacks of flour. We were eighteen-year-olds, and we carried hundred and fifty pound sacks of flour. Two of us would pick one up and carry it. Or forty loaves of bread on a plank. I, for instance, couldn't lift it.

Day and night by the oven, day and night. We'd finish kneading one tub, there's the next one waiting. There's a bombardment and we're baking bread . . .

Elena Nikiforovna Ievskaya
PRIVATE, LOGISTICS

And I spent the whole four years of the war on wheels . . . Went around following the signposts: "Shchukin Supply Corps," "Kozhuro Supply Corps." We would get tobacco, cigarettes, flints at the warehouse—all these things a soldier can't do without at the front—and off we'd go. Sometimes in trucks, sometimes in wagons, and often on foot with one or two soldiers. We carried it on our backs. You couldn't go to the trenches with a horse, the Germans would hear the creaking. We carried it. All on our backs, my dear . . .

Maria Alexeevna Remneva
SECOND LIEUTENANT, POSTAL WORKER

At the beginning of the war . . . I was nineteen years old . . . I lived in the town of Murom, in the Vladimir region. In October 1941 we Komsomol members were sent to build the Murom-Gorki-Kulebaki highway. When we returned from the labor front we were mobilized.

I was sent to the school of communications in Gorki, to the courses for postal workers. On finishing the courses, I was appointed to the active army, to the 60th Infantry Division. I served as an officer in the regimental mail. With my own eyes I saw people weep, kiss envelopes, when they received a letter at the front line. Many of their relations had been killed or lived on territory occupied by the enemy. They couldn't write. So we used to write letters from an Unknown Sender: "Dear soldier, it is an Unknown Girl writing to you. How is the fight with the enemy going? When will you come home with the Victory?" We sat at night writing . . . I wrote hundreds of those letters during the war . . .

OF THE SPECIAL "K" SOAP
AND THE GUARDHOUSE

Valentina Kuzminichna
Bratchikova-Borshchevskaya

LIEUTENANT, POLITICAL COMMISSAR
OF A FIELD LAUNDRY UNIT

On May 1 I got married . . . And on June 22 the war began. The first German planes came flying. I worked in an orphanage for Spanish children who had been brought to Kiev. That was 1937 . . . The civil war in Spain . . . We didn't know what to do, but the Spanish children began to dig trenches in the yard. They already knew everything . . . They were sent to the rear, and I went to the Penza region. I was given an assignment to organize courses for nurses. By the end of 1941 I personally held the exams for these courses, because all the doctors had left for the front. I handed out the certificates and also asked to be sent to the front. They sent me to Stalingrad, to an army field hospital. I was the oldest of the girls. My friend Sonia Udrugova—I'm still friends with her—was sixteen then, she had just finished ninth grade, plus these medical courses. We'd been at the front for three days, and I see Sonia sitting in the woods and crying. I go up to her: "Sonechka, why are you crying?"

"Don't you understand? I haven't seen mama for three days."

When I remind her of this incident now, she laughs.

At the Kursk Bulge I was transferred from the hospital to the field laundry unit as a political commissar. The laundresses were all hired help. We used to go somewhere in carts: there were basins, tubs sticking out, samovars to heat up water, and on top of all that the girls sat in red, green, blue, gray skirts. Everybody laughed, "Hey, there goes the laundry army!" They called me the "laundry commissar." Later on my girls got better dressed, "gussied themselves up," as they say.

The work was very hard. No mention of any washing machines. By hand . . . It was all done by women's hands . . . We arrive, they give us some cottage, or a dugout. We wash the underwear, and before we dry it we soak it in the special "K" soap to prevent lice. We had insect powder, but it didn't work. We used "K" soap, very stinky, it smelled awful. We used to dry the underwear in the same space where we did the laundry, and we also slept there. They gave us up to an ounce of soap to wash one soldier's underwear. The underwear was black as earth. Many girls got ruptures from the work, from carrying heavy things, from strain. "K" soap caused eczema, nails came off, we thought they'd never grow back. But even so, after two or three days of rest the girls had to go back and launder.

The girls obeyed me . . .

Once we came to a place where a whole unit of pilots was staying. They saw us, and we were all wearing dirty old things, and these boys scornfully said, "Look at the laundresses . . ."

My girls were almost crying. "Commissar, see what they . . ."

"Never mind, we'll show them."

We made an arrangement. In the evening my girls put on the best things they had and went to a meadow. One of our girls played the accordion, and they all danced. They had agreed, though, not to dance with the pilots. The pilots came and invited them to dance, but they didn't; they danced with each other the whole evening. The boys finally pleaded, "One fool said something, and you took offense at all of us . . ."

The rule was not to put hired hands in the guardhouse, but what could you do, if there were a hundred girls there together? We had curfew at eleven, and that was it. They tried to run away—well, girls will be girls. I used to send them to the guardhouse. Once some superiors came from another unit, and I had two girls in the guardhouse.

"What's this? You have hired hands in the guardhouse?" they asked.

I said calmly, "Comrade Colonel, write a report to headquarters. That's your business. But I have to fight for discipline. And I have exemplary order here."

With that they left.

The discipline was strict. Once I met a captain. He passed by my house just as I came out. He even stopped.

"My God! You're coming out of there, but do you know who lives there?"

"Yes."

"The political commissar lives there. Do you know how nasty she is?"

I told him I had never heard that.

"My God! She's so mean she never smiles."

"Would you like to make her acquaintance?"

"My God, no!"

Well, at that point I confessed, "Let me introduce myself, I'm the commissar!"

"No, it can't be! The things they've told me about her . . ."

I took care of my girls. We had a beautiful girl named Valya. I was once summoned away for ten days to headquarters. I came back and they told me that all those days Valya had come home late, that she was with some captain. If she was, she was, it's a bygone thing. Two months went by, I found out that Valya was pregnant. I summoned her. "Valya, how could this happen? Where are you going to go? Your stepmother" (she had no mother, she had a stepmother) "lives in a dugout." She cried and said to me, "It's your fault, if you hadn't gone away, nothing would have happened." I was like a mother, like an older sister to them.

She had a light coat, it was already cold, so I gave her my overcoat. Off she went, my Valya . . .

March 8, 1945. We organized a party for Women's Day. Tea. Some sort of candies we managed to get. My girls came out of their house and suddenly saw two Germans coming from the woods, dragging their submachine guns . . . Wounded . . . My girls surrounded them. Well, as the commissar, I wrote in a report that "today, May 8, the laundry women captured two Germans."

The next day we had a meeting of the commanders. The head of the political section said first thing, "Well, comrades, I want to give you some good news: the war will soon be over. Yesterday the laundry women from the 21st Field Laundry Unit captured two Germans."

Everybody applauded.

While the war went on, we received no awards, but when it was over, they told me, "Present two people for awards." I was indignant. I took the floor and said that I was the political commissar of the laundry unit, that the work of the laundresses was very hard, that many of them had ruptures and eczema on their hands and so on, that the girls were all young and worked more than trucks, than tractors. They asked me, "Can you present award-worthy material by tomorrow? We'll give more awards." And the commander of the unit and I sat all night over the lists. Many girls received medals "For Valor," "For Military Services," and one laundress was awarded the Order of the Red Star. She was the best laundress, she never left the tub: everybody was exhausted, falling off their feet, and she went on laundering. She was an older woman, her whole family had been killed.

When I had to send the girls home, I wanted to give them something. They were all from Belorussia and Ukraine, where everything was devastated, destroyed. How could I let them go empty-handed? We were stationed in some German village, and there was a sewing workshop in it. I went to look: luckily, the sewing machines were there, untouched. And so we prepared a present for each girl who was leaving. I was so glad, so happy. That was all I could do for my girls.

They all wanted to go home, and they were afraid to go. No one knew what awaited them there . . .

Tamara Lukyanovna Torop
PRIVATE, CONSTRUCTION ENGINEER

My papa . . . My beloved papa was a Communist, a holy man. I never met a better man in my life. He educated me: "Well, who would I be without Soviet power? A poor man. I'd be a hired hand for some rich kulak. Soviet power gave me everything. I received an education, I became an engineer, I build bridges. I owe everything to our own power."

I loved Soviet power. I loved Stalin. And Voroshilov. All our leaders. So my papa taught me.

The war was going on, I was growing up. In the evenings papa and I sang "The Internationale" and "The Holy War." Papa accompanied on the accordion. When I turned eighteen, he went with me to the recruiting office . . .

I wrote a letter home from the army telling him that I had built and defended bridges. What joy that was for our family. Papa made us all fall in love with bridges; we loved them from childhood. When I saw a destroyed bridge—bombed or exploded—I felt about it as about a living being, not a strategic object. I wept . . . On my way I encountered hundreds of destroyed bridges, big and small; during the war they were the first thing to be destroyed. Target number one. Whenever we went past the ruins, I always thought: how many years will it take to rebuild it all? War kills time, precious human time. I remembered well that papa spent several years building each bridge. He sat up nights over the drafts, even on weekends. The thing I was most sorry for during the war was the time. Papa's time . . .

Papa's long gone, but I continue to love him. I don't believe it when people say that men like him were stupid and blind—believing in Stalin. Fearing Stalin. Believing in Lenin's ideas. Everyone thought the same way. Believe me, they were good and honest people, they believed not in Lenin or Stalin, but in the Communist idea. In socialism with a human face, as they would call it later. In happiness for everybody. For each one. Dreamers, idealists—yes; blind—no. I'll never agree with that. Not for anything! In the middle of the war Russia began to produce excellent tanks and planes, good weapons, but even so, without faith we would never have overcome such a formidable enemy as Hitler's army—powerful, disciplined, which subjugated the whole of Europe. We wouldn't have broken its back. Our main weapon was faith, not fear. I give you my honest Party-member's word (I joined the Party during the war and am a Communist to this day). I'm not ashamed of my Party card and have not renounced it. My faith has never changed since 1941 . . .

Elena Ivanovna Babina

MILITIA FIGHTER

The German troops were stopped at Voronezh . . . They were unable to take Voronezh for a long time. They kept bombing and bombing it. The planes flew over our village, Moskovka. I still hadn't seen the enemy, I had only seen their planes. But very soon I learned what war was . . .

Our hospital was informed that a train had been bombed near Voronezh. We came to the place and saw . . . What did we see? Nothing but ground meat . . . I can't even talk about it . . . Aie, aie! The first one to come to his senses was our head doctor. He shouted loudly, "Stretchers!" I was the youngest, I had just turned sixteen, and everybody kept an eye on me in case I fainted.

We walked along the rails, went inside the cars. There was no one to put on the stretchers: the cars were burning, there was no moaning or screaming. There were no whole people. I clutched my heart, my eyes were closing from fright. When we returned to the hospital, we all collapsed wherever: one put her head on a table, another on a chair—and we fell asleep like that.

I finished my shift and went home. I came all in tears, lay down, and as soon as I closed my eyes, I saw it all again . . . Mama came home from work, Uncle Mitya came.

I hear mama's voice: "I don't know what will become of Lena. Look what's happened to her face since she went to work in the hospital. She doesn't look herself, she's quiet, doesn't speak to anyone, and she cries out during the night. Where's her smile, where's her laughter? You know how cheerful she used to be. Now she never jokes."

I listened to my mother and my tears poured down.

. . . When Voronezh was liberated in 1943, I joined the defense militia. There were only girls in it. They were all from seventeen to twenty years old. Young, beautiful, I've never seen so many beautiful girls together. The first one I got to know was Marusya Prokhorova; she was friends with Tanya Fedorova. They were from the same village. Tanya was a serious girl, she liked neatness and order. And Marusya liked to sing and dance. She sang naughty couplets. Most of all she liked to put on makeup. She'd spend hours sitting in front of the mirror. Tanya scolded her: "Instead of painting your face, you'd do better to iron your uniform and tidy up your bed." We also had Pasha Litavrina, a very feisty girl. She was friends with Shura Batishcheva. This Shura was shy and modest, the quietest of us all. Liusya Likhacheva liked to have her hair curled. She'd put her hair in curlers and take her guitar. She went to bed with the guitar and woke up with the guitar. The oldest of us was Polina Neverova; her husband was killed at the front, and she was always sad.

We all wore military uniforms. When mama saw me in uniform for the first time, she turned pale. "Have you decided to join the army?"

I set her at ease. "No, mama. I told you I keep watch on the bridges."

Mama wept. "Soon the war will be over. And you'll take off the army coat at once."

I thought so, too.

Two days after learning that the war was over, we had a meeting in the reading room. The head of the militia, Comrade Naumov, took the floor. "My dear combatants," he said, "the war is over. But yesterday I received an order saying that militia combatants are needed for the Western Road."

Someone in the audience shouted, "But Bandera's men are there!"*

Naumov paused and then said, "Yes, girls, Bandera's men are there. They're fighting against the Red Army. But an order is an order, it has to be carried out. Whoever wants to go, please apply to the head of the militia. Only volunteers will go."

We returned to the barrack, and each lay down on her bed. It became very, very quiet. No one wanted to go far from their native places. And no one wanted to die after the war was over. The next day they gathered us again. I sat at the presiding table; the table was covered with a red cloth. And I thought that this was the last time I'd be sitting at this table.

The head of the militia made a speech: "I knew, Babina, that you'd be the first to volunteer. And you are all fine girls, no cowards. The war is over, you could go back home, but you go to defend your Motherland."

Two days later we were leaving. They put us on a freight train. There was hay on the floors, and it smelled of grass.

I had never heard of the town of Stryy before, but that was where we were stationed now. I didn't like the town—it was small and frightening. Every day music played and someone was buried: a policeman, or a Communist, or a Komsomol member. Again we saw death.

---

* Stepan Bandera (1909–1959) is a controversial Ukrainian political figure. A nationalist and leader of a movement for independence of Ukraine from the Soviet Union, he led forces against the advancing Red Army in 1944 with aid from Germany. In 1959 he was assassinated by the Soviet secret police.

I made friends with Galya Korobkina. She was killed there. And another girl . . . She too was stabbed in the night . . . There I completely stopped joking and smiling . . .

OF MELTED BEARINGS AND RUSSIAN CURSES

Antonina Mironovna Lenkova

CAR MECHANIC IN A FIELD-CAR AND TANK REPAIR SHOP

I'm all my father . . . His daughter . . .

My father, Miron Lenkov, made his way from a simple illiterate lad to commander of a platoon in the Civil War. He was a real Communist. When he died, mama and I stayed in Leningrad. What is best in me I owe to this city. My passion was books. I sobbed over the novels of Lidia Charskaya,* read and reread Turgenev. I loved poetry . . .

The summer of 1941 . . . At the end of June we went to the Don to visit my grandmother. The war overtook us on the road. On the steppes mounted messengers immediately appeared, racing at breakneck speed, delivering summonses from the recruiting office. Cossack women sang, drank, and sobbed as they saw the Cossacks off to war. I went to the village of Bokovskaya, to the regional recruiting office. They said curtly and severely, "We don't take children to the front. Are you a Komsomol member? Excellent. Help the collective farm."

We shoveled piles of grain to save it from rotting inside. Then we harvested vegetables. Calluses hardened on my hands, my lips were

---

* Lidia Charskaya (1875–1938) was an actress at the prestigious Alexandrinsky Theater in St. Petersburg and a prolific writer of popular fiction. Her work was officially banned in 1920.

cracked, my face was covered with a steppe tan. And if I was in any way different from the farm girls, it was only in that I knew many poems and could recite them by heart all the long way home from the fields.

The war was coming closer. On October 17, the Germans occupied Taganrog. People began to evacuate. My grandmother stayed, but she sent me and my sister off: "You're young. Save yourselves." We spent five days walking to the Oblivskaya station. We had to throw out our sandals, and we entered the village barefoot. The stationmaster warned us, "Don't wait for a passenger train, get onto the flatcars, we'll bring the locomotive at once and send you to Stalingrad." We were lucky—we got onto a flatcar with oats. We sank our bare feet into the grain, covered ourselves with a shawl . . . Clinging close to each other, we dozed off. We'd long been out of bread and out of honey, too. The last few days Cossack women gave us food. We were embarrassed, we had no money to pay them, but they insisted, "Eat, poor things. It's bad for everybody now, we must help each other." I made a vow never to forget this human kindness. Never! Not for anything! And I haven't.

From Stalingrad we went by steamboat and then again by train, and reached the Medveditskoe station at two o'clock in the morning. A human wave carried us out onto the platform. Having turned into a pair of icicles, we were unable to move. We stood, supporting each other so as not to fall down, not to break into smithereens, as a frog did once in front of my eyes, taken out of liquid oxygen and thrown on the floor. Fortunately, someone we had traveled with remembered us. A carriage filled with people came, and we were tied behind it. They gave us padded jackets. They said, "Walk, otherwise you'll freeze. You won't be able to get warm. You can't be driven . . ." At first we kept falling, but we walked, then even ran. Ten miles . . .

The Frank settlement, the "First of May" kolkhoz. The chairman was very glad when he learned that I was from Leningrad and had finished ninth grade. "That's good. You'll help me here. With the accounting."

For a moment I was even glad. But then behind the chairman's back I saw a poster saying, "Girls, to the steering wheel!"

"I'm not going to sit in an office," I answered the chairman. "If they teach me, I'll be able to drive a tractor."

The tractors stood buried in snow. We dug them out, took them apart, burning our hands against the frozen metal, leaving pieces of skin stuck to them. The rusted, tightly screwed bolts seemed welded. When we didn't succeed in unscrewing them counterclockwise, we tried to do it clockwise. As luck would have it . . . just at that moment . . . as if from under the earth, the foreman Ivan Ivanovich Nikitin appeared, the only real tractor driver and our instructor. He clutched his head and couldn't keep from using good Russian foul language. Ah, fuck it all! His curses sounded like groans. But all the same I wept for once . . .

I rode out to the field backward; most of the gears in the gearbox of my STZ were "toothless." The thinking was simple: within fifteen miles, one of the tractors would break down and its gearbox would replace mine. That is what happened. A young tractor driver, a girl like me, Sarochka Gozenbuck, didn't notice that there was no water left in the radiator, and she ruined her motor. Ah, fuck it all . . .

Before the war I hadn't even learned to ride a bicycle, but here was a tractor. We spent a long time heating the motors—with open flames, in violation of all the rules. I also found out what overwinding was. And how do you start the motor after such a procedure: you couldn't turn the handle all the way, and halfway wasn't enough . . . The lubricants and the fuel were rationed by the war norms. You answered with your head for every drop, as well as for melted bearings. Ah, fuck it all . . . For every drop . . .

That day . . . Before going to the field I opened the crankcase to check the oil. Some sort of whey came out. I shouted to the foreman that I had to fill up with motor oil. He came, rubbed a drop in his hands, sniffed it for some reason, and said, "No fear! You can work one more day." I objected, "No, you yourself said . . ." He flew off the handle: "I said it, so now it's on my head—there's no escaping you. City dolls! Much too educated. Ah, fuck it all . . ." Drive, devil take it . . . I drove off. It was hot, the tractor smoked, impossible to breathe, but it was all nonsense. What about the bearings? I thought there was a bit of knocking. I stopped—there was nothing. I stepped on the pedal—there's knocking! Then all of a sudden right under the seat: bam, bam, bam!

I cut the motor, ran to the access hatch, opened it: two bearings on the connecting rod were completely melted!

I sank on the ground, put my arms around the wheel and—for the second time during the war—burst into tears. It was my fault: I had seen what kind of oil I had! I got scared of his foul mouth. I should have answered him in kind, but no, I'm too genteel for that.

I turned at some sounds. Well, well! The chairman of the kolkhoz, the director of the machine-tractor station, the head of the political section and, of course, our foreman. Who caused it all!

And he stands there and can't move. He understands it all. Says nothing. Ah, fuck it all . . .

The director of the MTS asks, "How many?"

"Two," I reply.

By the law of wartime I should go on trial for that. For negligence and sabotage.

The head of the political section turns to the foreman. "Why don't you look after your girls? How can I put this baby on trial!"

So it got settled. With just talk. And the foreman never again used foul language in front of me. And I learned from it, too . . . Ah, fuck it all . . . I could make a scene . . .

Then happiness came: we found our mama. She came, and we were a family again. Mama suddenly said, "I think you should go back to school."

I didn't understand right away what she meant. "Go where?"

"Who else is going to finish high school for you?"

After all that I had lived through, it was strange to find myself at a school desk, solving problems, writing compositions, memorizing German verbs, instead of fighting the fascists! At a time when the enemy had reached the Volga!

I didn't have very long to wait: in four months I would turn seventeen. Not eighteen yet, but at least seventeen. Then nobody could force me to go home! Nobody!

In the regional committee everything went smoothly, but in the recruiting office I had to put up a fight. Because of my age, because of my eyesight. But the first helped the second . . . When they brought up the question of my age, I called the commissar a bureaucrat . . . And started a hunger strike . . . I sat next to him and didn't budge for two days, refusing the offered slice of bread and a mug of boiled water. I threatened to die of hunger, but first to write who was guilty of my death. I don't think this frightened him, but even so he sent me for a medical exam. All this was taking place in the same room. Next to him. When the doctor, having checked my vision, spread her arms, the commissar laughed and said that my hunger strike was unnecessary. He felt sorry for me. I answered that I could see nothing because of the hunger strike. Having gone to the window and closer to the ill-favored eye chart, I burst into tears. I wept . . . For a long time . . . until I learned the lower lines by heart. Then I wiped my tears and said that I was ready to be examined again. I passed.

On November 10, 1942, having stocked up on food for ten days, as we had been told to, we (some twenty-five young girls) got into the back of a shabby truck, and began to sing "The Order Is Given," replacing the words "for the Civil War" with "to defend our country."

From Kamyshino, where we took the oath, we marched on foot along the left bank of the Volga to Kapustin Yar. There an auxiliary regiment was stationed. And there, among the thousands of men, we somehow got lost. There were "buyers" coming from various units to recruit reinforcements. They tried to ignore us. Passed us over all the time . . .

On the way I became friends with Annushka Rakshenko and Asya Bassina. Neither of them had any specialization, and I considered my own to be unmilitary. And therefore, whatever specialization was called out, the three of us together took three steps forward, thinking that we could master any specialization quickly, on the spot. But we were bypassed.

But when we stepped forward at the command, "Drivers, tractor drivers, mechanics—three steps forward!" the "buyer"—he was a young first lieutenant—didn't succeed in passing us over. I took not three steps but five, and he stopped.

"Why do you select only men? I, too, am a tractor driver!"

He was surprised. "It can't be. Tell me the assignment number for tractor work."

"One, three, four, two."

"Have you melted any bearings?"

I confessed honestly that I had completely melted two connecting rod bearings.

"Very well. I'll take you. For your honesty." He nodded and went on.

My girlfriends were standing with me. Next to me. The first lieutenant pretended that that's how it should be. Ah, fuck it all . . .

The commander of the unit, reviewing the reinforcements, asked the first lieutenant a question, "Why did you bring these girls?"

The man was embarrassed and replied that he felt sorry for us: we might wind up in some place where we'd be killed like partridges.

The commander sighed.

"Very well. One to the kitchen, one to the stockroom, the most educated one to the headquarters as a clerk." He paused and added, "A pity, such beautiful girls."

The "most educated one" was me, but to work as a clerk! And what did our beauty have to do with it? Forgetting about military discipline, I went through the roof: "We're volunteers! We came to defend the Motherland. We'll only go to the combat units . . ."

For some reason the colonel yielded at once. "All right, let it be combat. These two—to the letuchki, to work on the machines, and the one with the glib tongue—to engine assembly."

This is how our service in the 44th Automobile–Armored Vehicle Field Shop began. We were a factory on wheels. On special trucks, called letuchki, machines were installed for milling, boring, polishing, turning. There was an electric generator, casting, vulcanization. Each machine was worked by two persons. Twelve hours of work without a moment of rest. The partner stayed while the other went to eat dinner, supper, breakfast. If one's turn came to go on assignment, the other worked twenty-four hours. We worked in snow, in mud. Under bombardment. And no one told us again that we were beautiful. But beautiful girls were pitied at the war, more pitied. That's true. It was a pity to bury them . . . A pity to send the death notice to their mamas . . . Ah, fuck it all . . .

I often have dreams nowadays . . . I know I have them, but I rarely remember them. But I'm left with the impression that I have been somewhere . . . And come back . . . In a dream, what took years in real life takes just a second. And sometimes I confuse dream and reality . . . I think it was in Zimovniki, I just lay down for a couple of hours, when the bombardment began. Eh, you! Fuck it all . . . Better to be killed than spoil the pleasure of a two-hour nap. There was a big explosion somewhere nearby. The house rocked. But I still went on sleeping . . .

Fear was absent in me, there was no such feeling. I give you my word. Only after the most violent raids, I had a throbbing in a tooth that had a cavity. And that not for long. I might still consider myself terribly brave, if, a few years after the war, owing to constant, unbearable, and totally incomprehensible pains in various parts of my body, I hadn't had to consult specialists. And a very experienced neuropathologist, having asked my age, said in amazement, "To have ruined your whole vegetative nervous system by the age of twenty-four! How are you going to live?"

I replied that I was going to live quite well. First of all, I was alive! I had dreamed so much of surviving! Yes, I had survived, but after just a few months of my civilian life, my joints got swollen, my right arm refused to work and was in terrible pain, my vision deteriorated, one of my kidneys turned out to have descended, my liver was not in the right place, and, as it turned out later, my vegetative nervous system was completely ruined. But all through the war I had dreamed that I would study. And the university became like a second Stalingrad for me. I finished it a year early, otherwise I would have run out of energy. Four years in the same overcoat—winter, spring, autumn—and an army shirt so faded it looked white . . . Ah, fuck it all . . .

"THEY NEEDED SOLDIERS . . .
BUT WE ALSO WANTED
TO BE BEAUTIFUL . . ."

—

Over several years I recorded hundreds of stories . . . Hundreds of cassettes and thousands of typed pages are arranged on my bookshelves. I listen and read attentively . . .

The world of war reveals itself to me from an unexpected side. Never before did I ask myself the questions: How could one, for instance, sleep for years in shallow trenches or on the bare ground by a bonfire, go around in heavy boots and overcoats, and finally—not laugh and dance? Not wear summer dresses? Forget about shoes and flowers . . . They were eighteen or twenty years old! I was used to thinking that there was no room for a woman's life in the war. It is impossible there, almost forbidden. But I was wrong . . . Very soon, already during my first meetings with them, I noticed: whatever the women talked about, even if it was death, they always remembered (yes!) about beauty. It was the indestructible part of their existence: "She was so beautiful lying in the coffin . . . Like a bride . . ." (A. Strotseva, infantry soldier) or: "They were going to award me a medal, and I had an old army shirt. I sewed myself a collar out of gauze. Anyway it was white . . . It seemed to me at that moment that I was so beautiful. There was no mirror, I couldn't see myself. Everything got smashed during a bombardment . . ." (N. Ermakova, radio operator). They told cheerfully and willingly about their naïve girlish ruses, little secrets, invisible signs of how in the "male" everyday life of war and the "male" business of war they still wanted to remain themselves. Not to betray their nature. Their astonishing memory (after all, forty years had gone by) preserved a great number of small details of war life. Details, nuances, colors, and sounds. In their world everyday life and essential life joined together, and the flow of essential life had a value of its own. They recalled the war as a time of life. Not so much of action as of life. I observed more than once how in their conversations the small overrode the great, even history. "It's a pity that I was beautiful only during the war . . . My best years were spent there. Burned up. Afterward I aged quickly . . ." (Anna Galai, submachine gunner).

At a distance of many years some events suddenly grew bigger, others diminished. The human, the intimate grew bigger, becoming for me and, most curiously, even for them, more interesting and close. The human overcame the inhuman, if only because it was human. "Don't be afraid of my tears. Don't pity me. Let it be painful for me, but I'm grateful to you that I've recalled myself when I was young . . ." (K. S. Tikhonovich, sergeant, antiaircraft gunner).

I also did not know this war. And did not even suspect it . . .

OF MEN'S BOOTS AND
WOMEN'S HATS

Maria Nikolaevna Shchelokova
SERGEANT, COMMANDER OF A COMMUNICATIONS SECTION

We lived in the ground . . . like moles . . . But we did have some little trifles. In spring you would bring in a little sprig, set it up. Feel happy. Maybe tomorrow you won't be there—that's what we thought to ourselves. And you remember, remember . . . One girl received a woolen dress from home. We envied her, although wearing your own clothes wasn't allowed. The sergeant major—a man, that is—grumbled, "They'd do better to send you sheets. It's more useful." We had no sheets, no pillows. We slept on branches or on hay. But I had a pair of earrings stashed away; I'd put them on at night and sleep with them on . . .

When I got a concussion for the first time, I couldn't hear or speak. I said to myself, "If the voice doesn't come back, I'll throw myself under a train." I used to sing so well, and suddenly I had no voice. But my voice came back.

I was so happy, I put on my earrings. I arrived for duty and shouted with joy, "Comrade First Lieutenant, Sergeant Shchelokova reporting for duty . . ."

"And what's that?"

"What's what?"

"Get out of here!"

"What's the matter?"

"Pull the earrings off at once! What kind of soldier are you?"

This first lieutenant was very handsome. All our girls were a little in love with him. He used to tell us that in war soldiers were called for and only soldiers. They needed soldiers . . . But we also wanted to be beautiful . . . All through the war I was afraid that I'd be hit in the legs and get crippled. I had beautiful legs. What is it for a man? Even if he loses his legs, it's not so terrible. He's a hero anyway. He can marry! But if a woman is crippled, it's her destiny that's at stake. A woman's destiny . . .

Vera Vladimirovna Shevaldysheva

FIRST LIEUTENANT, SURGEON

I smiled all through the war . . . I figured that I had to smile as often as possible, because a woman should bring light. Before we left for the front, our old professor told us this: "You have to tell every wounded soldier that you love him. Your strongest medicine is love. Love protects, it gives the strength to survive." A wounded man lies there, he's in so much pain that he weeps, and you tell him, "There, my dearest.

There, my good one . . ." "Do you love me, nursie?" (They called all the young ones "nursie.") "Of course, I do. Only get well quickly." They could get offended, say bad things, but we never could. For one rude word they punished us with the guardhouse.

Hard . . . Of course it was hard . . . Even, say, climbing into a truck wearing a skirt, when there are only men around. Those were special ambulance trucks, very high ones. Climb to the very top! Just try it . . .

Nadezhda Vasilyevna Alexeeva
PRIVATE, TELEGRAPHER

They put us on a train . . . A freight train . . . We were twelve girls, the rest were all men. The train would go seven or ten miles and stop. Another seven or ten miles . . . Again a dead end. There was no water, no toilet . . . See?

Men would make a fire at a halt, shake out lice, get dry. And what were we to do? We would go to some nook and get undressed there. I wore a knitted sweater; lice sat on every sixteenth of an inch, on every stitch. I'd look and get sick. There are head lice, clothes lice, pubic lice . . . I had them all . . . What was I to do? I couldn't go and roast the lice together with the men. It was embarrassing. I threw the sweater out and stayed just in my dress. At some station an unknown woman gave me a jacket and some old shoes.

We rode for a long time, and then walked for a long time. It was freezing cold. I walked and kept looking in the mirror to see whether I was frostbitten. Toward evening I saw that my cheeks were frostbitten. I was so stupid . . . I'd heard that when the cheeks are frostbitten, they turn white. Mine were very red. I thought, let them stay frostbitten for good. But the next day they turned black . . .

Anastasia Petrovna Sheleg
JUNIOR SERGEANT, AEROSTAT OPERATOR

There were many pretty girls among us . . . We went to the bath-house, and there was a hairdresser's shop there. So, one after the other, we all dyed our eyebrows. The commander really gave it to us: "Have you come to fight or to a ball?" We spent the whole night crying and rubbing it off. In the morning he went around and repeated to each girl, "I need soldiers, not ladies. Ladies don't survive in war." A very strict commander. Before the war he had been a math teacher . . .

Stanislava Petrovna Volkova
SECOND LIEUTENANT, COMMANDER OF A SAPPER PLATOON

It seems to me as if I've lived two lives—a man's and a woman's . . .

When I came to training school, there was immediate military discipline. In class, at drill, in the barracks—everything was according to regulations. There were no allowances because we were girls. All we heard was, "Stop talking!" "Hey, you talkers!" In the evening we longed to sit and maybe do some embroidery . . . to recall something women do . . . It was strictly forbidden. We were all without a home, without domestic chores, and we felt out of sorts. We were given only one hour of rest: we could sit in the Lenin room, write letters, or stand at ease, talk. But without laughter or loudness—that wasn't allowed.

Could you sing songs?

No, we couldn't.

Why couldn't you?

It wasn't allowed. When you're on the march, you can sing, if the order is given. The order was, "Leader, strike up!"

So you couldn't just sing?

No, that was against regulations.

Was it hard to get used to?

I think I never really got used to it. You've just fallen asleep, and suddenly: "Reveille!" It was like the wind swept us off our beds. You begin to dress. A woman has more clothes than a man, you fuss with one thing, then another. Finally, belt in hand, you fly to the locker room. You grab your overcoat on the way and race to the armory room. There you put a cover on your shovel, hang it on your belt, attach a kit, buckle it anyhow. Grab a rifle, lock the bolt as you go, and literally roll down the stairs from the fourth floor. Once in line, you straighten yourself up. You're given a few minutes to do all that.

Now we're at the front . . . My boots are three sizes too big, deformed, engrained with dust. The woman I stay with brings me two eggs: "Take them for the road. You're so thin, you're about to snap in two." Quietly, so that she didn't see, I broke those two little eggs and cleaned my boots. I was hungry, of course, but the woman's instinct won out—I wanted to be pretty. You don't know how rough the overcoat is on the skin, how heavy it all is, these men's things: the belt and everything. I especially disliked the roughness of the overcoat on my neck, and also those boots. They changed your gait, changed everything . . .

I remember we were sad. We went around sad all the time . . .

Maria Nikolaevna Stepanova

MAJOR, HEAD OF COMMUNICATIONS IN AN INFANTRY BATTALION

It was not so easy to make soldiers out of us . . . Not so simple . . .

We were issued uniforms. The sergeant major formed us up: "Align your toes."

We align them. The toes are even, but we're not, because our boots are size twelve or fourteen. He keeps at it. "The toes, the toes!"

Then, "Cadets, even up your chests!"

That, of course, we can't manage, and he yells at the top of his voice, "What have you got in your shirt pockets?"

We laugh.

"Stop laughing," shouts the sergeant major.

To drill us in the precise and correct way of saluting, he made us salute everything—from chairs to posters on the walls. Oh, he had a hard time with us.

In some town we marched up to the bathhouse. The men went to the men's half, we to the women's. The women shout, cover themselves: "Soldiers are coming!" They couldn't tell we were girls: we had boys' haircuts and wore army uniforms. Another time we went to the toilet, and the women brought a policeman. We asked him, "So where do we go?"

He then shouted at those women, "These are girls!"

"What kind of girls, these are soldiers . . ."

Bella Isaakovna Epstein
SERGEANT, SNIPER

All I remember is the road. The road . . . Advancing, retreating . . .

When we arrived at the 2nd Belorussian Front, they wanted to have us stay at division headquarters. Meaning: you're women, why go to the front line? "No," we said, "we're snipers, send us where we're supposed to go." Then they said, "We'll send you to a regiment where there's a good commander, he takes care of girls." There were all sorts of commanders. So we were told.

This colonel met us with these words: "Look out, girls, you've come to fight, so fight, but don't get up to anything else. There are men around, and no women. Devil knows how else I can explain the thing to you. It's war, girls . . ." He understood that we were still very young things. The first time planes flew over, I crouched down and covered my head with my hands, then I thought, And what about my poor hands? I wasn't ready for death yet.

I remember how in Germany . . . Ah, this is funny! In one German village we were billeted for the night in a castle. There were many rooms, whole big halls. Such halls! The wardrobes were filled with beautiful clothes. Each girl chose a dress for herself. There was a yellow one that I liked, and also a house robe. I can't tell you what a beautiful house robe it was—long, light . . . like a fluff of down! We had to go to bed, because we were terribly tired. We put these dresses on and went to bed, and fell asleep at once. I lay in that dress and the robe on top of it . . .

Another time, in an abandoned milliner's shop, the girls each chose a hat for herself and slept all night sitting, so as to wear a hat at least for a little while. In the morning we got up . . . looked once more in the mirror . . . Then took everything off, and put on our army shirts and trousers. We never took anything. On the road even a needle is heavy. A spoon tucked into the boot top, that's all . . .

Zinaida Prokofyevna Gomareva

TELEGRAPHER

Men . . . They're so . . . They didn't always understand us . . .

But our Colonel Ptitsyn we loved very much. We called him "Daddy." He wasn't like the others, he understood our woman's soul. We're near Moscow, it's the retreat, the most difficult time, and he says to us, "Girls, Moscow is close by. I'll bring you a hairdresser. Dye your eyebrows, eyelashes, curl your hair. That's not in the rules, but I want you to be pretty. This will be a long war . . . It won't end soon . . ."

And he brought us a hairdresser. We had our hair curled, put on makeup. We were so happy . . .

Sofya Konstantinovna Dubniakova
MEDICAL ASSISTANT

We raced over the ice of Lake Ladoga . . . advancing . . . Right away we came under heavy shelling. There was water all around; a wounded man goes straight to the bottom. I'm crawling around, bandaging. I crawl up to one, his legs are broken, he's losing consciousness, but he pushes me away and tries to get into his sidor—his kit bag, that is. He's looking for his reserve rations. To eat, at least, before he dies . . . When we started to advance over the ice, we got some food supplies. I want to bandage him, but he wants his kit bag and nothing else: men had a very hard time enduring hunger. It was worse than death for them . . .

And about myself I remember this . . . At first you're afraid of death . . . Amazement and curiosity live side by side in you. Then they both vanish—from fatigue. You're at the limits of your strength. Beyond the limits. In the end only one fear remains—of being ugly after death. A woman's fear . . . Not to be torn to pieces by a shell . . . I saw it happen . . . I picked up those pieces . . .

Liubov Ivanovna Osmolovskaya
PRIVATE, SCOUT

It rained and rained . . . We ran over the mud, people fell into this mud. Wounded, killed. I didn't want to die in that swamp. A black swamp. For a young girl to lie in such mud . . . And another time, this was already in Belorussia . . . in the Orsha forests, there were small bushes of bird cherry. Blue snowdrops. A whole clearing covered with blue flowers . . . To perish among such flowers! To lie there . . . I was a silly goose, seventeen years old . . . That's how I imagined death . . .

I thought that to die was like flying off somewhere. Once during the night we talked about death, but only once. We were afraid to pronounce the word . . .

Alexandra Semyonovna Popova
LIEUTENANT OF THE GUARDS, PILOT

Our regiment was all women . . . We flew to the front in May 1942 . . .

The planes they gave us were Po-2s. Small, slow. They flew only at a low level. Hedge-hopping. Just over the ground! Before the war young people in flying clubs learned to fly in them, but no one could have imagined they would have any military use. The plane was constructed entirely of plywood, covered with aircraft fabric. In fact, with cheesecloth. One direct hit and it caught fire and burned up completely in the air, before reaching the ground. Like a match. The only solid metal part was the M-11 motor.

Later on, toward the end of the war, we were issued parachutes, and a machine gun was installed in the pilot's cabin, but before there had been no weapon, except for four bomb racks under the wings—that's all. Nowadays they'd call us kamikazes, and maybe we were kamikazes. Yes! We were! But victory was valued more than our lives. Victory!

You ask how we could endure it? I'll tell you . . .

Before I retired, I became ill from the very thought of how I could possibly not work. Why then had I completed a second degree in my fifties? I became a historian. I had been a geologist all my life. But a good geologist is always in the field, and I no longer had the strength for it. A doctor came, took a cardiogram, and asked, "When did you have a heart attack?"

"What heart attack?"

"Your heart is scarred all over."

I must have acquired those scars during the war. You approach a target, and you're shaking all over. Your whole body is shaking, because below it's all gunfire: fighter planes are shooting, antiaircraft guns are shooting . . . Several girls had to leave the regiment; they couldn't stand it. We flew mostly during the night. For a while they tried sending us on day missions, but gave it up at once. A rifle shot could bring down a Po-2 . . .

We did up to twelve flights a night. I saw the famous ace Pokryshkin when he returned from a fighting mission. He was a sturdy man, not twenty and not twenty-three like us. But while his plane was refueled, a technician took his shirt off and wrung it out. It was soaked as if he had been in the rain. So now you can easily imagine what it was like for us. You come back and you can't even get out of the cabin; they used to pull us out. We couldn't carry the chart case; we dragged it on the ground.

And the work our girl armorers did! They had to attach four bombs to the aircraft by hand—that meant eight hundred pounds. They did it all night: one plane takes off, another lands. The body reorganized itself so much during the war that we weren't women . . . We didn't have those women's things . . . Periods . . . You know . . . And after the war not all of us could have children.

We all smoked. I also smoked. It made you feel as if you'd calmed down a little. You come back to earth shaking all over, you light a cigarette—and you calm down. We wore leather jackets, trousers, army shirts, plus a fur jacket in winter. Like it or not something masculine appeared in your gait and your movements. When the war was over, they made us khaki-colored dresses. We suddenly felt we were young girls . . .

Sofya Adamovna Kuntsevich

**SERGEANT MAJOR, MEDICAL ASSISTANT
IN AN INFANTRY COMPANY**

They gave me a medal recently . . . from the Red Cross . . . The Florence Nightingale international gold medal. Everybody congratulates me and wonders, "How could you drag out 147 wounded men? You're such a diminutive girl in the wartime photos . . ." Well, maybe I dragged out two hundred, nobody was counting then. It never entered my head, we didn't understand it that way. A battle was going on, people were losing blood, so should I sit and take notes? I never waited for the attack to be over, I crawled around during the combat picking up the wounded. If a man had a shrapnel wound and I arrived an hour or two later, there would have been nothing for me to do, the man would have lost all his blood.

I was wounded three times and had a concussion three times. People dreamed of all sorts of things during the war: one of going back home, another of getting to Berlin, and I wished for just one thing—to live until my birthday, so as to turn eighteen. For some reason I was afraid to die without having lived at least eighteen years. I used to wear trousers, a forage cap, and I was always in tatters, because I always crawled on my knees, and under the weight of the wounded man. It was hard to believe that a day would come when I would be able to get up and walk, not crawl on the ground. That was my dream! One day a division commander arrived, saw me, and asked, "Who is this adolescent boy? Why do you keep him here? He should be sent to school . . ."

I remember when there weren't enough bandages . . . There were such terrible bullet wounds that each needed a whole package. I tore up all my underwear, and I told the boys, "Take off your long johns, your undershirts, I've got people dying here." They took everything off, tore it up. I wasn't embarrassed in front of them, they were like brothers to me, and I lived among them like a boy. We would march by three holding hands, and the middle one could sleep for an hour or two. Then we'd change places.

I got as far as Berlin. I put my signature on the Reichstag: "I, Sofya Kuntsevich, came here to kill war."

When I see a common grave, I kneel before it. Before every common grave . . . always on my knees . . .

OF A GIRLISH TREBLE AND
SAILORS' SUPERSTITIONS

Klara Semyonovna Tikhonovich
SERGEANT, ANTIAIRCRAFT GUNNER

I heard . . . words . . . Poison . . . Words like stones . . . It was men's desire—to go and fight. Can a woman kill?! Those were abnormal, defective women . . .

No! A thousand times no! No, it was a human desire. The war was going on, I lived my usual life. A girl's life . . . Then a neighbor received a letter: her husband was wounded and in the hospital. I thought, "He's wounded, and who will replace him?" One came without an arm—who will replace him? Another came back without a leg—who will go instead of him? I wrote letters, begged, pleaded to be taken into the army. That's how we were brought up, that nothing in our country should happen without us. We had been taught to love it. To admire it. Since there's a war, it's our duty to help in some way. There's a need for nurses, so we must become nurses. There's a need for antiaircraft gunners, so we must become antiaircraft gunners.

Did we want to resemble men at the front? At first we did, very much: we cut our hair short, we even changed our way of walking. But later, no, no way! Later we wanted to put on makeup, we saved sugar, instead of eating it, to stiffen our bangs. We were happy to get hold of a pot of water to wash our hair. During a long march we searched for soft grass. We tore up some grass and rubbed our legs . . . You see, we used the grass to wash off the . . . We were girls, we had our special needs . . . The army didn't think about it . . . Our legs were green . . . It was good if the sergeant major was an older man and understood everything, and didn't confiscate extra underwear from a kit bag. A young one was sure to throw it out. But it wasn't extra for a girl who had to change underwear twice a day. We used to tear sleeves from the undershirts, and we had only two, meaning only four sleeves . . .

Klara Vasilyevna Goncharova
PRIVATE, ANTIAIRCRAFT GUNNER

Before the war I loved everything military . . . Men's things . . . I wrote to the school of aviation requesting application forms. I looked good in a military uniform. I liked formation, precision, abrupt words of command. The response from the school was: "First finish high school."

Of course, when the war began, with my mood I couldn't stay home. But they wouldn't take me at the front. By no means, because I was sixteen. The military commissar said, Why, what will the enemy think of us, if the war has only just begun, and we're sending such children to the front—underaged girls!

"We must crush the enemy."

"We'll crush him without you."

I insisted that I was tall, that no one would know I was sixteen, that they'd think I was older. I stood in his office refusing to leave: "Write that I'm eighteen, not sixteen." "You say that now, and what will you think of me later?"

After the war I no longer wanted, I couldn't go into any sort of military specialization. I wanted to take off all the khaki color quickly . . . I detest trousers to this day. I won't wear them even to the forest to pick mushrooms or berries. I wanted to wear something ordinary, feminine . . .

Maria Nesterovna Kuzmenko
SERGEANT MAJOR, ARMORER

We felt the war at once . . . We graduated from professional school and the very same day the "buyers" came to us. That's what we called those who came to our school to recruit new people for the reorganized units. They were always men, and you could tell that they pitied us. We looked at them in one way, they looked at us in another. We tried to break the line, to step forward, to be taken, to be noticed, to show ourselves the sooner. They were tired and looked at us knowing where we were going to be sent. They understood everything.

Our regiment was all men, only twenty-two women. It was the 870th Long-range Artillery Regiment. We brought two or three changes of underwear from home, we couldn't take more. They bombarded us, and we were left with what we had on when we ran away. Men went to the depot and got a change of clothes. But there was nothing for us. They gave us footwraps, and we made panties and bras out of them. The commander found out and yelled at us.

Six months later . . . We were so overworked we ceased to be women . . . We stopped having . . . The biological cycle got thrown off . . . See? Very frightening! It's frightening to think that you'll never be a woman again . . .

Maria Semyonovna Kaliberda
SERGEANT, RADIO OPERATOR

We tried hard . . . We didn't want people to say of us, "Ah, these women!" And we made greater efforts than men did. We had to prove that we were no worse than men. For a long time there was this haughty, condescending attitude to us: "Some warriors, these women . . ."

But how could we be men? It was impossible. Our thoughts were one thing, our nature—another. Our biology . . .

We march . . . About two hundred girls, then about two hundred men. It's hot. A forced march of twenty miles. Twenty! We march, and leave these red spots behind us in the sand . . . red traces . . . The women's thing. How can you hide anything here? The soldiers come after us and pretend that they don't notice anything . . . don't look under their feet . . . Our trousers got dry on us and became sharp as glass. They'd cut us. We had wounds and there was always the smell of blood. The army didn't provide us with anything . . . We were on the lookout: when the soldiers hung their shirts on the bushes, we'd steal a couple . . . They figured it out and laughed. "Sergeant, give us spare underwear. The girls took ours." There wasn't enough cotton wool and bandaging for the wounded . . . And nothing for our . . . Women's underwear appeared maybe two years later. We wore men's underpants and tank tops. So, we march . . . In boots! Our feet are roasted, too. We march . . . To the crossing, where the ferries are waiting. We reach the crossing, and there the shelling begins. A dreadful shelling, the men all hide wherever they can. They call us . . . And we don't even hear the shelling, we can't be bothered, we quickly run to the river. Into the water . . . Water! Water! We sat in it till we soaked it off . . . Under the shrapnel . . . That's it . . . We were more afraid of shame than of death. Several girls were killed in the water . . .

Maybe for the first time then I wanted to be a man . . . For the first time . . .

Then—the Victory. At first I'd go down the street and not believe it was Victory. I'd sit at the table and not believe it was Victory. Victory! Our Victory . . .

Anna Nikolaevna Khrolovich
LIEUTENANT OF THE GUARDS, PARAMEDIC

We were already liberating Latvia . . . We were near Daugavpils. It was late at night, I was just about to lie down. I hear the sentinel call to someone, "Halt! Who goes there?" And literally ten minutes later

I'm summoned to the commander. I go to the commander's dugout, our comrades are there and some man in civilian dress. I remember this man well. All those years I saw only men in khaki, in army over-coats, and this one was in a black overcoat with a plush collar.

"I need your help," the man says to me. "My wife is giving birth a mile and a half from here. She's alone, there's no one in the house."

The commander hesitates. "It's in no-man's-land. You know it may be dangerous."

"A woman is giving birth. I must help her."

They gave me five riflemen. I packed a bag of bandage material, also a pair of new flannelette footwraps they issued me recently. We went. There was shelling all the time—now undershot, now over-shot. And the forest was so dark, we couldn't even see the moon. Fi-nally we saw the silhouette of some building. It was a farmstead. When we went into the house, I saw a woman. She was lying on the floor, all covered with some old rags. The husband at once began to curtain the windows. Two riflemen stood outside, two by the door, and one held the flashlight for me. The woman could barely keep from moaning; she was in great pain.

I kept begging her, "Bear with it, dearest. You mustn't cry. Bear with it."

It was no-man's-land. If the enemy noticed anything, they would rain shells down on us. But when the soldiers heard that the baby was born . . . "Hurray! Hurray!" Very soft, almost a whisper. A baby was born on the front line!

They brought water. There was nowhere to boil it, so I wiped the baby with cold water. Swaddled it in my footwraps. There was noth-ing in the house except the old rags the mother was lying on.

I slipped away to that farmstead for several nights. The last time I went was before we began to advance, and I said goodbye. "I can't come to you anymore, I'm leaving."

The woman asked her husband something in Latvian. He trans-lated, "My wife asks what your name is."

"Anna."

The woman said something else. The husband translated again, "She says it's a very beautiful name. We'll call our daughter Anna in your honor."

The woman raised herself a little—she still couldn't get up—and handed me a beautiful mother-of-pearl powder box. This was obviously the thing she cherished most. I opened the powder box, and the smell of the powder, when there was shooting around, explosions . . . It was something . . . I want to weep even now . . . The smell of the powder, that little mother-of-pearl lid . . . The little baby, a girl . . . Something homey, something from a real woman's life . . .

Taissia Petrovna Rudenko-Sheveleva

CAPTAIN, COMPANY COMMANDER IN THE MOSCOW FLEET, NOW A RETIRED LIEUTENANT COLONEL

A woman in the navy . . . That was something forbidden, even unnatural. People thought it would be bad luck for a ship. I was born near Fastov. In our village the women teased my mother to death: what did you give birth to—a girl or a boy? I wrote a letter to Voroshilov himself, asking to be accepted in the Leningrad Artillery School. They accepted me only on his personal order. The only girl.

When I finished the school, they still wanted me to stay on dry land. Then I stopped telling them that I was a woman. My Ukrainian last name, Rudenko, saved me.* But on one occasion I gave myself away. I was scrubbing the deck, suddenly heard a noise, and turned around: a sailor was chasing a cat that had ended up on the ship, no one knew how. There was a belief, probably from the earliest times, that cats and women bring bad luck at sea. The cat didn't want to quit the ship, and its dodges would have been the envy of a world-class football player. The whole ship was laughing. But when the cat nearly

---

* Most Russian family names have a feminine ending for women (Ivanov becomes Ivanova), but often Ukrainian names, such as Rudenko, do not.

fell into water, I got frightened and screamed. And it was evidently such a girlish treble that the men's laughter stopped at once. Silence fell.

I heard the commander's voice: "Watchman, is there a woman on board?"

"No, sir, Comrade Commander."

Panic again—there was a woman on board.

. . . I was the first woman to be a commissioned officer in the navy. During the war I was in charge of arming the ships and the naval infantry. Then an article appeared in the British press saying that some incomprehensible creature—neither man nor woman—was fighting in the Russian navy. And that no man would ever take this "lady with a dirk" for a wife. Not take me for a wife?! No, you're mistaken, my good sir, the most handsome officer will take me . . .

I was a happy wife and am still a happy mother and grandmother. It's not my fault that my husband was killed in the war. And I loved the navy all my life and still do . . .

Klavdia Vasilyevna Konovalova

JUNIOR SERGEANT, COMMANDER OF AN ANTIAIRCRAFT GUN

I worked in a factory . . . In a chain factory in our village of Mikhalchikovo, Kstovsky district, Gorki region. When men began to be recruited and sent to the front, I was transferred to a machine to do men's work. From there I was transferred to the forge shop as a hammerer, to make ship's chains.

I asked to be sent to the front, but the factory superiors used various pretexts to keep me there. Then I wrote to the district Komsomol committee and in March 1942 received a summons. I was leaving with several other girls, and the whole village came to see us off. We went on foot twenty miles to Gorki, and there they distributed us to various units. I was sent to the 784th Middle-caliber Antiaircraft Artillery Regiment.

Soon I was appointed number-one gunlayer. But that wasn't enough for me; I now wanted to become a loader. True, that was regarded as purely a man's job: you had to work with thirty-pound shells and carry out intense fire at a rate of one salvo every five seconds. It was not in vain that I had worked as a hammerer. Within a year I was promoted to the rank of junior sergeant and appointed commander of the second gun, which was serviced by two girls and four men. From the intense firing the gun barrels turned red-hot and it became dangerous to use them. We were forced, against all the rules, to cool them off with blankets moistened with water. The guns couldn't stand it, but people could. I was a tough, strong girl, but I know that in the war I was capable of doing more than in peaceful life. Even physically. An unknown strength surged up from somewhere . . .

Hearing about the Victory on the radio, I roused my team by sounding the alarm and gave my last command: "Azimuth—fifteen zero-zero. Angle of elevation—ten-zero. Detonator—hundred and twenty, pace—ten!"

I myself went to the breechblock and began a four-round salute in honor of our Victory after four years of war.

At these shots, everybody who was at the battery position came running, along with the battery commander, Slatvinsky. He ordered me put under arrest for the unauthorized action, but then canceled his decision. And we all went on saluting together from personal weapons, embracing and kissing each other. Drank vodka, sang songs. And then wept all night and all day . . .

Galina Yaroslavovna Dubovik

PARTISAN OF THE 12TH STALIN MOUNTED PARTISAN BRIGADE

I carry a handheld machine gun on my shoulder . . . I'll never admit it's heavy. Otherwise who would keep me as number two? Inadequate fighter, to be replaced. They'd send me to the kitchen. That's a disgrace. God forbid I should spend the whole war in the kitchen. I'd just cry . . .

Were women sent on missions equally with men?

They tried to spare us. You had to ask to be sent on a combat mission, or somehow to deserve it. To prove yourself. For that you needed boldness, desperateness of character. Not every girl was capable of it. We had a girl, Valya, working in the kitchen. She was so gentle, timid, you couldn't imagine her with a rifle. She would, of course, shoot in extremity, but she never yearned for action. Me? I yearned. I dreamed!

Yet in school I was a quiet girl . . . Inconspicuous . . .

Elena Ivanovna Variukhina
NURSE

The order: be in place within twenty-four hours . . . Assignment: to the 713th Mobile Field Hospital . . .

I remember I appeared in the hospital in a black marquisette dress and sandals, and over it I was wearing my husband's cape. They issued me a military uniform, but I refused to put it on, because everything was three or four sizes too big for me. They reported to the head of the hospital that I was insubordinate to army discipline. He didn't take any measures—let's just wait, in a few days she'll change clothes herself.

In a few days we were moving to another place, and came under heavy bombardment. We hid in a potato field, and it had rained just before. Can you imagine what became of my marquisette dress and what my sandals turned into? The next day I was dressed like a soldier. In full uniform.

Thus began my military path . . . All the way to Germany . . .

In the first days of January 1942 we entered the settlement of Afonevka, in the Kursk region. There was heavy frost. Two school buildings were chock-full of the wounded: they lay on stretchers, on the floor, on straw. There weren't enough trucks and fuel to evacuate them to the rear. The head of the hospital decided to make up a train of horse-drawn wagons from Afonevka and the neighboring settlements.

The next morning the train arrived. The horses were driven only by women. In the sledges lay hand-woven blankets, sheepskin coats, pillows. Some even brought featherbeds. To this day I can't remember without tears what happened then . . . Those scenes . . . Each woman chose a wounded man and began preparing him for the road and murmuring over him: "My dear little son!" "There, my dearest!" "There, my pretty one!" Each woman brought along a bit of home-cooked food, even warm potatoes. They wrapped the wounded in their homey things, put them carefully into the sledges. To this day it sits in my ear, this prayer, this soft women's murmuring: "There, my dearest," "There, my pretty one . . ." I'm sorry, and even feel remorse, that we didn't ask these women's last names then.

I also remember how we moved through liberated Belorussia and didn't meet any men in the villages. Only women met us. There were only women left . . .

OF THE SILENCE OF HORROR AND
THE BEAUTY OF FICTION

Anastasia Ivanovna Medvedkina
PRIVATE, MACHINE GUNNER

Can I find the right words? I can tell about how I shot. But about how I wept, I can't. That will be left untold. I know one thing: in war a human being becomes frightening and incomprehensible. How can one understand him?

You're a writer. Think up something yourself. Something beautiful. Without lice and filth, without vomit . . . Without the smell of vodka and blood . . . Not so frightening as life . . .

Anna Petrovna Kalyagina
SERGEANT, MEDICAL ASSISTANT

I don't know . . . No, I understand what you're asking about, but words fail me . . . I have no words . . . How can I describe it? I need . . . In order to . . . A spasm suffocated me, as it does now: at night I lie in the stillness and I suddenly remember. I suffocate. In shivers . . . Like this . . .

The words are somewhere . . . We need a poet . . . Like Dante . . .

Olga Nikitichna Zabelina

ARMY SURGEON

Sometimes I hear music . . . Or a song . . . a woman's voice . . . And there I find what I felt then. Something similar . . .

But I watch films about the war—not right. I read a book—not right. No, not it. It doesn't come off. I start talking, myself—that's also not it. Not as frightening and not as beautiful. Do you know how beautiful a morning at war can be? Before combat . . . You look and you know: this may be your last. The earth is so beautiful . . . And the air . . . And the dear sun . . .

Liubov Eduardovna Kresova

UNDERGROUND FIGHTER

We lived in the ghetto behind barbed wire . . . I even remember that this happened on a Tuesday. For some reason, I paid attention later that it had been Tuesday. Tuesday . . . I don't remember the date or the month. But it was Tuesday. I went up to the window by chance. Across the street from our house a boy and girl were sitting on a bench kissing. There were pogroms around, shootings. And they were kissing! I was astounded by this peaceful picture . . .

At the other end of the street, which was short, a German patrol appeared. They, too, saw it all, they had good eyesight. I had no time to think about anything. Of course I didn't . . . Shouting. Racket. Gunshots . . . I . . . No thoughts . . . The first feeling—fear. I only saw that the boy and the girl stood up—and had already fallen. They fell down together.

And then . . . A day passed, a second . . . a third . . . I was still thinking about it. You must understand: they didn't kiss at home, but outside. Why? They wanted to die like that . . . They knew they would die in the ghetto anyway, and they wanted to die differently.

Of course, this was love. What else? What else could it have been . . .
Only love.

So, I've told you . . . And, true, it came out well—beautiful. But
in reality? In reality I was horrified . . . Yes . . . What else? It just occurred to me . . . They were fighting . . . They wanted to die beautifully. That was their choice, I'm sure . . .

Irina Moiseevna Lepitskaya
PRIVATE, RIFLEMAN

Me? I don't want to talk . . . Although . . . In short . . . these things
can't be talked about . . .

Antonina Albertovna Vyzhutovich
PARTISAN NURSE

A mad woman wandered around the town . . . She never washed,
never combed her hair. Her five children had been killed. All of them.
And killed in different ways. One had been shot in the head, another
in the ear . . .

She used to come up to people in the street . . . anybody . . . And
say, "I'll tell you how my children were killed. Which one to begin
with? With Vasenka . . . They shot him in the ear! And Tolik in the
head . . . Well, which one?"

Everybody fled from her. She was crazy, that's why she could
tell . . .

Anna Mikhailovna Perepelka

SERGEANT, NURSE

I remember just one thing: the cry—victory! All day the cry rang out . . . Victory! Victory! Brothers! At first I didn't believe it, because we were already used to the war—as if that was life. Victory! We won . . . We were happy! Happy!

"YOUNG LADIES! DO YOU KNOW: THE COMMANDER OF A SAPPER PLATOON LIVES ONLY TWO MONTHS . . ."

———

I talk about the same thing all the time . . . In one way or another I keep coming back to it . . .

Most often I talk about death. About their relationships with death—it constantly circled around them. As close and as habitual as life itself. I try to understand, how was it possible to survive amid this endless experience of dying? To look at it day after day. To think. To try it on despite yourself.

Is it possible to talk about it? What lends itself to words and to our feelings? And what is ineffable? More and more questions arise for me, and fewer and fewer answers.

Sometimes I come home after these meetings with the thought that suffering is solitude. Total isolation. At other times it seems to me that suffering is a special kind of knowledge. There is something in human life that it is impossible to convey and preserve in any other way, especially among us. That is how the world is made; that is how we are made.

I met one of the heroines of this chapter in the auditorium of the Belorussian State University. The students were noisily and happily putting away their notebooks after the lecture.

"How were we then?" she replied to my first question with a question. "The same as these students of mine. Only dressed differently, and girls' jewelry was simpler. Steel rings, glass beads. Rubber sneakers. We didn't have these jeans and tape recorders."

I followed the hurrying students with my eyes, and the story was already beginning . . .

Stanislava Petrovna Volkova
SECOND LIEUTENANT, COMMANDER OF A SAPPER PLATOON

A girlfriend and I finished university before the war, and sapper's school during the war. We came to the front as officers . . . second lieutenants. They met us like this: "Good for you, girls! It's fine that you've come, girls. But we're not sending you anywhere. You'll be with us at headquarters." That was how they met us at the headquarters of the corps of engineers. We about-faced and went looking for Malinovsky, commander in chief of the front. While we went around, a rumor spread through the settlement that two girls were looking for the commander in chief.

An officer came up to us and said, "Show me your papers."

He examined them. "Why are you looking for the commander in chief? You're supposed to go to the headquarters of the corps of engineers."

"We were sent as commanders of sapper platoons, and they want to keep us at headquarters. But we insist on being only commanders of sapper platoons, and only at the front line."

Then this officer took us back to the headquarters of the engineer corps. For a long time they all talked and talked, there was a whole cottage full of people, and everybody gave advice and some laughed. But we held our ground, that we had an assignment, that we are supposed to be only commanders of sapper platoons.

Then the officer who brought us there got angry. "Young ladies! Do you know how long the commander of a sapper platoon lives? The commander of a sapper platoon lives only two months . . ."

"We know. That's why we want to go to the front line."

There was nothing to be done; they wrote out the assignment. "Well, all right, we'll send you to the 5th Shock Army. What a shock army is you probably know, the name itself tells you. Constantly on the front line . . ."

And they told us all sorts of horrors. We were glad.

"Agreed!"

We came to the headquarters of the 5th Shock Army. A cultivated captain was sitting there. He received us very nicely, but when he heard that we wanted to be commanders of sapper platoons, he clutched his head.

"No, no! What are you saying? We'll find work for you here at headquarters. Are you joking? There are only men there, and suddenly the commander's a woman—it's crazy. No, no!"

For two days they worked on us like that. I'm telling you . . . Persuading . . . We didn't budge: only commanders of sapper platoons. We didn't give an inch. That wasn't the end of it. Finally . . . Finally we got our assignments. I was brought to my platoon . . . The soldiers looked at me, one mockingly, another even angrily, yet another just shrugged his shoulders, which made everything clear at once. When the battalion commander said, "I present to you your new platoon commander," they suddenly howled: "Hoo-o-o . . ." One even spat: "Pfui!"

A year later, when I was awarded the Order of the Red Star, these same boys, those who were still alive, carried me on high to my dugout. They were proud of me.

If you ask what color war is, I'll tell you—the color of earth. For a sapper . . . The black, yellow, clayey color of earth . . .

We're on a march somewhere . . . Spend the night in the forest. We make a bonfire, and the bonfire burns, and everybody sits very quietly, some are already asleep. I'm falling asleep, looking at the fire. I sleep with my eyes open: some moths, some bugs fly into the fire, they fly all night long, without a sound, without a rustle, they silently disappear into this big fire. Others come flying after them . . . I'm telling you . . . Just like us. We marched and marched. Rolling like a stream.

Two months later I wasn't killed, I was wounded. My first wound was light. And I stopped thinking about death . . .

Appolina Nikonovna Litskevich-Bairak

SECOND LIEUTENANT, COMMANDER
OF A SAPPER-MINER PLATOON

In my childhood . . . I'll begin with my childhood . . . During the war I was afraid most of all to remember my childhood. Precisely childhood. One shouldn't recall the most tender things during a war . . . Not the most tender things . . . It's a taboo.

Well, so . . . In my childhood my father used to give me a crew cut with an electric hair clipper. I recalled it when we got our haircuts and suddenly turned into young soldiers. Some girls were frightened . . . But I easily got used to it. My element. Not for nothing did my father say, "It's a boy I've got here, not a girl." The blame for it all went to a passion of mine, for which I often got yelled at by my parents. In winter I used to jump down from a steep bank onto the snow-covered river Ob. After classes I would put on my father's old cotton-padded trousers and tie them over my felt boots. Tucked my thick jacket into the trousers and tightened the belt. On my head was a long-eared hat, tied under the chin. Bundled up like that, waddling clumsily like a bear, I went to the river. I ran as fast as I could and jumped off the cliff . . .

Ah! What a sensation, when you fell into the abyss and sank over your head in the snow! It takes your breath away! Other girls tried to do it with me, but they couldn't get it right: they'd sprain a leg, or hit their nose against the snow, or something else would happen. I was more adroit than the boys.

I mentioned childhood . . . Because I don't want to begin with blood . . . But I understand—of course it's important, of course. I like to read books. I understand . . .

We arrived in Moscow in September 1942 . . . For a whole week they drove us around the ring rail line. We stopped at the Kuntsevo, Perovo, Ochakovo stations, and everywhere some girls were taken off the train. The "buyers," that is, the commanders of various units and combat branches, came and persuaded us to become snipers, medical assistants, radio operators . . . None of it tempted me. Finally there were only thirteen girls left of the whole convoy. We were all put into one freight car. Just two cars stood on the side track: ours and the staff car. For two days no one came to us. We laughed and sang the song "Forgotten, Abandoned." At the end of the second day, toward evening, we saw three officers coming to our car together with the chief of the convoy.

The "buyers"! They were tall, trim, tightly belted. Spanking new overcoats, gleamingly polished boots with spurs. Really something! We hadn't seen their like yet. They went into the staff car, and we pressed up to the wall to hear what they were going to say. The chief showed them the list and gave a brief description of each of us: so-and-so, where from, education. In the end we heard: "They'll all do."

Then the chief came out of the car and ordered us to line up. They asked, "Do you want to study the art of war?" How could we not, of course we wanted to. Very much so! It was our dream! Not one of us even asked: study where and what? The order was: "First Lieutenant Mitropolsky, take the girls to the school." We shouldered our kit bags, formed a column of two, and the officer led us through the streets of Moscow. My beloved Moscow . . . the capital . . . Beautiful even in this difficult time. Our own . . . The officer walked quickly, with big strides, we could barely keep up with him. It was only at the thirtieth anniversary of the Victory, at the reunion in Moscow, that Sergei Fyodorovich Mitropolsky confessed to us, the former students of the Moscow Military-Engineering School, how ashamed he had been to lead us through Moscow. He tried to keep as far as possible from us, so as not to attract attention. To this herd of girls . . . We didn't know that and almost ran after him. We must have been quite a sight!

Well, so . . . In the first few days of studies I got extra duty twice: first I protested against the cold auditorium, then it was something else. Schoolgirl habits. So I got what I deserved: one extra duty, then another . . . More followed. Whenever I was posted in the street, the boys noticed me and began to laugh: our staff orderly. It was funny for them, of course, but I missed classes, didn't sleep nights. I spent the whole day standing by the door at the orderly post, and at night I polished the floors in the barrack with mastic. How did we do it then? I'll explain at once . . . In detail . . . It was not like now, when we have all sorts of brushes, floor polishers, and the like. Back then . . . After lights out you take your boots off, so you don't muck them up with mastic, wrap your feet in pieces of old overcoat, making a sort of peasant shoe tied with string. You scatter mastic over the floor and spread it with a brush, not a synthetic brush, but a natural one, so the clumps of hair stick to the floor, and only after that you start working with your feet. You have to polish it so it shines like a mirror. There's a whole night's dancing for you! Your feet are sore and numb, you can't straighten your back, sweat streams down your face and gets into your eyes. In the morning you're so tired you can't even shout "On your feet!" to your company. And during the day you can't sit down, because the orderly has to stand by the post all the time.

Once I had a mishap . . . It was funny . . . I had just finished cleaning the barrack and was standing by the orderly post. I was so sleepy, I felt I'd fall down any minute. I leaned on the post and dozed off. Suddenly I heard someone open the door to the barrack, I roused myself—the battalion duty officer was standing before me. I raised my hand in salute and reported, "Comrade First Lieutenant, the company is resting." He stared at me and I saw he could barely keep from laughing. Then I realized that, being left-handed and in a hurry, I had saluted him with my left hand. I quickly tried to switch to the right hand, but it was too late. Again I had made a slip . . .

It took me a long time to realize that this was not some sort of game and not a simple school, but a military academy. Preparation for war. A commander's order is law for a subordinate.

I remember the last question on the last exam: "How many times in his life does a sapper make a mistake?"

"A sapper makes a mistake once in his life."

"That's right, girl . . ."

And then the familiar: "Student Bairak, you may go."

And now—war. Real war . . .

I was brought to my platoon. I order, "Platoon, attention!" and the platoon doesn't even think of standing up. One man is lying down, another sits and smokes, yet another stretches himself till his bones crack: "E-eh!" They pretended not to notice me. These men were insulted that they, seasoned male scouts, had to obey a twenty-year-old girl. I realized it very well and was forced to give the command, "As you were!"

Just then shelling began . . . I jumped down into a ditch, and my overcoat was new, so I lay down not in the mud, but to the side on the unmelted snow. That's how it happens when you're young—the overcoat is dearer than life. Foolish girl! And my soldiers laughed.

Well, so . . . What was the engineer scouting that we conducted? During the night the soldiers dug a double hole in no-man's-land. Before dawn one of the unit commanders and I crawled to this little trench, and the soldiers camouflaged us. And we lay like that all day, afraid to stir. In an hour or two our hands and feet began to freeze, even if we were wearing felt boots and sheepskin jackets. Four hours—and you turn into an icicle. It snows . . . You turn into a snowman. That's in winter . . . In summer we had to lie in the heat or the rain. We'd spend the whole day watching everything attentively and drawing up a map of the observed front line and marking the places where changes in the surface of the terrain appeared. If we saw bumps on the ground or lumps of soil, dirty snow, trampled grass or dew smeared on the grass, that was what we were after . . . our goal . . . It was clear that German sappers had placed mines there. If they set up a wire fence, it was necessary to find out the length and breadth of the fence. What sort of mines they had put there: antitroop, antitank, or surprise mines. We marked the enemy's firing points . . .

Before our troops advanced, we worked during the night. We felt the ground inch by inch. Made corridors in the mine fields. All the work was done crawling . . . On your belly . . . I shuttled from one unit to another. There were always more of "my" mines.

I can tell many incidents . . . Enough for a movie . . . A serial.

Some officers invited me for breakfast. I accepted. Sappers weren't always served hot food; we mostly lived on whatever grub we could get. When everybody sat down at the kitchen table, I paid attention to the Russian stove with a closed door. I went over and began to examine the door. The officers poked fun at me: "You women imagine mines even in pots and pans." I joked back and then noticed that at the very bottom, to the left of the door, there was a small hole. I looked closer and saw a thin wire going into the stove. I quickly turned to those around the table: "The house is mined, I ask you to quit the premises." The officers fell silent and stared at me with mistrust; no one wanted to leave the table. It smelled of meat, fried potatoes. I repeated, "Clear the premises immediately." I set to work with the sappers. First we removed the door. Cut the wire with scissors. And there . . . There . . . In the stove lay several liter-sized enamel mugs tied together with string. A soldier's dream! Better than a mess tin. Then, in the depths of the stove, two big packages wrapped in black paper. About forty pounds of explosives. There's pots and pans for you . . .

We moved through Ukraine and came to the Stanislavskaya, now the Ivano-Frankovsky, region. Our platoon was given a mission: to urgently demine a sugar factory. Every minute counted: we didn't know how the factory had been mined. If there was a time bomb, we could expect an explosion at any moment. So we set out at quick march on our mission. The weather was warm, we traveled light. As we were passing a long-range artillery position, one of the soldiers suddenly ran out of the trench and shouted, "Heads up! What a chassis!" I raised my head and began to look for a "chassis" in the sky. There was no plane to be seen. Everything was quiet, not a sound. Where was the "chassis"? One of my sappers asked permission to leave the ranks. I saw him go to that artillerist and give him a good slap. Before I could figure anything out, the artillerist shouted, "Boys, they're beating us!" Other artillerists jumped out of the trench and surrounded our sapper. My platoon, without thinking for long, dropped their probes, mine detectors, kit bags, and rushed to help him. A fight began. I couldn't understand what was happening. Why did my platoon get mixed up in a fight? Every minute counted, and there they were scuffling.

I gave the order: "Platoon, fall in!" Nobody paid any attention to me. Then I drew my pistol and fired into the air. Some officers ran out of the blindage. It took quite a while to quiet everybody down. A captain came up to my platoon and asked, "Who is the senior officer here?" I saluted. He rolled his eyes; even he was at a loss. Then he asked, "What happened here?" I was unable to answer, because I really did not know the reason. Then my subcommander stepped forward and explained how it had all come about. Thus I learned that the word "chassis" was very offensive for a woman. Something like "whore." A frontline obscenity . . .

And you know . . . We're having a candid conversation . . . I tried not to think about love or about my childhood during the war. Or about death . . . Hm-m-m . . . We're having a candid conversation . . . Well, so . . . As I said: I forbade myself many things in order to survive. Especially everything gentle and tender. Even to think about it. To recall. I remember how we were given a few free evenings for the first time in liberated Lvov. For the first time during the whole war . . . The battalion watched a film in the city movie theater. In the beginning it felt somehow unusual to sit in soft chairs, to see a beautiful interior, to feel cozy and quiet. An orchestra played before the film, artistes performed. There were dances in the foyer. We danced the polka, the krakoviak, the *pas d'Espagne,* and finished with the inevitable "Russian." I was particularly affected by the music . . . It seemed unbelievable that there was shooting somewhere and that we would soon be on the front line again. That death was somewhere near.

But already a day later an order came for my platoon to comb the irregular terrain between a hamlet and a railroad. Several trucks had blown up there on mines . . . Scouts with mine detectors started moving along the highway. Cold rain sprinkled. We were all soaked to the skin. My boots swelled up and became as heavy as if they had iron soles. I tucked the skirts of my overcoat under the belt, so that they wouldn't hinder my walking. Ahead of me on a leash ran my dog Nelka. When she found a shell or a mine, she sat next to it and waited for it to be cleared. My faithful friend. So Nelka sat down . . . she waited and whined a bit . . . Suddenly I heard a command passed down the line: "Lieutenant, to the general." I looked around: a jeep was standing on the country road. I jumped over a ditch, untucked the skirts of my overcoat, straightened my belt and forage cap. Despite all that I looked shabby.

I ran up to the car, opened the door, and began to report: "Comrade General, at your orders . . ."

Before I finished, I heard, "As you were . . ."

I paused and stood at attention. The general did not even turn toward me, but was looking at the road through the windshield. He was getting nervous and looked frequently at his watch. I stood there. He turned to his orderly: "Where's that sapper commander?"

I again tried to report: "Comrade General . . ."

He finally turned to me and said vexedly, "What the devil do I need you for!"

I figured out what was the matter and almost burst out laughing. Then his orderly realized, "Comrade General, maybe she is the sapper commander?"

The general stared at me. "Who are you?"

"The commander of the sapper platoon, Comrade General."

"You—the platoon commander?" he said indignantly.

"Yes, Comrade General!"

"These are your sappers at work?"

"Yes, Comrade General."

"Quit saying 'general, general' . . . "

He got out of the car, took a few steps, then came back to me. Stood there, measuring me with his eyes. Then said to his orderly, "See that?"

Then he asked me, "How old are you, Lieutenant?"

"Twenty, Comrade General."

"Where are you from?"

"Siberia."

He kept questioning me for a long time, offered to transfer me to their tank unit. Was indignant about me looking so shabby: he wouldn't allow that. They needed sappers desperately. Then he took me aside and pointed to a little wood.

"My little crates are standing there. I want to send them along this railroad. The rails and the sleepers have been removed, but the road may be mined. Do my tankmen a favor, check the road. This is a closer and more convenient way to the front line. Do you know what a surprise attack is?"

"Yes, Comrade General."

"Well, goodbye, Lieutenant. Make sure you live till the victory, it will come soon. Understand!"

The railroad indeed turned out to be mined. We checked it.

We all wanted to live till the victory . . .

In October 1944 our battalion, being a part of the 210th demining Detachment, together with the troops of the 4th Ukrainian Front, entered the territory of Czechoslovakia. We were met joyfully everywhere. They threw us flowers, fruit, packs of cigarettes . . . Spread rugs on the pavement . . . The fact that a girl was commander of a platoon of men, and was herself a sapper-miner, became a sensation. I had a boy's haircut, wore trousers and an army jacket. I had adopted some male ways. In short, I looked like an adolescent boy. Sometimes I rode into a village on horseback, and then it was very hard to tell who I was, but women's intuition told them and they observed me attentively. Women's intuition . . . It was funny . . . Great! I'd come to the quarters where I was to be billeted, and the owners would be told that their lodger was an officer, but not a man. Many were so surprised that they just stood gaping . . . A silent movie! But I . . . Hmm-m-m . . . I even enjoyed it. I enjoyed surprising people that way. It was the same in Poland. I remember in one little village an old woman patted me on the head. I understood: "Is the *pani* trying to see if I have horns?" I asked in Polish. She became embarrassed and said she simply wanted to show pity for me, "such a young *panenka*."

And there were mines at every step. Many mines. Once we went into a house, and someone saw a pair of calfskin boots standing by a wardrobe. He was already reaching out to take them. "Don't you dare touch them!" I shouted. When I came up and began to study them, they turned out to be mined. There were mined armchairs, chests of drawers, sideboards, dolls, chandeliers . . . Peasants asked us to de-mine the rows of tomatoes, potatoes, cabbage. Once, in order to sam-ple some dumplings, our platoon went to a village to demine a field of wheat and even the flail for threshing the sheaves . . .

Well, so . . . I went through Czechoslovakia, Poland, Hungary, Romania, Germany . . . But few impressions have remained in my memory. Mostly I remember only visual images of the lay of the land. Boulders . . . Tall grass . . . Either it was really tall or it only seemed so to us because it was unbelievably difficult to go through it and work with our probes and mine detectors. Old grass . . . Burdock higher than bushes . . . I also remember many brooks and ravines. Dense forests, continuous wire fences with rotted stakes, overgrown minefields. Flowerbeds gone to seed. There were always mines hiding there; the Germans loved flowerbeds. Once there were people dig-ging potatoes in a field, and next to them we were digging mines . . .

In Romania, in the town of Dej, I stayed in the house of a young Romanian woman who spoke good Russian. It turned out her grand-mother was Russian. The woman had three children. Her husband had been killed at the front, in the Romanian volunteer division. Still, she liked to laugh and have fun. Once she invited me to go dancing with her. She offered me her outfits. The temptation was great. I put on trousers, an army shirt, calfskin boots, and on top of it all the Ro-manian national costume: a long embroidered linen blouse and a tight checkered skirt. Tied a black belt around my waist, threw a colorful shawl with long fringe over my head. To this should be added that, from crawling in the mountains all summer, I had a dark tan, only blond strands stuck out on my temples, and my nose was peeling— still it was hard to distinguish me from a real Romanian. A Romanian girl.

There was no club, the young people gathered in somebody's house. When we came, music was already playing, people were dancing. I saw almost all the officers of my battalion. At first I was afraid to be recognized and exposed, and so I sat in a far corner, without attracting attention, even covering myself with the shawl a little. At least I could see everything . . . From a distance . . . But after one of our officers invited me several times to dance without recognizing me with my lips and eyebrows painted, I began laughing and having fun. I was having a very good time . . . I liked to hear that I was beautiful. I heard compliments . . . I danced and danced . . .

The war ended, but we spent another whole year demining fields, lakes, rivers. During the war people dumped everything into the water; the main thing was to go ahead, to make it to the goal in time . . . But now we had to think about other things . . . About life . . . For the sappers the war ended several years later; they fought longer than everybody else. And what is it to wait for an explosion after the Victory? To wait for that moment . . . No, no! Death after the Victory was the most terrible. A double death.

Well, so . . . As a New Year's present in 1946 I was issued ten yards of red sateen. I laughed: "What do I need that for? Unless I make myself a red dress after demobilization. A Victory dress." As if I was reading the future . . . Soon the order came for my demobilization. As was customary, the battalion organized a festive farewell party for me. At the party the officers offered me a big, finely knitted dark blue shawl as a present. I had to redeem the shawl by singing a song about a blue shawl. I sang for them the whole evening.

On the train I developed a high fever. My face was swollen; I couldn't open my mouth. My wisdom teeth were growing . . . I was returning from the war . . .

"TO SEE HIM JUST ONCE . . ."

And now there will be a story about love . . .

Love is the only personal event in wartime. All the rest is common—even death.

What came unexpectedly for me? The fact that they spoke about love less candidly than about death. There was always this reticence, as if they were protecting themselves, stopping each time at a certain line. Guarding it vigilantly. There was an unspoken agreement among them—no further. The curtain fell. I understood what they were protecting themselves against: postwar insults and slander. And there was plenty of it! After the war they had to fight another war, no less terrible than the one they had returned from. If one of them resolved to be totally sincere, if a desperate confession escaped them, there was always a request at the end: "Change my last name," or "In our time it wasn't acceptable to talk about it aloud . . . indecent . . ." I heard more about the romantic and the tragic.

Of course, it is not the whole of life and not the whole truth. But it is their truth. As one of the writers of the war generation admitted honestly: "Cursed be the war—our stellar hour!" That is the watchword, the general epigraph to their lives.

But all the same, what was love like there? Near death . . .

OF A DAMNED WENCH AND
THE ROSES OF MAY

Efrosinya Grigoryevna Breus
CAPTAIN, DOCTOR

The war took my love from me . . . My only love . . .

The city was being bombed. My sister Nina came running to say goodbye. We thought we weren't going to see each other again. She said to me, "I'll join the medical volunteers, if only I can find them." I remember looking at her. It was summertime, she was wearing a light dress, and I saw a small birthmark on her left shoulder, here, by the neck. She was my sister, but it was the first time I noticed it. I looked and thought, "I'll recognize you anywhere."

And such a keen feeling . . . Such love . . . Heartrending . . .

Everybody was leaving Minsk. The roads were being shelled; we went through the forests . . . Somewhere a girl cried, "Mama, it's war!" Our unit was in retreat. We marched past a vast, wide field, the rye had come into ear, and there was a low peasant cottage by the road. It was already the Smolensk region . . . A woman was standing by the road, and it seemed as if this woman was taller than her house. She was wearing a linen dress embroidered with a national Russian pattern. Her arms were crossed on her chest; she kept bowing low. The soldiers marched past her, and she bowed to them and repeated, "May the Lord bring you home." She bowed to each of them and said the same thing. Everybody had tears in their eyes . . .

I remembered her all through the war . . . And another thing, this was in Germany, when we drove the Germans back. In some village . . . Two German women wearing bonnets were sitting in a courtyard having coffee . . . It looked as if there was no war . . . And

I thought, "My God, our country is in ruins, our people live in dug-outs and eat grass, and you sit here having coffee." Our trucks drive by, carrying our soldiers . . . And they drink coffee . . .

Then I rode through our land. And what did I see? All that remains of a village is a single stove. An old man sits there and three grandchildren stand behind him. He has evidently lost his son and daughter-in-law. The old woman collects dead coals to start the stove. She has hung up her coat, meaning she came from the forest. And there is nothing cooking in this stove . . .

And such a keen feeling . . . Such love . . .

. . . Our train stopped. I don't remember what it was—railroad repairs, or they changed the engine. I sit there with a nurse and next to us two soldiers are cooking kasha. From somewhere two German prisoners come to us and ask for food. We had some bread. We took a loaf, divided it and gave them some. I hear the soldiers who are cooking say, "Look how much bread our doctors gave to the enemy!" And then something like, "Ah, as if they know what real war is, they sit in their hospitals, how would they know . . ."

Some time later other prisoners came to those same soldiers who were cooking kasha. And the same soldier who disapproved of us just before says to a German, "What—want some grub?"

The man stands there . . . Waits. Our other soldier gives a loaf to his friend and says, "All right, cut him some."

The other cut them a slice each. The Germans take the bread and stand there—they see that there's kasha cooking.

"Well, all right," the one soldier says, "give him some kasha."

"It's not ready yet."

"You hear?"

And the Germans stand there as if they understand the language. Waiting. The soldiers added some lard to the kasha and gave it to them in empty tin cans.

There's the soul of a Russian soldier for you. First they denounced us, then they themselves gave the Germans bread and kasha as well, and only after adding some lard. I remember that . . .

And such a keen feeling . . . So strong . . .

The war was long over . . . I was going to a resort . . . Just then came the Caribbean crisis.* Again the world was uneasy. Everything became unstable. I packed my suitcase, put in dresses, blouses. So, did I forget anything? I fetched a folder with my papers in it and took out my army card. I thought, "If anything happens, I'll go straight to the recruiting office."

I was already on the seashore, resting, and I happened to tell someone at the table in the dining room that, in preparing to come here, I took along my army card. I said it without any ulterior motive or wish to show off. But a man at our table got all excited: "No, only a Russian woman can take her army card with her as she leaves for a resort, and think that if anything happens she'll go straight to the recruiting office."

I remember the man's ecstasy. His admiration. He looked at me the way my husband used to. With the same eyes . . .

Forgive me the long introduction . . . I don't know how to tell it in good order. My thoughts always jump, my feelings burst out . . .

My husband and I went to the front. The two of us together.

There's a lot I've forgotten. Though I think about it every day . . .

The end of a battle . . . It was so quiet, we could hardly believe it. He caressed the grass with his hands, it was so soft . . . and he looked at me. Looked . . . With those eyes . . .

He left with a reconnaissance team. We waited two days for them . . . I didn't sleep for two days . . . I dozed off. I woke up because he was sitting next to me and looking at me. "Go to sleep."

"It's a pity to sleep."

And such a keen feeling . . . Such love . . . Heartrending . . .

I've forgotten a lot, almost everything. I thought I wouldn't forget. Not for anything.

We were already passing through East Prussia, everybody was al-

---

* Known in the West as the Cuban Missile Crisis, a two-week standoff between the United States and the Soviet Union over the stationing of Soviet ballistic missiles in Cuba.

ready talking about Victory. He was killed . . . killed instantly . . . by shrapnel . . . An instant death. In a second. I was told they had all been brought, I came running . . . I put my arms around him, I wouldn't let them take him away. To be buried. They buried quickly during the war: the battle is over, they gather all those who were killed and dig a big hole. They cover them with earth. Another time it was just dry sand. And if you look at this sand for a long time, you think it's moving. Quivering. The sand heaves. Because there . . . For me they're alive, these people had just been alive . . . I see them, I talk with them . . . I don't believe . . . We go on walking, and don't believe yet that they're there . . . Where?

So I didn't allow them to bury him at once. I wanted us to have one more night. To sit next to him. To look . . . To caress . . .

Morning . . . I decided I would take him home. To Belarus. Several thousand miles away. War roads . . . Confusion . . . Everybody thought I'd lost my mind from grief. "You must calm down. Get some sleep." No! No! I went from one general to another and got as far as Rokossovsky, the commander in chief of the front.* At first he refused . . . Some sort of abnormal creature! So many men had been buried in common graves, in foreign lands . . .

I managed to obtain another meeting with him.

"Do you want me to kneel before you?"

"I understand you . . . But he's already dead . . ."

"We had no children. Our house burned down. No photographs are left. There's nothing. If I bring him home, there will at least be a grave. And I'll have somewhere to go back to after the war."

He said nothing. Paced the office. Paced.

"Have you ever loved, Comrade Marshal? I'm not burying my husband, I'm burying my love."

---

* Konstantin Rokossovsky (1896–1968) was a Polish-born Soviet officer. After serving with great distinction, he was arrested during the Great Purge and accused of treason. After being tortured and sent to the Gulag, he was rehabilitated, and during World War II became a key strategist in the major battles against the Germans. He was promoted to Marshal of the Soviet Union, and led the victory parade in Moscow in 1945.

He said nothing.

"Then I, too, want to die here. Why should I live without him?"

He said nothing for a long time. Then came up to me and kissed my hand.

I was given a special plane for one night. I boarded the plane . . . Put my arms around the coffin . . . And fainted . . .

Liubov Fominichna Fedosenko
PRIVATE, NURSE-AIDE

We were separated by the war . . . My husband was at the front. I was evacuated first to Kharkov, then to Tataria. Found a job there. Once I discovered they were looking for me. My maiden name was Lisovskaya. Everybody was shouting, "Sovskaya! Sovskaya!" I shouted, "It's me!" They told me, "Go to the NKVD, take a pass and go to Moscow." Why? Nobody told me anything, and I knew nothing. It was wartime . . . I thought maybe my husband had been wounded and they were summoning me to see him. I hadn't had any letters from him for four months. I was determined that if I found him crippled, without arms, without legs, I'd take him and go back home. We'd live somehow.

I arrived in Moscow and went to the appointed address. It says: CCCPB (Central Committee of the Communist Party of Belorussia) . . . That is, it was our Belorussian government, and there were many women there like myself. We asked, "What? Why? What had they summoned us for?" They said, "You'll find everything out." We were gathered in a big auditorium. Ponomarenko, the secretary of our Central Committee, is there, and other leaders. They ask me, "Do you want to go back where you come from?" Well, where I come from is Belorussia. Of course I want to. And they send me to a special school. To prepare me for going to the enemy's rear.

Today we finish training, tomorrow they put us in trucks and drive us to the front line. Then we walk. I didn't know what the front was and what "no-man's-land" meant. The order: "Ready! Fire number one." Bang! Flares were fired off. I saw the snow, very, very white, and then a row of people—it was us all suddenly lying down. There were lots of us. The flares died out, there was no shooting. A new command: "Run!" and we ran . . . And so we went through . . .

While I was in the partisan unit, I received a letter from my husband by some miracle. This was such a joy, so unexpected, because for two years I had heard nothing from him. And then a plane dropped some food, ammunition . . . And the mail . . . And in the mail, in this canvas bag, there was a letter—for me. Then I wrote a letter to the Central Committee. I wrote that I would do anything so long as my husband and I were together. I gave this letter to a pilot in secret from the commander of our unit. Soon there was news, sent by radio— once our mission was accomplished, our group was expected in Moscow. Our entire special group. We'd be sent to another place . . . Everybody must be on the flight, and especially Fedosenko.

We waited for the plane, it was nighttime and pitch-dark. And some sort of plane was circling over us, and then it dumped bombs on us. It was a Messerschmitt. The German had spotted our camp and circled back again. And at the same time our plane, a U-2, arrived and landed just by the fir tree where I was standing. The pilot barely landed and immediately began to take off again, because he saw that the German was circling back and would start shooting again. I took hold of the wing and shouted, "I must go to Moscow, I have permission." He even swore: "Get in!" And we flew together, just the two of us. There were no wounded . . . Nobody.

I was in Moscow in May and I went around in felt boots. I came to a theater in felt boots. It was wonderful anyway. I wrote to my husband: How are we going to meet? I'm in the reserves for now . . . But they promise . . . I ask everywhere: send me where my husband is, give me at least two days, just to look at him once, and then I'll come back, and you can send me wherever you like. Everybody shrugs. Still, I figured out from the postal code where my husband was fighting, and I went to him. First I go to the regional party committee, show my husband's address, the papers showing I'm his wife, and say that I want to see him. They tell me it's impossible, he's on the front line, go back, but I was so beaten down, so hungry, what was this—go back? I went to the military commandant. He looked at me and gave an order to issue me some sort of clothes. They gave me an army shirt, put a belt on me. And he began to talk me out of it.

"You know, it's very dangerous where your husband is . . ."

I sat there and wept, so he took pity on me and gave me the pass.

"Go out to the highway," he said. "There'll be a traffic controller, he'll tell you how to go."

I found the highway, found the traffic controller. He put me on a truck, and I went. I arrive at the unit, everybody's surprised, they're all military. "Who are you?" they ask. I couldn't say I was a wife. How could I say it? There were bombs exploding . . . I tell them—his sister. I don't even know why I said it. "Wait," they tell me, "it's a four-mile walk there." How could I wait, since I'd already traveled so far. Just then a car came from there to pick up food. There was a sergeant major with them, red-haired, freckled. He says, "Oh, I know Fedosenko. But he's in the trenches."

Well, I insisted and he took me. We drive, I can't see anything anywhere . . . There's a forest . . . A forest road . . . A new thing for me: the front line. But nobody anywhere. Only some shooting somewhere from time to time. We arrive. The sergeant asks, "Where's Fedosenko?"

They reply, "They went on a scouting mission yesterday. They stayed till daylight, and now they're waiting it out."

But they had communications. They told him that his sister had arrived. What sister? They say, "The redhead." His sister had black hair. So he figured out at once what sister. I don't know how he managed to crawl out of there, but he came soon, and he and I met. What joy . . .

I stayed one day, then two, and then decided: "Go to headquarters and report. I'm staying here with you."

He went to the superiors, and I held my breath: what if they tell

me to clear out within twenty-four hours? It's the front, I know that.
Suddenly I see the superiors coming to the dugout: the major, the
colonel. Everybody shakes my hand. Then, of course, we sat down in
the dugout, drank, and each of them said something about a wife
finding her husband in the trenches. That's a real wife, she has papers.
What a woman! Let me set eyes on such a woman! They said things
like that, and they all wept. I'll remember that evening all my life . . .
What else have I got left?

They enlisted me as a nurse-aide. I went on scouting missions with
him. A mortar fires, I see him fall down. "Killed or wounded?" I
think. I run there, the mortar goes on firing, and the commander
shouts, "Where do you think you're going, you damned wench!" I
crawled to him—he was alive . . . Alive!

By the Dnieper, on a moonlit night, they gave me the Order of the
Red Banner. The next day my husband was wounded, badly wounded.
We ran together, we waded together through some swamp, we
crawled together. The machine guns kept rattling, and we kept crawling, and he got wounded in the hip. With an exploding bullet, and try
bandaging that—it was in the buttock. It was all torn open, and mud
and dirt all over. We were encircled and tried to break out. There was
nowhere to take the wounded, and there were no medications. When
we did break through, I took my husband to the hospital. By the time
we got there, he had a general blood infection. It was the New Year . . .
1944 was beginning. He was dying . . . I knew he was dying . . . He
had many decorations; I took all his medals and put them next to him.
The doctor was making his rounds, and he was asleep.

The doctor came up. "You should leave here. He's already dead."

I reply, "Quiet, he's still alive."

My husband opened his eyes just then and said, "The ceiling has
turned blue."

I looked: "No, it's not blue, Vasya. The ceiling's white." But he
thought it was blue.

His neighbor says to him, "Well, Fedosenko, if you survive, you'll
have to carry your wife in your arms."

"And so I will," he agrees.

I don't know, he probably felt he was dying, because he took me by the hands, pulled me to him and kissed me. The way one kisses for the last time.

"Liubochka, what a pity, everybody's celebrating the New Year, and you and I are here . . . But don't be sorry, we'll still have everything . . ."

And when he had only a few hours left to live . . . He had an accident, and I had to change his bed . . . I gave him a clean sheet, bandaged his leg, but I had to pull him up to lay him on the pillow, and he was a man, he was heavy. I was pulling him up, I bent very low, and I felt that that was it, another minute or two and he'd be no more . . . It was in the evening. A quarter past ten . . . I remember it to the minute. I wanted to die myself . . . But I was carrying our child under my heart, and only that held me back. I survived those days. I buried him on January 1, and thirty-eight days later I gave birth to a son. He was born in 1944; he has children himself now. My husband's name was Vassily, my son is Vassily Vassilyevich, and I have a grandson, Vasya . . . Vassilek . . .

Vera Vladimirovna Shevaldysheva
FIRST LIEUTENANT, SURGEON

I saw . . . Every day . . . But I couldn't be reconciled to that. A young, handsome man dies . . . I wanted to hurry up and, well . . . and kiss him. To do something feminine, since I couldn't do anything as a doctor. At least to smile. To caress him. To take his hand . . .

Many years after the war a man confessed to me that he remembered my young smile. For me he was an ordinary wounded man, I didn't even remember him. He told me that my smile brought him back to life, from the other world, as they say . . . A woman's smile . . .

Sofya Krigel
SERGEANT MAJOR, SNIPER

We arrived at the 1st Belorussian Front . . . Twenty-seven girls. Men looked at us with admiration: "Not laundresses, not telephone operators, but sniper girls. It's the first time we've seen such girls. What girls!" The sergeant major composed a poem in our honor. The sense of it was that girls should be delicate, like roses in May, and the war shouldn't cripple their souls.

As we were leaving for the front, each of us gave an oath: there will be no romances there. It would all happen, if we survived, after the war. Before the war we didn't have time even to kiss. We looked at these things more strictly than young people nowadays. For us to kiss meant love for the rest of your life. At the front, love was forbidden. If the superiors found out about it, one of the couple as a rule was transferred to another unit. They were simply separated.

We cherished our love and kept it secret. We didn't keep our childish oaths . . . We loved . . .

I think that if I hadn't fallen in love at the war, I wouldn't have survived. Love saved us. It saved me . . .

Sofya K—vich
MEDICAL ASSISTANT

You ask about love? I'm not afraid of telling the truth . . . I was what's called a field campaign wife. A war wife . . . A second one. An unlawful one.

The first commander of the battalion . . .

I didn't love him. He was a good man, but I didn't love him. But I went to his dugout after several months. What else could I do? There were only men around, so it's better to live with one than to be afraid of them all. It was less frightening in battle than after battle, especially if we pulled back for a rest or re-formation. When there's shooting, gunfire, they call out, "Nurse! Dear nurse!" But after the battle each of them lies in wait for you . . . You can't get out of the dugout at night . . . Did other girls talk to you about that or did they not confess? They were ashamed, I think . . . Kept quiet. Proud! All sorts of things happened, because we didn't want to die. It's too bad to die when you're young . . . And for men it was hard to live for four years without women . . . There were no bordellos in our army, and there weren't any pills. Maybe somewhere they took care of those things. Not here. Four years . . . Commanders could allow themselves something, but not simple soldiers. Discipline. But no one talks about it . . . It's not done . . . I, for instance, was the only woman in the battalion. I lived in a common dugout with the men. They gave me a separate space, but what kind of space was it, if the whole dugout was twenty square feet. I used to wake up at night because I waved my arms—I'd slap one on the cheek, or the hands, then another. I was wounded and got into a hospital. I waved my arms there, too. A floor attendant woke me up in the night: "What's the matter?" How could I tell her?

The first commander was killed by a mine fragment.

The second commander of the battalion . . .

I loved him. I went into combat with him, I wanted to be near him. I loved him, and he had a beloved wife, two children. He showed me their photographs. And I knew that after the war, if he stayed alive, he would go back to them. To Kaluga. So what? We had such happy moments! We lived such happiness! Once we came back . . . A terrible battle . . . And we were alive. He wouldn't have had the same thing with anyone else! It wouldn't have worked! I knew it . . . I knew that without me he wouldn't be happy. He wouldn't be happy with anyone as we were happy together in the war. He wouldn't . . . Never!

At the end of the war I got pregnant. I wanted it . . . But I raised our daughter by myself, he didn't help me. Didn't lift a finger. Not a single present or letter . . . or postcard. The war ended, and love ended. Like a song . . . He went to his lawful wife and the children.

He left me his photo as a memento. I didn't want the war to end . . .
It's a terrible thing to say . . . to open my heart . . . I'm crazy. I was in
love! I knew that love would end together with the war. His love . . .
But even so I'm grateful to him for the feeling he gave me, and that I
had known with him. I've loved him all my life, I've kept my feeling
through the years. I have no need to lie. I'm an old woman. Yes,
through my whole life! And I don't regret it.

My daughter reproached me: "Mama, why do you love him?" Yet
I love him . . . I recently found out that he died. I wept a lot. Because
of it I even quarreled with my daughter: "Why do you weep? He's
been long dead for you." But I love him even now. I remember the
war as the best time of my life, I was happy then . . .

Only, please, don't give my last name. For my daughter's sake . . .

Ekaterina Nikitichna Sannikova
SERGEANT, RIFLEMAN

During the war . . .

I was brought to the unit . . . To the front line. The commander
met me with the words, "Take your hat off, please." I was surprised . . .
I took it off . . . In the recruiting office we were given crew cuts, but
while we were in the army camps, while we were going to the front,
my hair grew back a bit. It began to curl, I had curly hair. Tight
curls . . . You can't tell now, I'm already old . . . And so he looks and
looks at me: "I haven't seen a woman for two years. I just want to
look."

After the war . . .

I lived in a communal apartment. My neighbors were all married,
and they insulted me. They taunted me: "Ha-ha-ha . . . Tell us how
you whored around there with the men . . ." They used to put vinegar into my pot of boiled potatoes. Or add a tablespoon of salt . . .
Ha-ha-ha . . .

My commander was demobilized. He came to me and we got married. We went and got registered, that's all. Without a wedding. And a year later he left me for another woman, the director of our factory canteen: "She wears perfume, and you smell of army boots and foot-wraps."

So I live alone. I don't have anybody in the whole wide world. Thank you for coming . . .

Anastasia Leonidovna Zhardetskaya
CORPORAL, MEDICAL ASSISTANT

And my husband . . . It's good he isn't here, he's at work. He told me strictly . . . He knows I like to talk about our love . . . How I made my wedding dress out of bandages overnight. By myself. My friends and I spent a month collecting bandages. Trophy bandages . . . I had a real wedding dress! I still have a picture: I'm in this dress and boots, only you can't see the boots. But I remember I wore boots. I concocted a belt out of an old forage cap . . . An excellent little belt. But what am I . . . going on about my own things . . . My husband told me not to say a word about love—no, no, but to talk about the war. He's strict. He taught me with a map . . . For two days he taught me where each front was . . . Where our unit was . . . I'll tell you, I wrote it down. I'll read it . . .

Why are you laughing? What a nice laugh you have. I also laughed . . . What kind of historian am I! I'd better show you that photo, where I'm in that dress made of bandages.

I like myself so much in it . . . In a white dress . . .

OF A STRANGE SILENCE FACING
THE SKY AND A LOST RING

Maria Selivestrovna Bozhok
NURSE

I left Kazan for the front as a nineteen-year-old girl . . .

Six months later I wrote my mother that people thought I was twenty-five or twenty-seven. Every day is spent in fear, in terror. Shrapnel flies, you think your skin is torn off. And people die. They die every day, every hour, it feels like every minute. We didn't have enough sheets to cover them. We laid them out in their underwear. There was a strange silence in the wards. I don't remember such silence anywhere. When a man dies he always looks up, never to the side or at you, if you're next to him. Only up . . . At the ceiling . . . But as if he's looking into the sky . . .

And I kept telling myself that I wouldn't hear a single word of love in that hell. I wouldn't believe it. The war went on for so many years, and I don't even remember a single song. Not even the famous "Dugout." Not a single one . . . I only remember: when I was leaving home for the front, there were cherry trees blossoming in the garden. I walked and kept looking back . . . Later I probably came across gardens along the way, they must have blossomed during the war. But I don't remember . . . In school I was such a laugher, but here I never smiled. If I saw a girl pluck her eyebrows or use lipstick, I was indignant. I was categorically against it: how was it possible, how could she want to be attractive at such a time?

There were wounded around, there was moaning . . . Dead people have such yellow-green faces. How could I think of joy? Of my happiness? I didn't want to combine love with that. With those things . . .

It seemed to me that there, in those surroundings, love would perish instantly. What love can there be without festivity, without beauty? Once the war ends, there'll be a beautiful life. And love. But here . . . Here, no. What if I suddenly die, and the man who loves me suffers? Such a pity. That's how I felt . . .

My present husband courted me there; we met at the front. I didn't want to hear him: "No, no, when the war's over, only then will we be able to talk about it." I'll never forget how once, on returning from a battle, he asked me, "Do you have some nice little blouse? Please put it on. Let me see you in a blouse." But all I had was an army shirt.

I used to tell my girlfriend who got married at the front, "He didn't bring you flowers. Didn't court you. And suddenly—marriage. What kind of love is that?" I didn't approve of her feelings.

The war ended . . . We looked at each other and didn't believe that the war had ended and we were still alive. Now we were going to live . . . We were going to love . . . But we had forgotten all that, we didn't know how to do it. I came home, I went with mama to have a dress made. My first postwar dress.

My turn came and they asked me, "What kind of dress do you want?"

"I don't know."

"You come to a dressmaker, and you don't know what kind of a dress you want?"

"No, I don't . . ."

I hadn't seen a single dress in five years. I'd even forgotten how a dress is made. That there are all sorts of tucks, slits . . . Low waist, high waist . . . Incomprehensible to me. I bought a pair of high-heeled shoes, walked up and down the room, and took them off. I put them in the corner, thinking, "I'll never learn to walk in them . . ."

Elena Viktorovna Klenovskaya
PARTISAN

I want to remember . . . I want to tell what an extraordinarily beautiful feeling I brought away from the war. Almost no words can convey
with what rapture and admiration men regarded us. I lived in the same
dugouts with them, slept on the same bunks, went on the same missions, and when I froze so that I felt my spleen freeze in me, my tongue
freeze in my mouth, a little longer and I'd faint, I begged, "Misha,
undo your coat, warm me up." He'd do it: "Well, is that better?" "It
is."

I've never met with anything like it in my life. But it was impossible to think of anything personal when the Motherland was in danger.

But there was love?

Yes, there was. I encountered it . . . But you must forgive me,
maybe I'm not right, and this isn't quite natural, but in my heart I
disapproved of those people. I thought that it wasn't the time to be
concerned with love. Around us was evil. Hatred. It seems many
thought the same way . . .

And how were you before the war?

I liked to sing. To laugh. I wanted to be a pilot. I didn't even think
about love! It wasn't the main thing in my life. The main thing was—
the Motherland. Now I think we were naïve . . .

Svetlana Nikolaevna Liubich
MEDICAL VOLUNTEER

In the hospital . . . They were all happy. They were happy because
they were still alive. There was a twenty-year-old lieutenant who was
upset that he had lost a leg. But then, in the midst of universal grief, it
seemed like happiness: he was alive, and, just think, he was only
missing one leg. The main thing was—he was alive. He'd have love,

and he'd have a wife, and everything. Nowadays it's an awful thing to find yourself without a leg, but then they all hopped around, and smoked, and laughed. They were heroes and all that! Just think!

Did you fall in love there?

Of course, we were so young. As soon as the new wounded arrived, we always fell in love with somebody. My girlfriend fell in love with a first lieutenant, he was wounded all over. She pointed him out—there he is. So I, too, decided to fall in love with him. When he was taken away, he asked me for a photo. I had one photo taken somewhere at a train station. I took this photo to give to him, but then I thought: what if this isn't love, and I've given him the photo? They were already taking him away. I gave him my hand in which I clutched the photo, but I couldn't bring myself to open my fist. That's the whole of my love . . .

Then there was Pavlik, also a lieutenant. He was in great pain, so I put a chocolate under his pillow. And when we met, this was after the war, already twenty years after, he began to thank my friend, Lilya Drozdova, for this chocolate. Lilya said, "What chocolate?" Then I confessed that it was me . . . And he kissed me . . . After twenty years he kissed me . . .

Lilya Alexandrovskaya
ART SINGER

Once after a concert . . . In a big evacuation hospital . . . The head doctor came up to me and asked, "We have a badly wounded tankman here in a separate room. He reacts to almost nothing, maybe your singing will help him." I went to the ward. As long as I live, I'll never forget this man, who by some miracle got out of a burning tank, burned from head to foot. He lay motionless, stretched out on the bed, his face black, eyeless. My throat was seized with a spasm, and for a few moments I couldn't get hold of myself. Then I began to sing quietly . . . I saw the man's face stir slightly. He whispered something. I bent over and heard, "Sing more." I sang for him more and more, all my repertoire, till the doctor said, "It seems he's fallen asleep . . ."

Nina Leonidovna Mikhai
SERGEANT MAJOR, NURSE

Our battalion commander and the nurse Liuba Silina . . . They loved each other! Everybody could see that. He went to battle and she . . . She said she wouldn't forgive herself if he didn't die before her eyes, and she didn't see him in his last moment. "Let them kill us together. With the same shell." They wanted to die together or to live together. Our love was not divided into today and tomorrow, there was only today. Each of us knew that you love now, and the next moment either you or this man would be no more. In war everything happens more quickly: both life and death. In those few years we lived a whole life. I've never been able to explain it to anybody. Time is different there . . .

In one battle the commander was badly wounded, and Liuba lightly, just a scratch on a shoulder. He was sent to the rear, and she stayed on. She was pregnant, and he gave her a letter, "Go to my parents. Whatever happens to me, you're my wife. And we'll have our son or our daughter."

Later Liuba wrote to me that his parents didn't accept her and didn't recognize the child. And the commander died.

For many years I've been meaning . . . I wanted to go and visit her, but it didn't work out. We had been bosom friends. But to go so far—to the Altai. Recently a letter came telling me she had died. Now her son invites me to come and visit her grave . . .

I'd like to go . . .

Lilya Mikhailovna Butko

SURGICAL NURSE

Victory Day . . .

We gathered for our traditional reunion. I came out of the hotel, and the girls said to me, "Where have you been, Lilya? We cried our eyes out."

It turned out that a man had approached them, a Kazakh, and asked, "Where are you from, girls? What hospital?"

"Who are you looking for?"

"I come here every year looking for a nurse. She saved my life. I fell in love with her. I want to find her."

My girls laughed.

"You're looking for a nurse, but she's a granny by now."

"No . . ."

"You must have a wife? Children?"

"I have grandchildren, and I have children, and I have a wife. I've lost my soul . . . I have no soul . . ."

The girls told me that, and together we recalled: might he be that Kazakh of mine?

. . . They brought a young Kazakh boy. Really very young. We operated on him. He had seven or eight intestinal ruptures and was considered hopeless. He lay there so indifferently that I noticed him at once. Each time I had a spare moment I'd run to see him: "How are you doing?" I gave him intravenous injections, took his temperature, and he made it. He began to recover. Our hospital was on the front line, we didn't keep the wounded for long. We rendered first aid, tore them from the clutches of death, and sent them on. He was supposed to be taken away with the next party.

He lay on a stretcher, and they told me he had asked for me.

"Nurse, come closer to me."

"What is it? What do you want? You're fine. They're sending you to the rear. Everything will be all right. Count yourself among the living."

He says, "I beg you. I'm an only son. You've saved me." And he gave me a present—a ring, a small ring.

I didn't wear rings, for some reason I didn't like them. So I refused.

"I can't. I really can't."

He insisted. The wounded men supported him.

"Take it, it's from a pure heart."

"It's just my duty, don't you see?"

They persuaded me. To tell the truth, I lost that ring later on. It was too big for me, and once I fell asleep in a car, there was a jolt, and it fell off somewhere. I was very sorry.

Did you find that man?

No, we didn't meet. I don't know whether it was the same one. But the girls and I spent the whole day looking for him.

. . . In 1946 I returned home. They asked me, "Will you wear army clothes or civilian?" Army clothes, of course. It never even occurred to me to take them off. One evening I went to the Officers' House to a dance. Now you're going to hear what the attitude toward army girls was.

I put on shoes and a dress, and left the overcoat and boots at the cloakroom.

An officer comes up to me and invites me to dance.

"You must be from other parts," he says. "You're a very cultivated girl."

He spent the whole evening with me. Didn't let me get away. The dances were over, he says to me, "Give me your token."

He goes on ahead. They give him the boots and the overcoat from the cloakroom.

"These aren't mine . . ."

I come up: "No, they're mine."

"You didn't tell me you were at the front."

"Did you ask me?"

He was at a loss. Couldn't raise his eyes to me. He himself had just come back from the war . . .

"Why are you so surprised?"

"I couldn't imagine you had been in the army. You see, a girl at the front . . ."

"You're surprised that I was alone? Without a husband and not pregnant? Not wearing a padded jacket, not blowing strong cigarette smoke, and not using foul language?"

I didn't allow him to take me home.

I was always proud that I had been at the front. Defending the Motherland . . .

Liubov Mikhailovna Grozd
MEDICAL ASSISTANT

My first kiss . . .

Second Lieutenant Nikolai Belokhvostik . . . Ah, see, I'm blushing all over, and I'm already a grandmother. We were young then. Very young. I thought . . . I was sure . . . That . . . I didn't confess even to my girlfriend that I was in love with him. Head over heels. My first love . . . Maybe my only love? Who knows . . . I thought no one in our company had guessed. I had never liked anyone like that before! If I liked someone, it was not so much. But he . . . I walked around and thought about him all the time, every minute. That . . . It was real love. I felt it. By all the signs . . . Ah, see, I'm blushing . . .

We were burying him . . . He was lying on a tarpaulin; he had just been killed. The Germans were shelling us. We had to bury him quickly . . . Right away . . . We found some old birches; we chose one that stood a short way from an old oak. The biggest one. Next to it . . . I tried to remember, so I could come back and find this place afterward. The village ended there, there was a fork in the road . . . How to remember? How to remember if one of those birches was already burning right in front of our eyes . . . How? We began to take leave of him . . . They told me, "You go first." My heart leaped, I realized . . . That . . . It turned out everybody knew about my love. Everybody . . . The thought struck me: maybe he knew, too? See . . .

He's lying here . . . They'll put him into the ground now . . . a hole. They'll cover him with sand . . . But I was terribly glad at the thought that maybe he knew, too. And what if he liked me? As if he were alive and would now answer me . . . I remembered how he gave me a German chocolate bar for the New Year. I didn't eat it, I spent a month carrying it around in my pocket.

I've remembered it all my life . . . That moment . . . There were bombs falling around . . . He lay on a tarpaulin . . . That moment . . . I was happy . . . I stood smiling to myself. Crazy. I was happy that maybe he knew about my love . . .

I went up and kissed him. I'd never kissed a man before . . . That was the first time . . .

OF THE LONELINESS OF A BULLET AND A HUMAN BEING

Klavdia S—va

SNIPER

My story is a particular one . . . Prayers console me. I pray for my daughter . . .

I remember a saying of mama's. Mama liked to say, "A bullet's a fool; fate is a villain." She had this saying for all sorts of troubles. A bullet is alone, and man is alone; a bullet flies wherever it likes, and fate twists a man however it likes. This way and that, this way and that. A man is a feather, a sparrow's feather. You can never know your future. It's not given to us . . . We can't penetrate this mystery. When we were returning from the war, a Gypsy told me my future. She came up to me at the train station, called me aside . . . She predicted I would have a great love . . . I had a German watch; I took it off and gave it to her for this great love. I believed her.

And now I can't weep enough over that love . . .

I was going to the war happily. As a Komsomol girl. Along with everybody else. We traveled in freight cars. There were inscriptions on them in black mazut: "Forty persons/eight horses." There were a hundred of us stuffed in each car.

I became a sniper. I could have been a radio operator. It's a useful profession—both in the army and in peacetime. A woman's profession. But they told me they needed people to shoot, so I shot. I did it well. I have two Orders of Glory and four medals. For three years of war.

They shouted to us—Victory! They announced—Victory! I remember my first feeling—joy. And at once, that same moment—fear! Panic! Panic! How to live from here on? Papa had been killed at Stalingrad. My two older brothers had been missing in action since the beginning of the war. Mama and I were left. Two women. How were we to live? All our girls fell to thinking . . . We'd get together in the evening in a dugout . . . We discussed how our lives were only beginning. There was joy and fear. Before we had been afraid of death, and now—of life . . . It was equally frightening. It's true! We talked and talked, then sat and said nothing.

Will we get married or won't we? For love or without love? We told fortunes with daisies . . . We threw flower wreaths into the river, we melted wax . . . I remember in one village they showed us where a sorceress lived. We all rushed to her, even several officers. And all the girls. She told fortunes in water. By palm reading. Another time an organ-grinder had us draw paper lots. Tickets. I used to have lucky tickets . . . Where is that luck of mine?

How did the Motherland meet us? I can't speak without sobbing . . . It was forty years ago, but my cheeks still burn. The men said nothing, but the women . . . They shouted to us, "We know what you did there! You lured our men with your young c——! Army whores . . . Military bitches . . ." They insulted us in all possible ways . . . The Russian vocabulary is rich . . .

A fellow took me home from a dance; I suddenly felt really bad, my heart started fluttering. I walked and walked and then sat down in a snowdrift. "What's the matter?" "Never mind. Too much dancing." It was because of my two wounds. Because of the war . . . I had to learn to be tender. To be weak and fragile. But my feet were used to size ten boots. I wasn't used to being embraced. I was used to being responsible for myself. I waited for tender words, but I didn't understand them. To me they seemed childish. Among men at the front there were foul Russian curses. I was used to that. My girlfriend who worked in the library kept telling me, "Read poetry. Read Esenin."*

I quickly got married. A year later. To our factory engineer. I dreamed of love. I wanted to have a home and a family. I wanted my home to smell of small children. I smelled my first baby's diapers and was happy. The smell of happiness . . . A woman's happiness . . . In war there are no women's smells, they're all men's. War smells of men.

I have two children . . . A boy and a girl. First I had a boy. A good, intelligent boy. He finished university. An architect. But the girl . . . My girl . . . She began to walk when she was five, said her first word, "mama," at seven. Even now it comes out not "mama" but "moomo," not "papa" but "poopo." She . . . To this day I think it can't be true. It's some kind of a mistake. She's been in an insane asylum . . . For forty years. Since I retired, I go there every day. It's my sin . . .

For many years now, at the beginning of the school year I buy her a new primer. We spend a whole day reading the primer. Sometimes I come home from her, and it feels as if I've lost the ability to read and write. To talk. I don't need any of that. What for?

I've been punished . . . For what? Maybe for having killed people? I sometimes think so . . . You have a lot of time when you're old . . . I

---

* Sergei Esenin (1895–1925) was one of the major Russian lyric poets of the twentieth century.

think and think. In the morning I go on my knees, I look out the window. And I pray to God . . . I pray for everybody . . . I don't have a grudge against my husband, I forgave him long ago. The girl was born . . . He looked at us . . . He stayed for a while and left. Left with a reproach: "Would a normal woman have gone to the war? Learned to shoot? That's why you're unable to give birth to a normal child." I pray for him . . .

Maybe he's right? I sometimes think so . . . It's my sin . . .

I loved the Motherland more than anything in the world. I loved . . . Who can I tell it to now? To my girl . . . To her alone . . . I recall the war, and she thinks I'm telling her fairy tales. Children's fairy tales. Scary children's fairy tales . . .

Don't write my last name. No need to . . .

"ABOUT TINY POTATOES . . ."

There was yet another war . . .

In this war no one marked on the map where no-man's-land was, where the front line began. No one could count up all the soldiers. The numbers of weapons. People shot from antiaircraft batteries, machine guns, hunting rifles. From old Berdan rifles. There were no pauses, no general advances. Many fought single-handed. Died single-handed. It was not an army fighting—divisions, battalions, companies—but people, partisans and underground fighters: men young and old, women, children. Tolstoy called this many-faced surge "the cudgel of the people's war" and "the hidden warmth of patriotism," and Hitler (like Napoleon before him) complained to his generals that "Russians don't fight according to the rules."

To die in this war was not the most frightening thing. There was something else . . . Picture to yourself a soldier at the front, surrounded by his family— children, wife, old parents. He must be ready at every moment to sacrifice them, too. To send them to the slaughter. Courage, as well as betrayal, often had no witnesses.

In our villages on Victory Day there is weeping, not rejoicing. Many weep. They grieve. "It was so horrible . . . I buried all my family, I buried my soul in the war" (V. G. Androsik, underground fighter).

They begin to talk softly, and in the end almost all of them shout.

———

I am a witness . . .

I'll talk about the commander of our partisan unit . . . I won't name him, because his relations are still alive. It will pain them to read it . . .

The liaisons sent a message to the unit: the commander's family had been taken by the Gestapo—his wife, two small daughters, and the old mother. There were notices hanging everywhere, and distributed in the market: if the commander did not surrender, the family would be hanged. He was given two days to think it over. The *polizei* went around the villages and agitated among the people, saying that the Red commissars didn't pity their own children. They were monsters. Nothing was sacred for them. They scattered leaflets from a plane over the forest . . . The commander wanted to surrender, wanted to shoot himself. He wasn't left alone all this time, he was watched. He was capable of killing himself . . .

His unit got in touch with Moscow and reported the situation. They received instructions . . . The same day a party meeting of the unit was convened. The decision was made: not to yield to German provocation. As a Communist, our commander submitted to party discipline . . .

Two days later scouts were sent to the town. They brought terrible news: the whole family had been hanged. The commander was killed in the first battle after that . . . Killed somehow incomprehensibly. Accidentally. I think he wanted to die . . .

Instead of words I have tears . . . How can I persuade myself that I must speak? Who will believe it . . . People want to have a calm and pleasant life, not to listen to me and suffer . . . (V. Korotaeva, partisan).

I, too, try to persuade myself that I must go on . . .

OF A MINE AND A STUFFED TOY
IN A BASKET

Antonina Alexeevna Kondrashova
SCOUT FOR THE BYTOSHSKY PARTISAN BRIGADE

I carried out my mission . . . After that I couldn't stay in the village and went to join the detachment. A few days later my mother was taken by the Gestapo. My brother managed to escape, but my mother was taken away. They tortured her there, questioned her about her daughter's whereabouts. For two years she was held there. For two years, along with our other women, the fascists made her lead the way during their operations: they feared the partisan mines and always drove local people ahead of them—if there were mines, those people would be blown up, and the German soldiers would remain unharmed. A living shield. For two years they used my mother that way.

More than once, while waiting in ambush, we suddenly saw women followed by fascists. Once they came closer, you could see that your mother was there among them. And most frightful of all was waiting for your commander to give the order to fire. Everyone waited in fear for that order, because one would whisper, "There's my mother," another "And there's my sister," or someone would see their own child . . . My mama always went around in a white kerchief. She was tall, she was always the first to be noticed. Before I had time to notice her, someone would already report, "There goes your mother . . ." When they give the order to shoot, you shoot. And I myself didn't know where I was shooting; there was one thing in my head: "Don't lose sight of that white kerchief—is she alive, has she fallen?" A white kerchief . . . They all run away, fall down, and you don't know whether your mother has been killed or not. For the next two days or more, I walk around, beside myself, until the liaisons come back from the village to tell me she's alive. I can live again. Until the next time. I don't think I could stand it now . . . I hated them . . . My hatred helped me . . . To this day the scream of a child who is thrown down a well still rings in my ears. Have you ever heard that scream? The child is falling and screaming, screaming as if from somewhere under the ground, from the other world. It's not a child's scream, and not a man's either. And to see a young fellow cut up with a saw . . . Our partisan . . . After that, when you go on a mission, your heart seeks only one thing: to kill them, kill as many as possible, annihilate them in the cruelest way. When I saw fascist prisoners, I wanted to sink my claws into them one by one. To strangle them. To strangle them with my hands, to tear them with my teeth. I wouldn't have killed them, it would have been too easy a death for them. Not with weapons, not with a rifle . . .

Before their retreat, this was already in 1943, the fascists shot my mother. My mother was like this, she gave us her blessing: "Go, children, you have to live. Rather than just die. It's better not to just die . . ." Mama didn't say big words, she found simple women's words. She wanted us to live and study, especially to study.

The women who shared her cell said that each time she was led away, she begged, "Oh, my dears, I weep only for this: if I die, help my children!"

After the war, one of those women took me into her home, her family, even though she had two young children. The fascists burned our cottage, my younger brother died fighting with the partisans, my mother was shot, my father had been at the front. He came back from the front wounded, sick. He didn't survive much longer, he died soon. So, of my whole family, I was the only one left. That woman was poor herself, and what's more she had two young children. I decided to leave, to go away somewhere. But she wept and wouldn't let me.

When I discovered my mother had been shot, I lost my mind. I didn't know what to do with myself, I had no peace. I had to find her . . . But they had been shot and their grave, in a big antitank trench, had been leveled out by tractors. I was shown approximately where she stood, and I ran, dug there, turning corpses over. I recognized my mother by the ring on her hand . . . When I saw that ring, I cried out, and I remember nothing more. I remember nothing . . . Some women pulled her out, washed her from a tin can, and buried her. I still have that can.

At night I sometimes lie and think: my mother died because of me. No, not because of me . . . If, in fear for my loved ones, I hadn't gone to fight, and if another, a third and a fourth hadn't either, what is now wouldn't be. But to say to myself . . . To forget . . . How my mother walked . . . The sound of the order . . . I shot in the direction she came from. Her white kerchief. You can't imagine how hard it is to live with. And the longer I live, the harder it gets. Sometimes, at night, there's a sudden young laughter or voice outside the window, and you shudder, it suddenly sounds like a child crying, shouting. Sometimes you suddenly wake up feeling like you can't breathe. The smell of burning chokes you . . . You don't know the smell of a burning human body, especially in the summer. An anxious and sweet smell. With the job I have now, if there's a fire, I have to go there, write a report. But if they say that a farm is on fire, that there are dead animals, I never go, I'm not able . . . It reminds me . . . That smell . . . Like burning people . . . And so you wake up at night, run and fetch your cologne, and it seems that in the cologne, too, there's that smell. Everywhere . . .

For a long time I was afraid to get married. Afraid to have children. What if there's war suddenly, and I leave for the front? What about the children? Now I like to read books about life after death. What's there? Who will I meet? I want to meet mama, and I'm afraid of it. When I was young I wasn't afraid, but now I'm old . . .

Yadviga Mikhailovna Savitskaya

UNDERGROUND FIGHTER

My first impression . . . I saw a German . . . As if I'd been hit, my whole body hurt, every cell—how is it they're here? Hatred—it was stronger than fear for our near ones, our loved ones, and fear of our own death. Of course, we thought of our families, but we had no choice. The enemy had come with evil to our land . . . With fire and sword . . .

For instance, when it became known that they were going to arrest me, I left for the forest. To the partisans. I left, leaving at home my seventy-five-year-old mother, and alone at that. We agreed she would pretend to be blind, deaf, and they wouldn't harm her. Obviously, that was how I comforted myself.

The day after I left, fascists burst into my house. Mama pretended she was blind and couldn't hear, as we had agreed. They beat her badly, trying to extort from her where her daughter was. My mother was ill for a long time . . .

Alexandra Ivanovna Khramova

SECRETARY OF THE UNDERGROUND REGIONAL PARTY COMMITTEE OF ANTOPOL

I'll stay this way till the end . . . The way we used to be then. Yes, naïve; yes, romantic. Till my hair turns gray . . . But—that's me!

My friend Katya Simakova was a partisan liaison. She had two girls. Both girls were small—well, how old were they? Six or seven years old. She took those girls by the hands, went through the town and memorized what equipment stood where. A sentry would yell at her, and she would open her mouth, pretending to be simpleminded. She did it for several years . . . The mother sacrificed her daughters . . .

There was another woman, Zajarskaya. She had a daughter, Valeria; the girl was seven years old. We had to blow up the mess hall. We decided to plant a mine in the stove, but it had to be carried there. And the mother said her daughter would bring the mine. She put the mine in a basket and covered it with a couple of children's outfits, a stuffed toy, two dozen eggs, and some butter. And so the little girl brought the mine to the mess hall. People say that maternal instinct is stronger than anything. No, ideas are stronger! And faith is stronger! I think . . . I'm even certain that if it weren't for such a mama and such a girl, and they hadn't carried that mine, we wouldn't have been victorious. Yes, life—is a good thing. Excellent! But there are things that are dearer . . .

Paulina Kasperovich

PARTISAN

We had the Chimuk brothers in our detachment . . . They ran into an ambush in their village, took refuge in some barn, there was shooting, the barn was set on fire. They went on shooting till they ran out of cartridges . . . Then they came out, burned . . . They were driven around the villages in a cart to see who would recognize them as their own. So that people would give themselves away . . .

The entire village stood there. Their father and mother stood there, nobody made a sound. What a heart the mother must have had not to cry out. Not to call. She knew that if she began to weep, the whole village would be burned down. She wouldn't be killed alone. Everybody would be killed. For one German killed they used to burn an entire village. She knew . . . There exist awards for everything, but no award, not even the highest Star of the Hero of the Soviet Union is enough for that mother . . . For her silence . . .

Valentina Mikhailovna Ilkevich
PARTISAN LIAISON

I came to the partisans together with my mama . . . She did laundry for everyone and cooked. If she had to, she also stood watch. One day I left on a mission, and my mother was told I had been hanged. When I returned a few days later and my mother saw me, she became paralyzed; for several hours she couldn't speak. All of that had to be lived through . . .

We picked up a woman on the road. She was unconscious. She couldn't walk, she crawled and thought she was already dead. She felt blood streaming over her, but decided that she felt it in the other world, not in this one. When we shook her, and she regained some consciousness, we heard . . . She told us how they had been shot; she had been led out to be shot, she and her five children. As they were being led to the barn, the children were killed. They shot them and had fun doing it . . . Only one remained, a nursing baby boy. A fascist pointed at him: "Toss him up, I'm going to shoot him." The mother threw the child so as to kill him herself . . . Her own child . . . So the German wouldn't have time to shoot . . . She said she didn't want to live, that she couldn't live in this world after that, only in the other one . . . She didn't want to . . .

I didn't want to kill, I wasn't born to kill. I wanted to be a teacher. But I saw how they burned a village . . . I couldn't scream, I couldn't weep loudly: we were on a scouting mission and came close to that village. I could only bite my hands; I still have the scars; I bit them till they bled. Till the raw flesh showed. I remember how the people screamed . . . The cows screamed . . . The chickens screamed . . . It seemed to me they were all screaming with human voices. All of them alive. Burning and screaming . . .

This isn't me speaking, it's my grief speaking . . .

Valentina Pavlovna Kozhemyakina

PARTISAN

We knew . . . Everybody knew we had to win . . .

Later on people thought my father had stayed on an assignment from the Party. Nobody left him with any assignment. We ourselves decided to fight. I don't remember any panic in our family. There was great sorrow, yes. But no panic. We all believed that victory would be ours. On the first day the Germans entered our village, my father played "The Internationale" on his violin. He wanted to do something like that. Some sort of protest . . .

Two months went by, or three . . . Or . . .

There was a Jewish boy . . . A German leashed him to his bicycle, and the boy ran after him like a dog: *"Schnell! Schnell!"* He rode and laughed. A young German . . . Soon he grew tired of it, got off the bicycle, and gestured to the boy to kneel in front of him . . . On all fours . . . And creep like a dog . . . Leap . . . *"Hundik! Hundik!"* He threw a stick: fetch it! The boy stood up, ran, and brought the stick in his hands. The German got angry . . . Started beating him. Yelling at him. He showed him: leap on all fours and fetch it in your teeth. The boy fetched it in his teeth . . .

The German played with this boy for two hours. Then he leashed him to his bicycle again and they went back. The boy ran like a dog . . . Toward the ghetto . . .

And you ask why we began to fight? Why we learned to shoot . . .

Alexandra Nikiforovna Zakharova

PARTISAN COMMISSAR OF THE
225TH REGIMENT OF GOMEL PROVINCE

How could I forget . . . Wounded soldiers ate salt by the spoonful . . . A name is called, a soldier steps out of the ranks and collapses with his rifle from weakness. From hunger.

The people helped us. If they hadn't helped us, the partisan movement couldn't have existed. The people fought together with us. At times with tears, but still they gave: "Dear children, let's grieve together. Wait for victory."

They'd bring out the last tiny potatoes; they'd give us bread. Prepare sacks to take to the forest. One would say: "I'll give this much," another "This much." "How about you, Ivan?" "And you, Maria?" "I'll give, like everybody else, but I have children . . ."

What are we without our people? An entire army in the forest, but without them we would have died. They sowed, plowed, took care of us and of the children, clothed us all through the war. They plowed at night, when there was no shooting. I remember how we came to a village where an old man was being buried. He had been killed at night. Sowing wheat. He gripped the grain so hard we couldn't straighten his fingers. He was put in the ground with the grain . . .

We had weapons, we could defend ourselves. But they? For giving a loaf of bread to a partisan, they were shot. I stayed overnight and left, but if anyone gave away that I had spent the night in this cottage, they would all be shot. There was a woman there alone, without her husband, but with her three little children. She never drove us away when we came, but lit the stove and cleaned our clothes . . . She gave us all she had left, "Eat, lads." And the potatoes in spring are as tiny as peas. We're eating, and the children are sitting on the stove crying. Those were their last peas . . .

Vera Grigoryevna Sedova

UNDERGROUND FIGHTER

My first mission . . . They brought me leaflets. I sewed them into my pillow. Mama was making the bed and felt them. She ripped open the pillow and saw the leaflets. She began to cry. "You'll destroy yourself and me." But later she helped me.

The partisan liaisons came to us often. They'd unhitch the horses and come in. Do you think the neighbors didn't see? They saw and guessed. I said it was from my brother, from the country. But everybody knew very well that I had no brother in the country. I'm grateful to them; I should bow down to my entire street. One single word would have been enough for us all to die, my entire family. All they needed was to point a finger at us. But no one . . . Not a single person . . . During the war I came to love the people so much that I'll never be able to stop loving them . . .

After the liberation, I'd walk down the street and look around: I couldn't help being afraid, I couldn't calmly walk the streets. I counted the cars as I went, counted the trains at the station . . . It took me a while to get rid of that habit . . .

Vera Safronovna Davydova

PARTISAN

I'm already crying . . . The tears are pouring down . . .

We entered a house, there was nothing in it, just two bare, planed benches and a table. There wasn't even a mug, I think, to drink water. The people had nothing left but an icon in the corner, and an embroidered cloth draped over it.

An old man and an old woman were sitting there. One of our partisans took off his boots, his footwraps were so torn that he couldn't use them anymore. And the rain, and the dirt, and the torn boots. And this old woman goes to the icon, takes the embroidered cloth, and gives it to him: "Take it, child, or how can you go on?" There was nothing else in this cottage . . .

Vera Mitrofanovna Tolkacheva

PARTISAN LIAISON

In the early days . . . I picked up two wounded men outside the village . . . One was wounded in the head, and the other soldier had shrapnel in his leg. I pulled out the shrapnel myself, and poured kerosene in the wound. I didn't find anything else . . . I knew by then that kerosene was a disinfectant . . .

I took care of them and got them back on their feet. First one went off into the woods, then the other. The latter, as he was leaving, suddenly fell at my feet. He wanted to kiss my feet.

"Dear sister! You saved my life."

There were no names, nothing. Just sister and brother.

In the evening, the women gathered in my house. "They say the Germans have taken Moscow."

"Never!"

With these same women, after the war, we organized a kolkhoz, and I was appointed the chairwoman. There were also four old men and five boys, from ten to thirteen years old. Those were my plowmen. We had twenty horses. They all had scabies and needed treatment. That was all I had for farming. There were no wheels or yokes. The women turned the soil with shovels and did the harrowing with cows and bulls. The bullocks would lie down and refuse to get up— unless you all but tore their tails off. The boys harrowed by day, and in the evening, when they opened their little bundles, they all had the same food—potato prasnaki. You don't know what it is. Sorrel seeds, turnsole . . . You don't know it? There is such an herb. We picked clover. We ground it all in a mortar. And we cooked these prasnaki. A sort of bread . . . Bitter—very bitter . . .

In the fall came instructions: cut down 580 cubic meters of timber. Who with? I took my twelve-year-old boy and a ten-year-old girl with me. So did the other women. We delivered the timber . . .

———

Iosif Georgievich Yasukevich and his daughter Maria, partisan liaisons of the Petrakov Unit of the Rokossovsky Brigade during the war, tell the following story:

Iosif Georgievich

I gave away everything for the victory . . . My dearest things. My sons fought at the front. My two nephews were executed for communicating with the partisans. The fascists burned my sister, their mother. In their own house . . . People said that until the smoke covered her, she stood upright like a candle, holding an icon. After the war, whenever the sun goes down, I think something's burning . . .

Maria

I was young, thirteen years old. I knew my father helped the partisans. I understood. People would show up at night. They would leave something, take something. Often my father would take me along, put me onto the cart: "Sit and don't move from here." Once we got to the right place, he would pull out guns or leaflets.

Later he began sending me to the station. He taught me what I should remember. I would quietly sneak into the bushes and hide there until night, counting how many trains passed by. I memorized what they transported, you could see it: guns, tanks, or soldiers. Two or three times a day the Germans would shoot into the bushes.

But weren't you scared?

I was small, I always slipped through, and nobody would notice me. But that day . . . I remember it very well. My father tried twice to leave the farmstead where we lived. The partisans were waiting for him in the woods. Twice he went off and twice he was sent back by the patrols. It was getting dark. He called me: "Marika . . ." And my mother shouted, "I won't let our child go." She pulled me away from my father . . .

Still I ran through the woods, as he told me to. I knew all the paths by heart, but to tell the truth, I was afraid of the dark. I found the partisans, they were waiting, and I reported everything my father had told me. On my way back, it was already growing light. How was I to get around the German patrols? I circled through the forest, fell into the lake; my father's jacket and boots, everything sank. I got out of the hole in the ice . . . Ran barefoot over the snow . . . I fell ill and took to my bed and never got up. My legs were paralyzed. There were no doctors or medications. Mama treated me with herb infusions. Applied clay . . .

After the war they took me to doctors. But it was already too late. I remained bedridden . . . I can sit up a little, then I lie and look out the window . . . Remembering the war . . .

Iosif Georgievich

I carry her in my arms . . . For forty years. Like a little child . . . My wife died two years ago. "I forgive you everything," she said to me. "The sins of youth . . . Everything . . ." But not Marika. I saw it in her eyes . . . I'm afraid to die, because Marika will be left alone. Who will carry her? Who will cross her before going to bed? Who will ask God . . .

OF MOMMIES AND DADDIES

The village of Ratyntsy, Volozhinsky district, Minsk region. An hour's drive from the capital. An ordinary Belorussian village—wooden houses, flowers in the front gardens, chicken and geese in the streets. Children in sandboxes. Old women on the benches. I came to see one of them, but the whole street gathered. They started talking. Loudly, all at the same time.

Each about herself, but all about the same thing. How they plowed, sowed, baked bread for the partisans, took care of the children, went to diviners and Gypsies to interpret their dreams, and asked God to protect them. Waited for their husbands to come back from the war.

I wrote down the first three names: Elena Adamovna Velichko, Yustina Lukyanovna Grigorovich, Maria Fyodorovna Mazuro. After that I could no longer make them out because of the weeping . . .

—Ah, my darling daughter! My golden one! I don't like Victory Day. I weep! Ah, how I weep! Whenever I think, it all comes back. Happiness is beyond the mountains, but grief is just over your shoulder . . .

The Germans burned us down, picked us clean. We were left on a bare rock. We came back from the woods, there was nothing. Only the cats were still there. What did we eat? In the summer I went and gathered berries, mushrooms. The house was full of children.

When the war was over, we went to the kolkhoz. I reaped, and mowed, and threshed. We pulled the plow in place of horses. There were no horses; the Germans killed them. They shot all the dogs. My mother used to say: when I die, I don't know about my soul, but my hands will get some rest. My little girl was ten; she reaped with me. The brigadier came to see how such a little thing fulfilled the norm before evening. We reaped and reaped; the sun went down behind the forest, but we wanted it to stay higher. One day wasn't enough. We did two norms. We weren't paid anything; they just put down marks that counted as workdays. We spent the whole summer in the field and in the fall didn't get even a sack of flour. We raised the children on nothing but potatoes . . .

—So the war was over. I was alone. I was the cow, and the bull, and the woman, and the muzhik. Aie, aie, aie . . .

—War was woe . . . Only children in my cottage. Not a bench, not a trunk. Total nakedness. We ate acorns, in spring it was grass . . . When my girl went to school, I bought her her first pair of shoes. She slept in them, she didn't want to take them off. That's how we lived! Life is over, but there's nothing to remember. Only the war . . .

—A rumor went around that the Germans had brought our prisoners to a hamlet, and those who recognized their own could take them. Our women got up and ran! In the evening some brought back their own, others brought strangers, and what they told us was beyond belief: people were rotting alive, starving to death, ate all the leaves off trees . . . Ate grass . . . Dug roots from the ground . . . I ran there the next day, didn't find mine, and thought I might save someone else's son. I took a fancy to a swarthy one, his name was Sashko, like my little grandson. He was probably about eighteen years old. I gave the German some lard, eggs: "My brother." Crossed my heart. We came back home. He couldn't eat a whole egg, he was so weak. Before the month was out, a bastard turned up. He lived like all of us, married, two children . . . He went to the commandant's office and reported that we had taken in strangers. The next day the Germans came on their motorcycles. We begged and fell on our knees, but they deceived us by saying they would take them closer to their homes. I gave Sashko my grandfather's suit . . . I thought he would live . . .

But they were driven out of the village . . . All mowed down with machine guns . . . All of them. To a man . . . They were so young, young and good! And we decided, those who had taken them in—nine of us—to bury them. Five of us dragged them out of the pit, the other four looked around so the Germans wouldn't fall on us. We couldn't use our hands; it was very hot, and they had been lying there for four days . . . We were afraid of cutting them with our shovels . . . We put them on tablecloths and pulled . . . We drank water and covered our noses. So as not to faint . . . We dug a grave in the woods, and laid them down side by side. Covered their heads with sheets . . . Their feet . . .

For a year we never stopped mourning them. And each of us thought: Where is my husband or son? Are they alive? Because men do come back from war, but from under the sand—never . . . Aie, aie, aie . . .

—My husband was nice, kind. We only lived together for a year and a half. When he was leaving, I bore our baby in my bosom. But he didn't get to see our daughter, I gave birth to her without him. He left in the summer, and I gave birth to her in the fall.

I was still giving her the breast; she was less than a year old. I was sitting on the bed nursing her . . . A knock on the window: "Lena, a notice has come . . . About your husband . . ." (The women didn't let the postman come, they came to tell me themselves.) As I stood there holding my little girl to my breast, the milk spurted straight on the floor. My girl cried out, she got scared. She never took my breast again. It was precisely on the eve of Palm Sunday that I was told. In April . . . The sun was shining . . . I read in the notice that my Ivan had been killed in Poland. His grave is near the city of Gdansk. He died on March 17, 1945 . . . Such a small, thin scrap of paper . . . We were already expecting the Victory, our men were about to come home. The gardens were in bloom . . .

After this scare my girl was sick for a long time, till she went to school. A hard knock on the door or a shout—and she got sick. Cried during the night. I suffered over her for a long time, maybe for seven years I didn't see the sun, it didn't shine for me. Everything was dark in my eyes.

Victory!—they said. The men began to come home. But fewer returned than we sent out. Less than half. My brother Yusik came back first. Crippled, though. And he had a daughter just like mine. Four years old, or five . . . My daughter used to go to their house, but one day she came back crying: "I won't go anymore." "Why are you crying?" I asked. "Her daddy takes Olechka on his knees" (their daughter was called Olechka) "and comforts her. But I don't have a daddy. I only have a mommy." We hugged each other . . .

And so it went for two or three years. She would run home from outside: "Can I play at home? Or else daddy will come, and I'll be outside with the other kids. He won't recognize me. He's never seen me . . ." I couldn't chase her out of the house to the other kids. She sat at home for days. Waiting for daddy. But daddy never returned . . .

—Mine, as he was leaving for the war, cried so hard about leaving his little children. He was sorry. The children were so young they didn't know they had a father. Above all, they were all boys. I was carrying the smallest of them in my arms. He took him and pressed him to himself. I ran after him. They were already shouting "Fall in!" But he couldn't let go of him, he stood in the column with him . . . The commander yelled at him, and he was flooding the baby with tears. All the swaddling clothes got wet. We ran out of the village with the children; we ran for another three miles. Other women also ran along. My children were falling down, and I was barely able to carry the little one. And Volodya, that's my husband, turned to look, and I kept running. I was the last . . . The children stayed behind on the road. I was running with the little one . . .

A year later a notice came: your husband Vladimir Grigorovich was killed in Germany, near Berlin. I've never even seen his grave.

One of our neighbors came home perfectly healthy, another came home missing a leg. I grieved so much: let mine come back, even without legs, but alive. I'd have carried him in my arms . . .

—I was left with three little sons. I carried sheaves on my back, and wood from the forest, and potatoes and hay . . . All alone . . . I pulled the plow by myself, on my back, dragged the harrow. So what? In every second cottage of our village there was a widow or a soldier's wife. We were left without men. Without horses. The horses were also taken to the war. So I . . . I even received two awards as "best worker," and was once given ten yards of cotton. I was so happy! I sewed shirts for my boys, all three of them.

—After the war . . . The sons of those who had been killed were just becoming adolescents. Growing up. The boys were thirteen or fourteen years old, but they thought they were already adults. Wanted to marry. There weren't any men, but the women were all young . . .

If I had been told: give up your cow and there won't be any war, I'd have given it up! So that my children wouldn't have to endure what I have. Day and night I feel my sorrow . . .

—I look out the window, it's as if he's sitting there . . . Sometimes in the evening something seems to be there . . . I'm already old, but I always see him young. The way he was when he left. If I dream of him, he's also young. And I'm young, too . . .

The women all got death notices, but I got a scrap of paper— "Missing in action." Written in blue ink. For the first ten years I waited for him every day. I wait for him even now. As long as we live we can hope for anything . . .

———

—And how can a woman live alone? A man came, helped me or didn't. It's bad either way. Anyone can say what he likes . . . People talk, dogs bark . . . But if only Ivan had seen his five grandsons. Every once in a while I stand by his portrait and show him their photographs. I talk to him . . .

—Aie, aie, aie . . . Dear God . . . Merciful one . . .

—Just after the war I had a dream: I go out into the yard, and my husband is walking there . . . In a uniform . . . And he calls me, he keeps calling me. I leaped from under the blanket, opened the window . . . All's quiet. Even the birds aren't singing. They're asleep. Wind passes over the leaves . . . Whistling softly . . .

In the morning I took a dozen eggs and went to the Gypsy woman. "He's no more," she laid out the cards. "Don't wait in vain. It's his soul walking near the house." There had been love between us. Great love . . .

—A Gypsy woman taught me: "When everybody falls asleep, put on a black shawl and sit down by a big mirror. He'll appear in it . . . You shouldn't touch either him or his clothes. Just talk to him . . ." I sat up all night . . . Before morning he came . . . He said nothing, and his tears flowed. He appeared like that three times. I called him and he came. He wept. I stopped calling him. I felt sorry . . .

—And I'm waiting to meet mine . . . I'll tell him things day and night. I need nothing from him, only—let him listen. He's probably also grown old there. Like me.

———

—It's my native soil . . . I dig up potatoes, beetroots . . . He's there somewhere, and I'll come to him soon . . . My sister tells me: "Don't look in the ground, look at the sky. Upward. They're there." That's my cottage . . . Nearby . . . Stay with us. If you stay overnight you'll learn more. Blood isn't water, it's a pity to spill it, but it keeps flowing. I see it on television . . . every day . . .

You don't have to write about us . . . Better to remember . . . How you and I talked together. Wept. When you take leave of us, turn to look at us and our cottages. Not once, like a stranger, but twice, like our own. No need for anything more. Turn to look . . .

OF LITTLE LIFE AND A BIG IDEA

Thecla Fedorovna Struy
PARTISAN

I always believed . . . I believed Stalin . . . I believed the Communists. I myself was a Communist. I believed in Communism . . . I lived for that, I stayed alive for that. After Khrushchev's report at the Twentieth Congress, when he told about Stalin's errors, I became ill, I took to my bed. I couldn't believe it was true. During the war I also shouted, "For the Motherland! For Stalin!" Nobody made me do it . . . I believed . . . It's my life . . .

Here it is . . .

I fought with the partisans for two years . . . In my last battle, I was wounded in the legs, lost consciousness. It was freezing cold. When I came to, I felt my hands were frostbitten. Now they're alive, good hands, but then they were black . . . My feet, of course, were also frostbitten. If it weren't for the frost, it would have been possible to save my legs, but they were bloody and I lay there for a long time. When they found me, they put me with the other wounded; many of us were brought to one place, and the Germans encircled us again. Our unit escaped . . . Broke through . . . They stacked us onto sledges like firewood. There was no time for looking, for pitying; we were driven deeper into the forest. To hide. They drove and drove, and then reported to Moscow about my injury. You see, I was a deputy of the Supreme Soviet. A big person; they were proud of me. I was from the lowest, from a simple peasant family. I joined the Party very early . . .

My legs were gone . . . They amputated them . . . They did the surgery right there in the forest. The conditions were the most primitive. They put me on a table to operate, and there was no iodine; they sawed my legs off with a simple saw, both legs . . . They drove for four miles to get iodine from another village, while I lay on the table. Without anesthesia. Without . . . Instead of anesthesia—a bottle of moonshine. There was nothing but an ordinary saw . . . A carpenter's saw . . .

They contacted Moscow to request a plane. The plane flew over three times, circled and circled, but couldn't land. There was shooting all around. The fourth time, it landed, but both my legs were already amputated. Later, in Ivanovo and Tashkent, they performed four re-amputations; four times the gangrene came back. They cut away bit by bit, and it ended very high up. At first I wept . . . I sobbed . . . I imagined how I'd go crawling on the ground. I wouldn't be able to walk again, only crawl. I myself don't know what helped me, what held me back from . . . How I persuaded myself. Of course, I met good people. Many good people. We had a surgeon, also with no legs. He said this about me, the other doctors told me: "I admire her. I've operated on so many men, but I haven't seen anyone like her. She never made a sound." I controlled myself . . . I was used to being strong in front of people . . .

Then I went back to Disna. My native town. I came back on crutches.

Now I walk poorly, because I'm old, but back then I ran around town and went everywhere on foot. I ran around on my wooden legs; I traveled to the kolkhozes. They gave me the post of vice chairman of the district party committee. A big job. I never stayed in my office. I went around to the villages, the fields. I would get offended if I sensed some indulgence. There were few competent kolkhoz chairmen at the time, and if there was some responsible work, they sent representatives from the district committee. And so, every Monday we were summoned to the committee and dispatched here and there. I'd sit there in the morning, looking out the window; people kept coming to the committee, but I wasn't called. And it somehow pained me; I wanted to be like everybody else.

And at last the phone rings, the first secretary calls, "Thecla Fedorovna, report." How happy I was then, though it was very very hard for me to go from village to village. They would send me fifteen or twenty miles away, and sometimes I rode, sometimes I walked. I'd go somewhere through the forest, fall down, and be unable to get up. I'd steady myself against my bag, or cling to a tree, get up, and go on. And I received a pension, I could have lived for myself, for myself alone. But I wanted to live for others. I'm a Communist . . .

I have nothing of my own. Only orders, medals, and certificates of honor. My house was built by the state. It's a big house, because there are no children in it, so it seems quite big . . . And the ceilings are quite high . . . I live with my sister. She's my sister, my mama, my nurse. I'm old now . . . In the morning I can't get up by myself . . .

We live together, live by our past. We have a beautiful past. It was a hard life, but beautiful and honest, and I have no grudges. On account of my life . . . I lived honestly . . .

Sofya Mironovna Vereshchak

UNDERGROUND FIGHTER

Our time made us the way we were. We proved ourselves. There won't be another time like that. It won't be repeated. Our idea was young then, and we were young. Lenin had died recently. Stalin lived . . . How proud I was to wear a Pioneer neckerchief. A Komsomol badge . . .

And then—the war. And we were like that . . . Of course, we quickly organized an underground group in Zhitomir. I joined it at once, there was no discussion: to go or not to go, be afraid or not afraid. It wasn't even discussed . . .

After a few months our underground group was tracked down. It had been betrayed. I was seized by the Gestapo . . . Of course I was afraid. For me it was even more frightening than to die. I was afraid of torture . . . What if I couldn't stand it? We all thought that way . . . Alone . . . Since childhood, for instance, I had borne physical pain poorly. But we didn't know ourselves, we didn't know how strong we were . . .

At my last interrogation, after which for the third time I was put on the list to be shot . . . Here's what happened with my third interrogator, who told me he was a historian by education . . . This fascist wanted to understand why we were such people, why our ideas were so important to us. "Life is above any ideas," he said. I, of course, disagreed with that. He shouted, he beat me. "What? What makes you be this way? To calmly accept death? Why do Communists believe that Communism should conquer the whole world?" he asked. He spoke excellent Russian. So I decided to speak everything out, since I knew they'd kill me anyway—at least it would not be for nothing, and let him know that we were strong. For about four hours he questioned, and I answered, what I knew, what I had managed to learn in courses of Marxism-Leninism at school and at the university. Oh, what it did to him! He clutched his head, he ran around the room, stopped as if rooted to the spot and looked at me, but for once he didn't beat me . . .

I stood facing him . . . Half my hair had been torn out; I used to have two thick braids. Starving . . . At first I dreamed of a little, tiny piece of bread, then—at least of a crust, and later—of finding at least a few crumbs . . . So I stood facing him like that . . . With burning eyes . . . He listened to me for a long time. Listened and didn't beat me . . . No, he was not afraid yet, it was only 1943. But he already felt something . . . some kind of danger. He wanted to know—what kind? I answered him. But when I left, he put me on the list to be shot . . .

On the night before the execution, I looked back over my life, my short life . . .

The happiest day of my life was when my father and mother, after driving away from home under bombardment for several dozen miles, decided to come back. Not to leave. To stay home. I knew then that we would fight. It seemed to us that the victory would come so soon. Absolutely! The first thing we did was find and rescue the wounded. They were in the fields, in the grass, in the ditches, or had crept into someone's barn. I stepped out one morning to dig some potatoes and found one in our kitchen garden. He was dying . . . A young officer, he didn't even have enough strength to tell me his name. He whispered some words . . . I couldn't make them out . . . I remember my despair. But I think I've never been so happy as during those days. I acquired my parents for a second time. I used to think my father was not concerned with politics. He turned out to be a non-Party Bolshevik. My mother—an uneducated peasant, she believed in God. She prayed all through the war. But how? She fell on her knees before an icon: "Save the people! Save Stalin! Save the Communist Party from that monster Hitler." Every day while I was being interrogated by the Gestapo, I expected the door to open and my parents to come in. Papa and mama . . . I knew where I had come to, and I'm happy that I didn't betray anyone. We were more afraid to betray than to die. When

I was arrested, I understood that the time of suffering had come. I knew my spirit was strong, but what about my body?

I don't remember my first interrogation. I didn't lose consciousness . . . I only lost consciousness once, when they twisted my arms with some sort of wheel. I don't think I screamed, though they had shown me earlier how others screamed. During the following interrogations, I lost the sense of pain, my body became numb. Made of plywood. There was only one thought: no! I won't die in front of them. No! Only after it was over and they dragged me back to my cell, then I began to feel pain, I turned into a wound. I was a wound all over . . . My whole body . . . But I had to hold out. To hold out! So that my mother would know I died a human being, I betrayed no one. Mama!

They beat me, they hung me up. Always completely undressed. They photographed me. I could only cover my breasts with my hands . . . I saw people go mad. I saw how little Kolenka, he wasn't even a year old, we were teaching him to say "mama," when they were taking him from his mother, he understood in some supernatural way that he was losing her forever and shouted for the first time in his life, "Mama!" It wasn't a word, or wasn't only a word . . . I want to tell you . . . Tell you everything . . . Oh, such people I met there! They died in the basements of the Gestapo, and their courage was known only to the walls. And now, forty years later, I mentally kneel to them. "Dying is easiest of all," they used to say. But to live . . . How we wanted to live! We believed victory would come, we were only doubtful about one thing—would we survive until that great day?

In our cell there was a small window with a grille on it; somebody had to lift you up to look out of it—not even at a piece of sky, but at a piece of roof. But we were all so weak, we couldn't lift each other up. But we had Anya, a paratrooper. She was captured when they were being dropped from a plane in the rear, and her group was ambushed. And now, all bloodied up, battered, she suddenly asked, "Push me up, I'll look out at freedom. I want to be there!"

I want to—that's all. We lifted her together, and she shouted, "Girls, there's a little flower . . ." Then each of us started asking, "And me . . . And me . . ." And we found the strength somewhere to help each other. It was a dandelion. How it got to the roof and managed to stay there, I have no idea. And we all made a wish over this flower. I now think everyone's wish was: "Please get me out of this hell alive."

I used to love the spring so much . . . I loved it when the cherry trees were in bloom and near the lilac bushes there was the fragrance of lilac . . . Don't be surprised by my style, I used to write poetry. But now I don't like the spring. The war stands between us, between me and nature. When the cherry trees were in bloom, I saw fascists in my native Zhitomir . . .

I stayed alive by a miracle. I was saved by people who were grateful to my father. My father was a doctor. At the time that was a big thing. They pushed me out of the column, in the dark, as we were led out to be shot. I remembered nothing on account of the pain; I walked as if in sleep . . . I went where I was led . . . Then driven . . . They brought me home. I was all wounds. I immediately developed eczema from the stress. I couldn't even hear a human voice. I heard it and felt pain. Mama and papa talked in a whisper. I kept screaming, and fell silent only in hot water. I didn't allow my mother to leave me even for a second. She asked, "My dear, I have to go to the oven. To the garden . . ." But I clung to her. The moment I let go of her hand, it all descended on me again. Everything that had happened to me. To distract me, they brought me flowers. My favorite bluebells . . . Chestnut leaves . . . The smells distracted me . . . My mother kept the dress I wore when I was with the Gestapo. When she was dying, it was under her pillow. Until her last hour . . .

The first time I got up was when I saw our soldiers. Suddenly I, who had been lying in bed for over a year, leaped up and ran outside: "My dear ones! My darlings . . . You're back . . ." The soldiers carried me into the house. In my enthusiasm, on the second and third day, I ran to the recruitment office: "Give me a job!" They told my father, and he came for me: "My baby, how did you get here? Who helped you?" I held out for a few days . . . Then the pain came back . . . The suffering . . . I screamed for days. People passed by our cottage and begged, "Lord, either take her soul, or help her, so that she stops suffering."

The curative mud of Tskaltubo saved me. The will to live saved me. To live, live—nothing else. I went on living. I lived, like everybody else . . . Lived . . . For fourteen years I worked in a library. Those were happy years. The happiest. Now my life has become a continuous struggle with illnesses. Old age, whatever you say, is a nasty thing. Also the solitude. I remained completely alone. Papa and mama are long gone. These long sleepless nights . . . So many years have gone by, but my most frightening dream—I wake up in cold sweat. I don't remember Anya's last name . . . I don't remember whether she was from the Bryansk or the Smolensk region. I remember how she didn't want to die! She would put her plump white hands behind her head, look out the window through the grille, and shout, "I want to live!"

I never found her parents . . . I don't know who I should tell this story to . . .

Klara Vasilyevna Goncharova

ANTIAIRCRAFT GUNNER

After the war we learned about Auschwitz, Dachau . . . How to give birth after that? But I was already pregnant . . .

I was sent to a village to take subscriptions for a loan. The government needed money to rebuild plants and factories.

I arrived, there was no village, everybody was underground . . . Living in dugouts . . . A woman came out in some kind of terrible-looking clothing. I went into the dugout; three children were sitting there, all hungry. She was grinding something in a mortar for them, some kind of grass.

She asked me, "You came to take subscriptions for a loan?"

I said, "Yes."

She: "I have no money, but I have a chicken. Yesterday the neighbor wanted it. I'll go and ask her. If she buys it, I'll give you the money."

Even as I tell you this, I get a lump in my throat. Such people there were! Such people! Her husband was killed at the front. She was left with her three children, nothing else, just that chicken, and she was selling it to give me money. We were collecting cash then. She was ready to give away everything, just to have peace, for her children to stay alive. I remember her face. And all her children . . .

How did they grow up? I'd like to know . . . I'd like to find them and meet them . . .

"MAMA, WHAT'S A PAPA?"

———

I don't see the end of this road. The evil seems infinite to me. I can no longer treat it only as history. Who will answer me: what am I dealing with—time or human beings? Times change, but human beings? I think about the dull repetitiveness of life.

They've spoken as soldiers. As women. Many of them were mothers . . .

———

OF BATHING BABIES AND OF
A MAMA WHO LOOKS LIKE A PAPA

———

Lyubov Igorevna Rudkovskaya
PARTISAN

I run . . . Several of us are running. Running away . . . We're being chased. Shot at. And there's my mother already under fire. But she sees us running . . . And I hear her voice, she's shouting. People told me later how she was shouting. She shouted, "It's good that you put on a white dress . . . My dear daughter . . . There'll be no one to dress you . . ." She was convinced I'd be killed, and she was glad that I would lie all in white . . . Before this happened we were preparing to visit the neighboring village. For Easter . . . To see our relatives . . .

It was so quiet . . . They stopped firing. There was only my mother shouting . . . Maybe they were firing? I didn't hear . . .

My entire family was killed during the war. The war is over, and I have no one to wait for . . .

Raissa Grigoryevna Khosenevich

PARTISAN

They began to bomb Minsk.

I rushed to the kindergarten to get my son. My daughter was out of town. She had just turned two; she was at the day nursery, and they went out of town. I decided to pick up my son and bring him home, and then run for her. I wanted to gather them all quickly.

I reached the kindergarten, planes were flying over the city, bombing somewhere. I heard my son's voice over the fence; he was not quite four years old: "Don't worry, my mother says the Germans will be crushed."

I looked through the gate. There were many of them there, and he was reassuring the others like that. But when he saw me, he began to tremble and cry. It turned out he was terrified.

I brought him home, asked my mother-in-law to look after him, and went to get my daughter. I ran! I found no one where the nursery was supposed to be. The village women told me the children had been taken somewhere. Where? Who? Probably to the city, they said. There were two teachers with them; they didn't wait for the car and left on foot. The city was seven miles away . . . But they were such little children, from one to two years old. My dear, I looked for them for two weeks . . . In many villages . . . When I entered a house and they told me it was that very nursery, those kids, I didn't believe them. They were lying, forgive me, in their own excrement, feverish. As if dead . . . The director of the nursery was a very young woman; her hair had turned gray. It turned out that they had walked all the way to the city, got lost on the way, several children had died.

I walked among them and didn't recognize my daughter. The director comforted me, "Don't despair, look around. She must be here. I remember her."

I found my Ellochka only thanks to her shoes . . . Otherwise I would have never recognized her . . .

Then our house burned down . . . We were left on the street, in what we had on. German units had already entered the city. We had nowhere to go. I walked around the streets with my children for several days. I met Tamara Sergeevna Sinitsa; we had been slight acquaintances before the war. She heard me out and said, "Let's go to my place."

"My children are sick with whooping cough. How can I go with you?"

She also had little children; they might get infected. That's how it was then . . . There were no medications, hospitals no longer worked.

"No, let's go."

My dear, how could I ever forget it? They shared potato peelings with us. I sewed pants out of my old skirt for my son, to give him something for his birthday.

But we dreamed of fighting . . . Inactivity tormented us . . . What a joy it was when the opportunity came to join the underground workforce, and not sit around with folded arms, waiting. Just in case, I sent off my son, the older boy, to my mother-in-law. She made one condition: "I'll take my grandson, but you should no longer be seen in the house. We'll all get killed on account of you." For three years I didn't see my son; I was afraid to go near the house. And when the Germans already had an eye on me and picked up my trail, I took my daughter and we both went to the partisans. I carried her for thirty miles . . . Thirty miles. We walked for two weeks . . .

She stayed there with me for over a year . . . I often think: how did we survive that? If you asked me, I couldn't tell you. My dear, such things are impossible to endure. Even today my teeth chatter at the words "partisan blockade."

May 1943 . . . I was sent off with a typewriter to the neighboring partisan zone. Borisovskaya. They had our typewriter, with Russian characters, but they needed one with German characters, and we were the only ones to have such a typewriter. This was the typewriter I had carried out of occupied Minsk, following the underground committee's orders. When I got there, to Lake Palik, after a few days the blockade began. That's where I ended up . . .

I didn't come alone, I came with my daughter. When I went on a mission for a day or two, I left her with other people, but there was nowhere to leave her for longer periods. So of course I took my child with me. And we got caught in the blockade . . . The Germans encircled the partisan zone . . . They bombed us from the sky and shot at us from the ground . . . The men went around carrying rifles, but I carried a rifle, the typewriter, and Ellochka. As we walked, I tripped, she fell over me into a swamp. We went on, she fell again . . . And so on, for two months! I swore to myself, if I survived, I wouldn't go near that swamp again, I couldn't look at it anymore.

"I know why you don't lie down when they shoot. You want us both to get killed." That's what my four-year-old child would say to me. But I didn't have the strength to lie down; if I did, I'd never get up again.

Other times the partisans felt sorry for me.

"Enough. Let us carry your daughter."

But I didn't trust anyone. What if they start shelling, what if she gets killed without me, and I don't hear it? What if she gets lost . . .

I met the brigade commander Lopatin.

"What a woman!" He was amazed. "In those circumstances she carried her child, and didn't let go of the typewriter. Not every man could do that."

He took Ellochka in his arms, hugged her, kissed her. He emptied out all his pockets, gave her bread crumbs. She downed them with water from the swamp. And following his example, other partisans emptied their pockets and gave her crumbs.

When we got out of the encirclement, I was completely sick. I was covered with boils, my skin was peeling off. And I had a child on my hands . . . We were waiting for a plane from the mainland. They said that if it came, they would send off the most badly wounded, and they could take my Ellochka. And I remember that moment when I was sending her away. The wounded reached out for her: "Ellochka, to me." "Come to me. There's enough room . . ." They all knew her; in the hospital she sang for them: "Ah, if only I live till my wedding bells."

The pilot asked, "Who are you here with, little girl?"

"With mama. She stayed outside the cabin . . ."

"Call your mama, so she can fly with you."

"No, my mama can't leave. She has to fight the fascists."

That's how they were, our children. And I looked at her face and had spasms—will I see her again someday?

Let me tell you how my son and I were reunited . . . This was already after the liberation. I was walking to the house where my mother-in-law lived. My legs were like cotton wool. The women from the brigade, they were older, warned me, "If you see him, no matter what, don't reveal to him straightaway that you're his mother. Do you realize what he's lived through without you?"

A neighbor girl runs by: "Oh! Lenya's mother. Lenya's alive . . ."

My legs won't go any further: my son is alive. She told me that my mother-in-law had died of typhus, and a neighbor woman had taken Lenya in.

I walked into their yard. What was I wearing? A German army shirt, a patched-up, black padded jacket, and old boots. The neighbor immediately recognized me, but she said nothing. And my son sits there, barefoot, ragged.

"What's your name, boy?" I ask.

"Lenya . . ."

"And who do you live with?"

"I used to live with my grandmother. When she died, I buried her. I came to her every day and asked her to take me into her grave. I was afraid to sleep alone . . ."

"Where are your mama and papa?"

"My papa's alive, he's at the front. But mama was killed by the fascists. So my grandmother said . . ."

Two partisans were with me; they had come to bury their comrades. They listened to how he was answering, and wept.

I couldn't stand it any longer.

"Why don't you recognize your mama?"

He rushed to me. "Papa!!" I was wearing men's clothes and a hat. Then he hugged me and screamed, "Mama!!!"

It was such a scream! Such hysterics . . . For a month he didn't let me go anywhere, not even to work. I took him with me. It wasn't enough for him to see me, to see I was nearby, he had to hold on to me. If we sat down for lunch, he held me with one hand and ate with the other. He only called me "Mamochka." He still does . . . Mamochka . . . Mamulenka . . .

When we were reunited with my husband, a week wasn't enough to tell everything. We talked day and night . . .

Larissa Leontyevna Korotkaya

PARTISAN

War—it's always funerals . . . We often had to bury partisans. Either a group fell into an ambush, or they died in battle. I'll tell you about one funeral . . .

There was very heavy fighting. In that fighting we lost many people, and I was wounded. And after the battle came the funeral. Usually we gave short speeches over the grave. First came the commanders, then the friends. But here, among the dead, was a local fellow, and his mother had come to the funeral. She began to lament: "My little son! We prepared the house for you! You promised you would bring a young wife home! But you are marrying the earth . . ."

The unit stood there, silent, no one touched her. Then she lifted her head and saw that not only her son had been killed, but many other young ones were lying there, and she began to cry over those other sons: "My sons, my dear ones! Your mothers don't see you, they don't know you're being put in the ground! And the ground is so cold. The winter cold is cruel. I will weep instead of them, and pity all of you . . . My dear ones . . . Darlings . . ."

She just said, "I will pity all of you" and "my dear ones"—all the men began weeping aloud. No one could help it, no one had strength enough. The unit wept. Then the commander shouted, "Fire the salute!" And the salute silenced everything.

And I was so struck that I think of it even now, the greatness of a mother's heart. In such great grief, as her son was buried, she had enough heart to mourn for the other sons . . . Mourn for them like her own . . .

Maria Vasilyevna Pavlovets
PARTISAN DOCTOR

I went back to my village . . .

Children are playing outside our house. I look and think: "Which one is mine?" They all look alike. Shorn as sheep used to be—in rows. I didn't recognize my daughter and asked which one was Lusya. And I saw one of the kids in a long shirt up and run into the house. It was hard to tell who was a girl and who was a boy because of their clothing. I asked again, "So which one of you is Lusya?"

They pointed their fingers, meaning the one who ran off. And I realized that she was my daughter. After a moment my grandmother, my mother's mother, brought her out by the hand. She led her to meet me: "Come, come. We're going to give it to this mother now for leaving us."

I was wearing men's military clothes, a forage cap, and was riding a horse, and my daughter, of course, pictured her mother like a grandmother, like the other women. And here a soldier had arrived. For a long time she wouldn't come to my arms, she was scared. There was no point in feeling hurt—I hadn't raised her, she had grown up with grandmothers.

I had brought soap as a gift. At the time it was a fancy gift, and when I began washing her, she bit it with her teeth. She wanted to try and eat it. That's how they lived. I remembered my mother as a young woman, but it was an old woman who greeted me. They told her that her daughter had come back, and she flew out of her garden into the street. She saw me, spread her arms and ran. I recognized her and ran to her. She was a few steps away from me, and she fell down, exhausted. I fell next to her. I kissed my mother. I kissed the ground. I had so much love in my heart, and so much hatred.

I remember a wounded German soldier lying on the ground and clutching at it from pain, and our soldier came up to him: "Don't touch, this is my ground! Yours is there, where you came from . . ."

Antonina Grigoryevna Bondareva
LIEUTENANT OF THE GUARDS, SENIOR PILOT

I went to war after my husband . . .

I left my daughter with my mother-in-law, but she soon died. My husband had a sister, and she took my girl. And after the war, when I was demobilized, she didn't want to give my child back to me. She told me something like this: you can't have a daughter, since you abandoned her when she was little and went to war. How can a mother abandon her child, and such a helpless one at that? I came back from the war, my daughter was already seven years old; I had left her when she was three. I met a grown-up girl. When she was little, she didn't eat enough, didn't sleep enough. There was a hospital nearby; she would go there and act and dance, and they would give her some bread. She told me later . . . At first she waited for her papa and mama, but later—only for her mama. Her father had been killed . . . She understood . . .

I often remembered my daughter at the front, I never forgot her for a minute, I dreamed of her. I missed her a lot. I cried, knowing I wasn't the one telling her fairy tales at night. She fell asleep and woke up without me . . . Somebody else braided her hair . . . I wasn't upset with my sister-in-law. I understood . . . She was very fond of her brother. He was strong, handsome; it was unthinkable that such a man could be killed. But he died straight off, in the first months of the war . . . Their planes were bombed on the ground in the morning. In the first months and probably even in the first year of the war, the German pilots ruled the skies. And he died . . . She didn't want to let go of what was left from him. The last thing. She was one of those women for whom family, children, were the most important thing in life. Bombing, shelling, and all she can think of is, how come the child didn't get her bath today? I can't blame her . . .

She said I was cruel . . . had no woman's soul . . . But we suffered greatly at war. No family, no home, no children . . . Many of us left our children at home, I wasn't the only one. We would sit under a parachute, waiting for our assignment. The men smoked, played dominoes, and we, while waiting for a signal to take off, sat and embroidered handkerchiefs. We stayed women.

Here's something about my navigator. She wanted to send a picture home, so we tied a kerchief—someone had a kerchief—to hide her straps, and covered her army shirt with a blanket. And it was as if she was wearing a dress . . . And so we took the picture. It was her favorite picture . . .

My daughter and I became friends . . . We've been friends ever since . . .

OF LITTLE RED RIDING HOOD
AND THE JOY OF MEETING A CAT
DURING THE WAR

Lyubov Zakharovna Novik
NURSE

It took me a long time to get used to the war . . .

We were attacking. And when a wounded soldier came, bleeding from an artery . . . I had never seen such a wound, blood spurting out . . . I rushed for the doctor. But the wounded man shouted, "Where? Where are you going? Tie it with a belt!" Only then did I come to my senses . . .

What do I feel sorry about? One little boy . . . This seven-year-old kid was left without a mama. His mama had been killed. The boy was sitting on the road next to his dead mother. He didn't understand that she was already gone; he waited for her to wake up, and kept asking for food . . .

Our commander didn't leave the boy there, he took him along: "You have no mama, sonny, but you'll have lots of papas." So he grew up with us. As the son of the regiment. From the age of seven. He reloaded the cartridge disks of the PPSH-41 submachine gun.

When you leave, my husband will be angry. He doesn't like these kinds of conversations. He doesn't like the war. But he didn't go to war, he's young, younger than me. We don't have children. I always remember that boy. He could be my son . . .

After the war I felt sorry for everybody. For men . . . For roosters, for dogs . . . I still can't stand the pain of others. I worked in a hospital. The patients loved me because I was gentle. We have a big garden. I've never sold a single apple, a single berry. I just give them away, I

give them away to people . . . I remained like that after the war . . .
My heart's like that . . .

Lyudmila Mikhailovna Kashechkina

UNDERGROUND FIGHTER

I didn't cry then . . .

I was afraid of only one thing . . . When comrades were captured,
several days of unbearable waiting: would they stand firm under torture or not? If they didn't, there would be more arrests. After a certain
time, it became known that they would be executed. We had an assignment: to go and see who was to be hanged that day. You walk
down the street and you see: they're already preparing the rope . . .
You can't cry, you can't linger for an extra second, because there are
spies everywhere. And so much—this is the wrong word—courage,
so much mental strength was needed to keep silent. To pass by without tears.

I didn't cry then . . .

I knew what was coming, but I only understood, I only really felt
everything, when I was arrested. I was taken off to jail. They beat me
with boots, with whips. I learned what a fascist "manicure" was. Your
hands are put on a table and some sort of machine sticks needles under
your nails . . . Simultaneously under each nail . . . Hellish pain! You
immediately lose consciousness. I don't even remember, I know the
pain was horrible, but I don't remember it. I was drawn on logs.
Maybe that's not the word, maybe I've got it wrong. But this is what
I remember: there was a log here and a log there, and they put you in
between . . . Then some kind of machine is turned on . . . And you
hear how your bones crunch, get dislocated . . . Did it last long? I
don't remember that either . . . I was tortured on an electric chair . . .
That was when I spat in the face of one of the torturers . . . Young,
old, I don't remember anything. They stripped me naked, and that
one came up to me and grabbed me by the breast . . . I could only

spit . . . I couldn't do anything else. So I spat in his face. They sat me on the electric chair . . .

I've had very little tolerance for electricity ever since. I remember it just starts jolting you. Now I can't even iron my laundry . . . All my life it's been so. I start ironing, and I feel the current through my whole body. I can't do anything that's related to electricity. Maybe I needed some sort of psychotherapy after the war? I don't know. But I've already lived my life this way . . .

I don't know why I'm crying so much today. I didn't cry then . . .

They sentenced me to death by hanging. They put me in the cell for the condemned. There were two other women. You know, we didn't cry, we didn't panic: we knew what awaited us when we joined the underground fighters, and so we remained calm. We talked about poetry, remembered our favorite operas . . . We talked a lot about *Anna Karenina* . . . about love . . . We didn't even mention our children, we were afraid to mention them. We even smiled, cheered each other up. So we spent two and a half days . . . In the morning of the third day they called me. We said goodbye, kissed without tears. There was no fear. Apparently I was so used to the thought of death that the fear was already gone. And so were the tears. There was some sort of emptiness. I no longer thought of anyone . . .

We drove for a long time, I don't even remember how long. I was saying goodbye to life . . . But the truck stopped, and we . . . there were about twenty of us . . . We couldn't get out of the truck, we were so worn out. They threw us on the ground like sacks, and the commanding officer ordered us to crawl to the barracks. He urged us on with a whip . . . Near one of the barracks a woman was standing, breastfeeding her child. And somehow, you know . . . There were dogs and guards, all dumbfounded, standing there and not touching her. The commanding officer saw that scene . . . He rushed at her. He snatched the baby out of its mother's hands . . . And, you know, there was a pump there, a water pump, and so he smashed the child against that iron. His brains gushed out . . . Milk . . . And I see the mother fall . . . I understand, I'm a doctor . . . I understand that she's had heart failure . . .

. . . They led us to work. They led us through the city, through familiar streets. We just started to go down, there was a steep hill, and suddenly I hear a voice: "Mama, mamochka!" And I see my aunt Dasha standing there, and my daughter is running from the sidewalk. They happened to be walking down the street and saw me. My daughter ran and immediately threw herself on my neck. And just imagine, there were dogs, they were specially trained to attack people, but not a single dog moved from its place. They're trained to tear you to pieces if you come close, but here none of them moved. My daughter ran up to me, and I didn't cry, I only said, "My little daughter! Natashenka, don't cry. I'll come home soon." The guards stood there, and the dogs. Nobody touched her . . .

And I didn't cry then . . .

At the age of five my daughter read prayers, not poems. Aunt Dasha taught her to pray. She prayed for her papa and mama, for us to stay alive.

In 1944, on the thirteenth of February, I was sent off to a fascist hard-labor camp . . . I wound up in the Croisette concentration camp, on the shores of the English Channel.

Spring . . . On the day of the Paris Commune, the French organized our escape. I left and joined the maquis.[*]

I was awarded the French Order of the Croix de Guerre . . .

After the war, I came back home . . . I remember . . . The first stop on our land . . . We all jumped off the train and kissed the ground, embraced it. I remember I was wearing a white smock. I fell to the ground, kissed it, and put whole handfuls in my bosom. I thought to myself, surely I won't ever part with it again, my very own land . . .

I arrived in Minsk, but my husband wasn't home. My daughter

---

[*] The rural French underground resistance forces during the German occupation, from the word for "bush" or "scrubland."

was at Aunt Dasha's. My husband had been arrested by the NKVD; he was in prison. I went there . . . And what do I hear there? . . . They tell me, "Your husband is a traitor." But my husband and I worked together in the underground. The two of us. He was a brave, honest man. I realized that someone had denounced him . . . Slander . . . "No," I say, "my husband can't be a traitor. I believe him. He's a true Communist." His interrogator . . . He started yelling at me, "Silence, French prostitute! Silence!" He had lived under the occupation, had been captured, had been taken to Germany, had been in a fascist concentration camp—it was all suspicious. One question: how did he stay alive? Why didn't he die? Even the dead were under suspicion . . . Even them . . . And they didn't take into consideration that we fought, we sacrificed everything for the sake of victory. And we won . . . The people won! But Stalin still didn't trust the people. That was how our Motherland repaid us. For our love, for our blood . . .

I went everywhere . . . I wrote to all the authorities. My husband was released after six months. They broke one of his ribs, injured his kidney . . . When he was captured by the fascists, they smashed his skull, broke his arm. He turned gray there, and in 1945 the NKVD made him an invalid for good. I took care of him for years; I pulled him out of his illnesses. But I wasn't allowed to say anything against them; he wouldn't hear of it . . . "It was a mistake," that's all. The main thing, he thought, was that we won. That's all—period. And I believed him.

I didn't cry. I didn't cry then . . .

Nadezhda Vikentyevna Khatchenko
UNDERGROUND FIGHTER

How do you explain to a child? How do you explain death to him . . .

I was walking down the street with my son, and dead people were lying there, on one side and the other. I was telling him about Little Red Riding Hood, and around us were dead people. It was when we were returning from the evacuation. We arrived at my mother's, and he wasn't well. He crawled under his bed and sat there for whole days. He was five years old, and I couldn't get him to go outside . . .

For a year I struggled with him. I couldn't figure out what was the matter. We lived in a basement—when someone walked by in the street, we could only see his boots. And so one day he came out from under the bed, saw someone's boots out the window, and began to scream . . . Afterward I remembered that a fascist had hit him with his boot . . .

Somehow, in the end, it passed. He was playing in the yard with other kids, came home one evening and asked, "Mama, what's a papa?"

I explained to him, "He's fair, handsome, he's in the army."

And when Minsk was liberated, the first to burst into the city were the tanks. And so my son came running home crying: "My papa's not there! They are all dark, none of them are fair . . ." It was in July, and the tank crews were all young, tanned.

My husband came back from the war an invalid. He came back not young, but old, and I was in trouble: my son was used to thinking that his father was fair, handsome, but a sick old man came back. And for a long time my son didn't accept him as his father. He didn't know what to call him. I had to get them accustomed to each other.

My husband came home from work late, and I met him: "Why are you so late? Dima was worried: 'Where's my daddy?'"

He, too, after six years of war (he had also fought against the Japanese), had lost touch with his son. With his home.

And when I bought something, I said to my son, "Daddy bought this, he cares about you . . ."

Soon they became closer . . .

Maria Alexandrovna Arestova

ENGINEER

My biography . . .

Since 1929 I worked on the railroad. I was an assistant engineer. At the time there were no female locomotive engineers in the Soviet Union. But I dreamed. The head of the locomotive depot threw up his hands: "This girl, she just wants a man's profession." But I persevered. And in 1931 I became the first one . . . I was the first female engineer. You wouldn't believe it, when I was driving the locomotive, people gathered in the stations: "A girl is driving the locomotive."

Our engine was just undergoing a blowdown—that is, it was getting repaired. My husband and I took turns driving, because we already had a baby, and we settled on this: if he drove, I stayed with the baby; if I drove, he stayed home. On that very day, my husband had returned, and I was supposed to go. I woke up in the morning and heard something abnormal in the street, noisy. I turned on the radio: "War!"

I told my husband, "Lenya, get up! War! Get up, it's war!"

He ran to the depot and came back in tears: "War! War! Do you know what it is—war?"

What are we to do? What do we do with the baby?

I was evacuated along with my son to Ulyanovsk, to the rear. They gave us a two-room apartment. The apartment was nice, even now I don't have one like that. They took my son in the kindergarten. All was well. Everyone loved me. What else! A female engineer, and the first one . . . You won't believe it, I lived there a short time, less than half a year. I couldn't stay longer: how is it, everyone's defending the Motherland, and I sit at home!

My husband came. "So, Marusya, are you going to sit here in the rear?"

"No," I said, "let's go."

At the time they were organizing a special reserve unit servicing the front. My husband and I asked to join it. My husband was a senior engineer, and I was an engineer. For four years we drove a freight car, and our son with us. He didn't even get to see a cat during the entire war. When he got hold of a cat near Kiev, our train was being heavily bombarded, five planes were attacking us. He hugged her and said, "Dear kitty, I'm so glad I got to see you. I never see anyone. Come and sit with me, let me kiss you." A child . . . Children need children's things . . . He fell asleep saying, "Mama, we have a cat. Now we have a real home." You can't make up something like that . . . Don't leave it out . . . Be sure to write about the cat . . .

We were constantly being bombarded, shot at by machine guns. Their target was the locomotive; their main objective was to kill the engineer, to destroy the locomotive. The planes flew down and hit the freight car and the locomotive. And my son was sitting in the freight car. Above all, I was afraid for my son. I can't describe it . . . When they bombed us, I took him with me from the freight car to the locomotive. I grabbed him, pressed him to my heart: "Let us die from the same shrapnel." But could that be? Clearly, that's why we stayed alive. Write that down as well . . .

My locomotive was my life, my youth, the most beautiful thing in my life. Even now I wish I could drive trains, but they won't let me—I'm old . . .

How frightening to have a single child. How foolish . . . Now we live together with my son's family. He's a doctor, the head of his department. We have a small apartment. But I never go anywhere on holidays, I never go away on vacation . . . I can't describe it . . . I don't want to be away from my son, from my grandchildren. I'm afraid to part with them even for a day. And my son doesn't go anywhere. He's been working for nearly twenty-five years, and never once has he used a travel voucher. At work, they noticed he never asked for one. "Mama, I'd rather stay with you"—that's what he says. And my daughter-in-law is the same. I can't describe it . . . We don't own a country place only because we can't part, even for a few days. I can't live without them even for a minute.

Whoever has been to war knows what it is to part even for a day. For a single day . . .

OF THE SILENCE OF THOSE WHO
COULD NOW SPEAK

Valentina Evdokimovna M—va
PARTISAN LIAISON

To this day I speak in a whisper . . . About . . . That . . . In a whisper. After more than forty years . . .

I've forgotten the war . . . Because even after the war I lived in fear. I lived in hell.

Here was the Victory, here was joy. Here we were already gathering bricks, metal, and starting to clean up the city. We worked day and night; I don't remember when we slept or what we ate. We worked and worked.

September . . . It was a warm September, I remember a lot of sun. I remember the fruit. A lot of fruit. They sold bucketloads of Antonovka apples at the market. And that day . . . I was hanging the laundry on the balcony . . . I remember everything in detail, because from that day, everything changed in my life. Everything was shattered. Turned upside down. I was hanging the laundry . . . White bedsheets—I always had white sheets. My mother taught me how to wash them with sand instead of soap. We would go to the river to get sand, I knew a spot there. And so . . . The laundry . . . My neighbor called me from downstairs, shouting in a voice not her own, "Valya!! Valya!!" I rushed downstairs. My first thought was: where is my son? Back then, you know, the boys ran around in the ruins, played war and found real grenades, real mines. They blew up . . . They were left with no hands, no legs . . . I remember how we wouldn't let them go away from us, but they were young boys, they were curious. We yelled: stay home—five minutes later they were gone. They were attracted by weapons . . . Especially after the war . . . I rushed downstairs. I went out to the yard, and there was my husband . . . My Ivan . . . My dearest little husband . . . Vanechka!! He had come back . . . He had come back from the front! Alive! I kiss him, I touch him. I stroke his shirt, his hands. He had come back . . . My legs were weak . . . But he . . . He stands as if turned to stone. Well, he stands stiff as cardboard. He doesn't smile, he doesn't hug me. As if frozen. I got scared: he was probably shell-shocked, I thought. Maybe he's deaf. But never mind, the main thing is he's back. I'll look after him, I'll nurse him. I've seen so many other women living with such husbands, but everyone still envied them. All this flashed through my head in a second. My legs were weak from happiness. They trembled. He's alive! Oh, my dear, our women's lot . . .

The neighbors gathered at once. They were all happy, they all hugged each other. And he—a stone figure. Silent. They all noticed.

I said, "Vanya . . . Vanechka . . ."

"Let's go inside."

All right, let's go. I clung to his shoulder . . . Happy! I was full of joy and happiness. And proud! He sat down on a stool and remained silent.

"Vanya . . . Vanechka . . ."

"You know . . ." And he couldn't speak. He wept.

"Vanya . . ."

We had one night. Just one night.

The next day they came for him, knocking on the door in the morning. He was smoking and waiting; he already knew they would come. He told me very little . . . He didn't have time . . . He had gone through Romania, Czechoslovakia. He brought back honors, but he came in fear. He had already been questioned, had been through two government interrogations. He had been marked, because he had been a prisoner. In the first weeks of the war . . . He was captured near Smolensk, and was supposed to shoot himself. He wanted to, I know he wanted to . . . They had run out of bullets—not only to shoot, he had no bullets to kill himself. He was wounded in the leg, and was captured wounded. Before his very eyes, the commissar smashed his own head with a stone . . . The last bullet misfired . . . Before his very eyes . . . A Soviet officer doesn't surrender, we don't have captives, we have traitors. Thus spoke Comrade Stalin, who renounced his own son who had been captured. My husband . . . Mine . . . The interrogators yelled at him, "Why are you alive? Why did you stay alive?" He escaped from captivity . . . He escaped to the woods, to the Ukrainian partisans, and when Ukraine was liberated, he asked to go to the front. He was in Czechoslovakia on Victory Day. He was recommended for a decoration . . .

We had one night . . . If only I had known . . . I wanted to have another child, I wanted a daughter . . .

In the morning he was taken away . . . They took him out of bed . . . I sat down at the table in the kitchen and waited for our son to wake up. Our son had just turned eleven. I knew he would wake up, and the first thing he would ask would be, "Where is our papa?" What answer could I give him? How was I to explain to the neighbors? To my mother?

My husband came home seven years later . . . My son and I waited for him, through four years of war, and after the Victory, through another seven years of Kolyma.* Labor camp. Eleven years we waited. Our son grew up . . .

I learned to keep silent . . . Where is your husband? Who is your father? In every questionnaire there was this question: were any of your relatives in captivity? The school didn't accept me as a cleaning woman when I applied, they didn't trust me to clean the floors. I became an enemy of the people, the wife of an enemy of the people. A traitor. My entire life was a waste . . . Before the war I was a teacher, I graduated from teachers' college, but after the war I carried bricks at construction sites. Eh, my life . . . If this comes out incoherent, confused, forgive me. I rush . . . Sometimes, at night . . . How many

---

* The Kolyma region in far eastern Siberia, a vast, unsettled, subarctic territory, was made into a system of forced labor camps during the early 1930s. The prisoners were engaged in gold mining.

nights I spent lying alone and telling someone my story over and over. But in the daytime I kept silent.

Nowadays we can talk about everything. I want to . . . I want to ask: who is to blame that in the first months of the war millions of soldiers and officers were captured? I want to know . . . Who beheaded the army before the war, shooting and slandering the Red commanders—as German spies, as Japanese spies. I want to . . . Who trusted in the Budenny Cavalry back then, when Hitler was armed with tanks and planes? Who assured us, "Our border is secure . . ." Yet in the very first days, the army was counting its bullets . . .

I want . . . I can ask now . . . Where is my life? Our life? But I keep silent, and my husband keeps silent. We're afraid even now. We're frightened . . . And so we'll die scared. Bitter and ashamed . . .

"AND SHE PUTS HER HAND TO HER HEART . . ."

———

And finally—Victory . . .

If life for them used to be divided into peace and war, now it was into war and Victory.

Again two different worlds, two different lives. After learning to hate, they now had to learn to love again. To recall forgotten feelings. Forgotten words.

The person shaped by war had to be shaped by something that was not war.

OF THE LAST DAYS OF THE WAR, WHEN KILLING WAS REPUGNANT

Sofya Adamovna Kuntsevich
MEDICAL ASSISTANT

We were happy . . .

We crossed the border—the Motherland was free. Our land . . . I didn't recognize the soldiers, they were changed people. Everybody smiled. They put on clean shirts. They found flowers somewhere. I had never known such happy people. I had never seen it. I thought that when we entered Germany, I would have no pity for them, they would be shown no mercy. We had so much hatred stored up in our breasts! And hurt! Why should I feel sorry for his child? Why should I feel sorry for his mother? Why shouldn't I destroy his house? He didn't feel sorry . . . He killed . . . Burned . . . But I? I . . . I . . . I . . . Why? Why-y-y? I wanted to see their wives, their mothers, who had given birth to such sons. How would they look us in the eye? I wanted to look them in the eye . . .

I wondered: What will become of me? Of our soldiers? We all remember . . . How are we going to stand it? How much strength does it take to stand it? We came to some village; children were running around, hungry, miserable. Afraid of us . . . They hid . . . I, who swore I hated them all . . . I gathered from our soldiers all they had left of their rations, any piece of sugar, and gave it to the German children. Of course, I didn't forget . . . I remembered everything . . . But I couldn't calmly look into their hungry children's eyes. Early in the morning, German children stood in line near our kitchens, we gave them firsts and seconds.

Every child had a bag for bread slung over one shoulder, a can for soup at their belts, and something for seconds—kasha, peas. We fed them, treated them. We even caressed them . . . The first time I caressed one . . . I got scared . . . Me . . . Me! Caressing a German child . . .

My mouth went dry from agitation. But soon I got used to it. And they did too . . .

Nina Petrovna Sakova
LIEUTENANT, PARAMEDIC

I got to Germany . . . All the way from Moscow . . .

I was a senior paramedic in a tank regiment. We had T-34 tanks; they burned up quickly. Very scary. Before the war I had never even heard a gunshot. Once, when we were driving to the front, they were bombing some place very far away, and it felt to me as if all the ground was shaking. I was seventeen, I had just graduated from nursing school. And so it turned out, I just came and went straight into battle.

I got out of the tank . . . Fire . . . The sky was burning . . . The earth was burning . . . The metal was burning . . . Here were corpses, and there someone shouted, "Save me . . . Help me" . . . Such horror gripped me! I don't know how I didn't run away. How did I not flee the battlefield? It's so scary, there are no words, only feelings. Before I couldn't stand it, but now I can watch war movies, though I still cry.

I got to Germany . . .

The first thing I saw on German soil was a handmade sign, right by the road: "Here she is—accursed Germany!"

We entered a village . . . The shutters were all closed. They had dropped everything and fled on bicycles. Goebbels had persuaded them that the Russians would come and would hack, stab, slaughter. We opened the doors of the houses; there was no one, or they all lay killed or poisoned. Children lay there. Shot, poisoned . . . What did we feel? Joy, that we had defeated them, and that now they were suffering the way we did. A feeling of vengeance. But we felt sorry for the children . . .

We found an old woman.

I say to her, "We won."

She starts to cry: "I have two sons who died in Russia."

"And who is to blame? So many of us died!"

She answers, "Hitler . . ."

"Hitler didn't decide by himself. It's your children, husbands . . ."

Then she fell silent.

I got to Germany . . .

I wanted to tell my mother . . . But my mother died of starvation during the war. They had no bread, no salt, they had nothing. And my brother was lying in the hospital badly wounded. Only my sister waited for me at home. She wrote that when our troops entered Orel, she grabbed all the soldier girls by the overcoat. She thought I would surely be there. I had to come back . . .

Anastasia Vasilyevna Voropaeva
CORPORAL, SEARCHLIGHT OPERATOR

The roads of Victory . . .

You can't imagine the roads of Victory! Freed prisoners went with carts, bundles, national flags. Russians, Poles, French, Czechs . . . They all intermingled, each going his own way. They all embraced us. Kissed us.

I met some young Russian girls. I started talking to them, and they told me . . . One of them was pregnant. The prettiest one. She had been raped by the boss they worked for. He had forced her to live with him. She went along crying and beating her own stomach: "I won't bring a Fritz home! I won't!" They tried to reason with her . . . But she hanged herself . . . Along with her little Fritz . . .

It was back then that you should have listened to us—listened and recorded it. It's a pity that no one thought of hearing us out then; everyone just repeated the word "Victory," and the rest seemed unimportant.

One day a friend and I were riding bikes. A German woman was walking along; I believe she had three children—two in a baby carriage, one by her side, holding on to her skirt. She was so exhausted. And so, you see, she walks up to us, goes on her knees and bows. Like this . . . To the ground . . . We didn't understand what she said. And she puts her hand to her heart, and points at her children. We more or less understood, she was crying, bowing, and thanking us that her children had stayed alive . . .

She was somebody's wife. Her husband probably fought on the eastern front . . . In Russia . . .

A. Ratkina

JUNIOR SERGEANT, TELEPHONE OPERATOR

One of our officers fell in love with a German girl . . .

Our superiors heard about it . . . He was demoted and sent to the rear. If he had raped her . . . That . . . Of course, it happened . . . Not many write about it, but that's the law of war. The men spent so many years without women, and of course, there was hatred. When we entered a town or a village, for the first three days there was looting and . . . Well, in secret, naturally . . . You understand . . . After three days you could wind up in court. But in the heat of the moment . . . For three days they drank and . . . And here—love. The officer himself admitted it before the special section—love. Of course, that was treason . . . To fall in love with a German—the daughter or wife of the enemy? That's . . . And . . . Well, in short, they took away the photographs, her address. Of course . . .

I remember . . . Of course, I remember a German woman who had been raped. She was lying naked, with a grenade stuck between her legs . . . Now I feel ashamed, but then I didn't. Feelings change, of course. In the first days we had one feeling, and afterward another . . . After several months . . . Five German girls came to our battalion . . . To our commander. They were weeping . . . The gynecologist examined them: they had wounds. Jagged wounds. Their underwear was all bloody . . . They had been raped all night long. The soldiers stood in line . . .

Don't record this . . . Switch off the tape recorder . . . It's true! It's all true! . . . We formed up our battalion . . . We told those German girls: go and look, and if you recognize someone, we'll shoot him on the spot. We won't consider his rank. We're ashamed! But they sat there and wept. They didn't want to . . . They didn't want more blood. So they said . . . Then each one got a loaf of bread. Of course, all of this is war . . . Of course . . .

You think it was easy to forgive? To see intact . . . white . . . houses with tiled roofs. With roses . . . I myself wanted to hurt them . . . Of course . . . I wanted to see their tears . . . It was impossible to become good all at once. Fair and kind. As good as you are now. To pity them. That would take me dozens of years . . .

Aglaia Borisovna Nesteruk

SERGEANT, LIAISON

Our native land was liberated . . . Dying became totally unbearable, burials became totally unbearable. People died for a foreign land, were buried in a foreign land. They explained to us that the enemy had to be finished off. The enemy was still dangerous . . . We all understood . . . But it was such a pity to die . . . Nobody wanted to . . .

I remembered many signs along the road. They looked like crosses: "Here she is—accursed Germany!" Everybody remembered that sign . . .

And everybody was waiting for that moment . . . Now we'll understand . . . Now we'll see . . . Where do they come from? What is their land like, their houses? Could it be that they are ordinary people? That they lived ordinary lives? At the front, I couldn't imagine ever being able to read Heine's poems again. My beloved Goethe. I could never again listen to Wagner . . . Before the war, I grew up in a family of musicians, I loved German music—Bach, Beethoven. The great Bach! I crossed all of this out of my world. Then we saw, they showed us the crematoriums . . . Auschwitz . . . Heaps of women's clothing, children's shoes . . . Gray ash . . . They spread it on the fields, under the cabbage. Under the lettuce . . . I couldn't listen to German music anymore . . . A lot of time passed before I went back to Bach. Began to play Mozart.

Finally, we were on their land . . . The first thing that struck us was the good roads. The big farmhouses . . . Flowerpots, pretty curtains in the windows, even in the barns. White tablecloths in the houses. Expensive tableware. Porcelain. There I saw a washing machine for the first time . . . We couldn't understand why they had to fight if they lived so well. Our people huddled in dugouts, while they had white tablecloths. Coffee in small cups . . . I had only seen them in the museum. Those small cups . . . I forgot to tell you about one shocking thing, we were all shocked . . . We were attacking, and took the first German trenches . . . We jumped in, and there was still warm coffee in thermos bottles. The smell of coffee . . . Biscuits. White sheets. Clean towels. Toilet paper . . . We didn't have any of that. What sheets? We slept on straw, on sticks. Other times we went for two or three days without warm food. And our soldiers shot at those thermos bottles . . . At that coffee . . .

In German houses I saw coffee sets shattered by bullets. Flowerpots. Pillows . . . Baby carriages . . . But still we couldn't do to them what they had done to us. Force them to suffer the way we suffered.

It was hard for us to understand where their hatred came from. Ours was understandable. But theirs?

We got permission to send packages home. Soap, sugar . . . Someone sent shoes. Germans have sturdy shoes, watches, leather goods. Everybody looked for watches. I couldn't, I was disgusted. I didn't want to take anything from them, though I knew that my mother and my sisters were living with strangers. Our house had been burned down. When I returned home, I told my mother, and she hugged me: "I, too, couldn't have taken anything from them. They killed our papa."

Only dozens of years after the war did I take a small volume of Heine in my hands. And the recordings of German composers that I had loved before the war . . .

Albina Alexandrovna Gantimurova
SERGEANT MAJOR, SCOUT

This was already in Berlin . . . This incident happened to me: I was walking down the street, and a boy came running toward me with a submachine gun—a Volkssturm.* The war was already over. The last days. My hand was on my submachine gun. Ready. He looked at me, blinked, and burst into tears. I couldn't believe it—I was in tears, too. I felt so sorry for him; there was this kid standing with his stupid submachine gun. And I shoved him toward a wrecked building, under the gateway: "Hide," I said. He was afraid I was going to shoot him right then—I was wearing a hat, it wasn't clear if I was a girl or a man. He took my hand. He cried! I patted his head. He was dumbstruck. It was war after all . . . I was dumbstruck myself! I had hated them for the entire war! Fair or unfair, it's still disgusting to kill, especially in the last days of the war . . .

Lilya Mikhailovna Butko
SURGICAL NURSE

I regret . . . I didn't fulfill one request . . .

They brought a wounded German to our hospital. I think he was a pilot. His thigh was crushed, and gangrene had set in. Some kind of pity took hold of me. He lay there and kept silent.

I understood a little German. I asked him, "Do you want to drink?"

"No."

The other wounded men knew there was a wounded German in the ward. He was lying separately. I went to him, and they got indignant: "So you bring water to the enemy?"

"He's dying . . . I have to help him . . ."

His leg was all blue, nothing could be done. Infection devours a man in no time; the man burns out overnight.

I gave him water, and he looked at me and suddenly said, *"Hitler kaputt!"*

That was in 1942. We were encircled near Kharkov.

---

* The Volkssturm was a national militia organized by the Nazi Party during the last months of World War II. It drafted males between the ages of sixteen and sixty.

I asked, "Why?"

"Hitler kaputt!"

Then I answered, "That's what you say and think now, because you're lying here. But there you were killing . . ."

He: "I didn't shoot, I didn't kill. They made me. But I didn't shoot . . ."

"Everybody makes excuses like that when they're captured."

And suddenly he asks me, "I really . . . really . . . beg of you, Frau . . ." and he hands me a packet of photographs. He shows me: there is his mother, himself, his brother, sisters . . . A beautiful picture. He writes down an address on the other side. "You will get there. You will!" This was a German speaking, in 1942, near Kharkov. "So please drop this in the mailbox."

He wrote the address on one photograph, but he had an envelope full of them. And I carried those photographs around for a long time. I was upset when I lost them during a heavy bombardment. By the time we got to Germany, the envelope was gone . . .

Nina Vasilyevna Ilinskaya
NURSE

I remember a battle . . .

In that battle we captured many Germans. Some of them were wounded. We bandaged their wounds; they moaned like our lads did. And it was hot . . . Scorching hot! We found a teapot and gave them water. In the open. We were under fire. An order: quickly entrench and camouflage yourselves.

We started digging trenches. The Germans stared. We explained to them: so, help us dig, get to work. When they understood what we wanted from them, they looked at us with horror; they took it that once they dug those pits, we would stand them by those pits and shoot them. They expected . . . You should have seen their horrified looks as they dug . . . Their faces . . .

And when they saw that we bandaged them, gave them water, and told them to hide in the trenches they had dug, they couldn't come to their senses, they were at a loss . . . One German started crying . . . He was an older man. He cried and didn't hide his tears from anyone . . .

OF A COMPOSITION WITH CHILDISH
MISTAKES AND COMIC MOVIES

Vera Iosifovna Khoreva
ARMY SURGEON

The war was ending . . .

The political commissar called me. "Vera Iosifovna, you will have to work with the German wounded."

By that time my two brothers had already been killed. "I won't."

"But, you understand, it's necessary."

"I'm unable. I lost two brothers. I can't stand them, I'm ready to kill them, not treat them. Try to understand me . . ."

"It's an order."

"If it's an order, I'll obey. I'm a soldier."

I treated those wounded, did everything I had to, but it was hard for me. To touch them, to ease their pain. That's when I got my first gray hair. Right then. I did everything with them: operated, fed, anesthetized—everything I was supposed to. One thing only I couldn't do—that was the evening rounds. In the morning you had to bandage the wounded, take their pulse—in short, you proceeded like a doctor—but during the evening rounds you had to talk to the patients, ask how they felt. That I couldn't do. Bandage, operate—that

I could do, but talk with them—no. I warned the commissar straight off: "I won't do the evening rounds for them . . ."

Ekaterina Petrovna Shalygina
NURSE

In Germany . . . In our hospitals we already had many wounded Germans . . .

I remember my first wounded German. He had gangrene; we amputated his leg . . . And he lay in my ward . . .

In the evening, they said to me, "Katya, go check on your German."

I went. Maybe a hemorrhage, or something. He lay there, awake. He had no temperature, nothing. He just stared and stared, and then pulled out such a tiny pistol: "Here . . ."

He spoke German. I don't remember now, but back then I understood as much as I'd kept from my school lessons.

"Here . . ." he said. "I wanted to kill you, but now you kill me."

Meaning that we had saved him. He killed us, and we saved him. But I couldn't tell him the truth, that he was dying . . .

I left the ward and noticed unexpectedly that I was in tears . . .

Maria Anatolyevna Flerovskaya
POLITICAL WORKER

I might have had an encounter . . . I was afraid of that encounter . . .

When I was in school . . . I studied in a school with a German orientation . . . German school children would come to visit us. In Moscow. We went with them to the theater, we sang together. One of those German boys . . . He sang so well. We became friends. I even fell in love with him . . . And so, all through the war I thought: what if I meet him and recognize him? Could he also be among them? I'm very emotional, ever since I was a child, I'm very impressionable. Terribly!

One day I was walking in the field, the battle had just ended . . . We picked up our dead, only Germans were left . . . It seemed to me he was lying there . . . A similar-looking young man . . . On our land . . . I stood over him for a while . . .

A. C—va
ANTIAIRCRAFT GUNNER

You want to know the truth? I'm scared of it myself . . .

One of our soldiers . . . How can I explain this to you? His whole family had died. He . . . Nerves . . . Maybe he was drunk? The closer victory came, the more they drank. There was always wine to be found in the houses and basements. Schnapps. They drank and drank. He grabbed a submachine gun and ran into a German house . . . He unloaded the entire magazine . . . Nobody had time to stop him. We ran . . . But in the house, only corpses were left . . . Children lay there . . . They took away his submachine gun and tied him up. He cursed his head off: "Let me shoot myself!"

He was arrested and tried—and shot. I felt sorry for him. Everybody felt sorry for him. He had fought the entire war. As far as Berlin . . .

Are you allowed to write about this? Before, you weren't . . .

Xenia Klimentyevna Belko
LABOR-FRONT FIGHTER

The war waited for me . . .

Just as I turned eighteen . . . They brought me a written notice: present yourself to the district committee, bring three days' worth of food, a set of underwear, a mug, a spoon. It was called mobilization for the labor front.

They brought us to the town of Novotroitsk, in the Orenburg region. We started working in a factory. It was so freezing cold that my coat would freeze in our room; you took it and it was heavy as a log. We worked for four years without a vacation, without holidays.

We waited and waited for the war to end. Full stop. At three o'clock in the morning, there was noise in the dormitory; the director of the factory came, along with the other superiors. "Victory!" I didn't have the strength to get up from my bunk. They sat me up, but I fell back. For the whole day they couldn't get me up. I was paralyzed from joy, from strong emotions. I only stood up the next day . . . I went outside, I wanted to hug and kiss each and every one . . .

Elena Pavlovna Shalova
KOMSOMOL LEADER OF AN INFANTRY BATTALION

What a beautiful word—victory . . .

I wrote my name on the Reichstag . . . I wrote with charcoal, with what was at hand: "You were defeated by a Russian girl from Saratov." Everybody left something on the wall, some words. Confessions and curses . . .

Victory! My girlfriends asked me, "What do you want to be?" And we were so hungry during the war . . . Unbearably . . . We wanted to eat our fill at least once. I had a dream—when I got my first postwar salary, I would buy a big box of cookies. What do I want to be after the war? A cook, of course. I still work in the public food industry.

A second question: "When will you get married?" As soon as possible . . . I dreamed of kissing. I wanted terribly to kiss . . . I also wanted to sing. To sing! There . . .

Tamara Ustinovna Vorobeykova

UNDERGROUND FIGHTER

I learned how to shoot, throw grenades . . . Lay mines. Give first aid . . .

But in four years . . . During the war I forgot all the rules of grammar. The entire school program. I could disassemble a submachine gun with my eyes closed, but I wrote my application essay to the institute with childish mistakes and barely any commas. I was saved by my military decorations; I was accepted at the institute. I began to study. I read books and didn't understand them, read poems and didn't understand them. I'd forgotten those words . . .

At night I had nightmares: SS officers, dogs barking, cries of agony. When dying, men often whisper something, and that is even more frightening than their cries. Everything came back to me . . . A man was being led out to execution . . . In his eyes there was fear. You could see that he didn't believe it, until the last moment he didn't believe it. And curiosity, there was curiosity as well. He stood facing the submachine gun, and at the last moment he covered himself with his hands. He covered his face . . . In the mornings, my head was swollen from the shouting . . .

During the war I never thought about anything, but after it I began to think.

Going over it all . . . It all came back again and again . . . I couldn't sleep . . . The doctors forbade me to study. But the girls—my roommates in the dormitory—told me to forget about the doctors, and took me under their patronage. Every night they took turns dragging me to the movies to watch a comedy. "You have to learn to laugh. To laugh a lot." Whether I wanted or not, they dragged me. There weren't many comedies, and I watched each one a hundred times, a hundred times at a minimum. At first when I laughed it was like crying . . .

But the nightmares went away. I was able to study . . .

OF THE MOTHERLAND,
STALIN, AND RED CLOTH

Tamara Ivanovna Kuraeva

NURSE

It was spring . . .

Young boys died, they died in the spring . . . In March, in April . . .

I remember that in spring, at the time when the gardens were in bloom and everyone was waiting for victory, burying people was harder than ever. Even if others have already said it, write it down again. I remember it so well . . .

For two and a half years I was at the front. My hands bandaged and washed thousands of wounds . . . Bandages and more bandages . . . Once, as I went to change my headscarf, I leaned against the window frame and dozed off. I came to myself feeling refreshed. I ran into the doctor, and he started scolding me. I didn't understand anything . . . He went off, after giving me two extra assignments, and my workmate explained to me what it was about: I had been absent for over an hour. It turned out I had fallen asleep.

Nowadays I'm in poor health, my nerves are weak. When someone asks me, "What decorations did you receive?" I'm embarrassed to admit I don't have any decorations; there was no time to give me decorations. Maybe there was no time because many of us fought in the war and we each did what we could . . . We each did our best . . . How could everyone receive decorations? But we all received the greatest decoration of all—the ninth of May. Victory Day!

I remember an unusual death . . . At the time, no one could figure it out. We were busy with other things . . . But I remember . . . One of our captains died on the first day we set foot on German soil. We knew that his entire family had died during the occupation. He was a brave man, he was so looking forward to . . . He was afraid to die before that. Not to live till the day when he would see their land, their misery, their sorrow. See them cry, see them suffer . . . See broken stones in place of their homes . . . He died just like that, not wounded, nothing. He got there, looked—and died.

Even now, when I remember it, I wonder: why did he die?

Maria Yakovlevna Yezhova

LIEUTENANT OF THE GUARDS, COMMANDER OF A MEDICAL PLATOON

I asked to go to the front straight from the train . . . At once . . . A unit was leaving—I joined it. At the time, I figured that from the front, I would come home sooner, if only by a day, than from the rear. I left my mother at home. Even now, our girls remember: "She wouldn't stay at the medical platoon." And it's true, I would come to the medical platoon, wash up, grab some clean clothes—and go back to my trench. At the front line. I didn't think about myself. You crawl, you run . . . Only the smell of blood . . . I couldn't get used to the smell of blood . . .

After the war, I became a midwife in a maternity ward—but I didn't stay there for long. Not for long . . . For a short while . . . I'm allergic to the smell of blood; my body simply wouldn't accept it . . . I had seen so much blood during the war that I couldn't stand it anymore. My body wouldn't accept it anymore. I left Maternity and went to Emergency Aid. I got nettle rash, I was suffocating.

I sewed a blouse from a piece of red cloth, and by the next day some sort of red spots had spread all over my hands. Blisters. No red cloth, no red flowers—roses or carnations, my body wouldn't accept it. Nothing red, nothing that had the color of blood . . . Even now I have nothing red in my house. You won't find anything. Human blood is very bright, I have never seen such a bright color, not in nature, not in any painting. Pomegranate juice is somewhat similar, but not entirely. Ripe pomegranate . . .

Elena Borisovna Zvyagintseva
PRIVATE, ARMORER

Oh, oh, oh . . . Ah, ah, ah . . . Everybody oh'd and ah'd at how colorful I was. Jewelry all over. Even during the war I was like that. Not warlike. I wore all kinds of baubles . . . It's a good thing our commander was, as we'd say now, a democrat. Not from the barracks, but from the university. Just imagine, an assistant professor. With good manners. At that time . . . A rare bird . . . A rare bird had flown to us . . .

I love wearing rings, even cheap ones, so long as there are lots of them, on both hands. I like good perfume. Fashionable. All kinds of trinkets. Various and many. In our family they always laughed, "What should we give to our crazy Lenka for her birthday? A ring, of course." After the war, my brother made me my first ring out of a tin can. And a pendant out of a piece of green bottle glass that he polished. And another one of light brown glass.

I hang everything shiny on myself, like a magpie. Nobody believes that I was in the war. I myself can't believe it anymore. At this very moment, as we sit and talk, I don't believe it. But in that box lies the Order of the Red Star . . . The most elegant medal . . . Isn't it pretty? They gave it to me on purpose. Ha, ha, ha . . . To be serious . . . For history, right? This thing of yours is recording . . . So, it's for history . . . I'll say this: if you're not a woman, you can't survive war. I never envied men. Not in my childhood, not in my youth. Not during the war. I was always glad to be a woman. People say that weapons—submachine guns, pistols—are beautiful, that they conceal many human thoughts, passions, but I never found them beautiful. I've seen the admiration of men looking at a fine pistol; I find it incomprehensible. I'm a woman.

Why did I stay single? I had wooers. Wooers enough . . . But here I am single. I have fun by myself. All my friends are young. I love youth. I'm afraid of growing old more than of the war. You came too late . . . I think about old age now, not about the war . . .

So that thing of yours is recording? For history?

Rita Mikhailovna Okunevskaya

PRIVATE, SAPPER-MINER

I'm home . . . At home everybody is alive . . . Mama saved everybody: grandpa and grandma, my little sister and my brother. And I came back . . .

A year later our papa came back. Papa returned with great decorations; I brought back a decoration and two medals. But in our family we agree on this: the greatest hero was mama. She saved everybody. She saved our family, saved our home. She fought the most terrible war. Papa never wore his decorations and ribbons; he considered it shameful to show off in front of mama. Embarrassing. Mama doesn't have any awards . . .

Never in my life did I love anyone as I did my mama . . .

Bella Isaakovna Epstein

SERGEANT, SNIPER

I came back different . . . For a long time I had an abnormal relation with death. Strange, I would say . . .

They were inaugurating the first streetcar in Minsk, and I rode on that streetcar. Suddenly the streetcar stopped, everybody shouted, women cried, "A man's been killed! A man's been killed!" And I sat alone in the car. I couldn't understand why everybody was crying. I didn't feel it was terrible. I had seen so many people killed at the front . . . I didn't react. I got used to living among them. The dead were always nearby . . . We smoked near them, we ate. We talked. They were not somewhere out there, not in the ground, like in peacetime, but always right here. With us.

And then that feeling returned, again I felt frightened when I saw a dead man. In a coffin. After several years, that feeling returned. I became normal . . . Like the others . . .

Natalia Alexandrovna Kupriyanova

SURGICAL NURSE

This happened before the war . . .

I was at the theater. During the intermission, when the lights went on, I saw . . . Everyone saw him . . . There was a burst of applause. Thunder! Stalin was sitting in the government loge. My father had been arrested, my elder brother had disappeared in the camps, but despite that I felt so ecstatic that tears poured from my eyes. I was swooning with happiness! The whole room . . . The whole room stood up! We stood and applauded for ten minutes.

I came to the war like that. To fight. But during the war I heard quiet conversations . . . At night, the wounded smoked in the corridors. Some slept, some didn't sleep. They talked about Tukhachevsky, about Yakir . . . * Thousands had disappeared! Millions of people! Where? The Ukrainians told . . . How they had been driven into the kolkhozes. Forced to obey . . . How Stalin had organized famine; they themselves called it the "Death-by-Hunger." Golodomor. Mothers went mad and ate their own children . . . And the soil was so rich there that if you planted a twig, a willow would grow. German prisoners would put some in parcels and send it home. That soil was so rich. Meters deep of black earth. Of fertile soil. The conversations were quiet . . . In low voices . . . Those conversations never occurred

---

* Mikhail Tukhachevsky (1893–1937) and Iona Yakir (1896–1937) were two of the most important Soviet military leaders, theorists, and reformers. Both were arrested and shot during the purges of 1937.

in groups. Only if there were two people. A third was too many, the third one would have denounced . . .

I'll tell a joke . . . I'm telling it so as not to cry. It goes like this . . . It's nighttime. In the barracks. Prisoners are lying and talking. They ask each other, "Why were you locked up?" One says—for telling the truth. A second—because of my father . . . And a third answers, "For being lazy." What?! They're all surprised. He tells them, "We were sitting at a party in the evening, telling jokes. We got home late. My wife asked me, 'Should we go and denounce them now, or tomorrow?' 'Let's go tomorrow. I want to sleep.' But in the morning they came to take us . . ."

It's funny. But I don't feel like laughing. We should weep. Weep.

After the war . . . Everyone waited for their relatives to come back from the war, but we waited for them to come back from the camps. From Siberia . . . Of course! We were victorious, we had proved our loyalty, our love. Now they would believe us.

My brother came back in 1947, but we never found my father . . . Recently I visited my war friends from the front in Ukraine. They live in a big village near Odessa. Two obelisks stand in the center of the village: half the village died of starvation, and all the men died in the war. But how can we count them in all of Russia? People are still alive, go and ask them. We need hundreds like you, my girl, to tell our story. To describe all our sufferings. Our countless tears. My dear girl . . .

"SUDDENLY WE WANTED
DESPERATELY TO LIVE . . ."

The phone keeps ringing. I write down new addresses, receive new letters. And it's impossible to stop, because each time the truth is unbearable.

Tamara Stepanovna Umnyagina
JUNIOR SERGEANT IN THE GUARDS, MEDICAL ASSISTANT

Ah, my precious one . . .

All night I was remembering, collecting my memories . . .

I ran to the recruiting office: I had a hopsack skirt, white rubber sneakers on my feet—they were like shoes, with a buckle. All the fashion then. Here I was in that skirt, those sneakers, volunteering to go to the front, so they sent me there. I got into some sort of vehicle. I reached the unit, it was an infantry division, stationed near Minsk, but they told me I wasn't needed there. The men would be ashamed, they said, if seventeen-year-old girls started fighting. And anyhow we would soon crush the enemy. Go back to your mama, little girl. I was upset, of course, that they wouldn't let me fight. So what did I do? I went to see the commander in chief. He was sitting with that same colonel who had dismissed me, and I said, "Comrade even higher superior, allow me to disobey the comrade colonel. I won't go home anyway, I'll retreat with you. Where would I go, the Germans are already close." And after that they all called me "Comrade Even Higher Superior." It was the seventh day of the war. We began to retreat . . .

Soon we were drenched in blood. There were many wounded, but they were so calm, so patient, they wanted so much to live. Everybody wanted to survive until the day of victory. We waited: any day now . . . I remember, I was all soaked with blood—up to, up to, up to . . . My sneakers were torn; I already went barefoot. What did I see? The train station near Mogilev was being bombarded. And there was a train carrying children. They started throwing them out through the windows, little children—three or four years old. There was a forest nearby, so they ran toward the forest. The German tanks immediately drove out, and the tanks drove over the children. There was nothing left of those children . . . Even now you could lose your mind from that scene. But during the war, people held on. They lost their minds after the war. They got sick after the war. During the war gastric ulcers healed over. We slept in the snow, we had flimsy overcoats, and in the morning we didn't even have runny noses.

Later, our unit was encircled. I had so many wounded, and not a single truck was willing to stop. The Germans were right on our heels; any moment now they would trap us in their circle. Then a wounded lieutenant handed me his pistol: "Can you shoot?" How could I? I had only watched them shoot. But I took the pistol and went with him to the road, to stop trucks. There, for the first time, I cursed. Like a man. A nice, well-rounded curse . . . All the trucks passed by . . . I fired a first shot in the air . . . I knew that we couldn't carry the wounded in our arms. Impossible. They begged us, "Listen, boys, finish us off. Don't leave us like this." A second shot . . . I pierced the hood . . . "You fool!! Learn to shoot first." They stepped on the brakes. Helped us to load them.

But the most terrible was ahead of us, the most terrible— Stalingrad. What sort of battlefield is that? It's a city—streets, houses, basements. Try dragging the wounded out of there! My whole body was one single bruise. And my pants were covered with blood. Completely. The first sergeant scolded us, "Girls, we have no more spare pants, don't ask." And our pants would dry and get stiff. They don't get stiff from starch the way they do from blood; you could cut yourself on them. There wasn't a single clean spot; by spring there was nothing left to turn in. Everything burned. On the Volga, for instance, even the water burned. Even during the winter, the river didn't freeze, but burned. Everything burned . . . In Stalingrad there wasn't a single inch of dirt that wasn't soaked in human blood. Russian and German. And gasoline . . . And grease . . . They all realized there was nowhere left, we couldn't retreat. Either we would all die—the country, the Russian people—or we would be victorious. That became clear to everybody, we had reached such a moment. We didn't say it out loud, but everybody understood. Generals and soldiers both understood . . .

Reinforcements arrived. Such young, handsome fellows. Before the battle, you looked at them and knew they'd be killed. I was afraid of new people. I was afraid to get to know them, to talk to them. Because they were here, and then they were already gone. Two or three days . . . You kept looking at them before the battle . . . This was 1942—the worst, the hardest moment. One time, out of three hundred of us, only ten were left at the end of the day. And when we were the only ones left, when things calmed down, we began to kiss, to cry, because we were suddenly alive. We were all family for each other. We became family.

Before your eyes a man is dying . . . And you know, you can see, that you can't help him in any way; he only has a few minutes to live. You kiss him, caress him, speak tender words to him. You say goodbye. Well, you can't help him any other way . . . I still remember those faces. I see them all, all those boys. Somehow, as the years passed, I might have forgotten at least one of them, at least one face. But I didn't forget anyone, I remember them all . . . I see them all . . . We wanted to make graves for them, with our own hands, but it wasn't always possible. We left, and they stayed. You bandage his whole head, and under the bandages he's already died on you. And he gets buried with his head covered in bandages. Another one, if he died on the battlefield, at least he was looking to the sky. Or he dies and asks,

"Close my eyes, dear nurse, but carefully." The city is destroyed, the houses. Of course it's terrible, but when people are lying there, young men . . . You can't catch your breath, you run . . . To save them . . . It seems like you don't have the strength to go on for more than five minutes, you don't have enough . . . But you keep running . . . It's March, there's water under your feet . . . We weren't supposed to wear our felt boots, but I slipped them on and went. I crawled around all day wearing them, and in the evening they were so wet that I couldn't take them off. We had to cut them. But I didn't get sick . . . Can you believe it, my precious one?

When the fighting at Stalingrad ended, we were ordered to evacuate the most seriously wounded on steamboats and barges to Kazan, to Gorki. It was already spring, somewhere in March or April. But we found so many wounded, they were in the ground—in trenches, in dugouts, in basements. There were so many of them, I can't even tell you how many. It was horrible! We kept thinking, when we carried the wounded from the battlefield, that there would be no more, that we had evacuated them all, that there weren't any in Stalingrad itself. But when everything was over, it turned out that there were so many, it was unbelievable . . . Unimaginable . . . On the boat I was on we had gathered those with missing hands, missing legs, and hundreds sick with tuberculosis. We had to treat them, to encourage them with gentle words, comfort them with a smile. When they sent us, they promised we'd finally get to rest from battle; they said it was even like a reward, like an encouragement. But it turned out to be even worse than the Stalingrad hell. On the battlefield, you pulled a man out, gave him some aid, and handed him over—you had confidence that he was all right now, they had taken him away. You go on, you crawl after the next one. But here they're in front of your eyes all the time . . . There they wanted to live, they were eager to live: "Quick, nurse! Quick, dear!" But here they refused to eat, they wanted to die. They jumped off the steamboat. We had to watch them. Protect them. There was this one captain, I had to sit by his side even at night—he had lost both arms and wanted to put an end to his life. Once I forgot to warn the other nurse, I went out for a few minutes, and he threw himself overboard . . .

We brought them to Usolye, near Perm. There were already new, clean houses there, all especially for them. Like in a youth camp . . . We carried them on stretchers, but they were in agony. I felt like marrying any one of them. I'd have carried him in my arms. On the way back, the steamboat was empty. We could rest, but we didn't sleep. The girls lay there and suddenly started howling. We sat and wrote them letters every day. We designated who would write to whom. Three or four letters a day.

Here is a detail. After that trip, I began to hide my legs and face during battle. I had pretty legs; I was so worried they'd be mutilated. And I worried for my face. That's the detail . . .

After the war, for several years I couldn't get rid of the smell of blood; it followed me for a long, long time. I do the laundry—and I smell it. I cook dinner—again I smell it. Somebody made me a present of a red blouse, and back then it was a rarity, there wasn't much fabric, but I didn't wear it because it was red. I couldn't stand that color anymore. I couldn't go to the shop for groceries. The meat department. Especially in summer . . . And seeing chicken meat, you understand, it's very similar . . . As white as human flesh . . . My husband would go . . . In summer I couldn't stay in town at all, I tried at least to get away somewhere. As soon as summer came, it felt as if war was about to start. When the sun heated everything around—trees, houses, asphalt—everything had that smell. It smelled like blood to me. Whatever I ate or drank, I couldn't get away from that smell! Even clean bedsheets smelled like blood . . .

May 1945 . . . I remember we took a lot of pictures. We were very happy . . . The ninth of May—everybody shouted, "Victory! Victory!" Soldiers rolled in the grass—Victory! They tap-danced. Ayda-ya-a-a . . .

Fired into the air . . . Whatever we had, we fired it off . . .

"Cease fire at once!" ordered the commander.

"But there'll be ammunition left. What for?" We didn't understand.

Whatever people said, I heard only one word—Victory! And suddenly we wanted desperately to live! And how beautifully we'd begin to live now! I put on all my decorations and asked to be photographed. For some reason I wanted to be surrounded by flowers. They photographed me in some flowerbed.

The seventh of June was a happy day, it was my wedding. The unit organized a great feast for us. I had known my husband for a long time: he was a captain, a company commander. We swore to each other, if we survived, we'd get married after the war. They gave us a month's leave . . .

We went to Kineshma, that's in the Ivanovo region, to his parents. I went there as a heroine; I never thought a frontline girl could be greeted like that. We had been through so much, had saved so many children for their mothers, husbands for their wives. And suddenly . . . I learned about insults, I heard offensive words. Before that, all I heard was "dear nurse," "darling nurse." And I wasn't common-looking, I was pretty. I had a brand-new uniform.

In the evening, we sat down for tea. His mother took her son to the kitchen and wept, "Who have you married? A frontline girl . . . You have two younger sisters. Who will want to marry them now?" And today, when I remember that, I want to weep. Picture this: I had brought a record, I liked it a lot. It had these words: "and you sure have the right to go around in fancy shoes . . ." It's about a frontline girl. I played it, and the older sister came and broke it right in front of me, meaning, you have no rights. They destroyed all my photographs from the front . . . Ah, my precious one, I have no words for that. No words . . .

Back then, we had coupons for food, little cards. My husband and I gathered our coupons and went off to exchange them. We came, it was a special depot, there was already a line, we stood in it and waited. When my turn came, the man standing at the counter suddenly jumped over—straight to me, and started kissing me, embracing me and shouting, "Boys! Boys! I've found her. I recognized her. I really wanted to meet her, I really wanted to find her. Boys, she's the one who saved me!" And my husband was standing next to me. The man was a wounded man I had pulled out of a fire. While there was shooting. He remembered me, but I? How could I remember them, there were so many! Another time I met an invalid at the train station: "Nurse!" He recognized me. And he wept: "I always thought, if we met, I'd kneel to you . . ." But he had lost a leg . . .

We'd had enough, we frontline girls. And after the war we got more. After the war we had another war. Also terrible. For some reason, men abandoned us. They didn't shield us. At the front it was different. You crawl—a bullet or piece of shrapnel comes . . . The boys protected us . . . "Take cover, nurse!" someone would shout and fall on you, covering you with his body. And the bullet gets him . . . He would be dead or wounded. Three times I was saved like that.

We returned from Kineshma to the unit. We arrived and learned that our unit wasn't demobilizing, we were going to de-mine the fields. The land was to be given to the kolkhozes. For everyone else the war was over, but for the sappers it still went on. The mothers already knew we had won . . . the grass had grown very tall . . . But all around were mines, bombs. The people needed the land, so we had to be quick. Every day our comrades died. Every day, after the war, there were funerals . . . We left so many people there in the fields . . . So many . . . The land had already been given to the kolkhoz, a tractor comes along, somewhere there's a mine hidden, there were even anti-tank mines, and the tractor's blown up, the driver's blown up. And there weren't many tractors. There weren't many men left. To see those tears in the village, after the war now . . . Women howled . . . Children howled . . . I remember we had this soldier . . . Near Staraya Russa, I forget which village . . . He was from there himself, he went to de-mine his kolkhoz, his own fields, and died there. The village buried him there. He had fought the entire war, four years, and after the war he died in his native place, in his native fields.

As soon as I begin telling this story, I get sick again. I'm talking, my insides turn to jelly, everything is shaking. I see it all again, I picture it: how the dead lie—their mouths are open, they were shouting something and never finished shouting, their guts are ripped out. I saw fewer logs than dead men . . . And how frightening! How frightening is hand-to-hand combat, where men go at each other with bayonets . . . Bare bayonets. You start stammering, for several days you can't get the words out correctly. You lose speech. Can those who weren't there understand this? How do you tell about it? With what face? Well, answer me—with what face should I remember this? Others can somehow . . . They're able to . . . But me—no. I weep. Yet this must be preserved, it must. We must pass it on. Somewhere in the world they have to preserve our cry. Our howl . . .

I always look forward to our holiday. Victory Day . . . I look forward to it, and I dread it. For several weeks I purposely collect laundry, so that I'll have a lot of it, and I do the laundry all day. I have to keep busy with something, I have to be distracted for the whole day. And when we meet, we don't have enough handkerchiefs—that's how our front liners' gatherings go. A sea of tears . . . I don't like war toys, children's war toys. Tanks, machine guns . . . Who thought of that? It wrenches my soul. I never bought or gave war toys to children. Not to mine, not to others'. Once somebody brought a little warplane and a plastic machine gun into my house. I threw them out on the spot. Immediately! Because human life is such a gift . . . A great gift! Man himself is not the owner of that gift.

Do you know what thought we all had during the war? We dreamed: "If only we survive . . . People will be so happy after the war! Life will become so happy, so beautiful. People who have been through so much will feel sorry for each other. They'll love each other. They'll be changed people." We never doubted it. Not a bit.

My precious one . . . People still hate each other. They go on killing. That's the most incomprehensible thing to me . . . And who is it? Us . . . It's us . . .

Near Stalingrad . . . I was carrying two wounded men. I'd carry one for a bit, leave him, go back for the other. And so I carried them in turns. Because they were very badly wounded, I couldn't leave them. How can I explain this simply? They had both been hit high up on the legs; they were losing blood. Minutes were precious here, every minute. And suddenly, when I had crawled away from the battle and there was less smoke around, suddenly I realized I was carrying one of our tankmen and a German . . . I was horrified: our people are dying there, and I'm saving a German! I panicked . . . There, in the smoke, I hadn't realized . . . I see a man is dying, a man is shouting . . . A-a-a . . . They were both scorched, black. Identical. But then I made out a foreign medallion, a foreign watch, everything was foreign. That accursed uniform. So what now? I carried our wounded man and thought: "Should I go back for the German or not?" I knew that if I left him, he would die soon. From loss of blood . . . And I crawled back for him. I went on carrying both of them . . .

It was Stalingrad . . . The most terrible battles. The most, most terrible. My precious one . . . There can't be one heart for hatred and another for love. We only have one, and I always thought about how to save my heart.

For a long time after the war I was afraid of the sky, even of raising my head toward the sky. I was afraid of seeing plowed-up earth. But the rooks already walked calmly over it. The birds quickly forgot the war . . .

1978–2004

'. . . A largely irresistible story, complete with a big courtroom finish.' *Daily Mail*

'Uproarious . . . McKenna relates their astonishing story with meticulously researched relish . . . McKenna captures their arrest with the same *joie de vivre* as Stella and Fanny lived their tumultuous lives: a blur of petticoats, shrieks and confusion . . . It's a wonderful, gripping and moving story, including a pithy epilogue revealing what happened next to the major players. Tim Burton or Baz Luhrmann must make this into a film.' Tim Teeman, *The Times*

'Rich and absorbing . . . McKenna has done a tremendous job of recreating Victorian London's gay subculture, weaving newspaper reports, police documents and contemporary diaries into a jolly rollicking narrative. It would be an understatement to call it a colourful book . . . *Fanny and Stella* is a cracking read.' Dominic Sandbrook, *Sunday Times*

'McKenna does a masterful job of recreating the lives of Fanny and Stella . . . McKenna once again shows himself adept at meticulous research. He delivers a brilliant dissection of the plotting by authorities that led to the trial of Fanny and Stella. With his polished sense of narrative, McKenna's new book is a page-turner, rendered in felicitous, witty prose that makes the tragicomic lives of the two cross-dressers an unforgettable tale. In telling it, he provides a panoramic picture of a stratum of underworld queer English life in pre-Wilde days that is an important contribution to gay historiography . . . This fascinating account richly merits a place on your bookshelf.' Doug Ireland, *Gay City News*

'McKenna tells the whole story, from the shock of arrest, through flashbacks of the glorious careers of our heroines, to the drama of the trial, with remarkable verve and humor . . . It is a thoroughly delightful book.' Cheryl Morgan, *Lambda Literary*

'Gripping and novelistic history . . . McKenna has unearthed plentiful evidence.' *Sunday Telegraph*

'Neil McKenna pulls back the curtain on a city rife with poverty, disease, prostitution – and worry . . . Drawing on an avalanche of letters, court transcripts and newspaper articles, McKenna's description of the trial would be funny (and some bits are) if it weren't for the humiliation – medical examinations in particular – endured by these "two feather-pated young men . . . barely out of their teens." . . . McKenna's narrative – which traces post-trial lives too – ends on an unexpectedly upbeat note. Where we expect to find martyrs to Victorian hypocrisy, we find fully realized human beings: both Fanny and Stella are well worth our cheers.' Nancy Wigston, *Toronto Star*

---

by the same author

THE SECRET LIFE OF OSCAR WILDE

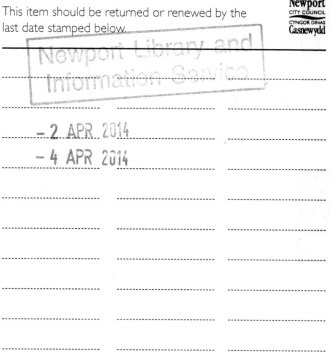

'The definitive account of the Boulton and Park story ... a fascinating tapestry of interrelated personal histories.' Richard Canning, *History Today*

'A most extraordinary tale ... a fascinating reminder that Victorian society was nowhere near as respectable as it liked to believe.' *Sunday Express*

'Neil McKenna could scarcely have chosen a subject better suited to his style. Deploying an extravagant wardrobe-full of voices and costumes, he practically writes in drag.' Minoo Dinshaw, *Financial Times*

'A fascinating slice of social history ... McKenna conjures the grubby glamour and camp excesses of Fanny and Stella's lives ... A lot of fun.' *Metro*

'Wonderful ... McKenna has developed the knack of writing in a Victorian style that makes us believe that the leading players of the drama are speaking to us today ... This is a great read. It will be made into a movie as sure as Neil McKenna is the greatest gay biographer of our era.' *QX Magazine*

'McKenna's style paints as thickly as his subjects, as full of flamboyant hyperbole and extravagant flourishes as the camp young fellows it portrays.' Terry Eagleton, *London Review of Books*

'Often jaw-dropping ... Faced with such terrific material, McKenna could easily have told the story straight (as it were). In the event, he puts in a performance easily as theatrical as his heroines in their pomp. While the basic research can't be faulted, he also gives us the inner thoughts of everybody concerned

FANNY AND STELLA

*The Young Men
Who Shocked
Victorian England*

NEIL MCKENNA

FABER & FABER

First published in 2013
by Faber and Faber Limited
Bloomsbury House,
74–77 Great Russell Street,
London WC1B 3DA
This paperback edition first published in 2014

Typeset by Faber and Faber Ltd
Printed in the UK by CPI Group, Croydon, CRO 4YY

A CIP record for this book
is available from the British Library

ISBN 978–0–571–23191–1

2 4 6 8 10 9 7 5 3 1

For
Dede Smith
companion-in-arms

Contents

List of Plates

Acknowledgements · xiii

1 Leading Ladies · 1

2 The Hapless Swain · 12

3 The Slap-Bum Polka · 24

4 In the Dock · 31

5 Foreign Bodies · 42

6 Wives and Daughters · 53

7 Becoming Fanny · 65

8 A Tale of Two Sisters · 79

9 Monstrous Erections · 88

10 A Dirty Business · 102

11 Getting Up Evidence · 114

12 A Victorian Romance · 126

13 Lord Arthur's Wife · 138

14 The Toast of the Town · 148

15 'Yr Affectionate Fanny'   159

16 The Dragon of Davies Street   167

17 'Come Love'   175

18 *Un Souvenir d'Amour*   187

19 The Battle of the Bottoms   198

20 He, She or It   210

21 A Bitches' Ball   223

22 The Wheels of Justice   235

23 Dead or Disappeared   246

24 This Slippery Sod   257

25 'Pestiferous and Pestilential'   269

26 The Ship of State   282

27 The Most Sensational Event   295

28 A Rout   309

29 'This Terrible Drama of Vice'   321

30 Clouds and Sunshine   336

Epilogue   353

Notes   361

Index   387

[x]

Plates

1   Fanny and Stella being led away, *The Days' Doings*
2   'Men in Women's Clothes: The Dressing Room', *The Illustrated Police News*
3   Stella Boulton, Scarborough, 1868 © Oliver Sarony/ Laurence Senelick Collection
4   Stella Boulton dressed as a man © Oliver Sarony/Laurence Senelick Collection
5   Fanny Park in white dress © Frederick Spalding/Essex Record Office
6   Fanny Park with unknown gentleman © Chelmsford, 1868, Frederick Spalding/Essex Record Office
7   Fanny Park © Frederick Spalding/Essex Record Office
8   Fanny Park, Stella Boulton and Lord Arthur Pelham-Clinton © Frederick Spalding/Essex Record Office
9   Fanny and Stella © Frederick Spalding/Essex Record Office
10 Charles Pavitt and Stella Boulton © Frederick Spalding/ Essex Record Office
11 'The Female Personators', *The Illustrated Police News*
12 The Comical Countess and Carlotta Gibbings, *The Illustrated Police News*
13 Stella Boulton © Napoleon Sarony/Laurence Senelick Collection
14 Stella Boulton © Mrs Williams of Northampton/Laurence

Senelick Collection

15 Fanny Park and Stella Boulton © Frederick Spalding/Essex
Record Office

Acknowledgements

This book could not have been written without consulting the materials on Fanny and Stella held by the National Archives in Kew, who were unfailingly helpful. I am also grateful to the British Library and the British Newspaper Library; to the Metropolitan Police Service Archive in London; to the National Archives of Scotland; to the Parliamentary Archives; to the Wellcome Institute Library; to the library of Imperial College, London; to the libraries of the Royal College of Surgeons in London and the Royal College of Surgeons in Edinburgh; to the Flintshire Record Office who hold the Hawarden MSS; to the Library of Nottingham University who hold the Newcastle Clumber MSS; to the Post Office Museum and Archive in London; to the Essex Record Office; to Michael Hussey of the National Archives and Records Administration in the United States; to Paul Stevens, librarian and archivist at Repton School; to Elizabeth Boardman, archivist at Brasenose College, Oxford; to Rob Petre, archivist at Oriel College, Oxford; to Robin Freeman, archivist at Hampshire Archives and Local Studies; to Andrew Dowsey, archivist at Fife Council; to the *Hamilton Advertiser* and the *Hampshire Chronicle*; to Lesmahagow Central Library; to Hamilton Central Library; and to the National Railway Museum in York.

I would also like to thank the many people who have helped in ways large and small: Dawn Ades, Val Allam,

Nuria Alvarez Vazquez, Carole Angier, Hans Arnold, Ruth Atkins, Susheel Basra, Diane Bennett, Mark Booth, Jamie Buxton, Michelle Carriger, Alan Clark, Sally Cline, Hope Cooke, Ania Corless, Eleanor Crow, Jim Davies, Moris Farhi, Peter Farrer, Edward Fenton, Paul Forbes, Simon Garfield, Nick Gilbert, Christopher Golding, Allister Hardiman, Terry Heath, Alex Holroyd, Charles Hurt, Maggie Iverson, Agnes Jones, Ellen Jones, Liane Jones, Peter Jones, Sian Jones, Marina Leopardi, Jules Lubbock, Vicky Manthorpe, Naomi May, Donald Mead, Naomi Narod, Rictor Norton, Robert Palmer, Patricia Pelham-Clinton-Hope, Carl Philpott, Jonathan Pimm, Gilly Poole, Monica Porter, Keith Raffan, Eleanor Rees, George Robb, Susan Ronald, Caroline Ross Pirie, Diane Samuels, Jane Scruton, Anne Sebba, Michael Seeney, Carole Seymour-Jones, Melanie Smith, David Souden, Diana Souhami, Linda Stratmann, Ben Summerskill, Sandy Suffield, Alex Sutherland, Matthew Sweet, Simon Watney, Caspar Wintermans.

I would particularly like to thank Jonathan Ned Katz for generously sharing his research on John Safford Fiske; Peter Swaab for his insights on Fanny and Stella; Anna Swan for her many helpful suggestions; Julie Wheelwright for her continuous support; Dr Stuart Flanagan for his medical knowledge; Professor Laurence Senelick for so generously allowing me to reproduce photographs of Fanny and Stella from his collection; Sue Fox for her inspired research in the US archives; Rina Gill for her enduring friendship and encouragement; and Will Atkinson for his generosity of spirit.

Dede Smith, to whom this book is dedicated, has been a tireless researcher and an enthusiastic advocate of Fanny and Stella, reading and re-reading the manuscript and suggesting countless improvements. I am very grateful for his friendship and for his wisdom.

I would like to express my very sincere thanks to my agent, Andrew Lownie, and to Julian Loose and Kate Murray-Browne, my editors at Faber, who have been everything that editors ought to be, and more besides.

Lastly, I would like to express my profound gratitude to Robert Jones without whose love and friendship this book could not have been written.

There was an old person of Sark
Who buggered a pig in the dark;
The swine in surprise
Murmured: 'God blast your eyes,
Do you take me for Boulton and Park?'

The Pearl, 1879

1

Leading Ladies

Thursday 28th April 1870

When they were seated in the stalls,
With their low-neck'd dresses and flowing shawls,
They were admired by one and all,
This pair of He-She ladies.
The gents at them would take a peep,
And say they are Duchesses at least,
Lor! what a fascinating pair,
Especially she with the curly hair.

'The Funny He-She Ladies'

Heads turned as the two strikingly handsome women swept imperiously into the pale-green and gilded foyer of the Strand Theatre and made their way to the private box, booked under the name of Mrs Fanny Graham, where two young men – Mr Hugh Mundell and Mr Cecil Thomas were the names they had given to the boxkeeper – were already waiting for them.

In the flurry of excitement, nobody noticed the three ordinary-looking, moustachioed men who had slipped quietly into the theatre on the heels of the two women and then quickly melted away into the darker recesses of the stalls and promenade.

The boxkeeper was excited. He thought that he recognised one of these two divinities as none other than the Duchess of Manchester, the great society beauty whom the Prime Minister, Mr Gladstone, just five days earlier at a state banquet, had praised as among 'the very fairest of our land'.

But the male members of the audience at the Strand Theatre were not so easily fooled. 'The general opinion throughout the house,' one observer reported, 'was that they were two fresh stars in the firmament of the demi-monde, and that their beauty, their fascination, and their paid-for smiles would, before the London season expired, cause many a poor dupe to curse the hour in which he had been born.'

The recently rebuilt Strand Theatre was one of London's largest, and seated over a thousand people. It was famous for three things: for the quality of its air, for its burlesque productions, and for its reputation as a place of successful sexual assignations. Air quality was a prime consideration. Most theatres and music halls reeked of unwashed humanity, a hot and heady mixture of sweat, body odour, pipe and cigar smoke, cheap scent and alcohol. When it was rebuilt in 1865 the Strand was the first theatre with a purposely designed ventilation system and the first to install an industrial-sized Rimmel's Vaporiser, invented by the *parfumier* Eugene Rimmel, which released clouds of perfumed steam to sanitise and deodorise the air.

London was in the grip of a new theatrical craze for burlesques and burlettas, for light operas, comedies, farces, melodramas and pantomimes where women dressed as men and men dressed as women. The pursuit of love with all its thorny and tangled turnings, all its comic and tragi-comic complications, was the proper subject of burlesque. That young women dressed as men fell in love with young men, and young men dressed as women fell in love with young women, far from confusing the audience, seemed to add a delightful *frisson* of sexual excitement to the proceedings. And the Strand Theatre was the very epicentre of burlesque mania, mounting a never-ending succession of 'Grand Burlesque Extravaganzas' which guaranteed full houses night after night.

Above and beyond its technical marvels and its burlesque extravaganzas, the Strand was notorious as a place where men could meet women for sex, and had been patronised on many occasions by no less a personage than the Prince of Wales. It was, as the cartoonist Alfred Bryan slyly insinuated, one of London's 'Noted Shops for Tarts', and a crude but popular limerick made explicit reference to the Strand's erotic reputation:

> There was a young man of St Paul's
> Possessed of the most useless of balls,
> Till at last, at the Strand,
> He managed a stand,
> And tossed himself off in the stalls.

If there was any lingering doubt that the two strikingly handsome women in Mrs Fanny Graham's box were expensively dressed whores, their behaviour soon put paid to such notions. They nonchalantly leaned over their box, waved their fans, twirled their handkerchiefs and 'lasciviously ogled the male occupants of the stalls'. They smoked, they giggled, they nodded and they winked as they waggled their tongues at men in such a way as to leave absolutely no doubt of their sexual intentions.

And they chirruped – so loudly that at one point some members of the audience complained that it quite drowned out the performance. Chirruping was a sucking noise, made with fluttering lips and usually reserved for babies and kittens, but used by whores and their punters alike to signal sexual desire. Sometimes chirrupers were arrested for causing a public nuisance. One persistent chirruper taken up by the police excused himself at the Lambeth Police Court by claiming 'he thought there was no harm in it'.

After half an hour or so Mrs Fanny Graham and her companion, Miss Stella Boulton, stood up, smiled and curtseyed to the gentlemen of the stalls and left their box to go to the theatre's refreshment bar, squired by Mr Mundell and Mr Thomas. Again, nobody paid the least attention to the three moustachioed men who had so unobtrusively followed them into the theatre and who now reappeared in the Strand's saloon bar looking for all the world as if they were fixtures there.

It was clear that Mrs Graham and Miss Boulton had already been drinking quite heavily, and they now proceeded to consume brandies and sherries at breakneck speed. They were immediately besieged by a gang of curious and admiring swells and gallants and some dubious and not-so-dubious gentlemen eager to sample the charms of these two dazzling demimondaines.

Miss Stella Boulton was seemingly the younger of the pair and was resplendent in a brilliant scarlet silk evening dress trimmed with white lace and draped with a white muslin shawl. She was more than just pretty. In the glittering, flattering, faceted lights of the Strand's saloon bar she was quite beautiful. She was tall and slender, with a narrow waist and a magnificent bosom, her finely shaped head topped by raven hair fashionably dressed in the Grecian style with coils of plaited hair held in place by a crosshatch of black velvet. Her pale face was captivating, with large liquid violet-blue eyes, just a becoming blush to her cheeks, perfect full ruby lips and pearly white teeth. She seemed to scintillate and shine like a star, and the men could hardly take their eyes off her. If she was indeed a whore, she was an exceptional whore. A veritable queen among whores.

By way of contrast, Mrs Fanny Graham was (and this was putting it charitably) on the plain side and was possessed of what the *Evening Standard* called, diplomatically, 'sterner features'. She seemed older, matronly and more worldly-wise, and her cascading flaxen curls seemed to sit oddly with her dark skin and dark eyes. She wore a rather unbecoming dark-green satin crinoline trimmed with black lace and a black lace mantilla. Her eyes were a little too small and closely set together, her nose a little too large, her brows a shade too heavy, and her cheeks more than a little jowly.

But Mrs Fanny Graham was withal a fine figure of a woman with an expression of great good humour and animation. She was handsome in a mannish sort of way. Her dark eyes sparkled when she spoke to her companion, whom she addressed variously as 'Stella', 'Stell', 'Sister' and 'Dear' in a loud theatrical voice which seemed to ricochet around the refreshment bar. Stella's voice, by contrast, was sweet and musical, though equally theatrical. She called her companion 'Fanny' and 'Sister dear'.

So Fanny and Stella were, it seemed, sisters both by birth and by profession, and if the men crowding around them had paused for thought, they might have reached some bracing conclusions about the cruelty of a bestowing fate which had endowed the one sister with such beauty and the other with such decided plainness. Both women were 'painted', Stella quite subtly and effectively, Fanny with considerably more artistic licence. And both wore rather a great deal of jewellery: necklaces, lockets, rings, earrings and bracelets.

Fanny and Stella were hard to fathom. They had behaved with such lewdness in their box in the stalls as to leave not the faintest shred of doubt in even the most disinterested observer that they were a pair of hardened and shameless whores. And yet, close up, Stella was revealed as a beautiful, almost aristocratic, young woman who showed flashes of an innate, and most decidedly un-whorelike, dignity and grace. One newspaper said later that she was 'charming as a star', another christened her 'Stella, Star of the Strand'. And despite all the opprobrium that would later be heaped upon her, despite all the mud that would be slung at her and all the mud that would stick to her, she never lost the mysterious aura of a great and stellar beauty.

Mrs Fanny Graham, too, was clearly a woman of some education and breeding, and was certainly very far removed from your common-or-garden whore. Here in the saloon bar, it seemed harder to reconcile their obvious quality with the ogling, tongue-waggling, chirruping lasciviousness of the stalls.

They spent half an hour or so in the refreshment bar. Before they left, Mrs Fanny Graham, unaware that she was being watched, betook herself to the Ladies' Retiring Room and asked the attendant there to pin the lace back to the hem of her crinoline where she had trodden on it. At a quarter past ten, Mr Hugh Mundell had been despatched in ringing tones by Mrs Graham to go and call for her carriage and soon afterwards the remainder of the party made a leisurely progress to the foyer and pushed their way through the noise and confusion of an emptying theatre to the waiting conveyance.

Just as the carriage was about to depart, one of the men who had been shadowing them all that evening jumped up and swung himself in through the door.

'I'm a police officer from Bow Street,' he said, producing his warrant card, 'and I have every reason to believe that you are men in female attire and you will have to come to Bow Street with me now.'

There was a moment's pause.

'How *dare* you address a Lady in that manner, Sir,' Mrs Fanny Graham demanded with frigid hauteur. For a second it seemed as if she might slap his face as a reward for such impudence.

Then all hell broke loose as Mr Cecil Thomas frantically struggled past the policeman, leapt out of the carriage and ran for dear life, elbowing his way through the bewildered crowds. Fanny and Stella were also contemplating flight and were already quietly edging themselves towards the opposite door of the carriage. Quite how fast they could run and quite how far they imagined they would get in their crinolines was anybody's guess. But their exit was firmly blocked by another burly policeman in plain clothes who appeared seemingly from nowhere. With a smart tap on the roof, the carriage set off at a rattle and a clatter away eastwards down the Strand.

The two women sat in shocked silence for a few moments. Stella looked as if she might be about to cry. Clearing her throat noisily, Fanny spoke, only this time her voice and demeanour had changed, miraculously transmuted into the voice of a well-bred young man about town.

'Look here, old fellow,' she said, 'it'll do you no good to take us to the station and if you'll let us go we'll give you anything you want.

'*Anything*,' she repeated with a knowing look.

'Anything you like to mention,' Stella echoed meaningfully, staring directly at the two policemen, and arching her eyebrows. '*Anything* you like to mention, you can have.'

'I'll do nothing of the sort,' said Detective Sergeant Frederick Kerley, gruffly. 'I must take you to the station.' Detective Officer William Chamberlain sat there in impenetrable silence.

It took rather less than five minutes to drive to Bow Street where Fanny and Stella were marched firmly into the police station and placed in a wooden dock to be formally questioned.

At thirty-five, Inspector James Thompson was one of the youngest and shrewdest senior police officers in London. Unlike many of his colleagues, he was an educated man, working as a clerk before joining the Metropolitan Police ten years earlier and rising quickly through the ranks to become Inspector of 'E' Division, one of the largest sections of the force, covering Holborn and the West End. Inspector Thompson's 195 police officers patrolled an exact total of forty miles and 869 yards of streets and roads and arrested around eight thousand people every year, a thousand or so of them prostitutes plying their trade on the busy thoroughfares of the West End.

Inspector Thompson had made his own way back from the Strand Theatre after giving the signal to Detective Sergeant Kerley and Detective Officer Chamberlain to arrest the two young men in women's clothes. Fanny and Stella were of course oblivious to the fact that this rather grave dark-haired policeman had been shadowing them all evening.

Under the flaring gas jets of Bow Street Police Station, they looked a pathetic pair. Stella's make-up was stained with tears, and the pearl powder that she and Fanny had so liberally applied to their *décolletages* had been shot through with sweat, revealing rather less lustrous skin beneath. Both Fanny's flaxen curls and Stella's Grecian plaits were starting to come away from the complex artificial architecture of their hair, giving them a faintly tipsy look. Inspector Thompson could see that their crinolines were long past their best, the antique lace borders grimy and torn. The flounces of their petticoats peeping out from under the crinolines were stained and decidedly grubby. He noticed that their hands were a shade too large, and their feet, encased in white kid boots, looked a shade too masculine. And beneath the peeling make-up, was that the merest shadow of a beard?

'Your name and address?' Inspector Thompson asked, looking at Stella severely. There was no reply. 'Your name and address?' he repeated.

'My name is Cecil Graham,' mumbled Stella, 'and I live at number 2 Bruton Crescent.' There was silence as Thompson wrote this down, the sound of his metal nib scraping the paper.

Stella suddenly decided that there was no point in lying to the police.

'Actually,' she interrupted quickly, 'my name is Ernest Boulton. I'm the son of a stockbroker and I live with my father at 23 Shirland Road, Maida Vale.' Thompson calmly scratched out 'Cecil Graham'.

'And I've just come back from Edinburgh,' Stella added lamely by way of an afterthought.

Inspector Thompson turned quizzically to Fanny.

'My name is Frederick William Park,' said Fanny wretchedly. 'I'm a law student and I lodge at number 13 Bruton Street, Berkeley Square.'

There was a long silence as Inspector Thompson slowly surveyed the pair, taking in every detail of their appearance.

'It seems a very extraordinary thing to me,' Thompson said quietly and deliberately, 'and I don't quite understand it. Will you give me some explanation for appearing in this dress?'

Fanny and Stella shifted about uncomfortably.

'We *are* men,' they mumbled miserably in unison. It had all been just 'a lark', 'a spree' that had got out of hand.

'And we are very, very sorry.'

A few minutes later Fanny and Stella found themselves in one of the chilly outdoor cells in the yard behind Bow Street. Detective Officer Chamberlain had ordered them to strip in the glare of the gas jets. The nightmare had started to unfold. They undressed slowly, reluctantly and awkwardly as Chamberlain and a crowd of other policemen watched with fascination and horror. There were jeers, whistles and sneers, followed by gasps as Fanny and Stella's crinolines fell to the floor revealing their undergarments.

'There were flannel petticoats,' Chamberlain testified later, 'and I believe calico petticoats; there were stays, a short white skirt, very short under the stays', and both of them had bosoms padded with wadding to make them appear 'very full'.

There was some confusion over whether or not Stella was wearing any drawers. Chamberlain was sure that she was not, a fact that he could only have ascertained by making Stella strip until she was completely naked and revealed as a slender young man with the face of a beautiful young woman.

Mr Hugh Mundell was not under arrest but he had insisted upon coming to the station. 'One of the police said he did not want me, that I could go,' Mundell said later. 'I said I had done nothing wrong.' He felt compelled, he said, to accompany Fanny and Stella to Bow Street. 'I did not want to desert them,' he said nobly. 'I wished to go and get bail for them. I thought they had been out on a lark, and that I might get bail for them.'

When Hugh Mundell joined them in the cell a little later, arrested for refusing to give his name and address, he found them very 'downspirited' and tried 'to keep them up'. It was hard work. Fanny and Stella were shivering and crying, their hair awry, their painted faces smudged with tears. They had been allowed to keep their underwear and were desperately trying to dress themselves and rearrange the wadding in their bosoms into some semblance of normality.

> Oh, was it not a cruel sell,
> That night they must remember well,
> When they had to pig in Bow Street cell,
> What a change for them he-she ladies.

It was the first of many public and not-so-public humiliations that Fanny and Stella would have to endure, and even the hard-nosed and even harder-hearted Detective Officer Chamberlain had to concede that Fanny and Stella were being 'so brave'.

2

The Hapless Swain

These young men appear to be very unfortunate,
for whenever they dressed in men's clothes they
were always taken for women, and when they were
attired in the dress of the fair sex they were always
taken for men. Under such unfortunate circumstances what were they to do?

Extraordinary Revelations, 1870

M r Hugh Alexander Mundell was the ardent, if hapless,
swain of Fanny and Stella, but his devotion had only recently been minted. He had met them just six days earlier,
having made his way to the Surrey Theatre, of low repute, in
the Blackfriars Road, in the hope of finding some female company. It was a regular haunt of his and, for just a shilling's
entrance, he could pass a pleasant evening in the companion-
able fug of humanity that thronged the theatre.

Though it aspired to be 'the nightly resort of all the Rank
and Fashion in London', the Surrey's fortunes had been in
decline for the last fifteen years and now its clientele was a
motley assemblage of working people from Lambeth and Ken-
nington sprinkled, according to Charles Dickens, with 'a few
pilgrims from the West End'. It was a rowdy, blowsy, familiar
sort of place, where the noise made by the audience frequently
drowned out the performance. It could be decidedly rough
both in and around the theatre.

Hugh Mundell was by his own reckoning exactly '23 years and a half old'. He was a remarkably naive, not to say gauche, young man, who later confessed in court that he had had 'very little experience' when it came to the ladies. He had never even corresponded with a lady, he admitted with a stammer and a blush. He described himself as a gentleman, but this was stretching the truth. He had no occupation and lived with his widowed father, a barrister of modest means, in Pimlico, a far from salubrious area. By his own admission he was leading an 'idle' sort of a life.

At the Surrey, Hugh Mundell wandered aimlessly around for an hour or so, then gravitated to the saloon bar, a glittering gilded temple of glass and mirrors. He was lounging against the long bar drinking a bumper of sherry with the theatre manager, a Mr Shelly, when he saw two extremely effeminate young men enter the saloon bar with perfect self-possession. They looked about the same age as himself, perhaps even a little younger. Their hair was rather longer than was usual and had the appearance of having been frizzed and teased into a mass of tight curls, perched upon which at a jaunty angle were tiny top hats of the sort fine ladies wore when riding to hounds. Both were clean-shaven, in an age when the absence of whiskers, moustaches and beards gave rise to the most terrible suspicions.

Their smooth skins seemed to shine and shimmer in the flaring gaslight of the buffet and Hugh Mundell wondered if they were wearing paint. Their jackets had astonishingly exaggerated revers and looked to have been specially nipped in to accentuate the smallness of their waists. Both young men wore large and exquisite flowers in their buttonholes and had small feet which seemed perfectly suited to the tiny, tottering, sashaying steps they took. They seemed to sway and ripple like reeds in the wind. And as they walked they talked in loud, affected, brittle voices and waved their beautifully manicured hands in elaborate gestures.

Hugh Mundell could hardly take his eyes off them.

Mr Shelly nudged him sharply. 'Those two are women dressed as men,' he said with a knowing wink and a leer, 'two gay women dressed up in men's clothes.' Hugh Mundell could well believe it. They were certainly unlike any men he had ever encountered. They had to be women. Women dressed as men. They walked like women and they talked like women. Their gestures were dainty and womanish. Their hair was curled like women's hair and surely only women wore paint.

'I took them to be women, and so did everyone else who was there,' Hugh Mundell said lamely. 'I was led blindfolded on. I was led away.'

Hugh Mundell could be forgiven for being so led away. It was not unusual for spirited young women to dress as fashionable young men about town and go on a spree. It gave them a thrill to penetrate the stag resorts, the traditional preserves of male privilege like the gentlemen's clubs and cigar divans, or go slumming to low taverns, to attend dog fights and cock fights, and bet on bare-knuckle pugilists.

After parading grandly around the saloon, the two young men swept out, announcing in loud and braying tones that they were going to a nearby public house. The dazzled Hugh Mundell felt himself compelled to follow, and in the pub he stared at them fixedly for twenty minutes, until they blushed.

'We think you're following us,' one of the young men observed 'in a joking manner'.

'I – I think I am,' Mundell managed to stammer and blush in reply.

The ice had been broken, and Hugh Mundell found himself talking to two of the most delightful people he had ever encountered. There was more than a little confusion about names. The young men introduced themselves as 'Ernest' and 'Frederick' but within minutes were addressing each other as 'Stella' and 'Fanny'. Hugh Mundell was thoroughly bewildered and gallantly started to call them 'Miss Stella' and 'Mrs Fanny', after Fanny announced that she was a married lady, a fact confirmed by the gold wedding band she wore.

Fanny and Stella clearly liked Hugh Mundell. He was tall and dark and moderately handsome. He was a puppy, to be sure, but a likeable puppy nevertheless. And, when he was not blushing and stammering with embarrassment, he was well-mannered and charming in a shy, spaniel-like way. Fanny and Stella had assumed that he was one of the many 'so' young men who hung around the theatres and music halls in the hopes of picking up other 'so' young men to have sex with. And his dogging of their footsteps and staring them out of countenance only strengthened their conviction that he was in hot – if mute – pursuit.

The problem of men looking for other men to have sex with had reached almost monstrous proportions in some London theatres. According to the pseudonymous author of *The Yokel's Preceptor*, a guide to the sexual pitfalls of London, 'these monsters in the shape of men, commonly designated Margeries, Pooffs, &c . . . flock to the Saloons and boxes of the theatres'. It was a particular problem in theatres like the Surrey, the Strand and the Lyceum which embraced burlesque and where every night 'so' young men could experience the erotic *frisson* of watching young men on stage apparently falling head over heels in love with each other and making passionate love to each other.

The evening passed in a kind of dream for Hugh Mundell. Before the show was over there were more drinks, more slow and stately promenades around the dress circle, and more intoxicating *badinage*. Everyone seemed to be looking wonderingly at this extraordinary pair of young men, and Mundell swelled with pride that he, beyond all others, was the object of their kindest attentions. As they left the Surrey Theatre, he gave an arm each to Fanny and Stella and escorted them to Waterloo Bridge, still convinced they were women.

'I talked to them as women,' Mundell recalled. 'I chaffed them in a quiet way about being women dressed in men's clothes. I did not carry it very far, though. I told them, when they walked, they ought to swing their arms a little more, like men when they walk.'

They parted on the friendliest of terms. Fanny and Stella extracted a promise that Hugh Mundell would meet them again at the Surrey on the following Tuesday evening so that they could watch the performance from beginning to end. 'I shall only be too happy,' he replied. And he meant it.

Hugh Mundell was walking on air as he made his way home to Pimlico. He had fallen suddenly and spectacularly in love with the beautiful and beguiling Miss Stella. And, amazingly, the beautiful and beguiling Miss Stella had accepted his advances, even going so far as to encourage them. But she had behaved that first evening with absolute propriety. 'There was never anything improper in her conduct,' he maintained stoutly. 'I thought her conduct was natural. I thought it was *womanly*.'

The next four days passed in an agony of anticipation for Hugh Mundell. He got to the Surrey Theatre early and had to wait over an hour, pacing up and down the dress circle, before the ladies arrived. He was clutching two red roses – one for Miss Stella and one for Mrs Fanny. This time they were dressed as women, resplendent in their finest crinolines, their hair elaborately coiffured, and dripping in glittering gaudy jewellery. They were quite dazzling. Pleasantries were exchanged.

'Will you come into our private box, Mr Mundell?' said Fanny, smilingly.

'Yes, I should be delighted,' he replied with a short bow, presenting each lady with a rose before rushing to get pins from the box attendant.

'While they were pinning the flowers, Miss Stella gave me a letter,' Mundell remembered. It was quite short and to the point. 'Dear Mr Mundell,' it began:

> You were telling us some stories the other night about a man dressing up as a woman. We are men, and we have put on women's dresses now to see what you think of our get up!

Hugh Mundell smiled to himself. 'It's a good joke,' he told them, 'but I don't for an instant believe it!'

'But it's quite true. We *are* men!' Fanny and Stella exclaimed in unison.

Mundell laughed. 'It's a good joke,' he repeated. 'A very good joke!'

Fanny and Stella shrugged. They had done their best. Their lovesick puppy was convinced they were women. Try as hard as they might to persuade him that they were in truth men, their adoring swain could not countenance it. It was a joke, it was a lark. Nothing more.

To almost everyone in the auditorium that night, it was clear that Fanny and Stella were, to put it bluntly, a pair of beautiful and dangerous young whores. But to the love-struck Hugh Mundell they represented something rather more complex, a strange and contradictory amalgam of the sacred and the profane; of pure love and impure lust.

Later in court, Mundell was asked about his behaviour towards Miss Stella on that evening.

'In what way did you treat her,' counsel for the prosecution demanded, 'as a lady or as a woman of the town?'

Mundell hesitated. He did not know how to answer. The truth was that he had treated Miss Stella as both a lady and as a whore. He was in love with her *and* in lust with her.

'Stella kept me from making any advances,' he mumbled at last, flushing scarlet. 'Whenever I made any advances, she kept me off. She resisted.'

'Describe what kind of advances you made to her,' counsel demanded.

'I put my arm round her neck once.' Mundell's reply was drowned out by laughter in the court, most loudly from Stella and Fanny. 'I might have gone further,' he said, provoking even more laughter. 'But we were not alone. A gentleman coming into the box stopped me.'

The evening ended with an invitation – almost an instruction – to call upon Fanny and Stella the day after next. Fanny handed him a card with the name of 'Frederick Park, 13 Bruton Street, Mayfair' engraved upon it.

'I shall ask for Mrs Park then,' Mundell said doubtfully to Fanny.

'You will not be let in if you do,' replied Fanny tartly.

'Well, if that's the case, I'll ask for *Mr* Park,' Mundell answered, and they all laughed.

Stella's feelings towards Hugh Mundell were, like his for her, a curious amalgam of lust and love. She wanted Hugh Mundell. She wanted to be loved by him, she wanted to be desired by him. She wanted to charm him and channel his love and his lust for her until he became her devoted slave, and she his coy, mercurial mistress. He was good-looking in a coltish sort of way, and his boyish naïveté and enthusiasm made a charming change from the usual run of men who fell in love with her.

There was, of course, the obvious hurdle that Stella was in truth a man. But that was a small matter and could usually be managed. Stella had, over the years, become very adept – an expert, in fact – at managing it. The trick was to make Hugh Mundell fall so deeply in love with her, so deeply in lust with her, to key him up to such a pitch of sexual desire that her surrender – when it finally came – was so looked for and so longed for that her gender became merely a matter of geography. Of course, when she was drunk and whoring, which was frequently, her drunken and whoring punters rarely noticed the difference. After all, most whores hardly ever took their clothes off, instead pulling up their skirts and using strategic slits in their drawers to allow entry.

And even on those rare occasions when the punters suspected she was a man dressed as a woman, or – even more rarely – when she had told them on a whim, or out of caprice, or from a desire to shock, that she was a man, when it came down to it, down to the nitty-gritty, down to the bump and grind of it, the offer of 'a bit of brown' or some 'back-door work', as it was called, was rarely refused and, truth be told, more often eagerly claimed as a prize beyond rubies and pearls.

Yes, Stella thought to herself, it most certainly could be managed.

Hugh Mundell deliberated long and hard on what exactly he should wear to pay a morning call on Miss Stella and Mrs Fanny. He arrived in Bruton Street promptly at eleven o'clock and rang the doorbell of number 13. It was answered by a small girl who took his proffered card and invited him to wait.

The gentlemen were at home, the small girl informed him, and he was shown into a spacious first-floor front. Fanny and Stella were playing the piano and singing a charming duet as he entered the room. If Hugh Mundell was a little disconcerted to find them dressed once again as young men, he did not show it. He noticed that the men's clothes they were wearing were identical to those they had worn six days earlier when he had first met them in the Surrey, and that the collars were none too clean.

To begin with, the conversation was a little stilted. Unlubricated by beer, sherry or other intoxicants, Hugh Mundell was more than usually tongue-tied and embarrassed. But Stella and Fanny's high spirits soon lifted the atmosphere, and before too long there were gales of laughter. Had he, by the bye, still got that letter they had given him the night before last at the Surrey Theatre, enquired Stella in her most playful tone.

'I said I had,' Mundell recalled. 'I took it out of my pocket and had it in my hand. They asked me to give it to them. I said I wouldn't. Then we had a little tussle for it.

'They both tried to get it from me,' he continued. 'They did not succeed. Afterwards I gave it to them and they returned it to me torn. I said, "I don't want it." I did not accept the pieces.'

Hugh Mundell's refusal to accept the fragments of the letter was a symbolic repudiation of an unwelcome truth. Deep down, in his heart of hearts, he may have suspected, may even have known, that Fanny and Stella were telling the truth when they said they were men. But how could he reconcile this with his powerful yearnings for Miss Stella? And if he could admit – did admit – that he loved Stella *and* that she was a man, he exposed a truth about himself too awful to contemplate.

Doubts were already beginning to assail him. If Mrs Fanny was really a woman, why did she have a card with the name Frederick Park engraved upon it? And why did the girl who answered the door talk about 'the gentlemen' being at home? Surely Miss Stella and Mrs Fanny only dressed up as men occasionally as a lark. It was all becoming very confusing.

Fortunately, there were more duets at the piano to take his mind away from such unwelcome contemplations. Stella gave her heart-rending version of 'Fading Away', a syrupy lament about the transience of life, quickly followed by a series of comic, not to say downright bawdy songs.

'They were talking constantly about performing and playing,' Mundell said later. An album was produced with photographs of their theatrical triumphs. Stella seemed to always play the young tragic heroine, the beautiful widow, the friendless girl cast adrift in a cruel world, while Fanny for the most part seemed to play old women, and 'principally dowagers'.

When it was decided that the party should go out to lunch, Fanny and Stella disappeared into a bedroom for the best part of an hour and came out dressed as ladies. It was like two butterflies emerging from their drab chrysalises, Hugh Mundell thought in a sudden flight of poetic fancy, though rather more prosaically he did notice that, in the unforgiving light of day, Fanny and Stella's frocks were worn and stained, and that the flounces of their petticoats were quite obviously in need of laundering.

Luncheon was a long and decidedly drunken affair during

which Fanny and Stella declared that if they did not go to the Strand Theatre to see the new Easter burlesque *St George and a Dragon* that evening, they would quite simply fade away and die.

At eight o'clock that evening Hugh Mundell found himself in a box at the Strand Theatre. Fanny and Stella were late and there was only one other gentleman to talk to. His name was Mr Amos Westropp Gibbings, a wealthy if rather effeminate young man with a pronounced lisp, who clearly knew Fanny and Stella very well.

'Who *are* they?' Hugh Mundell asked plaintively. 'I am quite in a myth about it. I sometimes think they are men, and sometimes that they are women.'

Mr Gibbings's reply was emphatic. Both Fanny and Stella were men, men who enjoyed dressing up as women.

'I have my doubts very much about Mrs Fanny,' Hugh Mundell retorted, 'but I am certain that Miss Stella is a woman.'

Much to his dismay, Fanny and Stella were clearly the worse for drink when they finally arrived, and their behaviour was considerably less than ladylike. It was not merely coarse, it was downright obscene. Hugh Mundell blushed and flushed and stammered and stuttered more than ever. The more he looked at Mrs Fanny, the more his doubts resolved themselves into certainties. Mrs Fanny *was* a man dressed as a woman. He felt sick.

And if Mrs Fanny was a man, where did that leave Miss Stella? Was it possible that this beautiful young woman really was, as she herself had consistently, insistently proclaimed, really a man? 'I am not a lady. I am a man,' she had kept repeating. 'I am not a lady. I am a man.'

In the gaudy, mirrored saloon bar of the Strand Theatre,

Hugh Mundell felt as if he had wandered into a waking night-mare, the distorted reflections of Fanny and Stella crowding in upon him, reproaching him, mocking him. He did not know what to do. He gulped his brandy and watched and waited while a gaggle of admirers surrounded Fanny and Stella. When Mrs Fanny commanded him in ringing tones to go and call a cab, it was a relief to get out into the chilly night air and try to clear his befuddled wits.

A few moments later all hell broke loose.

'There was a great deal of confusion,' Mundell recalled, 'and I hardly know what occurred, but I found myself in a cab on the road to Bow-street. I was very flurried. I don't know how it was.'

'I don't know how it was' was a metaphor for poor Hugh Mundell's life. He found it hard to make sense of the world. He was constantly in a quandary: confused and perplexed – 'quite in a myth', as he put it – about everything to do with Fanny and Stella. It was as if the world had connived and conspired against him, to mislead him and to misdirect him. Again and again his complaint was that he had been 'led on', 'led away', 'sold', told or otherwise persuaded that Fanny and Stella were really women when it was he and he alone who had convinced himself that they were women. No wonder he was flurried.

Barely a quarter of an hour later he was sharing a cell with two young men in female undergarments, trying to make some sense of the awful calamity that had overwhelmed him.

3

The Slap-Bum Polka

One day a cute detective chap,
Who of their game had smelt a rat.
Declared he would get on the track,
Of those two He-She ladies.
So he bolted up to Regent Square,
And soon espied this worthy pair.
They hailed a cab, who took his fare,
Says the police, 'I am after you my dear'.

'The Funny He-She Ladies'

At ten o'clock on the morning after the arrest of Fanny and Stella, in the first-floor front of an inconspicuous lodging house in Wakefield Street, Bloomsbury, Mr Amos Westropp Gibbings (known as Carlotta to all of her many friends) and Mr Martin Luther Cumming (or the Comical Countess) were in the middle of an extremely agitated conference with their landlady, Miss Martha Stacey, when they heard a loud and prolonged knocking on the front door.

They froze and looked at each other. Carlotta Gibbings tiptoed to the window and carefully peered out to see a man standing on the doorstep. She guessed he was a detective in plain clothes. She knew the type. Tallish, shabby, sharp-eyed and shifty with a self-important, bullying air about him. A nasty piece of work and, nine times out of ten, corrupt and corrupting.

'Police,' she mouthed silently.

There was an agonising wait while old Mrs Stacey, Martha's arthritic mother, shuffled up from the basement kitchen and fumbled awkwardly with the locks on the front door. When she finally managed to open the door she found a grim-faced man planted firmly on the doorstep who said he was a policeman. Before she knew it and with hardly so much as a beg-your-pardon or a by-your-leave, he had unceremoniously pushed his way past her into the narrow hallway and begun firing off a series of questions to which old Mrs Stacey, flustered and agitated as she was, could give no coherent answers.

Upstairs, Carlotta Gibbings and Martha Stacey looked at each other. The muffled exchanges from below were getting louder and more heated. Something had to be done. Martha Stacey nodded and, putting her finger to her lips, closed the door very quietly and went down the stairs to see what all the commotion was about.

Detective Officer Chamberlain curtly introduced himself to Martha Stacey. He had no time to waste, he said. There was urgent business, police business, that needed attending to.

'He asked whether two gentlemen lived there who dressed in female attire. He said they were in custody,' Martha Stacey recalled a week later. 'I forget the answer I gave but I said I was astonished.'

'What were they taken for?' she asked him.

'Either it was a freak or a lark,' Chamberlain replied shortly. 'Which room do they occupy?'

'I said they dressed in the one adjoining the ground floor,' recalled Martha Stacey. 'He went into the room and commenced searching it.

'Chamberlain did not show me any warrant, and I did not ask him for it,' she added. 'I was too confused.'

Once inside, Chamberlain began methodically opening boxes and portmanteaux, pulling out dresses and bonnets and boots, tipping out drawers, leafing through piles of papers and rummaging through boxes of jewellery.

'My mother remonstrated with him about it,' Martha Stacey testified. But Chamberlain merely shrugged his shoulders contemptuously. 'He said he had a right to do it and that he would take them away with him and *sell* them if he thought proper.

'He also took away some letters,' she continued. 'I can't say how many. Chamberlain looked at an album and took what portraits he thought proper out of it. He also took some more from another album. I should think about twenty in all.'

Clutching a pile of papers and photographs, Chamberlain locked the door and pocketed the key. No one, not a soul, was to enter those rooms under *any* circumstances, he said. There was important evidence which needed to be taken into custody. He would return in an hour or two.

Martha Stacey was in trouble and she knew it. 'Houses of accommodation' like hers were common in London and came in all shapes and sizes. They were not exactly brothels but they were places where people went to have sex, away from prying eyes and with no awkward questions asked. On the very lowest rung of the erotic ladder, they were places where for a shilling, sixpence or even less, streetwalkers could take their punters to a room where there would be a bed with filthy sheets, a verminous mattress and a bucket for the punters to wash in before and after doing the business. But at least there would be privacy. At the upper end of the scale, sumptuously appointed rooms or suites catered for wealthy gentlemen to pass an hour or two with a high-class whore.

Martha Stacey's house of accommodation was somewhere in the middle range. Though there was a problem with the whores in nearby Brunswick Square, Wakefield Street was, by and large, a respectable and quiet residential street, the ideal street for a respectable and quiet house of accommodation. The houses were very often owned and run by former prostitutes who in sharp contrast to the prevailing notion of the natural history of the profession – seduction, ruin, degradation, disease and premature death – had often saved a comfortable little nest egg from the game and wanted to invest it. Running a house of accommodation was a safe bet. They knew the business; they knew the girls; and they knew there would always be a demand for rooms from everyone from the poorest street-walker to the grandest concubine.

Martha Stacey was most likely a former prostitute herself. She was certainly not the shy, retiring or easily shocked type. Quite the opposite. Even old Mrs Stacey may have been in the business once. Prostitution ran in families, and successful prostitutes would teach their daughters the tricks of the trade. Even Frances Stacey, Martha Stacey's niece, who came in to help with the chores at Wakefield Street, may have been on the game some of the time.

Martha Stacey's establishment was, as far as she knew, unique in London, and its very uniqueness made it vulnerable and made it dangerous. It was a house of accommodation for young men who liked to dress up as young women and go out on the spree, for young men who liked to get themselves up 'in drag' – as Mr Gibbings used to call it, though for the life of her she couldn't see why.

Running her house for the 'so' young gentlemen who liked to drag themselves up had seemed like a good idea to Martha Stacey. They were certainly a cut above the professional Mary-Anns, or male whores, she had met. There was Mr Gibbings, Mr Thomas, Mr Boulton, Mr Park, Mr Cumming and Lord knows how many other young gentlemen who used to come to her house. They were clean, always polite to her, and ever so friendly. She liked her boys when they were boys and she liked her boys even more when they were girls. What a lark it all was! She had often joined in the 'laughing, chaffing and joking' when her boys were getting dragged up, and in the mornings when they recounted their adventures of the night before.

Besides, it was good business, very good business. They always paid on the nail. She charged five shillings a night, and a bit more besides if one of the young men entertained a gentleman – or two – overnight. She didn't know and she couldn't say, she was sure, how often this happened or if the young 'ladies' ever took money from their gentlemen callers. Her boys had their latchkeys and what they did in or out of their rooms was no concern of hers. She never saw anything – well, not much anyway. Mind you, she was quite ready to admit, you'd have to be deaf, dumb and blind not to have an inkling of what went on. Some nights there was an awful lot of to-ing and fro-ing; doors banging; moans and groans and giggles and screams. Judging from the state of the sheets, she had her suspicions – certainties, more like. Those boys certainly knew how to dance the 'Slap-Bum Polka'!

And for a modest charge of a few shillings a week she looked after the frocks, the wigs, the pots of paint, the unmentionables, the what-have-yous, the thingamajigs – and all the rest of the paraphernalia – and my goodness me there was enough of it; enough to open a shop nearly; enough to fill two rooms at Wakefield Street so tight you could barely squeeze your arse in. And for a few shillings more she wasn't averse to doing the odd bit of laundry if Frances was there to help her out. But now the police were involved and what a to-do it had all turned out to be. It was all ruined and spoilt and if she was not very careful, she would find herself in hot water, very hot water, and no mistake.

After twenty minutes or so of waiting, the stomping, thumping and banging from the room below stopped. Carlotta and the Comical Countess heard Chamberlain's muffled voice and then the thud of the front door shutting. He was gone and there was silence. Cautiously, Carlotta crept downstairs. Old Mrs Stacey and Martha were staring at the door of Fanny and Stella's room. They were plainly terrified. Chamberlain had locked it and he was coming back – and soon – with reinforcements.

Miss Carlotta Gibbings did not hesitate. Despite her 'very effeminate appearance' and her girlish lisp, Carlotta was determined and resourceful. She was the only person present not completely paralysed by fear. She guessed that Chamberlain had found plenty of material that would incriminate Fanny and Stella and might perhaps incriminate them all. But if there was anything that Chamberlain hadn't already grabbed, anything that he'd missed, anything that he'd overlooked, now was the time to remove it out of harm's way. She put her shoulder to the door and pushed hard; the lock burst open, and with a girlish shriek of surprise, Carlotta almost fell into the room.

It was a mess. Carlotta and the Comical Countess worked furiously. They could not be sure how long it would take Chamberlain to return. He might be back in an hour or two, as he had threatened; equally, he could be back in fifteen minutes or less with a couple of police constables requisitioned from the beat. Where should they start? Letters, papers, photographs, money and any jewellery of any value that Chamberlain hadn't already squeezed into his capacious pockets – anything that could incriminate them, anything that might incriminate others. It was all stuffed furiously into a carpet bag and a small portmanteau, together with two or three of Carlotta's 'handsomest frocks', some chignons, a bit of slap and two pairs of her favourite stays. And then they were gone, as if the devil himself were at their heels, the door left swinging open.

4

In the Dock

When first before the magistrate
Oh, what a crowd did them await,
It was a lark and no mistake,
To look at them He-She ladies.
Lor! how the people did go on,
With, 'I say I'll have your fine chignon,'
Another cried out, 'Stella dear,
Pull off those togs, and breeches wear.'

'The Funny He-She Ladies'

A night in the cells had done little to improve Fanny and Stella's bedraggled appearance. They had barely slept in the freezing cold, and spent most of the night crying and whimpering. They were very frightened, weak with hunger, and their heads ached with exhaustion and the effects of the numerous brandies and sherries they had knocked back the night before. A tin mug of weak tea and a hunk of cheap black bread made them feel only a little better.

Their dresses were returned to them at first light and they were gruffly instructed to make themselves decent, ready for their appearance before the beak. Fanny and Stella looked at each other in dismay. They had hoped and prayed that somehow or other a suit of men's clothes might be procured for them, that they would not have to appear in court wearing last night's frocks.

Although they did not know it, Carlotta Gibbings had already rushed to Bow Street Police Station early that morning with a change of clothes, calculating that they would stand more chance of getting off with a caution or a small fine if they appeared as respectably dressed young men rather than as two young men dressed as ladies of the night. But the officers had curtly turned Carlotta away.

Somehow or another, with a great deal of grumbling and a great deal of ingenuity, Fanny and Stella managed to tidy themselves up and recreate some faint echo of last night's finery. A handkerchief and some cold water from the ewer helped wipe away the dark tracks of their tears and the worst smudges of paint. Dressing themselves and repairing their toilette as best they could helped to lift their spirits. They looked very far from perfect but they were once again Mrs Fanny Graham and Miss Stella Boulton, stars of stage and street, and whatever the day might bring they hoped they would conduct themselves like ladies.

As Fanny and Stella waited in their cell, they could already hear the muffled hoots and yells of a mob swarming outside, and it took them some little time to realise that the mob was almost certainly assembled in their honour. They turned white with fear. When they left the police station, they would have to run the gauntlet as they crossed Bow Street to the courtroom opposite.

A loud roar went up as Fanny and Stella, followed by Hugh Mundell a few steps behind, came out of Bow Street Police Station flanked by half a dozen uniformed policemen. The diamanté star in Fanny's hair glinted in the thin April sunshine. Fanny and Stella seemed dazzled by the light and dazed by the mob of several hundred which milled and swirled around them trying to catch a glimpse of 'the Funny He-She Ladies'.

There were hoots, hisses, catcalls, whistles and a few ragged cheers. Where had they all come from? Fanny and Stella had been arrested at around eleven o'clock the night before, too late for the morning papers to carry the story. Who were these people? How had they found out? And why were they here? They heard their names, 'Fanny', 'Stella', shouted out in thin, raucous voices that seemed to float momentarily above the roar of the crowd. Voices that sounded familiar. Turning round they caught a few blurred glimpses of the smiling faces of friends and acquaintances frantically waving. They were not entirely friendless.

It took five minutes or more for the police to clear a path. Fanny and Stella were pushed and shoved and pinched and propelled forwards, backwards, sideways. Greedy, greasy fingers grabbed at their dresses and tried to touch and pull their hair. At first Fanny and Stella faltered, stumbled and almost fell. But they went on. And as they went on, they grew visibly taller, visibly stronger, more dignified. By the time they had crossed the road they were carrying themselves like a pair of duchesses attending a ball. They mounted the steps to the court, paused and turned to face the crowd, which had for a moment fallen silent. Fanny and Stella smiled gravely and – with the merest ghost of a curtsey – turned smartly on their heels and swept inside. The jeers and catcalls broke out again. But this time they were drowned out by a fusillade of cheers and whistles.

Mr James Flowers, Stipendiary Magistrate at Bow Street, had a reputation as one of the kindest men on the Bench. The tiny courtroom measured just thirty feet by twenty feet and 'was crowded with people eager to hear the charge', the

Illustrated Police News reported; 'crammed to suffocation' was the verdict of the *Evening News*. All eyes were on Fanny and Stella as they stepped into the wooden dock, followed by a rather sheepish Hugh Mundell, 'and great surprise was manifested at the admirable manner in which Boulton and Park had "made up" '. Fanny and Stella stood impassively, almost proudly, in the dock, as they surveyed the scene. Hugh Mundell looked anxious and fidgety as he stood alongside them.

Had this been a theatre rather than a court of law, a stage rather than a dock, Fanny and Stella would have been only too delighted to tread its hallowed boards. They liked nothing better than a house full to bursting and a rumbustious, restless and expectant audience ready to be quelled, ready to be charmed, ready to be dazzled by their performance. They could so easily have been appearing in *Retained for the Defence*, or one of the dozen or so other comediettas and one-act melodramas they had performed so often, together and separately, in which the beautiful and wronged young woman – invariably more convincingly played by Stella than by Fanny – would stand up before a jury of her peers and by the sheer power of her beauty and by the sheer force and passion of her rhetoric be declared innocent by acclamation. And even though Bow Street was a court and not a stage, Fanny and Stella felt a little of the familiar theatrical glamour stealing over them. They were dressed and they were ready. All they had to do now was to give the performance of their lives.

In the best traditions of burlesque there was not a little confusion and much laughter from the audience over the use of the personal pronoun. Were Fanny and Stella 'he's' or 'she's'? It was a vexed question. Clearly they were men dressed up as women and should, by rights, be referred to as 'he', but somehow it came more naturally to call them 'she'. The clerks who recorded the proceedings got into a terrible muddle, littering their transcripts with crossings-out and corrections, turning 'he's' into 'she's' – and vice versa. The witnesses were equally confused, stumbling and tying themselves in linguistic knots, usually ending up calling Fanny and Stella both 'she' and 'he' in the same sentence. Reporters for the *Daily Telegraph* and the *Illustrated London News* explained delicately to their readers that, though the defendants were emphatically young men, for the purposes of reporting the proceedings they had adopted the preponderant pronoun used in court – in this case 'she'. And Mr Flowers, the magistrate, got round the problem by referring to Fanny and Stella as 'these two women, as I may call them'.

The charges were read out by the Clerk of the Court to loud gasps from the crowded courtroom. Ernest Boulton and Frederick William Park were charged that they 'did with each and one another feloniously commit the abominable crime of buggery':

> further that they did unlawfully conspire together, and with divers other persons, feloniously, to commit the said crimes
>
> further that they did unlawfully conspire together, and with divers other persons to induce and incite other persons feloniously with them to commit the said crime
>
> and further that they being men, did unlawfully conspire together, and with divers others, to disguise themselves as women and to frequent places of public resort, so disguised, and to thereby openly and scandalously outrage public decency and corrupt public morals.

It was an extraordinary set of charges. Fanny and Stella paled and visibly trembled as they were read out. Only the last charge, that of disguising themselves as women and frequenting public places with the intention of outraging public decency and corrupting public morals, held any water. Although there was no statute in English law which specifically made it a criminal offence for men to dress up as women, by dressing up as women and behaving in an undeniably and extremely lewd manner at the Strand Theatre, Fanny and Stella had outraged public decency. On the substance of that charge and that charge alone, they were incontrovertibly guilty. It was a fair cop.

Crimes were divided into two categories: misdemeanours – less serious crimes usually dealt with by the stipendiary magistrates – and felonies, which were much more serious and were tried before a judge and a jury. Outraging public decency was a misdemeanour. If this were the only charge, Fanny and Stella would be well advised to plead guilty, throw themselves upon the mercy of the court and hope they could escape with a hefty fine and a good talking-to from Mr Flowers.

But the charge of buggery was much, much more serious. Until 1861, only nine years earlier, buggery had carried the death penalty. As it was, buggery still carried a prison sentence of penal servitude for life. Penal servitude meant, for murderers, rapists and sodomites, long hours of hard labour picking oakum, walking the treadmill, or working the dreaded crank, back-breaking work turning a handle to push a paddle through a vat of sand. No wonder Fanny and Stella turned pale.

Not only were they charged with buggery, they were charged with a catch-all *conspiracy* to commit buggery. In other words, the police were saying that not only had Fanny buggered Stella, and Stella buggered Fanny, but both of them had also buggered and been buggered by any number of 'divers persons'. Furthermore, they had each conspired with the other, and with any number of unknown, unnamed others 'to induce and incite' yet more men to commit buggery. It all conjured up an image of a vast, ever-spreading sodomitical spider's web with Fanny and Stella at its dark heart, controlling and directing, combining and confederating, to entrap and ensnare any and all men.

Seen through the prism of this conspiracy charge, Fanny and Stella's drunken double act in their box at the Strand Theatre, their ogling, tongue-waggling, chirruping invitations to the gentlemen in the stalls, took on an altogether darker and more menacing aspect. It could quite easily be construed as a conspiracy to incite and induce men to feloniously commit 'the abominable crime of buggery'.

There were only four witnesses produced for this preliminary hearing – all of them policemen. The evidence of Inspector Thompson and the evidence of Sergeant Kerley merely rehashed the events of the night before. Fanny and Stella listened, even smiled occasionally, but seemed largely uninterested in what they had to say. 'Both conducted themselves decorously,' the *Daily Telegraph* reported. 'While listening to the evidence, Boulton rested her head on her right hand but did not pay very particular attention.'

But everything changed when Detective Officer Chamberlain started to give his evidence.

'Last evening, about twenty minutes past eight, I saw the two prisoners dressed in female attire at 13, Wakefield-street, Regent-square.'

'You had followed them?' the Clerk of the Court asked.

'Yes,' Chamberlain replied simply.

Fanny and Stella looked at each other uneasily. This was a complete shock. Until now, they had assumed, perhaps naturally, that they had been arrested almost by accident, that the manager or some other dull functionary at the Strand Theatre had summoned the police when he saw what he suspected were two men dressed as women behaving obscenely and 'lasciviously ogling' the male occupants of the stalls.

Chamberlain's evidence changed everything. Neither Fanny nor Stella had breathed a word about 13 Wakefield Street to anyone. Not to Hugh Mundell, and certainly not to the police. Fanny had given her address as Bruton Street, and Stella had given the address of her mother and father in Maida Vale. Wakefield Street was a secret, their secret. So how did the police know about it? How was it that Chamberlain had been there last night, outside, watching for them, waiting for them, following them?

Chamberlain's next piece of evidence was even more alarming.

'I have been to 13, Wakefield Street, Regent-square this morning, and searched the parlours occupied by the prisoners Boulton and Park, and some other gentlemen,' he announced.

Fanny and Stella listened with increasing horror. Not only did Chamberlain know about their secret place, he had entered it, penetrated it, violated it. Their secret place, their place of safety.

'I found the photographs in the front parlour,' Chamberlain continued, using both hands to pass a tottering pile of photographs to the Clerk, who in turn handed them to Mr Flowers. 'They represent the two prisoners both in male and female attire.'

'Do you detect a likeness with either of the two prisoners

in female attire now, dressed both as male and female?' Mr Flowers asked.

Chamberlain squinted almost leeringly at Fanny and Stella in the dock.

'I do, Your Worship,' he said.

Chamberlain went on to reveal that he had been watching Fanny and Stella 'for a year past'. A whole year. And Police Constable Charles Walker, the fourth and last policeman from 'E' Division to give evidence that day, testified that he had been on constant surveillance duty outside Wakefield Street for the past fortnight and 'had seen both the prisoners go in and out at all hours of the night, repeatedly'. The neighbours, he said, had started to complain.

Fanny and Stella were in a state of shock. Their arrest, far from being almost accidental, far from being a bit of bad luck, now looked much more sinister. It had clearly been planned down to the last detail. Both by day and by night they had been watched, they had been followed, and their comings and goings recorded by a phalanx of policemen. And it had been going on for more than a year. Their sanctum in Wakefield Street had been discovered and turned over. Their photographs had already been produced in court, and they knew that there was more, much more, to come.

For a start there were the letters. Stella, in particular, wished that she could remember exactly which letters she had so carelessly strewn around Wakefield Street, and wished that she had been a little more careful, a little more discreet. Some of the letters – in truth, most of the letters – were in one way or another compromising, certainly to her, and more than likely to her friends. Those letters told the story of her life, and now that story was in the hands of the police.

Mr Abrams, the solicitor hired by Carlotta Gibbings to speak for Fanny and Stella in court, did his best, but he was clearly out of his depth. He was under the impression that he was to plead for two young men who had been caught out in a lark, a frolic, a call-it-what-you-will, but now he was confronted by something far more serious.

'Much of the evidence brought forward has taken me somewhat by surprise,' he told Mr Flowers, quite truthfully. 'But, so far as it goes, I respectfully submit that unless it can be clearly shown that these two persons were engaged on this evening in some unlawful purpose, no offence against the statute has been committed.'

It was a brave try but Mr Flowers was having none of it. 'The onus is rather thrown on them to allow that there was no unlawful purpose,' he retorted.

'I am not going to uphold their act, but I submit that it was . . .' and here Mr Abrams faltered, ' . . . that it was an act of folly.'

'This act of folly has been going on for a long time,' said Mr Flowers severely, and proceeded to remand Fanny and Stella in custody for seven days.

Fanny gave a start and Stella swayed a little. They both gripped the rail of the dock to support themselves. Stella looked as if she might faint. They were numb with shock. There seemed to be no end to the charges against them, nothing the police did not already know. The curtain had fallen on their first appearance and now there was a veil of darkness between them and the world they had once so joyously inhabited.

With their elbows firmly gripped by the court gaoler, they were forced to put one foot in front of the other and stagger out of the dock on their way to heaven-knows-where.

A prison or a scaffold. At that precise moment it was all the same to Fanny and Stella.

5

Foreign Bodies

EXAMINATION OF PEDERASTS: Place the suspect in a well-lit room and bend him forwards in such a way until his head is almost touching the floor. Part his buttocks with your hands and note the appearance of the anus. Then slowly insert a finger into the orifice to test fully the resistance of the sphincter.

Charles Vibert, *Précis de médicine légale*, 1893

D r Paul never was able to give a convincing explanation as to why he was loitering in the street immediately outside Bow Street Magistrates' Court just as the hearing inside was coming to an end. It was almost exactly one o'clock and he looked as if he were waiting for someone or something.

Though he later tried to suggest that it was a mere coincidence that he happened to be in Bow Street on that particular day, at that particular time – that he just happened to be passing – Dr Paul did not seem in the least surprised when a police constable touched him on the arm. In fact, he seemed almost to be expecting it: 'I was in the street,' Dr Paul said, 'and the policeman came and told me that Inspector Thompson wanted me.'

Dr James Thomas Paul was Divisional Surgeon to 'E' Division of the Metropolitan Police. He had been appointed in January 1864, and the salary the job afforded was a useful addition to the meagre income he earned from his practice as a surgeon. The work was repetitive rather than onerous. His job was to look after any and all of the medical needs of the 195 police officers of 'E' Division: their aches and pains, their cuts and bruises, their coughs and sneezes and wheezes, Dr Paul dealt with them all. If they were injured, he patched them up; if they were ill, he physicked them; and if they had the clap – and many of them did – he tried to cure them.

It was Dr Paul's job, too, to do what he could for the eight thousand or so dregs of humanity who washed up on the shores of Bow Street Police Station every year: the drunks and the whores; the thieves and the pickpockets; the mendicants and the mendacious; the mad, the sad and the bad. There were cuts and contusions to attend to, split lips and split heads to join together, the odd fracture, and all the accumulated and interacting diseases of poverty, overcrowding, poor air and even poorer diet. Dr Paul was not a bad man, and he did what little he could.

The constable guided Dr Paul through a warren of stairs and corridors to a small bare room at the back of the court building, lit only by a grimy skylight. It was a forlorn, out-of-the-way place, and it looked as if it had not been used for many a year. It smelt musty and stale. There was a desk, a stool and a tall screen. Inspector Thompson and two of his detectives, Chamberlain and Kerley, were waiting for him.

The door opened and Fanny and Stella were ushered in by the court gaoler. That they were badly frightened was only too evident from their chalk-white faces and the uncontrolled trembling of their bodies. It was barely ten minutes since Mr Flowers had remanded them in custody for seven days. Instead of being taken to the Black Maria to be transported to the

House of Detention, they had been herded along corridors and up and down stairs and now found themselves in this bleak place where the three policemen from the night before and an unknown fourth man were waiting for them, looking very grave.

Fanny and Stella thought they were in for a terrible beating – or even worse. They had heard about such things. It was common knowledge that some policemen liked to administer their punishments privately. It was common knowledge, too, that some policemen liked to take their pleasures privately. And sometimes they liked to do both at the same time.

Fanny and Stella stood in the dark and dingy little room shivering and trembling and imagining the worst when Dr Paul abruptly addressed Stella.

'Step inside here,' he said, pointing to the screen. 'Unfasten your things and drop them down, please to step out of them,' he ordered gruffly, clearing his throat. Stella started to undress: off came the dress and the petticoats, and lastly a curious arrangement: a pair of drawers with silk stockings sewn to them.

Dr Paul took a desk stool and pointed to it.

'Put yourself over that stool,' he said coldly.

'Without saying a word he did so,' Dr Paul said later when questioned in court. 'I did not use my hand with any violence. The prisoners did not offer any opposition to my examining them.'

This was bending the truth. Stella had been reluctant, fearful until Chamberlain or Kerley, one or the other, had said that if she did not comply, 'force would be used'.

Dr Paul claimed that he had been instructed by Inspector Thompson to examine Fanny and Stella to discover whether they were men or women. 'I examined them for the purposes of ascertaining their sex,' he declared baldly.

It was a lie, and not a very clever lie. There was no longer any possible doubt over Fanny and Stella's gender. The whole world knew that Fanny and Stella were men – except, apparently, Dr Paul. Inspector Thompson already knew for a fact that Fanny and Stella were men. They had told him so in no uncertain terms the night before. Ditto Detective Sergeant Kerley and Detective Officer Chamberlain. (It was Chamberlain who had watched, fascinated, as Fanny and Stella slowly stripped off their feminine finery the night before to reveal the shivering, slender bodies of two frightened young men.) The mob that had filled Bow Street that morning knew that they were men, the mob that was still milling around outside the court while Dr Paul was waiting, the mob that had chanted and cheered and jeered, the mob that had screamed filthy and lewd suggestions at Fanny and Stella. Every person present that sunny morning in Mr Flowers's courtroom knew that Fanny and Stella were men. The whole world knew that Fanny and Stella were men – except, apparently, Dr Paul. It was not the first lie that Dr Paul told, and it would not be the last.

When asked again, Dr Paul stuck to his guns.

'I examined them for the purposes of ascertaining their sex,' he answered, but this time adding one crucial qualification. 'I examined them for the purposes of ascertaining their sex, but not that only. I wished to ascertain something more, that was of my own accord, and my own idea.'

Something more. Dr Paul's career as a surgeon had hardly been glittering. He was hard-working enough, a belt-and-braces, run-of-the-mill surgeon with a barely adequate private practice and just his police work to keep the creditors at bay.

What set Dr Paul apart from the legions of other middle-aged, middle-of-the-road surgeons was that Dr Paul had an unusual hobby. He was interested – very interested – in sodomy and in sodomites. Dr Paul had been interested in sodomy and sodomites ever since he was a student, twenty years ago, when he had been taught by Dr Alfred Swaine Taylor, the celebrated and sometimes controversial father of English forensic medicine.

In one of his lectures to students at Guy's Hospital in 1850, Dr Taylor had spoken about a bizarre and disturbing case he had been involved in as a young doctor nearly twenty years earlier. It concerned the death of one Miss Eliza Edwards. On 23rd January 1833, Miss Eliza Edwards had roused her 'sister', seventeen-year-old Maria Edwards, who was sharing her bed, and complained of 'a wheezing in the throat'. It was clear to Maria and to the landlady of the 'house of doubtful repute' in Westminster that Eliza was very poorly indeed.

'Maria, I am dying,' Eliza whispered, gasping for every breath. 'It has pleased God to call me.'

Five minutes later Eliza Edwards was dead. She was just twenty-four, and the probable cause of death was consumption, though some were convinced that it was syphilis. For many years Eliza Edwards had made a name for herself as an actress of some repute, specialising in playing tragic young heroines. But the parts had dried up and, for the past three years, Eliza and Maria had been forced to work as prostitutes.

At an inquest held two days later no one claimed Eliza's body and the corpse was, in consequence, sold to Guy's Hospital for dissection. The dissection was to be carried out by Dr Alfred Swaine Taylor and was expected to be a routine affair, but when Eliza's nightclothes were removed, Dr Taylor discovered to his shock and amazement that the body of this young woman was in fact the body of a young man with a normal set of male organs strapped up with a bandage tied around the abdomen.

Outwardly, Eliza Edwards looked like a young woman.

'There was no appearance of a beard or whiskers,' Dr Taylor reported. 'The hairs on the face seemed to have been plucked out with tweezers. The hair was upwards of two feet in length, of a soft glossy texture. The features were of a feminine character.'

No one had suspected that Eliza was a man: not Maria, Eliza's supposed sister, who had lived with her since she was seven and who had worked with her as a prostitute; not Dr Somerville and not Dr Clutterbuck, both of whom had attended Eliza during her last illness; not the proprietress of the brothel in which Eliza and Maria lived and worked; and not, most of all, the succession of gentlemen callers who came, and came again, to pass an hour or so with the beautiful and talented Miss Edwards.

Pressing on with his examination, Dr Taylor noted that Eliza Edwards's anus was deformed. 'The state of the rectum left no doubt of the abominable practices to which this individual had been addicted,' he wrote. 'It was noticed by all present that the aperture of the anus was much wider and larger than natural.' Dr Taylor was also shocked to discover that 'the *rugae* or folds of skin which give the puckered appearance to the anal aperture had quite disappeared' – so much so, indeed, 'that this part resembled the labia of the female organs'.

Not only had Eliza Edwards dressed as a woman, acted as a woman, passed as a woman, she had, by the mysterious alchemy of sodomy, effectively *become* a woman.

This strange story of Eliza Edwards had fired the imagination of the young student doctor James Thomas Paul, and he had maintained an interest – verging on the obsessional – in sodomy and sodomites ever since. There was, he found, precious little information on the topic, but what there was Dr Paul had read. There was Dr Taylor's cautious and short section on the forensic aspects of sodomy in his book *The Principles and Practice of Medical Jurisprudence*. Then there was George Drysdale's hugely popular *The Elements of Social Science, or Physical, Sexual and Natural Religion*, first published in 1854 and running to no fewer than thirty-five editions, which was remarkably frank about the extent of sodomy in England, its causes and its cures.

Dr Paul's most recent and highly prized acquisition was a copy of Professor Ambroise Tardieu's *Étude médico-légale sur les attentats aux mœurs*, first published in Paris in 1857 and running into many editions. It was an astonishing work of urban anthropology, a physiological and psychological primer in sodomy. It professed to be a textbook telling the police, the medical profession and the legislature everything they had ever wanted to know about sodomy and sodomites, and much more besides. In it, Tardieu made a series of sensational claims about how the signs of sodomy were forensically written upon the body, indelibly inscribed, especially upon the anus and upon the penis.

Now, for the first time in his career, Dr Paul was about to examine two real-life sodomites. Dr Paul did not know what – if anything – he would find. Perhaps there would be nothing. The anuses of these two young men might prove to be no different from the hundreds, nay thousands, he had examined during his medical career. And in all these thousands of anuses never once had he seen any signs of sodomy – though it was, it must be said, *not* for the want of looking.

It was true that on a few occasions – several occasions, in fact – he had examined the anuses of women who had been buggered or 'abused by men', as he carefully and cautiously phrased it, and he had even given evidence in some of these cases. Dr Paul knew very well, as did every doctor worthy of the name, that buggery between men and women was much more common than most people dared to imagine.

Many men thought that having anal sex with a woman protected them in some way from syphilis and gonorrhoea – contagions and contaminations indissolubly associated with the spasms and miasmas of the vagina and its secretions. And there was a persistent folk belief that buggery with a woman would even effect a cure for clap, any sort of clap. Anal intercourse with a woman might be considered by some a 'special continental vice', an imported speciality of the swarms of decadent French whores who had flooded into London in the past twenty years, but in reality it was a widespread practice – not just a convenient form of birth control, but also a pleasurable end in itself.

Of course, as Dr Paul knew only too well, buggering a woman was – on paper at least – a serious crime: 'unnatural connexion with a woman' was the way the charge was usually, euphemistically, phrased. But was it not woman's ordained role in nature to be penetrated, to be a receptacle, for man? Anal sex was an unspoken part of that ordained role, unless, of course, there were special circumstances, like anal rape, which brought the crime to the attention of the police. Buggering a woman might be illegal, but the law more often than not turned a blind eye. Buggering a woman might be unnatural, but at least it was *naturally* unnatural – utterly unlike a man buggering another man or, God forbid, allowing himself to be buggered by a man.

That was quite another order of crime, an *unnaturally* unnatural connexion, a crime, an outrage upon Nature and an affront to God, an inversion, a blaspheming of the divinely ordained order of things.

Male and female created He them.

Only when he came to sum up his findings did Dr Paul betray the least emotion.

'I had never seen *anything* like it before,' he said in a shocked tone of voice. 'I have been in practice sixteen years, seven years out of that at the St Pancras General Dispensary, and I have on very many occasions examined the anuses of persons. I do not in my practice *ever* remember to have seen such an appearance of the anus, as those of the prisoners presented.

'I examined Boulton, and found him to be a man,' Dr Paul testified. 'The anus was dilated, and more dilatable, and the muscles surrounding the anus easily opened.'

Then it was Fanny's turn.

'Boulton was then removed, and the prisoner Park came behind the screen,' Dr Paul deposed. 'I said to him the same I had said to Boulton.'

Fanny stripped herself naked and bent herself over the same desk stool.

'The anus was *very* much dilated,' Dr Paul recounted almost by rote in court, 'and dilatable to a very great extent. The rectum was large, and there was some discoloration around the edge of the anus, caused probably by sores.'

The small puckering folds of skin around Fanny's anus – the *rugae* – he noticed were abnormal: 'I found them loose, and not in their normal state. I should say they were rough.'

There could, he said, be one – and only one – explanation

for the slackness of Fanny and Stella's bottoms. 'The insertion of a foreign body numerous times would account for those appearances,' he said.

Dr Paul was pressed as to exactly what he meant by 'the insertion of a foreign body numerous times'.

'The insertion of a man's person would cause the appearances I have described,' he replied. A 'man's person', a man's penis, or rather, men's penises – lots of men's penises – were the cause of the extraordinary state of Fanny and Stella's bottoms. They had, in Dr Paul's opinion, been so repeatedly sodomised by men that the anus had lost much if not most of its natural elasticity.

There was more. Dr Paul also examined Fanny and Stella's penises. Again he was shocked by what he found. Stella's penis and scrotum were 'of an inordinate length' and Fanny's 'private parts were elongated'. What, he was asked, might cause such an elongation of the penis?

'Traction,' Dr Paul replied solemnly. 'Traction might produce elongation of the penis and the testicles.'

It was an alarming comment, conjuring up an image of Fanny and Stella's penises physically distorted and elongated by the rigours of anal penetration. One of Dr Paul's treasured authorities on sodomy claimed that very often 'the dimensions of the penis of active pederasts were excessive in one way or another', that they were 'pointed and moulded to the funnel shape of the passive anus'. And sometimes they were 'twisted' – a consequence of 'the corkscrew motion required during anal sex'.

There was no doubt in Dr Paul's mind that the bodies of the two young men he had just examined bore all the hallmarks of sodomy. They might protest their innocence until they were blue in the face, but their sins were engraved in scarlet upon their flesh. It was proof, indisputable and unarguable scientific proof, of the charges against them that they 'did with each and one another and with divers other persons feloniously commit the abominable crime of buggery'.

6

Wives and Daughters

> Say, Stella, was Prometheus blind,
> And, forming you, mistook your kind?
> No; 'twas for you alone he stole
> The fire that forms a manly soul;
> Then, to complete it every way,
> He moulded it with female clay:
> To that you owe the nobler flame,
> To this the beauty of your frame.

> Jonathan Swift,
> 'To Stella, Visiting Me in My Sickness', 1720

Mrs Mary Ann Boulton was a devoted wife and an indulgent mother and she did not mind who knew it. Whatever adversity and misfortune they had as a family experienced (and, really, they had endured more than their fair share of adversity and misfortune), they were, she always maintained, a happy family. A very happy family.

Whatever sneers and snide asides there might be from those ignorant souls who looked down upon them because Mr Boulton was engaged in trade, she knew that she was every inch a lady. Her Papa had been a gentleman of 'independent means' and when they were in Dalston Terrace they had lived in quite some style. They were respected and respectable.

And her Papa had not ceased to be a gentleman just because the family had fallen on difficult times and had gone into manufacturing in a small way. Just as she had not ceased to be a lady because she had sought suitable employment as a governess, though she had never 'lived in'. She had been quite emphatic on that point. It was very hard for governesses who lived in not to be made to feel like servants.

Whatever people said about Tottenham, she had always found it most genteel. Indeed, it was her decided opinion that Tottenham, at one remove from the noise and the bustle of the metropolis, with its hedgerows and quaint cottages, was rather more genteel, more truly genteel, than many other parts of London famed for their gentility.

It was in Tottenham that she had been introduced to Mr Boulton. He was handsome, kindly and worldly-wise and six years older than herself – a perfect gap, she maintained. And he was called Thomas, which was her Uncle's name, and the coincidence had struck her as propitious. There seemed to be so many coincidences, so many good omens and portents: Thomas's Papa was a gentleman living in reduced circumstances (though perhaps not quite as gentlemanly as her own Papa), and Thomas, like herself, had cheerfully adapted to his altered condition and was making his way in the world. She knew little about stockbroking, but Thomas had assured her that it was a gentlemanly sort of occupation and that the prospects were excellent.

Thomas Boulton had paid his attentions to her very properly. They had quickly fallen in love, and when he proposed marriage she had accepted with alacrity. He had been undeterred by the absence of any fortune on her part, which, she must confess, had been something of a stumbling block on the road to matrimony. There had been times when she almost despaired of meeting a suitable husband. So on that blessed day when her Papa walked her down the aisle, she had been filled with an overwhelming sense of joy, not unmingled with relief.

Ernest was such a delicate boy from the very start. He was born in the bitterly cold December of 1848 and she worried that her baby, so small and pale and delicate and perfect, would not survive. He had a cough that would not go away, and she would lie awake at night, her heart in her mouth, listening out for him. There was consumption in Thomas's family and he had lost three brothers to it. So she fretted and nursed and prayed and coddled her darling baby boy, and by some miracle he survived that first harsh winter and she was grateful.

She remained grateful, even when her second baby son was called to God just days after he was born. She still had Ernest, her darling Ernest, and he was a joy and a comfort. He was such a lovely little boy, so pretty with his blue-violet eyes, large as saucers in his pale face, and his dark hair cascading in baby curls. People often mistook him for a baby girl.

By the time Gerard was born, when Ernest was four, Mr Boulton had left the stockbroking business and entered the wine trade, which was, by all accounts, a most gentlemanly profession and one in which he was bound to prosper, as it stood to reason that people would always want to drink wine. Mr B did indeed prosper – at least at first – and they moved to Greenwich, to a house in Queen Elizabeth Row.

Ernest was an extraordinary little boy. Extraordinary. He could sing before he could speak, with such a beautiful clear soprano voice. 'And Ernest was so fond of dressing up,' she recalled. 'From the age of six, before he could well speak, he was fond of dressing up and acting female parts.' He could play a maidservant or a little girl with ringlets and a lisp, or he could suddenly assume the airs and graces of a grand lady and then change, in the twinkling of an eye, to a rude, rough, drunken woman of the type they averted their eyes from in the streets. Nothing was lost on Ernest. He saw it all, he stored it all up.

She always remembered the time when her Mamma was staying with them in Queen Elizabeth Row and they were dining. Ernest came in, dressed to perfection as the parlourmaid, and waited upon her Mamma at table. He served the food and poured the wine and the water beautifully.

'Mamma did not recognise him in the least,' Mrs Mary Ann Boulton smiled indulgently at the memory. Indeed, her Mamma had been more than usually stern upon the subject. 'I wonder that, having sons, you have so flippant a girl about you,' she had said, after Ernest went out of the room.

Ernest was not what you might call a boyish boy, and had never exhibited the least interest in the sports and games that most boys liked to play. Mr Boulton had even gone so far as to suggest that Ernest was a trifle effeminate, something of a mollycoddle. They had had words. She would not dignify such an accusation with argument. Suffice it to say that Ernest had always been extremely delicate, and was extremely delicate still, and what mother worthy of the name would not cosset and coddle such a rare and delicate bloom?

It was, perhaps, a little unusual for a boy to make such a convincing girl and sing with such a beautiful soprano voice, but then Ernest was an unusual and talented boy. *She* had never worried about him dressing up as a woman to act and sing. *She* was not narrow. Was it not the rule in the Elizabethan theatre for beardless boys to act the parts of Shakespeare's heroines? If it was good enough for the Bard, it was surely good enough for her. When it came down to it, it was just dressing up and make-believe and, really, she did not see any harm in it then, and she still could not see any harm in it now – even though there had been all this unpleasantness, all these complications.

Dressing up and make-believe. Stella knew – she had always known, ever since she was a little girlish boy – exactly what she wanted for herself. She was to be an actress – a *great* actress, it went without saying – in musical comedies and in burlesque extravaganzas. She would be a dazzling dramatic actress, too, and men and women alike – but in her mind's eye, mostly men – would swoon and thrill as she sang sad songs of love in her perfect soprano voice and weep with pity and wonder at the pathos and power of her performances.

She was to be a queen of the stage: regal, gracious and greatly loved. She would hold her audiences in the palm of her hand. Night after night they would offer their loyalty and their devotion, and in return she would give herself to them, body and soul. Every time she made an entrance a tidal wave of applause would sweep through the auditorium and she would bathe in a rosy hue of love and adoration.

She would be a star. A star shining brightly and beautifully in the magical firmament of the stage. Her image would be etched and reproduced a million times in grainy black printer's ink in the popular newspapers. And theatregoers, from wealthy young sprigs of the aristocracy to spoony young men and rude shop boys, would queue up and pay two shillings and sixpence for a photographic portrait of her looking beautiful and soulful.

Then there would be her beaux, an endless line of love-struck admirers, those selfsame sprigs of the aristocracy, wealthy gentlemen and young officers in full dress uniform, all of them darkly, devastatingly handsome. They would send her lovesick notes written on thick creamy vellum and pretty gifts of hothouse flowers in boxes tied up with golden ribands. She would be duly grateful and duly gracious and send charming little notes of thanks written on delicate lace-edged paper scented with orange-flower water. She would try to be kind and try to be loving to each and every one of them. It was the very least she could do.

She had made her public debut at the age of fourteen playing Maria, the beautiful and tragic young heroine of *The Brigand*, where she sang very prettily and swooned very convincingly as she was abducted by swarthy moustachioed bandits who threatened to rob her of her virtue. She had been loudly applauded and there had been shouts of '*Brava! Brava!*' from the young men in the audience, and some of them even waved and smiled at her when she made her curtsey at the end, blushing very prettily under her greasepaint.

L ife, alas, did not run smooth for Mrs Mary Ann Boulton. The wine trade fell rather short of its early promise and the family was forced to retrench and to move to a smaller house in Peckham Rye.

With careful housekeeping, with much scrimping and scraping, with a great deal of ingenuity, and a few small godsends of gifts of money from her family, Mrs Mary Ann Boulton had just about managed to keep up appearances and ensure that Ernest and Gerard had 'everything they required', everything that two young men from a good family would expect and might be expected to have.

'I never allowed any cloud to fall upon my children,' she declared proudly. 'Whatever troubles we have had, I have always shielded them from everything.'

Things went from bad to worse. Mr Boulton continued to suffer 'reverses' – in truth, 'great reverses' – in business, so much so that he was obliged to cut his losses and look about him for a new opportunity. Only a small legacy from her departed Grandpapa kept the family afloat. The vexed question of Ernest's profession could not be put off for much longer. Ernest was nearly eighteen and had done very little since leaving school except act and sing and mope around the house. With things as they were, they could not afford articles for a profession, so what was Ernest to do with himself?

Ernest was adamant that he did not want to enter a dreary profession. He wanted to sing and to act. But his father was equally adamant that no son of his would ever work in the theatre. Dressing up and make-believe were no life for a boy, he said. Private theatricals were one thing. But he could not, would not, countenance the theatre as a profession. It was not a fit place for a young man starting out in the world.

Quite apart from the unsuitability of the theatre, it was a question of money. Ernest would always have a home with them, but a boy of his age needed money of his own.

'If he asked his father for anything, he always gave it,' Mrs Mary Ann Boulton said. 'I daresay he had upon an average, a pound a week pocket money and sometimes more.' It was a not inconsiderable sum, and it pressed hard upon their slender and straitened means. Mr Boulton said Ernest needed to earn his living, and the sooner he started work, the better.

As Ernest's mother, she found herself in a difficult position. Of course she agreed – she always agreed – with Mr Boulton. She had the greatest respect for his judgement. He knew the world and its manifold snares for the unwary and the naive. But it was hard to see Ernest so unhappy and so pale. There had been scenes and tears, and it was all very upsetting.

The London and County Bank in Islington was a very long way from Peckham, and each morning Stella would have to rise shortly after six to make the tiresome journey. Sometimes she would take the train from Lower Knights Hill to Victoria and then catch an omnibus, or when the weather was kind she would walk some of the way and pocket the money.

She had agreed, with the greatest reluctance, to become a clerk at the London and County Bank at a salary of £50 a year. Papa had arranged it. The prospects, her fellow clerks assured her, were excellent. In due course, Stella would become a fully fledged counter clerk and might eventually rise to the dizzy heights of a senior clerk. Stella could barely repress her yawns. If Mr Lewis, the chief clerk at the Islington branch, was anything to go by, she would rather die, she was sure, before turning into such a fussy, fiddling, pernickety dried-up stick of a man. She was bored and exhausted by the time she arrived in the morning, and she could hardly wait for the majestic mahogany timepiece to chime six times and let her make good her escape from the terrible clockwork monotony of the bank.

Mrs Mary Ann Boulton blamed herself for Ernest's illness. It was really very extraordinary that Ernest's ill-health should have so exactly coincided with his work at the bank. The hours were far too long, and there was that terrible journey, there and back, five – sometimes six – days a week, and in all seasons. It was all too much for him. He was delicate. 'He was consumptive – three doctors had said he was consumptive – and he had a constant cough,' she said. It was no wonder that

Ernest was so continually absent from the bank. And if the cough and the colds and the weakness of his chest were not enough, he developed that terrible abscess, that fistula, in such an unfortunate and indelicate area, which caused her poor boy so much pain and discomfort, so bravely borne.

In the end she put her foot down and insisted that Ernest could not continue. Which was just as well, because Mr Lewis had written a very serious letter to Mr Boulton about Ernest's absences and even suggested, none too tactfully, that he might be temperamentally unsuited to the London and County Bank. From the very moment he resigned, Ernest's spirits soared and he declared that he would devote his life to the theatre. There was little they could do to dissuade him.

'I was always rather opposed to his acting,' Mrs Mary Ann Boulton said later, her voice thin and querulous. 'But I did not forbid it. I would rather he would have done anything else, but he always had such a penchant for it that I was almost compelled to give my sanction.'

For as long as Stella could remember men had always taken notice of her. In school and out of school, at the theatre and at concerts, in church on a Sunday, on the streets, out shopping with Mamma, sitting on the omnibus and walking in the park, she had felt the hungry eyes of men of all types and all conditions upon her. There were the usual sniggerings, catcalls and whistles, and a quite bewildering array of lewd and shocking suggestions and gestures from the army of coarse and common young men thronging the streets as she made her way to and from the London and County Bank. She had been mortified at first and had cried into her pillow at night, but her Mamma had comforted her, smoothed her brow and lulled her into sleep.

And then she had started answering the rude men back, and sometimes she made them laugh. It did not take long to learn the difference between the hostile men and those whose suggestive banter was nothing more nor less than flirtation. She could see and feel the shiver and ache of desire in the flashing eyes of these young men. And some of them were quite handsome, really *very* handsome, in a common sort of way, and she was sometimes surprised to find that they provoked an answering shiver, an answering ache within herself.

Then there were the respectable men, mostly married, who would fall quite naturally into polite conversation with her at the bank and on the bus and in the park and at the concert hall. One thing would lead to another, and she would accept their invitation to luncheon, to tea or to supper. She would be modest and polite and smile boyishly or girlishly and sometimes look at them intensely from the depths of her blue-violet eyes and, when she saw them tremble, she knew what it was that they wanted.

And often, quite often – in fact, more often than not – she gave them what they wanted, in small, strange hotel rooms; in little out-of-the-way lodgings; in small houses where wives and children and maids-of-all-work were out; in parks and garden squares, after dark, behind trees and bushes; down alleyways, along towpaths; in closes, courtyards and crooked ways; in urinals and cubicles and public conveniences; in the dark, always hiding, always hidden; always watching, always fearing; always ready to fly when danger threatened.

Sometimes they told her that they loved her and they wanted her. Sometimes they said nothing. Only a few ever kissed her. Which disappointed her. Most only wanted one thing. They would hug and hold and squeeze her and then fumble clumsily with her trousers until they were down and off and then the deed was quickly accomplished. They would spend in her mouth or in her hand, and sometimes between her buttocks. If she felt like it, if she had that curious feeling, like an itch but not quite an itch, if they were not too big – or even if they were – she would let them penetrate her and spend in her bottom.

Afterwards they would wipe themselves and wash themselves vigorously, as if they were ashamed of what they had done. She was surprised at how many would start to cry. Sometimes they would kneel and pray for forgiveness from God. And sometimes they would hand her a golden sovereign and beg *her* forgiveness. Stella never knew what she had to forgive. But she said she forgave them nonetheless because it made them feel happier, and she always pocketed the golden sovereign.

Thankfully they were not all like that. Some men wanted to stay, to talk, to kiss, to embrace. And a few, more than a few, said they wanted to see her again and seemed to mean it. Such ardent swains could be very persistent and very cloying. Some of them begged her to share their lives, begged her, with tears in their eyes, for her love. But such love affairs were doomed, Stella concluded. They did not so much want to love her as to possess her, to own her as their plaything, as a china doll to be dressed up prettily in a suit or a satin gown.

Some of the coarse young men from the uncharted erotic swamp of nameless streets and alleyways, the working men, the soldiers and sailors and dark-skinned foreign men, just wanted to fuck her again and again until she could hardly bear the pain. She would leave drenched in the smell of their sweat and their seed and she would feel different. She would feel replete. And again and again she found herself drawn back to these men, drawn back by their feral bodies and their feral smells and, through the strange alchemy of lust, find rest and repose.

Stella loved them all. She knew that she could saunter on to the streets – in drag or out of drag, as Stella, Star of the Strand, or as plain Ernest Boulton – and that sooner or later a man, or several men, would proposition her. She drew notice. She compelled notice. They told her she was beautiful and that they desired her. They wanted her, they needed her. And Stella knew that it was within her power to make them happy.

In her mind, Stella compared going with men – for love or for money – with her life as a great actress. Were the two things *really* so very different? She was kind to men, she gave pleasure to men, to many men, to lonely and unhappy men. She brought joy to their lives, and they returned the favour with pretty gifts. She gave everything she had. She gave herself, body and soul. She performed – consummately – for each and every one. Each encounter was magical and memorable, and until the time came when she would find fame and fortune and marry the younger son of a Duke, she lived in a rosy hue of love and adulation.

7

Becoming Fanny

And all that's madly wild, or oddly gay,
We call it only pretty Fanny's way.

Thomas Parnell,
'An Elegy, to an Old Beauty', 1773

Number 35 Wimpole Street was a house of sorrow, and the early years and youth of Master Frederick William Park, or Miss Fanny Winifred Park as she invariably thought of herself, were tinged and tainted with grief.

Sometimes Fanny would sit quietly in the drawing room and solemnly turn the stiff, gilded leaves of the album of family photographs, and she would feel a lump in her throat and tears pricking at her eyes when she came to the photographs of those three of her brothers and two of her sisters who had died in their infancy. As the youngest of twelve children, she had not known these early departed brothers and sisters and she would often wonder how they would have been had they lived.

But Fanny had known her brother Atherton for all her short life. She was seven when the news of his death was received, and she could still recall how 35 Wimpole Street was plunged into a dark and terrible passage of grief, and how her Papa turned suddenly into a frail old man. Lieutenant Atherton Allan Park, so handsome in the full dress uniform of the 24th Bombay Native Infantry, so proud to serve his Queen and country, so cruelly cut down – hacked to death – at Jhansi under the burning Indian sun. Fanny shivered and shuddered at the thought.

Her tears would flow even more strongly when she looked at those precious few photographs of her poor Mamma, taken from them when Fanny was not yet three. Fanny herself could only remember her Mamma in fragments and feelings, as if from a half-waking dream. But Lucy, Sissy and Atherton (until he was so cruelly taken), and Alexander and Georgina – even Harry (though he was only seven at the time) – could all remember Mamma and could all tell Fanny about her and the way she was.

And then there was Mary Batson, who had nursed all twelve of them and had been her Mamma's nurse when *she* was a little girl. Mary Batson was still with them after all these years, and Mary knew everything there was to know about Mamma. Fanny would sit and listen to Mary's stories about the old days, about life in Merton Grove, when Wimbledon was a charming small village, about the balls, the parties and the love affairs, and about the time Papa and Mamma got married.

Everybody, from Mary Batson to Papa, to Lucy and Sissy and Georgina, agreed that her Mamma had been sweet-tempered and kind, with never a harsh word to say about anybody or anything.

She was also very devout, and it was she, Mary Batson said, who had introduced morning and evening prayers into the house. Even after Mamma's early departure from this world, the tradition had continued, though now only in the mornings, and for as long as she could remember Fanny had knelt in the crowded drawing room for what seemed like an age as Papa led the household in prayers of exhortation and supplication. (Not that any of it had done much good, Fanny reflected, given the catalogue of griefs and sorrows that had been inflicted upon them.)

Number 35 Wimpole Street was a house of women. Counting the servants, there were no fewer than thirteen women to three men and two boys. When he was at home, Papa was usually in his study. Atherton was away with the Army in India, and Alexander, who was eleven years older than Fanny, was away at school. Which left only herself and Harry in a houseful of women.

Lucy, who was nineteen when Mamma departed this life, had brought up the two boys, with the assistance of Mary Batson and the kindly interference of two elderly aunts. As the baby of the family, Fanny was showered with love and attention and was frankly a little spoilt. Indeed, both boys were spoilt. Harry was tall and handsome. He could charm the birds from the trees, a talent he used to talk his way out of hot water, in which commodity he frequently found himself immersed. Trouble followed Harry like a shadow, and Papa used to despair of him.

Frederick William, or Fanny Winifred, was altogether a different kettle of fish. He – or she – was quite unlike any of his siblings in looks or personality or demeanour. Mary Batson would nod and shake her head sagely over Freddy. It would often turn out this way, she was fond of saying, when the twelfth child was the last child and a boy-child. A changeling. A child of the fairy folk. And, indeed, for those with eyes to see there was something Puckish, something very sprite-like about Fanny, whose mischievous, joyous and playful nature made him into a regular Robin Goodfellow.

It was hard to be angry with Freddy for very long. He was an appealing if curious child, with large, fluid eyes, a mouth that seemed too big for his face, and an abundance of protruding teeth. He was slight and pale, altogether sickly-looking, and was disinclined to sports or exercise – other than walking the streets and promenading in Regent's Park – and he looked as if he needed a good dose of sunshine and fresh country air.

Most of all, Freddy liked to sing and to act and to dance. He liked to dress up as a soldier or a sailor or, better still, a lady, and would caper about the house as a Duchess or a drab and make jokes until the servants' sides ached with laughter. Or he and Harry would write plays and perform them for Lucy and for Papa and Mary Batson. Harry made a dashingly handsome hero, while Freddy would play the imperilled and lovesick heroine, and play her with such conviction and such verve that Lucy and Papa and Mary Batson would sometimes forget for more than a moment that Freddy was a little boy.

Quite when it was that Freddy became Fanny, she could not recollect. Suffice it to say that *she* had not changed. There had been no great or sudden revelation on the road to Damascus for *her* (always a favourite parable of Papa's). The Temple curtain was not rent asunder and nor had the scales fallen suddenly from *her* eyes. No. Becoming Fanny was a process of realisation, rather than revelation. For as long as she could remember, from before she had words to express it or explain it – before she had words at all – she had always been Fanny in her heart, she had always sensed she was different from other boys – but thankfully not from Harry. Never from Harry.

Fanny could not even remember when Harry stopped calling her Fred or Freddy and started to call her Fanny or Fan. It seemed just to happen, and once or twice Harry forgot himself and let it slip before Lucy, who frowned, and Papa who would turn pale and angry. And all the time Mary Batson would chuckle to herself and shake her head and talk nonsensically of changelings and fairy folk.

Becoming Fanny was a slow and painful process, and as she grew older, she became more and more aware that the world as currently constituted did not always look kindly upon those who were different, upon those who did not conform.

To this uncomprehending and uncaring world she was, she realised, an effeminate youth – an effeminate youth unrelieved by any conventional saving graces of beauty. Her head was too big for her body and her teeth were too big for her mouth; her skin was blotchy and inclined to pustules; her hair was wild and wiry; her eyes rather too close-set; her brows too dark; her nose decidedly too emphatic.

Fanny could not help it. She had tried and tried and tried to change, to become more manly, to be more like Atherton and Alexander. But however hard she tried, she always failed. She was never in step with the merry dance of manliness. It was like chasing her own shadow. It eluded her. It evaded her. However hard she sought it, she was destined and doomed never to find it – in this life at least – and there were many nights and many days over many months and many years when Fanny would weep with frustration, shame and misery, and wonder why it was that she had ever been born.

Why could she not be more like Harry, Fanny would often wonder in angry and bitter retrospects. They were cut from the same cloth, coined from the same mint. They were the same, but different. Harry passed. Nobody noticed and nobody guessed. He was just Harry, charming, handsome Harry, who fitted into the jigsaw of his life perfectly. Well, almost perfectly.

But when it came to herself, everybody noticed, everybody

guessed. Fanny could never pass, could never deceive, could never fit in. She was the odd one out, the ugly duckling, the cuckoo in the nest that nobody really wanted or knew what to do with. Nobody except Harry. And then she would weep afresh, with gratitude and love for Harry, and with sorrow that her Mamma was dead.

When the time came, Papa decided not to send Fanny to school. He insisted that she should be a scholar-at-home, taught by Lucy and by Miss Isabella Norris, the governess who had taught all the girls, and though Fanny could not at first fully understand why Papa did not send her away to board at school like Alexander, or be a day boy at a school like Harry, she began to apprehend that her Papa's decision was a strange amalgam of the best and worst of motives: best because he sought to spare her from the taunts and jibes of cruel boys who could not and would not understand her; and worst, because he wanted to hide her away from the world, to save himself and his family from owning to the shame of having Fanny as his child.

It was a dark day when Fanny finally realised that she was an affront to the world, that her very being offended the world in ways small and large. She was not entirely a man and not entirely a woman. To be sure, she had the body of a man. Harry, who seemed to know everything about the bodies of men, had assured her she was a man. There was no doubt about it, he said. But Fanny craved the company of women and she liked womanish things, like dresses and dances and beaux. She could sew, she could knit, and she was at her happiest at home with her sisters, sitting quietly together, or down in the basement with Mary Batson, listening to the reassuring drone of the servants' chitter-chatter.

There were times, however, when Fanny was obliged to ven-

ture beyond the grand portico of 35 Wimpole Street and go into the world that she so affronted. It was hard. Eyebrows would
be raised, gazes averted, backs abruptly turned. Sometimes she
would be stared out of countenance, stared at like an exhibit
in a museum, or like shoddy goods in a shop window. Glared
at with looks of such hatred that she trembled and felt fearful.
There would be muttered comments, whispered threats and
imprecations. Sometimes she was unceremoniously pushed or
shoved aside, spat upon. Or stones were thrown at her.
Urchins would hurl abuse, and furious red-faced gentlemen
would come up to her and deliver foul-mouthed volleys about
who she was and what she was and the terrible fate that would
soon befall her – from the noose to the fires of Hell. And she
would turn pale and tremble but stand her ground.

Thank goodness for Harry. It was Harry, of course, who so
patiently explained everything to her, though where and how
he found it all out, God only knew. If she was being truthful, it
was not so much of a shock, or even a surprise. Harry's disclosures only served to confirm what she already more than halfway
knew. Fanny knew that she liked men in ways that other boys
could not conceive of, and she knew that her feelings were like
those of her sisters. And she knew that Harry was the same.

Harry's disclosures made her feel she might, after all, have
some purpose in life, that she might eventually meet and fall
in love with a gentleman and live happily ever after. But in the
meantime, Harry told her, there were any number of men in
London – and not all of them gentlemen – who would want
to go with her. He would take her. He would show her. Fanny
listened with bright eyes. She felt a shiver of excitement and anticipation at the prospect.

Even though she and Harry both loved and desired men,

Harry was different. He had never evinced the least inclination to dress up as a lady or a serving wench or a fallen woman of the streets (and you did not have to venture very far from the front door of 35 Wimpole Street before stumbling across whores by the dozen plying their trade). Lucy, who had inherited her Mamma's compassion, called them sad creatures, though even she was discomfited by the more brazen types. The elderly spinster aunts merely stuck their noses in the air and hurried past as if to avoid a noxious emission.

But Fanny was fascinated and dazzled by the gaudy peacock colours of these women, by their blowsy ease and raucous laughter, by their painted faces and their billowing, untidy hair, by the smell of sweat and cheap scent which seemed to cling about them, and by other, strangely compulsive smells, which she would have thought she shouldn't like, but she did. And the whores were, by and large, nice to her. They would call her 'Dearie' or 'Margery' or 'Mary-Ann' or 'Miss Nancy', and most of the time it was not in a nasty way. Sometimes she would talk to them, and she found – to her surprise – that she was drawn to them and liked them more than she thought she would. They did not judge her like the others. They did not look down upon her. They would curse and cuss her in a friendly way, and then she would answer back with a haughty toss of her head and they would laugh uproariously.

That it was all wrong in the eyes of God, Fanny of course knew. Between those endless prayers and Bible readings at home and the droning, drowsy sermons in church on a Sunday, Fanny had come to understand the meaning of Sodom and Gomorrah. Harry had told her she was a sodomite (or she would be when the deed was accomplished). Fanny did not altogether care for the word. Sticks and stones, she said to herself, may break my bones, but names can never hurt me.

That it was all wrong under the laws of the land, she quickly discovered, and then wished that she had not. She was eleven or twelve when Harry first got into trouble with the police. The angry conversations went on for days behind the closed mahogany doors of 35 Wimpole Street. But Fanny heard enough about the wretched Italian boy, and Harry filled in the rest, swearing her to secrecy. Harry had been foolish and had fallen in love with a boy who abused his trust. Money was demanded and when no more was forthcoming, the boy carried out his threat. Harry was arrested and taken before the magistrate. It was all a pack of lies, he claimed, his handsome, honest face shining bright with righteous indignation. Fortunately his handsome, honest face carried the day and the case was dismissed.

And then, two or three years later, when Fanny was fifteen or sixteen – she could not properly recall – Harry was arrested in Weymouth Mews in the middle of the night and there was a great to-do and much weeping and wailing and talk of prisons and hard labour. It was a great and terrible scandal, made even worse by the fact that Papa was a very distinguished judge. Harry had shamed himself, shamed his family and shamed his Papa.

Harry was to go away, to disappear, and no one was supposed to know anything about it. And no one was ever to see him again, save for Papa, and perhaps Lucy (and Mary Batson, of course, as she was so old and it was thought that a permanent separation from her darling Harry would hasten her demise).

But as the months and years passed, Papa relented a little, and Harry the prodigal son would sometimes return from exile in Scotland to the bosom of his family, and the blood of fatted calves would be spilt. But only at the small villa in Isleworth, and never, ever in Wimpole Street, for fear of discovery. And through all the long years, despite the separation, the bond between herself and Harry was unbroken, and even strengthened.

What was to become of her? There were two, and only two, professions for the Parks: soldiering and the law. But the idea of Fanny going for a soldier was patently ludicrous. Even Papa had smiled at the idea. So law was the only option. Papa had decided that the best and most profitable – by which he meant morally profitable – course was for Fanny to be articled to a solicitor. He had a gentleman in mind, Mr Gepp of Chelmsford. A steady, slow, solid gentleman with a steady, slow, solid county-town practice.

Judge Alexander Park fervently hoped and prayed that a few steady, slow and solid years under the watchful eye of Mr Gepp would rub off on Frederick, that his enthusiasms would be curbed, that his manner would become graver and more manly, that he would grow some sense – and perhaps even some whiskers.

But the months and years passed and Frederick did not seem to be growing any sense at all. Quite the reverse. The older he got, the less manly, the more effeminate, the more extreme he became. There he would stand, a cigarette in his gloved left hand, his right leg bent slightly forwards, his hips tilted like a woman of the street. His hair would be teased and shined and curled, and he would reek of strong perfume. His face in repose was disdainful, but his eyes were like a lizard's, dark and glittering and restless. He did not have to speak. He did not have to act. His very being, his very presence proclaimed and declared to all the world the sodomite that he was.

It was a strange thing, but it was hard to imagine where Frederick had come from, or who he took after. Rack his brains as hard as he could, Judge Park could not recollect any family member on either side who bore even the remotest resemblance to Frederick. It was as if his son were undergoing a species of transformation from caterpillar to chrysalis to brilliant, gaudy butterfly, and there were times when he found himself half-believing Mary Batson's nonsense about changelings and fairy folk.

Frederick was now a gabbling, good-natured, prattling, gossiping, charming young man who seemed older – much older – and more worldly than his nineteen years, who caused heads to turn for all the wrong reasons whenever he entered a room. He was loud and lewd, and laughed uproariously at his own jokes. Ladies adored him, and he invariably had them in fits of hysterics. Men were either bewildered by him, or made uneasy or hostile by his otherness, by his difference (though a few, surprisingly, were flattered by his violent flirtatiousness).

'Theatrical' was the word, perhaps the only word (or at least the only decent word), to describe the young man that Frederick had turned into. He lived for the theatre. The theatre was his day and his night; his sun and moon and stars; his darkening storms and sunlit passages. There was little or no division between the dressing up and make-believe of the theatre and the dressing up and make-believe of his daily life. They were one and the same. All the world was his stage, and Frederick seemed to ricochet between melodrama, tragedy and comedy – especially comedy of the low and vulgar variety.

There were times when Judge Park had to pinch himself to

make sure that he was not dreaming, that he had not strayed into a fairy realm, or fallen down a rabbit hole and found himself in Wonderland, like the young heroine of Mr Lewis Carroll's story. Frederick's world – or that small portion of Frederick's world of which he had caught glimpses – struck him as decidedly odd. It was a grotesquerie where the men were more like women and the women, though seemingly rarer than unicorns, behaved like men. Nothing was straightforward. Nothing was serious. All was surface. Nothing was substance. It was amorphous, ephemeral and inconsequential and yet, for its denizens, at least, it seemed compelling and all-absorbing.

Of those denizens, from the few that he had met, Judge Park had formed a low opinion, a very low opinion. There was Mr Charles Pavitt, a plump miller's son from Chelmsford who was some sort of professional actor. Then there was the fat and florid Mr Martin Luther Cumming who giggled constantly. Mr Cumming was an Oxford man, supposedly, though he had yet to hear an intelligent remark from him. There was Mr Amos Westropp Gibbings, with a girlish lisp and more money than sense. And finally there was Mr Ernest Boulton, a delicately beautiful young man with sad eyes and a startlingly lovely soprano voice. Mr Boulton was apparently Frederick's best friend and boon companion and they spent hours closeted together, though how they had first met was a mystery that had never been satisfactorily unravelled. There were others, too, who came and went and went and came so often that they seemed to blur into one long, lingering shriek of effeminacy.

Frederick's passion for burlesque had led him into the deplorable habit, in Judge Park's view, of dressing up in women's attire and acting the parts of women. But even Judge Park had to concede that sometimes he did this with consummate skill, having a natural bent for playing domineering duchesses and dowagers of a certain age with great flair and an eye for comic detail that made his audiences laugh out loud.

What could he hope for, what hope was there, for this strange hybrid child, for his changeling son? He was under no illusions. His elder son Harry was tainted with sodomy. There could be no doubt about that and, however much Harry's version of the incident in Weymouth Mews differed from that of Police Constable George White, it was clear to everyone that sodomy was at the very heart of the transaction. And if Harry was so tainted, so stained with sodomy, then Judge Park feared that there could be very little doubt that Frederick was equally tainted, equally stained with the sins of the Cities of the Plain.

Judge Alexander Park was a devout Christian, 'sound in principles, firmly and zealously attached to the sound orthodox doctrines of the Church of England, and pure and correct in his morals'. But devout though he was, devout as his dear departed wife had been, neither of them were Christians of the hellfire and brimstone variety. With half of those children born to him already dead and buried, Judge Park loved and valued those still left to him. He sorrowed and grieved and prayed for Frederick, just as he sorrowed and grieved and prayed for Harry. He could not but despise and loathe the sin, but he could not help loving the sinners. How could he not love his sinful sons? They were the flesh of his flesh, the fruit of his loins. And if that fruit was rotten, then he must shoulder some of the blame and some of the burden and he must do whatever he had to do, whatever could be done, to help and protect them.

What could he hope for – what hope was there – for his errant sons? He could not bear to see them punished. The gravest penalty for sodomy had only been abolished a year or two ago, but ten years to life with hard labour was equally a sentence of certain death. Such a sentence would crush and break them within weeks, and their decline and death would be agonising and inevitable, and every night as he lay sleepless in bed he trembled at the prospect of the terrible fates that might befall his two sodomitic sons.

8

A Tale of Two Sisters

A SISTER'S LOVE : There is no holier feeling
than a sister's love – no affection purer and more
enduring than hers.

The Family Treasury, 1854

W hat could she say about Fanny? That she was a formidable actress? That she was funny? That she was
courageous? That she was loyal? That she drank too much,
spoke too much and laughed too loudly? That she was wise
beyond her years? That she looked older than her years? (And
Stella was sure that she was not being unkind when she said
this, as it was universally agreed that Fanny, with what might be
called her 'sterner features', certainly did look older, very much
older, than her years.) That she knew everything there was to
know about Mary-Anns (as well as knowing every Mary-Ann
on the pad in London)? That she was steeped, not to say
pickled, in the ancient mysteries and rituals of drag? That she
was generous, more than generous – generous to a fault, in fact
– with her favours? That despite the disadvantages of person
she laboured under, Fanny had, more often than not, snatched
erotic victory from the jaws of defeat by a combination of
charm, determination, guile and utter ruthlessness? That she
was a true friend? That she was a loyal sister, if not by ties of
consanguinity then by the most secret and the most sacred
bonds of sorority and of sodomy?

Miss Fanny Winifred Park was one of those young ladies who had blossomed into womanhood early. By the age of sixteen, when most well brought-up girls had but a dim apprehension of distant marriage and motherhood, Miss Fanny Winifred Park was already well schooled in the dark arts of seduction and sodomy. She was certainly no stranger to those thronged thoroughfares around Coventry Street and the Haymarket where the gay ladies of London plied their trade so vigorously. Indeed, Miss Fanny Winifred Park had made her professional debut, so to speak, on this particular West End stage, not far short of her seventeenth birthday, and by dint of assiduous application and hard practice had risen rapidly through the ranks of her chosen profession.

It was a curious thing, but she soon discovered that she was considerably more successful in selling herself when she was in drag than when she was out of drag. While it was certainly true that there were some men to whom a painted and effeminate youth strongly appealed, there were a great many more who were interested in her when she was dressed as a woman.

Miss Fanny Winifred Park was nothing if not a realist. Nature had not endowed her with an abundance of personal advantages. In matters of face, figure, complexion, teeth and hair, Nature had been less than generous (if not downright stingy), and she was only too well aware that in the hierarchy of painted effeminate youths working the streets, she barely reached the middle rank. Though there were some who had left their youth far behind them and now relied on paint slapped on like stucco, equally there were plenty of other, prettier boys who skimmed off the choicest punters and steamers. Not that she was complaining. After all, they were all God's creatures.

Fanny, however, when she was dressed in silk and suitably padded with a bustle and false bubbies, bewigged and with a generous application of paint, was transformed into what was generally termed a handsome woman. Not beautiful, certainly, but then not plain. Nor was there any of the blushing virgin nonsense about her. She was, she liked to think, very much a 'Girl of the Period', as the *Saturday Review* had so memorably phrased it: a fast girl, a girl who lived her life to the full, who drank and smoked, who went about and abroad and was curious about the world. A girl not trepidatious about life; a girl not startled by her own shadow; a girl not hidebound by convention and propriety and all those other suffocating corsets of the mind.

In her short span upon this mortal coil, Miss Fanny Winifred Park had certainly savoured life, and drunk deeply from the cup of Venus. She held her head high and was not ashamed to look men boldly in the eye and to give them what they wanted. Miss Fanny Winifred Park's favours usually came at a price, but she could be soft-hearted and sentimental. There were occasions when she felt it her duty to do what she could to console lonely men, especially soldiers and sailors in the service of the Queen – for whom she felt a particular *tendresse*.

Whatever her faults and virtues, Miss Fanny Winifred Park understood men. Like the best whores, she knew instinctively what men needed. She had the knack of making them happy. She was a good sport. She would dance with them and drink with them. She would listen to them and make them feel wanted. She understood, only too well, the intensity of the erotic abyss men so constantly struggled against and yet so constantly sought. She was their guide. She would take their trembling hands in hers and lead them to the dark side of the moon to assuage the desires that raged like a torrent within them till the pale dawn came and they would be released.

Most, if not all, of her customers laboured under the illusion that Miss Fanny Winifred Park was a woman, and why should they think otherwise? With her generous embonpoint, tweezered eyebrows, painted face and luxurious curls, she looked every inch the successful gay lady. Those gentlemen fortunate enough to enjoy her favours were generally more than satisfied with their purchase and left satiated and entirely un-aware that she was not quite what she seemed. And for the most part, the few who were entrusted with her secret, far from running away from her, seemed all the more excited by the idea. There would always be one or two who would recoil in horror, lash out with their fists or threaten her with the police. It was an occupational hazard, and Fanny was far from blind to the risks (look at her poor brother Harry, exiled to the wilds of Scotland). But she knew she could not live her life in any other way. She was young, she was strong and she was resourceful. She was more than a match for those who would try to do her harm.

Miss Fanny Winifred Park was all things to all men, switch-ing in the twinkling of an eye from the commonest of common whores to the grandest of *grandes dames*. One minute she could wallow and rejoice in filthy talk like a streetwalker, and the next she could delight and charm with small talk which would not disgrace the most refined London drawing rooms. She was welcoming, warm and funny, but when the occasion demanded it, could wither with one fell look. Though she still harboured hopes of a life in the theatre, fame and fortune on the London stage had so far eluded her. She had notched up some considerable successes in the provinces, playing principally dowagers, and her performance as Agatha De Windsor, a wronged woman of a certain age in *Retained for the Defence*, had astonished and delighted the audience in Chelmsford at a benefit for the Infirmary. It had been the high-water mark of her stage career. Never before (and sadly never since) had she experienced such storms of applause; never before (and sadly never since) had she so scaled the heights of Histronia; and never before (and sadly never since) had she been the recipient of one or two admiring letters and bouquets from gentlemen.

Not infrequently Fanny would sally forth dressed in the most impenetrable black with a stricken look upon her face. On such occasions she would be Mrs Fanny Winifred Graham (*née* Park). From the weeds she wore and the expression upon her face, it was assumed by her friends and acquaintances that Mrs Fanny Winifred Graham (*née* Park) was the worthy and dutiful relict of Mr Graham. But none of them could be certain. It was the one subject – in truth, the only subject – upon which Fanny never spoke. Her lips were sealed and if anyone was sufficiently unwise or unfeeling to attempt to resurrect – Lazarus-like – the memory of Mr Graham, Fanny's face would assume a tender expression. Dabbing a handkerchief to her eyes and clearing her throat noisily, she would beg her interrogator's pardon and swiftly change the subject to the latest fashions from Paris, the shocking price of bombazine, or the scandalous antics of the new French girls in Coventry Street.

There were those in Fanny's circle of candid friends, needless to say, who pooh-poohed the very idea of Mr Graham, who said that he was a figment of Fanny Park's fevered imagination, amiably remarking that she had never yet managed to keep a man for more than a night, let alone for long enough to lead him to the altar. These friends were further of the opinion that if Fanny Park really had got herself married, then the gentleman in question must have been very much advanced in years. He was probably senile, quite possibly blind, perhaps even crippled, or a combination of all three. There were many other such pleasantries. Through all these slings and arrows, Fanny would sail serenely on, tightly clasping the truth about the mysterious Mr Graham to her ample and womanly bosom.

'A Tale of Two Sisters'. It might have formed the plot of a burlesque melodrama; or been a story in an illustrated penny magazine; or even a front-page report in one of the more sensational weekly newspapers: by a terrible twist of Fate two sisters are separated at birth and grow to womanhood, each unaware of the existence of the other. Both sisters are sweet, kind and beautiful, and both of them are the object of many handsome and rich beaux. But both sisters are inexplicably sad; they feel a curious sense of being incomplete, of being one half of a whole; they sense a lack, an absence, a void in their lives. Something is missing, or is it *someone*?

Both sisters live useful, busy and fashionable lives in London, filling their time with society, shopping and good works. As they go about their daily business and as their paths inevitably cross (London society is, after all is said and done, not much more than a large, gossipy village), they sometimes have the strangest feeling of having met before. Fanny, the elder of the sisters, who speaks perfect French, uses the phrase *déjà vu*. Stella, who is musical, feels something similar, like a heard, familiar melody from the dim and distant past that she cannot quite place. After many vicissitudes, hair-raising escapades and improbable adventures, after some songs and dances and a few comic interludes, the scales fall from their eyes and a benignant

Fate reunites the two sisters who fall weeping upon each other's necks and vow never again to be parted on Earth or in Heaven.

So it was for the sistering of Fanny and Stella. The heavenly spheres were aligned, and Fanny and Stella had come together as sisters. Fate had brought them together, two halves of a whole, now united, now conjoined in joy. And having found each other, Fanny and Stella were loath to be parted.

By night and by day they did everything together and went everywhere together. To the theatre, to the halls; to the Boat Race, to Bond Street and to the Burlington Arcade; to parks and pleasure gardens; to dives and divans; to balls and cheap dances. Up and down, and down and up, they promenaded and paraded the streets of London, sometimes in drag and sometimes out of drag (and sometimes half-in and half-out, which confused and confounded everybody and meant that no one could be quite sure who or what they were). They hunted and searched and scoured the streets looking for men for love or for money, sometimes finding neither and sometimes finding both.

They wore the same clothes, the same paint and the same *coiffures*. They stood in the same way, their slender feet neatly pointing outwards like a ballet dancer's, their heads slightly thrown back, their gloved hands invariably holding a cigarette or a glass of champagne or a bumper of sherry. They walked arm-in-arm and alike: adopting a rapid, tittuping walk, with their noses stuck in the air, when they wished to have no truck with the world ('your mincing and theatrical walk', Louis Hurt, another of Stella's ardent swains, had once disparagingly and despairingly called it); or a slow, bottom-rolling, leering and lascivious royal progress which caused everyone – foes and friends alike – to stop and stare with a look of horror or delight, or a mixture of the two, upon their faces. Many, if not most, of those who encountered them thought they were either whores or actresses, or both, as – in the minds of most people – the two professions were indivisible. Their life was a performance. London was their stage. The world was their audience. They were exotic, extraordinary and quite magnificent.

'They always said the same thing,' was the hapless Hugh Mundell's attempt to explain the extraordinary manner in which Fanny and Stella spoke in concert. They said the same things at the same time. One would begin and the other would finish. Fanny would echo Stella, and Stella would echo Fanny. And when they spoke, they spoke with the same inflections, intonations and affectations. They used the same gestures, the same mannerisms and the same facial expressions. They laughed in the same way at the same jokes, and the same things displeased them, their brows contracting darkly in the same way. And though they spoke the Queen's English in loud and well-bred tones of command, they were also masters – or rather, mistresses – of common slang, of the argot of whores and the backslang of thieves and trampers and gypsies.

Above and beyond that, they had their own special language, a language into which only they and their confederates – the sodomites, the hermaphrodites and the God-only-knows-what-else-ites – had been initiated. It was called 'the Female Dialect' (or so Fanny, the fount of all wisdom on matters sod-omitical, had informed Stella), and it was as old as time, or nearly so. It was a strange and secret language; an upside-down, inside-out sort of dialect where 'she' meant 'he', and 'he' meant 'she'; where men were called by women's names, where Frederick was Fanny, Ernest was Stella, Amos was Car-lotta, and Cecil was Cecilia, or Sissy for short. Most of the men styled themselves just plain Miss and Mistress, but there was no shortage of those who liked to call themselves Lady This, the Countess of That or the Dowager Duchess of So and So. There was a positive glut of Princesses, and more Queens in the few square miles of London than there were kingdoms in the wide world for them to rule over.

They were sisters. Side by side and shoulder to shoulder. Sisters for better or for worse. Sisters in sickness and in health. Sisters in drag and sisters out of drag. They made a formidable and fearless pair. London stood before them, waiting to be conquered, ready to fall at their feet in a swoon.

9

Monstrous Erections

At Wakefield Street, near Regent Square,
There lived this rummy he-she pair,
And such a stock of togs was there,
To suit those he-she ladies.
There was bonnets & shawls, & pork pie hats,
Chignons and paints, and Jenny Lind caps.
False calves and drawers, to come out slap,
To tog them out, it is a fact.

'The Funny He-She Ladies'

A week to the day after their first appearance in Bow Street, Fanny and Stella were due in court again. 'The crowd outside was immense,' *Reynolds's Newspaper* reported, and 'completely blockaded the thoroughfares.' The police struggled to control the excited mob of a thousand or more who had come to gawp, to jeer and to cheer. Every window that commanded a view of the court was crowded with spectators, and dozens of people clung precariously to the roofs of cabs to try and catch a glimpse of these extraordinary men-women. Inspector Thompson and several detachments of his officers were hard-pressed to clear a way through the noisy, seething mass to allow the prison van to make its slow progress to the entrance of the court.

If the mob had expected Fanny and Stella to appear in all their feminine finery, they were disappointed. Instead of the gaudy, painted creatures they had hoped to see, two neatly dressed, clean-shaven young men stepped out nervously, evidently bewildered by the size and the noise of this largely good-natured crowd. Without paint and after a grim week on remand in the House of Detention in Coldbath Fields, they looked pale, frail and fragile. Even though they were out of drag, their plucked and tweezered eyebrows and their tightly fitting suits with nipped-in waists and exaggerated revers gave them a decidedly arch and feminine air.

The arrest of 'the Young Men Personating Women', 'the Hermaphrodite Gang', 'the Funny He-She Ladies', as they were called variously by the newspapers, had caused an unparalleled sensation. Every aspect of Fanny and Stella's lives – their arrest, their appearance, their clothes, their backgrounds – had been lovingly and lasciviously dilated upon and speculated over and, where facts were in short supply, cheerfully invented. 'It is suspected,' the *Daily Telegraph* breathlessly reported, 'that there are others, besides those in custody, who have for some time past been personating females in London. In fact it is stated that an association exists which numbers nearly thirty of these foolish young men.'

The *Illustrated Police News* went further and stated as a fact that a number of 'these foolish if not unnatural young men' had recently given a drag ball 'at a well-known hotel in the Strand, at which twelve of the party represented females and twenty of their companions the opposite sex'. There were rumblings and rumours too of important people – politicians and peers of the realm – who were implicated in the growing scandal, and heavy hints that mass arrests were imminent.

Every newspaper in the country had carried the story, and it would soon be making headlines in Europe and in the United

States. An enterprising publisher had already rushed out a penny pamphlet – *The Lives of Boulton and Park: Extraordinary Revelations* – which told the story so far, rehashing the testimony of Hugh Mundell and expressing many pious disapprovals of Fanny and Stella.

Of all the crimes Fanny and Stella were purported to have committed, by far the most heinous was Fanny's 'violation' of the Ladies' Retiring Room at the Strand Theatre on the night they were arrested. 'Nothing', the anonymous author of the penny pamphlet declared, more plainly showed 'the base and prurient natures which these misguided youths possess' than the 'unblushing impudence' of Fanny's application to the female attendant to pin up the gathers of her skirt which had become unfastened.

It was standing room only inside Bow Street and the courtroom was stiflingly hot. Some spectators had queued for five hours to see Fanny and Stella and to hear 'the filthy details' of the case. There was an unexpected air of jocularity and expectation, quite at odds with the severely moralising tone of the newspapers. One 'noble lord' spent the greater part of his day in Bow Street surveying Fanny and Stella through an opera glass. Many of those present were, as the newspapers reported, gentlemen belonging to the theatrical profession, and one of them, the manager of a popular theatre in the Strand, was heard to remark that if this sort of attraction was likely to last, it would be desirable to add another row of stalls to the court and 'allow seats to be booked a fortnight in advance'.

It was clear, too, that some friends of Fanny and Stella had queued for hours to get into court. 'Theatrical' covered a multitude of sins, and in addition to such leading comic actors as

Edward Askew Sothern and J. L. Toole, who had come to witness and wonder at the sport in Bow Street, there was an odd group of spectators who came to the court day in and day out. They were allsorts: young and old, tall and short, fat and thin – and all conditions in between. Some were well dressed, some sloppily dressed, and some were quite clearly mutton dressed up as lamb, wearing clothes that were too young, too fashionable or too tight. Some were decidedly effeminate with perfectly arched eyebrows that made them look permanently surprised, and some were sporting subtly dyed or not-so-subtly dyed curling locks. Many seemed to know one another and despite their very obvious differences there seemed to be a common weal between them. They were the very disparate parts of a curious whole, and there was a distinctly tribal quality about them.

As the case went on, this clique or claque of men formed a strange chorus, greeting much of the evidence – especially the evidence that favoured Fanny and Stella – with 'a most indecent manifestation of applause expressed by stamping and cheering' – much to the dismay of the magistrate, Mr Flowers, who entreated, most ineffectually, that 'such ebullitions of feeling should be restrained'. In the days that followed, as the witnesses for the prosecution took their turn in the box, many of them denounced these ardent supporters as sodomites, Mary-Anns and fellow he-she ladies.

Commencing proceedings, Mr Poland, the prosecuting attorney, stood up and brandished theatrically the detailed inventory of items seized at Wakefield Street by Detective Officer Chamberlain. Clearing his throat he proceeded to read it aloud to the accompaniment of much raucous laughter. Fanny and Stella could hardly repress their smiles. 'The list of articles in-

cluded the following,' Mr Poland said, drawing a deep breath
before plunging in:

Dresses:

Mauve satin, trimmed with black lace
White corded rep silk, trimmed with white lace
Pink satin, and tulle
White glacé, trimmed with blue satin and lace
White Japanese silk, pink stripe, trimmed with white lace
    and swansdown
Green cord silk
Violet glacé silk and white lace
Black satin, trimmed with mauve satin
Blue and white satin, piped with white satin
Mauve rep silk and green satin
Blue satin tunic
Pink tartalan
Muslin
Camlet costume
Cambric evening
Grey moiré antique
&c.

Here Mr Poland paused for breath. The list was exhaustive and
exhausting. 'Also,' he continued:

a number of skirts and petticoats, in tulle, tartalan, white
frilled cambric, white book muslin; frilled, check, plain
and coloured petticoats, crinolines, &c; cloaks, jackets
and bodices, opera cloaks, shawls, ermine jackets and

muff; crimson velvet and tunic; about a dozen pairs of
ladies' kid boots, shoes, &c; seven chignons (of various
kinds and colours), two long curls, ten plaits, and one
grey beard.

'The grey beard can hardly be called part of a woman's
costume,' a bemused Mr Flowers interjected.

'It may be part of a disguise,' Mr Poland snapped, clearly
irritated by the interruption. 'Curling irons, sunshades, six
pairs of stays,' he went on, 'one face press-over, two tulle falls,
chemisettes, garters, drawers, four boxes of violet powder, one
of bloom of roses, silk stockings, eight pairs of gloves, one
bottle of chloroform, artificial flowers and a great quantity of
wadding – used apparently for padding.'

D rag was not for the faint-hearted. It required discipline,
stamina and a great deal of ingenuity. Money helped, as
did plenty of space to store it all – which is where Martha Stacey's ground-floor dragging-up rooms came in so useful. The
sheer volume and complexity of the wardrobe of even the moderately well dressed young lady-about-town required a great
deal of time and attention.

Fanny and Stella's extensive drag wardrobe mirrored the
garish artificiality that was the fashionable order of the day.
Women of fashion laboured long and hard to present to the
world a brilliantly enamelled exterior of wasp-waists, heaving
bosoms and large bustling behinds. Nature was not enough.
It could be improved upon, altered, faked and falsified. Wasp-
waists required the tightest of tight-lacing, causing ladies
young and old to faint frequently and doctors repeatedly to
warn that prolonged tight-lacing could lead to permanent in-

ternal damage; bosoms were pushed and prodded and padded until they heaved; and the largest or smallest of behinds could be made to bustle by the use of a steel frame and half a dozen layers of flounced horsehair. An arsenal of false hair, false teeth, false bottoms, false breasts – and on at least one occasion, a false leg – was strategically deployed, along with a formidable battery of dyes and paints and an artillery of chemical processes to create the perfect woman. Beauty was made, not born. It was a commodity, manufactured, measured, sold and, above all, bought.

Acquiring the frocks, the petticoats, the stays, the undergarments, the shoes and all the other female accoutrements was no mean feat. It was hard, but not impossible, for men to buy dresses without arousing suspicion and hostility. Fanny and Stella had made daring trips in drag to the new emporia of Regent Street and Oxford Street where they had bought gloves and other accessories. Such was their airy disregard of convention, and so convincing their disguise, that Fanny and Stella could easily sweep into almost any gown shop in London and try on as many frocks and petticoats and cloaks and coats as they liked. Shopkeepers would naturally assume that they were a pair of soiled doves – extremely soiled doves – but then, many of their best customers were ladies of that sort, and morals rarely, if ever, got in the way of business.

Even if the doors of some of the most refined shops were firmly closed to Fanny and Stella, there were always alternatives. Like the irrepressibly cheerful young hero of the burlesque farce *A Sneaking Regard*, who breezily declares that he's off to 'a Theatrical Wardrobe Shop in Cross Street, to borrow the toggery, and equip myself well out in tip-top feminine style', Fanny and Stella would visit theatrical costumiers for wigs, for make-up, and, importantly, for boots and shoes which were hard to find in their sizes.

And if the need arose, there were any number of skilled needle-women in London – milliners, dressmakers, stay-makers, bonnet-makers and assorted lowly stitchers – who could barely support themselves and who had, more often than not, to turn to prostitution when times were hard. Many would happily turn a blind eye to measuring up and making up frocks and garments of a more intimate nature for young men for their 'private theatricals'.

Then there were the countless fripperers' shops, selling second-, third- and even fourth-hand finery, where a young man might purchase a dress for his wife or for his sweetheart – or for himself. And like thousands of women, Fanny and Stella may have taken advantage of the offer of sending '42 stamps' to Isabella and Samuel Beeton's *The Englishwoman's Domestic Magazine*, receiving in return a paper dress pattern of the latest French fashions. With a sewing machine and a little common sense, they could run up their own exquisite creations.

Since the 1850s there had been an explosion in the number of newspapers and magazines – and a corresponding explosion in advertising and mail order. By 1870, ladies and gentlemen could buy almost anything by mail order, particularly products the mere mention of which might bring an unbecoming blush to their cheeks. Publications groaned with advertisements for quack cures – pills, balms, cordials, panaceas, elixirs, specifics and tonics – for every ailment, real or imagined. Pages were crammed with advertisements for every kind of corset, stay, busk or truss; for undergarments of all conceivable varieties; for hair removers and hair improvers; for breast enlargers and breast re-ducers; and for a bewildering variety of cosmetics, creams and lotions to allow gentlemen and ladies – and would-be ladies – to transform themselves from ugly ducklings into fully fledged swans. Mail order was a godsend for Fanny and Stella, and no doubt a steady stream of packages addressed to Mrs Fanny Graham or Miss Stella Boulton would arrive at Wakefield Street or wherever else they happened to pitch their camp.

Hair was another vexed question. Hairstyles were heroic: towering, complex architectural follies involving one, two and sometimes as many as three chignons, hairpieces attached to a substructure called a frisette. Chignons and frisettes – these 'monstrous erections of dyed and false hair' – were heavy, often weighing two or three pounds. They were said to 'impose such a weight on the heads of these martyrs that they deserve pity rather than reproof', and the notorious procuress Madame Rachel wore such 'a whopper' of a chignon, ''twas said she was quite bandy-legged through the weight of her head'.

In the hysteria generated by Fanny and Stella's arrest, the *Graphic* claimed that there were 'hair-dressing establishments at the West End where a young gentleman, although previously bearded like the pard, may emerge within an hour's time so disguised by chignon, rouge and pearl-powder that his own mother would fail to recognise him'.

When she could afford to, in the days of plenty in 1868, Stella used to insist on twice-daily visits from a hairdresser in Brydges Street, Covent Garden. 'The hairdresser used to come in of a morning to clean Boulton's hair,' Maria Duffin, a maid, recounted, 'and if he was going to an evening party or to the theatre, the hairdresser used to come and arrange the chignon and the hair.'

But most of the time Fanny and Stella had to rely on their own resources. On the night of their arrest, Fanny and Stella had dressed each other's hair expertly. Stella wore hers *à la grecque*, with at least one – and probably two – chignons of elaborately curled and braided hair, while Fanny's was a profusion of tiny flaxen curls dressed with a diamanté star. Fanny, with her 'sterner features', also wore a Eugénie bandelette, a popular style of chignon, a fringe of curls worn across the forehead in the manner of the Empress Eugénie. It was said to soften the face.

Judging from the 'great quantity of wadding' found at Wakefield Street it was clear that Fanny and Stella used to pad their busts. They might as easily have resorted to 'The Registered Bust Improver', patented in 1849, which claimed to do away with the 'evident defects of pads made of Cotton and Wool'. Improvers were made from an 'air-proof' inflatable material, sold in boxes of half a dozen and available by post from Mr White of Gresham Street.

Fanny and Stella may have also followed the practice of French male prostitutes in drag, who wore false bosoms made from boiled sheep's lights – or lungs – cut to shape and then inflated. 'One of the prostitutes complained to me the other day,' the Parisian doctor François-Auguste Veyne reported, 'that a cat had eaten one of his breasts which he had left to cool down in his attic.' Stella had visited Paris in 1868 to perform in drag and would have met some of the city's formidable brigade of men who dressed as women and carried back to London the latest tips and fashions.

Facial hair was another headache. They could shave it, they could pluck it, or they could try to remove it permanently. Close shaving was effective but short-lived. However closely they shaved, a shadow of stubble would appear within hours, making kissing a little risky. This was a bigger problem for

Fanny, who was more hirsute than Stella. Plucking was painful, time-consuming and likely to lead to irritation. Some men swore by a weak solution of arsenic for removing facial hair or by hydrogen peroxide to inhibit beard growth.

Make-up was a vexed question too. There were those who saw any kind of 'paint' as an affront to Society, and the first vicious step on the road to ruin. Women who wore paint were no better than actresses or whores. But the fashion for paint grew steadily in popularity and by 1871 a ladies' magazine observed that 'no one who goes much into Society can fail to notice how common the use of paints, powders and cosmetics has become of late years.' Mrs H. R. Haweis was rather more forthright. 'If a girl has the trial of a complexion so bad that the sight of it gives one a turn,' she wrote in *The Art of Beauty*:

> it is a simple duty for her either not to go into Society at all, or, if she does, to conceal it, as she would not scruple to conceal lameness or leanness. You have no right to inflict your misfortune on everybody – it is an unpardonable offence against good taste.

The liberal application of paint helped cover a multitude of sins. Nearly all the witnesses who queued up to testify against Fanny and Stella spoke of them being heavily painted, though much of their make-up must have been hastily thrown into Carlotta Gibbings's carpet bag and spirited away from Wakefield Street. Detective Officer Chamberlain had only found a box of Bloom of Roses – liquid rouge made from the shell of the cochineal beetle – and four packs of violet powder. The writer and 'Practical Artist in Hair' Edwin Creer recommended violet powder as 'one of the most innocent and best preparations for whitening the skin' but warned against the plethora of 'pernicious compounds done up in a packet and labelled "Violet Powder"' which could be extremely injurious to health and sometimes cause death.

Among ladies, violet powder was widely used to dry out and deodorise the moister, more secret parts of the body – so much so that the *Pearl, a Monthly Journal of Facetiae and Voluptuous Reading* felt itself obliged to issue a 'CAUTION TO LADIES':

> A contributor wishes to remonstrate against the practice
> of a very nice young lady friend of his, who treats her
> quim as if it were a baby's arse. He says, 'a nice cunt is a
> delicious thing to suck, but damn the violet powder,
> which dries up all the natural juiciness'.

Then there was the mysterious bottle of chloroform found in Wakefield Street. By 1870, chloroform was in common use as a general anaesthetic and as a way of relieving pain. It was famously administered to Queen Victoria during the birth of Prince Leopold in 1853, and again at the birth of Princess Beatrice in 1857, creating outrage among many in the medical establishment who believed that the pangs of childbirth were divinely ordained and a painful but necessary rite of passage.

Chloroform also induced euphoria. Like laudanum, it was readily available without prescription from chemists' shops, and there were hundreds if not thousands of addicts who sought and found oblivion through inhalation of its sweet-smelling vapours. But it was highly addictive and too much could prove fatal.

Rather more alarmingly, chloroform was said to induce uncontrolled libidinous feelings. Mild inhalation had a strong aphrodisiac effect. When asleep under its influence both women and men reported dreams so vivid and so powerfully erotic that they felt as if they were real. There were in consequence many accusations of seduction and rape made by women against doctors and dentists who had administered the drug. Chloroform became inextricably bound up with the great moral panic over the white slave trade, stories of which had respectable young women travelling alone being waylaid, rendered unconscious, raped and then sold into sexual slavery in the far-flung corners of Empire.

Stella had been suffering for years from fistula, a painful abscess in the rectum, which by February 1869 had become so severe that surgery was the only solution. Chloroform was administered as an anaesthetic during this operation and Stella may well have been tempted to continue to use it as an effective analgesic. Chloroform vapours injected directly into the rectum were said to be highly efficacious for a variety of anal disorders.

Additionally, chloroform may have been a useful means of relieving pain and discomfort during anal sex, especially for Stella for whom it must have been a sore trial. Like amyl nitrite, which was discovered in 1844, chloroform dilated the blood vessels causing the involuntary muscles – especially the anal sphincter – to relax, making anal penetration much easier and rather less painful.

Chloroform's combined qualities as analgesic, aphrodisiac and anal dilator rendered it the drug of choice for Fanny and Stella. It might rouse the dormant passions of hesitant or reluctant lovers into vigorous life, at the same time as its vapours loosened and widened the sodomitic passages. And if it was used for nothing else, chloroform was the remedy of last resort for drunken, difficult or violent punters. They could be swiftly knocked out cold and dumped comatose in a back street or alleyway to wake up with a sore head and only a hazy recollection of the erotic misadventures of the night before.

10

A Dirty Business

Amenities of Leicester Square

Girl to Ponce: 'Go along, you bloody Mary-Ann, and tighten your arsehole with alum.'

English Whore to French Woman: 'Yah, you foreign bitches can only get a man by promising them a bottom-fuck!'

French Woman: 'Yes, I do let the English gentlemen have my arsehole, but my cunt I do keep for my husband.'

The Pearl, 1880

The dramatic arrest at the Strand Theatre was not the first time that Stella had been in trouble with the police. In 1867, when she was just eighteen, Stella had been arrested on at least two occasions in the Haymarket, the London thoroughfare synonymous with the very worst excesses of prostitution.

On the first occasion, Stella and her friend Martin Luther Cumming were both in drag, almost certainly drunk and plainly soliciting men – much to the indignation of half a dozen battle-scarred female streetwalkers who, as the *Daily Telegraph* delicately phrased it, 'considered they were interfering with their calling'.

A brawl quickly broke out between Stella and Cumming and the formidable old whores into whose tramp, or territory, they had dared to trespass. The altercation began with name-calling and threats and quickly escalated into violence. Stella and Cumming were promptly arrested by Police Constable Thomas Shillingford, as much for their own safety as for the offence of soliciting men.

Stella had met Martin Luther Cumming a year earlier, in June 1866, when she was invited to Oxford to perform in drag with 'The Shooting Stars', the university amateur theatrical troupe, in a burlesque double bill, *The Comical Countess* and *Lalla Rookh*. Though he was a little on the stout side, Cumming made an engagingly comic dowager, and *The Times* praised his 'admirable' performance as the Countess.

Stella and the Comical Countess became firm friends. They made a slightly ridiculous drag duet: Stella, beautiful, slender, soulful and, above all, a convincing girl; and Cumming the Comical Countess, plump and well-bred, comically camp, and quite clearly a man dressed in women's clothes.

In their drunken forays into the Haymarket, Stella would have stood more chance of getting away with soliciting had she been alone, though the whores of the Haymarket were notoriously protective of their patches and it was not uncommon for new girls to be badly beaten up, scratched and bitten, and sometimes scarred for life when they tried to muscle in on the best tramps. But the Comical Countess was so obviously a drunken toff in comic drag, that the whores straight away spotted him and Stella as a pair of interlopers.

Quite apart from the attempted trespass onto their hallowed tramps, the whores considered Stella and the Comical Countess unfair competition. It was one thing to compete against all the other girls on the street. The whores were used to that. They were even used to gaggles of Mary-Anns waggling their scrawny arses up and down the street. They didn't mind that so much because the steamers, or punters, that went with the Mary-Anns would hardly want a real woman. It stood to reason. But when it came to Mary-Anns dressed as women, and one of them properly beautiful, that was too much. It was downright deceitful. It wasn't right; it wasn't proper and it wasn't fair. It was taking the bread out of their mouths.

Though it hardly mattered to the Comical Countess, the money to be earned from whoring was no small matter for Stella. She needed it. She had just a pound a week for pocket money – and even that was not always assured, as Papa seemed to be forever in difficulties. She needed more than a paltry pound a week. She needed a wardrobe of silk and satins, of day gowns and evening gowns. She needed wigs and chignons. She needed stockings and shoes and boots and slippers. She needed powder and paint, muffs and capes, and hats and gloves and handkerchiefs. And more – much more – besides.

Stella could never remember if – let alone when – she had decided that going with men for money was the solution to her problems. It had somehow just happened. It had crept up on her. It had taken her from behind, you might almost say. Little and not-so-little gifts; half-a-sovereign here and a sovereign there; money pressed upon her whether she had asked for it or not; money baldly offered for sex; and money boldly taken for sex. Easy money. The easiest money. And she could take her pick. They were queuing up for her. It was a pleasure. Leastways, most of the time.

A few weeks after the incident with the Comical Countess, Stella was arrested in drag in the Haymarket again, this time in the company of a man named Campbell, better known as Lady Jane Grey, a notorious male prostitute in drag who was 'well-known to the police'. This time the case ended up in Marlborough Street Magistrates' Court, and Stella and Lady Jane Grey were fined and had their knuckles firmly rapped.

The courts dealt with a surprisingly large number of men who were arrested dressed as women. Usually they were charged with a breach of the Queen's peace, with creating a public nuisance, or with being drunk and disorderly, and let off with a small fine and a good talking-to. It was only if there was compelling evidence of some 'unlawful purpose' – of sodomy or prostitution, or both – that matters were treated more seriously.

Twenty years earlier, in the early hours of Saturday, 21st September 1850, Mr Bennett Martin, a clerk to a glass works, was on his way home from a party when he was accosted by a young woman dressed in a light cotton gown with stripes and wearing a straw bonnet and a veil.

'Are you good-natured, dear?' she enquired. It was the traditional opening gambit of London's whores. Mr Martin noticed that her voice was unusually husky and she had a strange singsong accent which for the life of him he was unable to place. But he was certainly very willing for a bit of slap and tickle, for a thrupenny stand-up, as it was called.

'I of course thought she was a woman,' Martin recalled. 'She certainly had a most feminine appearance and we walked together.'

But when the woman lifted her veil, Martin received two shocks. 'I observed to my utter astonishment that the face was that of a person of colour,' he said, 'and I soon suspected, from the growth of the beard, that I was speaking to a man.'

Martin seized hold of this 'woman' and dragged her along the street looking for a policeman.

An intimate examination at the police station confirmed that the woman, who gave her name as Eliza Scott, was in fact a man. In court, Eliza – or Elijah – Scott, speaking 'in a very mincing effeminate tone of voice', told the extraordinary story of her life. She claimed she had been sold by her aunt for a slave, escaped and, after many adventures, fetched up in the West Indies where she 'got her living by washing, ironing and cleaning, and attending people who are ill, more particularly those afflicted with rheumatism', whom she cured with the application of Indian herbs.

Many, if not most, arrests were accidental. When the routine nightly quotas of streetwalkers were rounded up, every so often one of them would turn out to be a man dressed as a woman. The police were at a loss as to how to deal with these strange apparitions. More often than not they were released with a caution. Willy Somerville, one of Stella's many admirers, wrote to her anxiously in 1868: 'Did you see a fellow had been taken up for being in drag but he was let off?' he enquired. 'Did you know him by name?'

Though politicians and preachers were quick to angrily deny its existence, male prostitution, especially among boys and young men, was widespread, not to say rife in London. 'There is a considerable amount of sodomy practised in London,' Howard Vincent, Director of the Criminal Investigation Department of the Metropolitan Police, told a Select Committee of the House of Lords in 1881. 'It is a fact, and it is an indisputable fact, there are boys and youths soliciting in the streets.'

'A great many brothel keepers lure young boys to their establishments,' Mr Talbot, Secretary of the London Society for the Prevention of Juvenile Prostitution, told the French socialist Flora Tristan. 'I believe I am correct in estimating that 2,000 out of 5,000 brothels encourage the prostitution of young boys.'

There was a veritable 'army' of male prostitutes in London, according to another observer. There were, he said,

> thousands of boys of precocious debauchery, either in the pay of mature male procurers and patrons, or 'working' by themselves, idle and corrupt youths in their late teens, young men in their twenties and thirties, older types (often of repulsive maturity), catamites of all ages, complexions, physiques, grades of cleanliness and decency.

And not only in London. When Inspector Silas Anniss of the Metropolitan Police raided brothels and bawdy houses in 1868 in the naval town of Devonport, he 'found seven or eight notorious houses specially the resort of boys and girls, from 12 to 17'. In just one house he found twenty-five boys available for sex. Different houses specialised in different sorts of boys. 'One house was frequented by butcher boys and errand boys; another by sailor boys; and another by drummer boys.'

Prostitution in drag was far less common but was still to be found on the streets of London. According to one observer, 'such types haunt the parks, public thoroughfares and so on, after nightfall', or could commonly be met with at the lowest cafés, bars and ballrooms.

A young man could make enormous sums of money, sometimes as much as £10, for sex with a man. But a sovereign or less, much less, sometimes as little as a shilling or two, was more usual. When the young male prostitute Jack Saul first came to London from Dublin in 1879 he was earning 'often-times as much as £8 and £9 a week' from selling himself. The work was easy and the punters plentiful.

Despite drunken disputes and brawls, relations between women on the game and the Mary-Anns, the men on the game, were usually cordial, often very cordial. After all, they were all in the same line of business. They were all in it together. Sometimes they fell in love and lived together and even got married. A male prostitute nicknamed Fair Eliza kept a 'fancy woman' in Westminster who did 'not scruple to live upon the fruits of his monstrous avocation'. Another 'notorious and shameless poof', known only as Betsey H—, married and fathered two sons, both of whom followed their father into male prostitution.

Charles Hammond, the lover and pimp of Jack Saul, lived very happily with a whore called Emily Barker for nearly three years before he met and married Madame Caroline, a buxom French whore with whom he set up a male brothel in Cleveland Street. Hammond was, by all accounts, a loving and considerate husband, though his affection for Madame Caroline did not prevent him taking one Frank Hewitt to his bed as his 'spooney boy'.

Lots of whores were quite happy to procure boys for men who occasionally fancied a bit of the other. 'Walter', the pseudonymous author of the autobiographical *My Secret Life*, recounts how a whore called Betsy Johnston easily procured an ageing and enthusiastic sodomite for his pleasure. Many years later, another of his favourite whores, Sarah, agreed to procure a boy for him. 'One man's prick stands and spends much like another, play with your own,' she had told him gruffly when he first mooted the idea. 'But if you want, I can get one easily enough, and I'll let him come here for you.' Sarah kept her promise and procured a young house decorator who had not been in employment for two months, who was desperate for money and prepared to have sex with a gentleman for a golden sovereign.

Relations between the police and the Mary-Anns were fraught with dangers – and sometimes with possibilities. On the night of their arrest outside the Strand Theatre, Fanny and Stella had arched their eyebrows and stared suggestively at Detective Sergeant Frederick Kerley and Detective Officer William Chamberlain. 'If you'll let us go we'll give you anything you want. *Anything*,' they had said, like a Greek chorus. 'Anything you like to mention. *Anything* you like to mention, you can have.' Money or sex or both.

Fanny and Stella were acting exactly as they had acted dozens of times before, as every whore – male or female – had acted countless times before. Whores would be arrested and, nine times out of ten, would be released after favours, financial or physical – or both – were forthcoming. As Fanny and Stella knew from experience, lots of policemen wanted to be gamahuched, to have their cocks sucked, while they were out on the beat, and they were never too particular about who did the sucking. Some of them wanted a bottom-fuck as well.

'I have been in the hands of the police (don't be frightened) or rather the other way round, the police have been in my hands so many times lately that my lily white hands have been trembling, and I am *utterly* fucked out,' wrote Malcolm Johnston joyously to his 'Pa' in Dublin. It was, he said, 'Such Camp!'

Malcolm Johnston was a Mary-Ann, who also liked to drag up. He was known to his friends and fellow Mary-Anns as 'The Maid of Athens'. Johnston was visiting London in the late

1870s and was making hay while the sun shone. 'Nearly all the police about here have been up in the evenings,' he confided to his Pa. 'Some I have done, others I have only kissed, a kissing one was up last night, and a fucking one two nights previous.'

After his arrest, Johnston helpfully amplified the meaning of certain phrases in his letter. 'Camp means amusement,' he explained to the police who were puzzled by the word. 'It might mean proper amusement or it might mean improper amusement,' he told them. 'The meaning of "some that I have done" is frigged off.'

But there was a darker side to this erotic moon. As Johnston's injunction – 'don't be frightened' – to his Pa suggested, there were some decidedly less 'camp' sides to relations between the Mary-Anns and the police. For the past twenty years the police had been arresting a steadily increasing quota of men for having sex with other men. Many hundreds, perhaps even thousands, were arrested and charged every year. The charges, most of them falling short of sodomy, were haphazardly and euphemistically reported as 'abominable offences', 'unnatural crimes', 'uncleanness' or 'unspeakable conduct' in the myriad local and national newspapers.

Some arrests resulted from tip-offs, others from complaints from men claiming they had been indecently assaulted by other men. Often these complaints were a ploy in the growing trade in blackmail and extortion. It was good business. Men who had sex with other men were usually too terrified to go to the police if they were being blackmailed. They reasoned, probably rightly, that once the police got wind of their proclivities, they themselves would be charged with a sexual offence. It was better to pay, and pay again and again and again, rather than face prosecution, prison and social ignominy.

Every man, no matter who he was, was potentially the target of blackmail and extortion. One fine Sunday evening in June 1868, Anthony Daly, a retired and highly respectable grocer from Walthamstow, went into the urinal at Mansion House Place to relieve himself. It was just after six o'clock in the evening and the only other person there was a snappily dressed youth, James Kean, who was just sixteen years old.

According to Daly, Kean behaved 'in a very extraordinary manner', attempting to touch his private parts. As they left the urinal, Kean asked Daly for sixpence and threatened him with an accusation of indecent assault if he did not pay up. But Anthony Daly was not going to allow himself to be blackmailed by a young male prostitute. He saw a police constable on the other side of the road and summoned him. After a chase, James Kean was arrested and it emerged that other gentlemen had made complaints about both his disgusting behaviour and his attempts at blackmail.

Anthony Daly was either very brave or very foolhardy. Mud stuck and many men in similar situations simply paid up. As the magistrate observed at Kean's trial, a charge of indecent assault was 'a charge which it was most difficult to rebut'. A few pence, a few shillings, a few pounds were nothing to the spectre of public ruin if the case came to court.

Increasingly, men were being arrested and charged as a direct consequence of police surveillance. By the 1860s, London's urinals and public water closets had become magnets for men who wanted to meet other men for sex. They had also become a target for the police. It was already an established and increasingly common practice to use policemen – sometimes in uniform and sometimes not – to keep watch in public lavatories for men loitering with sexual intent or for men actually committing indecent acts in the lavatory.

When a twenty-two-year-old carpenter, Benjamin Kersey, was charged with indecent exposure in a urinal in Hyde Park on 1st March 1871, the evidence was provided by Police Constable Farrier, A 289, who testified that he had 'been specially employed for the purpose of checking indecent practices in urinals' for the past eighteen months. After remarking on the frequency of such unpleasant cases, and on the difficulty of dealing with them, Mr Tyrwhitt, the magistrate, addressed some stern observations on the practice of using dedicated police constables to spy on men in public lavatories. 'The system is injurious to the public interest,' he said, 'and bad for the constables themselves, as after a time their minds become, as it were, diseased by being bent on the same point.'

But the practice continued unabated. Men who wanted to have sex with other men, men who loitered in parks and lavatories, were easy prey. They were usually too scared or too ashamed to resist arrest, most of them pleading guilty in the hope of landing a lighter sentence.

There were acquittals but many men charged with unnatural crimes or abominable offences were convicted. Sentences varied wildly, ranging from three months with hard labour to fifteen years' penal servitude. Some men chose to commit suicide rather than face the shame and ignominy of a conviction for a sexual offence with another man.

There was another side to relations between the police and men who wanted to have sex with men. It was a common practice for police constables on the beat to invite men to gamahuche them or to offer to bottom-fuck them down a dark alley. Once the deed was done, the constable would demand money. If it was not forthcoming – and even when it was – the constable would arrest the man and charge him with attempting to indecently assault a police officer.

The practice had become so common that learned tomes on medical jurisprudence urged caution.

> There cannot be the slightest doubt that false charges of this crime are more numerous than those of rape, and that this is too often a very successful mode of extortion. This is rather a legal than a medical question, but it is especially deserving of attention that these accusations are most frequently made by soldiers and policemen.

Fanny and Stella were only too well acquainted with this particular trick. Eight years earlier, in 1862, Fanny's older brother Harry had been arrested and charged with attempting to indecently assault Police Constable George White down a dark alleyway in the early hours of April Fool's Day. Harry appeared before the magistrate the next morning. As the eldest son of the respected and respectable Judge Alexander Park, Harry was granted bail set at a hefty £600, a small fortune. But once released from police custody, he disappeared for eight long years until, by a cruel twist of fate, Fanny and Stella's arrest would bring him face to face with Police Constable George White once again.

11

Getting Up Evidence

That if any witness or witnesses who shall be
examined by or before any justice or justices or
otherwise, upon oath, shall wilfully and corruptly
give false evidence, he, she, or they so giving false
evidence shall be subject to the same punishment
as if convicted of wilful and corrupt perjury.

A Compendious Abstract, 1823

Inspector Thompson was struggling to keep his head above
water amidst the deluge of information about the two young
men in women's clothes that had quickly started to flood in
after the arrest of Fanny and Stella and showed no sign of abate-
ment. The police had been 'literally inundated with
communication regarding this case from all parts of the country', *Reynolds's Newspaper* revealed.

'I have had a great deal of hard working on this case, and six
other officers with me,' Thompson remarked feelingly towards
the end of May, a month to the day after the sensational arrest
of Fanny and Stella. 'I have had fifty or sixty letters sent to me
about this case,' he continued. 'I have also had many letters,
not only affecting these prisoners, but other persons as well.'

It was a tidal wave of letters: letters of all shapes and sizes;
letters written in all hands from the most elegant to the barely
decipherable; misspelt, fulminating, incoherent, menacing,
damning, defending, and dark; letters expressing indignation,

outrage and horror; letters demanding severe – indeed, the severest – penalties to be inflicted; aimless, rambling, ranting letters on every subject from sodomy to prostitution to private theatricals; letters lamenting the sad decline in the standards of behaviour of young persons; letters with reported sightings of Fanny and Stella from the four corners of the world; letters enclosing smudgy clippings from newspapers with accounts of concerts and performances given by Fanny or Stella, in places as far apart as Chelmsford, Scarborough and Edinburgh; letters – many of them anonymous – voicing dark suspicions about alleged confederates of Fanny and Stella; and letters of accusation about countless other young men given over to this vice.

All these letters had to be read (and in some cases deciphered), understood, digested and acted upon – or not, as the case may be. New enquiries had to be initiated: leads followed, journeys undertaken, witnesses interviewed, statements taken, records kept. Almost every day there was a new development, and often more than one. Almost every day the net seemed to widen and another young man – and sometimes more than one – was implicated.

And then there were the personal callers at Bow Street Police Station: a steady stream of men and women from all stations and conditions of life, hesitant, apologetic, indignant, apoplectic, who had something to say or something to tell and felt compelled to do so in person. It really was no wonder that Inspector Thompson and the six officers helping him were beginning to feel the strain of such a long and complex investigation which seemed to be growing daily ever larger.

Most of those who called at Bow Street in person could add very little to the substance of the investigation. They were there because they wanted to call the attention of the police to supposed sightings of Fanny or Stella going back years; to reported cases of importuning by gay ladies who were, in the indignant opinion of the importuned, not ladies at all, but men; and to every kind of suspicious behaviour by young men, including some direct and not so direct allegations of effeminacy, sodomy and other dark crimes, not to be named among Christians.

Most could be safely ignored. Some might provide useful intelligence. A few were more promising. And one or two were crucial. One of the most important witnesses to come forward was Mr John Reeve, Staff Supervisor at the Royal Alhambra Palace in Leicester Square. And then there was Mr George Smith, Beadle of the Burlington Arcade, who was an entirely different kettle of fish.

Mr John Reeve was a tall, well-made man in his middle years. He was a man of few words, and what words he spoke were spoken gravely and chosen with great care. Reeve had been most reluctant to put pen to paper, as he was more than a little ashamed of his sprawling and ill-formed – almost childish – handwriting, and he would go to any lengths to avoid writing letters. He much preferred to call in person at Bow Street and tell Inspector Thompson what he knew about this dirty business.

In the five years and five months he had been at the Alhambra, Reeve said, he had fought a running battle with these painted young men who, no matter how many times they were turned out, forbidden to return or threatened with the police, nevertheless fetched up again and again like a bagful of bad pennies. Boulton and Park were two of the worst offenders; two of the most persistent, two of the most badly behaved.

'I have known Park three years, and Boulton nearly as long,

upwards of two,' Reeve told the court in Bow Street.

> I have seen them at the Alhambra many, many times – at
> least twenty times. My attention was first called to them
> about two years ago. I saw them walking about as
> women, looking over their shoulders at men as if enticing
> them. I went to them and desired them to leave.

Fanny and Stella would not give up. They were soon back, this time dressed as men, though, as Reeve reported, it was a very strange form of male attire. 'They were walking about together, their faces painted up, their necks powdered, their shirt collars much lower than they are now, and their waistcoats were very open.' They were openly flirting with gentlemen, John Reeve spluttered. 'They looked at people as they passed and their mannerisms were more feminine than masculine. People round them were saying they are two women dressed in men's clothes. I had observed them looking at a gentleman in a manner that I thought highly improper.'

In fact, Fanny and Stella had been at the Alhambra within the last six weeks. 'They were in a Private Box, and dressed as men. They were painted up. They wore pink coloured flowers and hung their pink gloves over the box.'

> I saw the people looking up at the box they were in and
> rising from their seats to get a better view of them. I saw
> that they were playing all sorts of frivolous games with
> each other: they were looking down in front of the box,
> handing cigarettes backwards and forwards to each other
> and lighting them by the gaslight. I went to the box and
> told them they must leave.

Fanny and Stella were decidedly the worse for wear.

'They asked to have more soda and brandy,' John Reeve remembered. '"No," I said, "I've told you to keep out of the place many times," and I marched them out. I told the Box Keeper to be very particular about admitting them again.'

The worst part of it, Reeve said, was that they came in company with a great gaggle, a great tribe of similar young men. 'I have seen about twenty young men at the Alhambra with their faces powdered in company with Boulton and Park.' Painted and powdered and perfumed young men, with shrieking voices and tweezered eyebrows and curled hair. It was bewildering and confusing, and John Reeve did not mind admitting it. Sometimes they came dressed as women, and sometimes they were dressed as men, or rather as young women might look if they had dressed themselves as men.

'I could not tell whether they were men or women,' he said. 'Sometimes I thought they were women, and sometimes I thought they were men.'

The very thought of what these young men had in mind for the gentlemen they ogled and chirruped at turned his stomach. Despite his best endeavours, these young men continued to plague the Alhambra, seemingly in greater numbers and with more perseverance than any other music hall or theatre that he knew of. Nothing seemed to deter them. They were more than a nuisance. They were a veritable plague. He had made 'frequent complaints to the Police about these men'. Nobody had seemed interested. Nothing was done. And then, to his very great surprise, there in the newspapers, were the two worst offenders, caught red-handed in wickedness.

He had of course gone to see Inspector Thompson at Bow Street as soon as he found out about the arrest of Park and

Boulton, as he discovered they were called. He had only ever heard them referred to by foolish girls' names – Jane and Fanny and Stella and a whole host of other pretty names. Inspector Thompson was very interested. He told him he was to go and quietly observe them in the Magistrates' Court in Bow Street to confirm that they were the very same young men who had so plagued the Alhambra. If they were indeed one and the same then John Reeve was to go straight away to Whitehall, to the offices of the Treasury Solicitor who, since 1661, had been in charge of all serious public prosecutions, and tell Mr John Greenwood himself everything he knew.

Whether Inspector Thompson was always strictly truthful about what went on behind the scenes of the investigation into the Young Men in Women's Clothes was thrown into some doubt by the testimony of Mr George Smith, the genial and beaming Beadle of the Burlington Arcade. A former constable with eight years of more or less unblemished service in the Metropolitan Police, Mr George Smith had, according to Thompson, been most eager to offer every assistance to the police.

Mr George Smith knew a great deal about Fanny and Stella and about the Mary-Anns that walked the Burlington Arcade, the hollow-eyed, hungry young and not-so-young men with their tawdry, gaudy, cheap clothes and their oh-so-tight trousers, marching and mincing up and down the Arcade and glaring and staring at every man who walked by. Some of them were painted like women, and some of them were even dressed like women.

One of the worst offenders was, according to Mr George Smith, the youth called Boulton. A pretty fellow, to be sure, in every sense of the word. Sometimes he was dressed as a man (or rather how a lady might look dressed as a man), and at other times he would be dressed as a gay lady, looking every inch the part, from the wig on his head to the kid boots on his feet. Mr George Smith had kept a particular and close eye on this one, who would come on his own or in company with one or two others. 'I noticed his face,' Smith declared in Bow Street Magistrates' Court.

> It was painted very thickly with rouge and everything else on. He always caused such a commotion when he came into the Arcade. Everybody was looking at him . . . I saw him *wink* at a gentleman and turn his head in a sly manner. He winked his eye and put his face on one side, and did like *that*, the same as a lady would do, the same as a woman would do.

And here George Smith paused and, to much laughter, made a passable stab at contorting his manly visage into the lascivious come-hither nods and winks he had witnessed. He was rather less successful when it came to attempting to reproduce chirruping, that particular and peculiar sound made by the most depraved and desperate of streetwalkers and common prostitutes when they were enticing passing gentlemen to buy their jaded wares.

'I dare say I do not do it so well as they can,' was his rueful verdict.

Mr George Smith could speak to one infamous afternoon, in 1868 or thereabouts, when Boulton had come up close to him, so close that he could see the paint thickly caked upon his phiz, and actually tried it on with him.

'Oh, you sweet little dear!' said Boulton, leaning forward and lisping and whispering in his ear. 'Oh, you nice little dear!'

Mr George Smith was, he was quite ready to admit, quite taken aback. He was surprised and he was shocked. Such a thing had never happened to him before, and he was obliged to stop and pause. It had been quite a facer for him, and no mistake. Of course, the youth was drunk or deranged, or both. By the time Mr George Smith had recovered himself and found out Constable Holden, Boulton was nowhere to be seen. He had scarpered.

A few days, or even a few weeks, later, Boulton was back in the Burlington Arcade in company with a plump and florid youth prone to fits of giggling. 'I saw Boulton turn his head to two gentleman, smile at them, and again make a noise with his mouth, the same as a woman would for enticement.'

Mr George Smith did not hesitate. He marched straight up to them and said, 'I've received several complaints about you, and you remember what you said to me a week or two ago. I've seen enough of your conduct to consider you to be an improper person to be in the Arcade. You must leave at once.'

'Take no notice of that fellow,' Boulton told his companion, in 'a feminine manner'. The pair of them tried to push past the solid and majestic bulk of Mr George Smith. But that gentleman was having none of it. He took hold of Boulton and frogmarched him to the gates at the Piccadilly end. 'You're as bad as the other,' he told him, 'you leave the Arcade at once,' before grabbing him and flinging him down on the pavement outside.

Just three days after this episode, Boulton was back, this time with a flint-faced Mary-Ann called Park with whom Smith was already acquainted, having seen him a dozen or so times before, alone and in company with various other Mary-Anns.

'They used to walk the Arcade arm-in-arm with such an effem-inate walk that it used to cause the notice of everyone,' Smith recalled. 'On seeing me they directly walked into a hosier's shop kept by Mr Lord.'

Mr George Smith waited outside Mr Lord's hosiery shop. And he waited and he waited, for an hour or more, until at last the pair of them emerged with their noses stuck in the air as if they were fine ladies out for an afternoon's shopping.

'I've cautioned you not to come here,' he said to Boulton. 'You'll leave the Arcade at once.'

'I shall go where I like,' Boulton haughtily replied.

'You'll do nothing of the sort. You'll go out.' They tried to walk on, but Mr George Smith seized the pair of them by the scruffs of their necks and violently ejected them onto the pavement.

And so the skirmishing went on. There was no rhyme or reason to this siege of the Burlington Arcade. Sometimes they were there, and sometimes there was no sign of them. A week or a month might pass and Mr George Smith would not see a Mary-Ann from one day's end or one week's end to the next. But on other days, in other weeks, they were ever present, an army of angry, buzzing flies. Swat as many as he liked (and Mr George Smith did like), it made no difference. They came back, again and again and again. They would try and catch him off his guard, watching and waiting for him to go off for his din-ner or for a refresher in the tavern next door. Then they would sail in, bold as brass, and when he got back he would have to chase them out all over again.

This happy state of antagonism might have continued in-definitely had it not been brought to an end by Mr George Smith's abrupt dismissal for the trivial offence of accepting tips from some of the gay ladies who patronised the Arcade.

Out on his ear and out on his arse. No warning, no notice, nothing. Nothing but his wages to date and barely the price of a glass of beer in his pocket. As Beadle, he received a wage of a guinea a week, but that was nothing compared to the tips he collected. In a good week he could easily expect to make £5, and he had been known, on high days and holy days, to pocket that much in a day if business was brisk.

'I don't think it a disgrace to have taken money for drink,' Smith declared. 'Everyone does it. I am not ashamed of it. If a lady offered you half-a-crown, wouldn't you take it?'

Stripped of his Beadle's rank and denuded of his Beadle's blue frogged greatcoat and shiny top hat, Mr George Smith made a less than impressive witness for the prosecution when he went into the box at Bow Street. Matters were not at all helped by the fact that it was obvious to everyone that he had been drinking and it was not yet even noon.

'Have you been drinking today?' counsel for the defence demanded.

'Yes I have,' replied Smith defiantly. 'I have had two or three half-pints of ale.' But judging from Mr George Smith's florid complexion and his 'flippant and impertinent' manner, which seemed to verge on insolence, it was clear to one and all that he had imbibed at least double that quantity, and perhaps a tot or two of brandy as well.

That same drink which made Mr George Smith so combative, so flippant and so impertinent in court also made him loquacious and incautious. He had a great deal to say about the circumstances of the investigation into the young men in women's clothes, a great deal too much to say.

Smith claimed he went to see Inspector Thompson in a

positive frenzy of public-spiritedness. But then he let slip a shocking admission.

'I have been getting up evidence for the police in this little affair,' he boasted. 'They asked me to do so on Sunday, 24th April. I told Inspector Thompson what I knew about the defendants.'

Mr George Smith's revelations caused rather more than a murmur or a ripple of surprise in Bow Street. They caused a minor sensation. After all, Miss Stella Boulton and Miss Fanny Park had been arrested only on 28th April, fully four days *after* Mr George Smith's meeting with Inspector Thompson. And though he corrected himself later on – 'I see now I have made a mistake as to the date' – it was hard for anyone present in Bow Street Magistrates' Court to believe that there was any conceivable confusion or ambiguity concerning Sunday 24th April, about which Mr George Smith had been so emphatic.

Not only that. Smith's choice of words was particularly unfortunate. 'Getting up evidence' was a phrase commonly understood to mean contriving and fabricating evidence to incriminate the innocent. It sounded rather as if Mr George Smith had been toiling away, poking his reddened nose into dark corners, sniffing out odds and sods of information, putting two and two together and making ten.

'I have been seen at the Treasury-office,' he continued in a bragging sort of way. 'I gave the same evidence as I gave to Thompson, with one or two corrects caused by thinking over the matter again –' and here Mr George Smith abruptly paused, as he caught sight of Inspector Thompson's darkening, thunderous face. 'I – I mean additions,' he added lamely.

'I *may* be paid by Mr Thompson for attending this court,' Mr George Smith added injudiciously. 'He said I should be paid for my trouble in giving evidence and I shall not object. I should not object to a situation if the Treasury should give me one.'

Taken all in all, the testimony of Mr George Smith was disastrous for the prosecution. He was like a bull in a china shop, a drunken, blundering, crashing, self-serving oaf. He was vain, greedy and corruptible. He freely admitted to helping the police gather evidence against Fanny and Stella in return for money or for help with a situation, or both, and he appeared to give the impression that at least some, if not all, of the evidence against them was 'got up'. With his various 'additions', 'corrects' and contradictions, it was clear to everyone that Mr George Smith was a liar, and a bad liar at that.

But out of this treacherous swamp of lies, certain truths began to emerge vaporously. The arrest of the two young men in women's clothes was not as haphazard or accidental as the police and the prosecution liked to make out. Taken together with the evidence of Police Constable Charles Walker, who said he had been covertly watching the movements of Fanny and Stella in and out of Wakefield Street for a fortnight before their arrest, and the evidence of Detective Officer Chamberlain, who said he had been keeping his beady eye on them for a year past, the arrest of the young men in women's clothes took on a very different complexion. Clearly, it had been planned and schemed over and thought about for some time in advance, and things were not quite so simple, not quite so cut and dried as first they might appear.

12

A Victorian Romance

At length I am a bride! Lord Arthur was so pathetic, and appealed so earnestly to every sentiment of my love, that I could not do otherwise than entrust my happiness to his keeping, and agree to a speedy marriage. I need hardly tell you how the thoughts of becoming a bride fluttered my virgin heart, only to think of being naked in bed with a fine fellow like Arthur, who I only too truly guessed would be formidably armed with a Cupid's spear commensurate with the very ominous bunch in his trousers, which always had a peculiar fascination to me. So rather more than a week ago we were made man and wife.

Letters from Laura and Eveline, 1903

Like all the best love affairs it had been as accidental as it had been unexpected.

For well over a year now, Louis Hurt had been Stella's ardent and devoted swain, and she was only too well aware that her Mamma thoroughly approved of him. Indeed, Mrs Mary Ann Boulton was doing everything in her power to promote the match. Louis was constantly at the house, invited to luncheons and dinners, and frequently asked to spend weekends with the family. On one occasion he had stayed for an entire fortnight.

Stella liked Louis and sometimes she even fancied herself

a little in love. He was predictable, gentlemanly, hard-working and, most importantly, utterly devoted to her. But these virtues were also his vices. Louis wanted her, but he wanted her on his own terms. His spaniel-like attentions could be irksome and he was possessive to the point of jealousy when it came to other beaux, which meant that Stella was very sensibly rather less than frank with him about her nocturnal escapades in the West End.

Truth be told, dear Louis was really rather dull and disapproving. He was not at all in favour of fun or frivolity, and he was very decidedly against dragging up. It was only on very rare occasions, on high days and holy days, that he could be persuaded to consent to accompany her to the theatre or to a ball or a party in her full drag glory.

And though he certainly had considerable charm of manner and equally considerable charm of person, his conversation could be dreary and repetitive. When he was not droning on about his work with the Post Office, he would talk about Alderwasley, about his ten brothers and his four sisters, until her poor head ached with trying to keep up and sort the one from the other. And he spoke rather too much about 'Mother', who sounded very formidable and dragon-like and not at all the sort of person that Stella felt she would like as her Mamma-in-law.

Louis was never in the right place at the right time. Whenever she did want him he would be away – in Wales or Wiltshire or Worcestershire or some other wild place – and when she did not want him, there he was, with his fine grey eyes which seemed to be imploring and beseeching her, and yet at the same time judging her, reproaching her, constraining her. So much so that Stella found herself looking forward to his long absences, and dreading his returns.

For Mrs Mary Ann Boulton these were the happiest of happy days, and 1867 the happiest of happy years. Ever since Ernest, at her behest – nay, upon her insistence – had given up work in the January, he had blossomed forth. He seemed happier than he had ever been, and the dark, gloomy days of the London and County Bank were quickly forgotten. His health still gave her cause for concern. She still fretted and worried that he was consumptive (there was a decided propensity to consumption on Mr Boulton's side), and he was often pale and exhausted.

But Ernest had such a gift for friendship, and she so much enjoyed meeting his friends and helping them in their little theatrical enterprises. There was Mr Frederick Park, Mr Martin Cumming, Mr Charles Pavitt, Mr Cecil Thomas, Mr Albert Wight and half a dozen others whose names she could not possibly be expected to remember. They were constantly at the house. Indeed, Frederick, or Fred, or even 'Fanny' as the others had called him in jest, was so much with them that he seemed almost like a brother to Ernest.

Boys would be boys, and there was much joshing and many colt-like high spirits. And why ever not? She had been highly amused when Ernest first told her about his new name. 'He laughed and told me that he did go by the nickname of "Stella".' Stella. In Latin, star. Most pretty and most appropriate, and when the boys were gathered together in her home, sometimes she could not help herself from joining in the fun and addressing him as 'Stella' too, to hoots and whoops of delight.

They were all mad for the theatre, and constantly singing and playing and dressing up and putting on little private theatricals. She had never seen anything as comical as plump Mr Cumming playing a dowager duchess, and Fanny and Stella, as she now started to think of them, made extremely convincing ladies. Fanny, it was true, made a handsome – rather than a beautiful – woman, and looked older than his years, unlike her Stella, who utterly astonished and silenced all and sundry with his beauty, his conspicuous beauty, as a young woman.

Mrs Mary Ann Boulton was much in demand as prompter, stage manager and wardrobe mistress. 'On one or two occasions I gave a dress,' she said later. In truth, it was more like a dozen dresses when she added them all up in her mind, but who was counting? It was a little embarrassing for the boys to procure dresses for private theatricals, and yet so easy for her to help with buying bits and pieces, pinning and sewing, making and altering. Besides, she enjoyed being a part of it all. But she needed all her skills of diplomacy to smooth and soothe those little differences of opinion which seemed to flare up with alarming frequency. It was not for nothing, she had begun to realise, that acting was also called the histrionic art.

Then in the autumn of 1867 came an invitation to dinner at the home of Mr and Mrs Richards. The invitation was not especially unusual or unexpected. Mr Richards was a stockbroker, a friend of Mr Boulton's and connected to him by way of business. But when Mrs Richards had whispered so confidentially to Mrs Boulton that a personage, none other than Lord Arthur Clinton, the Honourable Member for Newark, and son (but not heir) to His Grace, the late Duke of Newcastle, was attending she had got herself into one of her states and dressed herself with the utmost ceremony for the occasion, almost as if she were going to be presented at court.

For some reason – which Stella could not now recall –

neither her Papa nor Gerard were able to go with them to the Richards's. It was to be just Mamma and herself. Of course, she was only too well aware that she would be expected to sing for her supper. But she was quite happy to do so.

Stella was, she freely admitted, more than a little intrigued at the prospect of meeting Lord Arthur. As far as she was aware, she had never met a real Lord before, and it would be interesting to do so. She had no idea of what to expect. He might be ninety years old and deaf as a post. Or, like so many of the men she met, he might want to talk about huntin', shootin' and fishin' all night, and she would have to sit there and politely try to stifle her yawns.

Lord Arthur Pelham-Clinton could not be described as handsome in any conventional sense. He was of the middle height, slightly built and inclined to stoop. He wore a small, neat moustache and long side-whiskers. The top of his head was already as bald as an egg, a fact he cleverly disguised by combing over the hair from one side of his head to the other and plastering it down with plenty of Rowland's Macassar Oil, a remarkable product guaranteed, it was said, to 'nourish and preserve the hair, and make it grow thickly on all bald patches'.

Lord Arthur seemed older and wiser than his years. There were dark shadows under his eyes, and his lips were full and red, making a strange and not unpleasing contrast with the pallor of his complexion. There was something about him that caught Stella's attention from the moment they were introduced, a certain gleam in his eyes, a certain vigour in his handshake, a certain smile, a certain intense gaze, a certain *je ne sais quoi*, as Fanny would have it with her cheap French phrases.

Stella blushed and smiled, and smiled and blushed, and

was suitably modest when she felt that modesty was called for, and suitably bold when she needed to be bold. Sometimes she would look up and catch him gazing at her appreciatively and would find herself colouring under the penetrating scrutiny of his dark eyes.

Lord Arthur made a special effort to put her at her ease. He begged her to call him Arthur, asking her for her opinion and asking her questions about herself before hastening everybody into the drawing room to hear, he said with a smile that melted her heart, young Mr Boulton sing. And so Stella had sung the hauntingly sad 'Fading Away', and sung it with such sweetness and with so much intensity that she felt the first prickings of a tear or two in her large and very beautiful blue-violet eyes.

> Rose of the garden,
> Blushing and gay,
> E'en as we pluck thee,
> Fading away!
>
> Beams of the morning,
> Promise of day,
> While we are gazing,
> Fading away!

As she took her bow, which was really more of a curtsey, she looked over to Lord Arthur and thought she saw the glint and glimmer of an answering tear in his eyes. And then she was certain.

Her friendship with Lord Arthur had, to use her Mamma's phrase, very quickly 'ripened into intimacy'. Arthur, as she must now learn to call him, had asked her Mamma that very night if he might call upon them in Dulwich, and naturally Mamma was in transports of delight at the prospect, though Dulwich was, of course, just another of Mamma's pretty fictions, as their house was firmly within the rather less genteel borders of Peckham Rye.

The household was thrown into a feverish frenzy of expectation and preparation. Though Papa very manfully decreed that Lord Arthur must take them as he found them, Mamma worked herself up into a state of the greatest excitement and the greatest agitation. Within a day or two of their first meeting, she had told anyone and everyone in Peckham Rye about Lord Arthur, and was happily discoursing about the late and dear Duke as if they had been on terms of the most intimate acquaintance.

When, upon Arthur's first visit, it became clear that Stella was his particular object, all thoughts of Louis Hurt flew the rickety coop of her Mamma's mind. With a variety of sage nods and winks, knowing looks and sighs, and with many significant shakings of her artificial curls, she gave Stella to understand that she, and therefore her Papa (though Stella had never known him to give an opinion upon any of her beaux), thoroughly approved of her new suitor. Where once 'dear Louis' had held sway, now 'Lord Arthur' reigned supreme. Though pressed repeatedly to call him Arthur, Mrs Mary Ann Boulton invariably used his title, laying particular and empathic stress upon the word '*Lord*'.

There were luncheons, dinners, evening parties and musical parties. Arthur's public passions were theatrical. He could play and sing and act, and though his talents in these arenas could in no way compare with Stella's, they were complementary. He would play her accompaniments, sing duets with her, and act the part of the handsome hero to her dazzling heroine in the two-handed drawing-room entertainments that Stella loved to perform.

Lord Arthur was constantly at Peckham Rye. He was shown off, like a prize ox, casually displayed for the delectation and edification of Mrs Mary Ann Boulton's friends and neighbours, who had, she felt, never fully appreciated her or her family's true gentility. Quite apart from what he could and would do for Ernest, Lord Arthur, with his social and political connections, would, she thought, be of immense help to Mr Boulton and his business, and no doubt he would be able to put something in Gerard's way when the time came. At last, she thought to herself, things are finally coming right.

But the path of true love did not always run smoothly. Within weeks of their first meeting, there were those two unfortunate and disagreeable episodes to contend with.

Ernest and Mr Cumming were arrested in the Haymarket. It was all a mistake, a lark. In an excess of youthful zeal, and perhaps even a little in their cups, they had donned their stage costumes and gone out to carouse among the gay ladies. They had meant no harm, and it was of course completely preposterous of those ladies of the night to assume that either Ernest or Mr Cumming was – and here Mrs Mary Ann Boulton shuddered – 'interfering with their calling'. And then, by a terrible fluke, the same thing had happened again, this time with Ernest's friend, Mr Campbell, a gentleman with whom she was not acquainted (and frankly with whom she had no wish to be acquainted).

Mr Campbell was apparently 'a man perfectly well-known to the police', though of course Ernest could not possibly have been aware of that fact. How the police and the newspapers dared to insinuate what they did was beyond her. They had

had the temerity to suggest that Ernest and Mr Campbell were 'apparently plying for men, so much so that a disturbance ensued'. Thankfully Mr Boulton had arranged matters, and Ernest had been released with a small fine and a stern talking-to. They had decided as a family that it had been much ado about nothing, a comedy of errors – a conclusion which, fortunately and very much to her relief, Lord Arthur Clinton seemed to share.

Mrs Mary Ann Boulton's ears had pricked up with alarm when, during the early days of the courtship (for surely no other construction could be placed upon it?), Lord Arthur casually made a reference to 'my fiancée'. And she had bristled defensively a week or so later when she read in *The Times* that 'a marriage is arranged to take place between Lord Arthur Clinton, M.P., and Miss Matthews'.

Love or money? It sounded like the title of one of the plays that Ernest and his young friends were so fond of performing. Mrs Mary Ann Boulton knew that in the world of the theatre love would always triumph in the end, but away from the limelight, in the dark and difficult present, she feared that gross Mammon often won the day. She trembled at the thought. All she could do was hope and pray, and double and redouble her efforts to snare Lord Arthur for Ernest. Fortunately, her fears proved groundless when Lord Arthur announced that he had relinquished his engagement to Miss Matthews, or as some of the less savoury newspapers hinted, Miss Matthews had shown him the door.

And then there was the question of Lord Arthur's bankruptcy. Mrs Mary Ann Boulton's poor fuddled head could not understand the ins and outs of it all, but it appeared from the crumbs that Lord Arthur let drop, and from what was reported in the newspapers, which she could not keep herself from reading avidly, that he had been ill advised – not to say wilfully misled – over money matters by unscrupulous people and had got himself into difficulties. It was so easily done, so very easily done, and she had every sympathy, though debts of £34,134 did seem extraordinarily excessive and beyond her ability to comprehend.

There were some unsavoury details: Lord Arthur, it seemed, had unfortunately availed himself of the services of a pawn-broker, a Mr Attenborough, and pledged a number of items with him, the tickets for which, she had read with incredulity, had been stolen by a servant. It was very much to Lord Arthur's credit, she reflected, that in the absence of proof, Lord Arthur had not informed the police of the theft nor, indeed, dismissed the man in question.

It appeared that Lord Arthur had a generous nature – Mrs Mary Ann Boulton might even go so far as to say an *over*-generous nature. The sum of £1,694 owed to Messrs Ortner, Houle and Co. for items of jewellery given as presents was very considerably more than what she herself spent annually on keeping house. She was surprised to discover that Lord Arthur had given his intended bride 'in all, five diamond rings'. She could not help comparing – a little uneasily, it had to be said – the cost of one of these diamond rings, apparently £75, with the huge sum of £210 for 'a chest containing plate and cutlery' given as a gift to one Lieutenant Jones, a fellow officer of Lord Arthur, which bespoke a deal of manly friendship and affection existing between them.

It was unfortunate, it had to be said, that Lord Arthur's generosity, his over-generosity, cast a slight shadow over Ernest's coming-of-age party in the December of 1867. Mrs Mary Ann

Boulton had been planning it for months, if not years. A supper party for family and friends in their house in Dulwich to celebrate her darling boy's majority. There was to be champagne, a full supper, presents and surprises, and entertainments, both musical and dramatic. Naturally, she wrote to Lord Arthur first as guest of honour, and she received a charming reply:

> My dear Mrs Boulton,
>   Pray accept my most sincere thanks for your most kind invitation which I accept with the greatest pleasure, especially as it is to celebrate the coming of age of your son, Ernest, for whom I entertain the most sincere regard. Believe me to remain
>   Sincerely yours,
>   Arthur Pelham-Clinton

'*Your son, Ernest, for whom I entertain the most sincere regard.*' Mrs Mary Ann Boulton savoured those words over and over again.

Then, at the very last minute, Ernest had informed her that Arthur had 'said he would be very pleased to send any little thing down to supper if Ernest would like him to do so'. When she finally got to the bottom of things, she was horrified. It seemed that Lord Arthur had ordered and intended to pay for an entire supper from Buck's the Caterers. Apart from throwing her into complete disarray (and how typical of menfolk to be so oblivious of her existing arrangements), Mr Boulton had put his foot down and decreed that they could not accept such a gift, especially when Lord Arthur had been declared a bankrupt barely a fortnight earlier.

Mrs Mary Ann Boulton asked Ernest to most politely decline Lord Arthur's offer. 'My answer to my son when he told me of having received the letter was: "Then write and tell Lord Arthur that it would not do for you to name such a thing to your Mother or she would be offended." Those were my words,' Mrs Mary Ann Boulton declared. 'Everything was provided.'

But matters had not ended there.

'When I was dressing for the evening on my son's birthday, two persons arrived from Buck's and said they had been desired by Lord Clinton to provide a supper and my words were these: "I feel sure that Lord Arthur means this kindly but it is a mistake."'

Lord Arthur wrote her a very pretty letter of apology: 'I fear I offended and caused annoyance to you on Friday last – if so pray let me offer my sincerest apologies &c &c.' And so the matter was forgotten, and the perfectly smooth surface of their relations polished back to full lustre. When she reflected upon the incident, there was, she concluded, more to delight than to dismay. It had all sprung from Lord Arthur's 'most sincere regard' for Ernest, from an ebullition, from an excess, of those manly feelings of affection towards her darling boy.

And really, what on earth could be wrong with that?

13

Lord Arthur's Wife

MARRY! If you are for pleasure, marry; if you prize rosy health, marry; and even if money be your object, marry. A good wife is Heaven's last, best gift to man, his angel and minister of graces innumerable, his gem of many virtues, his casket of jewels. Her voice, the sweetest music; her smiles, his brightest day; her kiss, the guardian of his safety, the balsam of his life; her industry, his surest wealth; her economy, his safest steward; her lips, his faithful councillors; her bosom, the softest pillow of his cares; and her prayers, the ablest advocates of Heaven's blessings on his head.

The Ladies' Treasury, March 1867

Fanny could not give two hoots for the law, for Chelmsford, or for the firm of Gepp and Sons. But her allowance from Papa depended on her sticking her articles out. Fortunately Mr Gepp Senior was not a harsh taskmaster. Indeed, it sometimes struck her rather forcibly that Mr Gepp Senior was as eager to see the back of her as she was to see the back of him. Fanny's absences from the firm multiplied. Her recent and severe bout of scarlet fever had meant blessed months away from Gepp and Sons, and even then she was still as weak as a kitten and would often feel unwell and unable to face her duties. Weekends were stretched and stretched until they almost joined up. Then there were holidays to be taken, and of course rehearsals. End-less rehearsals. Mr Gepp rarely questioned her absences, and her pleas to be excused – so she could rehearse or perform or have a costume fitted for such worthy causes as the Benefit for the Infirmary – were greeted with a combination of bewilder-ment, resignation and, truth be told, sighs of relief.

Fanny ended up spending rather more time in London than she did in Chelmsford. She was in London almost every week-end, and when Stella fell in love with Lord Arthur Pelham-Clinton and they moved into Mrs Peck's establishment in Southampton Street, Fanny was a regular and welcome visitor. She slept in the little dressing room which opened off Stella and Arthur's bedroom. It was not an entirely satisfactory solu-tion from either of their points of view. It was perfectly un-derstandable that a young married couple in the first flush of passion needed privacy, and Fanny had no perverse wish to listen to Stella squealing like a stuck pig every time she brought a steamer home or Arthur chose to exercise his conjugal rights. It was all *most* unladylike.

Equally, the same problems arose on those rather less fre-quent occasions when Fanny wished to entertain a gentleman overnight, or just for an hour or two. Indeed, there were times when Mrs Peck's first-floor front bore a passable resemblance to a cheap knocking shop, and come the morning Fanny was never sure who she would find there in various and interesting states of *déshabille* and disarray, and it would require all her reserves of skill and cunning to smuggle out these waifs and strays without either Sharp-eyed Maria or Slow Eliza from Norfolk spotting them.

There were other difficulties to contend with. As the older, unmarried and – she was not ashamed to admit it – plainer sister, living with her quite exceptionally beautiful younger sister and her sister's aristocratic husband in the cramped surroundings of Mrs Peck's first-floor front, Fanny sometimes felt that she was playing gooseberry to Stella and Arthur, that she was in the way, that she was under their feet. But when she voiced these nagging concerns, Stella would fly into a fit of hysterics and declare that she could not, she would not, do without her dearest Fanny; that they could never, would never, be parted.

There was much muttering and much speculation in the servants' hall of 36 Southampton Street about the new tenants on the drawing-room floor. By common consent, it was felt the *he* was all right. At least he was polite and nearly always said please and thank you and the like. And even if he didn't have two farthings to rub together, it was still something to have a *real* Lord, the son of a Duke, in the house after so many to-ings and fro-ings of plain and ordinary Misters.

But young Mr Boulton was another kettle of fish altogether. He might be called Mr Boulton, but everyone was convinced that he was, in truth, a she.

Secretly, Eliza Clark rather liked Mr or Miss Boulton. He was only a year or two older than herself and, if he was in the mood, he would chat to her in a friendly, interested sort of a way and ask her questions about her life in Norfolk before she came to London; about her previous service; and about her sweethearts. Eliza could always tell straight away what sort of mood he was in. Some mornings he would smile and bustle about and sometimes even give her a hand with the dusting or the bed-making. On other days he would sit silently, scowling, lost in his own angry thoughts, furiously smoking thin cigarettes or cigars.

'I thought Boulton was a female all the time he was there,' Eliza said later. It was the small things that convinced her, like the fact that he (or she) 'used powder to her face' and sang very prettily with 'a womanish voice'.

One thing she did puzzle over was the dresses that Mr Boulton and Mr Park wore when they went out in all their finery in the evening. They were not the sort of dresses that respectable ladies wore. Quite the opposite. 'I have been to the Theatre and have seen Ladies dressed as Boulton and Park were,' was the only way she could blushingly phrase it in court; she could not bring herself to speak the word 'whore' in front of gentlemen. 'When they went out dressed as Ladies, Boulton wore white muslin, and Park, black silk, made low, and like ladies wear.'

'I used to accuse him of being a female,' Eliza said. As the weeks went by, she had become quite bold, and as she bottomed out the rooms every morning, she used to think of a dozen different ways of getting him to admit that he was in truth a she. It was their little bit of fun. But she could never get a straight answer. 'He used to pass it off as a joke.'

Maria Duffin, by contrast, was a sharp-eyed, sharp-tongued, inquisitive, clever sort of a girl, a cockney girl who had seen far more of the world than was strictly good for her, and quite the opposite of Slow Eliza. 'I never could satisfy myself whether Boulton was a man or a woman,' Maria said. And it was true. Sometimes she was convinced that he was a woman in disguise. At other times she was not so sure, and she sometimes suspected that he was a man, a man who dressed up as a woman.

'Boulton generally dressed as a Lady,' Maria said. In the mornings he would wear a loose flowing gown or wrapper, the kind of gown, she was reliably informed, that gay ladies wore to their 'work' inside houses of ill-repute. 'When he went out with Lord Arthur in an evening he always dressed in women's clothes. I have seen him only once or twice dressed in gentlemen's clothes.'

And then there was Mr Park, Boulton's particular friend, who used to come at the weekends, regular as clockwork, and stay two or three nights. Here was more perplexity, more bewilderment, more confusion. What exactly was Mr Park? Was he a man or a woman? Maria was not sure. Sometimes he would be dressed as a man and sometimes as a woman.

Certainly, the sleeping arrangements had struck Maria as decidedly odd. 'When Boulton was there he slept in the same room, and in the same bed with Lord Arthur Clinton,' she said, frowning at the memory. 'There was a small dressing room leading out of Lord Arthur's bedroom. There was a bed in that room, and Park slept in that bed. The entrance to the dressing room was only through Lord Arthur's bedroom. There was no other door to the dressing room. When Park was away, Boulton did not occupy that bed, but continued to sleep with Lord Arthur Clinton.'

Maria Duffin knew this because it was her job to take the hot water into the bedroom every morning. Of course she would give a cursory knock and, with barely a second's pause, enter the bedchamber. It was a game. She wanted to catch them out, she wanted to catch them at it, to find out once and for all whether Boulton was a man or a woman or some sort of in-between. And there they would be, huddled together, half-asleep and half-entwined, and quickly covering themselves over with the bedclothes.

It was she who first saw the card with 'Lady Arthur Clinton' engraved upon it. It was true that at the time she was poking and prying about the room while Lord Arthur and Boulton were absent – she could not remember exactly when – but most likely when they were away in Scarborough in the October. When she pointed it out to Eliza, she of course had taken it as proof positive of what the household had suspected all along: that Boulton was a lady dressed up as a man.

But still Maria's doubts persisted. There was something not quite right, something that did not fit. But she could not, for the life of her, put her finger on what it was. One morning, as she was making the beds, Maria decided to come right out and ask him.

'I beg your pardon,' she said, 'but I really think you are a man.'

Boulton had looked at her a little oddly and then laughed gaily.

'I am *Lady* Clinton', Stella had said grandly, '– Lord Arthur's *wife*,' laying particular stress on the word 'wife'. Then she waggled the fingers of her left hand in front of Maria's face and invited her to look at her wedding ring and keeper. Maria had looked, and she knew that that should have settled matters. But she was still left feeling uneasy and confused. Despite Lady Clinton's dramatic revelation, she was still all at sea, still uncertain, and had a feeling deep down that Lady Clinton was not a Lady at all. Turning it over and over in her mind, she felt very uncomfortable. She would take her mother's advice and leave this house. Perhaps Mr Lindley in Catherine Street would take her back.

F anny and Stella had sworn that they would never let Arthur come between them, but of course he did. It had all begun innocently enough and with the best of intentions.

Fanny was used to listening to both sides of the story. It seemed to help both Stella and Arthur to have a third party, a confidential friend, a sister, a sister-in-law, someone to whom they could pour out their troubles, who would do her best to try to smooth out their differences. And what troubles and what differences! There were a thousand and one irritations, a thousand and one little altercations peppering every day. To be quite candid, Stella was highly strung. At her worst, she was a hissing, spitting Virago, and there were raised voices, slammed doors and flouncings-out at least half a dozen times a day.

If she was not spitting venom, Stella would sit with a darkening face in a darkened room, gazing into nothingness, contemplating the unfathomable abyss of her own mind. She was not getting on with Arthur. She wondered if they had ever got on. And more importantly, she questioned whether they ever would get on and whether it had been doomed before it had even begun.

She was very much afraid that Arthur had misled her, if not deceived her. His courtship had been assiduous. He had flattered her and attended her and bombarded her with expensive trifles and *bijouterie*. He had made out that he was a man of means, prepared to take her to wife and keep her in a style befitting Stella, Lady Clinton.

But she had been sold a pup – or rather, a puppy. Arthur was a declared bankrupt. He was a wastrel, a feckless profligate drowning in an ocean of debt so vast and so deep that it was improbable, if not impossible, that he would ever escape. And still his debts mounted. Still he spent money like water. Still he borrowed. They were sinking lower and lower, and the bitter irony of it all was that it was she who had to venture forth nightly and sell her arse to passing trade to put food on the table and pay the rent. She should have listened to and profited from those endless and tedious lessons about the importance of money that dear, dull Louis Hurt had tried to drum into her.

Of course, if Stella had bothered to ask Fanny for her opinion before rushing headlong into matrimony, Fanny could and would have told her that marriage was not a state to be entered into unadvisedly, lightly or wantonly, as she believed the Form of the Sodomisation of Matrimony ran, but reverently, discreetly, advisedly and soberly. (On this last point, Fanny could testify that Stella was certainly not sober before her marriage to Arthur, and had rarely been sober since. Not that she was judging her. If Fanny had a sovereign for every time she herself had fallen down dead drunk, she would be a rich woman.) But Stella had been so determined to have Arthur's ring on her finger that she was deaf, dumb and blind to all advice and sisterly counsel.

Stella was wilful, vain, moody, petulant and quarrelsome. At the same time she was loyal, brave, exciting and beautiful. Stella's beauty was her greatest gift and her greatest curse. She was a perfect beauty, and that meant she could get more or less whatever she wanted simply by snapping her fingers or fluttering her eyelashes.

In Fanny's considered opinion, Stella's account of Arthur's courtship was partial and jaundiced. It was certainly true that Arthur had laid siege to her, but only because she had *wanted* him to lay siege to her. From the moment she first met Arthur, Stella had set her cap at him. Her ambition knew no bounds. She wanted to be Stella, Lady Clinton. And more. If Fate so decreed that his two older brothers were to die suddenly and without issue, Arthur would be Duke of Newcastle and she his beautiful Duchess, and then the whole world would have to bow and scrape and curtsey to her. She had visions of living at Clumber, or in the grand town house in Pall Mall, and driving in the park in an open carriage emblazoned with her personal cipher.

But, upon reflection, Arthur was a far from ideal husband for Stella. Stella was too volatile, too explosive. She needed a strong man, a man who would stand for no nonsense, a man with a firm hand who would give her a good slap (as Fanny herself had had to do upon occasion) when she got out of control. Stella was utterly oblivious to Arthur's finer qualities: to his kindness and his thoughtfulness, to his loyalty and his devotion. It was true that Arthur had not been quite honest with Stella; true that he was mired in the most terrible debt; true that he lacked direction and drive; but Stella's withering contempt, her constant carpings and criticisms had reduced him and diminished him. She had humiliated and emasculated him. And what – Fanny asked herself with a rhetorical flourish – had it profited her?

Arthur, it was clear, needed the love and support of a good woman. He needed a wife who would encourage him, a wife who could organise him, a wife who could direct him. A wife who was a helpmeet to her husband; a quiet, good, kind wife, but a wife nonetheless who could stand beside her husband as an equal; a wife who could mingle effortlessly with his family and friends, at ease in the drawing rooms of London and at home in the country. A knuckling-down sort of wife, unafraid of hard work and hard times. A wife, in short, like the kind of wife that Fanny thought *she* would make. There. She had dared to think it. She had dared to whisper it. And once thought, once whispered, she could not unthink it, she could not unwhisper it.

Fanny, Lady Clinton. It had, she thought, a certain ring about it. Really, quite a definite ring about it.

14

The Toast of the Town

Oh! the dresses, neat, eccentric,
Individualised and queer;
Oh! the dresses various coloured,
As the flowers that deck the year;
Oh! the dresses, breezy, airy,
Most expansive, startling, grand;
Oh! the dresses, quite peculiar,
As the fossils on the strand.

'Cantab', 'The Spa at Scarborough:
A Reminiscence', 1864

The *Scarborough Gazette and Weekly List of Visitors* (founder, publisher and proprietor: Mr Solomon Wilkinson Theakston) was the most venerable and the most select of the dozen or so newspapers that served the genteel resort and spa of Scarborough.

Those with a curiosity to discover what was going on in the wider world – in, for instance, the North Riding of Yorkshire; in England, Wales, Ireland and Scotland; in Continental Europe; or in far-flung countries sweltering under scorching suns – did *not* turn to the *Scarborough Gazette and Weekly List of Visitors*. Nor did those who wished to read of war and revolution, of famine and pestilence, of great adventures and daring deeds, give themselves the bother of consulting the *Scarborough Gazette and Weekly List of Visitors*. And those Mr

Gradgrinds from the world of manufacturing, trade and commerce who needed hard facts and adamantine figures as mental grist for their dark Satanic mills were emphatically not subscribers to the *Scarborough Gazette and Weekly List of Visitors*.

The *Gazette* (the abbreviation used by all but its most particular readers) held no truck with such worldly events. News was an unwelcome and unpleasant intrusion into its elegant and serene pages. It had been published, week in and week out, since 1845, which was the very year that the railway came to Scarborough and the very year that the town's first built-for-purpose hotel – the Crown Spa Hotel – opened for business.

Vulgar rivals and cheap imitators had periodically attempted to usurp the position of the *Gazette* as the town's social lodestar, as its finely calibrated chronometer of gentility. The *Scarborough Advertiser and List of Visitors* had lasted a mere four months, while the grandly named *James Greasley's Scarborough Times and Weekly List of Visitors* survived just a matter of weeks. It was true that the *Scarborough Herald and Weekly List of Visitors* had mounted a more sustained siege, lasting, much to everyone's surprise, for two years and two months, before withering on the vine. The *Scarborough Gazette and Weekly List of Visitors* sailed on, unperturbed and imperturbable, through rough seas, storm and tempest, as Scarborough's ship of social state.

The entire purpose of the *Gazette*, its beginning, middle and end, was polite society and the social round. Week in, week out, the *Gazette* would appear at exactly the same time on a Thursday morning with two or three, and sometimes more, pages devoted to listing those visitors to Scarborough considered to fall within the pale of polite society. For ease of social gradation visitors were grouped together according to which hotel, apartment or other establishment they were residing in during their stay, and these selfsame hotels, apartments and other establishments would be listed in strictly *de*scending order of gentility.

Scarborough's long season stretched from March to almost the end of November, and every day of every week the train would shudder slowly to a halt alongside the railway station's famously long platform, and from its first-class carriages would be disgorged and deposited, like the shining pebbles washed up on the Strand, a fresh batch of distinguished visitors to make new patternings in Scarborough's endlessly shifting social sands.

And what pebbles, what patterns, what sands! When Royalty, in the ample figure of the Prince of Wales, graced the town with a visit in 1869, the news caused much fluttering in the breasts of the ladies of Scarborough. Some were propelled into a positive frenzy of excitement and gave themselves up to endlessly promenading the fashionable shopping streets, or genteelly loitering in the gardens and parades in their best bonnets, in the forlorn hope of dropping a curtsey to His Royal Highness.

The Peerage was well represented, with a fair sprinkling of Dukes and Duchesses and Dowagers, Lord This's and Lady That's, as well as a baker's dozen of baronets or their relicts. There were any number of Honourables, and an even larger number of assorted, untitled relations: annuitarians of all shapes and sizes; cousins of multiple and dizzying removes; swathes of elderly maiden aunts and blustering port-nosed uncles; and plenty of plain – in the fullest sense of the word – Misses. Almost without exception these assorted relations were as poor as church mice – poorer even, if such a thing were possible – but they kept up appearances wonderfully well and never ceased bragging about and basking in the reflected glory of their wealthier kin.

Then there were those from the middle ranks of society: an abundance of elderly and wealthy widows; plenty of plump ladies of a certain age richly dressed in Macclesfield silks garnished with gold and diamonds; ruddy-faced gentleman farmers and their ruddy-faced lady wives, who always looked a little uncomfortable in their Sunday best; surgeons, lawyers and portly parsons and lean preachers with their wives and children, as well as the odd Collector or lesser-ranking official of the East India Company spending his six months' home leave by the sea. Without any particular distinguished connexion but with plenty of money, they had managed to establish a precarious toehold in Scarborough society by dint of lavish hospitality and a willingness, bordering on the slavish, to flatter and praise and pander to their social betters.

Scarborough prided itself on not being narrow, on not being hidebound. The wealthy, as well as the well-born, all had their contribution to make and it would be foolish to make too many hard and fast rules. All were meticulously recorded in the hallowed pages of the *Scarborough Gazette and Weekly List of Visitors* as if it were the Book of Life itself.

Apart from those invalids – real and imagined – who came in search of a cure and assiduously drank the vinegary, brown chalybeate waters famed for their aperient properties – 'it strengthens and exhilarates the bowel,' according to *Theakston's Guide to Scarborough* (author and publisher: Mr Solomon Wilkinson Theakston) – and discovered by the enterprising Mrs Thomasin Farrer in the reign of good King Charles, matrimony was the main purpose and preoccupation of Scarborough's visiting gentlefolk. Like a vast flock of migratory birds that each year flew to the farthest shores to seek out a mate, so the distinguished and the not-so-distinguished, the rich and the poor, the plain and the beautiful, the old and the young, the hopeful and the hopeless, those with a past and those with a future, flocked to Scarborough for the annual mating season where rich and brilliant plumage, elaborate courtship rituals, dancing and singing, struttings, couplings, feints and sleights made it a sight to behold.

There was a mild flutter of anticipation among the readers of the *Gazette* of Thursday, 15th October 1868 when that august organ, struggling gallantly with the spelling of Stella's given name, announced that 'Lord Arthur Pelham-Clinton, M.P. and Mr Earnest Boulton, Esquire' would be appearing next Tuesday and Wednesday at the Spa Saloon, Scarborough in a dramatic double bill, *A Morning Call* and *Love and Rain*.

The subsequent sudden and dramatic postponement of the entertainment at the Spa Saloon took everybody by surprise. Mr George Reeve Smith, the manager, took the unusual step of publishing the text of the terse telegram he had received from Lord Arthur:

> Oct. 20, 1868. – Clinton, London, to Smith, Spar.
>   Ernest Boulton very unwell. Cannot leave London
> to-day. Will start by nine train to-night. Pray postpone
> entertainment until Wednesday.

It was felt by everyone to be a most gentlemanly telegram, and there was widespread speculation as to what the sudden indisposition of Mr Ernest Boulton might be. It was to be hoped that it was neither serious nor contagious (especially not the latter, in case Lord Arthur contracted the contagion, and then who knew what might happen). But the anxious matrons of Scarborough were reassured by the fact that Mr Boulton would clearly be well enough to travel later the same day, though everyone knew that travelling through the night was ruinous to health. Indeed, there was such a wave of sympathetic interest in the wellbeing of these two young men that when they arrived in Scarborough bleary-eyed and half-asleep early on the Wednesday morning, both performances were completely sold out.

In its edition of Thursday, 22nd October 1868, the *Gazette* recorded, erroneously, the names of the two distinguished visitors who had arrived the day before: 'Pelham-Clinton, Lord Arthur M.P.' and 'Belton, Ernest Esq.' They were staying at the Royal Hotel, where the startlingly named 'Mr D. Anus' was also listed as residing. Though considerably less expensive than the newly built Grand Hotel with its 365 bedrooms (one for every day of the year), the Royal was nevertheless highly regarded by *Crosby's Guide* as 'the oldest and most aristocratic' of the Scarborough hotels.

The more enthusiastic readers of the *Gazette* were curious, more than a little curious, to see Lord Arthur Pelham-Clinton in the flesh. Apart from being the third son of a very distinguished Duke, he had been, it was said, quite a hero during the dreadful Indian Uprising, though no one could remember the exact details of his gallantry. More to the point, he was the Member for Newark (and quite a rising Member, it was said, with the patronage of Mr Gladstone assured by virtue of being his godson).

It was a trifle unusual, Scarborough conceded, for a rising Member to tread the boards so enthusiastically; such theatrical propensities seemed more than a little odd, especially as the interests of most gentlemen from similar stock began and ended with blood sports. But whether there was any impropriety in it was quite another matter. Scarborough noted that Lord Arthur had appeared on the professional stage alongside the Marquis Townshend's troupe of 'Noble Amateurs', and so as far as society was concerned that was the end of it. Any endeavour, theatrical or otherwise, which numbered in its ranks at least one Marquis must be a highly respectable, if not positively praiseworthy, pastime.

There was one aspect of Lord Arthur's life in which Scarborough took a particular and kindly interest. He was known to be unmarried at the present time, and in the eyes of Scarborough society an unmarried Lord was an unmarried Lord and therefore an extremely desirable commodity for their many unmarried daughters. Though there had been rumours of engagements, indeed of several engagements, none of them had fruited into matrimony. It could well be that Lord Arthur was currently engaged. Scarborough would cross that bridge when – and if – it came to it. But a man was innocent until proven guilty. Scarborough would therefore treat Lord Arthur as *not* engaged to be married – and go on treating him as such until proof positive was offered to the contrary.

According to the well-thumbed copy of *Dod's Peerage, Baronetage and Knightage of Great Britain and Ireland* in Mr Theakston's Library (founder and proprietor: Mr Solomon Wilkinson Theakston), Lord Arthur Pelham-Clinton was twenty-eight years of age – the perfect age, in the opinion of many, for a man to marry; an age when the impetuosity of youth gives way to manly maturity, when wild oats have been sown (and sometimes unfortunately reaped), and when most men are soberly considering taking a well-brought-up wife with a comfortable fortune.

Then, of course, Lord Arthur was a bankrupt and his name had been in the newspapers. Though the shame and stigma of bankruptcy might well damage the chances of other, lesser, men in the matrimonial market, the wealthy matrons of Scarborough with spinster daughters on their hands saw it as a positive advantage. It was a truth universally acknowledged that a single man *not* in possession of a good fortune must be in want of a rich wife. And the same could surely be said for Lord Arthur's theatrical consort, Mr Boulton or Mr Belton (the *Gazette*, puzzlingly, had it both ways), who was very likely a most superior sort of young man, although rigorous interrogations of the pages of *Dod's Peerage* had not, as yet, borne fruit.

Stella played the roles of Fanny Chillingtone and Lady Jane Desmond to the hilt, with plenty of stage whispers and alouds and asides, managing half a dozen lightning-quick costume changes which delighted the audience and brought forth storms of applause. She was beautiful and she was fascinating, and the audience could not keep their eyes off her. She effortlessly ran through the gamut of emotions, being, by turns, thrillingly bitter and bitingly sarcastic, aristocratically haughty, foot-stampingly impatient and curl-tossingly petulant. She was mischievous, worldly, calculating, but could switch in a flash to vulnerable, fearful and tearful. She simpered, she flirted, she smiled and she was coy. She was compelling and she was dazzling. She sparkled and she shone like the diamonds she wore on stage, reflecting and refracting all the wonderful, the multifarious, the flashing and the fleeting moods of Woman Incarnate. The audience loved her.

Unsurprisingly, the *Gazette* was positively fawning in its praise of the actors. The Spa was 'honoured' and its frequenters 'delighted' by the 'two charming little drawing-room pieces'. The *Gazette* was especially in awe of 'the very easy "at home" character of the acting' which quite obviously reflected 'the *au fait* acquired by the social position of the actors'.

Lord Arthur and his companion were invited to attend the sumptuous studios of Mr Oliver Sarony in order that a series of photographic likenesses might be taken. In the commodious dressing rooms of Sarony's studios ('an establishment with every convenience for carrying out Photography to perfection', his advertisements in the *Gazette* proclaimed), they were to dress themselves as Sir Edward Ardent and Mrs Chillingtone. Mr Sarony took no fewer than thirty-four different negatives for a sequence entitled 'Man and Wife'. In a long and exhausting session, Stella was also prevailed upon to pose in other attitudes and costumes, including as a nun at prayer, which made a most striking and soulful image.

The photographs sold like hot cakes, and Mr Oliver Sarony struggled to keep up.

'Was there a popular demand for these photographs?' Stella's barrister asked him in court nearly three years later.

'Yes,' the photographer replied. 'There was a great demand.'

'They sold freely to the Gentlemen and visitors in Scarborough?'

'Very fast, as fast as we could print them.'

The most popular photographs were those of Stella alone, and were purchased, in the main, by admiring and incredulous gentlemen. Lord Arthur may have been the most sought-after bachelor by the matrons of Scarborough, but it was Stella who caused the greatest excitement among the gentlemen of the place. Encouraged by the warmth of her reception, which seemed to verge on adulation, Stella determined to venture out in full drag in the town, where her presence created a most extraordinary commotion – especially among the gentlemen. Hats were doffed. Bows were made. Introductions were effected. Arms were proffered and eager invitations to luncheon, to tea and to dinner fell like confetti at her feet. Scarborough had never seen anything quite like it. She was the toast of the town, and seemingly all eyes were upon her.

They were not always friendly eyes. Despite her conquering the hearts of most of the gentlemen in Scarborough, there were a few who obstinately refused to succumb to Stella's many and various charms, a few who manifested hostility towards her, towards the very idea of her, who brindled and bridled at the very mention of her name. One such was Mr Wybert Reeve, 'lessee and manager' of the long-established Theatre Royal in Scarborough, a sworn and bitter rival of the Spa Saloon and the Spa Theatre, which had in recent years leeched his audiences away.

When Lord Arthur and Stella decided to attend a performance at the Theatre Royal, Mr Wybert Reeve felt compelled to call the police.

Lord Arthur had the impertinence to introduce Ernest Boulton *in female attire*, and sit with him in a prominent place among the Ladies and Gentlemen assembled in the dress circle in my theatre.

On hearing of it I at once desired the police, if possible, to take them into custody. They, however, contrived to leave the theatre with the crowd.

The next morning I wrote to Lord Arthur Clinton, expressing in strong terms my annoyance, and explaining the order I had given to the police if he dared to repeat the offence.

Notwithstanding this, and my refusal to accept an apology, he afterwards applied to me to allow them both to appear in a piece entitled *A Morning Call* on the stage of this theatre, which I at once decidedly refused.

It was a narrow escape for Lord Arthur and Stella. Mr Wybert Reeve's visceral anger and animosity towards them was a stark reminder, a warning, that not all gentlemen could be beguiled, dazzled and seduced by Stella's beauty and by Stella's charms. Burlesque on stage was one thing: acceptable to some, offensive to others. But it was quite another thing when men dressed as women walked the streets; when they dared to take their places – their *prominent* places – among the serried ranks of ladies and gentlemen in the Dress Circle; when they smirked and simpered and giggled and flirted with gentlemen as if they were real women. It was all wrong. It was more than wrong. It was unnatural and it was criminal, and (in the opinion of Mr Wybert Reeve and many other gentlemen with whom he had discussed the matter with much huffing and puffing) if there was not a law against such goings-on, there ought to be. Lord Arthur and his catamite may have evaded capture for now. But such creatures should take heed, they said. They will get their comeuppance. It was only a matter of time.

15

'Yr Affectionate Fanny'

Don't be too particular
When you come to woo;
Lay aside your spectacles
Worthy bachelors, do!
When wives are young and dutiful
Honeymoon's pleasures abound;
But who would wish for a beautiful
Honeymoon all the year round?
Then don't be too particular!

John Orlando Parry, 1843

Everyone was agreed. Stella was impossible. Quite impossible. Completely, absolutely and utterly impossible.

Not just annoying. Not just irritating. But infuriating, exasperating, maddening. She was entirely selfish and entirely self-absorbed. She was easily bored and took no pains to conceal her boredom. She was frequently rude and often offensive, especially when she was in her cups, a condition which was the rule rather than the exception.

Stella never listened and she never learned. She was impatient and intolerant. She was dismissive of the feelings of others, belittling and humiliating them as and when the mood took her.

Stella demanded everything as her right and as her due. She took, took and took again. But she gave nothing in return.

There were rarely any pleases, and even fewer thank-yous, no gratitude, no recognition of a service rendered, of a gift given or a compliment bestowed. Nothing, not even a smile.

And she was quick to take umbrage over the slightest slight, real or imagined. She could sulk for days or weeks. She was even quicker to anger. Her tempers and her tantrums were things frightening to behold: sudden and violent sea tempests that wrought a terrible havoc and then blew themselves out as swiftly and as bewilderingly as they had blown up. Afterwards, Stella would in some mysterious fashion be calmed and cleansed, drained and purified of the poison within her, while Arthur and all those around her were left clinging to the flotsam and jetsam of their wrecked lives and emotions.

Stella was a prolific writer of letters, though notes might be a better word to describe the shower of missives that assailed Arthur by every post. She was not much given to writing love letters (though of course she delighted in receiving them). Her letters tended to be short and to the point, ranging in tone from the firm and instructive to the impatient and irritable, with only very occasional oases of affection and regard in between.

Arthur could usually tell what sort of mood Stella was in from the way she signed her letters. 'Stell' was a rare and good augury. It was her comfortable name, her familiar name. It meant that she was at one with the world, at her ease, in her wrapper, with her stays loosened, her stockings rolled down and her curling papers in.

'Stella' was almost as good. Stella was a great and formal beauty. Stella was the cold light of the moon and the stars in the sky, and her love burned with the hard, clear flame of eternity. Stella was poetic and soulful, the dark and mysterious muse of Spenser or of Swift. Stella's love was pure and untainted. An alabaster love, smooth and icily beautiful.

'Ernest' or 'Ernest Boulton', 'E' or 'E.B.' were admirably brisk and determinedly businesslike. They were common-sensical, down-to-earth, feet-on-the-ground names and they spoke of wanting to get things organised, of wanting to get things done. Ernest and Ernest Boulton, E and E.B., were often exasperated and irritated, angry and annoyed, and some-times driven to distraction or to drink, or both, by Arthur's enduring and ever-expanding catalogue of failings and inadequacies.

'Stella Clinton', on the other hand, was decidedly inaus-picious. Stella Clinton was a stormy-petrel sort of a name, a name presaging destruction and disaster; a threatening, lower-ing, darkening sky of a name. Stella Clinton was a shot across the bows, or the rumour and rumble of approaching cannon. Stella Clinton was regal and haughty, imperious and imperial, a Roman matron, a Boadicea, a Bess of Hardwick, a Virgin Queen. Stella Clinton was glorious, and Stella Clinton was magnificent. But woe betide those who dared to cross her, for there was no escape from her vengeance, no escape from her cold fury.

On rare occasions there was no signature at all, just an angry full stop jabbed and stabbed onto the page. When in receipt of one of these anonymous missives, Arthur knew that a terrible storm was about to break above his head and that if he had any sense he would run for cover.

Stella bombarded Arthur with letters and notes. At the time of leaving Mrs Peck's establishment in Southampton Street – and it was a moot point as to whether they left of their own ac-cord or whether they were evicted by that good lady – things between himself and Stella went from bad to worse, and in the course of a week, or even less, he received not so much a flurry as an avalanche of letters by almost every post.

Arthur staggered under the weight of these letters instructing him to do this, ordering him to do that. Peremptory and insolent notes, reproaching him and rebuking him, telling him he was good for nothing and interrogating him about actual and alleged infractions. And these said instructions, injunctions and orders, once executed, were immediately and abruptly countermanded, usually without explanation or apology. No wonder Arthur sometimes did not know whether he was coming or going.

'My dear Arthur,' Stella's missives invariably began:

'I am just off to Chelmsford with Fanny where I shall stay till Monday. We are going to a party there tomorrow night . . .' 'We were very drunk last night, consequently I forgot to write to you . . .' 'I am very tired and seedy.'

'How *can* you be so absurd?' . . . 'I must of course trust to you about the things you promised . . .' 'Now no promises please, as this is *no* joke.'

'A game pie or two might be nice as a little present to me . . .' 'If you have any coin I could do with a little . . .' 'Send me some money, Wretch . . .' 'I wanted the money so it's rather a bore.'

'I shall leave here by the 10.40 train. Meet me . . .' 'Why *cannot* you tell me the truth for once and say you did not come to the station at all? . . . ' 'It is now five o'clock and no letter for me, of course, not that I expected them, but your everlasting promises are *sickening* . . .' 'When you write let it be a very proper letter.'

'I have waited in for you just two hours and a half. I need not tell you I am extremely put out about it . . .' 'I do not like to be treated with such rudeness and if you had any feelings of a gentleman you would know that to be impunctual shows great ill breeding.'

'I am quite tired of waiting and shall not return tonight, nor at all if I am to be treated in this way. I will call tomorrow at one o'clock and shall expect you to be in . . .' 'We cannot go on in this way . . .' 'I am most annoyed.'

'I am consoling myself for your absence by getting screwed . . .' 'And now, dear, I must shut up.'

'We cannot go on in this way,' Stella had written. Arthur entirely agreed. He was exhausted. He yearned for some respite and some repose from the terrible strain of living with Stella. Never had he stood in greater need of a confidential friend, and it was with some relief that he turned to Fanny for guidance and support. Fanny, the older, wiser, calmer sister. Fanny, who knew Stella inside-out and upside-down. Fanny the diplomat, smoother of passages and privy counsellor to the secrets of Stella's heart.

After one particularly epic and exhausting confrontation, which ended as usual with Stella flouncing out, he wrote despairingly to Fanny, who replied by return. 'My Dearest Arthur,' she began on her familiar blue notepaper, emblazoned with the monogram 'F.W.P' in gilt lettering (so very clever and so very economical a device, used with equal facility by Frederick William Park *and* by Fanny Winifred Park).

'My Dearest Arthur,' she wrote, 'You must really excuse me from interfering in matrimonial squabbles (for I am sure the present is no more than that) and tho' I am as you say Stella's *confidante* in most things, that which you wish to know she keeps locked in her own breast.

'My own opinion on the subject varies fifty times a day when

I see you together,' Fanny continued.

> She may sometimes treat you brusquely, but on the other
> hand see how she stands up for your dignity and
> position, so that really I cannot form an opinion on the
> subject.
>
> As to all the things she said to you the other night, she
> may have been tight and she did not know what she was
> saying, so that by the time you get my answer you will
> both be laughing over the whole affair – as Stella and I
> did when we quarrelled and fought down here. Don't
> you remember when I slapped her face?

Arthur of course remembered that day very clearly. As he understood it, it was not the first time that Fanny had slapped Stella's face (or indeed, the first time that Stella had slapped Fanny's).

'Do not think me unkind, Dear, as really I have told you all I know and have not an opinion worth having to offer you,' Fanny concluded. 'Goodbye Dear, Ever yrs, Fan.'

Arthur's correspondence with Fanny was not all gloom and agonisings over Stella. He wrote her a charming letter offering his congratulations on the occasion of her twenty-first birthday and promising a suitably handsome gift – funds permitting. It prompted a gushing reply:

'My dearest Arthur,' Fanny wrote:

> How *very* kind of you to think of me on my birthday. *I*
> require *no* remembrance of my Sister's husband as the
> many *kindnesses* he has bestowed upon me will make me
> remember him for many a year and the Birthday present

he is so kind as to promise me will only be one addition
to the heap of little favours I already treasure up.

'I cannot echo your wish that I should live to be a hundred,'
Fanny continued archly, in reply to Arthur's earnestly expressed hopes, 'though I should like to live to a green old age –
green! did I say? *Oh Ciel!*, the amount of paint that will be required to hide that very unbecoming tint!

'My "campish" undertakings are not at present meeting with
the success which they deserve,' she confided, 'whatever I do
seems to get me into hot water somewhere but *n'importe*,
what's the odds so long as you're happy? Once more with
many many thanks, believe me, Your affectionate Sister-in-law,
Fanny Winifred Park.'

'What's the odds so long as you're happy?' It was a joyous
sentiment, and so typical of Fanny. It was an attitude of mind in
contrast, in marked contrast, Arthur could not but help thinking, to the sullen moods and gloomy introspections of Stella.
Fanny lived for the moment. She was careless of tomorrow. If
she got into hot water, as she called it, she would laugh gaily
and simply shrug it off. It was, Arthur reflected, a very appealing quality, a very attractive quality.

'Is the handle of my umbrella mended yet?' Fanny jovially
enquired. 'If so, I wish you would kindly send it to me, as the
weather has turned so showery that I can't go out without a
dread of my back hair coming out of curl. Let me hear from you
at any time,' she concluded. 'I am always glad to do so, Ever yr
affectionate Fanny.'

'Ever yr affectionate Fanny.' These words stayed with him.
To be sure, they were innocent and innocuous enough, but
for reasons he could not immediately fathom, the words took

root in his mind and he was surprised to feel a curious lightness in his heart when he thought of them, as if Fanny's joyous spirit had in some mysterious fashion entered into his soul.

16

The Dragon of Davies Street

Ann Empson, a lady of determined appearance,
who eyed the prisoners with no friendly aspect.

Reynolds's Newspaper, 5th June 1870

M iss Ann Empson was a lady of singular, not to say startling, appearance. She was tall and spare and grey, and
she scowled a great deal. And when she was not scowling, her
face wore a fell and determined expression, as if life were a
battle that must be fought to the bitterest of bitter ends.

Miss Ann Empson was conspicuously unmarried, and it was
clear from the very severe and resolute tone with which she
declared her state of spinsterhood in court that she had never contemplated matrimony and never would, which came as
something of a relief to London's eligible bachelors as Miss
Empson was not an easy person. Not at all an easy person.

Miss Ann Empson maintained a small establishment at number 46 Davies Street, in the fashionable environs of Bond
Street, where she condescended to let lodgings – chambers, as
she grandly termed them – to suitable single gentlemen with
an irreproachable character. But such suitable single gentlemen
rarely stayed for long after they discovered, in very short order,
that Miss Ann Empson was a fire-breathing Dragon, clearly
descended from a long and distinguished line of fire-breathing
Dragons.

There were long lists of rules and regulations, strictly enforced and invigilated by the indefatigable Miss Empson her-self, who policed and patrolled her kingdom with admirable – if fearsome – zeal. Infringements and infractions rarely, if ever, escaped detection, and were invariably punished by a vigorous tongue-lashing or by summary expulsion from her kingdom, and very often by both.

Miss Ann Empson constantly seethed and was always out of temper. If it was not this, it was that. If it was not one thing, it was another. If it was not some*thing*, then it was some*one* giving her cause for complaint. She fumed and smouldered and burned with perpetual indignation and rage at the world, so much so that there were those who swore they detected a faint bituminous odour about her, though it was more likely that these sulphurous exhalations were a consequence of the numerous nips of brandy she felt it necessary to imbibe throughout the day to help settle her stomach.

Miss Ann Empson was still seething, still fuming, even after all this time. It was disgusting. There was no other word for it. She felt physically sick every time she thought about it. Under her roof. In her bed. (Not *her* bed, exactly, but near enough.)

It had all begun so well. Lord Arthur Pelham-Clinton seemed to fit the bill perfectly. Blood, after all, was Blood, and having little or none of that commodity coursing in her own veins, Miss Empson was all the more eager to have a resident gentleman of irreproachable Bloodstock. Lord Arthur was a Lord, the son of the late Duke of Newcastle, no less, and an Honourable Member to boot.

What with it being so close to Christmas, Miss Empson had been resigned to not getting a let for the drawing-room floor until after the festive season had passed. And then Lord Arthur had turned up out of the blue and charmed and delighted her so much that she was putty – yes, *putty* – in his hands. Indeed, so charming and so delightful had he been that she had waived her usual month's deposit, and even advanced him the not inconsiderable sum of ten golden sovereigns on a note of hand. In retrospect, she thought that she must have taken temporary leave of her senses. Either that, or Lord Arthur had unusual powers of Mesmerism which he had exercised in order to make her agree to things that went so very much against the grain.

Matters had not stopped there. Incredibly, given her strict and sacred injunctions against overnight visitors in any shape or form, Miss Empson found herself weakly agreeing to allow Lord Arthur's country cousin, a Mr Ernest Boulton, to stay in Davies Street on those occasions when he was up in town, and she was even persuaded to buy – yes, *buy* – a single bed for that express purpose. As she said, she was putty in his hands. *Putty*.

Things started to go wrong almost immediately. Lord Arthur moved in, and within a day she had smelt a rat. Or rather, two rats, in the form of the two young men – though that was rather a loose description – who arrived very shortly after him. One of them was Mr Boulton, the country cousin, the other a Mr Park – but she could not remember which was which, which was not at all surprising as they seemed to be two peas from more or less the same pod. All she could say with any certainty was that one was dark and one was fair, and that one was pretty and the other plain.

The manner of Miss Ann Empson's giving evidence at Bow Street Magistrates' Court was refreshingly bracing.

'Are you married?' Mr Straight, for the defence, gently enquired of her after she was sworn.

'Certainly not!' she replied with a snort of contempt. 'I am a *single* woman,' she said, glaring at the assembled multitude, daring any or all to contradict her.

It was clear from her abrasive tone that Miss Empson was angry and aggrieved and spoiling for a fight.

Mr Straight tried another tack. 'Have you been drinking this morning?' he asked.

It was a reasonable enough question. The unhealthy pallor that so many fashionable young ladies struggled to achieve by dint of draughts of strong vinegar and copious quantities of ingested chalk was emphatically not exhibited by Miss Ann Empson. She spurned such fashionable conceits and instead defiantly sported a ruddy and flushed complexion entirely congruent with numerous nips of brandy. There was something, too, about the way she slurred certain words, about the gleam and the glaze of her eyes, and about the fixity of her fell expression, which suggested she had not, for the time being at least, taken the Pledge.

'Have you been drinking this morning?' Mr Straight asked again.

'I could not speak so well as I do if I had,' Miss Empson replied combatively. There was loud laughter. For some reason, the spectators crammed into Bow Street appeared to find Miss Empson funny, and she had barely to open her mouth before guffaws of laughter broke out. Miss Empson was simultaneously offended and pleased by the laughter and played up to it wonderfully.

'You had better answer the question,' Mr Flowers the magistrate sternly interjected.

'Have you been to a public house to-day?' demanded Mr Straight.

'On my oath I have not,' answered Miss Empson, swaying slightly. 'I have not had any drink at home. A policeman brought me here in a cab, but I don't know who it was.'

There was much more in the same vein, but slowly, with much difficulty, Mr Straight got down to the meat and drink of Miss Ann Empson's evidence. Lord Arthur Clinton had lodged with her for a fortnight before she was obliged to evict him. Shortly after he had taken possession of his rooms, his young cousin from the country had turned up and enjoyed 'a mutton chop and bitter beer at Lord Arthur's expense' and had stayed that night. So far, so good.

Miss Empson rarely hesitated when it came to exercising her ancient rights and privileges as a landlady and regularly entered her tenants' apartments for a good snoop around while they were out. So on the morning after his country cousin had spent the night, Miss Empson found herself in Lord Arthur's bed-room feeling puzzled and perplexed.

'I was surprised,' she said, 'to see that the new bed I had bought had not been slept in.' Had Lord Arthur's cousin changed his mind and returned to the country? It was possible. But a thorough examination of the bedding suggested that the country cousin had 'slept with Lord Arthur in the same bed', which raised some unpleasant, some very unpleasant, speculations in her mind.

A night or two later, while on one of her regular patrols, Miss Empson had seen a woman coming out of Lord Arthur's rooms, which was strictly forbidden under the draconian laws of the establishment.

'I saw Lord Arthur go on tiptoe to let her out,' she said.

'I saw him through the kitchen stairs letting a lady out, as I considered.

'I complained to Lord Arthur that he had brought a woman to my house. He said it was a man. Lord Arthur assured me it was a man. He represented him as his cousin.' But Miss Empson was quite certain of what she had seen. There was no two ways about it. It was a woman.

'I complained of it as an abuse of my latch-key,' Miss Empson declared indignantly, much to the amusement of the public gallery. But, shocking and disgusting as the presence of this woman in her house was, at least it put paid to those earlier and very unpleasant speculations.

A day or so later, she had caught the two young men, Mr Boulton and Mr Park, in the very act of moving in, which again was strictly forbidden. This sort of cheap trick might pass unnoticed in certain common lodging houses, but it would not do in Davies Street. It would not do at all. There they were, bold as brass, in Lord Arthur's rooms with their boxes just brought up and about to be unpacked. Miss Empson confronted them.

'I said to them, "You have brought your boxes up, and I will make you take them down." I did so. One of them turned round and said, "I wish never to see your house again," and I replied "I'll take good care you don't."

'He said, "Why not?" and I replied, "Because I let the rooms to Lord Arthur Pelham Clinton."'

'I'm not having this,' she told them in no uncertain terms. 'I *will* not have it. I *shall* not have it.'

Miss Empson was ruddy with the glow of this remembered triumph and glared out defiantly at the courtroom, armed and ready to repel all boarders, doubters and naysayers.

Not long after this, Miss Empson mounted an expedition

deep into the heart of Lord Arthur's territory. No stone was to be left unturned, no drawer unopened, no letter unread. She went through everything with a fine-tooth comb. She pried and probed and poked about her, and she was rewarded, if that was the right word, by the discovery of an entire wardrobe of 'lady's wearing apparel: bracelets, necklets, chignons and the like, silk dresses, shawls and everything that ladies wear, kid boots and more'. There were pots of paint and rouge and powder, and an assortment of other feminine necessities, the particulars of which she felt it indecorous to enter into.

Miss Empson put two and two together. It dawned upon her that when Lord Arthur said that the woman he had surreptitiously let out was a man, he was almost certainly telling the truth. Miss Empson was shocked and revolted. Under her roof, in her bed. If that was their pretty game then they were out, out on their ears, that very night. Of one thing she was sure. She would need a nip or two of brandy – and probably several nips – before her stomach could be settled that night.

In Bow Street Magistrates' Court, Miss Empson was confused. Boulton and Park were there in the dock and she recognised them both as the two young men she had turned out. One was dark and one was fair. One was plain and one was pretty (though not so pretty now, she noticed with satisfaction). But which was Boulton and which was Park? Lord Arthur had told her that his country cousin was called Boulton, but surely this could not be so. In court, Boulton had been identified as the dark, pretty one, but she was as sure as sixpence that the young man who had spent the night in Lord Arthur's bed, the young man whom she had seen dressed as a woman, was the plain, fair one. She pointed to him in the dock.

'The prisoner nearest to me – Park – who I call Boulton, is

the one who slept with Lord Arthur,' she said. 'That is the one. It was the one with the golden hair.'

Fanny shifted uncomfortably on the hard wooden bench of the dock as she was fingered by the redoubtable Miss Empson. She did not like to be reminded so graphically of her all-too-brief and doomed liaison with her sister's husband. Needless to say, Arthur had fallen at the first fence. Under interrogation by Stella he had crumpled and confessed all, and even tried to save his own sorry and scrawny neck by implying that it was Fanny who had made all the running.

Stella had been incandescent with rage. She did not know which was worse: Arthur's infidelity or Fanny's betrayal. But if she blamed anyone, she blamed Fanny. Arthur was weak, indecisive and painfully susceptible to flattery. Stella could well imagine how Fanny had flattered and simpered, and simpered and flattered until poor foolish Arthur did not know whether he was coming or going, at which point Fanny would have pounced like a cat on its unsuspecting prey.

There had been tears and tantrums, scenes and slappings. Arthur was devastated and appalled. Fanny could only hang her head in shame and beg her sister's forgiveness. But Stella was adamant. She renounced her husband, disowned her sister and did what all sensible married women should do in such circumstances: she went home to her Mamma.

17

'Come Love'

Love is a pretty pedlar
Whose pack is fraught with sorrows,
With doubts and fears,
With sighs and tears,
Some joys – but those he borrows.

Robert Jones,
'The Muses Gardin for Delights', 1610

Why Stella had even bothered to keep this short note was a mystery. It had been hurriedly scrawled in pencil on a torn and crumpled half-sheet of paper. Stella was not much given to keeping billets-doux. She was so accustomed to receiving letters from ardent swains and besotted beaux that she had become careless of such epistolary declarations. And in comparison to so many of the epic letters of love and adoration and despair that she received from young and not-so-young gentlemen, this short note barely ranked as a Valentine.

It was addressed in a decidedly shaky script to 'Mr Ernest Boulton at Mrs Dickson's, 118 Princes Street, Edinburgh' and contained the briefest of brief messages:

Darling Erné,
 Do come up tonight. Everybody is too drunk to mind.
Donald is here and wants to see you. Come love.

Always for ever thine.

JSF

Bring Mr P.

'JSF' were the initials of Mr John Safford Fiske, the United States Consul in Edinburgh, who had recently fallen head over heels in love with Stella Boulton. 'Donald' was Donald Sinclair, a friend and fellow sodomite of John Safford Fiske. And the mysterious 'Mr P.' of the postscript was Harry Park, Fanny Park's older brother, who was spending a few days in Edinburgh with Stella. Eight years earlier, Harry had fled a charge of 'having indecently exposed himself and trying to incite a Police-Constable to commit an indecent offence'. Now, as 'Mr Charles Ferguson', Harry was living quietly in the out-of-the-way and unpronounceable small town of Lesmahagow in Lanarkshire, or Abbey Green, as its more anglicised and prosperous residents preferred to call it.

T he year 1869 had not been kind to Miss Stella Boulton. In fact, it was decidedly cruel, beginning with her startling discovery of a brazen and heartless infidelity on the part of her *caro sposo*, Lord Arthur Clinton, with none other than her beloved sister, Mrs Fanny Winifred Graham (*née* Park).

It had, according to Arthur, only happened the once, in fearsome Miss Ann Empson's drawing-room floor in Davies Street. But once was enough. Of course, she blamed Fanny. Arthur was easily led and it was not the first time that he had had his head turned by the tricks and wiles of a designing and unscrupulous woman.

It was a bitter blow. She tore up the cards engraved with that luminous title 'Lady Arthur Clinton' and reverted to her maiden name. She was now just plain Miss Stella Boulton (though her many gallant admirers would protest vociferously at the epithet 'plain' when applied to the lovely Miss Stella).

It was perhaps as well that she had returned home to Peckham Rye. Within weeks she was ill. Very ill. Gravely ill. It had all begun a year or so earlier with a nasty suppurating boil on her anus (or her 'arse-quim' as Fanny was fond of calling it). She had been under the care of Dr Hughes, who treated the sore with the vigorous application of poultices, ointments, antiseptics, douches, injections, disinfectants and dressings, as well as supplying her with a formidable battery of different medicines. Nothing seemed to work.

She had suffered from it almost constantly while she was living with Arthur, and, really, was it any wonder that she was so often out of sorts, short-tempered and snappish? But Stella had winced and grimaced with the pain and carried on as if nothing was the matter. Someone, after all, had to pay the rent and put food on the table, and as Arthur was so mired in debt and seemingly so incapable of earning money, it was left to her to manage matters as best she could. So Stella still had to go out on the pad, tattered and torn, and instead of moaning with pleasure, real or simulated, she moaned with pain. It was all the same to the punters. Stella sighed. The things she did for love.

Dr Hughes had been called to the house and his manner had been very grave and subdued. He said that the boil had turned into an abscess and now the abscess had turned into a *fistula in ano*. Stella was not exactly sure what a *fistula in ano* was. All that she knew was that it was agonisingly painful, and that the longer it went on, the worse it became. Dr Hughes said if Stella did not submit to the knife, he would not answer for the consequences. Indeed, matters had reached such a pass that even with an operation, there was no guarantee of success. Any delay would be fatal.

The operation was a success. Within a fortnight Stella was feeling better, and the pain was very much diminished. In time, Dr Hughes assured her, it would disappear altogether.

One consequence of this near brush with death was that Fanny was forgiven and the sisters were reconciled. Upon being informed of the gravity of Stella's illness, Fanny rushed to her sister's bed of sickness and begged for forgiveness. It was graciously granted. Stella was not one to hold a grudge. Besides, she missed Fanny more than she cared to admit. Husbands and lovers might come and go, but when all was said and done, the love of a sister was rarer and more precious than rubies and pearls.

As the spring turned to summer, and the summer turned to autumn, Stella was very much improved in health. But she felt increasingly restless in Peckham Rye. Having been mistress of her own establishment, such as it was, in Southampton Street, it was hard for her to bow to the superior claims of her Mamma to be mistress in her own house. So when, in late September, Louis Hurt invited her to go and spend a few months with him in Edinburgh for a change of air, Stella accepted with alacrity. However dark and damp and dour Edinburgh in the winter might be, at least she would be free, like a bird set free from a gilded cage.

During her convalescence, there had been moments of reflection and introspection when she questioned whether she had done the right thing in giving Louis up. There was much to recommend him. He was tall and handsome. He was from a good family. Like Arthur he had been educated at Eton, but unlike Arthur, he had made his own way in the world. He was hard-working, sensible and solvent. His prospects were good, and most importantly of all, he was utterly devoted to her.

Louis had courted her assiduously and her Mamma, always determined – over-determined, perhaps – to see her marry well, had entertained the highest hopes for the match. Louis was always a welcome visitor at Peckham Rye, often spending as much as a fortnight with them before rushing off to remote and rustic places to inspect post offices.

But Stella had always had her doubts. In truth, Louis was more than a little dull. He was strict and strait-laced. He did not approve of her career. He did not approve of drag. He did not approve of her campish ways. He did not approve of her going out on the pad. He did not approve of unpaid bills, un-made beds, dirt, disorder or disarray.

Louis was reluctant to call her Stella. He called her Ernest, or Ernie, but never Stella. And though he never exactly put it into words, Stella sensed that he disapproved of her friendship with Fanny. All he wanted her to do was to behave herself, to conform, to grow her moustache, to be more manly and mas-culine, to be less mincing and to try to be Ernest Boulton, the beloved boy of Louis Hurt. Now, at a time when she felt weak and helpless, Louis's strong arms, his unfaltering love and his certainty seemed very appealing.

Stella's worst fears about Edinburgh were not fully realised. It was certainly dark and damp and dour, but it was also austerely beautiful, and the cold winds from the North Sea were refreshing and invigorating after the fugs and smogs of London. Louis had been there for a year or more and had com-fortable chambers in Princes Street, in the very heart of the city.

Mrs Dickson, the landlady, seemed to be a good soul, and mercifully there was none of that poking and prying about of uppity servant girls that had so plagued Stella at Mrs Peck's in Southampton Street.

There was bound to be a fly in the ointment, though, and this time the people who lived above were being tedious, as people who live above generally are, and had complained about the noise of the piano, most especially about her 'playing weekday tunes on the Sabbath'. Mrs Dickson had tactfully requested Stella to 'leave it off on a Sunday'.

There was much to discover, much to learn and much to enjoy. Stella professed herself charmed by everything she found, even though in her heart of hearts she still sometimes hankered after London, after Coventry Street and the Haymarket, after the Alhambra and the Burlington Arcade, after the theatres and the streets and the shops, after that great erotic tide that bore down upon her and engulfed her, sweeping her up and taking her where it willed.

Stella had only to set foot in the streets of Edinburgh to draw gasps and stares. Many, but by no means all, of these gasps and stares were hostile. The rest were of the bewildered, the curious, the frankly interested and the downright flirtatious variety. Stella revelled in the attention. 'Nothing like him had ever been seen in Edinburgh before,' Mr John Doig, a colleague of Louis's, declared. 'He was spoken about a great deal, and a great number of people expressed doubts about his sex.'

There was no shortage of gentlemen callers. In fact, there was a surfeit. Stella's debut in Edinburgh caused quite a stir in certain circles and in no time at all she was besieged on all fronts by beaux. There was that roguish rough diamond, Mr John Jameson Jim, who, after a severe bout of brain fever (brought on, he confessed, 'by drinking and girls'), had seen the light and abruptly transferred his gruff and manly attentions to Stella, falling for her hook, line and sinker. 'Have you the same love as ever for me?' he would write in the plaintive and pleading tone of a lovesick youth.

Or there was plain and honest Jack from the small town of Musselburgh, just outside Edinburgh, who, not to put too fine a point on it, was desperate to pass a night with Stella, and not solely for the charm of her conversation. Plain and honest Jack favoured a bold and direct approach when it came to matters of the heart. '*Will* you stay tonight?' he demanded in pencil. 'You are a *great* cow if you don't.'

Or the very charming and helpful young man behind the counter at Messrs Kensington and Jenner who had been so understanding and so accommodating in the matter of a new gown in silk moiré for Stella which she ordered on the last day of March. He had given her such a knowing look, a loaded look so redolent of meaning, that Stella blushed and hardly knew where to put herself.

And finally there was Mr John Safford Fiske, who was as fine a specimen of American manhood as she had yet met. He was tall, but not too tall; muscular, athletic and lithe; manly and masculine, with sensual lips and large soulful eyes which melted her heart – as well as various other organs – when their loving gaze turned upon her.

Fortune had always smiled upon Mr John Safford Fiske. He had led a charmed and happy existence and was, in consequence, charming and happy. From the moment of his birth to parents of modest means in the small and unexceptional town of Ashtabula on the shore of Lake Erie, a benevolent Fate had steered John Safford Fiske safely through the treacherous waters of life. All those who knew him (or knew of him) were convinced that he was destined for great things.

His talents were prodigious. At Yale he had demonstrated a facility for languages, both living and dead, and for history, ancient and modern. He had a passion for literature, especially for poetry, and was conspicuously widely and well read. But he was no dry and dreary scholar, slowly desiccating in his tower of ivory. Here was a manly man, a man of strong ruddy flesh and bright ruby blood, fleet of foot, sound in wind and limb, a man well-endowed with strength and courage as well as virtue and learning.

When, after a distinguished career at Yale, John Safford Fiske accepted the position of Deputy Clerk for the New York State Senate in Albany, there were those who prophesied a bright future in the world of politics or the world of diplomacy, or both. He exuded trust and integrity, and he effortlessly married an innate authority with an easy charm. People looked to him and up to him. They relied on him to frame arguments, suggest solutions, resolve disputes and generally make the world a better place.

John Safford Fiske himself entirely concurred with all these estimations and expectations of greatness to come. He had always held that Fortune and Fate helped those who helped themselves, which was why, in the summer of 1867, he had not hesitated to take the bold step of writing directly to Mr William H. Seward, United States Secretary of State, to ask, quite charmingly, for the position of United States Consul in Edinburgh. He was supported in his application by Judge Joseph Mullin of Watertown, New York, who praised his protégé as 'a young man of unblemished character, perfect integrity and unquestionable ability'.

Appointing Mr Fiske as United States Consul, Judge Mullin wrote, 'will do no discredit to the department or the country' and will 'aid a young man who is destined to do honour to both'. Mr Fiske 'intends devoting himself to literature', Judge Mullin continued, and 'seeks a place abroad with the aim of extending his knowledge of man'.

The application was successful and so, in the autumn of 1867, the twenty-nine-year-old Mr John Safford Fiske arrived in the New Athens ready and eager to take up his consular duties. They were not especially arduous. Much of his work was ceremonial. Going here and going there. Attending this and attending that. Receptions, banquets, balls and dinners. Listening, smiling, being charming. He was admirably suited to such duties. With his strength, wisdom, youth and vigour allied to an absolute certainty of his own destiny, Mr John Safford Fiske was the perfect embodiment of his young nation's values and aspirations, of its sense of its own importance and of its coming greatness.

John Safford Fiske had a plan. He wanted to marry, and to marry well. He would need a wife, a wife with a fortune to place at his disposal so that he could fulfil his literary and his political ambitions. His present means were more than adequate to meet his needs, but even in the great democracy of the United States, it was money that talked, and talked the loudest; money that opened doors; money that made the world turn; money that bought influence and brought power. He needed money, and the fastest and easiest way to acquire money, and lots of it, was to marry, and to marry well.

In fact, Mr John Safford Fiske was preparing to surrender himself to matrimony. Fortune and Fate had again smiled upon him and provided him with a young, beautiful and charmingly dressed heiress. She was American, born and bred into one of the best and oldest families on the East Coast, so he could be quite sure of her pedigree.

She was coming to Edinburgh in the spring. She was coming to see him. She was expecting him to propose to her and he was determined to do so. They would marry that summer and then, after a year or two in Edinburgh, he would be appointed ambassador, perhaps to London or to Paris, where he would live in splendour and serve with distinction before returning to Washington and the Senate.

John Safford Fiske's attitude to marriage was modelled on that of the Ancient Greeks. Marriage was a duty and a necessity. The world must turn, children must be born and the sacred cycle of nature perpetuated. Men needed wives for dynastic purposes and for domestic harmony. But he would reserve his love and his lust for boys and for young men, as he had done, carefully, discreetly and quietly, throughout most of his adult life. Women for duty, but boys for pleasure.

Of course there would be curbs on his freedoms. As a married man, he would have responsibilities towards his bride, but as soon as the children came, he hoped that he might be left alone to pursue young men. 'After we were married I could do pretty much as I pleased,' he mused. 'People don't mind what one does on £30,000 a year, and the Lady wouldn't much mind as she hasn't brains enough to trouble herself about much beyond her dresses, her carriage etc.'

From the moment of his arrival in Edinburgh he had sought out 'adventures', as he called them, and had established a delightful network of charming and handsome young men, including the brothers Donald and Robbie Sinclair. It was Robbie to whom he felt closest, Robbie with 'his smiling face', his 'clear gray eyes' and the 'vivid roses' in his cheeks – or so it was until the fateful moment when Stella Boulton swept into Edinburgh like the devouring North Wind and turned his world upon its head.

There were women and there were men and then there was Stella. John Safford Fiske had never before met anyone like her and he knew for a certainty that he would never do so again. She was fascinating. She was compelling. She seemed to him to be half-man and half-woman, but more, infinitely more, than the sum of her two parts. Stella was, he wrote, 'Laïs and Antinous in one'. An amalgam, a coalescence, of Laïs the Corinthian, the most famous, the most beautiful and the most expensive courtesan of the Ancient World, the muse of Demosthenes, and Antinous, the most beautiful and most beloved boy of the Emperor Hadrian. It was, he wrote, 'a ravishing thought'.

Who could fail to fall in love with two such beings, united in one perfect body? Fiske knew he was powerless to resist. It was more than love, more than lust. It was a kind of madness. A rapture. He could not sleep and he could not eat. Thoughts of Stella, in drag or out of drag, as a man, as a woman or as a hermaphrodite, filled his waking and sleeping hours. His chambers became a secret shrine to Stella, where he would worship her votive images in the privacy of his bedroom and hold her four carelessly written little notes about inconsequentialities in a bundle to his heart and feel a terrible joy and exultation.

He wanted her. More than he wanted anything else. More than he wanted a wife and a fortune. More than he wanted power and glory. More, perhaps, than life itself. He knew only too well that the more he wanted her, the more he risked all. But he was prepared to give up everything for her.

'Come love,' John Safford Fiske hastily wrote in pencil to Stella. 'Always for ever thine.' Despite its brevity, despite its drunken scrawl, this torn and crumpled half-sheet of paper was nonetheless as ardent and authentic a declaration of enduring love as Stella had yet received, which was perhaps why she treasured this brief note so much and kept it clasped to her breast.

18

Un Souvenir d'Amour

All Cracks are found so full of Ails
A *New Society* prevails
Call'd Sodomites; Men worse than Goats,
Who dress themselves in Petticoats.

John Dunton, *The He-Strumpets:*
A Satyr on the Sodomite-Club,
1707

Miss Fanny Winifred Park, also known as Mrs Fanny Graham, as Miss Vivian Gray (and by a variety of names unfit for polite ears), was beginning to feel decidedly worried. The sore on her bottom which had first appeared in January had not gone away. If anything, it was getting worse and becoming more painful. At first she had assumed, quite naturally and quite reasonably, that it was a mere wound of love; a passing soreness and discomfort; a consequence of being rather too energetically sodomised. In any event, she had decided to rest up for a few days and be deliciously *hors de combat*. She would allow things to settle, to right themselves, before venturing forth again with renewed vigour and renewed appetite. Not that her appetite in that department could ever be described as feeble. *Quite* the reverse. But the soreness had not gone away, and now she was feeling extremely uncomfortable and very low.

It was a nuisance that both Stella and Harry – the two people who might best advise her – were in Scotland: Stella selfishly still ensconced in Edinburgh with her former paramour, Louis Hurt, and Harry officially still in disgrace and in hiding, though Stella had confidentially informed her that Harry was being *very* indiscreet. Short of travelling all the way to *l'Ecosse*, she had no one to give her counsel. One or two friends, though, had bravely hazarded a look at her bottom, and amid some extremely vulgar and very unwelcome general observations, the particulars of which she need not enter into, said they thought that her poor cunny looked *very* sore.

What was she to do? If it was – horror of horrors – the pox, she could hardly go to the family doctor, explain that she had been sodomised to the point of insensibility and was now suffering from *un souvenir d'amour*. She was not sure she could trust him to keep quiet, and if it got out it would kill her poor Papa. Even if she went to another doctor, there might well be tiresome questions, and there was no guarantee that the police would not be dragged in.

Chancre of the anus or a pox in the arse was rather more common – at least in women – than most doctors either knew or cared to admit. It was a distasteful aspect of an already disagreeable branch of diagnosis. National honour no less than national decency was at stake. William Allingham, a doctor specialising in diseases of the rectum, was, like many others, convinced that anal sex (and in consequence, anal syphilis) was altogether a Continental, and specifically a French, phenomenon. 'In France this cannot be uncommon,' he asserted. 'I trust it is not common in America. I cannot say that in this country it is altogether unknown, but I hope and think it is infrequent.'

William Acton, the most celebrated venereologist of the age, agreed. Appearances were deceptive. The 'immense preval-ence' of anal warts in female prostitutes in the metropolis of London might lead some to conclude that there was an equally immense prevalence of anal sex. 'Foreigners noticing these ap-pearances in our foul wards go away fully convinced that un-natural crimes are very common in London,' he wrote. But 'a greater error than this cannot occur'. According to Acton, anal warts in female prostitutes were simply vaginal warts that had migrated.

This theory of migration was equally useful to Acton and his colleagues in explaining away those cases of anal syphilis which did present themselves. Syphilis in the vagina migrated to the anus either by discharges from syphilitic chancres in the vagina 'running down' to the anus, or through menstrual fluids following the same route. Sometimes anal syphilis might be the consequence of accidental or stray contact between the penis and the female anus, of the sort that might reasonably be expec-ted to occasionally occur in the throes of passion. But the most obvious explanation, that anal syphilis was a consequence of anal sex, was an unwanted and unwelcome truth, a truth better buried than bruited abroad.

In a break with tradition, George Drysdale, a doctor and pi-oneering sexologist, was considerably more frank than most of his English colleagues when he stated that anal syphilis was 'frequently to be seen in the female venereal hospitals'. Anal sex was, he said, commonplace among female prostitutes. 'There are very few of the older prostitutes', he said, 'who do not lend themselves to these practices, as well as many of the younger ones; however, they always maintain an obstinate si-lence when questioned on this point.'

There was a long-held suspicion that some men turned to

sodomy as a way of avoiding venereal disease. As early as 1707, in *The He-Strumpets: A Satyr on the Sodomite-Club*, the playwright John Dunton attributed the growing popularity of sodomy to an epidemic of the clap among female prostitutes. The poem 'Don Leon', a paean in praise of sodomy supposedly written by Lord Byron, suggested that sodomy with boys was a specific against being 'infected with rank disease'. And the anonymous author of *Extraordinary Revelations*, the penny pamphlet about Fanny and Stella, described sodomy as an 'abomination by which lust defies disease'.

Although reports of rectal syphilis and gonorrhoea in men were uncommon, they were not unheard of. In 1851, the French syphilologist Philippe Ricord recounted the cautionary tale of 'G—', a young man of twenty-five, 'of a good constitution, and enjoying excellent health', who consulted him about 'a recent cutaneous eruption' of ulcers around his anus 'for which he pretended he could assign no cause'. Ricord was convinced that these ulcers were syphilitic chancres. He cross-questioned the young man who finally confessed that:

> after a dinner party, when too liberal a quantity of
> generous wine had made him lose his reason and forget
> his manliness, he had slept with a friend, to whose
> beastly appetite he had sacrificed himself. He
> remembered having suffered greatly during the
> connection, and having passed blood on the following
> and subsequent days.

George Drysdale was once again out of step with his colleagues when, in 1861, he asserted that 'sodomy is common enough, especially in the prisons, where the most uneducated and degraded of the community, being shut up together, and left in idleness, take this mode of passing the listless hours':

> Instances now and then occur of gonorrhoea and chancre of the anus, which the patients, when pressed hard, either confess, or tacitly admit to having been contracted by these unnatural practices, though at first they always deny that the disease has such an origin, and ascribe it to an unclean water-closet &c.

Henry James Johnson, a former surgeon at the London Lock Hospital, which specialised in treating venereal diseases in female prostitutes and among the poor, had come across a very severe case of chancre of the anus in a man which strongly suggested that it was a consequence of anal sex. 'I saw one case which I did not doubt must have been a case of that description,' he testified at Fanny and Stella's trial. The state of this man's anus could, he said, admit of no other explanation but that he had been 'repeatedly' sodomised. 'At the time we were perfectly convinced of it.'

Desperate circumstances called for desperate measures. Miss Fanny Winifred Park was by now all but certain that she had contracted the pox. She still hoped for the best, at the same time fearing the worst. It was just conceivable that it might yet turn out to be some kind of local irritation, an ulcerating pile, perhaps, or something akin to Stella's fistula. But Fanny had an awful feeling that it was syphilis. The pain from the sore was excruciating; she could not sit and she could not sleep. That she needed to see a doctor, and sharpish, was not in dispute. But which doctor?

She had heard from friends that sometimes the doctors in the hospitals and the dispensaries asked fewer questions when confronted by young men with problems in their bottoms. Getting the required letter of recommendation from a subscriber to the hospital's charitable fund was the easy part. That was not difficult to obtain if you mixed in the right society and made up a story about some respectable young man of your acquaintance who had fallen upon hard times and could not afford to see a doctor.

Armed with her ticket-of-admission letter, Fanny would transform herself into that respectable young man. She would dress herself up in appropriate clothing, not her own well-cut suits from her Papa's tailor, but the sort of clothes that would have come from a fripperer's shop; second-, or third- or fourth-hand; frayed and worn and cheap, and probably none too clean. It was like dragging up, Fanny thought to herself, only in reverse.

Renowned as she was for playing 'principally dowagers' on the amateur and semi-professional stage, Fanny was convinced that she could give this particular role her all. After all, she had had plenty of experience of young men from the lower strata of society. Like her older brother Harry, she had a decided and definite penchant for the working men of London; a fascination, a reverence for their animal instincts, for their strangely hesitant and yet passionate approach to the business of fucking which so exactly coincided with her own needs. She knew them inside-out. She knew what clothes they wore, down to their undergarments; she knew how they spoke, how they acted, how they smelt. She would give the performance of her life.

She would become that shy young man, a mercer's clerk,

perhaps, who had unaccountably got this sore on his bottom. If the doctor asked point-blank how she – or rather, he – had acquired it he/she would blush and hang his/her head in shame and say that he/she had been drunk and could remember nothing at all. If there was any funny business, if there was the least sign of the police being called, she could leg it. All the hospital would have was a false name and a description of a shabbily dressed young man who might have been a clerk.

Fanny turned up at Charing Cross Hospital one afternoon in mid-February dressed in an old cutaway coat and 'wearing a pair of shabby plaid trousers'. As part of her disguise she had not shaved for two or three days. The hospital was very busy, and clearly she would have to wait for a long time. She paced up and down, down and up the long stone corridor waiting to be called. She could not sit still on the hard wooden benches that lined both sides of the corridor, partly because of the pain of the sore on her bottom, and partly because of nerves. She was always nervous before a performance.

'He was walking backwards and forwards in the passages,' the hospital hall porter, George Layton, recalled, 'which is contrary to the rules of the hospital and I asked him to take a seat.' Fanny was on the point of issuing the sharpest of sharp retorts, but recollecting where she was and why she was there, bit her lip and duly took a seat on a wooden bench.

S omething very strange had happened this year. Not one, not two, but *three* young men – three in almost as many weeks – had presented themselves in Dr Richard Barwell's consulting room at Charing Cross Hospital with afflictions of the rectum. Was it a coincidence, or was there something more singular going on – something more sinister? He had dealt with the first case summarily. The young man – a rather common specimen and gaudily dressed – had turned up one afternoon in early February complaining of a sore on his bottom. Dr Barwell's suspicions were aroused by the young man's rather affected, effeminate way of speaking. Naturally he had enquired of this young man how long he had had this sore and how it might have come about. Was it some sort of injury? The young man hesitated. In a manner of speaking, yes, he said, it was a sort of injury. He smiled a confiding sort of smile. And then he admitted everything.

'He confessed to the act of sodomy,' Dr Barwell recounted indignantly in court. 'He confessed how he had got this sore, so cynically – almost *boastfully*, or *jauntily*, I should rather have said – that I would have nothing to do with him. I drove him away.'

Dr Barwell rarely lost his temper, but on this occasion with this young man, he had lost his temper badly, very badly indeed. He had, quite literally, driven this young sodomite away, pushing the frightened youth out of his consulting room and propelling him down the corridor while people looked curiously on. He had thought about it many times since and always with revulsion. It was not so much the affliction that he objected to. He had seen dozens of cases of syphilis of the anus before, invariably in women, and he had shrugged his shoulders and treated them. Such things went on, and he would not sit in judgement. Even the fact that this was a case of syphilis of the anus in a young man, revolting as that was, rare as that was – for he had never seen another case – even that fact was not the cause of his loss of control. Nor was it simply the absence of any remorse, any sense of shame, on the part of the young man, shocking as that was. No, what had made him lose his reason, what had driven him over the edge, was this young man's evident *pleasure* – pleasure which seemed to be commingled with *pride* – pride in the act of sodomy; a pleasure that he had the temerity to boast about; a pleasure that he assumed, that he presumed, others would understand and somehow share. That was what had made Dr Barwell see such violent red.

In just a matter of days, another man had fetched up in his consulting room. Dr Barwell had asked what the matter was, and after some hesitation the man said he thought he was suffering from 'a gonorrhoeal discharge, as he himself called it, from the anus'. Dr Barwell was taken aback. The man was nondescript; neither young nor old, not obviously effeminate, and he clearly had some education. Most of Dr Barwell's patients would never even have heard of the word 'gonorrhoea', let alone use the word in front of him. The man was civil and had the grace to look somewhat ashamed of himself. Dr Barwell decided that he would treat him.

Dr Barwell could not now believe that yet a third man had turned up with a venereal affliction of the rectum. The young man sitting nervously in front of him was dressed in 'rather common clothing' which was a little too tight upon his slim frame. He had a sore bottom, he explained, or rather, a sore upon his bottom that would not heal or go away. Dr Barwell looked at him sharply. The young man seemed reluctant to meet his eyes and hung his head as if he were ashamed of himself. How had this sore originated, he asked, and for how long had he had it? The young man hesitated. About three or four weeks, he thought. And he had no idea how he came by it. Dr Barwell could tell he was lying but said nothing.

S o far, so good, thought Fanny to herself. The rather stern-looking doctor had given her one or two very penetrating glances before asking her to bend over and drop her trousers. That, at least, was something she was well practised in. She wanted to giggle but repressed herself sternly. At least he was examining her and would, presumably, treat her. It was all going according to plan. She winced with pain as the doctor parted her buttocks.

'I examined him and found a syphilitic sore upon the anus, a primary sore,' Dr Barwell recalled. 'It was an open sore, called a chancre, and the anus gaped sufficiently to show the mucous membrane, and the sore upon it. The sore was at the back part of the anus, on the edge of the margin of the mucous membrane.'

There was no doubt in Dr Barwell's mind that this young man's chancre 'would have been communicated by a person who had the disease, and not by slight or mere contact'. While he could not be absolutely certain that this young man had been sodomised (though the gaping anus strongly suggested that he had), at the very least there had been direct and prolonged sexual contact between a syphilitic penis and this young man's anus.

The sore was not the worst he had ever seen, but nor was it slight either. 'With energetic treatment such a sore would be healed in two months or ten weeks, sometimes much sooner,' Dr Barwell said. He gave Fanny a battery of medicines: iodide of mercury, bichloride of mercury, iodide of potash and a weak solution of carbolic acid as a mild disinfectant.

Twice a week, every week, as winter turned into spring, Fanny put on the same old cutaway coat and the same shabby plaid trousers and attended Dr Barwell's surgery at Charing

Cross Hospital in character as a poor but respectable clerk. Dr Barwell remained stern and aloof, and Fanny knew better than to engage him in conversation. Sometimes he would examine her bottom and sometimes merely take her own account. Mercifully, the sore was healing, and Fanny learnt to recognise the little grunt of approval Dr Barwell made when things were progressing well.

In April 1870, after almost two months of treatment, Fanny's visits to the hospital abruptly ceased. Dr Barwell was mildly surprised, as this person had been assiduous in keeping his appointments. But it was common for attendance to fall off once the sore had healed. This young man was almost cured, though not quite, and Dr Barwell would have liked to have continued seeing him for a few more weeks yet.

But before he knew it there were two policemen standing on the doorstep of his house on a Saturday morning in the middle of May. A young man had been arrested upon suspicion of sodomy, they said, and they 'insisted upon his accompanying them to see if he could identify his patient'. Dr Barwell refused. He was a doctor, not a policeman, and he would have no part in these proceedings if he could help it. He had strong professional obligations of confidentiality, even to avowed or suspected sodomites, and he was, he said, 'most unwilling to be mixed up in such an unpleasant business'. But the policemen would not take no for an answer. If Dr Barwell refused, they would apply to Mr Flowers for a summons, forcing him to make the identification. And if he refused to answer that summons, he would be in contempt of court and they would arrest him. He had no choice in the matter.

'And so,' as the *Lancet* reported, 'Dr Barwell was thus most unwillingly made a witness for the Crown.'

19

The Battle of the Bottoms

An Awkward Question

'Mamma dear,' said the youth, 'what is the meaning of the word bugger?'

'Bugger, my child? Why do you ask?'

'Because I heard my tutor call the coachman a damn bugger.'

'Well, my child,' replied the Marchioness, 'a bugger is a person who does his fellow an injury behind his back.' Cough.

The Pearl, 1880

The consulting room at Newgate Gaol had rarely been so crowded. Crammed inside along with Fanny and Stella, there were no fewer than six doctors, four prison warders, three detectives, two medical orderlies, Mr Abrams the solicitor and a gentleman from the Treasury who was there to represent the public interest. There was barely room to swing a cat.

That afternoon in early June was especially fine and warm, which was all very well outside in God's fresh air, but in the dank and airless confines of Newgate, with its unmistakable and pervasive smell of prison rot – a rank combination of unwashed bodies, disease, sewage, despair and hopelessness – the stench and the heat were overwhelming. Several of the gentlemen in attendance felt decidedly faint, and only the strong odour of carbolic in the consulting room prevented them from actually keeling over.

Fanny and Stella had been transferred to Newgate at the end of May. As the web of conspiracy seemed to grow ever larger, and the case against them assumed greater and greater seriousness, the House of Detention in Coldbath Fields was deemed inadequate to contain such dangerous prisoners.

In Newgate they could be held 'in close prison', or solitary confinement, so that the contagion of sodomy and effeminacy which they both carried within their bodies would not taint the other prisoners. 'We are of the opinion that there is much danger of contamination among younger prisoners,' a Report by the Departmental Committee on Prisons had concluded when considering this very subject. 'They are of an age when curiosity stimulates the inherited or acquired depravity which is so often found in young criminals.'

The extraordinary scene in the consulting room at Newgate Gaol was the consequence of an impasse between the Crown, who wanted unambiguous and unarguable forensic proof that Fanny and Stella had been repeatedly sodomised, and the defence, who wanted to prove the exact opposite.

As things stood, the defence appeared to be at a slight advantage, having already despatched Dr Hughes, Dr Harvey and the splendidly named Dr Le Gros Clark to examine Ernest Boulton and Frederick Park in the House of Detention a fortnight earlier. Their conclusions, reached after a very thorough examination, were the very opposite of those reached by Dr Paul, the police surgeon who had examined Boulton and Park the morning after their arrest, and by Dr Barwell, who said he had treated Park for syphilis of the anus. According to Dr Hughes, Dr Harvey and Dr Le Gros Clark, there was nothing abnormal about these two young men's penises, and nothing in, on or around their anuses or rectums which betrayed any evidence of unnatural crime – just a small scar, a cicatrix, on the outside of Stella's anus where she had been operated upon for *fistula in ano* early in 1869.

Now half a dozen 'eminent medical gentlemen' – from both sides, and from no side, of the argument – would examine these young men for forensic signs of sodomy. And to ensure that everything was above board and out in the open, the examinations would be conducted while they were all assembled together in the consulting room of Newgate Gaol. According to the newspapers the examinations were to take place 'by the direction of the Government', a decision taken at the highest levels, and it was said that the Attorney-General himself had taken personal charge of the case.

'Eminent medical gentlemen' was how they were described in the newspapers, though there was medical eminence and there was medical eminence. The undoubted star of their troupe was Dr Alfred Swaine Taylor of Guy's Hospital. He was remarkable for the fact that he was a Professor twice over, simultaneously holding two chairs at Guy's: in chemistry and in medical jurisprudence. He was the most celebrated medical jurist of his day, having almost single-handedly pioneered the science of forensic medicine.

Dr Taylor's first book, *A Manual of Medical Jurisprudence*, was published in 1836, when he was just thirty years old, and had already run to eight editions. He had appeared as an expert witness in over four hundred trials, and he was feared and loved in equal measure by the guilty and the innocent.

With his shock of dark hair, now streaked with silver, Dr Taylor looked much younger than his sixty-four years. He was insatiably curious about everything, a polymath, with interests ranging from the physics of geology to the chemistry of photography. He was an expert in poisons and in the classification of gunshot wounds, and an early pioneer in the use of chloroform. By a strange coincidence, it was Dr Taylor who had administered chloroform to Ernest Boulton during the operation for *fistula in ano* performed by Dr Hughes at the Boulton family home in Peckham Rye in February 1869.

By an even stranger coincidence, it was Dr Taylor who, thirty-six years earlier, had performed the post-mortem dissection on the young actress Eliza Edwards, and made a startling, not to say disturbing, discovery: Eliza Edwards was in fact a man – of sorts.

By a third bizarre coincidence it was as a student at Dr Taylor's celebrated series of lectures, in the early 1850s, that Dr James Thomas Paul had first heard about sodomy and sodomites, and about young men who dressed as young women. He had been inspired, if that was the right word, to discover more, and it became quite a passion with him. The wheel had turned full circle, but Dr Paul would not be there to meet his old mentor. The defence were adamant. They would not brook his presence.

Hot on the heels of Dr Taylor in the stakes of medical eminence came Dr Frederick Le Gros Clark, Fellow of the Royal College of Surgeons, Examiner of the University of London, Chair of Surgery at St Thomas's Hospital, Examiner of Surgeons to the Royal College of Physicians and so on and so forth. Dr Le Gros Clark was already well acquainted with the private parts of the two young men in women's clothes, having examined them just a fortnight earlier in company with Dr

Hughes and Dr Harvey. None of them could find any sign of sodomy, insertive or receptive, so Dr Le Gros Clark could be counted as a witness for the defence.

The third medical gentleman who could justly lay claim to eminence was Dr Henry James Johnson, a distinguished surgeon who for the best part of forty years had specialised in *les souvenirs d'amour*, the diseases of love. Now nearly seventy, Dr Johnson was still remarkably upright and remarkably active. He had a large private practice in Suffolk Place, off Trafalgar Square, and those gentlemen unfortunate enough to contract a dose would hasten in a closed carriage to his consulting rooms where they could be assured of the best and most up-to-date treatment for their condition.

For two years, from 1832 to 1833, he was the House Surgeon at the old London Lock Hospital, which had been set up in 1746 to provide free treatment for syphilis and other such afflictions to the poor, and it was here that he had developed his formidable knowledge and expertise in all diseases venereal.

In 1851, after recovering from a long illness from which he fully expected to die, he published *Gonorrhoea and Its Consequences*, which was among the first books to argue that gonorrhoea was an infectious disease in its own right: not a local irritation; not a weakened form of syphilis; and emphatically not an unfortunate consequence for the male of the species of those constricting 'vaginal spasms' experienced by women (especially prostitutes) when overly aroused during sexual intercourse.

With Dr Johnson, the real medical eminence of their group ended. Dr William Hughes, who was also one of the party, was of course a highly respected and respectable doctor in general practice in Fenchurch Street, but he could lay no conceivable claim to expertise on the subject of sodomy or post-sodomitic symptoms. Dr Hughes was there for one reason only: having operated on Boulton's fistula a year earlier, he was privy to the pertinent medical history of one of the young men in question.

Equally, Dr Barwell was under no illusions about the reasons for his own presence in the consulting room at Newgate Gaol on this sticky afternoon in June. He was there because, like Dr Hughes, he had compelling and pertinent medical knowledge of one of the defendants: the young man he now knew to be called Frederick Park. Having treated this young man for an unambiguous and unarguable chancre of the anus, he supposed himself to be a witness for the prosecution.

Dr John Rowland Gibson, the Surgeon of Newgate Gaol, was the sixth and final member of this medical troupe. It would have been an impossible professional discourtesy for him not to be present in his own consulting room while the two prisoner-patients under his care and control were examined by colleagues. By any standard of medical etiquette, he had to be present and he had to participate in the proceedings.

To give him his due, Dr Gibson's many years of experience of attending to the medical needs of the very worst of God's creatures must have given him insights into the dark depravities and feralities of the criminal body and the criminal mind, insights not usually granted to doctors. Among Dr Gibson's many duties was to testify as to the sanity – or otherwise – of murderers and rapists and other hardened criminals, and to certify that those executed within the prison walls were properly dead when taken down from the gibbet. With such a rare and unusually solemn practice, Dr Gibson might be expected to detect those outward bodily signs and deformations – visible only to the trained eye – which betrayed the inner diseased pathology of the criminal and the degenerate.

Likewise, with his long experience of criminals, Dr Gibson might well be able to intuit certain incorporeal qualities about his patients, such as patterns of lying, auras of deceit, miasmas of criminality, airs of guilt – or even innocence. In any and in all events, Dr Gibson would bring something different and strange to these very different and very strange proceedings.

Notwithstanding the eminence of the six medical gentlemen present, only three of them had any actual experience of the signs and symptoms of sodomy: Professor Taylor with Eliza Edwards, almost forty years previously; Dr Johnson, who claimed to have seen one certain case of receptive sodomy among the outpatients of the Lock Hospital – again, almost forty years earlier; and Dr Barwell himself, who, after a lifetime of professional innocence in such matters, had this very year seen three young men with afflictions of the rectum in as many weeks. With the best part of 150 years' combined knowledge and experience, these six doctors had examined the back passages of just five confirmed sodomites.

British doctors laboured under a disadvantage when it came to trying to determine whether or not Ernest Boulton and Frederick Park had been sodomised. If it was the case indeed, as one and all were only too ready to proclaim, that sodomy was a rare and alien fungoid in the sexual flora of the British Isles, then it stood to reason that British doctors would neither have, nor need to have, forensic knowledge or experience of the tell-tale signs of sodomy.

It was widely felt that any disagreement between the six eminent medical gentlemen on whether or not these two young men had been sodomised would be detrimental to the reputation of the medical profession. The *Lancet* confessed to 'a feeling of apprehension lest a new scandal may be caused by directly conflicting medical testimony' in 'this very grave case' and felt sufficiently exercised to devote an entire editorial to the delicate subject of knowledge (or rather, the lack of knowledge) of sodomy among English doctors.

So how could a fair verdict be reached, a verdict based on sound scientific principles and on observable forensic evidence? The *Lancet* felt 'most strongly' that the Government 'should place the medical evidence for the prosecution in the hands of a select committee of medical men'. Given the dearth of home-grown experience in 'this very repulsive subject', the *Lancet* urged the Government to recruit the two leading French specialists in sodomy, Monsieur Ricord and Monsieur Tardieu, to work in coalition 'with two English medical men of the highest eminence'.

In the consulting room at Newgate, Fanny and Stella lay upon identical couches, their nakedness covered by coarse brownish sheets with the words 'Newgate Prison' emblazoned in letters three inches high. Both of them were sorry sights now: pale, unshaven and undernourished. Their plucked and tweezered eyebrows were beginning to grow out of shape, and their eyes were dull. Neither of them appeared to evince any surprise at the presence of so many people in the consulting room. Mr Abrams had no doubt warned them what they must expect, and they waited patiently for what they knew must happen.

Apart from the mandatory bath in filthy water upon admission to Newgate Gaol, facilities for washing were almost non-existent. 'The two things most neglected in Her Majesty's prisons are cleanliness and godliness,' recorded one inmate of Newgate. Apart from a damp rag and the occasional basin of brackish water grudgingly allowed before a court appearance, prisoners were unable to keep themselves clean. Fanny and Stella had done their best, but their private parts and their backsides were in an unwashed and decidedly unpleasant state.

Quite apart from the closeness of the room, the malodorous state of Fanny and Stella and the overwhelming stench of prison rot (to which only Dr Gibson seemed oblivious), the atmosphere in the room was tense. As the *Lancet* had prophesied, the medical gentlemen present were in profound and uncomfortable disagreement. The hospitable preliminaries of Dr Gibson had fallen flat, and even Dr Le Gros Clark's fabled 'dignified courtesy of manner' failed to ease the tension.

Each medical gentleman took his turn to examine the two young men. Their genitalia would be looked at first: penis, testicles and scrotum lifted, pulled, squeezed and peered at; foreskin rolled back; and the meatus, the lips of the urethra, pinched and prised apart to see if there was any discharge. Then they would be asked to turn over and lie flat while their buttocks were carefully parted and scrutinised, before they were instructed to stand up and bend over the couch while their anuses were minutely examined.

Dr Johnson had bought with him a large and powerful lens for the purpose of magnification, and also a speculum, the hugely unpopular and painful device shaped like the beak of a duck used to force open the vaginas of prostitutes suspected of being diseased. Which in a way was entirely right and proper, if it was true that these young men had so unmanned themselves, so unsexed themselves, that they had allowed men to use them as common prostitutes.

E ven if they had not actually read the controversial works of the sodomite-hunter Professor Ambroise Tardieu, or the marginally less rabid, marginally more rational discourse of his recently deceased German colleague Dr Johann Ludwig Casper, most of the medical gentlemen present had a broad idea of what they were looking for.

There were, Professor Tardieu had decreed, three 'characteristic signs of passive pederasty'. First, *infundibulum*, or a funnel-shaped depression of the anal cleft caused by the intense pressure applied by the penis of the insertive sodomite to the anus of the receptive partner in order to gain ingress.

Second, erasure of the *rugae*, the characteristic puckerings and ridges around the anus. The mechanics of sodomy eroded and erased these *rugae*, literally wore them away, partially or completely, and when such erasure was present, sodomy must be presumed to have been the cause. When, as a young man, Professor Taylor had examined the anus of 'Miss Eliza' Edwards post-mortem, the *rugae* had been entirely obliterated. Such was the alchemy of sodomy that the anus resembled female labia.

Third and most tellingly, excessive or extreme dilation of the anus was invariably apparent to the naked eye. Again, at the post mortem of Eliza Edwards in 1833, it had been 'noticed by all present' that his/her 'anal aperture' was greatly enlarged, 'much wider and larger than natural'.

But in cases where anal dilation was not immediately apparent to the naked eye, it was necessary to test the dilatability of the anus, to discover how quickly it would dilate when stimulated by the repeated insertion of the physician's lubricated finger, imitating, in so far as it was possible, the repeated insertion of the sodomite's erect *membrum virile*. The quicker the dilation, the greater the likelihood that sodomy had been practised.

'Beware,' Tardieu warned doctors. Some sodomites were skilled in evading the detection of anal dilation. 'They clench their buttocks, but it will suffice to quickly change position, or put them on their knees in a kneeling position, or simply prolong the examination until they tire of contracting their muscles, to triumph over this gross fraud.'

There could have been little danger of Fanny and Stella clenching their buttocks so as to deceive the doctors. Six doctors, six fingers, and multiple insertions by each doctor meant that by the end of the examinations, which lasted well over two hours, the dilatability or otherwise of their anal sphincters became almost meaningless.

The examinations were conducted in almost complete silence. There was no discussion, no commentary, no exchanges of opinion, save one when Dr Barwell pointed out to Dr Johnson a scar on the prisoner Park's anus which, he said in a triumphant tone, was the scar left behind by the syphilitic chancre he had treated some months earlier.

But Dr Johnson politely begged to differ. 'No,' he said. 'That is only a small varix,' a varicose vein. 'It was quite small. It was not so big as a marrow fat pea – hardly so large as an ordinary garden pea,' he said later.

Dr Johnson used his magnifying glass and examined the supposed scar more closely. 'What you see is nothing but the light reflected from the glistening side of the varix. There is no scar whatever,' he told Dr Barwell. 'I then handed him the glass to look for himself and he declined it, implying that he could see as well, I suppose, without a magnifying glass as with one. At any rate he declined it.'

By the time the examinations were completed, the heads of all those nineteen persons present were spinning with the heat and the stench and the strangeness of the task they had been engaged in.

Of the six doctors present, five were agreed that there were no signs of sodomy present upon the bodies of the prisoners, no scars or cicatrices consequent upon a syphilitic chancre, no evidence to suggest unnatural practices – apart from a certain feyness, a certain delicacy, a certain femininity (more marked in Boulton than in Park, but nonetheless present in both). Dr Barwell alone dissented.

All six were however agreed that the *rugae* had been partially obliterated around Park's anus, with five of them reading little or nothing into this state of partial destruction, and Dr Barwell again dissenting. Equally, all six agreed about the presence of a crop of condylomatous warts around both young men's anuses, but disagreed as to the origins and meaning of these warts, with Dr Barwell, as usual, dissenting most violently.

Unpleasant, humiliating and painful as the prolonged examinations had been, this was good news for Fanny and Stella. A majority of the six eminent medical gentlemen had found in their favour. 'It may be relied upon as a positive fact,' *Reynolds's Newspaper* reported breathlessly, 'that the result of this examination undoubtedly tended to throw some doubt upon the medical evidence adduced before the police magistrate.' It now seemed doubtful, at least to *Reynolds's Newspaper* and to some others, that the prosecutions of these two young men could or should proceed. For a brief, shining moment it almost seemed possible – perhaps even likely – that Fanny and Stella might be released without charge.

20

He, She or It

There is not the slightest doubt that England is
hastening towards the border which divides the
sexes; already persons have over-stepped and stand
alone, hated and despised.

The Englishwoman's Domestic Magazine, 1871

D r Henry James Johnson, one of the six eminent medical
gentlemen who examined Fanny and Stella in Newgate
Gaol, had been most forcibly struck by the startling, the really
quite startling, *womanliness* of their bodies, especially about
their bottoms. They were men, and yet they were not men.
They were women, and yet not women. They were something
indeterminate, somewhere in-between. The whiteness and
smoothness and translucency of their skin, with their slender
waists, the gentle curve of their hips and their shapely buttocks,
all bespoke womanliness. Above and beyond the womanliness
of their bodies, there was an indefinable aura of femininity
about them, he could not put it more precisely than that, which
was all the more powerful because it was so mysterious, so hard
to pin down.

Of course Dr Johnson was only too well aware that these
young men had regularly dressed themselves as women, wearing corsets to give themselves wasp-waists and tight-laced bodices to squeeze and push their breasts upwards and outwards.

They had tweezered their eyebrows and plucked their beards and used every artifice: wigs, paint, pads and God only knew what else to create a convincing illusion of womanliness. There could be no doubt that such practices, long adhered to, long indulged in, might very well lend a permanent air of womanliness to any young man. Constant tight-lacing, quite apart from constricting and deforming the disposition of the internal organs to an alarming and dangerous degree, did have the effect of permanently altering the bodies of young women, giving them impossibly small waists and shapely hips and buttocks. But even making allowances for the effect of such practices, Dr Johnson still found these young men troublingly womanly.

'The smallness of the anus, the tightness of the sphincter, and the smallness of the rectum' were all, Dr Johnson said, what he might expect to find in a healthy young woman. These characteristics were, he added, most marked in Frederick Park's posterior, 'if possible more so even than in Boulton'.

Was it possible that the womanliness of Fanny and Stella was actual, rather than assumed? Could there be a biological explanation for the troubling emanations of femininity that both these creatures exuded? Were they, perhaps, a species of hermaphrodite? An amalgam of male and female? Not masculine and not feminine, but a combination of the two genders commingled to produce a strange hybrid?

From the moment of Fanny and Stella's arrest, attitudes were divided, like the Red Sea. There were those who regarded them as wicked and wilful sodomites, all the more wicked and all the more wilful because they deceived, they tricked men into thinking that they were women. And then there were those who took the view that Fanny and Stella were indeed hermaphrodites, bodily or mentally, or most probably a mixture of both: degraded certainly, but also unfortunate and to be pitied, because their actions – however reprehensible and however offensive – were the consequence of instincts ordained by a freakish and perverse Nature.

As the details of the case against them began to unfold, *Reynolds's Newspaper* had gone from calling them 'the Young Gentlemen in Woman's Clothes' to describing them as part of 'the Hermaphrodite Clique' and 'the Hermaphrodite Gang'. Other newspapers implied their innate duality by calling them 'men-women' or 'he-she ladies' or variations on this theme. Even before their arrest, many found it impossible to believe that Fanny and Stella – particularly and most especially Stella – were men. Wherever they went, whoever they met, in drag, or out of drag, as Fanny and Stella, or as Frederick and Ernest, there were always those who had their doubts as to their exact gender. Were they men? Or were they women? Or were they a rare and remarkable matched pair of hermaphrodites?

In January of the previous year, Fanny and Stella, in company with Charles Pavitt, had formed a small touring theatrical company called 'Her Majesty's Servants'. They made their debut on 27th January 1869 at the tiny but grandly named Theatre Royal in the small Essex town of Stock. 'By special request', the actors performed 'Mr. H. J. Byron's comedy of *One Hundred Thousand Pounds*, the characters of Alice and Mrs. Barlow being played respectively by Boulton and Park, who are designated in the programme, Miss Ernestine Edwards and Miss Mabel Foster'.

'During the piece Miss Edwards sang "Fading Away" with a care and taste that brought down the house,' the *Essex Herald* reported, clearly not able to fully grasp the fact that Miss Ernestine Edwards was, in truth, Mr Ernest Boulton. Other newspaper correspondents could only marvel at the perfect illusion of femininity that Stella/Ernestine created: 'Listening to his extraordinary voice, and criticising, however narrowly, his wonderfully feminine appearance and manner, it is really difficult for a moment to believe that he is not a really charming girl.' Indeed, Miss Ernestine Edwards was so perfect and so charming that the anonymous correspondent went on to hint orotundly that Miss Edwards had to be a species of hermaphrodite. 'Certainly,' he declared, 'if some of Nature's journeymen had not been at work, "Mister" Boulton, we hesitate almost to write this prefix, would have incontestably been a woman.'

Later that same year, Stella and Charles Pavitt toured Essex and Hertfordshire with *A Drawing-Room Entertainment*, devised and written by themselves and designed to be performed in country-house drawing rooms, assembly rooms and village halls. 'We agreed to share the profits and divide the expenses,' Charles Pavitt recalled. 'The entertainment usually comprised a short opera, a humorous dialogue, and a laughable sketch. In all these the ladies' characters were represented by Ernest Boulton.' Sadly, there was no role for poor Fanny.

Wherever they went, Stella shone, and even though the playbills unambiguously declared that all the female parts were performed by Mr Ernest Boulton, all who saw her could hardly believe that she was not in reality a beautiful and charming girl. 'We may add that Mr. Boulton very cleverly personates female characters,' wrote one reviewer, 'and that it is difficult for a spectator to realise the fact that he is a "make-up" for the occasion. His song, "Fading Away" is exceedingly feminine.'

Off stage, as well as on stage, Stella had more than her fair share of admirers who seemed unable to comprehend that the beautiful young woman they saw singing and swooning on stage was in reality a young man. Bouquets were invariably the order of the day.

'On one evening,' Charles Pavitt recalled, 'Boulton had as many as *fourteen* bouquets thrown to him.' And there were any number of invitations to supper from gentlemen, and from ladies. All of them wanted Stella to attend 'in his female costume', and 'several sporting gentlemen wanted him to go in his lady's costume into the hunting-field, but he would not go.'

Even when Stella was dressed as a man, even when she introduced herself as Ernest, even when she shook hands as manfully as she could and spoke as gruffly as she could manage, many men simply refused to accept that she was a man. The delicacy of her body, the softness of her voice, the brilliancy of her eyes, the smoothness of her skin, the lustre of her hair, the sweetness of her scent, the smallness of her hands and the daintiness of her feet were all, and in every way, female, feminine, womanly.

Quite apart from those gentlemen admirers who simply could not or would not believe that Stella was a man, even when it was written in black and white, even when Stella protested that she was indeed a man, even when she dressed in men's clothing, there were also those with no conceivable amatory interest in her who were equally convinced that she was a woman.

A few weeks before her arrest, dear, dull Louis Hurt wrote to Stella from a remote inn in Scotland, where they had spent a night or two in the course of Louis's interminable inspections of post offices. Stella had worn male clothing, but had signally failed to convince anyone that she was a man. 'My darling Ernie,' Louis began:

> The landlord of the inn from which I write tells me that all the men whom we saw here the other day were positive you are a woman. He assured them you were not, although he seems not to have been certain himself. He said you moved about and stood like one but that your thighs, which he examined when you were going upstairs, were not so plump as a woman's.

No doubt it reminded them both of an unfortunate incident eighteen months earlier when Louis had dragged a reluctant Stella off on a tour of post offices in Wales and the West Country – for the good of her health, he said. The 'rustics in Devizes and Newport' had taken it upon themselves to write to the Postmaster-General himself accusing his roving inspector of travelling upon official business with a woman disguised as a man in tow. If it had not been so serious, it would have been funny, especially when the said rustics intimated their belief that Mr Hurt's companion was a woman of low repute, little realising how close they had come to hitting that particular nail on the head. It had taken the urgent intervention of Lord Arthur Clinton, MP, to clear matters up.

Mr Flowers, the magistrate at Bow Street, also appeared to be convinced that Fanny and Stella were in fact women, or some variation on a womanly theme, despite the weight of evidence and despite their own assertions and protestations: 'I really thought they were women, and I expressed that opinion at the time,' Mr Flowers said in court some three weeks after Fanny and Stella's first appearance there. 'I was in hopes that the defence would be that they were women.'

Of course, there were some men whom Stella was quite happy *not* to tell: steamers or punters, the men *she* picked up (because she was nothing if not choosy) in the Haymarket and round and about, the men who paid her money, and good money too, thinking she was a beautiful young whore, so different from the usual run of ruined and raddled harridans. It was easier for them not to know, and it was not hard to keep them in the dark. Most were so drunk they didn't know whether they were coming or going, let alone by the front or the back door, and even if they were sober, they hardly cared.

Some of them, of course, knew she was a man because they had had her before, or they had guessed, or they had groped her and found something they were not expecting. Or she had told them on an impulse or out of caprice to see what, if anything, would happen. Usually they carried on regardless; most were past the point of no return. A few even seemed curious and asked if she was one of those rare and wonderful creatures that was man and woman in one, the very idea seeming to arouse them sexually.

In his riotous and unreliable *Recollections*, Jack Saul, the celebrated Mary-Ann, recounts Stella confiding in him that she once seduced a handsome gentleman by the name of Mr Bruce in the Star and Garter Hotel in Richmond by purporting to be a hermaphrodite.

> 'I pretended to resist his attempts to get at my cunny,'
> Stella said, 'and at last blushingly told him that I was one
> of those unfortunate beings (which perhaps he had heard
> of) who had a malformation, something like the male
> instrument – in fact, it was capable of stiffening, and

always did so under excitement, exactly as a man's would do.'

'But, darling,' Stella said, addressing herself to Mr Bruce, 'It is quite harmless, and can do no mischief like the real male affair. Now you, I know, will be too disgusted to want to kiss me, although I am dying for you to afford me that pleasure.'

Mr Bruce assured Stella that he had often heard of hermaphrodites and was curious to know more.

But despite Stella's many triumphs in the endless battle of love, there were occasional defeats. Another admirer who believed, at first at least, Stella to be a woman was Mr Francis Kegan Cox – or Captain Cox as he preferred to be called. Captain Cox was every inch the swell. He was a partner in the auctioneering line, having had what might tactfully be termed a chequered past. After nine years in the army he had sold his commission and spent the several years knocking around Australia and New Zealand looking for opportunities, of which none presented themselves.

Back in London, he landed on his feet and secured an enviable position as Secretary to the Civil Service Club.

'I resigned that office voluntarily,' Captain Cox admitted in court. 'There was a complaint made against me.'

'Like mistakes in arithmetic?' Mr Straight, for the defence, enquired sarcastically.

Captain Cox cleared his throat and swallowed hard. 'Sums were entered into the books without names, carelessly,' he countered.

From the debacle of the Civil Service Club, Captain Cox

found his way to the City where he and an unnamed gentleman set themselves up as auctioneers. In September 1868, Stella was sitting at luncheon in the Guildhall Tavern, Leadenhall Street, in company with Lord Arthur Clinton and Mr W. H. Roberts, Lord Arthur's solicitor, loan arranger and general fixer, when the Captain walked in.

It transpired that Captain Cox and Mr Roberts were previously acquainted. Introductions to Lord Arthur and Stella were effected, and Captain Cox was invited to join the luncheon party. He needed no pressing. He was strangely and powerfully drawn to the young man who had been introduced to him as Mr Ernest Boulton, but Captain Cox was dashed and damned and blowed if he believed that for an instant. Even though 'he' was dressed from top to toe in male attire, it was clear to him that Boulton was a girl, a very pretty girl, and a very flirtatious girl at that. There could be no doubt about it. She was coming on exceedingly strong to him.

'It was from the manner Boulton's hair was done, and from the smallness of his hands and feet, as well as his general manners, that I formed an opinion he was a woman,' the Captain said later in Bow Street.

Stella was equally smitten. The Captain was a fine, swaggering figure of a man and, at thirty-five years old, in the prime of his life. He was the cock of the walk. Tall, strong, upright and confident in matters of the heart (and other organs), he did not scruple to indicate in every possible way that he was very taken with Stella.

Stella, in turn, was flattered, flirtatious and on flamboyant form.

'Oh you City birds have good fun in your offices', Stella said in a tone of mock complaint, 'and you have champagne!'

The Captain rose gallantly to the bait.

'You had better come over and see,' he replied meaningfully, and that very afternoon a radiant Stella and a less than effervescent Lord Arthur Clinton turned up at 1 Gresham's Buildings, being the Captain's flashy rented offices.

'My partner arrived whilst we were there and we had champagne,' Captain Cox continued. Lord Arthur's nose was clearly out of joint. After all, he and Stella were living together as man and wife, and he had not long since ordered – but not yet paid for – engraved cards bearing the legend 'Lady Arthur Clinton'. Of course, Arthur knew that Stella frequently went out on the pad to sell herself to men for much-needed cash to keep them afloat. Though he was not exactly happy about this arrangement, he could see the advantages. What he did not care for, not one jot, was being made to play the cuckold in public. And after one particularly loaded exchange between Stella and this man Cox, he left the room and slammed the door, and went for a walk to cool his heels and cool his head while the flirtation continued apace.

'I treated Boulton as a fascinating woman,' Cox said later.

'Have you had a large experience in fascinating women?' asked the sarcastic Mr Straight. Captain Cox objected to this question, very strongly. But Mr Straight was not to be deflected. 'Have you had a large experience in fascinating women?' he repeated.

'I have known a great many women in my time,' was the guarded reply.

'Were you in the habit of making advances of this sort on your first acquaintance?'

'It would always depend whether there was an advance made,' the Captain answered.

'Do you state that there was an advance made by him?'

'I do. Boulton went on in a flirting manner with me, and I kissed him, she or it, at the time believing he was a woman.'

There. He had said it. He had kissed Ernest Boulton.

Captain Cox's confession brought forth gasps and giggles from the public gallery.

'But you don't mean to say Boulton kissed you?'

'Well, he did something very like it,' Captain Cox replied.

'You anyhow kissed him?'

'I certainly did.' (Laughter.) 'Shortly after that Boulton complained of being chilly. My partner whipped the cloth off the table, put him in an armchair, and wrapped up his feet in the cloth.'

A few days later, Lord Arthur and Stella attended one of the Captain's auction sales at the Roebuck Tavern in Turnham Green. Lord Arthur's spirits seemed entirely restored and a jolly time was had by all. There was a piano in the public bar and Stella sat down and sang divinely, later taking the opportunity to slyly slip the handsome Captain a photograph of herself in men's clothes.

As in all the best romances, the dashing Captain Cox had sealed his love with a kiss and it was left to the imagination of the gentle reader, or, in this case, the minds of the coarse-grained, foul-mouthed chorus that comprised the public gallery of Bow Street Magistrates' Court, to determine if the love affair between Captain Cox and Stella was ever consummated. And if the raucous laughter, squints, leers and half-mumbled lewd comments emanating from that quarter were anything to go by, the public gallery had already reached its unanimous verdict.

There was an unhappy coda to the romance. Somehow or other Captain Cox got wind of Stella's true gender.

'I afterwards heard something about Boulton's sex,' Captain Cox told the court, carefully avoiding naming who it was who had tipped him off, though the odds were on the dubious Mr Roberts who was simultaneously trying to prevent Lord Arthur from being cuckolded and the Captain from being cruelly duped. When he found out, Captain Cox was incandescent with rage.

'After this I went to Evans's. I saw Boulton there. Park and Lord Arthur Clinton were with him. I went up to the table where Boulton, Park and Lord Arthur were sitting, and used abusive language. "You — infernal scoundrels," I said. "You ought to be kicked out of the place." I said more to the same purport, and kept walking up and down by the table. I afterwards promised not to create a disturbance, and left.'

M r Pollard, the most senior solicitor at the Treasury, had been very sympathetic and understanding. With scrupulous politeness he had called him Captain at every possible opportunity, tut-tutted over his treatment at the hands of the Civil Service Club and listened to stories of his army life and his Antipodean adventures with every appearance of animated interest.

It was with the greatest delicacy and the greatest difficulty that Mr Pollard brought the conversation round to the vexed topic of his giving evidence. Captain Cox shuddered and shivered. He was understandably reluctant to appear as a witness and admit to kissing – if that was all it was – a woman dressed as a man who turned out to be a man after all. He was a former officer and still some sort of gentleman.

Mr Pollard urged and persuaded. In cases like this, he said, cases of interest and importance to the Crown, cases which reflected on the national character and the national honour, there would of course be expenses. *Generous* expenses. Mr Pollard underlined the word 'generous'. A man like Captain Cox could hardly be expected to neglect or abandon his important business to help secure the conviction of two pernicious sodomites without some adequate disbursement from the Crown for his time and his trouble. And so it had been agreed. A dusty Treasury ledger records the receipt of 'a letter from Captain Cox applying for his expenses as a witness'.

Sadly, Captain Cox did not live to collect his disbursement from the Treasury, though his widow and his children were no doubt very grateful. The gallant Captain died two weeks to the day after he gave his evidence in Bow Street, of smallpox, the death certificate stated, and also quite possibly of shame.

21

A Bitches' Ball

I have heard of 'a bitches' ball'. It might mean two
things. It might be a ball for prostitutes, and it
might be a ball for men prostitutes. I have taken
part in a ball for male prostitutes at my father's
house about two years ago.

Malcolm Johnston, also known
as The Maid of Athens, 1884

Miss Carlotta Westropp Gibbings requests the pleasure
of your company at a Ball at Haxell's Hotel, West Strand
on Friday, 7th April at 9 o'clock.

There was the greatest excitement about Carlotta's ball. It
went without saying that it was to be the most perfect
and the most dazzling ball ever given. A brilliant ball to launch
a brilliant season, the most brilliant season they had ever
known – and by the end of it none of the young men who liked
to dress as young ladies expected anything less than to be engaged to be married to a peer of the realm or a prince from
foreign parts.

It would most emphatically not be one of those poky, secret-
ive, sad little balls they sometimes attended, in a room above a
public house or in a low tavern in some out-of-the-way place
no one had ever heard of, with a solitary pianist picking out ancient waltzes on a rickety piano and the air thick with cheap

tobacco smoke, beer and sweat. And there was to be no riff-raff, only the *crème de la crème* of gentlemen and the choicest ladies from their circle. Certainly no trollops off the streets (though, strictly speaking, this meant that many, if not most, of their friends would face disqualification).

No, Carlotta's ball was going to be held in a proper ballroom, on the second floor of Haxell's Hotel, which, if not the biggest ballroom in London, was one of the most elegantly appointed. There was to be a small orchestra. There was to be champagne and a proper supper served at the stroke of midnight. And there were to be at least two dressing rooms for the ladies and a smoking room for the gentlemen. And between the dances, there were to be musical interludes and singing. Everything, absolutely everything, was to be, as Fanny said at least a dozen times a day, *comme il faut*.

Best of all, Stella had been prevailed upon to return from her exile in Edinburgh and grace the proceedings with some songs. She was to come a few days early and stay in Haxell's Hotel as Carlotta's guest. It would be the first time Fanny had seen her sister for six months and there was a great deal of catching up to do.

Fanny was in a whirl of excitement and expectation. She was in her element, advising her dearest Carlotta on every aspect of the ball. They had planned it together, down to the last detail, and it was to be all perfection. By rights, of course, it should have been Carlotta's Mamma who organised this ball to launch her daughter upon an unsuspecting world, but her Mamma was in Clifton, Carlotta had explained, and was dour and sour and rather too fond of going to Mr Charlesworth's church. So Fanny had stepped in and become Carlotta's trusted and truest friend; her wisest counsel; an older sister and a maiden aunt rolled into one. *Tante Fanny*. She rather liked the sound of that.

Carlotta was Fanny's newest and, with the exception of Stella, her most intimate friend. They had met quite recently, just before Christmas, at a *bal masqué* at Highbury Barn, one of the few places where young men dressed as young ladies were welcome and where they had formed quite a little society of friends.

Fanny and Carlotta had hit it off immediately and had become more or less inseparable. Almost like sisters. They had much in common. Like Fanny, Carlotta had been dragging up since she was fourteen or fifteen years old. 'I have known the slang term "drag" about five months,' Carlotta later proclaimed in court to gasps and giggles. 'I have gone about dressed as a woman but I *never* went out so dressed with the intention of walking in the street.'

Which was, perhaps, just as well, Fanny mused to herself charitably, for her sweet-natured Carlotta was no oil painting. In fact, she was decidedly plain, labouring under the multiple disadvantages of an overly long neck, broad and most unwomanly shoulders and a complete absence – a perfect desert – of chin which, to be frank, made her look a little simple.

Fanny could sympathise. She, too, had once laboured – and indeed laboured still – under some disadvantages of the person, and yet she had turned these disadvantages to triumphs, winning many victories in the endless battle of love. Personality counted for much, but there was a great deal she could teach her dear Carlotta about the dark arts of dressing well, of painting herself, of arranging her coiffure, and generally making a little go a very long way. Every pot has its lid, thought Fanny, and properly dressed and properly lit – the dimmer the better, dare she say it! – even Carlotta might appear to advantage and prove irresistible to the gentlemen at her ball.

D rag balls were a regular feature of life in London, though few aspired to – or indeed, achieved – the brilliance and opulence of Miss Carlotta Westropp Gibbings's ball. There was a clear distinction to be made between public and private drag balls. Many advertised themselves publicly as masquerade balls, as fancy dress balls, or, like the entertainments at High-bury Barn, as *bals masqués* and were open to all comers.

In April 1864, the diarist Arthur Munby 'chanced to see an advertisement of a masked ball at some pleasure gardens in Camberwell: admission *one shilling*'. Munby was intrigued. 'Who would be attracted by such a ball?' he asked himself and decided to find out. He was hoping, perhaps, to strike a rich new vein of the working-class women he loved to encounter and to write about obsessively in his diaries. 'Only about fifty or sixty people were present,' Mundy recorded, 'most of them in fancy dress of a tawdry kind.' The ball was held in a large wooden shed.

> Several of the girls were drest in men's clothing, as sailors and so on: one, as a volunteer in uniform, I took for a man until someone called her Jenny.
>
> Moreover, not a few of the youths were elaborately disguised as *women* of various kinds; some so well, that only their voices showed they were not girls – and pretty girls.

'This is a thing new to me,' Munby wrote censoriously, 'and is simply disgusting.'

Private drag balls were a very different kettle of fish. They were strictly by invitation, and entry was usually by password only. They were often small, hole-in-the-wall affairs, with not more than a dozen or so dancers, and held in an odd assortment of venues: in rooms above taverns; in out-of-the-way halls and assembly rooms; in cellars, stables and barns; and sometimes in private houses.

Drag balls were held regularly at the Druids' Hall in Turn-again Place in the City of London. Even though the hall was unlicensed for drinking and dancing, the police seemed happy to turn a blind eye until the summer of 1854 when two men were arrested in full drag. John Challis, aged sixty, was 'dressed in the pastoral garb of a shepherdess of the golden age', while his companion George Campbell was 'completely equipped in the female attire of the present day', a court heard. 'There were about a hundred persons present,' Inspector Teague told the magistrate, Sir Robert Carden, 'and from eight to ten men were dressed as females.' Challis and Campbell had, he said, 'rendered themselves very conspicuous by their disgusting and filthy conduct'. Challis in particular was 'behaving with two men as if he were a common prostitute'.

A few years after Fanny and Stella's arrest, no fewer than forty-seven men were arrested when police burst in on a private drag ball at the Temperance Hall in Hulme, a desperately poor district of Manchester. The organisers had gone to considerable lengths to keep out prying eyes, fastening lengths of black crepe over the windows and employing a blind accordionist as the only musician. But Detective Sergeant Jerome Caminada had been tipped off, and he and his officers had climbed onto the roof of an adjacent building in order to spy on the proceedings. What they saw amazed them. Half the men were in drag and the other half in a variety of exotic costumes. The men in drag were performing, Caminada testified, 'a sort of dance to very quick time, which my experience has taught me is called the "Can-Can"'.

Admission to the ball was by password only but Detective Sergeant Caminada had somehow found it out. Knocking on the door of the Temperance Hall, he uttered the word 'Sister' in a mincing voice and the door opened to reveal a man dressed as a nun. Then there was panic as policemen and local volunteers rushed in to round up the revellers.

Things had got off to a less than perfect start, Carlotta thought irritably. She had always intended that her ball should be small and select, with no more than a dozen couple at most. The whole thing was to be an austerely beautiful and romantic affair, untainted by the sort of brutish behaviour which characterised so many low drag balls.

She had to confess that she was very far from pleased to discover that Fanny had been dispensing invitations broadcast to the ragtag and bobtail of her acquaintance and then had the nerve to tell *her* that this one and that one simply had to attend, or that she had already promised so-and-so that they could come. The upshot was that there were now forty-eight guests, quite double the original number. She was sure that she did not know half of them, and equally sure that she would not *wish* to know them.

Mr Edward Haxell, the jovial proprietor of Haxell's Hotel, was in his element. Young Mr Gibbings's ball was going swimmingly and all the young men and the young men dressed as ladies seemed to be enjoying themselves enormously. 'They changed partners for the dances,' he recalled later, 'and there was nothing wrong in any way during the whole night.

'There was no impropriety of attitude that I saw in the room, not a *vestige*,' he insisted. 'I heard the observation made about how well the young men were acting.' It was true that some of the young men – the young men dressed as young men, that is – had danced with each other, which was a little odd when you first saw it, but after a while it seemed perfectly natural, indeed, rather charming, and Mr Haxell wondered idly to himself why this did not happen more often in situations where there was a dearth of ladies.

He had counted thirteen young men dressed as ladies, though there might of course have been more. It was some-times hard to tell the real thing from the fake. Miss Gibbings, Miss Boulton and Mrs Graham of course he knew well. And he had been previously introduced to Miss Cumming and Miss Thomas. Miss Peel he knew by reputation only as Mr Percival Peel, rumoured to be nephew to the late Sir Robert Peel, the former Prime Minister.

Miss Stella Boulton – or Lady Stella Clinton, as he had heard her referred to more than once – made an utterly convincing young lady. When she had first arrived at Haxell's a few days before the ball, Miss Gibbings introduced her as 'the best amateur actress off the boards', and Mr Haxell could well believe it. She seemed to light up even the dullest room from the moment she entered. She was, in the truest sense, enchanting. No wonder everyone seemed to fall instantly under her spell. He was even a little in love with her himself.

'I heard Boulton sing his popular song "Fainting Away", I think three times, with great *éclat*,' he said later in court. (Or was it 'Fading Away'? He could not be sure.) 'I spoke to the Master of the Band about Boulton's singing, and when he sang a second time, he went straight up to him and said, "It is the most perfect man's soprano voice that I *ever* heard!" '

Of course, when the police started nosing around and asking questions, everyone was falling over themselves to say how Carlotta's ball had all gone off so perfectly, with so much propriety, with so much sweetness and light. Everyone, that is, apart from Jack Saul, whose bawdy recollections of that night were closer to the bone, in every sense.

On the surface, he said, everything about the ball seemed to be above board. Both the gentlemen and the ladies conducted themselves, for the first hour or two at least, with the greatest propriety. But as the evening wore on, and more and more champagne was consumed, the ball started to turn into a bacchanal, and the ballroom became a brothel.

'There seems to be,' Jack Saul mused with some relish, 'such a peculiar fascination to gentlemen in the idea of having a beautiful creature, such as an ordinary observer would take for a beautiful lady, to dance and flirt with, knowing all the while that his inamorata is a youthful man in disguise.'

The gentlemen could hardly contain themselves at the sight of so many young-men-dressed-as-ladies and even those who were long past the first flush of youth, those with sterner features, like Fanny Park, or those with stouter builds were positively chased around the ballroom. Jack Saul noticed Mr Haxell nodding and smiling and encouraging his guests to enjoy themselves, seemingly unaware of what was going on under his very nose. 'No doubt the proprietor was quite innocent of any idea of what our fun really was,' Saul wrote, 'but there were two or three dressing rooms into which the company could retire at pleasure.'

These dressing rooms which Carlotta had insisted upon

were supposed to be intimate retreats for the young men dressed as ladies to refresh themselves and to repair their toilette. But in reality they resembled nothing so much as dimly lit bordellos where drunken guests fumbled and frolicked with each other.

Tiring of drinking and dancing, Jack Saul recalled, 'I sat for a while on a sofa by myself, watching the dancers and taking notice of all the little freedoms they so constantly exchanged with one another.'

Both Fanny and Stella caught his eye. Fanny was 'dancing with a gentleman from the City, a very handsome Greek merchant', while Stella was enjoying the attentions of Lord Arthur Clinton who, Jack Saul observed, 'was very spooney upon her'.

> During the evening I noticed them slip away together, and made my mind up to try and get a peep at their little game. So I followed them as quietly as possible, and saw them pass down a corridor to another apartment, not one of the dressing rooms which I knew had been provided for the use of the party, but one which I suppose his Lordship had secured for his own personal use.
>
> I was close enough behind them to hear the key turned in the lock. Foiled thus for a moment, I turned the handle of the next door, which admitted me to an unoccupied room, and to my great delight a beam of bright light streamed from the keyhole of the door of communication between that and the one in which my birds had taken refuge.

Jack Saul knelt down and put his eye to the keyhole. He could see and hear everything. 'Lord Arthur and Boulton were standing before a large mirror,' he recalled. Stella was busy unbuttoning Lord Arthur's trousers. 'Soon she let out a beautiful specimen of the *arbor vitae*, at least nine inches long and very thick. It was in glorious condition, with a great, glowing red head.'

Stella 'at once knelt down and kissed this jewel of love and would, I believe, have sucked him to a spend, but Lord Arthur was too impatient.' Picking Stella up, Lord Arthur flung her down backwards on the bed to reveal 'a beautiful pair of legs enveloped within lovely knicker-bocker drawers. They were prettily trimmed with the finest lace, and I could also see pink silk stockings and the most fascinating little shoes with silver buckles.'

Matters proceeded apace. Lord Arthur quickly put his hands into Stella's drawers and 'soon brought to light as manly a weapon as any lady could desire to see, and very different from the crinkum-crankum one usually expects when one throws up a lady's petticoats and proceeds to take liberties with her'.

'What's this beautiful plaything, darling?' Lord Arthur asked in an erotic frenzy 'as he fondled and caressed Boulton's prick, passing his hand up and down the ivory-white shaft and kissing the dark, ruby-coloured head every time it was un-covered'.

'Are you a hermaphrodite, my love?' he demanded. 'Oh I must kiss it: it's such a treasure!'

Jack Saul was riveted. 'How excited I became at the sight you may be sure,' he recorded. 'I was determined not to frig myself, as I was sure of finding a nice partner when I returned to the ball-room. Still, I would rather have had Boulton than anyone else. His make-up was so sweetly pretty that I longed to have him, and him have me.'

Jack Saul could see how Stella's body seemed to shake and spasm as Lord Arthur's finger 'postillioned her bottomhole'.

Seeing how agitated he had made her, he took that splendid prick fairly into his mouth and sucked away with all the ardour of a male gamahucher; his eyes almost emitted sparks as the crisis seemed to come, and he must have swallowed every drop of that creamy emission he had worked so hard to obtain.

After a minute or two Lord Arthur wiped his mouth, and turned Stella around so that her bottom was in the air.

Opening the drawers from behind, he kissed each cheek of the lovely white bum, and tickled the little hole with his tongue. But he was too impatient to waste much time in kissing, so at once he presented his prick to Boulton's fundament, as he held the two cheeks of his pretty arse open with his hands.

Although such a fine cock, it did not seem to have a very difficult task to get in, and he was so excited that he very nearly came at once. But keeping his place, he soon commenced a proper bottom fuck, which both of them gave signs of enjoying intensely, for I could fairly hear his belly flop against Boulton's buttocks at every home push, whilst each of them called the other by the most endearing terms such as:

'What a darling you are! Tell me, love, that you love me! Tell me it's a nice fuck!'

And then the other would exclaim:

'Tush; push; fuck me; ram your darling prick in as fast

as it will go. Oh! Oh! Quicker, quicker: Do come now,
dearest Arthur; my love, my pet! Oh! Oh!! Oh!!!'

22

The Wheels of Justice

We hope and believe that not one winding of this filthy business will be left unexplored, nor one of those concerned in it be left unexposed or unpunished. Now that we have got our hand on the cockatrice's den it is of the utmost moment that we should not take it away until we have cleared out its last recesses and subjected every one of its inmates to the just penalty of his guilt.

Pall Mall Gazette, 8th June 1870

For Louis Hurt in Edinburgh, the dramatic arrest of Fanny and Stella had come as a bolt from the blue. He was struggling to make sense of what had happened. Events seemed to be moving so swiftly and, apart from the extensive and salacious reports in the newspapers, which were already a day or more old by the time he saw them, he had no way of knowing what was happening. Of course, he had written and telegraphed to Mr and Mrs Boulton, but they appeared to be almost as much in the dark as himself.

Louis was angry and confused. He had warned Ernie over and over again about the undesirability – let alone the dangers – of dressing up as a woman. 'I am rather sorry to hear of your going around in Drag so much,' he had told him sternly just days before. 'You know my sentiments.'

Stella was only too well aware of Louis's sentiments on

the subject of 'Drag', which he always spoke of and wrote of with a large capital D, as if to emphasise his disgust and his disdain. His pompous pronouncements, his admonitions and his injunctions on Drag were endlessly repeated.

Though Louis was a trifle dull (in truth, rather more than a trifle), he more than made up for it with his spaniel-like loyalty and devotion to his Ernie. Within a week of Fanny and Stella's arrest he had asked for, and been granted, a leave of absence from the Post Office, but was also in receipt of a terse request from the Postmaster General himself to provide a full written explanation of his relations with the young men in women's clothes. 'I suppose I shall be called up to resign,' he gloomily confided to John Safford Fiske.

Louis's plan was to go to London and do what he could. If it was at all possible, he would visit Ernie in prison. He would certainly go and see Mr and Mrs Boulton at Shirland Road in Maida Vale and offer what help he was able. And he would rally Ernie's friends and acquaintances and see what could be done. Lastly, he would find out what the implications were for himself.

Louis feared the worst. The newspapers were full of rumours and speculations about cliques and claques of young men who dressed as women, of peers and politicians, of scandal and disgrace, of imminent arrests and round-ups. The police were no fools. It would not take them long to realise that Ernie had spent the past six months living with him in Edinburgh. Ernie was always so careless. Letters would be found. Compromising letters. Letters to 'My darling Ernie' from 'Your loving Louis', and whatever else he had committed to paper in his dark and lonely moments. He would be arrested and quite possibly – quite probably – charged with sodomy. Mrs Dickson would be questioned. He turned pale at the prospect.

For the moment, however, he was free: free to find out what exactly the police knew, and perhaps more importantly what they did not know – yet; and free, for the moment, to flee if matters should take a turn for the worse. 'Do you advise my going to New York?' he enquired of John Safford Fiske.

It was almost certain that Fiske would be implicated too, along with Harry Park and Donald Sinclair and John Jameson Jim and all the others in their little society of friends. All except poor Robbie Sinclair, who was now beyond the reach of the police, dead of consumption at just twenty-three.

Once he was in London, Louis began to feel reassured. He had spoken to Abrams, the solicitor, who said the situation was grave, certainly, but not perhaps as grave as he had first imagined. His opinion, his hope, was that the Metropolitan Police and the Treasury had overreached themselves. They had levelled grave and grandiloquent charges of sodomy and conspiracy to commit sodomy. But such grave and grandiloquent charges required clear and unambiguous evidence. And so far, the Metropolitan Police and the Treasury had signally failed to produce any evidence worthy of the name. There was – as yet – no evidence of sodomy; and no evidence of invitations to sodomy; no evidence of any attempts to induce, incite, entice or inveigle any other men into committing sodomy.

Even the evidence of the chief prosecution witness, a young man named Hugh Mundell, had gone to their credit. 'Miss Stella' and 'Mrs Fanny', as he persisted in calling them, had made efforts, strenuous efforts, to inform that gullible young man that they were, in fact, men dressed up as women, even penning a note to that effect. It had made not a ha'p'orth of difference. Mr Hugh Mundell still refused to accept that they were men. Really, if this callow young man was the best that the

Metropolitan Police and the Treasury could muster, then the defence was, according to the optimistic Mr Abrams, almost home and dry.

The medical evidence of sodomy, which had at first seemed so compelling and so convincing, also failed to hold water. It was certainly true that Dr Paul, the police doctor, had detected alarming signs of sodomy written upon the bodies of Fanny and Stella. And Dr Barwell, from the Charing Cross Hospital, had sworn on oath that he had treated Frederick Park for a syphilitic chancre upon his anus which could only have been the consequence of sodomy.

Powerful as this evidence was, it had been weakened – mortally weakened – by the mass examinations of the parts of Ernie and Fred which had taken place at Newgate Gaol. Five out of the six eminent medical men present could find no signs of sodomy, not a shadow, not even a trace – insertive or receptive – upon either of them.

Louis was feeling altogether more sanguine. 'I am heartily glad that I came here,' he told Fiske in the middle of May. 'Case looks well at present. Abrams says there is no warrant issued against me. I have just seen a crowd standing round Ernest and Park's photos in a shop.'

By Herculean endeavours, Louis managed to squeeze and push himself into the public gallery in Bow Street. 'I was in Court and rather regretted going when I saw how pale and worn poor little Ernie looked,' he wrote to Fiske. 'It made me so unhappy. I managed to say a word or two to him. Tomorrow I hope to have a short interview with him.'

'My dear John,' Louis wrote to Fiske after his short and unhappy interview in Newgate with his poor little Ernie, pale and wan and half-frightened to death, but still putting a brave face on it all, 'Ernest begs you will destroy any letters from him you may have. I hope you will if you have not already done so.'

Fiske had already burned all Stella's letters in his possession. But unfortunately his love letters to Stella were already in the hands of the police. The last and most passionate of these had been posted just twelve days before the arrest of Fanny and Stella. It was addressed to '*un ange qu'on nomme Erné*', an angel named Erné, and no one who read it could have the slightest doubt of his feelings towards Stella:

My darling Ernie,

I have eleven photographs of you (and expecting more tomorrow) which I look at over and over again – I have four little notes which I have sealed up in a packet. I have a heart full of love and longing – and my photographs, my four little notes and my memory are all that I have of you – when are you going to give me more? When are you going to write a dozen lines of four words each to say that all the world is over head and ears in love with you and that you are so tired of adoration and compliments that you turn to your humdrum friend as a relief. Will it be tomorrow? Or will it be next week? Believe me, darling, a word of remembrance from you can never come amiss, only the sooner it comes the better.

Yours always
jusqu'à la mort
John S Fiske

It did not take long for the newspapers to obtain the text of this damning letter, though when the contents were published most people felt it was foolish rather than filthy. 'I have just seen a

copy of the letter,' Louis wrote to Fiske. 'There is nothing indecent in it (of course) but it is in the most high flown language.
After this letter, I can't understand why your rooms haven't
been searched; perhaps because you have been Consul. Post
going — Yours, L.'

It was certainly true – and not a little surprising – that neither
Louis Hurt nor Fiske had yet been interviewed by the police
in connection with the case, especially given the furore surrounding it. Fiske's diplomatic status as United States Consul
in Edinburgh may well have given the police pause for thought
and protected him, at least in the short run, from Inspector
Thompson's unwelcome attentions.

But Mr Abrams was firmly of the opinion that prevention
was better than cure. Both Mr Hurt and Mr Fiske would be
well advised to make themselves available for interview by the
Metropolitan Police. Such a move would clearly demonstrate
candour and help dissipate the cloud of suspicion hovering
above them. Inspector Thompson's enquiries were far from
concluded. Putting themselves forward for voluntary interview
was a hundred times, nay a thousand times, preferable to waiting for Thompson to arrest them.

Louis was firmly persuaded by the urgings of Mr Abrams,
but Fiske hesitated. He still hoped against hope that it might
all go away. After all, the very worst the police had against him
was that foolish letter he had written to Erné and, as Louis said,
there was nothing actually indecent in it. It was hardly compelling evidence of sodomy. It was unfortunate that his letter had
damaged Erné's case. But he could not help that. He had himself to think about now.

It was quite possible, perhaps even probable, that the police
would leave well alone. Scotland was a different jurisdiction

from England, and there would be all sorts of legal complexities to surmount.

Finally, however, on 3rd June, Fiske decided to come to London to see if matters could not be resolved. He would not countenance an interview with Inspector Thompson. But he would call on Mr Poland, the barrister leading the prosecution against Erné and Fred Park. He would tell Mr Poland that his letter was utter nonsense. It would be a frank and a manly chat. He would tell Mr Poland that he was about to be married and that these unfortunate and unfounded allegations risked his future happiness. And Mr Poland would listen sympathetically and nod his head wisely and all would yet be well.

One of Fiske's most urgent tasks the day after he arrived was also far from congenial. It was downright distasteful. The indefatigable Mr Abrams had opined that both he and Louis Hurt should take the precaution of being examined for signs of sodomy by an eminent medical man. Though Mr Abrams remained optimistic, if the worst came to the worst, it might prove very useful, very useful indeed, to have irrefutable medical evidence that neither he nor Louis had ever indulged in sodomy. Dr Alfred Harvey was the man he had in mind. He had already minutely examined Boulton and Park and detected no signs of sodomy.

Fiske's next task was equally uncongenial. He had to call at the Legation of the United States for a painful interview with Mr John Lothrop Motley, United States Minister in London. 'Mr Fiske called at the Legation on the 4th instant,' Motley wrote in a confidential memorandum to the Secretary of State in Washington:

in order to communicate the fact that his name was implicated in the disgraceful affair of the men in women's clothes, and to request some introduction in writing from the Legation to the Counsel charged with their prosecution. He thought he could make explanations to that personage which might relieve him from the suspicions resting upon him.

In the course of the interview, Fiske revealed the extent of his friendship with Erné.

He admitted that he had made the acquaintance of the prisoner Boulton at Edinburgh, that he had introduced himself to him, that he had requested him to put on his female attire, that he had received him familiarly at his own house (not in women's clothes, however) by invitation eight times, and that he had written letters to him, three of which were in the hands of the prosecution.

Fiske turned up at Mr Poland's chambers the following day to request an interview, only to be sent word through his clerk that Mr Poland regretted that such an interview between a prosecuting barrister and a potential witness – and perhaps even a potential defendant – was impossible and unthinkable.

Fiske was left reeling. It was a serious and unexpected reversal. Had the twin goddesses of Fortune and Fate ceased to smile upon him? He shivered and – as he returned to Edinburgh – for the first time in his life he was frightened of what the future might hold.

The Wheels of Justice

The wheels of justice might grind slowly but they ground inexorably. Inspector Thompson's telegram was handed to Detective Officer Roderick Gollan of the Edinburgh City Police on the morning of 9th June, kindly requesting him to call upon Mr John Safford Fiske at his chambers at 136 George Street and search the premises for any evidence, written or photographic, that might connect him to Ernest Boulton.

Fiske was still at home when Detective Officer Gollan called at George Street mid-morning. He did not appear to be at all surprised by the policeman's visit. In fact, he seemed to be expecting it. Gollan began to methodically work his way through the cupboards and drawers in the sitting room and the bedroom, slowly and thoroughly reading every letter he came across. In the pen drawer of his desk he found three letters and two telegrams signed 'Louis', and concealed in a hatbox in the bedroom were a dozen or so photographs of young men (rather effeminate young men, it seemed to Detective Officer Gollan) and some newspaper cuttings about the case of the Young Men in Women's Clothes.

'I asked Mr Fiske if there was anything else,' Gollan testified in court later. 'After a little hesitation he said if I would leave the room he would produce the remainder that he had that could refer to the case.'

'What did you say to that?'

'I said I would not leave.'

'What took place then?'

'He said, "I will admit to you my weakness", and he went and produced from behind the grate of the chimney piece a box containing an album containing a number of *cartes de visite*.'

'Had you seen it when you were searching?'

'No.'

'What further took place?'

'He said, "I have got a number of letters from Mr Boulton, but I have destroyed them."'

'Did he say anything further?'

'He said, "I have written some foolish notes to Boulton but meant no harm by them."'

Detective Officer Gollan left George Street having spent almost two hours searching. He sent a telegram to Inspector Thompson listing what he had found and awaited further instructions. They were not long in coming. At around 4 p.m. the same day, John Safford Fiske heard a loud knock at the front door. Detective Officer Gollan had come to arrest him and to take him into custody.

Mr John Lothrop Motley despatched a confidential memorandum to the Secretary of State in Washington:

In cipher:

Mr Fiske – Facts as to his imprisonment in London and application for bail.

I have now to state that John S. Fiske, United States Consul in Edinburgh, was on the 9th instant arrested at that place and brought to London the next day. He is now held in Newgate on a Bench Warrant awaiting his trial.

He was required to find bail in four sureties of £500 each. He has employed able counsel as I am informed for his defence, and I have requested the United States Vice-Consul General at London privately to watch the case.

Mr Fiske of course hopes to establish his entire innocence of any misdemeanour, but he does not, as I understand, deny familiar acquaintance with Boulton, one of the men in women's clothes indicted for felony, for conspiracy and for misdemeanour, nor the authorship of certain letters to him now in the hands of the prosecution.

I am informed that he wishes to send in his resignation, but if his letter to that effect can only be written on Newgate paper, I have caused it to be intimated to him that it should not be written.

For John Safford Fiske, Fortune and Fate had turned into the Furies and wreaked their wrath upon him. If convicted he would face many years in a filthy English prison, and if he emerged at all, he would be a broken man. Even if he were to prove his innocence, such as it was, there would be no return to the life of hopes and dreams and vaunting ambition.

If there was one consolation, it was that he was not entirely alone in his ordeal. Erné Boulton and Fred Park were in Newgate too, though there were bitter feelings in his heart towards Erné, once his ravishing and beloved Laïs and Antinous in one, now the spring and the source of this terrible nightmare in which he found himself trapped. Even cautious, clever, charming Louis Hurt had been arrested at the same time on the same charges and was also in Newgate. They made a strange quartet. They were tied together by dark and invisible threads of lust and love and they would stand, or most likely fall, together.

23

Dead or Disappeared

We have it on the authority of a usually well-in-
formed daily contemporary, that peers of the realm
are implicated with the dirty proceedings that will
shortly come prominently before the public in a
court of justice.

Reynolds's Newspaper, 26th June 1870

V ery few people were surprised when the warrant for Lord
Arthur Pelham-Clinton's arrest was finally issued in early
June, five weeks after the arrest of Fanny and Stella. Indeed, the
only surprise was that it had taken so long, given that Lord
Arthur had been so publicly implicated in the scandal of the
Young Men in Women's Clothes from the very start.

As the weeks went by, there had been mounting public indignation over what was seen as deliberate foot-dragging on
the part of the authorities in bringing Lord Arthur to justice.
Rumours began to circulate that powerful forces were at work
on his behalf. As the son of the fifth Duke of Newcastle, who
had been Secretary of State for War, and as godson to Mr Gladstone, the current Prime Minister, the recently retired Honourable Member for Newark, it was said, was being shielded from
prosecution.

As the evidence unfolded, it was clear to everybody that
Lord Arthur was up to his aristocratic neck in the scandal. He
knew both Boulton and Park: he had performed in public with

Boulton and lived with him in private, apparently and astonishingly as man and wife. There were compromising letters, suggestive photographs, and at least two dozen sworn statements that put Lord Arthur at the dark heart of this wicked sodomitic conspiracy.

But the powers that be still hesitated, still delayed. Why? There were mutterings that Lord Arthur was being given time to settle his affairs and make good his escape; that he was about to flee abroad; indeed, that he had already flown and was now safely beyond the clutches of the Metropolitan Police.

Some newspapers, like the *Pall Mall Gazette*, were convinced that Lord Arthur knew too much. If he was arrested and brought to justice, there was a danger that he would implicate others – peers and politicians and personages – in the vast spider's web of sodomy and scandal, and that the cankerous corruption at the heart of the ruling class would be exposed. 'Peers of the realm are implicated with the dirty proceedings' was the unambiguous verdict of *Reynolds's Newspaper*, which prided itself on taking up the cudgels for ordinary folk against the bastions of birth and privilege.

The *Pall Mall Gazette* called for steely 'resolution on the part of the Government' not to yield to the influence of 'the highest classes of society' who were 'on the side of hushing up a scandal of this magnitude'.

The suspicions of those who believed that the Government was intent on hushing up the scandal were strengthened, rather than diminished, when, on the day that the long-looked-for warrant was belatedly issued for his arrest, Lord Arthur Clinton was nowhere to be found. He had vanished off the face of the earth, leaving not a trace.

The last person to have seen Lord Arthur was a cabman. At around two o'clock on the afternoon of Saturday, 28th May, Lord Arthur hailed a cab and told the cabman that he would need him to drive him around upon a variety of errands until that evening.

'I took up my fare at the Opera Hotel, Bow-street,' said the cabman, 'and on depositing him at the same hotel at night I was sent to Long's Hotel with a letter addressed to a gentleman stopping there. But the gentleman had gone abroad (so I was informed), and when I got back to the Opera Hotel to report the result, and to get my money, I was informed that Lord Arthur had gone also.'

And that was the last sighting of Lord Arthur Pelham-Clinton, at least as far as Inspector Thompson and his detectives could establish. The ports were being watched and his description had been circulated. But where he had gone was a mystery.

For those with a suspicious turn of mind, like Inspector Thompson, there was something not quite right about Lord Arthur's six-hour cab journey around London. Why would a man who was about to disappear, seemingly in a puff of smoke, go to the trouble of bilking a cabman for a fare of £1? And why, if you were going to bilk a cabman, would you be at pains to reveal that your name was Lord Arthur Clinton and that you were residing at the Opera Hotel, Bow Street?

Inspector Thompson could smell a rat. He had a nose for such things. He suspected that this seemingly aimless, six-hour cab journey was nothing more and nothing less than a diversion, a clever and cunning attempt to lay a false trail. The police would be trying to trace the movements of the man claiming to be Lord Arthur from the time the cabman deposited him at the Opera Hotel around eight o'clock. But what if the real Lord Arthur had crept away hours or perhaps even days before?

Speculation was rife. 'We understand the police believe that Lord Arthur Clinton has gone to America,' the *Weekly Times* reported. The *Observer* agreed, but added that 'there are people who have affirmed that His Lordship has been seen in London, and notably at Ascot'.

Rumours of the death of Lord Arthur Clinton first began to filter through to Fleet Street during the afternoon of Saturday 18th June, just in time for the final editions of the evening papers. Facts were in short supply but it appeared that the troubled Lord Arthur had died in the remote village of Muddeford in Hampshire. Or was it Huddeford, as the *Illustrated Police News* reported? Or Nuddeford, as the *Weekly Times* had it?

There was speculation – hope even – that, as an officer and a gentleman, Lord Arthur had done the decent thing and shot himself through the head with a single silver bullet. Such a course of action was very much to be desired. It would have been Lord Arthur's admission of guilt and a demonstration of his remorse. A clean and contrite conclusion to a sodomitic conspiracy which had caused a convulsion of the national mind. No washing of aristocratic dirty linen in public. No risk of further revelations. No need for a damaging and debilitating trial to further sap the nation's sense of strength and virility.

But such sanguine – not to say sanguinary – hopes were dashed when it emerged that Lord Arthur had died of natural causes just a few days short of his thirtieth birthday. 'The rumour which was current late on Saturday regarding the death of Lord Arthur Clinton is confirmed,' the *Daily Telegraph* reported two days later. Lord Arthur, it appeared, 'had been in the neighbourhood of Christchurch for some time, on a fishing excursion, passing under the title of Captain Edward Gray'.

Over the following week, more details of Lord Arthur's final days and hours emerged. 'We are in a position to give a trustworthy account of Lord Arthur Pelham Clinton's fatal illness,' the *Lancet* confided to its readers (though quite why the *Lancet* should take such an interest in Lord Arthur's untimely death was curious, to say the least).

On Monday, 13th June, doctors attending Lord Arthur 'found him suffering from sore throat and other symptoms of Scarlet Fever, which has been widely prevalent in the neighbourhood', the *Lancet* continued. 'Lodgings in the village were procured for him, and thither he was safely removed. The disease, though virulent, ran a normal course, and the patient appeared to be gaining ground.' But complications set in on the morning of Thursday, 16th June, and Lord Arthur was unable to void urine. 'The patient', the *Lancet* reported, 'had sunk very low, and, in spite of the free administration of stimulants, failed to rally. Telegrams were immediately despatched to his friends, and at five minutes past one on Saturday morning he died.'

Among those 'friends' of Lord Arthur who were telegraphed when his condition worsened was the ubiquitous and unsavoury Mr W. H. Roberts, his solicitor, who arrived in Muddeford early on the Friday morning to find his client still conscious and still rational, but in a state of 'utter prostration'.

Just hours after Lord Arthur expired, Roberts took the extraordinary step of releasing a letter purportedly dictated by him from his 'bed of sickness'. It was a deathbed denial of the accusations of sodomy made against him. 'Nothing', Lord

Arthur declared, 'can be laid to my charge other than the foolish continuation of the impersonation of theatrical characters which arose from a simple frolic in which I permitted myself to become an actor.'

If Mr Roberts and the late Lord Arthur (wherever he may be, looking down hopefully, or up, more probably, given the general dissipation of his short life) thought that this deathbed declaration of innocence would, to use a vulgar phrase, 'wash' with a hostile and sceptical public, they were much mistaken. The letter was greeted with universal incredulity and howls of raucous laughter.

On the 'sad and wasted' life of Lord Arthur Clinton, the *Daily Telegraph* confined itself to a few choice words. 'There was nothing specially notable in his Lordship's career,' it wrote, 'and it is expressing only the bare truth to say, that what was known reflected on him no credit whatever.' Under the banner headline 'A MIS-SPENT LIFE', *Reynolds's Newspaper* denounced him as 'dissolute, debauched, reckless, and brainless', 'the disreputable scion of the Newcastle family' and 'a blackguard Lord'.

'Lord Arthur's inclinations', the *Porcupine* wrote, 'seem to have led him into the worst society, into the maelstrom of London dissipation, and he ended in being charged (wrongfully, let us hope) with one of the most abominable of crimes.' The *Porcupine* concluded its moral spasm with a homily which might have been taken directly from the pages of the Old Testament. 'Verily,' it intoned piously, 'those of us who are apt to envy the lot of high-born personages may take the lesson of Lord Clinton's life and death profitably, though painfully, to heart.'

Lord Arthur's funeral took place on what would have been his thirtieth birthday. 'The funeral was unusually plain,' the

Weekly Times reported, 'and the grave, though in a secluded spot was a common one.' The main mourners present were Lord Arthur's older brother, the present Duke of Newcastle, his uncle, Lord Thomas Clinton, and the ever-present Mr Roberts.

It was, in the opinion of many, a decidedly hole-and-corner affair, conducted with a mere nod to ceremony and with almost indecent haste. Lord Arthur's family, it seemed, were falling over themselves to bury both his memory and his mortal remains as deep in the Hampshire earth as they possibly could.

Lord Arthur's corpse was enclosed in no fewer than three coffins, one of them rumoured to be made of lead, a precaution for the prevention of contagion which struck some observers as really quite excessive. Engraved under the figure of Our Blessed Lord on the silver breastplate of Lord Arthur's outer coffin was the simple text: 'He hath borne our griefs and carried our sorrows.' Opinion was divided as to whether this text was a reference to Christ in his capacity as Redeemer, or whether it was the family's sad and poignant commentary on Lord Arthur's short and dissolute life.

Even before the coffin was lowered into the yawning and hungry grave, there were those who openly doubted whether Lord Arthur was dead at all. The *Nottingham Daily Guardian*, which might be thought sympathetic to the Clinton family because of the local connection with the family seat of Clumber, reported that certain 'persons of the critical and legal cast of mind profess to doubt the authenticity of Lord Arthur Clinton's death'. 'Is Lord Arthur Clinton really dead and buried?' the *Porcupine* asked, speaking for many. 'It is no secret that persons of a suspicious mind have been heard to say that the death of Lord Arthur is "all moonshine".'

The sudden and strange disappearance and death of Lord Arthur Clinton raised more questions than answers. Why had he gone to ground in the small town of Christchurch, taking the *nom de guerre* of Captain Edward Gray? If he was, as he proclaimed, as innocent as the day is long, then why misdesignate himself in this way? It was a suspicious thing to do and plainly suggested that he did not wish to be found.

And why Christchurch? Mr Roberts's assertion that Lord Arthur had gone there for a fishing holiday was unconvincing. Though the fishing in and around Christchurch was reputed to be excellent, anybody who knew Lord Arthur would swear that his passions were theatrical, and emphatically not piscatorial. Indeed, it was said that he did not know one end of a rod from the other and he thought that a reel was an Irish jig.

For stern logicians like Inspector Thompson, the whole affair was baffling and bewildering. 'It is understood', the *Daily Telegraph* confided, 'that Inspector Thompson has been specially employed to inquire into the circumstances of Lord Arthur Clinton's decease.' Clearly there were doubts, strong doubts, within the Metropolitan Police, within the Treasury, and quite possibly within 10 Downing Street, where Lord Arthur's affectionate godfather, Mr Gladstone, still held sway.

But there were certain immutabilities that Inspector Thompson could grip hold of. Either Lord Arthur Clinton was dead or he was alive. If he was dead, he had died of natural causes, or he had taken his own life, or he had been murdered. Of these three possibilities, Inspector Thompson discounted murder. With the exception of poisoning, which could be tricky to detect, murder usually meant blood and gore and signs of violence. And there was not a scrap of evidence to suggest that Lord Arthur had been done away with.

Natural causes or suicide were both possibilities, but Inspector Thompson was unpersuaded. In his experience, the Lord Arthurs of this world did not willingly resign themselves to death or to doing the decent thing. And if Lord Arthur had planned to take his own life, why had he gone to the bother of disappearing and living under an assumed name? Why not simply blow his brains out in the comfort of his own home?

No. There were too many inconsistencies, too many contradictions. In Inspector Thompson's experience, death was starkly factual and rarely admitted to the confusion and fancy footwork which characterised this particular case. Nothing was quite right, nothing seemed to fit: the strange six-hour cab ride, 'Captain Edward Gray', the posthumous letter, and the three coffins, one of lead – to make assurance triply sure? It might be supposed that this latter was a certain means to prevent poisonous miasmas leaching out from the corpse and spreading the contagion. On the other hand, it might equally be a clever means of keeping prying eyes out of the coffin and keeping Nosy Parkers, like himself, at bay.

Lord Arthur had died in Prospect Cottage in Muddeford, attended, at the hour of his death, by only a boy. It was odd, too, that the death was notified to the authorities by this boy, Sambrooke Newlyn, the son of a coal merchant-cum-hotel proprietor. It seemed a heavy responsibility for one so young. No fewer than three doctors had attended the gentleman in Prospect Cottage suffering from scarlet fever. But curiously, not one of them could say that they actually saw him die.

Inspector Thompson's instinct told him that it was a put-up job, that Lord Arthur had not died, but merely staged his own disappearance. He doubted that the theatre-loving Lord had the necessary low cunning to carry out so audacious a plan. But

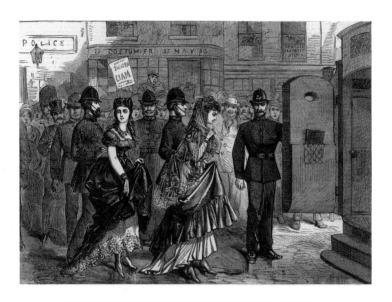

29th April 1870: An excited crowd looks on as Ernest Boulton and Frederick Park in full drag leave Bow Street Magistrates' Court the morning after their arrest at the Strand Theatre

'And such a stock of togs was there.' The police raid Fanny and Stella's secret dressing-rooms in Wakefield Street and confiscate their entire drag wardrobe

Stella Boulton, 'the most wonderful impersonator of female character ever before the public' with 'the most perfect soprano voice', photographed in Scarborough in October, 1868

'Rose of the Garden, blushing and gay' – the captivating Stella Boulton dressed as a man

Dressed in silk and suitably padded, bewigged and with a very generous application of paint, Fanny made a handsome woman

Fanny (left) – 'a gabbling, good-natured, prattling, gossiping, charming young man', photographed with an unknown gentleman in Chelmsford in 1868

Fanny, with her 'sterner features', had a natural bent for playing domineering duchesses and dowagers of a certain age

A love triangle: Fanny (standing) and Stella (front) with Lord Arthur Pelham -Clinton

Stella and Fanny dressed in character in the sort of drawing-room entertainment they toured to small country houses and market-town assembly rooms

Stella and Charles Pavitt on tour in Essex in 1869

The shocking case of 'The Female Personators' was front-page news all over the country

The Comical Countess and Carlotta Gibbings

Stella, now blonde, in New York circa 1875, in a portrait by the celebrity photographer Napoleon Sarony

Stella as a shepherdess of the golden age, circa 1880

Sisters. Side by side and shoulder to shoulder. Sisters for better or for worse: Stella rests her head on her beloved Fanny's breast

Mr Roberts was, in his opinion, more than capable of conceiving and executing such an elaborate scheme. Roberts was here, there and everywhere, with a finger in every pie and a perfect – too perfect – answer to every question. He was the spider at the centre of this very strange web of lies and deceit.

Short of exhuming the body encased in its three coffins, Inspector Thompson would never know whether Lord Arthur Clinton was dead, whether he had left for America or Paris or Buenos Aires, or indeed, whether the coffin was filled with a sack of sawdust. In any event, an exhumation based on a hunch would never be permitted.

Lord Arthur Clinton had evaded the law. He had escaped with help from his family and from his friends in high places. There was a forlorn hope that justice might still be done. Lord Arthur might make a mistake. He might one day return and be recognised in the street, in the theatre, or at Ascot.

Inspector Thompson smiled to himself. He could wait.

I n his offices in Moorgate only a day or so after Lord Arthur's funeral, Mr Roberts also smiled to himself as he sealed the envelope addressed to Mr Ouvry, the Pelham-Clinton family solicitor. Mr Roberts specialised in trouble. It was his stock in trade, his meat and drink. He was never very far from trouble, it followed him and found him out. He delighted in trouble, in solving trouble, in making trouble disappear, and making troublesome peers vanish, as if by magic. Lord Arthur was gone, and though not quite forgotten, would soon gently fade from memory like a watercolour left in the sun.

Mr Ouvry tut-tutted to himself when he opened Mr Roberts's missive. He was, he had to confess, a little taken aback by the promptitude – a promptitude verging on indecent haste – of Mr Roberts's bill for £251 of 'expenses' incurred on behalf of Lord Arthur Clinton. Not even a week had passed since Lord Arthur's interment. But Mr Roberts's claim was special, not to say unique. Mr Ouvry immediately advanced the sum of £50 but was unable to settle the bill in full because, as he explained in a private letter to Mr Gladstone, now Lord Arthur's executor, 'nothing was coming to Lord Arthur's estate'. Unfortunately, Lord Arthur's debts had not died with him and his estate was besieged on every side by angry creditors.

But in Mr Ouvry's opinion, this bill was a debt of honour that must be met by the family. 'It is impossible that the family should allow Mr Roberts who has really behaved most kindly in this matter to be out of pocket,' he wrote confidentially to Gladstone. Lord Arthur's father, the late and unfortunate Duke of Newcastle, Mr Ouvry said, 'would have paid for getting him abroad, and I would have thought would not have hesitated to meet this claim'.

There it was, in black ink on white paper, in the crabbed hand of the respected and respectable Mr Ouvry. There could be no doubt about it. Mr Roberts had got Lord Arthur abroad, he had spirited him out of the country to start a new life free from debt, free from taint, and free from the best endeavours of Inspector Thompson and his detectives. All for the not inconsiderable but still very reasonable sum of £251.

And the beauty of it all, at least from Mr Roberts's point of view, was that everyone – or almost everyone – believed that at that very moment the worms of Hampshire were feasting upon what remained of Lord Arthur's fleshly being.

24

This Slippery Sod

The management of the case for the prosecution on
the part of the police is entitled to the utmost
praise. Inspector Thompson, of Bow-street, has
displayed throughout an acuteness, tact, and
shrewdness reflecting the greatest credit on that
officer. 'Involuntary' witnesses have been ferreted
out, subpoenaed, and placed in the box, with a
celerity that perfectly astounded them.

Reynolds's Newspaper, 29th May 1870

M r Charles Ferguson of Abbey Green in Lanarkshire gave
an involuntary start when he heard the doorknocker so
vigorously engaged. It was not yet nine o'clock and he was not
expecting visitors, especially at so uncivilised an hour. He had
not yet breakfasted and was still *en déshabille*. Visitors were the
very last thing he wanted or needed today or, indeed, any day.

If Fanny and Stella's troubles were not enough to be going
on with, enough to worrit him and fret him and make him feel
ill, John Safford Fiske and Louis Hurt had been taken into custody four weeks ago. The net seemed to be closing, the noose
was tightening, and he could not help wondering how many
more friends, how many more acquaintances, would be rounded up, let alone whether he would be among their number.

The mere thought of nets and nooses gave him palpitations
and made him feel faint. He had not been sleeping at all well

– in truth, hardly at all – and he was at a loss to know what to do or where to go. Should he stay? After all, there was no reason why the police should ever pay a call upon Mr Charles Ferguson of Abbey Green: the respectable, retiring, irreproachable Mr Charles Ferguson of Abbey Green who travelled a great deal on business and who was hardly known by his neighbours except as a young man who kept himself very much to himself.

Or should he flee? Pack a valise with his clothes and his papers and abandon Abbey Green for ever. And go where? With the hue and cry raging in London, and the police sniffing the scent like bloodhounds in Edinburgh, the two places where he had friends and family were closed to him. But there were any number of other places he could go to. Out-of-the-way places, ordinary, very slightly dreary places, like the small town of Abbey Green (or the unpronounceable Lesmahagow, as the locals would have it), which he had chosen so carefully because no one, other than its denizens, had ever heard of it.

Or there were the cities. The best places to hide, he had been told, were the large cities, like Leeds and Manchester and Liverpool, cities where a solitary young man could settle himself quietly in a small hotel or in a suite of rooms; where his presence would be unremarkable and unremarked; where he might come and go as he pleased until the dogs were called off and he could think more clearly.

Or then again there was Paris. Arthur and Louis and Stella had so constantly sung its praises, had so constantly recounted their adventures there that he had a great longing to visit this city where the streets were paved with erotic gold. And what did it matter that his French was so poor? Love was a universal language, and he had always prided himself on having the gift of tongues.

Sometimes he would be on the point of going, his bags packed and at the door, and then he would hesitate. Something always held him back. He could not explain it. It was a strange combination of fear – fear of leaving, fear of starting afresh – and optimism: was there really any need to up sticks and travel to the ends of the earth – to Paris, at least – to escape a fate that was by no means certain? There was no reason to run. No one here knew him as anyone other than Charles Ferguson. The money from his father had always come by a highly circuitous route. It would be impossible to trace him that way. And even if the police found any of his letters, they would be hard-pushed to find him as he had always been so scrupulous about never writing down his address – though Fanny and Stella, and one or two others, of course, knew where to write to him. No, it would take a very skilled hunter to beard him in his lair.

This terrible business with Fanny and Stella and John and Louis had brought it all back. Everything he had tried to forget, everything he thought he had forgotten. All back with terrible, terrifying clarity. Asleep and awake. Every detail, every sensation played out again and again. Cold sweats. Heart pounding. Nausea in the pit of his stomach. The sensation of having been punched violently in the gut. He trembled at the very thought.

He was barely seventeen the first time it had happened, with that foolish Italian boy. He had naively fallen into the trap. It was all too good to be true and he was surprised when the boy demanded money, and kept demanding money. When he had no money left to give, the boy, true to his word, had gone to the police. Much to his shame and chagrin, he had been very publicly arrested in his father's house in Wimpole Street, and every servant in the street had talked about it for a year and a day.

Fortunately, he had been acquitted. It was his word against the boy's. The well-spoken word of a well-educated young gentleman, the son of a respected and respectable judge, against the accusations of a young Italian immigrant who had no business to be here and who seemed to be entangled in all sorts of dubious endeavours.

Mr Charles Ferguson loosened his cravat and poured himself a drink. He had been drinking rather heavily, more heavily than usual, since Fanny and Stella's arrest, and it was not the first time these past weeks that he had breakfasted upon a glass of whisky or a brandy and soda. It calmed his nerves but clouded his judgement.

Drink had been the cause of his downfall eight years before in the early hours of April Fool's Day. He was eighteen and had been drinking heavily all evening as he scoured the streets and the public houses of London looking for a man, with a signal lack of success. Sometimes it was like that. You could go for hours with nothing doing. Other times, it was there on a plate, just waiting to be eaten.

Of course, if he had wanted to pay for it, there were any number of Mary-Anns on the pad in the warren of alleys around Leicester Square who would go with him for a few shillings – plump and prosperous Mary-Anns; hungry, desperate Mary-Anns with haggard and drawn faces; handsome, dangerous Mary-Anns who were not real Mary-Anns at all, but ruffians and blackmailers who would rob you as soon as look at you.

But he did not want Mary-Anns that night. He wanted real men, strong men. Soldiers, sailors, porters, working men. Men who smelt like men. Men who fucked women. Men who would treat him as a woman. Men who would make him gamahuche them until he choked. Men who would fuck him. Brutally. No quarter given. And none expected. Men who would make him pay for the privilege.

The night had been an unmitigated disaster. In the early hours of the morning, drunk and exhausted, he had finally admitted defeat and was on his way home to Wimpole Street when he noticed the policeman standing at the top of Weymouth Mews looking at him. Staring him out of countenance. Not another soul was abroad. He may have been drunk but not drunk enough to mistake what it was the policeman wanted. It was obvious. Obvious from the way he spoke to him, obvious from the way he so manifestly adjusted his crotch, obvious from the trembling intensity of his voice. There could be no doubt about it. He could feel it. He could smell it. It was like a great galvanic wave of electricity passing between them. Wordlessly they walked into the sheltering, darkness of Weymouth Mews.

S omewhere between three and four o'clock in the morning, Police Constable George White was, he said, walking his regular beat in Weymouth Street, just north of Oxford Circus, when a clean-shaven young man of 'a rather effeminate appearance' accosted him.

'Policeman, I want to speak to you,' he said.

'I walked with him to the corner of Weymouth Mews,' Constable White recalled, 'which was only a few yards off, and went down.

'I expected that the prisoner was going to give me some important information about a burglary,' White continued. 'Instead of doing so, however, he got his arm around my neck, kissed me, and pinned me against the wall with his left knee. Then he exposed his person and otherwise acted improperly.'

Constable White responded by charging the youth with 'disgusting conduct' and said he was going to take him into custody.

According to White's testimony in court, the boy had looked as if he was about to faint. 'Oh! pray don't arrest me!' he had exclaimed. 'Have mercy on me; it nearly broke my father's heart when a charge was made against me on a former occasion. I'm sure it will be the death of him now.'

The young man struggled ineffectually to escape, White claimed, but by now another policeman, Acting Sergeant Edwin Dibdin, had appeared to lend a hand. The young man tried another tack. 'Come with me to my father's house in Wimpole Street and he'll give you twenty pounds apiece and my watch and chain,' he said in a wheedling, pleading voice. But the bribe was refused – at least according to the testimonies of White and Dibdin – and the terrified boy, white as a sheet, trembling and sobbing, was marched to Marylebone Police Station where he gave his name as Charles Ferguson, aged nineteen, and was formally charged with 'having indecently exposed himself and trying to incite a Police-Constable to commit an indecent offence'.

Charles Ferguson appeared before Mr Yardley, the magistrate, the next day, whereupon he shamefacedly admitted that his real name was Edward Henry Park, the son of Judge Alexander Park. 'I am ashamed to say,' he told Mr Yardley, 'but I never was more drunk in all my life. I have no recollection of anything that passed.'

It was a clever defence. A young man, blind drunk, larking around, clumsy and stumbling, needs to empty his bladder urgently, exposes his person in front of a passing police constable and accidentally falls upon said police constable. A clever defence which was to fail dismally. Harry Park was committed for trial. With the evidence against him he could expect a hefty prison sentence. Bail was set at the enormous sum of six hundred pounds. But it was a price worth paying, Judge Alexander Park reasoned, if it meant his beloved son's freedom.

No sooner was Harry released than he forfeited bail and disappeared from the face of the earth, and was to remain disappeared for eight long years.

Inspector Thompson permitted himself a rare smile of satisfaction, gazing out of the window of the train as it chugged northwards through a landscape of soot-blackened red-brick factories and chimneys belching forth giant clouds of mephitic vapours.

Thompson had every reason to be satisfied. He had four in the bag, which was not a bad day's work, all things considered. He knew that dozens, perhaps even hundreds more had been arrested up and down the land, and those who had fled abroad or gone to ground would not dare to flaunt themselves in public again any time soon. He had, as yet, failed to apprehend Cumming and Thomas, but there was plenty of time to turn his attention to those young men. Only Lord Arthur Clinton, the biggest prize of them all, was beyond his reach after conveniently – rather too conveniently, he thought – dropping dead of the scarlet fever.

This one he was after now was by way of a bonus. An unexpected but nevertheless most satisfying catch who had cleverly evaded detection for eight long years. By tomorrow this slippery sod would be safely in custody and, if Inspector

Thompson got his way, he would go to prison for a very long time.

Inspector Thompson turned his attention to his travelling companion, who was an altogether unprepossessing specimen. George White looked as if he was in his forties, but was probably younger. He was tall, burly and running to fat now. But eight years ago, when he would have been a little slimmer, a little more upright in his smart police uniform with gleaming buttons, the Margeries and the Mary-Anns must have seen him as a fine figure of a man.

Inspector Thompson did not know, and did not wish to know, exactly what it was that White had done. All he knew was that he had left the police force under a cloud. It must have been something bad because, even under the new broom, corruption was still rife and still tolerated. No doubt White had been stupid or greedy, or both, and got caught red-handed.

It was that one letter, one among many hundreds of letters, that had caught Inspector Thompson's eye and led him to this forlorn and forgotten corner of Lanarkshire in vigorous pursuit of his prey. It was in a trunkful of papers belonging to Lord Arthur Clinton which the fearsome Miss Ann Empson, Lord Arthur's splenetic former landlady, had commandeered until the rent was paid in full. Miss Empson was still spitting pins when she got in touch with him and said she had important information about those funny He-She Ladies (though, in *her* humble opinion, they were very far from being ladies).

That one letter had stood out from all the rest:

> Dear Stella,
>   You can easily imagine how dull I am and disinclined to write. I hope you will have much fun tonight and both

you and Dan must send me news as soon as is convenient. I left the two ladies a few moments after you departed but met them again at 12. Bob never turned up but Stenney came at 3 o'c. I forgot all about the photos and he never mentioned them – he saw me to the Station. I came from Holytown with George and James Tudthorpe.

Today is Glasgow Fast. I will positively write again soon but at this present I *cannot*,

Love to Fanny

Yours ever

Harry

PS: Of course I have as ever left a few little things behind such as the Glycerine – *that* don't matter but I cannot find (oh horror!) those filthy photographs nor Louis's likeness. I do hope they are not lying about your rooms.

No address, no date and signed only 'Harry'. Inspector Thompson knew that any letter addressed to 'Stella' was most likely written by a fellow votary of the Hermaphrodite Clique. The postscript gave the game away: it was obvious what 'Harry' meant when he referred to 'those filthy photographs'. 'Oh horror!' indeed. Inspector Thompson was only too painfully aware of the vast trade in indecent and obscene photographs that went on under the very noses of the police, including photographs of the most depraved and disgusting acts of sodomy between men.

Rather more recondite was the reference to 'Glycerine'. At first sight it seemed innocuous enough, but to any policeman like himself, with a working knowledge of sodomy and sodomites, it spoke scarlet volumes. From plain old-fashioned spittle to cold cream, lard and butter, he knew they needed these lubricating agents in furtherance of their filthy games. Glycerine was the very latest thing, he had been told. It was quite the rage amongst them. He shuddered at the very thought.

Whatever the shortcomings of the Metropolitan Police Detective Force – and they were legion – it excelled at the administrative apparatus of criminality, at keeping lists, records, photographs of suspected and convicted criminals alike. These records revealed that Park had an older brother, Edward Henry Park, also known as Charles Ferguson, who had been charged with attempted indecency upon a police officer eight years ago.

Henry or Harry? Was it possible? No address. No date. No surname. But adrift in the tumultuous sea of paper in Lord Arthur's trunk there was an envelope and upon that envelope there was a postmark. He had never heard of Abbey Green but he understood it to be somewhere in Lanarkshire. A telegram to Glasgow. Discreet enquiries undertaken. They were looking for a Mr Park or a Mr Ferguson (or any other young Englishman of effeminate appearance aged around twenty-six) living in or around Abbey Green. It was a long shot, but it had proved to be a lucky shot, a very lucky shot.

Mr Charles Ferguson of Abbey Green was not entirely sober. Truth be told, he was some considerable distance from sobriety, but he carried his drink very well and could muster enough gentlemanly self-possession to instruct the girl to show his visitors in. He felt a familiar churning in the pit of his stomach as he recognised the unmistakable presence, the unmistakable smell of a policeman, though neither of his two visitors were dressed as such.

George White spoke first.

'Mr Edward Henry Park?' It was as a much a statement of fact as it was a question.

'Will you have something to drink?' Charles Ferguson countered, fumbling with the decanter.

George White nodded to Inspector Thompson. Yes, they had the right man.

'You are wanted for absconding from bail,' Inspector Thompson said calmly, 'while awaiting trial for serious offences.'

Harry Park turned to face his visitors.

'Not likely,' he replied. 'It's so long ago. They had the "tin", had they not?'

Inspector Thompson turned and looked at George White disdainfully. He knew full well what Harry Park meant by the 'tin'. It meant money paid for sex, money extorted after sex. So that was it. George White and Edwin Dibdin. They were in it together. A racket. White would entice the sodomites. Something disgusting would take place. Money demanded with menaces. Money handed over. And then the poor sod would still be arrested. He almost felt sorry for Harry Park and for the others – for there would have been others, you could be sure of that.

Three days later, on the day Fanny and Stella were released on bail, Harry Park, 'a tall, stylishly-dressed young man, who had an effeminate aspect, no beard or whiskers, slight moustache, and hair carefully parted in the centre', was back in Marylebone Police Court. 'The bench and court were densely crowded with persons anxious to hear the trial,' the *Illustrated Police News* reported. Harry Park had nothing to say for himself, except his name and his address and that he left the case entirely in the hands of his solicitor.

In court, Mr Sergeant Parry was eloquent in his plea of mitigation.

'I am here at the earnest request of a broken-hearted father. Where Park has learnt such degrading practices it is utterly impossible to surmise or guess, and the father's anguish must be the greater in thinking that all his care and anxiety should meet with this sad result.

'Many persons are of the opinion that the perpetration of such offences in itself shows something wanting in mind and feeling which indicates that the offender is not in full possession of his faculties, and that such cases would be far better treated in a lunatic asylum than in a court of Justice.'

But Mr Sergeant Parry's oratory fell on deaf ears. The magistrate, Mr D'Eyncourt, was not to be swayed by pleas for mercy or intimations of insanity. He sentenced Harry Park to twelve months' imprisonment with hard labour, the heaviest sentence he was able to impose under the law, he said. Harry Park remained impassive as the sentence was handed down, but his frail-looking father, Judge Alexander Park, was seen to stagger under the weight of the blow.

25

'Pestiferous and Pestilential'

What words can paint the infamy of such Hellish
proceedings on the part of men towards those of
their own sex?

Extraordinary Revelations, 1870

At the time of Fanny and Stella's arrest in April 1870, the
subjects of Queen Victoria could be forgiven for thinking
that their world was under siege from an army of threats: internal and external, visible and invisible, actual and imagined.
Things seemed to be getting worse rather than better, and
many thought that they could hear the not-so-distant thunder
of the hooves of the Horsemen of the Apocalypse: pestilence,
war, famine and death.

The nation was in a state of flux, of transformation. The
world seemed to be changing almost daily. New ideas, new
inventions and new ideologies were everywhere. There were
threats of war, revolts and revolutions at home and abroad. The
Fenians were bringing terror to the streets of London, Liverpool and Manchester, and nobody knew where they might
strike next. And there were no less important revolutions of the
mind, revolutions which seemed to shake and shatter the old
certainties. Mr Charles Darwin seemed to be suggesting that
Man was not created by God in His own image, but was actually descended from the bestial ape, and might very well revert
to that bestial state.

Contagious diseases had become virtually endemic, and frequently erupted into epidemics: smallpox, consumption, cholera, typhus, typhoid, scarletina, diphtheria, influenza, measles and the whooping cough killed off large swathes of the population, especially infants and children, and debilitated those who survived.

And there were other contagions, no less dangerous, no less threatening to the nation's health. There were the multiple and interlinked contagions of poverty, crime, disorder, immorality and vice. Especially vice. Prostitution was everywhere, with some experts positing that there were no fewer than a hundred thousand prostitutes working in London, or one prostitute to every ten men. Marriage was on the wane, and yet the numbers of children born – especially to the very poor – just grew and grew. As the poor became more numerous, the slums of the cities expanded, becoming the breeding grounds for all the spoken and unspoken ills of society.

The certainties and clarities of a divinely ordered hierarchical society where all men – and women – knew their station had been replaced by an anarchic world driven by instinct and appetite, by lust and by greed; a random, rudderless and unfixed world where the old bastions of religion, law, custom and morality were buffeted and besieged by forces so dark and so primal they could barely be apprehended, let alone understood.

Doubt – a corrosive, contagious and cancerous doubt – had entered into the heart and soul of the nation. Fears, anxieties and uncertainties seemed to swirl about the landscape of the national psyche like a London pea-souper, casting strange new shapes and shadows upon a once familiar landscape. Much of this doubt seemed to coalesce and dwell upon the human body, upon its sexual frailties and deviations, and upon the concomitant afflictions which – many thought – were visited upon the land as divine retribution for sins of the flesh.

Of all these sexual contagions, syphilis – silent, creeping, invisible and ultimately deadly – was the most feared. Many believed that syphilis was causing degeneration in the wider population. If syphilis continued to spread unchecked, then future generations would be enfeebled and made even more prone to disease and early death. Mr William Henry Sloggett, a noted surgeon, was in deadly earnest when he told a Royal Commission that he was convinced that 'the effect of venereal disease is to deteriorate and sometimes to produce the gradual *extinction* of a race, as is the case of the South Sea Islanders'.

Everyone was agreed that something had to be done to stem the rising tide of filth, immorality and disease that threatened to inundate and destroy Britannia and all that she stood for. What was needed was 'a grand movement . . . to improve the social and moral condition of the inhabitants of this country', a newspaper editorial rousingly declared. It was to be a vast sanitary and social engineering endeavour, a modern crusade, designed not merely to reclaim Jerusalem from the infidel, but to remake it, to build a new Jerusalem for the modern world.

Innumerable commissions of the great and the good were established to enquire minutely into every aspect of life, most especially into the lives of the poor: into their housing, their sanitation, their children, their diet, their health, their leisure, their habits and their work. There were grand plans afoot to clear slums and eradicate overcrowding; to provide sewers and clean drinking water; to set standards of hygiene in common lodging houses; to have compulsory education and compulsory vaccination for children; to regulate working conditions in factories; reform the legal system; and stop the adulteration of food. Innumerable charities were established with the stated aim of reclaiming prostitutes, encouraging temperance and promoting sexual continence.

If the lives and habits of the poor could be regulated and controlled, if they could be sanitised, the entire nation would benefit. Just as the children of the poor would be vaccinated against disease, society would be inoculated against the evils of crime and disorder, plague and pestilence, revolt, revolution and degeneration.

Sex between men had long been a target for those who wanted to cleanse society of its vices. And sodomy with its clear associations with excrement lay at the very confluence of potent fears, both old and new, about sex, dirt, disease and death which haunted the national psyche.

Sodomy was both an old and a new vice. It was as old as sin, as old as the Old Testament itself, as old as the horrible fate of the Cities of the Plain, Sodom and Gomorrah, destroyed by fire and brimstone.

From the Middle Ages onwards, there was a widely held belief that sodomy, even the least toleration of sodomy, would bring down divine retribution upon an entire nation. Sodomy was, as the illustrious jurist Edward Coke wrote, '*contra ordinationem Creatoris et naturae ordinem*', contrary to the commandments of God and the order of Nature.

Even to speak the very word was dangerous. Sodomy was the '*crimen inter Christianos non nominandum*', the crime not to be named among Christians. To say the word was to invoke the diabolical deed and bring calamity in its wake. In 1642 Governor Bradford of New England spoke of sodomy and buggery as 'things fearful to name'.

Sir Robert Heath, the Attorney-General who, in 1631, pro-secuted the Earl of Castlehaven in a state trial in Westminster Hall for committing sodomy with his servants, warned that the Earl's crimes were 'of that pestiferous and pestilential nature that if they be not punished they will draw from Heaven heavy judgements upon this Kingdom'.

'Pestiferous and pestilential' was more than mere rhetoric on the part of Sir Robert Heath. He meant exactly what he said: sodomy was literally plague-bringing. If even a single case of sodomy went unpunished, the Kingdom would be collectively and divinely punished by plagues, contagions and pestilences. 'By these abominations the land is defiled,' he declared, 'there-fore the Lord does visit this Land for the iniquity thereof.'

In his masque *Sodom*, John Wilmot, Earl of Rochester and celebrated Restoration rake, wrote of the imaginary Kingdom of Sodom ruled by King Bolloxinion and Queen Cunitigratia. Advised by Borastus, his 'Buggermaster-General', and encour-aged by Buggeranthos, General of the Army, Bolloxinion de-crees, in a fit of pique, that sodomy is to be the new order of the day:

> Henceforth, Borastus, set the Nation free,
> Let conscience have its force of Liberty,
> I do proclaim, that Buggery may be us'd
> Through all the Land, so Cunt be not abus'd.

The Kingdom of Sodom is turned upon its head. All is in 'hugger-mugger': topsy-turvy, upside-down and inside-out. Death and disease stalk the land; children are stillborn; crops fail; and the people are 'raving and mad'. Sodom totters on the edge of a dark abyss. A despairing Flux, the King's Physician and 'Man of Philosophy', beseeches Bolloxinion to reverse his decree in an effort to cure the 'epidemical' and 'tortur'd pains your Nation doth endure'. But Flux's pleas falls on deaf ears. 'I'll reign and bugger still,' a defiant Bolloxinion proclaims, provoking a horrible chorus of 'firy demons' to rise up in a cloud of 'fire, brimstone and smoke'. It is Hell upon earth.

When, in February and March 1750, two earthquakes shook London, Thomas Sherlock, the Bishop of London, declared them divine retribution for the rise of sodomy in the city:

> The unnatural Lewdness, of which we have heard so much of late, is something more than Brutish and can hardly be mentioned without offending chaste Ears, and yet cannot be passed over entirely in Silence, because of the particular Mark of Divine Vengeance set upon it in the Destruction of *Sodom* by Fire from Heaven. Dreadful Example!

In the 1840s and 1850s there had been shocking revelations about the prevalence of sodomy and the rape of boys in the convict barracks of New South Wales and in the mines of Van Diemen's Land. Questions had been asked in Parliament.

By the 1860s, sodomy was a vice that was once again beginning to exercise, to agitate, to vex society. Hardly a week passed without some veiled – and often not so veiled – references to unnatural or abominable crimes in local and national newspapers.

In January 1866 the journalist James Greenwood anonymously published three articles in the *Pall Mall Gazette*. 'A Night in the Workhouse' was Greenwood's sensational account of the night he passed in the casual ward of the Lambeth workhouse, the locked male ward where the dispossessed and the dislocated could pass the night; all the vagrants, trampers, ex-convicts and assorted riff-raff who had fetched up hungry and homeless and hopeless on the streets of Lambeth.

It was a shocking revelation of human degradation; of poverty, dirt, disease and, most shockingly of all, of raw and unrestrained – almost feral – sodomy between men and between men and boys. As he witnessed naked 'great hulking ruffians' and 'dirty scoundrels' seeking bedmates for the night, as he lay in the dark listening to the 'infamous' sexual noises of the night, Greenwood 'could not help thinking of the fate of Sodom'.

There was new knowledge of old sins; new scientific facts were being formulated. In *Hard Times*, Charles Dickens's novel of industrial life, Thomas Gradgrind, the cruel factory owner, is a man obsessed with facts:

> 'Now, what I want is Facts,' said Mr Gradgrind. 'Teach
> these boys and girls nothing but Facts. Facts alone are
> wanted in life. Plant nothing else, and root out
> everything else. You can only form the minds of
> reasoning animals upon Facts: nothing else will ever be
> of service to them . . . Stick to Facts, sir!'

Facts, facts and more facts were the intellectual *lingua franca* of the nineteenth century. Victorians were obsessed with facts and the classification of facts. Taxonomy, or the science of 'classification, of putting things in their proper order', according to an anonymous lexicographer in 1839, first made its appearance in relation to botanical and mineral samples in the early part of the nineteenth century. By the 1850s, taxonomy had become not so much a method of classification as a potent guiding principle. The Victorian world-view was dominated by a need – a need verging on a compulsion – to order, to classify, to list and to designate; to establish relationships, formulate hierarchies and assign values. Nothing escaped this minute taxonomic enquiry. Everything was grist to the great mill of knowledge which ground out the meal of the modern world.

And now this great taxonomic enterprise was turning its attention to sodomy and sodomites. Learned tomes on medical jurisprudence began for the first time to describe the symptoms of sodomy. Articles and books started to appear – in France and Germany at first, but soon imported to Britain – which attempted to define and classify the sodomite, by his ways, his wiles and his physical characteristics. Experts included Casper in Germany, translated into English in 1864, and Tardieu in France (whose 1857 treatise on sodomy would find its way into the eager hands of Dr Paul). There were new names for old sinners, like 'Uranian', first coined in 1864, and 'homosexual', invented in 1869. There were even the slow, steady rumblings of medical and legal debate about the rights and wrongs of sex between men.

In 1867, three years before the arrest of Fanny and Stella, the *Medical Times and Gazette* had published an article by an anonymous 'alienist', a new breed of doctor who sought to bridge the physiological and the psychological, the sexual and the social. Entitled 'Aberrations of the Sexual Instinct', the article was a comprehensive catalogue, a complete taxonomy of unnatural behaviour, singling out for especial concern and condemnation the linked vices of masturbation, androgyny and sodomy.

By the 1860s, the dangers of masturbation had become a

national obsession verging on mass hysteria. Masturbation in girls and women – or 'peripheral excitement' as the distinguished obstetric surgeon Isaac Baker Brown termed it – was thought to be responsible for a raft of female ailments including painful menstruation, melancholia, hysteria, epilepsy, nymphomania, dementia and death.

Boys who masturbated or who were deemed at risk of masturbating were isolated and variously beaten, clamped, bound, bathed, exercised, physicked, hectored and lectured. Not only did masturbation lead to a bewilderingly wide variety of diseases from spermatorrhea to blindness, it also sapped vitality, weakening and destroying the healthy male body. But most seriously of all, masturbation inexorably led by paths secret and mysterious to sodomy.

Masturbation also sapped virility, making men biologically and psychologically less manly, more androgynous, more effeminate, dangerously closer to that weaker vessel, woman. 'Androgynism', the *Medical Times and Gazette* declared, 'may be taken to mean the intrusion of either sex, voluntarily or not, into the province of the other; to wit, when a woman dissects a dead body, or a man measures a young woman for a pair of stays.'

There was growing concern and complaint about the increasing visibility of masculine women and effeminate men. 'There is not the slightest doubt', a carefully worded editorial in the *Englishwoman's Domestic Magazine* announced, 'that England is hastening towards the border which divides the sexes; already persons have over-stepped and stand alone, hated and despised.' The *Pall Mall Gazette* launched a lengthy diatribe against the 'unsexed' masculine woman who seeks to 'usurp' the place of men:

She has probably learned to smoke, and she takes kindly to a little strong drink; she talks slang, perhaps she bets, perhaps dabbles in the share market. She pants for excitement of a fierce and manly kind – for excitement that will stimulate her, that will satisfy her – for excitement that will unsex her.

As early as 1857, *The Times* was fulminating about a new breed of smirking and 'respectable young men who serve in drapers' shops': 'For our own part we would far rather see any son of ours wielding the saw or the trowel, or even standing side by side with navvies on parade, than mincing and bowing and rubbing his hands to "carriage people" during the best days of an effeminate life.'

'Smirking, mincing and effeminate': it was clear that the Thunderer's ire was directed at what it saw as the emergence of a new class or type of young men, men who were neither one thing nor the other, neither fish, nor fowl, nor good red meat, not men and not women, in-between men, 'mistakes', androgynous, effeminate men, sodomites by instinct and inclination, young men in fact very much cast in the mould of Fanny and Stella.

It was not for nothing that in 1851 the Registrar-General described the shortage of men over twenty years of age as 'unnatural'. Marriage was waning, healthy young men were in short supply and yet androgynous, epicene young men seemed to be on the increase. Something was wrong. Very wrong.

There was a widespread feeling of unease that sodomy was spreading. 'The increase of these monsters in the shape of men commonly designated as Margeries, Pooffs, &c, of late years, in the great metropolis, renders it necessary for the safety of the public, that they should be made known,' *The Yokel's Preceptor* warned in the 1850s.

After the arrest of Fanny and Stella, simmering public anxiety and indignation at the spread of sodomy reached a crescendo. Fanny and Stella were, it seemed, the tiny, visible tip of a vast iceberg. For every sodomite 'who is known, innumerable persons unknown offend in a similar way', reported the *Daily Telegraph*. The *Saturday Review* heartily agreed. 'It is certain that the numbers are far more numerous than it is pleasant to imagine.'

Not only was sodomy on the increase, but rather more seriously, sodomites were becoming more visible, and more flagrant. 'A certain form of iniquity has, within the last year or two, been thrust more openly than of old on the attention of the public,' claimed the *Daily Telegraph*. Sodomites were organised and confederated. They were a gang; they were part of 'a doubtful fellowship'; they formed a 'clique', and, most worryingly of all, a class.

The newspapers worried where it all might end if left unchecked. 'Vice,' the *Daily Telegraph* warned, 'emboldened by impunity, will at length stalk forth boldly from its secret haunts, and flaunt about in public places in a way that must compel attention.' *The Times* went even further: 'There is no saying how far things might go in a year or two,' it prophesied. '"Drag" might become quite an institution, and open carriages might display their disguised occupants without suspicion.'

What was to be done, what could be done in the face of this tidal wave of sodomy? *Reynolds's Newspaper* drew an explicit comparison with Sodom and Gomorrah. 'This London of ours is as foul a sink of iniquity as were certain Jewish cities of old, which, for their flagrant wickedness, met with retributive destruction by fire from heaven.' Clearly, the fate of London, of Britain, and of its empire-in-all-but-name hung by a sodomitic thread. The only solution was to root out and destroy sodomy before 'fire, brimstone and smoke' engulfed the nation.

That the contagion of sodomy had spread, was spreading, and had infected all levels of society was not in doubt. The question was how far had it already spread, and how much further might it spread. There was, the *Pall Mall Gazette* thought, a strong sense of 'organisation and concert' involved in this sodomitic 'conspiracy'. Sodomites were essentially vampiric. In order to survive, they were driven and compelled to corrupt the innocent and, in so doing, create even more sodomites. 'It is essential for its continuance that it should go on enlisting fresh members,' the paper warned.

It was this idea of a deliberate and purposeful conspiracy to spread the contagion of sodomy, to infect – and by infecting, re-cruit – new sodomites which so frightened the authorities. The very words used in the indictment against Fanny and Stella – conspiring, confederating, combining, agreeing 'with divers other persons whose names are unknown' – revealed the fear of a contagion that was turning into an epidemic, a veritable plague.

As sodomites, especially as effeminate sodomites, disguised as women, and prostituting themselves, Fanny and Stella and everything they stood for touched some of society's deepest and darkest fears of dirt, degeneration, syphilis, excrement, poverty, violence and effeminisation.

Sodomites had to be identified and stopped, though where to start? The arrest of Fanny and Stella was just the beginning. With the sanction of religion, law and custom, and with the support of a modern and powerful police, the lines of battle were drawn. It was nothing less than a crusade, a great and grand design to discover, defeat and destroy the dark Kingdom of Sodom, to banish it, once and for all, from this green and pleasant land.

26

The Ship of State

'Herald, read the accusation!' said the King. On
this the White Rabbit blew three blasts on the
trumpet, and then unrolled the parchment scroll,
and read as follows:

    'The Queen of Hearts, she made some tarts,

    'All on a summer day:

    'The Knave of Hearts, he stole those tarts,

    'And took them quite away!'

    'Consider your verdict,' the King said to the jury.

Alice's Adventures in Wonderland, 1865

'To judge from the crowd assembled in Westminster Hall
at an early hour,' the *Daily Telegraph* reported, 'there
has been no falling-off of the public interest in this twice-told
tale.' It was almost a year to the day since the arrest of Fanny
and Stella in drag outside the Strand Theatre, and a large
crowd had gathered in Palace Yard this brilliant May morning
to catch a glimpse of the defendants as they arrived. Many of
them were hoping to squeeze into the public gallery to watch
what they hoped would be the trial of the decade, if not the
century.

The trial of the Young Men in Women's Clothes was a trial
that some had predicted would never take place, especially
after the Attorney-General himself had suddenly and dramatically intervened in early July 1870 and withdrawn all charges of

sodomy against Ernest Boulton and Frederick Park. Fanny and Stella (along with Louis Hurt and John Safford Fiske, against whom charges of sodomy had also been withdrawn) were released on bail quietly and without fanfare, and it was generally assumed that that was that and the entire dismal and disturbing affair would gently fade from public memory, like a photograph left out in the sun. The *Porcupine* was confident that 'the public are not likely to be troubled much further in this matter'. The *Penny Illustrated* agreed: 'It is thought nothing more will be heard of the Young Men in Women's Clothes.'

To all intents and purposes, Fanny and Stella had vanished off the face of the earth. There had been neither sight nor sound of them since they were released on bail in July 1870. The months had gone by and not a squeak, not a whimper, not a whisper had been heard from them or about them. It was, perhaps, too much to hope that they were dead. Too much to hope that they had done the decent thing and died by their own hand. Or that they were dead from natural – or rather, *un*natural – causes, from the foul contagions that their course of life must necessarily have inflicted upon them. Or – vain hope! – that they had died from shame and remorse (though neither of them had yet exhibited the least bit – not a morsel, not a scrap, not a crumb – of these worthy Christian virtues).

If not death, then it was profoundly to be hoped that their disappearance was for good (in every sense of the word), that they had had the sense to flee these islands, never again to return and so disturb and upset the nation's equanimity. More prosaically and more probably, they had gone to ground and were merely lying low. Even if they wanted to flee, or 'scarper' as their slang talk had it, good Inspector Thompson and his team of detectives were no doubt alert to that possibility and would be watching their every move, just as they had watched their every move for a year or more before their arrest.

All that might be said by way of mitigation and by way of compassion was that the families of Boulton and Park had exercised and demonstrated the most Christian charity and forbearance in giving these hunted and cornered beasts shelter and food, though a sound birching and a fatal dose of prussic acid might have been more to the point.

So it had come as a shock and a jolt after all these months to discover that Fanny and Stella and their confederates – eight of them in all – still had a case to answer and were to answer that case in the Court of Queen's Bench, the highest court in the land, before the highest judge in land, the Lord Chief Justice, and a special jury.

Just before ten o'clock Fanny and Stella made their way with some difficulty through the crammed courtroom towards the plain and simple wooden bench where defendants and counsel alike would sit for the duration of the case. Both Fanny and Stella had flowers – 'a bouquet of flowers' – in their button-holes and both were dressed, according to one of the witnesses, 'somewhat more tastily' than was quite common with young men.

'Boulton was scarcely altered in looks since his appearance at Bow Street and, except for the faint shade of a moustache, he might still easily have been taken for a girl in boy's clothes,' the *Daily Telegraph* breathlessly reported. 'Park, on the other hand, has grown stout, and his large whiskers have so altered his face as completely to deprive it of the feminine look which it wore a year ago.'

If Fanny and Stella were nervous, they did not show it. But they were subdued. Indeed, their demeanour was quite different from that bravado, that defiant jocularity which had so characterised – and in the opinion of many, so disfigured – their many appearances at Bow Street a year ago. Now, they had every appearance of being sober, serious and dignified young men. Fanny's stoutness and luxuriant dark whiskers proclaimed her masculinity, and even Stella had made her nod to maleness with the 'faint shade of a moustache' that dear, dull Louis Hurt had begged her, in vain, to grow.

Gone, too, were those 'campish' ways of theirs: the constantly darting eyes, the cocked eyebrows, the pursed lips and the theatrically expressive faces. There was no more playing to the gallery. There was no more giggling or flirting or ogling or chirruping. There were no more hissing sibilants; no more contemptuous snorts; no more withering looks; no more tossings of actual or imaginary curls; no more flutterings of eyelashes; no more swishings of metaphorical bombazines. Every detail of Fanny and Stella's outward appearance in the Court of Queen's Bench that morning proclaimed them to be elegant, educated and civilised young gentlemen. This transformation, this miraculous migration from vicious effeminacy to virtuous manhood, was the work of one man: their new solicitor, Mr George Lewis.

Mr George Lewis was a very different kettle of fish from the beleaguered Mr Abrams who had single-handedly and with great gallantry acted as the Forlorn Hope of Fanny and Stella's defence from the moment of their arrest, but who, it had quickly become apparent, was floundering badly in the face of the magnitude and complexity of the charges levelled against them. Mr George Lewis was ferocious and formidable. He was a force to be reckoned with, provoking fear and love in equal measure. He was an implacable prosecutor and a determined defender, and he had a growing reputation as the man to turn to when scandal threatened. The Prince of Wales himself had consulted him when he was named as a lover – as one of several lovers – of Lady Harriet Mordaunt in the sensational action for divorce brought by her husband, Sir Charles Mordaunt. Mr George Lewis had advised His Royal Highness to go into the witness box and had, by all accounts, so perfectly coached him in what to say and how to say it that he was credited with saving not only the Prince's tattered reputation, but also the institution of the Monarchy itself.

Mr George Lewis was a different sort of a solicitor from the commonality of solicitors. More of a general: a Marlborough or a Wellington or a Napoleon. He was obsessed with each and every detail of a case. Nothing, however small, however insignificant, escaped his notice, and yet he always kept his eye on the great game. He would tell his clients what to wear, what to say, how to act – in court and outside court. His clients were his puppets, they were putty in his extraordinary hands.

In person, Mr George Lewis was quiet, polite, unassuming. Indeed, most of those present in Westminster Hall for Fanny and Stella's trial hardly noticed this young-looking, slightly built man, prematurely grey and with abundant Dundreary whiskers who accompanied them into court. He looked like a clerk and he liked it that way. He did not want to stand out from the crowd. He liked to be unobtrusive and self-effacing. He liked to beaver away behind the scenes, delving and digging, dissecting and directing.

Mr George Lewis was nothing if not rigorous. Rigour was the beginning, the middle and the end of his work as a solicitor.

He left nothing to chance. He would devour depositions and scour witness statements looking for errors, anomalies, contradictions. And he made sure that he read everything himself. Indeed, shortly after taking on the case of the Young Men in Women's Clothes, he had presented himself at Mr Pollard's office at the Treasury and insisted on reading through each and every deposition and document, each and every letter and note and report connected with the case.

Mr George Lewis wanted to find out everything there was to know, and more besides. His methods were said to be as unorthodox as they were audacious. He had an extensive and unrivalled network of informants – 'a spider's web of narks and spies', as one disgruntled observer put it – which he would use to devastating effect in turning up new evidence that the police would never have found in a month of Sundays. He revelled in theatrical flourishes, producing surprise new witnesses, like a magician pulling rabbits out of a hat.

Mr George Lewis disliked injustice in any shape or form. The case of Boulton and Park, friendless, despised and beleaguered, and with all the apparatus and power of a merciless State ranged against them, may have touched a chord of sympathy and compassion within him and prompted him to offer his services. That and the fact that the case was widely regarded not just as unwinnable, but also as toxic, a case that would infect and poison all those who had dealings with it. Whatever the reason, now that he had taken the case, Mr George Lewis let it be known to one and all that he would fight for Fanny and Stella with every fibre of his being. He would fight and he would win.

Of the eight men whose names were listed in the Indictment, only four were present in court. Lord Arthur Clinton was dead and buried, supposedly of scarlet fever, but there were many who thought he was merely playing dead, that he was comfortably ensconced abroad, cocking a snook at the police and at the public morals. Three of the defendants, Martin Luther Cumming (the Comical Countess), William Somerville and Cecil 'Sissy' Thomas, had never been interviewed, let alone apprehended, and were to be tried in their absence. That left just four defendants who were there in the flesh: Ernest Boulton, Frederick Park, Louis Hurt and John Safford Fiske.

Many if not most of those who had managed to push and squeeze themselves into the small courtroom found themselves not a little baffled and bewildered by the charges. It appeared that none of the defendants were charged with *actual* acts of buggery or sodomy, nor even with acts falling short of buggery or sodomy. No, they were charged with 'conspiracy to solicit, induce, procure and endeavour to persuade persons unknown to commit buggery'. It struck many present that morning, from the highest to the lowest, that such a charge was somehow incomplete and rather lopsided. Was it really possible to convict persons for the thought but not for the deed? It was like bread without butter, cakes without ale, pie without mash. How could you prove the intention without the act? And where would it all end? If minds were now to be read, if private thoughts and whims and wishes and fancies were now constituted crimes, who then was safe from the long arm of the law?

Fanny and Stella (and the absent Comical Countess) were also charged with a second offence: that they 'unlawfully and wickedly did conspire, confederate, combine' to 'openly and publicly pretend and hold themselves out and appear to be women and thereby to inveigle, induce and incite divers of the male subjects of Her Majesty improperly, lewdly and indecently to fondle and toy with them as women and thereby openly and scandalously to outrage public decency and to offend against public morals'.

(Not that anyone could ever have been fooled – even for a moment – by the Comical Countess. Miss Martin Luther Cumming might publicly pretend and hold herself out to be a woman until she was blue in the face, but, in her case, wishes were emphatically not kisses. She was and would always be a clownish and clowning fat young man, blowsily and badly dressed as a woman, an object of fascination, repulsion, ridicule and – strangely – sometimes pity.)

Here again, some of those present in Westminster Hall had the unworthy thought that when all was said and done, this second charge of conspiracy and confederation amounted to not much more than dressing up in drag and flirting with gentlemen.

Not to put too fine a point on it, the case against the four young men was all at sea. Everything was upside-down and inside-out and back-to-front. The judicial cart was being put before the horse. Instead of being tried for the crimes they had committed, these four young men were on trial for crimes they had yet to commit, for crimes they might have thought about, or talked about, or imagined for a moment in their mind's eye – or not, as the case may be. No wonder that some were reminded of nothing so much as the strange topsy-turvy trial of the Knave of Hearts for stealing the tarts in Mr Lewis Carroll's curious and entertaining book, *Alice's Adventures in Wonderland*.

All the might and main of the great Ship of State had been brought to bear upon the Young Men in Women's

Clothes. Every cannon had been primed and loaded and trained and targeted upon Fanny and Stella, ready to fire a deadly broadside. The Attorney-General himself was to lead the charge, which was a rare and notable occurrence, usually reserved for only the gravest of grave cases, for the most serious of seditioners and for the highest of high treasoners. And even then, it had been many a long year – long beyond the memory of most there that day – since the Attorney-General had stripped down to his long drawers and stepped into the ring for a bare-knuckle, bloody fight, ably seconded by the Solicitor-General brandishing a sponge soaked in vinegar. And it had been centuries, quite literally, since an Attorney-General had personally prosecuted a case of sodomy – two hundred and forty years, almost to the day, in fact, since Sir Robert Heath, Attorney-General to Charles I, had stood up in Westminster Hall to denounce the Earl of Castlehaven for multiple acts of sodomy with his servants.

Defending Fanny and Stella (and Louis Hurt and John Safford Fiske, who might just as well have been numbered among the absentee and absconded defendants for all the notice anyone took of them) was the flower of the British Bar, if that was not too great a stretch of the imagination to describe the half-dozen or so overstuffed, barrel-chested, bewhiskered and be-wigged barristers who formed the thin red line bravely holding back the massed and powerful armies of an outraged Britannia.

Any prosecuting counsel worth his salt (and the Attorney-General was generally allowed to be well worth his salt) knew only too well that his opening address to the jury could make or break the case. A good opening speech was half the battle won, it was the first and most deadly salvo, ripping through the defence with devastating accuracy. A clever prosecutor was like a skilled general, carefully choosing his ground, exploiting the topography and marshalling his forces to maximum advantage. Indeed, a clever prosecutor could often outwit his adversary and win his case by the brilliance and vigour of his opening address.

But today, as he stood up to deliver his opening speech, it was clear that the Attorney-General was not his usual self. He was not comfortable, he was not confident and he was not easy. It was plain to all that Sir Robert Collier would rather be anywhere than in the Court of Queen's Bench in Westminster Hall leading the prosecution in a trial about which he clearly had his doubts. For all the rhetorical flourishes and folderols of his opening address, it was evident that his heart was not really in it. His speech was weak and colourless, the thinnest of thin gruel, insubstantial to the point of incorporeality. It was not so much what Sir Robert said, or even the way he said it, it was simply that he lacked conviction. And, because he lacked conviction, his words fell on stony ground.

It did not take long before the causes of his unease became apparent. 'This is a prosecution that I open with peculiar *reluctance*,' Sir Robert began rather unpromisingly, going on to explain that he had 'no choice' in the matter. With much beating about the bush and with a great deal of umming and aahing and ahemming, Sir Robert let it be known that the prosecution was at the request and at the behest of the Home Secretary, Mr Henry Bruce. That worthy gentleman, Sir Robert said, had 'felt it his bounden duty to undertake the most searching investigation in order to ascertain as far as possible whether an apprehension – a popular apprehension – that a crime held in peculiar detestation in this country had been committed was a well-founded apprehension'.

Sir Robert had bewildered and confused the court almost before he had begun. No one in court was quite sure of his exact meaning. 'An investigation to ascertain whether an apprehension that a crime had been committed was a well-founded apprehension.' It did not seem to make any sense. And that was putting it politely. Who, or rather what, was on trial here? Was it the perpetrators of the crime itself, the crime 'held in peculiar detestation in this country' (by which, presumably, Sir Robert meant sodomy)? Was it Boulton and Park and Hurt and Fiske, and all the divers other sodomites, named and unnamed, alive and dead, known or unknown, who were on trial? Or was it the 'popular apprehension' of sodomy that was on trial? Was it Sir Robert's task to test the truth of the widespread belief that sodomy had gained a foothold – more than a foothold – in England? Was he there to prove that sodomites were daily becoming bolder and more brazen? That they were daily becoming proselytisers? That by their tricks and their ways and their wiles, and especially by their dressing and passing as women, they were daily deceiving, corrupting and recruiting the flower of English manhood? That their sodomitic stalking-ground, mission field and battlefield all rolled into one was England's green and pleasant land?

The answer appeared to be that everything and everyone was on trial. Sodomy in thought and sodomy in deed was on trial. Sodomites in particular and sodomites in general. Effeminate men and men who dressed as women. England's manhood and England's morality and England's masculinity. They were all on trial. So the trial was not really a trial at all but an investigation and a deliberation, and the defendants were not really defendants but symbols and representatives of the fearful sodomitic threat that hovered darkly over fair Albion.

It was clear that Sir Robert Collier hoped, perversely, that the evidence would lead to an acquittal. 'Perhaps I am not going too far,' Sir Robert declared, 'when I say that you and I and all of us will experience a sense of relief if we come to the conclusion that the popular apprehension was unfounded.' If Boulton and Park and Hurt and Fiske were found to be not guilty then there could and would be general rejoicing that our island nation, our granite fortress sailing serenely in a silver sea, had repelled the piratical and parasitical sodomitic boarders, that it had fought off the sodomitic threat from without.

'But,' Sir Robert gravely warned the Jury,

> if the evidence leads you to the conclusion that the
> prisoners are guilty, you will not hesitate to perform a
> public duty than which nothing can be more important.
> You will do what in you lies to stop this plague which, if
> allowed to spread without check or hindrance, might
> lead to a serious contamination of our national morals.

A guilty verdict would mean that sodomy had broken forth in the land, that the contagion had been unleashed and was spreading silently, infecting and contaminating all who came into contact with it. A guilty verdict would mean that all of them – Fanny and Stella, Louis Hurt and John Safford Fiske, the absconded Comical Countess, Miss Sissy Thomas and the mysterious Mr Somerville, even the dead-and-buried Lord Arthur Clinton, even the 'divers others' and the 'persons unknown' of the indictment; all the sodomites and all the buggers and all the Mary-Anns; all the He-She's and the She-He's; all the effeminate men and masculine women; all the young men in women's clothes and all the young women in men's clothes; all the androgynes and all the hermaphrodites and the in-betweens – all of them must be punished. All of them must be purged. All of them must be prevented from spreading the taint and poison of sodomy. A guilty verdict would mean the preaching of a new national crusade to hunt down and extirpate the sodomites from the nation's midst.

It was almost too terrible a prospect to contemplate, and it was no wonder that all those present in the Ancient and Honourable Court of Queen's Bench felt a sudden and collective shudder of horror, as if someone or something had walked across their graves.

27

The Most Sensational Event

By sometimes dressing in female costume, sometimes in male costume, with a studied air of
effeminacy, powdering their necks, painting their
faces, by amatory airs and gestures, the Defendants
endeavoured to excite each other's passions, and to
make themselves objects of desire to persons of
their own class.

Opening speech of the Attorney-General, 9th
May 1871

Who was the strikingly handsome young man who made
his way into the court in the company of the eminent
and silver-tongued barrister Sir John Karslake on the second
morning of the trial? Was this dark and soulful-looking young
man one of the missing defendants in the case? William
Somerville, perhaps? Or Cecil Thomas? Or Martin Luther
Cumming?

Rather more sensationally, might it be a contrite Lord Arthur Clinton, back from the dead; back from foreign parts; back
from whichever hole he had crawled into to hide after leaving
his catamite to face the music? Such a spectacular resurrection
and return of this missing-declared-dead peer and politician
would greatly add drama and piquancy to a trial that already
seemed to be listing and foundering under the freight of its own
expectations.

Much to the disappointment of some, Mr Simeon Solomon was neither an absconded defendant nor a revivified Lord Arthur. He was an artist and a man of self-confessed 'irregular affections', and his presence in the Court of Queen's Bench that morning could be attributed to an admixture of vulgar and prurient curiosity to see Lady Stella Clinton and Miss Fanny Winifred Park in the flesh, a strong sense of solidarity in adversity with them, and an overwhelming fear that his own name, or the name of his intimate friend and fellow sodomite – or 'Dolomite', as they were fond of calling each other – Mr Algernon Charles Swinburne, the infamous young poet, might come up.

'Boulton is very remarkable,' Simeon Solomon wrote to Swinburne. 'He is not quite beautiful. But supremely pretty, a perfect figure, manner and voice. Altogether, I was agreeably surprised at him.' Solomon was less impressed by John Safford Fiske, 'the writer of those highly effusive letters', who 'looks rather humdrum'.

In his preliminary canter through the evidence, the Attorney-General had made much of the mass of epistolary evidence available to him in this case and insisted on reading aloud, and in full, no fewer than thirty-one letters. Many of these letters had already been aired in Bow Street a year earlier and subsequently widely reproduced in the newspapers, much to the dismay of Mr Collette of the Society for the Suppression of Vice, who fretted that evidence of such 'a very revolting nature' might inadvertently be read by ladies at the breakfast table.

But if Sir Robert Collier hoped that these letters would be the first deadly salvo in the battle to come, that they would leave the lines of the defence rent and tattered, he was disappointed. Many, if not most, of the letters seemed to fall somewhat short of the mark or to miss their target completely. It was surprising how quickly the host of 'My Dears' and 'My Darlings' and the endless and ardent declarations of love had lost their power to shock. Most of those present had heard it all or read it all before. And, regrettably, Sir Robert's sonorous style of recitation hindered rather than helped matters. Sir Robert was no Mr Poland. He lacked that rotund gentleman's vulgar quality of showmanship and his ability to lubriciously underscore and point up certain phrases in the letters, which had added greatly to the gaiety of nations.

Sir Robert's slow and deliberate readings added a good hour to the length of his address and, though the case had barely begun, there was already a distinct air of ennui and a palpable sense of impatience in the court. When would the Attorney-General get to the point? When would he get to the meat and drink of the case? It was all very well to listen to these endless ejaculations of love and friendship, but it was sodomy and buggery that were the order of the day and where were they? The tedious wait reminded those present of the fabled dinner where guests were first tantalised and then tortured by the delicious smells of a promised feast that never materialised.

It was true that Sir Robert had up his sleeve a few new letters which, like the vigorous application of birch twigs on the posterior parts, helped to stimulate – momentarily – the flagging passions of the court. There was the intriguing letter to 'Dear Stella' from Mr Edward Henry Park – or 'Harry' as he signed himself – the older brother of Frederick or Fanny Park, a letter which seemed to suggest that he was no stranger to sodomy. He had written, in that incautious postscript, of the 'Glycerine' and 'filthy photos' he had left with Boulton, but surprisingly,

Sir Robert Collier made no attempt to amplify the meaning nor explain – let alone exploit – the significance of these comments, much to the frustration of his auditors.

Then there were two letters from the absconded defendant Mr William Somerville, addressed to his 'Dearest Stella' and signed 'Willy' with his 'fondest love' and 'many kisses'. 'You imagine I do not love you,' he had written. 'I wish to God it was so, but tell me how I can prove it and I will willingly do so.'

These letters from Harry Park and Willy Somerville served only to illustrate one of the very central contradictions of the case: why was it that some young men were indicted on the slightest of slight evidence while others, against whom the evidence seemed much stronger, were not? Willy Somerville had been named as a conspirator in this plot to inveigle the flower of the nation's manhood to knowingly or unknowingly engage in sodomy – and yet the only evidence offered against him was these two letters, the letters of one lovesick youth to another, of so bland a character as to send everyone soundly to sleep.

In sharp contrast, Harry Park's name had not figured in the indictment. And yet it was clear, crystal clear, that Harry Park was up to his elbows in this sodomitic conspiracy. He had spoken of 'Glycerine' and 'filthy photographs' and even the purest of pure minds could not fail to apprehend (at least in part) his meaning. Besides, as everyone knew only too well, Harry Park was currently detained at Her Majesty's pleasure, having been convicted of indecently assaulting Police Constable George White. So why had his name not been added to the roster of conspirators? It seemed an inexplicable omission.

And then there was the presence of Mr Cecil 'Sissy' Thomas on the indictment. No letters from him or to him were presented as evidence. Indeed, the only 'evidence' against him was hearsay. It was alleged that he was the young man in the company of Fanny and Stella on the night they were arrested, the young man who had, in the sodomitic slang, 'scarpered' when the police reared their ugly heads. And he had supposedly dressed in drag once or twice at Wakefield Street with his intimate friend Amos Westropp Gibbings, known to his friends as 'Carlotta'.

If Sissy Thomas was part of this alleged conspiracy, then why had Carlotta Gibbings not been fingered too? The morning after the arrest of Fanny and Stella, Carlotta had cleared the rooms at Wakefield Street of incriminating materials and fled to France, clutching two pairs of her favourite stays. Then she had come back and stood up in Bow Street and declared that she had been out and about 'in drag' on many occasions, to theatres, to restaurants and, famously, to the Boat Race, complete with parasol and picnic. She had even thrown a ball for twenty-four couple at Haxell's Hotel where Heaven knows what had gone on in the Ladies' Retiring Room, in darkened corners and in back passages.

T he trio of letters from Miss Fanny Winifred Park to Lord Arthur Clinton were by far the most revealing and the most entertaining of the letters read out by Sir Robert Collier. They were also the most bewildering and required a considerable stretch of the imagination on the part of the twelve Jurymen to think themselves into the upside-down, back-to-front, inside-out world of these young men. Everything was at once familiar and yet at the same time strange. Black was white, and white was black. Men were women, wives and sisters, with lovers, husbands and brothers. Ernest, or rather Stella, was the 'sister' of Frederick or Fanny. Stella was the 'wife' of Lord Arthur Clinton, which made her Lady Stella Clinton, and which in turn made Miss Fanny Winifred Park Lord Arthur's 'sister-in-law'. It was an altogether unsettling experience, like gazing into a distorting mirror. It was a world within a world, hidden, unsuspected and compelling.

The court was frankly baffled by some portions of Miss Fanny Winifred Park's letters. 'My cawfish undertakings are not at present meeting with the success which they deserve,' she had confided to Lord Arthur, 'whatever I do seems to get me into hot water somewhere but *n'importe*, what's the odds so long as you're happy?'

'Cawfish?' It was an odd word to use, unless it was a misspelling for crawfish, and was a reference to the small lobster-like decapod commonly called a crayfish or a crawdad. Was Miss Fanny Winifred Park exhibiting signs of a growing (and manly) interest in angling? Or was she appealing, shamelessly, to one of Lord Arthur's sporting passions?

Mr Straight, who was assisting Mr Sergeant Parry in Miss Fanny Winifred Park's defence, was of the opinion that the word was 'campish', but Mr Sergeant Parry overruled him peremptorily. 'It is "cawfish" in my copy,' he declared emphatically. 'What "campish" means I cannot understand, but if he had written "scampish" he would not, I think, have been using an improper word.'

The Lord Chief Justice felt that matters were drifting dangerously off the point. 'Whatever it may mean it is certainly "campish",' he decreed firmly.

The Attorney-General had marshalled no fewer than thirty-one witnesses for the prosecution, an impressive array by any standards and one which held the promise of exciting and extraordinary revelations. First to go into the witness box was Mr Hugh Mundell, who had barely changed in the course of a year, except that he blushed and stammered and swallowed and hesitated more than ever. Why the Attorney-General had chosen this bumbling young man, who seemed rather younger than his years, as his star witness whose testimony would encapsulate and exemplify all the sodomitic evils of Fanny and Stella was beyond comprehension.

He was there, in theory at least, to confirm the very worst suspicions about 'Miss Stella' and 'Mrs Fanny', as he insisted on calling them. He was there to state in no uncertain terms how Miss Stella and Mrs Fanny, sometimes dressed as women and sometimes as men, had by 'painting their faces' and 'powdering their necks', by their 'studied air of effeminacy' and by their 'amatory airs and gestures' conspired to induce and inveigle him to fondle and toy with them, conspired to dupe and deceive him into committing sodomy. In theory at least.

But Hugh Mundell turned out to be a witness for the defence. Miss Stella and Mrs Fanny had, he said, for the avoidance of doubt, informed him repeatedly, verbally and in writing, that they were men dressed as women, but he had wilfully refused to believe them. And far from inducing and inveigling him to fondle and toy with them, when, unprompted and with no encouragement, he had attempted to take indecent liberties with Miss Stella, she had most firmly rebuffed him.

From the way his eyes shone when he spoke, it was apparent to everybody that Mr Hugh Mundell was still more than half in love with Miss Stella and would not hear a word said against her, let alone speak ill of her himself. It was a dismal, not to say disastrous, beginning to the case for the prosecution, and it was universally agreed that Sir Robert Collier would have to work very hard if he was to save his ship from crashing onto the rocks.

There was a surprising number of new witnesses, among them some eminent medical gentlemen and a positive phalanx of new witnesses from Scotland, including Mrs Agnes Dickson, Louis Hurt's landlady, and Detective Officer Roderick Gollan of the Edinburgh City Police, who had discovered the cache of compromising photographs and *cartes de visite* hidden in the chambers of Mr John Safford Fiske.

There was Police Constable Thomas Shillingford who, in 1867, had arrested – or more properly, rescued – the young and very beautiful Miss Stella Boulton and her companion, the young and not-at-all-beautiful Martin Luther Cumming, from a mob of battle-scarred and very angry whores in the Haymarket. Both Stella and the Comical Countess were in drag and had aroused the rightful ire of the Haymarket whores by daring to trespass on their hallowed pads and patches.

Mrs Jane Cox, the widow of Mr Francis Kegan Cox, the gentleman who had so unadvisedly and so passionately kissed Ernest Boulton full on the lips in his office in the City, had bravely agreed to stand in her shamed spouse's shoes, and her dignity in the witness box as she listened with a stricken face to her late husband's deposition elicited many fitting murmurs of sympathy.

Miss Eleanor Colton, a most ladylike attendant at the Lyceum Theatre, told how Stella, dressed in mauve satin, had used the convenience in the Ladies' Retiring Room to relieve herself while Fanny stood guard at the door. Miss Colton's testimony aroused feelings of righteous indignation and utter revulsion. It was one thing to dress up as a woman and dupe and deceive unsuspecting men, but to violate and pollute so sacred a sanctum as the Ladies' Retiring Room made the blood of every true Englishman boil over with anger. 'If every *roué* can by assuming feminine garb enforce his way with impunity into the chambers set apart for our countrywomen,' one editorialist declared, 'then we call upon Law and Justice to aid us in exposing these outrages on decency.'

Mr William Kay, of the long-established firm of Outfitters and Dressmakers that bore his name in Russell Square, was called to give his expert opinion on the costumes confiscated at Wakefield Street. A number of portmanteaux, baskets and boxes were brought into court and disgorged a dazzling array of feminine attire. There were no fewer than seventeen dresses and gowns; quantities of skirts and petticoats; bodices and blouses; cloaks and shawls; shoes and boots and gloves; a bewildering assortment of ladies' unmentionables; a single muff; seven chignons, two long curls, ten plaits and – sitting rather oddly like a cuckoo in this nest of femininity – that artificial grey beard.

By the time everything was unpacked and laid out for the consideration of the Jurymen, the court resembled nothing so much as a fripperer's shop in one of the less salubrious parts of the city. After their long incarceration in those assorted portmanteaux, baskets and boxes, the clothes showed 'the crush and spoil of age', as Mr Digby Seymour, defending counsel for Stella, most poetically put it. They were fusty and frowsy, and there was that decidedly unpleasant smell that always pervades shops dealing in second-, third- and fourth-hand clothing, a smell of unwashed bodies and unwashed linen, of dirt and want and overcrowding, of cheap scent and cheap sex, of unfulfilled dreams, disappointments and death.

Mr Kay had, he said, 'thoroughly' examined each and every item of clothing and declared them 'very much tumbled about' and 'not as clean as they might have been' (which was a polite way of saying they were filthy). In consequence, they were of little or no value. 'I wouldn't have them as a gift,' he declared contemptuously.

A cheap and theatrical stunt it may have been, but this display of tawdry feminine finery did its work well. 'A thrill of horror ran through the jury box,' reported the *Daily Telegraph*, as the clothes were unpacked and displayed. To be told that Fanny and Stella had dressed as women and walked the streets was one thing. To see the very clothes they had worn while so promenading was quite another. All the letters of love and longing in the world could not state the case so concisely and so compellingly as these tumbled-about women's clothes had done.

Then there were those witnesses who had already appeared at Bow Street Magistrates' Court and who were now obliged to stand again in the witness box, like Slow Eliza from Norfolk and Sharp-eyed Maria, the bickering housemaids of 36 Southampton Street, where Lord Arthur and Stella had lived as man and wife. Mr John Reeve, the taciturn and gloomy staff supervisor at the Royal Alhambra Palace, spoke to the scandalous and shocking behaviour of Fanny and Stella and of the accompanying gaggle of other like-minded painted and powdered young gentlemen when they regularly descended upon the Alhambra and wreaked moral havoc with their oglings and their chirrupings and their tongue-wagglings.

And then there was Miss Martha Stacey who, in company with her elderly mother, ran the infamous house of accommodation in Wakefield Street where Fanny and Stella and Carlotta and Sissy had lodged and dressed, and where, it was strongly suspected, they 'entertained' – for want of a better word

– 'gentlemen' – again for want of a better word – even though nobody could prove it. If Miss Martha Stacey knew of the gentlemen callers at her establishment, she was most certainly not saying so. She was not saying very much at all, and her frequent glances towards Mr George Lewis sitting inconspicuously at the bar might have suggested – to a suspicious mind – that that gentleman had coached her in what and what not to say.

Martha Stacey exemplified a curious feature of this trial. To the very evident frustration of the Attorney-General, the testimony of several witnesses for the prosecution seemed to have changed subtly. What had been established facts and adamantine certainties at Bow Street a year earlier were now something less than established, something less than adamantine. A small and almost imperceptible degree of doubt had crept into the testimonies of Miss Martha Stacey, Mrs Louisa Peck (the chatelaine of Southampton Street) and Mr Arthur Gladwell, the occupier of the second-floor front in Southampton Street (and now the proud husband of Mrs Peck's sister, Sarah Jane). None of them had done anything as obvious as retract or change their evidence, but now they seemed fractionally more hesitant, more ready to believe in the possibility that they may have been mistaken in their observations. It was enough to unsettle and undermine the case for the prosecution and to lead to the unworthy thought that the £5,000 so generously put up for Fanny and Stella's defence (reputedly by the wealthy Miss Carlotta Westropp Gibbings) had been well spent by Mr George Lewis on bribes.

There was, however, no such hesitation, no such doubt on the part of the formidable Miss Ann Empson. Back by popular demand, Miss Empson delighted her audience by reprising her role as the fearsome and fire-breathing Dragon of Davies

Street. She fumed and smouldered with indignation, she scowled and snorted with rage, and she so frequently spat out small balls of fire and brimstone in the general direction of Fanny and Stella that those two young gentlemen must surely have felt themselves fortunate not to go up in flames like the citizens of Sodom and Gomorrah. When Miss Empson turned her eye upon any particular gentleman in the courtroom, he was seen to step back and stumble, and even the Lord Chief Justice himself appeared to recoil from Miss Empson's Gorgon-like gaze.

B ut 'the most sensational event of the day', according to the *Daily Telegraph*, 'was the cross-examination of the ex-beadle of the Burlington Arcade'. It was a barnstorming *tour de force* by the policeman-turned-beadle-turned-loafer, a man who had begun his career with high and manly ideals and who, over the years, had progressively sunk to his present unfortunate state, a slave to the demon drink, living off the largesse of his mother-in-law at best, and at worst, off the immoral earnings of prostitutes.

His performance melded tragedy and comedy in equal measure and was full of self-delusion and self-pity. One minute he was the cock of the walk, a braggart and a blusterer, his chest puffed out like a pigeon's with manly self-importance; the next, his voice was choking with emotion, and tears were running down his reddened cheeks as he was made to confront the depth and depravity of the abyss he had fallen into.

Mr George Smith was a liar. An habitual liar. He lied, and he lied, and he lied again. He lied to cover up his lies. He lied so much that he forgot what he was lying about, and then would accidentally reveal the startling truth his lies were designed to

conceal. There were 'roars of laughter' as he was caught out –
again and again and again – in deceit and dishonesty, as 'one
damaging confession after another was wrung out of him' in
cross-examination.

It seemed that Mr George Smith had taken money in the
form of tips and bribes from almost everyone: from the gay
ladies in the Burlington Arcade he was supposed to keep out;
from the wealthy gentlemen he introduced to those selfsame
gay ladies; from the shopkeepers in the Burlington Arcade who
tipped him to encourage those gay ladies and their gentlemen
followers to patronise their establishments; from his mother-
in-law and from his friends; from Inspector Thompson; from
the Treasury Solicitor; and from anyone else who was prepared
to pay him. Indeed, the only persons that Smith had not taken
money from were Fanny and Stella, or so he said.

It was left to the Lord Chief Justice to bring Mr George
Smith's devastating cross-examination to an end. 'Do you
think it is possible', he asked Mr Sergeant Parry with withering
irony, 'to prove this witness to be less credible than you have
shown him to be already?'

It was a disaster, there was no other word for it, a downright
disaster. Even if Smith was telling the truth about the haunting
of the Burlington Arcade by Fanny and Stella, by Sissy
Thomas and the Comical Countess, and by all the other
painted and powdered young men looking for wealthy gentlemen, no one would believe him, no one could believe him.

The case for the prosecution was in tatters. Apart from the
coup de théâtre of producing Fanny and Stella's extensive wardrobe of feminine finery in court, the Attorney-General had yet
to make any sort of a case against them or the other six defendants, present, absconded or dead. His star witness, the hapless

Hugh Mundell, had effectively been a witness for the defence. Martha Stacey, Louisa Peck and others had cleverly sown seeds of doubt about their own testimony, and George Smith had, quite literally, been laughed out of court.

It was clear that the tide was beginning to turn. When Fanny and Stella emerged from Westminster Hall at the end of the second day's proceedings, the large waiting crowd in Palace Yard cheered and clapped them, drowning out the feeble chorus of boos and hisses.

After spending the day observing the trial, it was not surprising that Simeon Solomon was in no doubt about the outcome. 'Of course they will be acquitted,' he told Swinburne.

As Fanny and Stella were whirled away in their cab, Stella, wreathed in smiles and looking radiant, blew kisses to all and sundry.

28

A Rout

The conception of criminal justice which the atmosphere of Scotland Yard fosters is pretty much the same as that which has existed for countless ages in the empire of China. If a crime has been discovered, the majesty of the law must be vindicated by the punishment of somebody. But it is a minor consideration who that somebody shall be. The police have in a great measure lost the faculty of seeing things as they are, and not as they wish them to be.

The Times, 25th July 1871

The Attorney-General knew that his last and best hope of a conviction in this case was the evidence of the two medical men: Dr Richard Barwell and Dr James Paul. Never mind that five of the six doctors who had so minutely examined the parts of Boulton and Park in Newgate Gaol were of the opinion that there were no signs of sodomy present. Those five doctors had examined the young men only after they had been in custody for almost six weeks, six long weeks during which the worst of their sodomitic injuries, if the Attorney-General could so phrase it, would have had the opportunity to heal and fade from view.

But Dr Barwell had treated Frederick Park for chancre of the anus at Charing Cross Hospital when that young man had come in using a false name and disguised as a respectable clerk from the poorer classes. He had seen him week in and week out over a period of three months and he could and would speak authoritatively to the extraordinary state of sodomitic disease that obtained in this young man's posterior parts.

Dr Paul was the police doctor who had examined Fanny and Stella in a dingy room at the back of Bow Street Magistrates' Court on the morning after their arrest. He had been shocked and horrified – indeed he had been turned quite pale – by the gaping anuses and the deformed and elongated penises of these young men, signs and symptoms which, according to the texts on the subject, could only have been caused by persistent sodomitic indulgence on a scale which beggared belief.

Both these medical gentlemen had seen the signs and symptoms of sodomy written in scarlet upon the bodies of these two young men in exceptional and in intimate detail. Surely a jury of twelve Englishmen good and true would be obliged to give credence to the testimony of Dr Paul and Dr Barwell over that of five doctors who had examined Boulton and Park only long after their sodomitic crimes had been forcibly ceased?

For his part, Dr Barwell was indignant. Indignant still, a year on, that he had been forced, under threat of a summons, to testify in this case against his wishes and against what he considered to be his professional duty of confidence to his patients, even patients like the three young sodomites who had attended his clinic in as many weeks. And newly indignant that his word as to the identity of the young man he had treated for the syphilitic affliction of the anus was now being so heavily challenged by counsel for the defence. Those legal gentlemen thought themselves very clever, so very clever (and no doubt they were) in the way they sowed their seeds of confusion and uncertainty in the minds of the Jurymen; so very clever in the way they tried to trip him up; so very clever in the way they tried to make out that *he* was confused, mistaken or misled – if not actually lying under oath. And he was well aware that the more indignant and the more insistent he became, the less credible he appeared. But *he* knew, beyond any doubt, that the young man Park standing in the dock – though stouter now, better dressed and sporting manly whiskers – was the same young man who had stood trembling before him in his room at Charing Cross Hospital with an affliction of the anus and mutely pleading for help.

When his turn came, Dr Paul stood up in Westminster Hall manfully and repeated his shocking findings as to the state of the orifices of evacuation and the organs of generation of Ernest Boulton and Frederick Park. There was no denying that his account was clear, concise and compelling. He had been the first doctor to examine these youths just hours after they were taken from the streets and it was clear that they had both recently engaged in sodomitical activities. So far Dr Paul was proving to be a strong witness, perhaps the strongest witness for the prosecution, and the Attorney-General was well pleased.

'What is that book in your pocket?' demanded Mr Digby Seymour. It was a curious and abrupt way to open a cross-examination.

'This?' replied Dr Paul, pulling the book from his coat pocket and feeling surprised and not a little flustered by the question. 'This is a work of Tardieu's.'

The book in question was Professor Ambroise Tardieu's *Étude médico-légale sur les attentats aux mœurs*, a famous work of scientific observation upon the ways and wiles of sodomites in Paris, a manual intended for doctors, especially police doctors like Dr Paul, on how to read the unmistakable signs of sodomy which the good professor believed were forensically engraved upon the bodies of sodomites.

'Have you been studying Tardieu lately?' Mr Seymour enquired, with an ever so slight and sarcastic emphasis on the word 'studying'.

'I have read it today,' Dr Paul replied, reddening. 'I have had it fifteen months.'

Fifteen months? Indeed? Mr Seymour seized on this like a ferret. 'That would be about the time you bought it with reference to this case?' he suggested.

Dr Paul opened his mouth to reply but no words came forth.

'Not so long ago as fifteen months,' he said after an embarrassingly long pause. 'I never heard of it until I had given evidence in this case.'

'Who told you of it?'

'An – an anonymous letter that I received,' he stuttered out after another pause.

It was clear to all that Dr Paul was lying. But why had he lied under oath, on such a subject, and lied so palpably, and so badly? And why had he come up with the barely credible story that an anonymous admirer had written to alert him to the existence of the book? Surely the date when he actually read the book was of little or no moment? February or May 1870. Two months before the arrest of Fanny or Stella. Or two months afterwards. Did it really matter all that much?

It mattered a great deal. If Dr Paul's first answer was true – if indeed he had acquired his copy of Tardieu in February 1870, a full two months before the arrest of Fanny and Stella – then it meant that something was amiss. It meant that there was more to the arrest of Fanny and Stella than met the eye.

It meant that Dr Paul had, in short, been priming himself and preparing himself for the day when he would examine Fanny and Stella for signs of sodomy.

There was more.

Mr Sergeant Parry, defending Fanny Park, dragged from a very reluctant Dr Paul the curious admission that he had met with Inspector Thompson on the Sunday *before* the arrest of Fanny and Stella.

'Just attend to me,' Mr Sergeant Parry instructed Dr Paul, whose attention appeared to be wandering. 'You say Inspector Thompson called on you on the Sunday before. This is before these young men were apprehended?'

'Exactly,' Dr Paul replied with a certainty he clearly did not feel.

'Did he tell you he was on the watch for them?'

'Certainly not.' Dr Paul's reply was just a little too emphatic, a little too shrill, to be convincing.

'He did not communicate with you on that subject?' Mr Sergeant Parry enquired with a note of evident surprise.

'Not in the least.'

'Then he called to pay you a *friendly* visit?' Mr Sergeant Parry's sarcasm was undisguised.

'No, it was something about the attendance on some man,' Dr Paul replied falteringly, conveniently forgetting that he had just said he saw Inspector Thompson every day – or almost every day – at Bow Street and that it was as unlikely as it was inconvenient that Inspector Thompson would journey halfway across London on a Sunday to discuss Dr Paul's attendance on 'some man'.

'It was not in reference to this case at all?' persisted Mr Sergeant Parry.

'Not in the least,' Dr Paul answered with as much certainty as he could muster.

It was again clear to everyone present that Dr Paul was lying, and that Inspector Thompson's highly unusual house call was in some unfathomable way connected with the arrest four days later of the Young Men in Women's Clothes.

And was it really a coincidence, Mr Sergeant Parry wanted to know, a mere accident, as Dr Paul tried to suggest, that he just happened to be passing, just happened to be loitering without intent, outside the entrance to Bow Street Magistrates' Court at exactly one o'clock in the afternoon on Friday, 29th April, the day after Fanny and Stella's arrest, at precisely the same time as Fanny and Stella were leaving Mr Flowers's courtroom? And again, was it really a coincidence that, at that very moment, he was spotted by an unnamed and lowly police constable who just happened to have been sent by Inspector Thompson to see if he could find Dr Paul to ask him to come and examine the Funny He-She Ladies?

And what of the examination itself? On this thorny subject the wretched Dr Paul was subjected to a devastating catechism and chastisement at the hands of Mr Digby Seymour, who questioned the legitimacy, and indeed the legality, of such an examination.

'Had you received any Magistrate's order or any authority to make this examination?' Mr Digby Seymour enquired.

'I was in the street and the policeman came and told me that Inspector Thompson wanted me,' Dr Paul answered shakily. 'When I got there Inspector Thompson said, "Sir Thomas Henry has ordered that you are to examine these men."' Sir Thomas Henry was the senior Stipendiary Magistrate at Bow Street.

'Have you ever stated before that there was any order from Sir Thomas Henry?' asked Mr Digby Seymour. 'Have you not always said that you acted upon your own responsibility?'

Dr Paul mumbled a confused reply to the effect that he had never been allowed to explain himself properly.

'Did it occur to you', Mr Digby Seymour concluded, 'that it would be a matter of simple fairness to have a medical man representing Boulton present when this examination was going on?'

There was another long and unfortunate pause.

'No,' Dr Paul replied in a stricken voice.

It was left to the Lord Chief Justice to destroy what little credibility remained to Dr Paul. 'You should be more careful in future or you may find yourself involved in very unpleasant consequences,' he warned Dr Paul sternly. 'I am not aware that the mere fact of your being Surgeon to the Police Force entitles you to send a man behind a screen and examine him for any purpose you may think necessary. You had no more authority to call upon these young men to undergo this revolting examination,' he continued, 'than if you had sought a man in the street and asked him to unbutton his breeches.'

Something very curious was happening. As one conspiracy seemed to melt away like the morning mist, a new and very different conspiracy was emerging from the shadows. The steady stream of damaging revelations and admissions from other prosecution witnesses, taken together with Dr Paul's transparent lies, strongly suggested that the police, the politicians and the powers that be in the Treasury had conspired together in preparing the arrest and prosecution of Fanny and Stella.

Mr George Smith, the ex-Beadle of the Burlington Arcade, had boastfully claimed that he had been 'getting up evidence for the police in this little affair', a most unfortunate choice of words. And he had admitted to meeting with Inspector Thompson fully four days *before* the arrest of Fanny and Stella, which to a suspicious mind might suggest that the arrest was planned and premeditated.

More damaging still was Smith's claim that Inspector Thompson had promised to 'pay him for his trouble'. That and the fact that he received the sum of fourteen shillings from Mr William Pollard, the Assistant Treasury Solicitor, who had so energetically and assiduously interviewed all the witnesses in this case before they appeared in court (which was in itself a highly unusual proceeding). To make matters worse (if they could be made any worse), the loquacious Mr Smith had hinted that some sort of promise had been held out to him of 'a situation at the Treasury', a prospect which Smith declared he would most certainly 'not object to'.

Then there were the admissions from certain police officers of 'E' Division that Fanny and Stella had been under continuous and extensive police surveillance. 'I have watched them for a year past,' Detective Officer Chamberlain had asserted. 'I have seen them at the Casino in Holborn, and I have seen them in Brunswick Square, and in Southampton Row.' Stella's return from Edinburgh, three weeks before the arrest, had triggered day-and-night surveillance of Martha Stacey's house of accommodation in Wakefield Street by Police Constable Charles Walker, who said he had watched the house for a marathon twenty days and twenty nights.

Surveillance by plain-clothes officers was a new weapon in the armoury of the police. Sir Richard Mayne, the zealous and authoritarian Commissioner of the Metropolitan Police, had established an unofficial special branch in the 1860s to engage in spying and surveillance. Plain-clothes detective officers were sent all over London to report back to the Commissioner on those considered a threat to the nation's security, threats which ranged from the serious to the faintly ridiculous.

Anything or anyone that had the potential to threaten the state was relentlessly surveilled. The Trade Unions were regularly spied upon, as were 'meetings of the unemployed', both seen as potential hotbeds of revolutionary change. One detective had filed a report on a meeting he attended in Soho Square on the subject of 'Maladministration of the Law'. Another reported on 'a speech made by Mr Bradlaugh at the New Hall of Science, Old Street, on Percy Bysshe Shelley'. Charles Bradlaugh was a declared atheist and was thus seen as a threat to the status quo.

Day-and-night surveillance was expensive and was usually restricted to master criminals, anarchists, Fenian conspirators and foreign spies. It seemed decidedly odd to place the activities of two feather-pated young men like Fanny and Stella, barely out of their teens, on a par with the Fenian bombers. Their frivolous chitter-chatter and their endless forays in drag might be immoral (most would say disgusting, unmanly and un-Christian to boot), but it was not – as yet – a crime to dress up as a woman.

Mr Digby Seymour and the entire defence counsel were at very considerable pains to stress the youthfulness and the boyishness of Fanny and Stella. They were 'young Mr Boulton' and 'young Mr Park'; they were 'boys' or 'little more than boys'; they were 'youths' and 'young men'; they were 'dainty lads' and 'pleasing boys': unformed and unfinished, prone to larks and high spirits, as all boys are. And certainly, they were sometimes foolish, sometimes thoughtless, and sometimes heedless of the consequences of their actions – as all boys are. But foolishness should not be confused with wickedness, nor folly conflated with vice.

And even if there had been goings-on, sodomitical shilly-shallyings, between these two foolish young men and others in their circle, what of it? Did their sordid sexual misadventures really merit such lavish attention from the Metropolitan Police? Hardly a week went by without one or more prurient reports of trials for 'abominable' and 'unnatural' offences between men committed throughout the length and breadth of the land. So, what, if anything, was special about Fanny and Stella?

There were more uncomfortable disclosures. Mr William Pollard confirmed that the Treasury Solicitor, Mr John Greenwood, had from the very beginning taken personal charge of the prosecution until his untimely death two months earlier. Surely this very eminent and very important gentleman had bigger fish to fry? Surely he had better things to do than busy himself with the doings of two young men who liked to dress as women?

And how was it that the conspiracy charges against Fanny and Stella were ready and waiting for them on the morning after their arrest? In the normal course of events, such an indictment would have taken weeks, if not months, to prepare. Reports of surveillance would have had to be written and submitted, summaries of evidence prepared and considered, and senior police officers like Inspector Thompson – and perhaps even the Commissioner himself – quizzed before the final indictment could be drafted.

Such a serious prosecution would certainly require the knowledge and approval not only of Mr John Greenwood himself, but quite probably of the other senior Government law officers, the Solicitor-General and the Attorney-General, and perhaps even beyond. Sir Robert Collier had already let slip that the Home Secretary had taken a strong personal interest in this case and was driving the relentless prosecution of these two young men.

Then there were the secret and not-so-secret payments to witnesses for the prosecution. George Smith freely admitted that he had received fourteen shillings, even though there was no record of this payment in the Treasury Register. But the Treasury Register *did* record payments to Francis Kegan Cox and to Maria George, *née* Duffin, via Inspector Thompson: '679 – Dec 1870 – R. v Boulton and Park – Direct payment to Inspector Thompson of amounts paid to Maria Duffin – I authorise further advances as may be necessary.'

It was all very worrying. Why should Mr Cox receive payment for doing his public duty and testifying to criminal acts? And why was Inspector Thompson making payments, payments *plural*, to Maria George, *née* Duffin? There was indisputable evidence that three witnesses were being paid. How many more witnesses were being paid? And for what? Something was wrong.

More worrying still was the entry in the Treasury Register detailing payments to the three policemen most closely connected with this case: '492 – Dec 1870 – R. v Boulton and Park – To pay £5 – £3 – £2 to Inspector Thompson, Sergeant Kerley, and Detective Officer Chamberlain.'

It was almost unheard of for officers of the Metropolitan Police to receive a gratuity in the ordinary course of their duty.

Gratuities were only ever given upon retirement from the force. There might be exceptional circumstances when the Commissioner might advance a small sum to relieve hardship, but such payments were rare. Why, then, was the Treasury doling out these 'rewards', as Mr Digby Seymour contemptuously termed them, to salaried officers of the Metropolitan Police? It was all very irregular.

Spying, surveillance, bribery, collusion, corruption and political interference at the highest levels. What on earth was going on? Could it be that this prosecution was in some way political? Had it something to do with the late Lord Arthur Clinton? Or was it an ill-conceived and badly executed attempt to extirpate the scourge of sodomy from the land by holding a solemn state trial which would serve as a terrible example and warning to any and all young men tempted to indulge in this criminal folly?

Whatever the motives, the prosecution was in utter disarray. It was a rout, there was no other word for it. All that remained was the ugly stench of conspiracy and corruption and the abhorrent spectacle of justice being seen to be *un*done.

29

'This Terrible Drama of Vice'

> She watches, if his cheek grows pale,
> She watches, if his glad smile fail,
> She watches, if a sigh he breathes,
> And if he sorrows, then she grieves;
> She watches for his safe return,
> Through life, the mother watches on.
>
> Fanny Fales, 'A Mother's Love', 1853

Mrs Mary Ann Boulton was the object of the greatest curiosity and the greatest compassion as she stepped into the witness box to speak in defence of her beloved and beleaguered son.

Mrs Mary Ann Boulton looked frail and she looked old, though she could not have been much more than fifty, if that. That there had been trials in her life – quite apart from this latest great and grand trial – was evident from the lines etched upon her face. She looked worn out by cares and worries. Nevertheless, she was sombrely and respectfully dressed in deference to the solemnity of the occasion, though she had taken care to follow Mr George Lewis's sage advice not to wear black in case it looked as if she were already in mourning for Ernest. Her eyes were red and swollen as if from recent tears, and her voice was a little hoarse as though she were labouring under great emotion.

But here she stood, proud and unafraid. She was not here to apologise or to explain. She was not here to beg or to plead. She was here to speak truth to power, to tell the highest judge in the land in the highest court in the land that Ernest was innocent of the terrible crimes and dark conspiracies imputed to him. She was here to tell the world about her son, about her 'own beloved Child'. The thought of him made her eyes prick again with hot tears and her chest swell with a mother's love.

It was obvious that Mrs Mary Ann Boulton was not a well woman, that she was some sort of invalid, though the nature of her affliction was not known. Her doctor had, of course, warned her not to appear. She badly 'wanted strength', he had said. The ordeal would be too much for her. It could set her back. But she had dismissed his concerns and ignored the butterfly flutterings of her heart and steeled herself to fight for her child, like a tigress defending her young. And so when Mr Digby Seymour asked, 'Are you the mother of Mr Ernest Boulton?' she had answered in a clear voice replete with strength and pride and love.

'I am,' she declared.

It was a powerful beginning.

But where was Mr Thomas Boulton? That was the unspoken question on everyone's lips. Surely as a husband and a father he should have been in court in the stead of his wife in this hour of need. Why must Mrs Mary Ann Boulton endure such a terrible ordeal alone and unprotected? But if there was a ripple of indignation it was quickly followed by a wave of sympathy for the bravery and courage of this frail woman so ready and so willing to fight in hand-to-hand combat for her beloved son.

Which was exactly what Mr George Lewis had had in his

mind when he persuaded Mrs Mary Ann Boulton that she, and she alone – unencumbered by her husband – was Ernest's best hope of acquittal. A mother's love, a mother's loyalty was more powerful and more potent in the eyes and in the hearts of a jury of twelve Englishmen good and true than all the legal arguments in the world.

So Mr Boulton had been despatched to the Cape of Good Hope on some ship-broking errand which would brook no delay. He was, in consequence, safely out of the way, leaving the stage clear for what promised to be the greatest performance of Mrs Mary Ann Boulton's entire life.

Mrs Mary Ann Boulton still clung to the sweetly pretty fashions of her youth and wore her hair in the same girlish bunched ringlets which had so captivated Thomas Boulton during their courtship. In those distant, happier days, her ringlets softly shook like the May blossom on the trees when she laughed or when she sang. And even though, today, these same ringlets trembled with suppressed pain, passion and emotion, Mrs Mary Ann Boulton still recalled to the minds of those present a happier and more certain age, a less cynical and less sordid age of bluer skies and brighter promise.

Who could not but be impressed by the admirable Mrs Mary Ann Boulton? She was all courtesy and all attention. She had a very particular and refreshingly pleasing way of inclining her head in mute respect and deference to her gentlemanly interlocutors, as if bowing to their superior knowledge. When questions were put to her, she listened hard (and was seen to listen hard), and when she replied to those selfsame questions she did not so much answer as wholeheartedly agree. 'Exactly so', she would answer. 'Entirely so', 'Quite so', and 'Certainly', she would say with a reassuring nod and an eager smile.

And sometimes when it fell to her to recall the happy days and the sad days, a tear would glint like a diamond in her eye, and there would be a fresh rush of sympathy and love for this frail but strong Mother among Mothers. Counsel for the prosecution and the defence alike, even the Lord Chief Justice himself, treated her with kid gloves. Consequently, she got away with murder, or as good as. Difficult questions that really demanded a clear and direct answer were brushed aside or answered instead with a fondly recalled family anecdote.

If all else failed, Mrs Mary Ann Boulton could rely on her memory, or rather, her lack of a memory. 'I have not at all a retentive memory,' she would say. 'I cannot remember', 'I do not remember at all', 'I may have forgotten', 'I should be afraid to say exactly' and 'I could not say positively' were endlessly combined and confederated and given out with such charming conviction that it would have been hard – not to say heartless – to insist on pursuing the fox to the kill.

Mrs Mary Ann Boulton had a very confiding and a very including manner of expressing herself, a manner that drew people in, and once she had begun to speak she could not stop. She told Ernest's life story (and much of her own) in a series of sweetly charming vignettes which she acted out before the court. She would recall and repeat entire conversations and then pause and look about her to see the effect of her words. She conjured up the past so naturally, so guilelessly, that the entire court was transfixed and transported. When she swelled with pride or shuddered with dread, the court swelled and shuddered with her. When she smiled or she laughed, or was indignant or angry, the court smiled and laughed, and was equally indignant, equally angry.

Ernest: A Story of Sweetness and Light. It might have been

the title of a sentimental tract upon the sanctity of a mother's love for a son. And a son's devotion to his mother. A tract upon courage and fortitude in the face of suffering. A tract upon hope, faith and perseverance. Most of all it was a tract upon innocence – innocence of heart, innocence of deed and innocence of thought.

Ernest. A much-wanted and much-loved child, weak and sickly from birth. So weak and so sickly that Mrs Mary Ann Boulton had had to fret and fuss over her boy. A delicate, fragile boy who delighted in dressing up and in acting. And yes, they had rather encouraged it, as it seemed to make him happy. (And who could deny a sickly child those few precious moments of happiness?)

Ernest. Such a clever, funny child. A little boy who had dressed up as the maidservant and waited at table, even fooling his Grandmamma. Ernest, with the voice of an angel, who would make grown men weep when he sang.

Life had not been easy. Mr Boulton's business affairs, never on the firmest of footings, had gone from bad to worse, and they had experienced great reverses. Not that she had ever allowed any shadow to fall on her two boys. *She* would go without – indeed she had gone without – rather than let her sons suffer in any way.

Ernest had gone out to work, but his health could not cope with the rigours of the London and County Bank. So *she* had put her foot down, and Ernest had resigned, to devote himself to performing. He had performed at charitable benefits in town, and toured the county of Essex with Mr Pavitt, where his reception had been something wonderful. Bouquets, some dozens of bouquets, had been thrown upon the stage. He had performed professionally in Scarborough with Lord Arthur

Clinton. And yes, she had kept every single programme, every single newspaper clipping and every photograph of Ernest in character. What Mother worthy of the name would not swell with pride at her son's successes?

Then a shadow had fallen. Her worst fears had been re-alised. Ernest's health deteriorated. He got worse and after a year of the *greatest* anxiety they were told that he must have an operation to save his life. She had never known such dread. But she had put a brave face on it. She had smiled and laughed and told Ernest to take no notice of his silly old Mamma weeping over a trifle.

It was all most affecting, and there were tears in Mrs Mary Ann Boulton's eyes as she spoke, and lumps in the throats of many of those present in court.

'Ernest has been a most dutiful and affectionate son,' she proclaimed, smiling radiantly across the courtroom at him. 'The *only* fault he ever had was a love of admiration which has been fed by the gross flattery of *some* very foolish people.' She would go no further than that. She would not name names. *They* knew who they were and that was enough. It was because of *them* that her dear darling boy was standing where he was today.

There was barely a dry eye in the house, and if the Ancient and Honourable Court of Queen's Bench had been a theatre (which in a way it was), then Mrs Mary Ann Boulton would most certainly have received a standing ovation, and bouquets – some dozens of bouquets – would have been thrown. As it was, there was an appreciative hum, with much noisy clearing of throats and many blowings of noses.

Mr Digby Seymour bore more than a passing resemblance to a well-fed cat. He was sleek and smooth and shiny with luxuriant white whiskers. Though rotund, he was surprisingly nimble on his feet, and his voice, with just a touch of his native Irish brogue, was soothing and calming and altogether reassuring. But his eyes were sharp and ever watchful, and he could turn in an instant to snarl and scratch and rend and tear, as the unfortunate Dr Paul had discovered to his cost.

Mr Digby Seymour rubbed his hands together and positively purred. He had taken Mrs Mary Ann Boulton by the hand and with the greatest courtesy, charm and solicitude guided that good lady through her testimony. It had all gone very well. Better than he had dared to hope.

Mrs Mary Ann Boulton had held the court spellbound. Her account of Ernest's life had been as compelling as it was consistent, and it had swept all before it. No matter that it was sugary and sentimental, almost to the point of sickliness. No matter that it was partial and incomplete. No matter that her memory had so consistently and conveniently failed her. She had risen above the morass and mire of claim and counterclaim, of truths, untruths and half-truths, of opinion, conjecture and speculation, and revealed the higher and the greater truth of a mother's love for her son. Mrs Mary Ann Boulton had convinced herself of the truth of her testimony, and in consequence she had convinced everyone else.

Mr Digby Seymour knew that the lacklustre performance of his esteemed colleague and friend the Attorney-General had signally failed to prove the case for the prosecution. But it did not necessarily follow that the trial would result in an acquittal. Juries were fickle, frightened creatures who turned this way and that depending on the direction of the wind and the scent in their nostrils. They needed certainty and they needed convincement: commodities which, fortunately for the defence,

Mrs Mary Ann Boulton had provided in spades with her Authorised Version of Ernest's life. From now on hers would be the gold standard of truth against which every other scrap of evidence must be weighed and measured and judged.

Mrs Mary Ann Boulton was invoked at every possible opportunity by Mr Digby Seymour: 'We know as a fact from Mrs Boulton,' he would say. 'We have it proved by Mrs Boulton' and 'Mrs Boulton swears' and so on and so forth. For every alleged crime and misdemeanour, for every fact and circumstance that told against her son, Mrs Boulton's seemingly guileless, garrulous testimony was a perfect and complete antidote. She was a universal panacea, a potent remedy of last resort.

Almost every plank of the case for the prosecution was upended and demolished by the asseverations of Mrs Mary Ann Boulton. All was open and above board. She knew about everything and everyone, and everything and everyone had met with her approval. She knew nearly all the defendants in this alleged conspiracy. She knew Mr Frederick Park as her son's intimate friend and fellow enthusiast for the theatre. Frederick often stayed with them and had stoically and devotedly helped to nurse Ernest back to health after his terrible surgical ordeal. She approved of the friendship between these two young men, and why on earth should she not?

Mr Louis Hurt was 'a friend that we esteemed'. He had been a frequent guest at their home. It was not at all a secret that Mr Hurt and her son corresponded – in fact, Ernest always read Mr Hurt's entertaining letters aloud to her and there was never so much as a *hint* of impropriety in them. She had encouraged Ernest to accept Mr Hurt's kind invitation to spend a few weeks recuperating in the bracing air of Edinburgh after his operation. She had supplied Ernest with more than adequate

funds for this visit. Indeed, Ernest had always been well supplied with funds. (So why, Mr Digby Seymour was at pains to
point out to the Jury, would there be any need for him to prostitute himself to men for money?)

Mrs Mary Ann Boulton had been no less approving of
Ernest's friendship with the late Lord Arthur Pelham-Clinton.
The acquaintance had been formed in circumstances of the
utmost respectability. She herself had been present on the
occasion of a dinner given by Mr and Mrs Richards at which
Lord Arthur was also a guest. He had become a friend of the
family and visited them in Dulwich on occasions too numerous
to mention.

Yes, she was fully aware that Ernest personated women in
private theatricals, on the amateur stage, and latterly on the
professional stage. Ernest had her full sanction and approval.
Indeed, she had even given him one or two of her old dresses.

If Ernest Boulton's own mother did not object to these theatrical *jeunesses*, to these burlesques, to these dressings-up in
women's clothes, so Mr Digby Seymour's persuasive argument
ran, if *she* could not see the harm in this play-acting and panto-
miming and make-believe, then was it not reasonable to assume
there was no *real* harm in the behaviour of these young men?

Mrs Mary Ann Boulton knew, too, that her Ernest's friends
and fellow enthusiasts for all things theatrical – Mr Park, Mr
Cumming, Mr Thomas, the late Lord Arthur Clinton and
others whose names she could not presently recall – used to
call her son 'Stella' by way of a nickname. There was nothing
sinister or secret about it. It was merely a jest and a joke among
boys and she had laughed along with them.

Now, Mr Digby Seymour argued, if there had been anything
untoward, anything unsavoury, anything indicative of unnatur-

al vice in the use of this nickname (as the prosecution had most odiously suggested), then surely Mrs Boulton would have recoiled from its use, as if from the serpent's kiss itself?

As to the photographs of young Mr Boulton attired in female costume, what of them? The Attorney-General had made much of them, suggesting that they were in some way indicative of a tendency towards unnatural vice. 'But there is nothing indecent or indelicate in these photographs, nothing to shock the most critical morality, nothing to disturb the most refined taste,' Mr Digby Seymour protested. Had not Mrs Boulton been shown each and every one of these photographs of her son so attired? 'My son sent me every one,' she had said, more than once. And had she not collected them in an album and kept them, along with the theatrical programmes, the newspaper notices and other related ephemera as memoranda of her son's growing success and fame?

If these photographs were what the Attorney-General so filthily suggested, was it conceivable that a son would dare to expose them to the gaze of his mother, or that Mrs Boulton could have borne to look at (let alone collect and keep) such photographs without revulsion?

And this led Mr Digby Seymour on quite naturally to the whole subject of openness and concealment which went to the very heart of the matter. He did not and could not constitute himself an expert in the ways and means of the dark vice imputed to the defendants, but it struck him forcibly, most forcibly indeed, that the very openness of Boulton and Park's conduct told strongly in their favour. There was no concealment, no attempt at concealment. On the contrary, there was flaunting and there was display – in theatres, in casinos and in public places. These young men went to any and all lengths to draw attention to themselves, to advertise themselves, to announce themselves to the world.

'You would expect a different kind of conduct,' said Mr Digby Seymour, 'you would expect a secret hiding from the sight of men and women. They would try to avoid exciting the suspicions of others. They would shrink and hide away and draw over themselves and their horrible deeds a pall of darkness.' 'Would young men engaged in the exchange of wicked and accursed embraces put on the dresses of women and go to theatres and public places for the purpose of exciting each other to the commission of this outrageous crime?' he asked theatrically.

'Gentlemen,' he answered himself solemnly, 'the very *absurdity* of the suggestion is its own refutation.'

Lastly and with the greatest reluctance, Mr Digby Seymour was obliged to turn to the medical part of the evidence.

'Ernest Boulton comes accused of being the principal actor, or rather, Gentlemen, the principal *sufferer* in yielding to the habitual embraces of others in this terrible drama of vice,' he began. But a majority – five out of six – of the eminent medical men, 'men of the highest position in their profession', who examined the state of this young man's parts in Newgate Gaol, 'were strong and emphatic that there is not one trace, from beginning to end, not one particle of evidence in favour of his guilt'.

'Not one trace and not one particle,' he repeated.

That left just two medical gentlemen, Dr Richard Barwell and Dr James Paul, whose testimony suggested that young Mr Boulton had indulged in these 'vile and wicked practices'. But under cross-examination Dr Barwell had reluctantly admitted that he could not be absolutely certain that the condition of the parts of Ernest Boulton was the consequence of unnatural acts.

His was a conjecture merely, a speculation, no doubt arrived at with the best of intentions, but still a conclusion that was subjective and open to contest and to challenge.

And then there was Dr Paul. Well, the less said about *that* gentleman the better. And with that, Mr Digby Seymour assumed an expression of dignified contempt. 'Dr Paul who gave us a story so absurd, after an examination so unsatisfactory, that I shall not say another word about it.'

Besides, Mrs Boulton had given a compelling account of the very serious illness suffered by her son which culminated, after many months of severe – the severest – pain, in an operation to save his life. No one who had listened to her deeply affecting account could be in any doubt as to its veracity.

Mr Digby Seymour wished to deal with and dispose of the medical evidence once and for all. Throughout the entire period when, according to the Attorney-General, young Mr Boulton was the willing pathic, if he could so term it, of Lord Arthur Clinton, of Mr Louis Hurt and Mr John Safford Fiske, throughout the period when he was, apparently, being sodomised by dozens – perhaps even hundreds – of unknown and unnamed men, it was an indisputable and an undeniable fact that he was suffering from (or latterly recovering from) the terrible and painful affliction of *fistula in ano* and was, in consequence, 'morbidly sensible to pain'.

Was it conceivable, was it credible, that this young man, already in agony in those delicate parts, would consent to further add to that agony, to further augment it, by allowing himself to be sodomised – as the Attorney-General alleged – at every possible opportunity, when such acts must have created 'the most exquisite torture'?

Mr Digby Seymour threw himself upon the common sense

of the Jury. 'Surely, Gentlemen,' he reasoned, 'you will say that Ernest Boulton was the very *last* being alive as to whom you would entertain the suspicion that he would be the suffering and the yielding party to the perpetration of such an offence? I put it before you almost as a *physical impossibility*.'

Mr Digby Seymour had made his point well. There were murmurs and nods of agreement, and the Gentlemen of the Jury shifted uncomfortably on their hard benches, their eyes positively watering at the very thought of such exquisite torture.

Mr Digby Seymour knew that he bore a heavy burden of responsibility. Perhaps the heaviest burden. The Attorney-General had roped together, as it were, all the defendants, which meant that if one fell, they all fell. And if one was found innocent, all were innocent.

But it was *his* client, young Ernest Boulton, who bore the brunt of the prosecution. He was at the dark heart of this spider's web of sodomy and corruption. He was the lynchpin and the king-post of this conspiracy. All roads led to him and all roads led from him. Stella, the shining star to whom all were drawn. Stella, the glittering sun around whom all orbited. Four of the defendants were Ernest Boulton's paramours, the remaining three his friends and fellow female personators. Without Ernest Boulton there could be no conspiracy. Without Ernest Boulton there was no case. All the evidence, all the evidence that really mattered – the letters and photographs; the tittle-tattle of servants and landladies and ladies' retiring-room attendants; the observations and insinuations of Dr Paul – all of it was focused and concentrated on Ernest Boulton. Acquit Ernest Boulton, and all would be acquitted.

There were what looked like tears in Mr Digby Seymour's

eyes and there was a break in his voice as he imploringly invoked the image of Mrs Mary Ann Boulton one last time. He beseeched the Jury to acquit this mother's child, this mother's most dutiful and most affectionate son. A young man who could so inspire the love and loyalty and admiration of this Mother among Mothers could surely not be 'capable of plunging at his young age into the depths of this terrible defilement'.

'Pronounce by your verdict that there may be folly, but not guilt,' Mr Digby Seymour enjoined, his oratory beginning to soar like a lark on the wing. 'Pronounce by your verdict that there may be extravagance; that there may be madness, if you please, in the indulgence of this fancy on the part of my client. But you will require stronger evidence than this before you come to the conclusion that these men are guilty of the terrible charge made against them.'

Mr Digby Seymour paused and took a deep and portentous breath before his final peroration.

'I say that, in a case like this, I trust your verdict will establish that the moral atmosphere of England is not yet tainted with the impurities of continental cities, and from our island position we are insulated from these outrages upon Decency, Morality and Nature itself.

'I trust that you will pronounce by your verdict that London is not cursed with the sins of Sodom, or Westminster tainted with the vices of Gomorrah.'

And with that powerful and patriotic rallying call to reject and renounce the very idea of sodomy and sodomites stalking England's green and pleasant land, Mr Digby Seymour abruptly and dramatically sat down.

I t was a few minutes before five o'clock when the Jurymen filed back into the Ancient and Honourable Court of Queen's Bench. It had taken them just fifty-three minutes to consider their verdict. Such a short deliberation was extremely unusual, especially in a case so complex and important.

According to the collective wisdom of the counsel assembled in Westminster Hall that afternoon, such a perfunctory consideration meant one of two things: either the guilt of the defendants was so evident, or their innocence so shining, that little or no discussion was needed to reach a verdict.

'Gentlemen, are you all agreed?' the Clerk of the Court asked the Jurymen. 'Do you find the defendants guilty or not guilty?'

'*Not* guilty,' replied the Foreman emphatically, at which there was an outbreak of wild cheers and whistles and loud cries of 'Bravo!'

'Upon all counts of the indictment?' the Lord Chief Justice asked, struggling to make himself heard above the din.

'Yes, my Lord. Not guilty on *all* the counts.'

As all eyes turned towards the defendants, Stella, with perfect timing, swayed melodramatically, and fell into a dead faint.

30

Clouds and Sunshine

Rose of the garden,
Blushing and gay. . .
E'en as we pluck thee,
Fading away!

Anne Fricker, 'Fading Away', 1854

MR ERNEST BOULTON begs to thank those managers
who have offered engagements, but intends to resume the
Drawing-Room Entertainment in which he originally
appeared. He is desirous of meeting with a gentleman
who is musical, has a good voice, and who could take one
of the leading parts in the entertainment — Address, &c.

Reynolds's Newspaper, 6th August 1871

Just two months after her sensational acquittal at Westminster Hall, Stella was eager to be back in the theatrical saddle. Though the trial had taken a very considerable toll upon her fragile health and strength, she was nevertheless resolved to return to the stage at any and at all costs.

Besides, what choice did she have? A respectable life was closed to her for ever. Who would marry her now? The stench and taint of sodomy was upon her and she was now so notorious that even going on the pad was unthinkable. She would be recognised at once and hauled straight back to court.

Of course, she could always scarper abroad, as so many of her friends and acquaintance had done, like rats fleeing a sinking ship. But Miss Stella Boulton was made of sterner stuff. She had not come this far, through tribulations and through trials, through fire and through flame, to turn and run, to hide herself away from the light of day and live a haunted and hunted life.

No matter that she was notorious. No matter that her name was on everyone's lips – for all the wrong reasons. Miss Stella Boulton was defiant. She would snatch victory from the jaws of defeat. She would steal fame from infamy. She would take up where she had left off, return to the stage and be a shining star. The world had most certainly not heard the last of Miss Stella Boulton.

But Stella had a problem. She needed a leading man.

Lord Arthur Clinton was dead and buried (though that strange story had more than its fair share of doubters and disbelievers). Dead or alive, Lord Arthur was, in any event, no longer at liberty to play Sir Edward Ardent to her Fanny Chillingtone.

So Stella took the bold and unusual step of advertising for a leading man. She had no idea how many – if any – applicants there would be. But at least one, Mr Louis Munro, a gentleman in the prime of life, rose to the challenge, and by the early autumn of 1871 Stella and her dashingly handsome new leading man (off stage as well as on stage) were embarked on an ambitious tour of the Midlands and the North.

'Mr Ernest Boulton in his Drawing-Room Entertainment,' the advertisement in the *Liverpool Mercury* proclaimed. 'Mr Ernest Boulton in his unrivalled impersonation of the Female Character. As played before the Mayors of Oldham, Macclesfield and Other Towns to Crowded Houses.'

According to a gushing review in that organ, 'Mr Boulton displayed considerable ability, particularly in the character of the four female cousins, in which the rapidity of change of dress and the alterations of voice, gesture, and general appearance were very striking. There was a numerous audience, and the entertainment gave the most unqualified satisfaction.'

Not all towns and cities were as enthusiastic as Oldham, Macclesfield and Liverpool, however. Towns in the South of England were considerably less enamoured of the theatrical and womanly charms of Ernest Boulton. In May 1872 the following announcement appeared in the *Hampshire Telegraph and Sussex Chronicle*:

PORTLAND HALL, SOUTHSEA
FOR TWO NIGHTS ONLY

Mr Ernest Boulton, assisted by Mr Louis Munro, will have the honour of giving his Select, Varied and Refined Drawing-Room Entertainment in which he will appear in those Wonderful Impersonations of Female Character which have won him world-wide celebrity.

The Entertainment will commence with a Fashionable Sketch, entitled 'A CHARMING WIDOW' (with the celebrated song 'Fading Away' sung by Mr E. Boulton)

To be followed by an Original Operetta (in ten minutes) composed expressly for Mr Boulton, and entitled 'THE POWER OF GOLD'

To conclude with the Domestic Person Entertainment, entitled 'CLOUDS AND SUNSHINE'. (Constance, Mr Ernest Boulton, Ferdinand, Mr Louis Munro)

It was a dismal flop. 'The beauty of the song, "The Fair Gipsy Maid", was entirely destroyed by Mr Boulton, who, of course, was the Fair Gipsy Maid, singing far too loudly and without the slightest attempt at pathos,' a scathing notice in the *Hampshire Telegraph* read. Mr Louis Munro 'sang in a very wretched manner', and taking everything together, the *Telegraph* concluded, 'this is an entertainment which is scarcely one we can recommend'.

Other newspapers were even more damning. 'This so-called "entertainment" is one of which we feel we cannot too strongly disapprove,' the *Hampshire Advertiser* opined sternly in an editorial. 'It is a class of performance pandering to a vitiated taste, and ought therefore to be discouraged in every possible way.'

Things went from bad to worse. Two months later a performance had to be abandoned amid scenes of near riot:

> Ernest Boulton, of Boulton and Park notoriety, was to have given an entertainment at Aldershot on Monday evening but was prevented by a number of officers and others, who determined they would not hear him, and a regular row ensued, in the midst of which the gas was turned out, and the principal performer was glad to make his escape as best he could.

There were simmering private and professional tensions, too, and a few weeks after the debacle of Aldershot, Stella and the dashingly handsome Mr Louis Munro acrimoniously parted company.

As far as Stella was concerned it was good riddance. There would be no difficulty in replacing Louis Munro. Her good-looking and manly brother, Gerard, was shaping up very nicely and would be the perfect foil to her leading lady.

Stella and Gerard continued to tour the North of England, generally to great acclaim, though there were periodic ejaculations and expostulations of surprise and ire that the notorious Ernest Boulton was continuing to perform in drag and seemingly making a good living from it.

> Beams of the morning,
> Promise of day,
> While we are gazing,
> Fading away!

Despite Stella's many professional triumphs, the past always came back to haunt her. When she was appearing in York, the *Pall Mall Gazette* fulminated against 'the impudence of aged sinners' performing in a cathedral city. And whenever any young man was arrested in drag, the name of Ernest Boulton was always brought up.

Stella was weary of it. And so at the end of 1873, she made two momentous decisions. She would change her stage name to Ernest Byne and she would go to America to find the fame and fortune that still eluded her in England. Besides, she was missing Fanny dreadfully and wanted to see her.

When Judge Alexander Park had stood up in Westminster Hall to give evidence on Fanny's behalf, it was painfully obvious to everyone that he was a very sick man, and it came as no surprise when he died just six months later. Fanny and Harry, who had been released from prison in July 1871, were with him to the end.

Now there was nothing to keep either of them in England.

America would be a fresh start. They would make a new life for themselves, where no one knew them, where they would be free, in so far as it was possible, of the past. They had money, more than enough money, to live comfortably, and if the stories Fanny had heard about America were true, there would be no shortage of handsome American beaux for Harry and herself.

Much as she loved Stella, Fanny had always felt overshadowed by her sister's beauty and by her talent. It was not that she resented Stella. She most certainly did not. But it was hard sometimes not to feel a little piqued when Stella was so determinedly hogging all the limelight, and she herself so constantly standing in the wings. In America she would have the chance to make her own way, to prove herself on the New York stage and find fame and fortune.

As Fred Fenton, 'comedian', Fanny carved out a modest career for herself in the 'small business' of the theatre: walk-on parts and character roles, nearly always in drag. She excelled, as she always had, at playing elderly and eccentric English dowagers, and for a short and glorious period she was resident at the famous Fifth Avenue Theater in New York. It was the closest she ever came to stardom.

S tella and Gerard arrived in New York in the spring of 1874. One of their first engagements was at the Theatre Comique where they reprised their successful English comedietta *The Four Cousins*, attracting favourable notices: 'Ernest Byne in the character of Ellen, a domestic young lady, sang with much effort "A Pretty Girl Milking Her Cow", and at the close of the piece, with Gerard in a duet entitled "Now With Joy My Bosom Bounds".'

'Two gentlemen who sat next to us', the reviewer for the *New York Clipper* breathlessly confided, 'discussed in audible tones the merits of Ernest Byne, believing him to be a woman. After enjoying their conversation, we took the liberty of informing them of the sex of the supposed lady, and handed them a programme to substantiate it, whereupon they were completely *astonished* and *confused*.'

Colonel T. Allston Brown, one of New York's most flamboyant – and shrewdest – agents and managers, took Stella on and mounted a vigorous press campaign to announce his newest signing: 'ERNEST BYNE, pronounced by the entire press of New York, Boston and London to be the most WONDERFUL impersonator of female character ever before the public, and whose debut in New York has met with such unparalleled SUCCESS.' A selection of 'OPINIONS OF THE PRESS' followed, including an entirely fictitious quote from '*The Times of London*' which declared that 'anything more marvellous and clever than Ernest Byne's impersonations cannot be conceived, the difficulty being in believing that he is not acting real life'.

In New York, Stella was a star, perhaps not of the first magnitude, but celebrated enough to have her likeness taken by the society photographer Napoleon Sarony, the brother of Oliver Sarony, the Scarborough photographer who had taken no fewer than thirty-four studies of herself and Lord Arthur after they had performed *A Morning Call* to great acclaim in that genteel spa.

In 1876, the *New York Clipper* was moved to hymn Ernest Byne in doggerel:

> Your airs and graces make us all
> Believe you must be feminine:
> Your arts, though you're no *Harlequin*,
> Do well deserve a *column*, *Byne*.

As well as the joy of seeing Fanny and Harry again, it was quite possible – probable even – that in New York Stella was reunited with Lord Arthur Clinton, apparently back from the dead.

Ever since Lord Arthur's sudden and convenient death from scarlet fever just days before the police closed in on him, there had been sightings of him here, there and everywhere. He was shooting in Scotland or racing at Ascot. He had been spotted in town, at the theatre, in fashionable restaurants, strolling in Hyde Park. Or he was living abroad, under an assumed name, in Paris, in Sydney, in New York. Especially New York. According to *Reynolds's Newspaper* in October 1872, the dissolute peer was alive and well and living there: 'Lord Arthur Clinton who was mixed up in the Boulton and Park business, and was reported dead, has been recognised several times at some of the New York Theatres and clearly identified.'

Three years later, in September 1875, the *Northern Echo* in Darlington reported that Lord Arthur Clinton was amongst the mourners at the funeral of his sister, Lady Susan Vane-Tempest, and the following year the *Morning Post* said that he was present in Dublin 'at the Installation of the Duke of Connaught as Great Prior of the Irish Masons'.

In 1879, the grandly named Australian newspaper the *Clarence and Richmond Examiner and New South Wales Advertiser* proclaimed that 'My Lord Arthur Clinton' was not dead at all. He had, in fact, 'only temporarily died to oblige his family', the paper revealed, and now, after an absence of some years, he 'has just appeared in the arena of London society alive and hearty' having spent the past eight years in hiding in Australia.

S tella and Gerard returned to England in early 1877 and resumed touring as 'The Wonderful Bynes'. With 'Elegant Parisian Clothes and Costly Appointments', the Wonderful Bynes offered a varied programme of 'Songs, Eccentricities, Duets, Operettas &c'. All in all, it was 'a most marvellous entertainment', the theatrical bible the *Era* declared. 'The Bynes are the talk of Grimsby'.

But the past could still catch up with Stella. In April 1879, 'AN INDIGNANT NONCONFORMIST' in Cardiff wrote to the *Western Mail* to complain about some 'disgustingly suggestive' posters placarded across the town announcing the forthcoming engagement at the Stuart Hall of 'The Wonderful Bynes Company' featuring 'Mr Ernest Byne, the Unequalled Impersonator of Lady Characters': 'Will either Mr. John or Mr. Richard Cory, who are part-owners of the Stuart-hall, kindly inform the public who this "unequalled impersonator of lady characters" is, and also whether "the Wonderful Bynes Company" include Boulton and Park, or either of that notorious pair?'

In 1881, the Wonderful Bynes were in London. According to the census taken that year, Ernest Byne, 'actor', was living in lodgings at 21 Euston Street in Somers Town. Stella was thirty-two but she defied the advancing years by the simple expedient of knocking five years off her true age and proclaiming herself to be twenty-seven. She was still a fine figure of a woman and if she could get away with it, why should she not?

Spring's fairest blossoms.
Summer's bright day . . .
Autumn's rich cluster,
Fading away!

Just five days before Stella passed herself off as a still-blooming twenty-seven-year-old, Mrs Fanny Winifred Graham (*née* Park) breathed her last in Newark, New Jersey, where she had been looked after for some years past by Mr Oliver Hagen, a watchmaker, and his wife, Catherine. No cause of death was listed on her death certificate, a tactful omission which usually meant that syphilis and its fearsome complications were responsible.

The syphilitic sore on Fanny's bottom, the sore that would not go away, the sore that had forced her to seek grudging treatment from the forbidding figure of Dr Richard Barwell at the Charing Cross Hospital, had finally caught up with her. Dr Barwell had managed to heal the sore, but he could not eradicate the syphilis from her body. As the years passed, the syphilitic poison slowly but surely gnawed away at Fanny's body and Fanny's mind until, at the last, half-mad and half-blind, racked with pain and paralysed, Fanny died aged thirty-four.

Dear garrulous, gossiping, glorious Fanny. Fanny: stout of heart, stern of feature and sweet of nature. Fanny: with her campish ways, her braying laugh and her low cunning. Fanny: not beautiful, certainly; frequently foolish; uncommonly lewd; invariably lustful. Fanny: always kind, utterly charming and generous to a fault, especially with her favours.

In her short span, Fanny had perfectly realised her true self. She had fashioned herself from the most unlikely and the most unpromising of clays. She had formed herself and shaped herself with nothing but the ingenuity of her own hands. She had stitched and sewn, knitted and glued, pinned, tied, taped and laced herself to miraculously contrive the strange and gaudy creature that was Mrs Fanny Winifred Graham (*née* Park).

Not for Fanny the uncertainties and the insouciances of youth or beauty. There was no delicate, blushing springtime, no clustering blossom – other than artificial – on the bough. Fanny had been delivered of herself in her prime. She was a woman of a certain age, a woman of the world. Clever, knowing, witty and wise, it was no wonder she played principally dowagers and duchesses. She *was* one.

Defiant, determined, brave and fearless, Fanny did not flinch and she did not flee. 'How *dare* you address a Lady in that manner, Sir?' Fanny had challenged Detective Officer Chamberlain with superb aplomb and frigid hauteur on the night of the arrest. Her courage never failed her, even in her darkest hours.

So Mrs Fanny Winfred Graham (*née* Park) lived and died. '*N'importe*,' she would often say. 'What's the odds as long as you're happy?' It could have been her epitaph.

Fanny was laid to rest in Rochester, New York, alongside her beloved brother, Harry, who had died five years earlier in October 1876. A year's imprisonment with hard labour in the House of Correction in Coldbath Fields was generally considered to be a sentence of death by another name. Appalling food, lack of sanitation and back-breaking work – designed to subjugate the strongest will – reduced even the most robust of men to physical wrecks. Harry died a broken man, but it was no small consolation that he died a free man.

At the time of her death, Fanny was neither rich nor poor, but comfortably placed and living off the income from her capital. Her estate was to be divided between the widow of her older brother Alexander and the devoted Catherine Hagen, who had nursed Fanny through her last, long illness. There was one other bequest: 'I give, devise and bequeath the sum of £500 and also my Topaz ring now worn by me unto my friend Henry B. Warner, now of the City of San Francisco, California.'

Who was Henry B. Warner? Was he that handsome American beau that Fanny had hoped to meet, that ardent swain she had been searching for all the days of her life and thought she would never find? Was he the great love of her life? Had Henry B. Warner perhaps given Fanny the topaz ring as a love token? The ring was clearly important. It was the ring 'now worn by me', as Fanny had so scrupulously written in her last will and testament. Two years later, in the St James Hotel in St Louis, the legacy was given over to Henry B. Warner who signed a receipt for it in a shaky hand, as though he were labouring under great emotion.

> Song of the wild-bird,
> Heart-stirring lay. . .
> E'en as we listen,
> Fading away!

The year after Fanny's death, Stella and Gerard became Ernest and Eden Blair, and for the next twenty-two years would tour as The Brothers Blair, with a staple of two short drawing-room comediettas, *My New Housekeeper* and the 'Society absurdity' *Complications*. It was a tried and tested formula. To Gerard's handsome male lead Stella would appear in various comic female incarnations: an argumentative Irish washerwoman, a giddy young widow and a haughty and acidulated peeress of the realm. 'The performer who undertakes the female characters is very good, without being vulgar in the slightest degree,' the *Era* noted in 1891.

Touring the length and breadth of the country was arduous. Bookings were steady rather than spectacular, and reviews were lukewarm rather than lavish. 'The Brothers Blair are artistes of a high order,' the *Belfast News-Letter* wrote in 1896, 'and their drawing-room sketch caused much amusement.' They found themselves performing mostly in provincial music halls, often in small, out-of-the-way places like Douglas on the Isle of Man and Margate in Kent. Occasionally they got a booking in London, which was useful for Gerard as by this time he was married with a wife and son living in Camberwell.

It was not quite hand-to-mouth, but it was an erratic, irregular existence, punctuated by worrying periods with no work. The bright promise of Stella's youth, the bright promise of her beauty and her talent, had slowly tarnished with the passing years. The brilliant future that she had envisioned for herself had faded, faded away.

Stella rarely complained now. The dark moods and thunderous faces of her younger self were gone, replaced by a quiet joy and a deep sense of gratitude. She was grateful for the life she had; grateful that she was not rotting in some dark and dank prison cell; grateful to be working in the theatre; grateful to be alive. And if, for a moment, she was ever ungrateful or disappointed or dissatisfied with her lot, if she was ever sharp or impatient or petulant, she had only to turn her thoughts to poor dear Fanny so cruelly taken from them in her prime.

Of course there were still followers and beaux and gentleman callers (though to be strictly accurate, only a very few of her gentleman callers were gentlemen, or anything much approaching gentlemen).

Still they came, though she was no longer young and no longer beautiful. But she was, after all, Miss Stella Boulton-Byne-Blair and she could no more stop followers from following, beaux from coming and gentleman callers from calling than she could stop the rain from falling or the wind from blowing.

Still they came, like the endless waves breaking upon the shore: young men and old, fat men and thin, tall men and short. Shy working men in stiff collars and Sunday-best suits, who spoke in strange accents and came to ask her to walk out with them. Callow youths who blushed and stammered and poured their love out in a scalding torrent of words, and cocky, cheeky youths who flirted with her violently.

Soldiers and sailors, vagabonds and ruffians. Men of middling rank and men of no rank at all. Poor men aplenty and rich men (though in truth, these days rich men were at something of a premium). Still they came, to fete Stella, to admire her, to desire her, to court her, to fall in love with her, and sometimes, sweetly and seriously, to propose marriage to her.

Stella loved them all. And she was kind to them all. What else could she do? How else could she be? She must be tender. She must give them comfort and she must give them love. She must tend to their bruised and broken hearts. She must fledge them and make them strong. She must teach them courage and she must teach them to endure against all hazard and against all hardship, just as she herself had learned these bitter lessons.

She must give them hope, even when hope could hardly be imagined, let alone grasped. Most of all she must transmit to them the strange and secret joy that was special to their kind and to their commonwealth. The same strange and secret joy that poor dear Fanny had found. The small, flickering flame of joy that must be painfully and carefully nursed from feeble, sickly ignition into clear and vigorous combustion.

It was her mission and her purpose. Stella knew that the path stretched out endlessly before her. Not in her lifetime, certainly. Nor in the lifetimes of those that followed. But perhaps in the lifetimes of their children's children, the first glimmerings of this burgeoning flame of joy would pierce the dark and cruel night, like the breaking of a rosy dawn on a summer's morn.

> Hope's fairy promise,
> Charms to betray,
> All that is earthly,
> Fadeth away . . .

S tella had seen in the new century and she had outlived the old Queen. In the autumn of 1903, she fell ill, seriously ill, with an affliction of the brain. The doctors said it was a cerebral neoplasm, a growth in the brain, and most probably a consequence of syphilis. It was a long illness, bravely born. After a life of quite extraordinary incident, Stella passed away peacefully a year later, aged fifty-four, with Gerard by her side.

There was just enough money to bury Stella, but not enough to raise a headstone to mark her grave. Only a handful of mourners were there to witness her passing.

> But there's a land,
> Where nought shall decay,

Where there's no sorrow,
No fading away!

The sky was bright with heavenly light as they gathered above Stella's unmarked grave. All of them. A great celestial host of bougers, bowgards and buggers, of catamites and Ganymedes, of ingles, pathics and poofs, of Mollies, Margeries and Mary-Anns. All the sad young men and all the sad old men. All the he-she's and the she-he's; all the effeminate men and all the masculine women; all the young men in women's clothes and all the young women in men's clothes. All the androgynes and the hermaphrodites and the in-betweens. All the generations of numberless and nameless sodomites, of martyrs, outcasts and outlaws, of the lost, the lonely and the unloved. All of them, in serried ranks, gathered together, a great and joyful host, there to raise her up, to throne her and to coronate her, with gladsome laudings and praisings, as Stella, Queen of Queens, Star of the Heavens.

Epilogue

On Wednesday 15th June 1870, the *Echo* reported a sighting of Martin Luther Cumming.

> Mr. Cumming, against whom a warrant has been issued in connection with the charge of personating women, went to Brussels immediately after the arrest of Park and Boulton, and put up at one of the best hotels. As, however, he had no papers, and could not give evidence as to his means of existence, he was requested to leave the country. When he was called upon he had his hair in curl papers, and portraits in which he and a friend were represented in women's clothes were found in his rooms.

And that was the last time that anyone saw or heard of the Comical Countess.

Dr James Paul, who had squirmed with shame and embarrassment at the Lord Chief Justice's stern and stinging criticisms of his conduct in the case, continued to be gainfully employed as Surgeon to 'E' Division of the Metropolitan Police until his premature death in 1877.

Malcolm Johnston, the Maid of Athens, was arrested in Dublin in 1884 after the exposure of a sodomitic scandal in Dublin Castle, the seat of English rule in Ireland. He was tried and sent to prison for sodomy and was never heard of again.

Jack Saul, the infamous male prostitute, was also caught up in the Dublin Castle Scandal of 1884 but managed to avoid prison. In August 1890, Jack was interviewed by Inspector Abberline of the Metropolitan Police in connection with the Cleveland Street Scandal. 'I am still a professional Mary-Ann,' he told Inspector Abberline. 'I have lost my character and cannot get otherwise.' Later that year, Jack Saul testified in court that he had been picked up in the street by no less a personage than the Earl of Euston and gone back with him to the male brothel at 19 Cleveland Street. 'Lord Euston was not an actual sodomite,' Jack deposed. 'He likes to play with you and "spend" on your belly.'

Miss Carlotta Westropp Gibbings took up with Louis Munro, Stella's short-lived leading man, and together they scraped a precarious living touring the South Coast with 'A Drawing-Room Entertainment' almost identical to that offered to the public by Stella. In 1873, Carlotta and Louis were arrested and charged with 'uttering a fictitious cheque' for a watch they later pawned. By a miracle they were acquitted. Penniless and friendless, Carlotta had no choice but to return to Cheltenham and live with her forbidding Mamma. Carlotta died in 1890, aged forty-one, from 'congestion of the lungs'.

The dogged and determined Inspector Thompson continued to serve in 'E' Division of the Metropolitan Police until his retirement in 1890. He died seven years later, aged sixty-two.
Both Detective Sergeant Frederick Kerley and Detective Officer William Chamberlain retired early from the Metropolitan Police and became private detectives. In 1895, Kerley put his knowledge and experience of London's sodomitic under-

world to good use when he was employed, alongside the famous Inspector Littlechild, by the Marquis of Queensberry to find male prostitutes willing to testify against Oscar Wilde.

George Lewis's career continued to prosper. In 1895, he was employed to defend Queensberry against a charge of criminal libel brought by Wilde. Lewis worked tirelessly for reform of the divorce laws and he was instrumental in the creation of the Court of Criminal Appeal. He was knighted in 1893 and died in 1911 at the age of seventy-eight.

Two years after attending Fanny and Stella's trial in Westminster Hall, the young Pre-Raphaelite painter Simeon Solomon was arrested with George Roberts, a sixty-year-old stableman, in a public lavatory in Oxford Street. They were charged with attempting to commit sodomy. Roberts was sentenced to eighteen months' imprisonment with hard labour, while Solomon's sentence of eighteen months' imprisonment with light labour was reduced on appeal to a term of police supervision. A year later, Solomon was arrested with another man in a *pissoir* in Paris and sentenced to three months' imprisonment.

'Cecil Graham', the false name given by Stella to Inspector Thompson on the night she was arrested, reappeared in 1892 as the name of a character in Oscar Wilde's first society comedy, *Lady Windermere's Fan*. Wilde's Cecil Graham is a sharp, brittle and witty man about town who easily mixes in high – and in low – society. Wilde insisted that Cecil Graham wear a green carnation on stage on the first night. Although Wilde later claimed that the mystic green carnation was his own idea – 'I invented that magnificent flower,' he said – he had, in fact, merely borrowed the idea from the sodomites and cross-dressers of Paris who wore the green carnation as a badge of their sexuality. Was Wilde's fey and effeminate Cecil Graham a secret homage to Stella Boulton? Wilde certainly knew of Fanny and Stella, having read the explicit account of some of their sexual exploits in Jack Saul's *The Sins of the Cities of the Plain* (1881). But had they met? Wilde lived in London between 1878 and 1895, years in which Stella and Gerard regularly performed in the capital, and it is entirely possible that the famous Oscar Wilde encountered the infamous Miss Stella Boulton in London's sodomitic underworld and listened with rapt attention and shining eyes to Stella's account of her scandalous life and extraordinary trials.

Hugh Mundell, Stella's Hapless Swain, renounced the world together with all its snares and temptations and became a chiropodist instead. He was still practising this useful profession in 1901, at the age of fifty-four, in the parish of St George's, Hanover Square. He never married.

Miss Ann Empson, the Dragon of Davies Street, remained true to her Vestal Vows and never married. A year after the trial of Fanny and Stella, she retired to Croydon to keep house for her half-brother, Mr Alexander Sidebottom, where she died, aged sixty.

Cecil 'Sissy' Thomas became an underwriter at Lloyd's. He never married and lived for most of his life with his sister in circumstances of the utmost respectability.

John Reeve left the Alhambra and became the landlord of the

Union Flag, a public house on the Lambeth Road. The Union Flag also became a theatrical boarding house, accommodating music-hall turns as diverse as a French trapeze artiste, a low comedian and a pantomime dame.

Charles Pavitt spent most of the rest of his working life writing comic songs for music halls. Among his most popular were 'The Gretna Green Galop' and the ever so slightly *risqué* 'I've Got a Peep-Show', the refrain of which ran:

> For I've got a Peep-Show, a Peep-Show, a Peep-Show,
> I've got a Peep-Show, a penny for a peep.

Mr Edward Nelson Haxell, the jovial hotel keeper, built himself a castellated gothic fantasy of a house in the pretty rural village of Kingsbury on the outskirts of London. He died in 1899, at the age of seventy-nine. In the 1920s, Haxell's Hotel, the scene of Carlotta's famous drag ball, became part of what is now the Strand Palace Hotel.

Dr Richard Barwell's career prospered and he continued to work until he was nearly seventy. In his retirement he was an enthusiastic skater and remained hale and hearty into his late eighties. He died in Norfolk, the county of his birth, in December 1916, aged eighty-nine.

Maria George (*née* Duffin) married and buried two husbands. In 1911, she was a widow and living in Hampstead with her younger sister, Hannah, a council lavatory attendant. Maria died in 1931 aged eighty.

Mrs Mary Ann Boulton, Mother of Mothers, died peacefully on a summer's day in 1889 aged sixty-seven. To the very end she continued to assiduously collect every playbill, every newspaper clipping and every photograph of her darling boys, and she would boast about them and their career on the stage to anyone and everyone who would listen. Mrs Mary Ann Boulton died in the sure and certain knowledge that she had done her duty by her sons and never, as she had so proudly proclaimed in court, 'allowed any cloud to fall upon my children'. And when the time came, Stella was laid to rest beside her.

John Safford Fiske took himself off to Europe where he spent most of the rest of his life painting, writing and cultivating his 'large and beautiful garden' in Alassio, in north-west Italy, 'where the rose blooms the whole winter'. In 1905 he wrote, 'I think I may claim that, in an unpretending way, I have shaped for myself a life that is agreeable enough in the living.' He died in 1907, aged fifty-seven. He left his carefully catalogued library of four thousand volumes, including Oscar Wilde's *The Picture of Dorian Gray* and an edition of Walt Whitman's poems, to Hobart College in New York State. His carefully concealed photographs of Stella (and one or two of Fanny, as well), which were unearthed by Detective Officer Roderick Gollan of the Edinburgh City Police on the morning of 9th June 1870, were taken into custody and pasted into the Linlithgowshire Rogues' Gallery, where they can still be seen today in Edinburgh City Archives.

Dear, dull Louis Hurt left London immediately after his acquittal and spent the next five years wandering Europe, visiting

Paris, St Petersburg and Rome before eventually settling in Vienna in 1876. He was appointed Professor of English at the Wiener Handelsakademie and also taught at the Theresianum, a semi-military school for royalty and aristocrats where, according to his obituary in the *Wirksworth Parish Magazine*, the last Khedive of Egypt, Abbas Hilmi Pasha II, and Ferdinand of Coburg, later King of Bulgaria, 'passed through his hands'. He died in Vienna in 1936, at the remarkable age of ninety-one.

After a flurry of real and imagined sightings of Lord Arthur Clinton in the 1870s, nothing was heard of him ever again. Was he dead? Or had he, like Louis Hurt and John Safford Fiske, taken himself off to the kindlier climes of Europe? In the will of Henry, seventh Duke of Newcastle, drawn up in 1927, there is a curious and beguiling reference to 'my uncle, Lord Arthur Pelham-Clinton (a person reputed to be dead and as to the proof of whose death some question might arise)'. *Some question might arise.* Was this cryptic legalese the closest that the family would ever come to admitting that Lord Arthur had not died of scarlet fever in 1870, but had been helped to escape the ends of justice? The clause in the seventh Duke's will effectively disinherits Lord Arthur – and (improbably) 'any of his male issue' – 'as if the said Lord Arthur Pelham-Clinton had died in my lifetime'. Either Lord Arthur had died in the seventh Duke's lifetime, or he had not. If he was still alive in 1927, as the seventh Duke's will seems to hint that he was, he would have been eighty-seven.

Gerard Boulton gave up the stage after Stella died and moved to Winchester with his wife, Matilda, and their son. Gerard kept the name 'Eden Blair', and for many years he was the manager of the Regent Theatre in Winchester. 'His charming manner earned him the respect of all, and especially of children,' his obituary in the *Hampshire Chronicle* recorded. In his later years he was a stalwart of the Spiritualist Church in Hyde Abbey Road. He died on 26th January 1940 aged eighty-six. Gerard was just sixteen when the scandal of the Young Men in Women's Clothes erupted in 1870, and with him died the last living memories of Fanny and Stella.

Notes

Every word of the sensational six-day trial of Fanny and Stella in May 1871 was assiduously taken down by a team of short-hand writers from Messrs Walsh and Son of Little George Street, Westminster. The entire trial was then transcribed in longhand in at least a dozen clerkly hands (of varying legibility), and bound together in one enormous volume. *The Queen v Boulton and Others before the Lord Chief Justice and a Special Jury: Proceedings on the Trial of the Indictment* is a remarkable document, not least because it has survived intact when so many other transcripts of major Victorian trials have been lost or destroyed. The trial transcript is in the care of the National Archives in Kew, along with the bundle of thirty-one depositions given by witnesses at Bow Street Magistrates' Court in April and May 1870 and some thirty letters, just a tiny fraction of the two thousand documents handed over to Inspector Thompson by Miss Ann Empson, the Dragon of Davies Street.

Much of the material in this book is drawn directly from the trial transcript (DPP 4/6), the depositions (KB6/3) and the letters (KB6/3, part I) in the National Archives, and designated in the notes as 'Trial', 'Deposition' and 'Letters'. I have relied heavily on contemporary newspaper reports of the trial and its aftermath, all of which can be consulted at British Library Newspapers in Colindale, London.

1 *Leading Ladies*

1 'When they were seated' – 'The Funny He-She Ladies', *Curiosities of Street Literature, Comprising Cocks and Catchpennies* (London, 1871).

2 'the very fairest' – *Echo*, 3 May 1870.

2 'The general opinion' – *The Lives of Boulton and Park: Extraordinary Revelations* (London, 1870).

3 'There was a young man' – *The Pearl*, November 1879.

3 'lasciviously ogled' – *Extraordinary Revelations*.

4 'no harm in it' – *Pall Mall Gazette*, 6 March 1881.

5 'sterner features' – *Evening Standard*, 2 May 1870.

6 'charming as a star' – Quoted in the opening speech of Sir John Karslake, Trial.

6 'Stella, Star of the Strand' – *Extraordinary Revelations*.

7 'I'm a police officer' – *Daily Telegraph*, 30 April 1870.

7 'How *dare* you' – *Evening Standard*, 2 May 1870.

7 'Look here' – Deposition of Detective Sergeant Kerley/*Reynolds's Newspaper*, 14 May 1871.

9 'Your name and address?' – Trial testimony of Inspector Thompson.

10 'There were flannel petticoats' – Trial testimony of Detective Officer Chamberlain.

10 'One of the police' – Deposition of Hugh Mundell/*Daily Telegraph*, 7 May 1870.

11 'a cruel sell' – 'The Funny He-She Ladies'.

11 'so brave' – Trial testimony of Detective Officer Chamberlain.

2 *The Hapless Swain*

12 'These young men' – *Extraordinary Revelations*.

12 'the nightly resort' – Jim Davis and Victor Emeljanow, *Reflecting the Audience: London Theatregoing, 1840–1880* (Hatfield, 2001).

12 'a few pilgrims' – *All the Year Round* (19 May 1877) quoted in Davis
    and Emeljanow, *Reflecting the Audience*.

12 '23 years and a half' – *Daily Telegraph*, 7 May 1870.

13 'very little experience' – Deposition of Hugh Mundell.

13 'an "idle" sort of a life' – *ibid*.

14 'Those two are women' – *ibid*.

14 'I took them to be women' – *Daily Telegraph*, 7 May 1870.

14 'We think you're following us' – Trial testimony of Hugh Mundell.

15 'these monsters' – 'H. Smith', *The Yokel's Preceptor: Or, More Sprees
    in London!* (London, *c*.1850).

16 'I talked to them' – *Daily Telegraph*, 7 May 1870.

16 'only be too happy' – Deposition of Hugh Mundell.

16 'never anything improper' – *Daily Telegraph*, 7 May 1870.

17 'our private box' – Trial testimony of Hugh Mundell.

17 'Dear Mr Mundell' – *ibid*.

17 'It's a good joke' – *ibid*.

18 'In what way' – *Daily Telegraph*, 7 May 1870.

18 'I shall ask for Mrs Park' – Trial testimony of Hugh Mundell.

19 'a bit of brown' – 'Walter', *My Secret Life* (Amsterdam, *c*.1880).

19 'back-door work' – *The Pearl*, 1880.

20 'I said I had' – Trial testimony of Hugh Mundell/*Daily Telegraph*, 7
    May 1870.

21 'They were talking' – *Extraordinary Revelations*.

21 'principally dowagers' – Deposition of Amos Westropp Gibbings.

22 'Who *are* they?' – *Daily Telegraph*, 7 May 1870.

22 'I have my doubts' – Trial testimony of Hugh Mundell.

23 'I am not a lady' – *ibid*.

23 'There was a great deal of confusion' – *The Times*, 7 May 1870/ *Ex-
    traordinary Revelations*.

23 'quite in a myth' – Trial testimony of Hugh Mundell.

23 'led on' – *ibid*.

3 The Slap-Bum Polka

24 'a cute detective chap' – 'The Funny He-She Ladies'.

25 'He asked whether two gentlemen' – Deposition of Martha Stacey.

26 'My mother remonstrated' – *ibid.*

27 'in drag' – Deposition of Amos Westropp Gibbings.

28 'laughing, chaffing' – Deposition of Martha Stacey.

28 'Slap-Bum Polka' – Jack Saul, *The Sins of the Cities of the Plain* (London, 1881).

29 'very effeminate' – *Reynolds's Newspaper*, 5 June 1870.

30 'handsomest frocks' – Trial testimony of Detective Officer Chamberlain.

4 In the Dock

31 'When first before' – 'The Funny He-She Ladies'.

33 'was crowded' – *Illustrated Police News*, 7 May 1870.

34 'crammed' – *Evening News*, 30 April 1870.

34 'great surprise' – *Daily Telegraph*, 30 April 1870.

35 'these two women' – *ibid.*

35 'did with each' – KB6/3, The National Archives.

37 'Both conducted' – *Daily Telegraph,* 30 April 1870.

37 'Last evening' – *ibid.*

38 'lasciviously ogling' – *Extraordinary Revelations.*

38 'I have been' – Deposition of Detective Officer Chamberlain.

38 'I found' – *Daily Telegraph*, 30 April 1870.

39 'for a year past' – *ibid.*

39 'seen both the prisoners' – Deposition of Police Constable Walker.

40 'Much of the evidence' – *Daily Telegraph*, 30 April 1870.

40 'The onus' – *ibid.*

5 *Foreign Bodies*

42 'EXAMINATION OF PEDERASTS' – Charles Vibert, *Précis de médicine légale* (Paris, 1893, translated by Dede Smith).

42 'I was in the street' – Trial testimony of Dr James Paul.

44 'Step inside' – Deposition of Dr Paul.

44 'Unfasten' – *ibid*.

44 'Without saying' – *ibid*.

44 'I did not use' – *ibid*.

44 'force' – *ibid*.

44 'I examined them' – *ibid*.

46 'a wheezing' – C. J. S. Thompson, *Ladies or Gentlemen? Women Who Posed as Men and Men Who Impersonated Women* (New York, 1993).

46 'doubtful repute' – *Observer*, 22 May 1870.

46 'Maria' – Thompson, *Ladies or Gentlemen?*

47 'no appearance of a beard' – Alfred Swaine Taylor, *The Principles and Practice of Medical Jurisprudence* (London, 1861).

47 'The state of the rectum' – *ibid*.

49 'abused by men' – Deposition of Dr Paul.

49 'special continental vice' – *The Leader*, 18 September 1858.

50 'I had never seen' – Trial testimony of Dr Paul.

50 'I examined Boulton' – Deposition of Dr Paul.

50 'Boulton was then removed' – *ibid*.

50 'The anus was *very*' – *ibid*.

51 'a foreign body' – Deposition of Dr Paul.

51 'an inordinate length' – *ibid*.

51 'Traction' – *ibid*.

51 'the dimensions' – Ambroise Tardieu, *Étude médico-légale sur les attentats aux mœurs* (Paris, 1857, and seventh edition, 1878, translated by Dede Smith).

6 Wives and Daughters

53 'Say Stella' – Jonathan Swift, 'To Stella, Visiting Me in My
      Sickness', 1720.

53 'independent means' – entry in the 1841 Census.

53 'And Ernest was' – Trial testimony of Mrs Mary Ann Boulton.

56 'Mamma' – *ibid.*

58 'everything' – *ibid.*

59 'reverses' – *ibid.*

59 'If he asked his father' – *ibid.*

60 'consumptive' – *ibid.*

61 'I was always' – *ibid.*

7 Becoming Fanny

65 'And all that's madly wild' – Thomas Parnell, *Poems upon Several
      Occasions* (London, 1773).

77 'sound in principles' – Sir James Park, *Some Account of Myself*,
      unpublished and undated MS, *c.*1835.

8 A Tale of Two Sisters

79 'A SISTER'S LOVE' – Jethro Jackson, *The Family Treasury of
      Western Literature, Science and Art* (London, 1854).

79 'sterner features' – *Evening Standard*, 2 May 1870.

85 'your mincing' – Louis Hurt to Ernest Boulton, 8 April 1870, Trial.

86 'They always said' – Trial testimony of Hugh Mundell.

9 Monstrous Erections

88 'At Wakefield Street' – 'The Funny He-She Ladies'.

88 'The crowd' – *Reynolds's Newspaper*, 15 May 1870.

89 'It is suspected' – *Daily Telegraph*, 30 April 1870.

Notes

89 'these foolish if not unnatural' – *Illustrated Police News*, 7 May 1870.

90 'Nothing' – *Extraordinary Revelations*.

90 'the filthy details' – *Reynolds's Newspaper*, 29 May 1870.

90 'noble lord' – *ibid*.

90 'allow seats' – *Evening Standard*, 6 May 1870.

91 'a most indecent' – *The Times*, 30 May 1870.

91 'such ebullitions' – *ibid*.

91 'The list' – *The Times*, 16 May 1870.

94 'a Theatrical' – Jim Davis, 'Androgynous Cliques and Epicene Colleges: Gender Transgression On and Off the Victorian Stage', *Nineteenth Century Theatre*, Vol. 26, No. 1 (Summer 1998).

95 '42 stamps' – *The Englishwoman's Domestic Magazine*, 1861.

96 'monstrous erections' – C. Willett Cunnington, *Feminine Attitudes in the Nineteenth Century* (London, 1935).

96 'a whopper' – *Curiosities of Street Literature, Comprising Cocks and Catchpennies* (London, 1871).

96 'hair-dressing establishments' – *Graphic*, 7 May 1870.

96 'The hairdresser' – Deposition of Maria Duffin.

97 'sterner features' – *Evening Standard*, 2 May 1870.

97 'great quantity' – *The Times*, 16 May 1870.

97 'evident defects' – Cunnington, *Feminine Attitudes*.

97 'One of the prostitutes' – Reay Tannahill, *Sex in History* (London, 1980).

98 'no one who goes' – *Godey's Lady's Book and Magazine*, 1871.

98 'If a girl' – Mrs H. R. Haweis, *The Art of Beauty* (London, 1878).

98 'one of the most innocent' – Edwin Creer, *A Popular Treatise on the Human Hair* (London, 1865).

99 'CAUTION TO LADIES' – *The Pearl*, April 1880.

10 A Dirty Business

102 '*Amenities of Leicester Square*' – *The Pearl*, 1880.

102 'considered' – *Daily Telegraph*, 10 May 1871.

103 'admirable' – in Alan Mackinnon, *The Oxford Amateurs: A Short History of Theatricals at the University* (London, 1910).

104 'well-known' – *Daily Telegraph*, 10 May 1871.

105 'Are you good-natured' – *The Times*, 24 September 1850.

106 'in a very mincing' – *The Times*, 25 October 1850.

106 'Did you see' – Willy Somerville to Stella Boulton, no date but *c*.1868, Letters.

106 'There is a considerable' – Evidence of Howard Vincent, 19 July 1881, *Minutes of Evidence of the Select Committee of the House of Lords on the Protection of Young Girls*, Parliamentary Papers, 1881.

106 'A great many' – *Flora Tristan's London Journal*, translated by Denis Palmer and Giselle Pincetl (London, 1980).

107 'army' – 'Xavier Mayne', *The Intersexes: A History of Simisexualism as a Problem in Social Life* (Rome, 1908).

107 'seven or eight' – 'Evidence of Silas Rendell Anniss, 27 February 1871', in *Analysis of the Evidence Given Before the Contagious Diseases Commission*, prepared by J. Salusbury Trelawny (London, 1872).

107 'such types' – 'Xavier Mayne', *The Intersexes*.

107 'oftentimes' – Statements of Jack Saul to Inspector Abberline of the Metropolitan Police, 10 and 12 August 1889, The National Archives.

108 'fancy woman' – 'H. Smith', *Yokel's Preceptor*.

108 'notorious' – *ibid.*

108 'spooney boy' – Statements of Jack Saul to Inspector Abberline.

108 'One man's prick' – 'Walter', *My Secret Life*.

109 'If you'll let us go' – Deposition of Detective Sergeant Kerley/*Reynolds's Newspaper*, 14 May 1871.

109 'I have been in the hands' – Letter from Malcolm Johnston, Dublin Commission Court – The Queen v Cornwall and Others, August 1884.

109 'Nearly all ' – *ibid*.

110 'Camp' – Statement of Malcolm Johnston, Dublin Commission Court.

111 'in a very extraordinary' – *Morning Post*, 23 June 1868.

111 'a charge' – *ibid*.

112 'been specially employed' – *Birmingham Daily Post*, 10 March 1871.

112 'the system' – *Freeman's Journal*, 9 March 1871.

113 'the slightest doubt' – Alfred Swaine Taylor, *Medical Jurisprudence* (London, 1846).

11 Getting Up Evidence

114 'That if any witness' – *A Compendious Abstract of the Public General Acts of the United Kingdom of Great Britain and Ireland* (London, 1823).

114 'literally inundated' – *Reynolds's Newspaper*, 15 May 1870.

114 'I have had a great deal' – *Daily Telegraph*, 30 May 1870.

116 'I have known Park' – Deposition of John Reeve.

117 'They were walking' – *ibid*.

118 'I have seen about twenty' – *ibid*.

118 'frequent complaints' – *ibid*.

120 'I noticed' – Deposition of George Smith.

120 'I saw him *wink*' – Trial testimony of George Smith.

120 'I dare say' – *Daily Telegraph*, 14 May 1870.

120 'Oh, you sweet little dear!' – Deposition of George Smith.

121 'I saw Boulton' – *ibid*.

121 'I've received' – *ibid*.

121 'Take no notice' – *ibid*.

121 'You're as bad' – *ibid*.

121 'They used to walk' – Trial testimony of George Smith.

122 'I've cautioned' – Deposition of George Smith.

123 'I don't think' – *The Times*, 14 May 1870.

123 'Have you been drinking' – *Daily Telegraph*, 14 May 1870.

123 'flippant' – *ibid*.

124 'getting up evidence' – Deposition of George Smith.

124 'a mistake as to the date' – *ibid*.

124 'at the Treasury-office' – *The Times*, 14 May 1870.

124 'I *may* be paid' – Deposition of George Smith/Trial testimony of George Smith/*The Times*, 14 May 1870.

124 'additions' – *The Times*, 14 May 1870.

12 *A Victorian Romance*

126 'At length I am a bride!' – *Letters from Laura and Eveline, Giving an Account of Their Mock-Marriage, Wedding Trip, Etc.,* (London, 1903).

128 'He laughed' – Trial testimony of Mary Ann Boulton.

129 'On one or two occasions' – *ibid*.

130 'nourish' – 1876 advertisement for Rowland's Macassar Oil.

131 'Rose of the garden' – Anne Fricker, 'Fading Away', 1854.

131 'ripened' – Trial testimony of Mary Ann Boulton.

133 'interfering' – *Daily Telegraph*, 10 May 1871.

133 'a man perfectly well-known' – Opening speech of the Attorney-General, Trial.

133 'apparently plying' – *ibid*.

134 'a marriage' – *The Times*, 6 June 1868.

135 'in all, five' – *The Times*, 10 November 1869.

135 'a chest' – *ibid*.

136 'My dear Mrs Boulton' – Lord Arthur Clinton to Mrs Boulton, 11 December 1868, Letters.

136 'said he would be very pleased' – Trial testimony of Mary Ann Boulton.

136 'My answer' – *ibid*.

137 'When I was dressing' – *ibid*.

137 'I fear I offended' – Lord Arthur Clinton to Mrs Boulton, 12

October 1868, Trial.

13 Lord Arthur's Wife

138 'MARRY!' – *The Ladies' Treasury*, March 1867.

140 'I thought Boulton' – Deposition of Eliza Clark.

141 'I have been' – *ibid*.

141 'I used to accuse' – *ibid*.

141 'I never could satisfy myself' – *Evening Standard*, 30 May 1870.

141 'Boulton generally dressed' – Deposition of Maria Duffin.

142 'When Boulton was there' – *ibid*.

143 'I beg your pardon' – Trial testimony of Maria George (*née* Duffin).

14 The Toast of the Town

148 'Oh! the dresses' – 'Cantab', 'The Spa at Scarborough: A Reminiscence' in *The Lovers' Dictionary: A Poetical Treasury of Lovers' Thoughts, Fancies, Addresses and Dilemmas* (London, 1867).

151 'it strengthens' – *Theakston's Guide to Scarborough* (Scarborough, 1868).

152 'Lord Arthur Pelham-Clinton, M.P.' – *Scarborough Gazette and Weekly List of Visitors*, 15 October 1868.

152 'Oct. 20, 1868.' – *Daily Telegraph*, 13 May 1871.

153 'the oldest' – George Crosby, *Crosby's Guide to Scarborough* (Scarborough, *c*.1850).

155 'honoured' – *Scarborough Gazette and Weekly List of Visitors*, 22 October 1868.

156 'an establishment' – *Scarborough Gazette and Weekly List of Visitors*, 15 October 1868.

156 'a popular demand' – Trial testimony of Oliver Sarony.

157 'Lord Arthur had' – Wybert Reeve to the Editor of the *Daily Telegraph*, 3 June 1870.

15 *'Yr Affectionate Fanny'*

159 'Don't be too particular' – words and music by John Orlando Parry, 1843.

162 'I am just off' – Ernest Boulton to Lord Arthur Clinton, 4 December 1868, Letters.

162 'We were very drunk' – Ernest Boulton to Lord Arthur Clinton, late 1868, letters read in evidence, Trial.

162 'tired and seedy' – *ibid.*

162 'How *can* you' – *ibid.*

162 'I must of course trust' – *ibid.*

162 'Now no promises' – *ibid.*

162 'A game pie' – *ibid.*

162 'If you have any coin' – *ibid.*

162 'Send me some money' – Ernest Boulton to Lord Arthur Clinton, 4 December 1868, Letters.

162 'I wanted the money' – Ernest Boulton to Lord Arthur Clinton, late 1868, letters read in evidence, Trial.

162 'I shall leave here' – *ibid.*

162 'Why *cannot* you' – *ibid.*

162 'It is now five o'clock' – *ibid.*

162 'When you write' – *ibid.*

162 'I have waited' – *ibid.*

162 'I do not like' – *ibid.*

163 'I am quite tired' – *ibid.*

163 'We cannot go on' – *ibid.*

163 'I am most annoyed' – *ibid.*

163 'I am consoling' – *ibid.*

163 'And now, dear' – *ibid.*

163 'My Dearest Arthur' – Frederick Park to Lord Arthur Clinton, 22 November 1868, Letters.

164 'How *very* kind' – Frederick Park to Lord Arthur Clinton, 21

November 1868, Letters.

165 'Is the handle' – Frederick Park to Lord Arthur Clinton, late 1868, Letters.

16 *The Dragon of Davies Street*

167 'Ann Empson' – *Reynolds's Newspaper*, 5 June 1870.

169 'Are you married?' – *Reynolds's Newspaper*, 5 June 1870.

170 'Have you been drinking' – *The Times*, 30 May 1870.

171 'a mutton chop' – Deposition of Ann Empson.

171 'I was surprised' – *ibid*.

171 'I saw Lord Arthur' – Deposition of Ann Empson/*The Times*, 30 May 1870.

171 'I complained' – Deposition of Ann Empson.

172 'as an abuse' – *ibid*.

172 'I said to them' – *ibid*.

173 'lady's wearing apparel' – Trial Testimony of Ann Empson.

173 'The prisoner nearest' – *ibid*.

17 *'Come Love'*

175 'Love is a pretty pedlar' – Robert Jones, 'The Muses Gardin for Delights', 1610.

175 'Mr Ernest Boulton' – John Safford Fiske to Ernest Boulton, March/April 1870, Letters.

176 'having indecently' – *Illustrated Police News*, 16 July 1870.

177 'arse-quim' – *Letters from Laura and Eveline*.

180 'playing weekday tunes' – Trial testimony of Agnes Dickson

180 'Nothing like him' – Trial testimony of John Doig.

180 'by drinking' – John Jameson Jim to Ernest Boulton, February or March 1870, Letters.

181 'Have you the same love' – John Jameson Jim to Ernest Boulton, 8 April 1870, Letters.

181 '*Will* you stay' – 'Jack', to Ernest Boulton, 4 April 1870, Letters.

182 'of unblemished character' – Joseph Mullin to William H. Seward, 26 August 1867, 'Letters of Application and Recommendation During the Administrations of Abraham Lincoln and Andrew Jackson, 1861 to 1869', Microfilm M650, US National Archives and Records Administration.

184 'After we were married' – John Safford Fiske to Ernest Boulton, 20 April 1870, Letters.

184 'adventures' – John Safford Fiske to Ernest Boulton, 18 April 1870, Letters.

185 'his smiling face' – *ibid*.

185 'Laïs and Antinous' – *ibid*.

185 'ravishing' – *ibid*.

185 'Come love' – John Safford Fiske to Ernest Boulton, March/April 1870, Letters.

18 Un Souvenir d'Amour

187 'All Cracks are so full of Ails' – John Dunton, *The He-Strumpets: A Satyr on the Sodomite Club*, 1707, in Rictor Norton, *Mother Clap's Molly House* (London, 2006).

188 'In France' – William Allingham, *Fistula, Haemorrhoids, Painful Ulcers, Stricture, Prolapsus, and Other Painful Diseases of the Rectum* (London, 1871).

188 'immense prevalence' – William Acton, *A Complete Practical Treatise on the Diseases of the Urinary and Generative Organs*, (London, 1860).

189 'running down' – *ibid*.

189 'frequently to be seen' – George Drysdale, *The Elements of Social Science; or, Physical, Sexual and Natural Religion* (London, 1867).

190 'infected' – attributed to Lord Byron, 'Don Leon', *c*.1830.

190 'abomination' – *Extraordinary Revelations*.

190 'G—' – Philippe Ricord, *Illustrations of Syphilitic Disease*, translated by T. F. Belton (Philadelphia, 1851).

190 'sodomy' – Drysdale, *Elements*.

191 'I saw one case' – Trial testimony of Dr Henry James Johnson.

192 'principally dowagers' – Deposition of Amos Westropp Gibbings.

193 'shabby plaid trousers' – Deposition of Dr Richard Barwell.

193 'He was walking' – Trial testimony of George Layton.

194 'He confessed' – Trial testimony of Dr Richard Barwell.

195 'a gonorrhoeal discharge' – *ibid*.

195 'rather common clothing' – *ibid*.

196 'I examined him' – *ibid*.

197 'insisted' – *Lancet*, 28 May 1870.

197 'And so' – *Lancet*, 28 May 1870.

19 *The Battle of the Bottoms*

198 'An Awkward Question' – *The Pearl*, 1880.

199 'in close prison' – Opening address by Mr Digby Seymour, Trial.

199 'We are of the opinion' – *Report From the Departmental Committee on Prisons*, Prisons Committee (London, 1895).

200 'eminent medical gentlemen' – *Daily Telegraph*, 15 May 1871.

200 'by the direction' – *Reynolds's Newspaper*, 19 June 1870.

202 'vaginal spasms' – Evidence of Dr David McLoughlin to the Skey Committee on Pathology and Treatment of Venereal Disease, 6 December 1864.

205 'a feeling' – *Lancet*, 25 June 1870.

205 'The two things' – D— S— , *Eighteen Months' Imprisonment* (London, 1883).

206 'dignified courtesy' – Obituary notice of Dr Frederick Le Gros Clark, *British Medical Journal*, 6 August 1892.

207 'characteristic signs' –Tardieu, *Étude médico-légale*.

207 'noticed by all present' – Taylor, *Medical Jurisprudence* (1873 edition).

208 'Beware' – Tardieu, *Étude médico-légale*.

208 'a small varix' – Trial testimony of Dr Johnson.

209 'It may be relied upon' – *Reynolds's Newspaper*, 19 June 1870.

20 *He, She or It*

210 'There is not the slightest doubt' – *The Englishwoman's Domestic Magazine*, 1871.

211 'the smallness of the anus' – *Trial Testimony of Dr Johnson*.

212 'the Hermaphrodite Clique' – *Reynolds's Newspaper,* 5 June 1870.

212 'the Hermaphrodite Gang' – *Reynolds's Newspaper,* 12 June 1870.

212 'By special request' – *Extraordinary Revelations*.

212 'During the piece' – *Essex Herald*, 2 January 1869, in *Daily Telegraph*, 9 May 1870.

213 'Listening' – anonymous newspaper report in *Extraordinary Revelations*.

213 'We agreed' – *Daily Telegraph*, 13 May 1871.

213 'We may add' – *Extraordinary Revelations*.

214 'On one evening' – *Daily Telegraph*, 13 May 1871.

214 'My darling Ernie' – Louis Hurt to Ernest Boulton, 4 April 1870, read in evidence, Trial.

215 'rustics' – Louis Hurt to Lord Arthur Clinton, 9 October 1868, read in evidence, Trial.

215 'I really thought' – *Daily Telegraph*, 21 May 1870.

216 'I pretended to resist' – Saul, *Sins of the Cities*.

217 'I resigned' – *Daily Telegraph*, 21 May 1870.

218 'It was from the manner' – Deposition of Francis Kegan Cox.

218 'Oh you City birds' – *Daily Telegraph*, 21 May 1870.

219 'I treated Boulton' – *ibid*.

220 'I afterwards heard' – *ibid*.

222 'a letter from Captain Cox' – '657 – December 1870', Treasury Solicitor's Account Books, TS 40 14, The National Archives.

21 *A Bitches' Ball*

223 'a bitches' ball' – Statement of Malcolm Johnston, Dublin Commission Court.

225 'the slang term "drag"' – Deposition of Amos Westropp Gibbings.

226 'chanced to see' – Arthur Munby's diary entry for 13 April 1864, in Derek Hudson, *Munby: Man of Two Worlds* (London, 1974).

227 'dressed in the pastoral garb' – *The Times*, 1 August 1854.

227 'a hundred persons' – *ibid*.

227 'a sort of dance' – *Illustrated Police News*, 2 October 1880, in H. G. Cocks, *Nameless Offences: Homosexual Desire in the Nineteenth Century* (London, 2003).

228 'Sister' – *ibid*.

228 'They changed partners' – Deposition of Edward Nelson Haxell.

229 'the best amateur actress' – *ibid*.

229 'I heard Boulton sing' – *ibid*.

230 'There seems to be' – Jack Saul, *Sins of the Cities*.

230 'No doubt the proprietor' – *ibid*.

231 'I sat for a while' – *ibid*.

231 'dancing with a gentleman from the City' – *ibid*.

231 'During the evening' – *ibid*.

231 'Lord Arthur and Boulton' – *ibid*.

232 'at once knelt down' – *ibid*.

232 'soon brought to light' – *ibid*.

232 'How excited I became' – *ibid*.

232 'postillioned her bottomhole' – *ibid*.

233 'Opening her drawers' – *ibid*.

22 *The Wheels of Justice*

235 'We hope and believe' – *Pall Mall Gazette*, 8 June 1870.

235 'I am rather sorry' – Louis Hurt to Ernest Boulton, 17 April 1870,

Letters.

236 'I suppose' – Louis Hurt to John Safford Fiske, 29 May 1870, Trial.

236 'My darling Ernie' – Louis Hurt to Ernest Boulton, 8 April 1870, Letters.

237 'Do you advise' – Louis Hurt to John Safford Fiske, 29 May 1870, Trial.

238 'heartily glad' – Louis Hurt to John Safford Fiske, 18 May 1870, Trial.

238 'I was in Court' – Louis Hurt to John Safford Fiske, 29 May 1870, Trial.

238 'My dear John' – Louis Hurt to John Safford Fiske, 18 May 1870, Trial.

239 '*un ange*' – John Safford Fiske to Ernest Boulton, 18 April 1870, Letters.

239 'I have just seen' – Louis Hurt to John Safford Fiske, May 1870, Trial.

241 'Mr Fiske called' – Confidential Memorandum No 353: John Lothrop Motley to Hamilton Fisk, Secretary of State, London, 11 June 1870, in 'Despatches from U.S. Ministers to Great Britain, 1791–1906', US National Archives and Records Administration.

243 'I asked Mr Fiske' – Trial testimony of Detective Officer Gollan.

244 'Mr Fiske – Facts' – Confidential Memorandum No 357.

23 Dead or Disappeared

246 'We have it on the authority' – *Reynolds's Newspaper*, 26 June 1870.

247 'Peers' – *ibid*.

247 'resolution' – *Pall Mall Gazette*, 8 June 1870.

248 'I took up my fare' – *Reynolds's Newspaper*, 12 June 1870.

249 'We understand' – *Weekly Times*, 12 June 1870.

249 'there are people' – *Observer*, 26 June 1870.

249 'The rumour' – *Daily Telegraph*, 20 June 1870.

250 'We are in a position' – *Lancet*, 25 June 1870.

250 'utter prostration' – *Evening Standard*, 20 June 1870.

250 'bed of sickness' – *ibid.*

250 'Nothing' – *ibid.*

251 'sad and wasted' – *Daily Telegraph*, 21 June 1870.

251 'A MIS-SPENT LIFE' – *Reynolds's Newspaper*, 26 June 1870.

251 'Lord Arthur's' – *Porcupine*, 25 June 1870.

251 'Verily' – *ibid.*

251 'The funeral' – *Weekly Times*, 26 June 1870.

252 'He hath borne' – *Echo*, 24 June 1870.

252 'persons' – *Nottingham Daily Guardian*, 22 June 1870.

252 'Is Lord Arthur' – *Porcupine*, 25 June 1870.

253 'It is understood' – *Daily Telegraph*, 10 May 1871.

256 'nothing' – Mr Ouvry to William Gladstone, 29 June 1870, folio 3011, Glynne Gladstone MSS.

256 'It is impossible' – *ibid.*

24 *This Slippery Sod*

257 'The management' – *Reynolds's Newspaper*, 29 May 1870.

261 'a rather effeminate' – *Illustrated Police News*, 30 July 1870.

261 'I walked' – *The Times*, 2 April 1870.

261 'Oh! pray don't' – *ibid.*

262 'Come with me' – *The Times*, 26 July 1870.

262 'I am ashamed' – *ibid.*

264 'Dear Stella' – Harry Park to Stella Boulton, early 1871, Letters.

266 'Mr Edward Henry Park?' – *Illustrated Police News*, 30 July 1870.

267 'a tall, stylishly-dressed' – *ibid.*

267 'The bench and court' – *ibid.*

268 'I am here' – *The Times*, 26 July 1870.

25 *'Pestiferous and Pestilential'*

269 'What words can paint' – *Extraordinary Revelations.*

271 'venereal disease' – 'Evidence of William Henry Sloggett, 30 January 1871', *Analysis of the Evidence Given Before the Contagious Diseases Commission.*

271 'a grand movement' – *London Entr'acte*, 23 January 1871.

272 *'contra'* – Sir Edward Coke, *Third Part of the Institutes of the Laws of England* (London, 1797).

272 'things fearful' – William Bradford, *Of Plymouth Plantation*, written between 1620 and 1647, in Jonathan Katz, *Gay American History* (New York, 1978).

273 'pestiferous' – in Richard Davenport-Hines, *Sex, Death and Punishment: Attitudes to Sex and Sexuality in Britain since the Renaissance* (London, 1991).

273 'abominations' – in Alan Bray, *Homosexuality in Renaissance England* (London, 1982).

273 'Henceforth, Borastus' – John Wilmot, *Sodom, or The Quintessence of Debauchery* (Paris, 1957).

273 'hugger-mugger' – *ibid.*

274 'The unnatural Lewdness' – Thomas Sherlock, *A Letter from the Lord Bishop of London to the Clergy and People of London and Westminster; on Occasion of the Late Earthquakes* (London, 1750).

275 'great hulking ruffians' – James Greenwood, 'A Night in the Workhouse', *Pall Mall Gazette*, 13 January 1866.

275 'Facts' – Charles Dickens, *Hard Times* (London, 1854).

275 'classification' – George Roberts, *An Etymological and Explanatory Dictionary of the Terms and Language of Geology* (London, 1839).

275 'peripheral excitement' – Isaac Baker Brown, *On the Curability of Certain Forms of Insanity, Epilepsy, Catalepsy, and Hysteria in*

Females (London, 1866).

277 'Androgynism' – *Medical Times and Gazette*, 9 February 1868.

277 'the slightest doubt' – Cunnington, *Feminine Attitudes*.

277 'unsexed' – *Pall Mall Gazette*, 29 June 1870.

278 'respectable young men' – *The Times*, 25 September 1857.

278 'Smirking' – *ibid.*

278 'unnatural' – in Michael Mason, *The Making of Victorian Sexuality* (Oxford, 1995).

278 'The increase' – 'H. Smith', *Yokel's Preceptor* c.1850

279 'who is known' – *Daily Telegraph*, 31 May 1870.

279 'It is certain' – *Saturday Review*, 20 May 1871.

279 'A certain form of iniquity' – *Daily Telegraph*, 31 May 1870.

279 'a doubtful fellowship' – *Daily Telegraph*, 31 May 1870.

279 'clique' – *Reynolds's Newspaper*, 5 June 1870.

279 'Vice' – *Daily Telegraph*, 31 May 1870.

279 'There is no saying how far things might go' – *The Times*, 31 May 1870.

279 'This London of ours' – *Reynolds's Newspaper*, 5 June 1870.

280 'organisation and concert' – *The Pall Mall Gazette*, 8 June 1870.

26 The Ship of State

282 'Herald, read the accusation!' – Lewis Carroll, *Alice's Adventures in Wonderland* (1865).

282 'To judge' – *Daily Telegraph*, 10 May 1871.

283 'the public' – *Porcupine*, 9 July 1870.

283 'It is thought' – *Penny Illustrated*, 11 December 1870.

284 'a bouquet' – *Illustrated Police News*, 13 May 1871.

284 'tastily' – *Daily Telegraph*, 10 May 1871.

284 'scarcely altered' – *ibid.*

285 'campish' – Frederick Park to Lord Arthur Clinton, 21 November 1868, Letters.

286 'a spider's web' – in John Juxon, *Lewis and Lewis: The Life and*

Times of a Victorian Solicitor (London, 1983).

286 'conspiracy to solicit' – 9 May 1871, DPP 4/6, The National Archives.

288 'unlawfully' – *ibid*.

288 'openly and publicly' – *ibid*.

291 'This is a prosecution' – Opening speech of the Attorney-General, Trial.

291 'his bounden duty' – *ibid*.

293 'Perhaps I am not going' – *ibid*.

293 'But' – *ibid*.

27 *The Most Sensational Event*

295 'By sometimes dressing' – Opening speech of the Attorney-General, Trial.

296 'irregular affections' – Solomon to Swinburne, 1862, in Jean Overton Fuller, *Swinburne: A Critical Biography* (London, 1968).

296 'Dolomite' – Solomon to Swinburne, 10 May 1871, in John Y. LeBourgeois, 'Swinburne and Simeon Solomon', *Notes and Queries*, March 1973.

296 'Boulton is very remarkable' – Solomon to Swinburne, 15 May 1871, in LeBourgeois, 'Swinburne and Simeon Solomon'.

296 'a very revolting' – *Illustrated Police News*, 4 June 1870.

297 'Dear Stella' – Harry Park to Stella Boulton, Letters.

298 'Dearest Stella' – Willy Somerville to Stella Boulton, Letters.

300 'My cawfish' – Opening speech of Sir John Karslake, Trial.

300 'It is cawfish' – *ibid*.

301 'Whatever it may mean' – *ibid*.

301 'painting their faces' – Opening speech of the Attorney-General, Trial.

302 'If every *roué*' – *Extraordinary Revelations*.

303 'crush and spoil' – Opening speech of Mr Digby Seymour, Trial.

303 'thoroughly' – Trial testimony of William Kay.

304 'A thrill' – *Daily Telegraph*, 13 May 1871.

306 'the most sensational' – *Daily Telegraph*, 10 May 1871.

306 'roars of laughter' – *ibid*.

307 'Do you think' – *ibid*.

308 'acquitted' – Solomon to Swinburne, 15 May 1871, in LeBourgeois, 'Swinburne and Simeon Solomon'.

28 *A Rout*

309 'The conception' – *The Times*, 25 July 1871.

311 'What is that book' – Trial testimony of Dr James Paul.

313 'Just attend to me' – *ibid*.

314 'any Magistrate's order' – *ibid*.

315 'You should be more careful' – *ibid*.

315 'getting up evidence' – Deposition of George Smith.

316 'pay him' – Trial testimony of George Smith.

316 'a situation' – *The Times*, 14 May 1870.

316 'I have watched them' – *Daily Telegraph*, 30 April 1870.

317 'the unemployed' – Letter Book of the Commissioner of the Metropolitan Police, MEPO 1/48, The National Archives.

317 'Maladministration' – *ibid*.

317 'Mr Bradlaugh' – *ibid*.

317 'young Mr Boulton' – Opening address of Mr Digby Seymour, Trial.

319 '679 – Dec 1870' – Treasury Solicitor's Account Books, TS 40 14, The National Archives.

319 '492 – Dec 1870' – *ibid*.

320 'rewards' – Opening speech of Mr Digby Seymour, Trial.

29 *'This Terrible Drama of Vice'*

321 'She watches' – Fanny Fales (Mrs Frances Elizabeth Swift), *Voices*

of the Heart (Boston, 1853).

322 'own beloved Child' – Mary Ann Boulton to Ernest Boulton, Letters.

322 'wanted strength' – *ibid*.

322 'Are you the mother' – Trial testimony of Mary Ann Boulton.

322 'Exactly so' – *ibid*.

324 'a retentive memory' – *ibid*.

326 'Ernest has been' – *ibid*.

328 'We know as a fact' – Closing speech of Mr Digby Seymour, Trial.

328 'a friend' – Trial testimony of Mary Ann Boulton.

330 'nothing indecent' – Closing speech of Mr Digby Seymour, Trial.

330 'My son sent me' – Trial testimony of Mary Ann Boulton.

331 'You would expect' – Closing speech of Mr Digby Seymour, Trial. 'Ernest Boulton' – *ibid*.

331 'vile and wicked' – *ibid*.

332 'Dr Paul' – *ibid*.

332 'morbidly sensible' – Opening address of Mr Digby Seymour, Trial.

332 'the most exquisite torture' – *ibid*.

332 'Surely, Gentlemen' – Closing speech of Mr Digby Seymour, Trial.

334 'capable of plunging' – *ibid*.

335 'Gentlemen' – *Lloyd's Weekly Newspaper*, 21 May 1871.

30 Clouds and Sunshine

336 'Rose of the garden' – Fricker, 'Fading Away'.

336 'MR ERNEST BOULTON' – *Reynolds's Newspaper*, 6 August 1871, quoting from the *Era*, late July 1871.

337 'his Drawing-Room Entertainment' – *Liverpool Mercury*, 14 November/21 November 1871.

337 'Mr Boulton displayed' – *Liverpool Mercury*, 9 September 1873.

338 'PORTLAND HALL' – *Hampshire Telegraph and Sussex Chronicle*, 29 May 1872.

338 'The beauty' – *Hampshire Telegraph and Sussex Chronicle*, 5 June 1872.

339 'This so-called' – *Hampshire Advertiser*, 15 June 1872.

339 'notoriety' – *Birmingham Daily Post*, 17 June 1872.

339 'Beams of the morning' – Fricker, 'Fading Away'.

340 'the impudence' – *Pall Mall Gazette*, 18 October 1873.

341 'comedian' – *New York Clipper*, 9 April 1881.

341 'Ernest Byne' – *New York Clipper*, 11 April 1874.

341 'Two gentlemen' – *ibid*.

342 'ERNEST BYNE, pronounced' – *New York Clipper*, 25 April 1874.

342 'Your airs' – quoted in Laurence Senelick, *The Changing Room: Sex, Drag and Theatre* (London, 2000).

343 'Lord Arthur Clinton' – *Reynolds's Newspaper*, 20 October 1872.

343 'at the Installation' – *Morning Post*, 30 January 1878.

343 'My Lord Arthur Clinton' – *Clarence and Richmond Examiner and New South Wales Advertiser*, 25 February 1879.

344 'Elegant Parisian Clothes' – *Era*, 24 June 1877.

344 'Songs, Eccentricities' – *Era*, 10 March 1878.

344 'a most marvellous' – *Era*, 24 June 1877.

344 'The Bynes are' – *Era*, 22 July 1877.

344 'AN INDIGNANT NONCONFORMIST" – *Western Mail*, 14 April 1879.

344 'actor' – Census of 1881.

344 'Spring's fairest blossoms' – Fricker, 'Fading Away'.

346 'How *dare* you' – *Evening Standard*, 2 May 1870.

346 'N'importe' – Frederick Park to Lord Arthur Clinton, 21 November 1868, Letters.

346 'I give, devise' – Last Will and Testament of Frederick William Park, 17 July 1878.

347 'Song of the wild-bird' – Fricker, 'Fading Away'.

347 'Society absurdity' – *Era*, 22 December 1891.

348 'The performer' – *Era*, 13 June 1891.

348 'The Brothers Blair' – *Belfast News-Letter*, 13 June 1896.

350 'Hope's fairy promise' – Fricker, 'Fading Away'.

350 'But there's a land' – *ibid*.

Epilogue

354 'a professional Mary-Ann' – Statements of Jack Saul to Inspector Abberline.

354 'Lord Euston' – *ibid*.

354 'uttering a fictitious cheque' – *Hampshire Telegraph and Sussex Chronicle*, 25 January 1873.

354 'congestion' – Death certificate of Amos Westropp Gibbings, 29 March 1890.

355 'I invented' – Oscar Wilde to the Editor of the *Pall Mall Gazette*, 1 October 1894, in Merlin Holland and Rupert Hart-Davis, *The Complete Letters of Oscar Wilde* (London, 2000).

357 'For I've got a Peep-Show' – C. J. Pavitt, 'I've Got a Peep-Show' (*c*.1875).

357 'allowed any cloud ' – Trial testimony of Mary Ann Boulton.

358 'large and beautiful garden' – unsigned autobiographical essay by John Safford Fiske, *History of the Class of 1863 Yale College* (New Haven, Connecticut, 1905), in Jonathan Ned Katz, *Love Stories: Sex Between Men Before Homosexuality* (Chicago, 2001).

358 'passed through his hands' – *Wirksworth Parish Magazine*, October 1936, in Derek Wain, *The Hurts of Derbyshire* (Ashbourne, Derbyshire, 2002).

359 'my uncle' – Will of the Most Noble Henry Pelham Archibald Douglas Duke of Newcastle, 1927.

359 'His charming manner' – *Hampshire Chronicle*, 19 February 1940.

Index

Abberline, Inspector, 354

Abbey Green, Lanarkshire, 257–60, 266

Abrams (solicitor): acts for Fanny and Stella, 40, 198, 205, 285; advises Hurt and Fiske, 237–8, 240–1

Acton, William, 188–9

Alhambra *see* Royal Alhambra Palace

Allingham, William, 188

anal sex *see* sodomy

Anniss, Inspector Silas, 107

Attenborough, Mr (pawnbroker), 135

Attorney-General *see* Collier, Sir Robert

Barker, Emily, 108

Barwell, Dr Richard: examines and treats Fanny for syphilis, 193–7, 199, 203–4, 208–9, 238, 310–11; gives evidence at trial, 309–10, 331; later career and death, 357

Batson, Mary, 66–8, 70, 75

Beeton, Isabella and Samuel, 95

Belfast News-Letter, 348

Betsey H— (male prostitute), 108

Blair, Ernest and Eden (stage names of Stella and Gerard Boulton), 347

Boulton, Gerard (Stella's brother): birth and childhood, 55, 58; and Lord Arthur Clinton, 133; partners Stella as leading man, 340, 344, 347; in America, 341–2; returns to England, 344; adopts name Eden Blair, 347, 360; marriage and son, 348; with

Stella at death, 350; manages theatre in Winchester and death (1940), 360

Boulton, Mary Ann (Stella's mother): character and qualities, 51; marriage, 54–5; and Stella's dressing up as child, 56–7; decline in fortunes, 58–9; and Stella's poor health, 60–1, 128, 332; encourages Louis Hurt's interest in Stella, 126, 179, 328; and Stella's friends, 128–9; and Stella's relations with Lord Arthur Clinton, 131–7, 325–6, 329; and Stella's arrests, 133–4, 235; Louis Hurt offers support to, 236; testifies at Stella's trial, 321–30, 332, 334; death, 358

Boulton, Ernest *see* Boulton, Stella

Boulton, Stella: appearance and dress, 4–6, 13, 129, 141, 284, 296; at Strand Theatre, 4–6; arrested (1870), 7–11; gives name as Ernest Boulton, 9; Mundell meets and falls for, 12–23; appears before Bow Street magistrate and charged, 34–7; remanded in custody, 40–1; examined by Dr Paul, 44, 50–1, 310; birth and childhood, 55–6; singing, 55–7, 59, 131, 212–13, 220, 224, 229, 338–9, 341–2; dressing up as girl, 56–7; acting ambitions and performances, 57–9, 61, 212–14, 325; banking career, 59–60; attractive to men,

61–4; friendship with Fanny, 76, 79, 84–7; second court appearance, 88–91; drag wardrobe and accoutrements, 92–8; operation for fistula, 100, 177–8, 201; earlier arrests, 102–5, 133; acts in Oxford with Cumming, 103; earnings from prostitution, 104; testimonies and evidence against, 114–25; Louis Hurt courts, 126–7, 178–9; relations with Lord Arthur Clinton, 130–7, 139, 142–6; coming-of-age party (1867), 135–6; shares lodgings with Lord Arthur, 139, 142; character and behaviour, 144–5, 159–60; stage appearance in Scarborough, 152, 155–8; writes notes to Lord Arthur, 160–3; stays with Lord Arthur at Miss Empson's in Davies Street, 169, 172; and Lord Arthur's infidelity with Fanny, 174, 176; letter from Fiske, 175–6, 186; reconciliation with Fanny, 178; in Edinburgh, 179–81, 185; in Newgate Gaol, 198–9, 205–6, 245; medically examined in prison, 199–200, 204, 206, 208–9, 238; feminine appearance of body, 210–11, 214; supposed hermaphroditism, 211–17; dalliance with Captain Cox, 218–20; attends Carlotta's ball, 224, 229, 231–3; released on bail, 267, 283; trial before Lord Chief Justice, 282, 284, 291–2, 308; charges of sodomy withdrawn, 283; grows moustache, 284–5; criminal charges, 288–9; under police surveillance, 316–17; mother testifies for at trial, 324–6, 328–9; found not guilty, 335; resumes theatrical career after acquittal, 336–44, 347–8; changes name to Ernest Byne and moves to America, 340–1; returns to England, 344; as Ernest Blair, 347; male admirers in later years, 348–50; final illness, death and burial, 350–1, 358

Boulton, Thomas (Stella's father): marriage, 54–5; business reverses, 59, 325; and Lord Arthur Clinton, 132–3; Stella's arrest, 235; Louis Hurt offers support to, 236; absent from Stella's trial, 322–3

Bow Street Magistrates' Court, 33–4, 90, 169, 173

Bow Street Police Station, 8, 32, 115

Bradford, William, Governor of New England, 272

Bradlaugh, Charles, 317

Britain: social problems and change, 269–72

brothels, male, 107

Brown, Isaac Baker, 277

Brown, Colonel T. Allston, 342

Bruce, Henry, 291

Bryan, Alfred, 3

buggery see sodomy

Burlington Arcade, Piccadilly, 116, 119, 121–2, 306–7

Byne, Ernest (stage name of Boulton, Stella) see Boulton, Stella

Byron, George Gordon, 6th Baron: 'Don Leon', 190

Byron, H.J.: One Hundred Thousand Pounds (play), 212

Caminada, Detective Sergeant Jerome, 227–8

Campbell, George, 227

Campbell ('Lady Jane Grey'), 104–5, 133

Carden, Sir Robert, 227

Carlotta *see* Gibbings, Amos Westropp

Caroline, Madame, 108

Carroll, Lewis: *Alice's Adventures in Wonderland*, 289

Casper, Dr Johann Ludwig, 207, 276

Castlehaven, Mervin Touchet, 2nd Earl of, 273, 290

Challis, John, 227

Chamberlain, Detective Officer William: and arrest of Fanny and Stella, 8, 10–11, 45, 109, 346; calls at Martha Stacey's house, 25–6, 29, 91, 98; testifies against Fanny and Stella, 37–9, 125; and medical examination of Fanny and Stella, 43–4; admits to surveillance of Fanny and Stella, 316; payments to, 319; retires from Metropolitan police and becomes private detective, 354

Charing Cross Hospital: Fanny attends for anal syphilis, 193

chirruping, 3–4

chloroform, 99–100

Clarence and Richmond Examiner and New South Wales Advertiser, 343

Clark, Eliza, 140–1, 143, 304

Coldbath Fields, House of Correction, 346

Cleveland Street Scandal (1890), 354

Clinton, Lord Arthur *see* Pelham–Clinton, Lord Arthur

Clinton, Lord Thomas, 252

Clutterbuck, Dr, 47

Cockburn Sir Alexander (Lord Chief Justice), 284

Coke, Sir Edward, 272

Collette, Charles Hastings (The Society for the Suppression of Vice), 296

Collier, Sir Robert (Attorney–General): prosecutes Fanny and Stella, 290–3, 296–300, 307, 327; calls witnesses, 300–5; on Home Secretary's interest in trial, 319

Colton, Eleanor, 302

Cox, Captain Francis Kegan, 217–22, 319

Cox, Jane, 302

Creer, Edwin, 98

Cumming, Martin Luther ('the Comical Countess'): uses Wakefield Street house, 24, 29; friendship with Fanny, 76, 128; arrested with Stella, 102–3, 133, 302; acting, 103, 129; attends Carlotta's ball, 229; Inspector Thomas pursues, 263; tried in absence, 288; appearance, 289; last sighting in Brussels, 353

Daily Telegraph, 35, 89, 102, 249, 251, 253, 279, 282, 284, 304, 306

Daly, Anthony, 111

Darwin, Charles, 269

Davies Street, London, 167, 169, 176

Departmental Committee on Prisons, 199

D'Eyncourt, Mr (magistrate), 268

Dibdin, Acting Sergeant Edwin, 262, 267

Dickens, Charles: on Surrey Theatre, 12; *Hard Times*, 275

Dickson, Mrs Agnes, 180, 236, 302

Doig, John, 180

Druid's Hall, City of London, 227

Drag balls, 226–30

Drysdale, George, 189–90; *The Elements of Social Science*, 48

Dublin Castle Scandal (1884), 353–4

Duffin, Hannah, 357

Duffin, Maria (*later* George), 96, 141–3, 304, 319, 357–8

Dunton, John: *The He-Strumpets*, 190

Edinburgh, 176, 178–81, 183–5

Edward, Prince of Wales: at Strand Theatre, 3; visits Scarborough, 150; in Mordaunt divorce case, 286

Edwards, Eliza, 46–7, 201, 204, 207

Edwards, Maria, 46–7

Empson, Ann, 167–73, 264, 305–6, 356

Englishwoman's Domestic Magazine, The, 95, 277

Era (theatrical newspaper), 344, 348

Essex Herald, 212

Euston, Henry James FitzRoy, Earl of, 354

Evening News, 34

Extraordinary Revelations see Lives of Boulton and Park, The: Extraordinary Revelations (anonymous pamphlet), 190

Fair Eliza (male prostitute), 108

Fanny see Park, Fanny Winifred

Farrer, Mrs Thomasin, 151

Farrier, Police Constable, 112

Fenians, 269, 317

Fenton, Fred see Park, Fanny Winifred

Ferguson, Charles see Park, Harry

Fiske, John Safford: in Edinburgh, 176, 181, 184; background and career, 182–3; infatuation with Stella, 185–6; and Louis Hurt, 236–8; letters to Stella in police hands, 239–40; visits London to explain relations with Stella, 241–2; premises searched by police, 243–4, 302; arrested and held in Newgate, 244–5, 257; charges of sodomy withdrawn, 283; trial, 288, 290, 292; Simeon Solomon describes, 296; retirement to Italy and death, 358

Flowers, James, 33, 35, 38–40, 43, 91, 93, 170, 197, 215

France: cross-dressers, 97

George, Maria *see* Duffin, Maria

Gepp and Sons (Chelmsford solicitors), 74, 138

Gibbings, Amos Westropp ('Carlotta'): meets Mundell, 22; uses Martha Stacey's Wakefield Street house of accommodation, 24–5, 27, 299; removes incriminating matter from Wakefield Street, 29, 98, 299; takes men's clothes to police station for Fanny and Stella, 32; engages solicitor for Fanny and Stella, 40; friendship with Fanny, 76; hosts ball at Haxell's Hotel, 223–4, 226, 228–30, 299; relations with Fanny, 224–5; appearance, 225; friendship with Sissy Thomas, 299; supposedly finances Fanny and Stella's

defence, 305; tours with Louis
Munro, 354; death, 354
Gibson, Dr John Rowland, 203–4,
206
Gladstone, William Ewart: on
Duchess of Manchester, 2; as
godfather, guardian and political
patron of Lord Arthur, 153; and
settling of Mr Roberts's bill,
256
Gladwell, Arthur, 305
Gollan, Detective Officer Roderick,
243–4, 302, 358
gonorrhoea, 202
Graham, Fanny Winifred *see* Park,
Fanny Winifred
Graphic (newspaper), 96
Greenwood, James, 274–5
Greenwood, John, 119, 318–19

H—, Betsey *see* Betsey H—
Hagen, Catherine, 345, 347
Hagen, Oliver, 345
hairstyles, 96
Hammond, Charles, 108
Hampshire Advertiser, 339
*Hampshire Telegraph and Sussex
Chronicle*, 338–9
Harvey, Dr Alfred, 199–200, 202,
241
Haweis, Mrs H.R.: *The Art of Beauty*,
98
Haxell, Edward Nelson, 228–30, 357
Haxell's Hotel, West Strand: ball,
223–4, 228–9; incorporated into
Strand Palace Hotel, 357
Haymarket, London, 102
Heath, Sir Robert, 243, 290
Henry, Sir Thomas, 314–15
hermaphrodites, 211–12
Hewitt, Frank, 108

Highbury Barn *see* drag balls
homosexual: as term, 276
houses of accommodation, 26–7
House of Correction *see* Coldbath
Fields, House of Correction
Hughes, Dr William, 177–8,
199–203
Hulme, Manchester, 227
Hurt, Louis: on Stella's mincing walk,
85; courts Stella, 126–7, 132,
179; invites Stella to Edinburgh,
178–9, 188; background and
character, 179; on Stella's
feminine appearance, 214–15,
285; and arrest of Stella and
Fanny, 235–6; devotion to Stella,
236; visits police, 240; arrested
and confined in Newgate, 245,
257; charges of sodomy
withdrawn, 283; trial, 288, 290;
Mrs Boulton testifies about, 328;
later career and death, 358–9

Illustrated London News, 35
Illustrated Police News, 34, 89, 249,
267

Jim, John Jameson, 180, 237
Johnson, Dr Henry James, 191, 202,
204, 208, 210–11; *Gonorrhoea
and Its Consequences*, 202
Johnston, Betsy, 108
Johnston, Malcolm ('the Maid of
Athens'), 109–10, 223, 3533
Jones, Lieutenant (friend of Lord
Arthur Clinton), 135

Karslake, Sir John, 295
Kay, William, 303
Kean, James, 111
Kerley, Detective Sergeant Frederick,

8, 37, 43–5, 109, 319, 354–5
Kersey, Benjamin, 112

Lancet (journal), 197, 205–6, 250
Layton, George, 193
Le Gros Clark, Dr Frederick,
    199–202, 206
Leopold, Prince: birth, 99
Lesmahagow, Lanarkshire *see* Abbey
    Green
Lewis, Mr George: acts for Fanny and
    Stella, 285–7; character and style,
    286–7; and Martha Stacey, 305;
    advises Stella's mother as witness,
    321–2; later career and
    knighthood, 355
Lewis, Mr (chief clerk in bank), 60–1
Littlechild, Inspector, 355
Liverpool Mercury, 337
Lives of Boulton and Park:
    Extraordinary Revelations
    (pamphlet), 90
London and County Bank, Islington,
    60
London Lock Hospital, 202
Lord Chief Justice *see* Cockburn, Sir
    Alexander (Lord Chief Justice)
Lyceum Theatre, London, 15

Martin, Bennett, 105
masturbation, 276–7
Mayne, Sir Richard (Metropolitan
    Police Commissioner), 316
Medical Times and Gazette, 276
Metropolitan Police: special branch
    and surveillance, 317–18
Motley, John Lothrop, 241, 244
Mullin, Judge Joseph, 182–3
Munby, Arthur, 226
Mundell, Hugh: at Strand Theatre, 1,
    4, 6; accompanies Fanny and

Stella to police station, 10–11, 23,
    32; meets Fanny and Stella,
    12–23; appears in Bow Street
    Magistrates' Court, 33–4, 90; on
    bond between Fanny and Stella,
    86; as chief prosecution witness,
    237, 301, 308; later career as
    chiropodist, 356
Munro, Louis: as Stella's leading
    man, 337–9; takes up with
    Carlotta Gibbings, 354

New York, 341
New York Clipper (newspaper), 342
Newcastle, Henry Pelham Alexander
    Pelham-Clinton, 6th Duke of, 252
Newcastle, Henry Pelham Archibald
    Pelham-Clinton, 7th Duke of, 359
Newgate Gaol, 198–9, 205–6, 245
Newlyn, Sambrooke, 254
Norris, Isabella, 70
Northern Echo, 343
Nottingham Daily Guardian, 252

Observer (newspaper), 249
Ortner, Houle & Co., Messrs, 135
Ouvry, Mr (solicitor), 255–6

Pall Mall Gazette, 247, 274, 277,
    280, 340
Paris: cross-dressers, 97
Park, Judge Alexander (Fanny's
    father), 74–7, 263, 268, 340
Park, Lieut. Atherton Allan (Fanny's
    brother), 65, 67
Park, Fanny Winifred: at Strand
    Theatre, 1, 3, 6; appearance and
    dress, 5, 13, 74, 80–2, 129,
    141–2, 284; arrested, 7–11, 31;
    gives name as Frederick William
    Park, 9; Mundell meets, 12–23;

appears before Bow Street magistrate and charged, 34–7; remanded in custody, 40–1; examined by Dr Paul, 50–1, 310; family background and upbringing, 65–6; character and looks, 67–70, 79–82, 345–6; effeminacy, 68–70, 74; home schooled, 70; liking for men, 71–3; articled to solicitor, 75, 138; behaviour and manner, 75–6; acting, 76–7, 82–3, 212; Stella's view of, 79; early sexual experience, 80–1; pretends to widowhood, 83–4; friendship with Stella, 84–7, 128; second court appearance, 88–91; drag wardrobe and accoutrements, 92–8; hair care, 96–7; beard problem, 97–8; testimonies and evidence against, 114–18, 121–5; absences from Gepp & Sons (solicitors), 138–9, 148–9; at Stella's Southampton Street lodgings with Lord Arthur, 139–40, 142; and Stella's relations with Lord Arthur, 144–6; hopes for marriage to Lord Arthur, 146–7; correspondence and confidences with Lord Arthur, 163–6; at Miss Empson's in Davies Street, 169, 172, 174; Lord Arthur sleeps with, 174, 176; reconciliation with Stella, 178; treated for syphilis, 187–8, 191–3, 196–7, 203, 238, 309–11, 345; trial before Lord Chief Justice, 191–2, 282, 284, 308; in Newgate Gaol, 198–9, 205–6, 245; medically examined in prison, 199–200,

204, 206, 208–9, 238; femininity of body, 210–11; supposed hermaphroditism, 211–12, 215; relations with Carlotta Gibbings, 224–5; attends Carlotta's ball, 224, 228–31; released on bail, 267, 283; charges of sodomy withdrawn, 283; grows beard, 284–5; criminal charges, 288; letters to Lord Arthur read out in court, 299–300; under police surveillance, 316–17; in Mrs Boulton's testimony, 328; and father's death, 340–1; acting in America as 'Fred Fenton', 341; death from syphilis, 345; estate and will, 347

Park, Harry (Fanny's brother): and Fanny's home life, 66–70; sexual relations with men, 71–2, 77; arrested and absconds to Scotland, 73–4, 82, 113, 187–8, 261–3; bond with Fanny, 74; in Edinburgh, 176; propensity for working men, 192; prospective arrest, 237; lies low (as Charles Ferguson) in Abbey Green, Lanarkshire, 257–60, 266; sexual adventures in London, 260–2; letter to Stella, 264–5, 297–8; rearrested by Thompson, 267–8; and sentenced to twelve months' hard labour, 267–8, 298; and father's death, 341

Park, Frederick William *see* Park, Fanny Winifred

Park, Lucy (Fanny's sister), 66–8, 70, 72

Parry, Mr Sergeant, 268, 300, 307, 313–14

Paul, Dr James Thomas: duties as

police surgeon, 42–3; examines
Fanny and Stella, 44–5, 50–1,
199, 238, 310, 315; interest in
sodomy, 46, 48–50, 201, 276;
studies under Alfred Swaine
Taylor, 201; gives evidence and
cross-examined at trial, 309,
311–15, 327, 331–2; later career
and death, 353
Pavitt, Charles, 76, 128, 212–14,
325, 357
*Pearl, The: a Monthly Journal of
Facetiae and Voluptuous Reading*,
99
Peck, Louisa, 139–40, 161, 180, 305,
308
Peel, Percival, 229
Pelham-Clinton, Lord Arthur: Stella's
relations with, 129–37, 139,
142–6, 218; theatrical interests,
132–3; engagement to Miss
Matthews collapses, 134; financial
difficulties, 134–6, 144, 155;
offers to provide catering for
Stella's coming-of-age party,
136–7; comes between Stella and
Fanny, 143; Fanny hopes to
marry, 146–7; visits Scarborough
with Stella, 152–4, 156–8, 325–6;
and Stella's moods and demands,
160–3; correspondence and
confidences with Fanny, 163–6;
lodges at Miss Empson's in
Davies Street, 168–9, 171–3;
sleeps with Fanny, 174, 176;
confirms Stella is a man, 215; and
Stella's dalliance with Captain
Cox, 218–21; with Stella at
Carlotta's ball, 231–3; arrest
delayed, 246–7; disappearance
and reported death and burial,
247–56, 287, 337; letters from
Fanny read out in court, 299–300;
Mrs Boulton approves of, 329;
reported reappearances in New
York and Australia, 343–4;
question of death unsolved, 359
Penny Illustrated, 283
Poland, Mr (prosecuting attorney),
91–2, 241–2, 297
Pollard, William (Assistant Treasury
Solicitor), 221, 287, 316, 318
Porcupine (journal), 251–2, 283
prostitutes, male: prevalence, 104–7;
payments for, 107–8; marry, 108;
relations with police, 109–13;
blackmailed, 110–11
prostitution: in Britain, 270

Queensberry, John Sholto Douglas,
8th Marquis of, 355

Reeve, John, 116–19, 304, 357
Reeve, Wybert, 157–8
Reynolds's Newspaper, 88, 114, 209,
247, 251, 279, 343
Richards, Mr & Mrs (of Dulwich),
129–30, 329
Ricord, Philippe, 190, 205
Rimmel, Eugene, 2
Roberts, George, 355
Roberts, W.H., 218, 221, 250–2, 255
Rochester, John Wilmot, 2nd Earl of:
Sodom, 273
Royal Alhambra Palace, Leicester
Square, 116–18, 304

Sarah (whore), 108–9
Sarony, Napoleon, 342
Sarony, Oliver, 156
Saturday Review, 81, 279
Saul, Jack: earnings as prostitute,

107–8; on attraction to men of cross-dressers, 230; observes Stella and Lord Arthur at Carlotta's ball, 231–3; in Cleveland Street scandal (1890), 354; *The Sins of the Cities of the Plain*, 216, 356

Scarborough: social life, 148–52; Stella and Lord Arthur visit, 162–7

Scarborough Gazette and Weekly List of Visitors, 148–9, 151–3

Scott, Eliza (or Elijah), 106

Seward, William H., 182

Seymour, William Digby: defends Stella at trial, 303, 311, 314–15, 317, 320, 322, 326–7, 329–34

Shelly, Mr (manager of Surrey Theatre), 13–14

Sherlock, Thomas, Bishop of London, 274

Shillingford, Police Constable Thomas, 103, 302

Sidebottom, Alexander, 356

Sinclair, Donald, 175–6, 184, 237

Sinclair, Robbie, 184, 237

'Sissy' *see* Thomas, Cecil

Sloggett, William Henry, 271

Smith, George, 116, 119–25, 306–8, 316, 319

Sneaking Regard, A (burlesque farce), 94

Sodomy (buggery): as criminal offence, 36–7; medical evidence and experience of, 47–9, 204–5, 207, 238; between men and women, 49; penalty for, 78; and syphilis, 189–90, 193–7; defined, 198, 276; seen as social evil, 272–6, 278–81; as issue in Fanny and Stella trial, 292–4, 320

Solomon, Simeon, 296, 308, 355

Somerville, Dr, 47

Somerville, William, 106, 288, 298

Sothern, Edward Askew, 91

Southampton Street, London: Stella and Lord Arthur lodge in, 139–41; Stella and Lord Arthur leave, 161

Stacey, Frances (Martha's niece), 27, 29

Stacey, Martha, 24–9, 93, 304–5, 308, 316

Stacey, Mrs (Martha's mother), 25, 27

Stella *see* Boulton, Stella

Stock, Essex *see* Theatre Royal

Straight, Mr (defence lawyer), 170–1, 217, 219, 300

Strand Theatre, London, 1–3, 15, 22, 38

Surrey Theatre, London, 12–13, 15–16

Swinburne, Algernon Charles, 296

syphilis, 188–9, 193–5; feared, 271

Talbot, James Beard, 106

Tardieu, Ambroise, 205, 207–8; *Étude médico-légale sur les attentats aux moeurs*, 48, 276, 311–12

Taylor, Dr Alfred Swaine, 46–8, 200–1, 204, 207; *A Manual of Medical Jurisprudence*, 200

Teague, Inspector, 227

Theakston, Solomon Wilkinson, 148, 151, 154

Theakston's Guide to Scarborough, 151

Theatre Royal, Stock, Essex, 212

Thomas, Cecil ('Sissy'): at Strand Theatre, 1, 4, 7; friendship with

Stella, 128; Inspector Thomas pursues, 263; tried *in absentia*, 288, 298; later career, 356

Thompson, Inspector James: and arrest of Fanny and Stella, 8–9, 37, 42–3, 45, 88; overwhelmed with testimonies, 114–15, 118–19, 124; and Fiske's status as Consul, 240; requests search of Fiske's premises in Edinburgh, 243; and disappearance of Lord Arthur, 248, 253–5, 263; travels to Scotland to apprehend Harry Park, 263–4, 266–7; and Fanny and Stella's lying-low on bail, 283; payments to George Smith, 307; meets Dr Paul before arrest of Fanny and Stella, 313–14; conspires to bring charges, 316, 318–19; retirement and death, 354

Times, The, 278–9

Toole, J.L. (actor), 91

Tottenham, 54

Treasury: payments to witnesses and police officers, 319–20

Tristan, Flora, 107

Tyrwhitt, Mr (magistrate), 112

Vane-Tempest, Lady Susan, 343

Veyne, Dr François-Auguste, 97

Victoria, Queen, 99

Vincent, Howard, 106

Wakefield Street: house investigated by police, 24–5, 29–30, 38–9, 91, 299, 304

Walker, Police Constable Charles, 39, 125, 316

'Walter': *My Secret Life*, 108

Warner, Henry B., 347

Weekly Times, 249, 252

Western Mail, 344

Westminster Hall, 282

White, Police Constable George, 77, 113, 261–2, 264, 267, 298

White, Mr (of Gresham Street), 97

Wight, Albert, 128

Wilde, Oscar, 355; *Lady Windermere's Fan*, 355–6

Wimpole Street, 65, 67

Yardley, Mr (magistrate), 262

Yokel's Preceptor, The, 15, 279